CONTINENTAL DRIFTING

For Nancy —
I hope you like it — the
book gets "birdier" as it
progresses. When are we going
birding —

Regards,
Darwin
12/00

By Darwin Wile

CONTINENTAL DRIFTING

By Darwin Wile

First Printing
© Copyright 2000, Darwin Wile

ISBN: 1-891118-39-0

Published by
Wind Canyon Books, Inc.
P.O. Box 1445
Niceville, FL 32588-1445
1-800-952-7007
e-mail: books@windcanyon.com
www.windcanyon.com & www.aviation-heritage.com

Layout/Design: Becky Jaquith
Cover Design: **Wind Canyon Books, Inc.** ©2000
Cover photo courtesy of Darwin Wile

To Lynette:

Come live with me, and be my love.

Christopher Marlowe

ACKNOWLEDGEMENTS

Venasque, France – May 9, 2000
   This charming hilltop village has witnessed centuries of history. Just a few years ago, Greg Lamond lived here while he trained for the Tour De France. Sitting on the rooftop terrace of our rented apartment, I feel the warmth of a glass of *vin rouge* as well as the late afternoon sun on my left shoulder. A dark cloud is trying to smother Mt. Ventoux in the north. An hour from now, a Pygmy Owl will begin calling from its chimney perch across ancient Rue St. Paul.

   Continental Drifting is ready for printing, as George Jaquith has just assured me on the phone, and I'm thinking about the people who, knowingly or not, played an important part in one man's dream. Certainly there is George—he understood what we did and took a chance on *Continental Drifting* when lots of other publishers had no interest in the book. I'm thinking also of my friend, Warren Adler. Without his encouragement and help this book would have made it no further than my computer's memory. To Warren and George, I am forever indebted.

   Hundreds of people like Dori and Karl, George and Karin, Heidi and Louis, Barb and Ed, Rosemary and Russ, Juul and Jan, and Jean and Dick not only made the story better, but were there when we needed them. They are in my thoughts frequently.

   Many people helped us in other ways—Suzanne and Jeff, Sally and Elgin, Carole Lee and Ron, Lucille and Dick, Tom, Brock and Ann, and Virgil. We thank them all.

   Mike Wile and Kristen Meckem ("Mikey" and "Krissie") are busy crafting their life stories with families of their own. Nevertheless, the best memories from our years of drifting are those in which our cherished children participated. I feel limitless gratitude to them for being who they are.

   Finally, to Lynette: She signed on for the ride—sometimes reluctantly, but always with faith in me. *Toujours, je t'aimerai. A moi, toujours tu seras belle.*

ABOUT THE AUTHOR

Darwin Wile has been a resident of Jackson Hole, Wyoming since 1987. He was born in Lancaster, Pennsylvania in 1940 and grew up near-by in Middletown. He graduated with a B.A. (cum laude) from Harvard in 1962, where he played football and won All-American mention, and he also holds an M.B.A. from New York University. He married Lynette Orwig in 1963. The couple has 2 married children and 6 grandchildren.

Darwin is retired from the newspaper business. From 1989 to 1993, he was President and Chief Operating Officer of American Cities Business Journals, the largest publisher of business journals in the U.S. Before that, he was a Vice President and Group Publisher for Capital Cities Communications, a large media company which included the ABC Television Network.

Darwin retired from active business pursuits at a relatively young age to follow other interests. In Volkswagen campers, he and his wife, Lynette, have camped their way around the world while traveling extensively in North and South America, Europe, Africa, Australia and Asia. In addition to *Continental Drifting,* he has written and published three books in the field of natural history.* His newspaper column, "Continental Drifter," appears in the *Jackson Hole Guide.*

Finding the Birds of Jackson Hole, 1994; *Teton Trails,* 1995; *Identifying and Finding the Mammals of Jackson Hole,* 1996.

PROLOGUE

Alice Springs, Australia, somewhere in the Red Desert, September 4, 1994

From my notes: The moon will rise later; now millions of stars fill the dark sky. High in the south, Alpha and Beta Centauri point to the Southern Cross. An enormous, bright filmy cloud stretches across the nighttime desert firmament—the Milky Way. A campfire burns in the distance. Around it dark figures move slowly, occasionally gesticulating—Aborigines, presumably passing along legends from the Dreamtime.

Spent much of the day thinking about writing a book, bringing our odysseys together. Seeing the world has become an obsession occupying much of my adult life. Our adventures began in 1973 and 1974—a young family driving a Volkswagen camper through Central and South America, Europe, and Morocco. Then came Alaska and Canada in 1987, Africa in 1988, and now Australia. Asia remains. When we return home, I think it will be time to begin writing.

Would anyone want to read a book about traveling around the world in a camper? Many people talk about leaving their conventional life and following a dream—sailing around the world, moving to the woods or an island, or just retiring early enough to be able to do the things you want. Few do it. Following a dream may occupy a lot more time than most have or are willing to take. It may involve discomfort, the ubiquitous unknown, and even occasional danger. And while you don't have to be rich, it does require a spirit of independence and adventure. That said, I think more than a few people would relish the pursuit of their dreams. Unfortunately, the inertia and perceived responsibilities of conventional, everyday life conspire to prevent them from trying it. Perhaps these people would find such a book interesting. But, if wise publishers decide there's no market for this book, that's O.K. I'll write it anyway and print out a few computer copies for our grandchildren to read some day. Maybe they'll find it interesting enough. For some, the concept of an afterlife exists only in memories. Hopefully, reading this book will teach our children and grandchildren something about us and leave them with a few good memories.

I journeyed fur, I journeyed fas';
I glad I foun' de place at las'!
Uncle Remus

Jackson Hole, Wyoming, 1995

We've owned a home in Jackson Hole since 1987 when, at the age of forty-six, I retired for the first time. Prior to that, we had a condominium in Jackson, using it for summer vacations and winter ski trips.

For much of the 19th century, this valley below the Tetons was the land of mountain men—guys like John Coulter, Jim Bridger, Jedediah Smith, and Davy Jackson—and hardly anyone else. The valley, actually a depression surrounded by mountains and called a "hole" by the trappers, lies south of the Yellowstone Plateau and north of the Hoback and Snake mountain ranges. The Gros Ventres Mountains seal off the east, while the glacially carved, snow capped Tetons dominate the landscape to the west. Jackson Hole was Davy Jackson's favorite beaver trapping "digs" and became his namesake.

The Rocky Mountains are relatively young, geologically, as mountain ranges go. And the Tetons are the babes of the Rockies, having been pushed up during the last ten million years, a span of time representing less than one quarter of one per cent of the Earth's geologic history. During this brief time, the forces of wind, water, and gravity sculpted the youthful Tetons to a rich ruggedness.

The "Hole" stretches sixty miles north and south and varies in width from six to twelve miles. Cottonwoods, spruce, and willows line the meandering banks of the cutthroat trout-filled Snake River and its tributaries as they wind through the valley. Otherwise, with the exception of a few buttes mantled with aspens and conifers, sagebrush covers much of the valley's mostly flat terrain.

In numbers and variety of wildlife, Jackson Hole may come closest in North America to rivaling Africa's Serengeti. As many as fifteen thousand elk winter in the valley, half of them in the National Elk Refuge just outside the town of Jackson. Wolves, moose, deer, black and grizzly bears, pronghorns, coyotes, bighorn sheep, and mountain lions freely roam the valley and hills. Beavers, otters, badgers, and many other smaller mammals swim and scamper about their respective habitats. Eagles and hawks ride the thermals; swans and pelicans glide across ponds; geese and cranes nest in the wetlands.

Jackson Hole lies remote from a still distant outside world. Residents take pride in their spirit of rough individualism. They love the natural world. And they feel special. I can't think of a place I'd rather live. Nor can I think of a better place to write a book.

I'll tell the piper what to play
Until the Fates my thread have spun!
Death never takes a holiday —
It's time to get some living done!

From: *There Still Is Time* by Walther Buchen, 1940

CONTENTS

Chapter	Page

Chapter One

Who Is This Guy, And Why Is He Always Quitting His Job And Buying Volkswagen Campers?

I shall be telling this with a sigh
Somewhere ages and ages hence:
Two roads diverged in a wood, and I—
I took the one less traveled by,
And that has made all the difference.
From: *The Road Not Taken,* by Robert Frost

Crossing Lake Titicaca.

I was born in Lancaster, the heart of the Pennsylvania Dutch country, in 1940. My parents had little money. Initially, we lived with my grandparents in the settlement of Eden, a small natural paradise on the banks of the Conestoga Creek near Lancaster. The war began, and my dad landed a job as an airplane mechanic at an air force base near Middletown, Pennsylvania, where we settled. I grew up in a hunting and fishing culture. Today Middletown is best known for its proximity to Three Mile Island, a large island in the Susquehanna River that was the site of the infamous 1979 nuclear accident. When we were growing up, nuclear power plants were unknown, and the only structures on Three Mile Island were fishing huts. Speaking of fishing, Middletown also is the home of Bob Clouser, a world renown fishing guide and fly tier. More important, his sister, Dolly, was

1

my ninth grade girlfriend! The only other remarkable thing about Middletown is Kuppy's Diner, a fourth generation eatery (owned and operated by my pals, Greg and Carol Kupp) and worth a detour of a few miles if you're ever in the area.

My parents' education was limited. This never prevented them from trying to instill good values in my brother and me. My mother taught me to be honest and to respect girls. My dad insisted, from the time I entered school as a six-year old, that I get good grades and learn to play football well enough to be offered a college scholarship. He knew he would never be able to afford to send me to school, and, in those days, Pennsylvania was a hot recruiting ground for football players. My parents involved us in church activities, even though they seldom attended church themselves, and they encouraged our involvement in scouting. Much of my boyhood revolved around camping and hiking, and I managed to become an Eagle Scout. I'll always remember those times, sitting around a campfire with my friends (after a supper of Dinty Moore beef stew and baked corn-on-the-cob filched from a nearby field), talking about planets and stars, rock and roll, or girls, and wondering how life could ever get any better than this.

I'm not sure what made me want to see the world, but perhaps Mike Roksandic had something to do with it. "Rock" was a rough around the edges, twinkly-eyed tough guy from Steelton, Pennsylvania. He spent most of his autumn afternoons trying to teach us junior high school boys how to block and tackle. I suppose most of my friends remember Rock primarily in that context—friend and football coach. While I learned a lot about football from Rock, I remember him especially in what others considered his incidental role, our geography teacher. I don't know if he ever left the state of Pennsylvania, but somehow he had a knack for impressing me with the mystique of other lands. When he talked about the Sahara, I could feel the sand in my shoes. He had me climbing the Himalayas, sailing the South Pacific, canoeing the Amazon, and searching for the North Pole. He brought to life the nomads, farmers, hunters, fishermen and other peoples populating the diverse cultures of the world and scratching out an existence in whatever way made sense in their environment. Looking back now, I wonder if I didn't become a closet vagabond even in those days.

The responsibilities of my education and then marriage dictated focusing on a career rather than indulging any interest I might have had in exploring the globe. Eventually, however, circumstances unfolded in such a way that permitted the Roksandic inspired wanderlust to escape from the closet. But I'm getting ahead of myself.

Following Dad's direction, I maintained good grades in school and learned to play football well enough to receive scholarship offers from a number of colleges. Harvard's football coach had previously coached at my high school and was held in high regard by the people of Middletown, including my dad. There was little doubt where Dad wanted me to go to college. With a tuition scholarship in hand, I left for Cambridge in the fall of 1958 to attend Harvard where I played football with some distinction and eventually graduated with honors.

Thoughts of distant places seldom occupied my college life. The first two years were very difficult for me academically. When I wasn't in the classroom, I was usually in the library. Any spare time was filled with part-time jobs and sports. When one of my roommates announced he was going to spend the summer traveling in Ireland, I remember that the idea did not appeal to me—summer employment awaited. My dad had taken a second job to help offset the non-tuition expenses of sending me to college, and there was no question of my not working during summer vacations. I pumped gas and changed tires on the Pennsylvania Turnpike during the week and had a cushy job as a lifeguard at the local swimming pool on weekends.

Today steel companies probably find it difficult to entice young people to spend their careers in a declining industry. Back in the '50s, however, a lot of Pennsylvanians were employed in some aspect of producing steel, and the business still retained a bit of the glamour surrounding heavy industry. In the spring of my senior year, I was offered a chance to go to Chicago and work for a large steel company. I had never been farther west than Pittsburgh, and the salary seemed pretty good at the time.

Six guys were chosen for a management training program that was to last nine months. At the end of the program each of us was to be assigned to one of the company's operating divisions. "Vertical integration" was big in those days, and this steel producer owned its sources of raw materials (iron ore, limestone, and coal mines) as well as some of its largest customers (steel warehousing and fabrication, steel container manufacturing, and steel building contracting). We visited many of these locations, but spent most of our time learning the business in the company's Indiana Harbor mills south of Chicago.

Another trainee and I were the only two bachelors. He had been a football player at the Air Force Academy and had gotten an MBA from Michigan. We decided to share an apartment in Hammond, Indiana, so we would be close to the mills. The convenience of being close to work was sadly offset by the deficiency of eligible young women hanging around the mills. My roomie and I involuntarily settled into a rather monastic life.

Our unexciting lifestyle sometimes seemed to bother the other fellows in the training program at least as much as it did us. One trainee and his wife had gone to DePauw, a university in Greencastle, Indiana. (Today this guy is Chairman of the Board of that same steel company.) His wife had a sorority friend whom she was dying to fix up with my roomie. She thought they were destined for each other and planned a magnificent dinner at their apartment to bring the couple together. Almost as an afterthought, probably so I wouldn't feel left out, they invited another one of their sorority friends for me. A wonderful evening was had by all, but sometimes love works its magic capriciously. The couple "made for one another" dated four or five more times before they split up. Eight months later, the other friend, Lynette, and I were married.

Lynette aroused more than a few desires in me, including the allure of other lands. She had majored in French in college and had traveled over much of Europe. I admired her photos and stories of Europe, and we often talked about travel. Reality required, however, that we assign a relatively low priority to our interest in places beyond. We both had a lot on our platter: two children came along quickly. I had been assigned to the company's steel container division and transferred to the New York area where, in addition to my daytime job, I was busy at night finishing a master's degree and fulfilling my U.S. Army Reserve obligation. Nevertheless, Lynette continued to remind me of faraway places, hoping one day circumstances would be such that our travel interests, time available, and financial wherewithal would converge. Eventually they did.

Salary increases were slow in coming and modest, at best, in the steel business. Meanwhile, our expenses were going up. Living in the New York area with two children and paying tuition for graduate school was expensive. After a couple of years, I left the steel business and found a job selling electronic accounting machines on commission. The first year our income nearly tripled. The second year I did even better, leading the division in sales and receiving a promotion to sales manager in Minneapolis.

Not long after we moved to Minneapolis, our division was acquired by a large local computer company. I was asked to work in marketing at the home office. This was during the late sixties when it was quite common for small, specialized companies to spring up and go public. Soon after I arrived, my boss and some of his friends left the company and formed a data input company. They asked me to come along to run the sales and marketing operations. The lure was stock options. Lynnie and I invested all the cash we could spare in the young company, and, for a while, we seemed to be flying high. Unfortunately, our balloon was burst by a recession combined with some of our competitors releasing products the marketplace preferred to those we were selling. We rolled the dice and lost. It was a learning experience.

One lasting impression of that experience had little to do with my business career. The job required travel to South America and Europe, and some of Mike Roksandic's stories about the world began to come to life for me. Flying from Lima to Buenos Aires, I looked down and saw breath-taking Lake Titicaca perched two miles up in the Andes, the world's highest navigable lake surrounded by some of its highest mountain peaks—and promised myself to return for a closer look. I made sales calls in serious Sao Paulo and frivolous Rio de Janeiro. Lynette joined me in London, Geneva, and romantic Paris. We eschewed the touristy beaten track in favor of the haunts of locals. Talking with people, seeing how they lived, learning what they thought, their history, their character; all served to whet my appetite. I was determined to come back for more.

Our little company soon failed, and I was looking for a job. One day I got a call from a man who owned a chain of community newspapers. He needed someone to run his advertising department, and I thought the newspaper business sounded interesting. We got along well, and he soon promoted me to general manager. Nevertheless, the subject of serious travel was coming up more frequently in conversations between Lynette and me.

One conversation in particular occurred on a short vacation in San Francisco, our first time there. We were in a bar at the top of the Mark Hopkins Hotel and were due to return to Minneapolis the next morning. We had spent the past few days riding gravity-defying cable cars, visiting mysterious Chinatown, and eating succulent abalone steak in a little restaurant on Fisherman's Wharf. We had driven to Stanford and Berkeley, crossed the Golden Gate, gazed at the venerable redwoods in Muir Woods, watched the Sausalito houseboats bobbing in the bay, and wandered aimlessly around the Monterey Peninsula. This evening was the culmination of it all. We ate slowly at the Fairmount Hotel, letting a good French wine and the Irish tenor voice of John Gary condition us for whatever else we would think or say that last intimate evening. Then we walked across the street to the Mark Hopkins for a nightcap and a final look at the marvelous city by the Golden Gate. All of this and the uninhibiting impact of the wine created a philosophic atmosphere in which my persuasiveness as well as Lynette's vulnerability to the lure of romantic places were enhanced.

"Let's chuck it all and take off for a year or two."

"What about your job? You can't just quit your job!"

"Why not? I'm only thirty. I can easily get another job when we come back. We can sell our house and live on the equity."

"What about the children?"

"We'll take them out of school. They'll learn a lot more traveling than they will in school."

"Where will we go?"

"Let's start in South America. Then we'll do Europe. If we're having fun, we'll go on and do the rest of the world."

Back home we talked about South America often. I don't know why we locked in on South America rather than Europe, Asia, or Africa. But there was no question that it was to be South America. That continent became a symbol to us. Talking about going to South America lifted us from the ruts we all inevitably find ourselves in—jobs that have lost their challenges, suburban living that has become too comfortable, and, the most frightening rut of all, the responsibilities of life preventing you from living your dreams.

In the spring of 1973, we made the decision to go to South America. I asked the owner of the newspaper company to have dinner with me. This man had trouble keeping his executives over the years, and I wanted to handle my leaving just right. I explained that this desire to travel had been building up over the years and that the decision to leave in no way suggested there was anything wrong with our relationship. I told him he could pick any time within the next year for me to leave, whenever it was best for him. He suggested that, instead of leaving permanently, I should take a leave of absence, go to South America, and see if we wanted to continue traveling. Perhaps after a few months we would grow tired of living in a small camper, and then my job would be waiting for me. This sounded like an arrangement in everyone's best interest, so I agreed to it. His proposal was so reasonable, I commited to returning to work there after the leave of absence, at least for a reasonable period of time. We decided I would leave at the end of the calendar year after the pre-Christmas advertising rush.

In December of 1973, Lynette and I packed what we needed, along with our nine-year-old son and our six-year-old daughter (Lynette and I were thirty-three), in a Volkswagen pop-top camper and started driving south. Through Mexico and Central America and down the west coast of South America we motored. Several months later, when we returned to Minneapolis, I learned that my boss had hired someone else for my job. So we sold our home, flew to Luxembourg, picked up another VW camper, and toured Europe. Fifteen months later we returned to the United States.

In many ways, making the decisions to leave for South America and then Europe was more difficult, especially for Lynette, than similar decisions we made one or two decades later. Not only did we have to sell our house and leave our friends, but we had to consider the additional responsibility of educating two young children. Besides, leaving the conventional life seemed more risky the first time around. Our parents and friends thought we were certifiably demented. To temper all of this in our own minds, and to provide Lynette an out, we agreed we would give it six weeks. She would stick it out that long, but when that time expired, if she had enough, I agreed that we would come home.

We left Minneapolis on a blustry December morning and drove to Lynette's parents' home near Chicago where we spent Christmas. Winter clutched most of the country in its grip. A few days later we sprinted south past Memphis, Little Rock, and Dallas, trying to escape the snow and ice. The weather eventually improved as we drove south through Texas, and we crossed the border at Laredo under a bright, warm sun. We followed the Pan American Highway south through Mexico and Central America, stopping wherever we chose to see towns, cities, archeological sites, markets, festivals, and just to talk with the people. After a few weeks of this, I summoned the courage to ask Lynette how things were going.

"Well, what do you think?"

"About what?"

"The trip! The adventure! What we're doing!"

"Oh, that. It's fine."

"You mean you're enjoying it?"

"It's wonderful. I look forward to getting up every morning. There's always something new. And interesting. Or exciting."

"Then you're not thinking of going back after six weeks?"

"Heavens, no! Whatever gave you that idea?"

About a year later, we were camped on a wonderful, sunny beach in Estepona, Spain. President Nixon had resigned a few months before. The economic scene seemed dismal as the United States slid into a recession. We had planned to drive south along the coast of Spain and cross from Gibraltar to Morocco. After dinner we walked slowly along the beach, sipping the instant coffee we had by now become accustomed to. A clear, star-studded, night sky covered the Mediterranean. The children, presumably, studied back in the camper. I broke the silence.

"Things don't look so good back home."

"What do you mean?"

"The economy. It's getting worse."

"So what?"

"Maybe we should go home."

"Why?"

"I'm concerned about being able to get a job. When the economy's bad, people don't hire."

"So let's take another year and do Africa and Asia. Probably then the economy will be better, and it will be easier to find a job."

Now, keep in mind, this was the woman who, not much more than a year earlier, wasn't sure she wanted to leave home and pretty much demanded a six week trial period. How the tables had turned! I was wimping out, and Lynette had become the intrepid adventurer.

Chapter Two
A Breaking-In Period:
Blissful Adventures In South America

Over the Andes
High in Peru,
I need a Valentine.
Do you?

Krissie at Tula

PREPARATIONS

In many ways, we had been thinking about and preparing for this trip for several years. All four family members were experienced campers, veterans of the Boundary Waters of northern Minnesota. We read back issues of *National Geographic* containing articles on Latin American countries and subscribed to *Americas*, a magazine published by the Organization of American States, which contained historical and political background as well as travel information. Lynette and I belonged to a University of Minnesota affiliated international discussion group which included several members from Latin America. While most South American travel guides offered limited utility outside the major cities, we pored over AAA's maps and guidebooks, Jahn's *Latin American Travel Guide* and Jacobs' *South American*

Travel Digest.

Choosing a camper was easy. We bought a 1973 Volkswagen with a Westphalia camping conversion, because of its relatively low cost, efficient design, and serviceability throughout Latin America. A pop-top feature enabled the roof to be elevated when the camper was parked, providing more head room and a cot in which our nine-year-old son, Mike, slept. Our six-year-old daughter, Krissie, slept in another removable cot that stretched across the driver's compartment. Lynette and I slept on a small double bed that appeared when the rear seat was unhitched and pulled out flat. These sleeping arrangements were comfortable once we were in our respective beds, but it did take a while to develop a routine that lent some efficiency in getting into bed at night and out in the morning. A small, removable dining table, several storage areas, and an icebox and sink were included in the camper's amenities. Some of our friends recoiled at the idea of four people living in such a small space. We didn't look at it that way—our "living room" was the beach, mountainside, or village where we happened to be parked.

Before leaving we underwent complete physical examinations and the series of inoculations recommended by the Minnesota Department of Health. We also assembled a rather sophisticated first aid kit.

Taking the children out of school was no problem, because the administration and teachers were totally cooperative, recommending our working with Mike and Krissie on reading and math and giving us textbooks and workbooks on those subjects. We left an itinerary with the school so the teachers could notify us if they perceived from the tests and other material we mailed back that the children were falling behind or needed additional work in any area.

Because I was on a leave of absence and planned to return to Minneapolis after touring South America, we rented our home furnished rather than selling it. A couple whose house had been destroyed in a fire rented it and treated it well.

We applied for passports and visas where needed and, through AAA, arranged for a *carnet de passage* on our camper. A "carnet" is essentially a passport for a motor vehicle which assures the countries through which you're traveling that you won't sell the car without paying import duty.

Having studied Spanish in school, Lynette and I took an evening refresher course. One friend agreed to pay our bills and collect our mail. Another boarded our cat. I'm sure we prepared for our adventure in other ways I've long since forgotten.

A Little Background

A few hundred million years ago, all the land on earth was joined in one gigantic supercontinent. Tremendous pressures built up by entrapped heat in the center of the earth. These pressures were released at relatively weak points in the Earth's crust, creating fractures or rifts. Thus, the supercontinent broke up along these rifts more than 100 million years ago, and large segments began a long, slow drifting journey across the Earth's surface. A northern land mass, containing what would become Europe, Asia and North America, broke away from a southern land mass consisting of future Africa, South America, Australia and Antarctica. Subsequently, North America broke away from Eurasia; Australia and Antarctica drifted away from Africa and South America and then from one another; India tore away from Africa and slowly slammed into Asia, pushing up the Himalayas; and South America broke away from Africa and began its journey across what would eventually be called the Atlantic Ocean.

For more than 50 million years the great continent of South America remained an island. As it slowly plowed its way west, the western edge of the continent wrinkled under the pressure of the collision with that segment of the Earth's crust lying under the Pacific Ocean. Thus was born the great Andean chain of mountains.

During the millions of years that South America was an island, its plant and animal life evolved in isolation from organisms elsewhere on the planet. Sloths, anteaters, armadillos, monkeys, and various rodents and marsupials became unique citizens of this huge island. Not until two or three million years ago when the middle American isthmus rose out of the seas and linked the two great continents of the western hemisphere did prehistoric North American cats, tapirs, deer, and raccoons appear in South America.

Probably 85% of the animals in South America today are endemic. These animals live in a land more extremely varied than any other on Earth. The Andes mountain chain contains many peaks over 20,000 feet and is geothermally very active with many live volcanoes and frequent earthquakes. Lakes high in the Andes, less than 100 miles from the Pacific, are the source of the Amazon River which drains an area larger than that of the continental United States and ultimately pours into the Atlantic Ocean 3000 miles away. The huge Amazon basin, which waters the world's largest tropical rain forest, was an inland sea millions of years ago. Successful adaptations of life-forms from that time still exist in the lakes and rivers of the enormous drainage area—fresh water skates, rays, dolphins and manatees.

A thin strip of desert lies west of the Andes along much of the coast of Peru and Chile where rain virtually never falls. The mountains are barriers to winds from the east, and the cold Humboldt Current prevents moisture-laden air from the Pacific from reaching the continent. Other major natural habitats supporting extensive ecosystems in South America include high elevation altiplanos, grassy prairies, and fertile plains.

Middle America was the cradle of civilization in the western hemisphere. From 1200 to 900 BC, the Olmec culture thrived on the northern gulf shore of Mexico. Primarily corn farmers, these people were also intellectually sophisticated, building religious centers, large plazas and reservoirs and developing an accurate calendar. Olmec religious and artistic influence spread widely throughout Mesoamerica. Themes common in later cultures such as bloodletting, human sacrifice, ritual ball games, and jaguar deities all traced their origin to the Olmec culture.

In 600 BC, ancestors of the Zapotecs built Monte Alban near present day Oaxaca in southern Mexico. Later, around the birth of Christ, the Zapotecs developed a vibrant culture at Monte Alban. Also around 600 BC, in Guatemala, the Mayans built the magnificent city of Tikal. The Mayan culture, centered in the Yucatan Peninsula and the city of Chichen Itza, became the bulwark of the Classic Period (300-900 AD) in Middle America, a time marked by political stability and intellectual advancement in the arts, sciences, architecture and religion. Another important culture during this period thrived near present day Mexico City at Teotihuacan. Intellectually sophisticated architects and farmers, these people built enormous pyramids and used irrigation as early as 500 AD. They prospered until 750 AD when barbaric tribes from the north destroyed their culture.

Crop failures, peasant revolts, and the rise of military states bent on empire building ushered in a time of trouble. By 900 AD, all the great cultures had disintegrated. Teotihuacan fell. Monte Alban and the Zapotec culture were lost to Mixtec invaders. The marauding Toltecs conquered much of Mesoamerica, including the Mayans, in the name of their war gods whose images resided in their capital city of Tula. Wars continued throughout Middle America until 1200 AD, and most of Mexico was divided into small city states with no political unity.

Somewhere in the north of Mexico was a land, the exact location of which is lost to history, called Aztlan. Its inhabitants were bloodthirsty barbarians who began arriving in Central Mexico in the thirteenth century. At first, they worked for the more civilized tribes near Lake Texcoco upon which modern Mexico City is built. Then they became mercenaries for the warring Tepanecs, before long turning on the Tepanecs and conquering them. By the sixteenth century, they had spread their conquests to all of Mexico and Guatemala and developed a culture that was a collection of customs and ideas from earlier civilizations. Religion dominated their lives. The conquest of other peoples was necessary both to support their rich standard of living and to provide sacrificial victims for their voracious gods, most of whom were borrowed from the Toltecs, a people they venerated for their warlike ways.

Thus was the rise of the Aztecs to power. Few resisted them. The Miztecs, who had displaced the Zapotecs at Monte Alban, allied with their old enemies and successfully defended themselves against the Aztecs. But few others prevailed against these terrorists. By 1519, the Aztec culture reached its zenith. This was the year many omens said that their great fair-skinned god, Quetzalcoatl, would manifest himself to them. Fair-skinned Hernando Cortez appeared instead.

While great cultures evolved in Middle America, civilization in South America was not far behind. As early as 1500 BC, inhabitants of Sechin (Peru) became sophisticated farmers, weavers, potters, and architects. From 900 to 200 BC, the Chavin culture reached its peak. These people were cultists whose art reflected their religious beliefs. Jaguars and alligators dominated their art, betraying a cultural contact with another people (possibly the Olmecs of Central America), since there were no alligators and jaguars in the desert of northern Peru. The Chavin influence in art spread over Peru, providing the first evidence of unity among the South American tribes.

From 200 BC to 600 AD, Peruvian civilization continued to advance. The arts and architecture flourished. The Mochicas in the north built Huaca del Sol and Huaca del Luna, two giant pyramid temples dedicated to the sun and the moon. In the south, Nazca astronomers and potters spread their culture along the coast. Empire building took place between 600 AD and 1000 AD with centers located at Huari in the north and Tiahuanaco near present day LaPaz, Bolivia, in the south. Culture linked the diverse tribes in these two empires covering all of Peru and parts of neighboring countries.

Between 1000 AD and the late fifteenth century there was little political unity. The area was divided into regional kingdoms which tended to keep to themselves. The most important of these kingdoms was Chimor, controlling 200 miles of Peruvian coastal region. The capital of the Chimu kingdom was Chan Chan, the largest city in ancient Peru with a population of more than 50,000 people. The Chimus built forts along the coast for protection and inhabited the fertile river valleys and oases in the Peruvian desert. Not until the fifteenth century, when conquerors cleverly diverted Chan Chan's water supply, were the Chimus subdued.

Many years ago, when the great creator god, Viracocha, decided that man should inhabit Earth, he brought his son, Manco Capac, and his daughter, Mama Ocllo, out from an island of the great mountain lake, Titicaca. Viracocha directed his children to find the center of the earth. Manco Capac and Mama Ocllo did as bid and searched for the sacred valley of which Viracocha spoke. They found this beautiful valley in the center of the Earth, built a city there, and called it Cusco. Thus was the Capaccuna culture established by their first ruler, or Inca, Manco Capac and his sister, Mama Ocllo.

For centuries, the Capaccuna remained a small, peaceful Andean civilization. Then, in 1438, from across the Apurimac River, came the Chancas. The Chancas feared their Inca neighbors and determined to defeat them in a surprise attack on Cusco. The old Inca ruler was near death and put up little resistance, and the Chancas burned and looted the royal city. Later, the old man's son, Pachacuti, abruptly put an end to the celebration of the victorious Chancas. With regrouped forces, Pachacuti attacked the city and routed his enemy.

Pachacuti—*Earthshaker!* This greatest Inca truly shook the Earth. He began the Incan expansion in all directions. He conquered by diplomacy, and, where diplomacy did not work, he used force. But he conquered all the tribes and kingdoms in his path, establishing laws and efficiently organizing the empire. He imposed Quechua, the Inca language, on all the land and maintained communications by an efficient system of runners, or Chasquis, who could relay a message from Cusco to Quito, over twelve hundred miles, in five days and who could keep Cusco supplied with fresh fish from the Pacific two hundred miles away. Pachacuti resolved that his city would never again be taken defenseless. He began construction on Sacsahuaman, an impregnable fortress overlooking Cusco, and containing granite stones weighing as much as three hundred tons.

Expansion of the empire was continued by Pachacuti's son, Topa Incan. He defeated the Cajamarcas to the north, opening the way for a march of conquest all the way to Quito. Having gained control of the highlands, Topa Incan now turned toward the sea. Chan Chan's aqueducts were fed by rivers from the mountains. Topa Incan diverted these waters and brought the desert kingdom of the Chimus to its knees.

At its peak, the Inca empire rivaled any other in history. It stretched over three thousand miles along the Andes from Colombia to Chile and ruled five million people. This civilization built roads spanning the empire, buildings and cities that withstood earthquakes and bridges crossing torrential rivers raging through deep canyons. Effective social organization saw to it that there was little crime or hunger. And then, incredibly, this powerful empire, these five million people of the Sun, surrendered without a fight to less than two hundred men with seventy-five horses led by a little white man with a black beard, Francisco Pizarro.

Interstate 94, between Minneapolis and Chicago, December 21, 1973

The thermometer registered a negative five degrees Fahrenheit at 8:30 a.m. when we left home for Illinois. Lynette's parents lived in Winnetka, near Chicago, and we planned to spend Christmas with them before heading south. The United States was in the middle of an energy crisis; a national speed limit of fifty miles per hour turned what was normally a six hour drive into nine hours. We crossed the frozen Mississippi at LaCrosse, Wisconsin. The family conversation turned to a discussion of the world's longest rivers. Five-year-old Kristen was certain the Pacific Ocean was the world's longest river. Months later, while swimming off one of the Galapagos Islands six hundred miles from the coast of Ecuador, it occurred to me that, in a sense,

Krissie had a point. The Humboldt Current is an ocean "river" flowing from the Antarctic Ocean north along the Pacific coast of South America past Peru and then curving west through the Galapagos and far out into the ocean.

The next few days were, as always, pleasant visiting Lynette's parents. We played bridge, watched football games, went ice skating, and shopped for Christmas gifts. Lynette's dad and I found time to polish our winter bird watching skills. In the evenings, we chatted around the fireplace. Grandmother rubbed Lynette's feet and Grandfather played Kings' Corners and Crazy 8's with Mike and Krissie.

Lynette's parents were gentle people who never interfered with our lives. But, on this visit, I sensed Grandfather was troubled by our adventurous decision. We didn't talk about it, however, until years later when he brought up the subject. We sat with our binoculars on a park bench overlooking Lake Michigan.

"Darwin, there's something I've wanted to tell you for a long time."

"What is it?"

"When you went to South America in a camper, I was concerned about what you were doing—leaving your job, taking the children out of school, all of that. I guess I thought it was more than a little irresponsible."

"I knew you felt that way."

"I was wrong. Now I understand what you did. I can see the effect it had on the kiddies and on Lynette and you. I think what you did was special, and I want you to know that."

Lynette's dad died soon after that. He was one of the most important people in my life. Getting approval for my actions doesn't register very high on my needs list. But I can't tell you how good it felt to hear those words of vindication from this special man.

My parents also expressed concern about the wisdom of this adventure. We made both sets of parents feel a bit more comfortable by explaining in detail where we were going and leaving them the addresses of embassies at which we would stop to pick up mail. We also committed to write frequently.

Lynette's brother and his family lived only a few blocks from her parents. Santa left everyone's gifts at his house where we planned to celebrate Christmas. On the big day we opened presents, sang carols, played ping pong and had a contest to see who could pitch the most playing cards into a fedora across the room. Grandfather won. Dinner included wild rice, fried potatoes, hearts of palm salad, roast beef and a Christmas goose, with ice cream puffs for dessert. Months would go by before we ate like that again.

We left Winnetka early the next morning and drove through a blizzard in southern Illinois and Missouri. There seemed to be as many cars stranded in roadside ditches as there were driving on the road. The snow continued falling until we were well into Arkansas where we spent our first night camping in a motel parking lot near Little Rock. We awakened shivering, and, rather than eating breakfast in the cold camper, drove to Sambo's and ordered hot cakes. Afterwards, on the drive west, ice covered the flooded lowlands, and large numbers of hawks, vultures and ravens perched on fence posts and power poles and in trees waiting for the sun's warmth. An impromptu count numbered 83 hawks in a one mile stretch. The children played license plate games, Lynette sang "Remember the Red River Valley" when we crossed the Red River, and, later, we ate catfish and grits at a roadside diner.

Carole Lee and Ron Randall and their two children, good friends from Minnesota, were visiting Carole Lee's parents, the Clarks, in Dallas and had invited us to stop on our way through. We arrived late in the afternoon and had a lot of laughs over cocktails. The grandparents were incredulous that the four of us would spend the next few months living in such cramped quarters. The Vikings and Cowboys were playing on Sunday, and Mr. Clark teased Mike Randall and Mike Wile, pretending he didn't know who Fran Tarkenton was, calling him "Frank Tickleton." Kristen turned six the next day, and, after a dinner of roast beef, pickled carrots and corn pudding, we celebrated her birthday with cake and ice cream. She looked at me, smiled, and, to the obvious consternation of the Randall's and Clarks, said, "Happy half-birthday, Daddy." Lynette cleared up the confusion by explaining Krissie's and her dad's birthdays are exactly six months apart. That night, Mike and his sister slept inside with Mike and Amy Randall, while Lynette and I camped in our friends' driveway.

The drive south to San Antonio took us through some stiff winds, but, otherwise, the weather had improved. Lynette extricated her ukulele from somewhere in back of the camper and sang a medley of Texas songs, including "The Yellow Rose of Texas" and "Deep in the Heart of Texas." After visiting the Alamo, I related the Mexican rendition of the battle which characterized Santa Ana as a hero and Bill Travis, Davy Crockett, Jim Bowie and the boys as cowards who begged to have their lives spared. Lynette characterized their version rather succinctly—"Tripe!," while Mike attributed it all to Mexican propaganda, an attempt to put Santa Ana's defeat at San Jacinto in a better light. That night Venus, Mars and Jupiter passed in review over the KOA campground while we watched *Bedknobs and Broomsticks* on their outdoor movie screen. In the morning we drove to Laredo and crossed the border into Mexico.

Nuevo Laredo, Mexico, December 30, 1973

Crossing the border between Laredo, Texas, and Nuevo Laredo, Mexico, turned into a two hour ordeal, much of which involved a thorough search of our camper. If we had hidden something illegal, the Mexican authorities certainly would have found it.

At last—Latin America! Certainly southern Texas often has a Mexican flavor, but nothing that prepares you for the dramatic and immediate difference between the two countries. Images which would become typical greeted us that first day of driving through the Mexican desert—coyotes trotting through mesquite and cactus, a great horned owl on a telephone pole, black vultures perched on Joshua trees waiting..., cowboys checking fence lines on horseback, an old bearded man in a little wooden cart being pulled by a burro, women walking and carrying firewood while their husbands rode on burros, and poverty.

We spent our first night in Mexico in the town of Sabinas Hildago and ate our first Mexican dinner—tacos, enchiladas and chili—at a small restaurant called El Tampico. The friendly owner joined us at our table. He had lived in Milwaukee for several years where he learned to cook and speak English. I asked him how he had come to own the restaurant, and he told us a sinister story about the previous owner having fallen out of favor with the local unions and being forced to sell to him. He said we could safely spend the night camped in the restaurant parking lot and insisted one of his daughters, a pretty little girl named Juanita, show us around town. Juanita approached her assigned task with lots of enthusiasm but no knowledge of English. With our limited Spanish we soon determined she wanted to take us to a municipal park with a small waterfall. The evening was pleasant, and so was our stroll around town with little Juanita. Back at the camper, Mexican music blared from a nearby tavern, but we drifted off to sleep long before the trumpets and guitars stopped playing.

Our camper climbed out of the desert valley over twenty-three hundred-foot Mamulique Pass onto a plateau paralleling the foothills of the Sierra Madres. Now we would be in sight of mountains for the next several months. Driving through the small towns and countryside, we observed the simple, bucolic life of the Mexicans, and I had the feeling that here humans lived as their environment allowed. Later, as we descended toward the village of Cienaga de Flores, the red pollution from the distant Monterey steel mills contradicted my impression, revealing that, even in Mexico, humans controlled their environment.

We refueled in Monterey, and, after convincing the attendant he had shortchanged me ten pesos, continued on to Villa Santiago, a lovely town with pastel colored adobe homes, a picturesque church and a quiet, pleasant park. Nearby, a waterfalls appropriately named Cola de Caballo, gushed over the brink of an eighty-foot cliff, fanning out to both sides and resembling the tail of a horse. Lynette drove as the road passed through fields of corn and citrus groves. Many of the plants had been killed by a recent frost, apparently the first one experienced for many years. We stopped for fresh orange juice at a restaurant surrounded by gardens of colorful flowers and owned by a widow from Chicago. Near Linares we almost hit a goat, reminding us that here livestock own the right of way.

Despite their often squalid surroundings, the Mexican people displayed a clean appearance. School children had a scrubbed look in their white blouses and shirts. Homes along the road were built with sticks, adobe bricks and thatched roofs. Near Montemorales we bought tangerines for a penny each. Fields became lush. Women washed their clothes and bathed their children in green-blue streams flowing through cypress-lined arroyos.

We pulled into a campground near the small city of Victoria. A man strode toward us with a wave and a smile.

"Hi! Name's Burrows, Russ Burrows. What's yours?"

"Wile. Darwin. You speak English."

"Yep. From Wisconsin. Just came down here to get away from the rat race."

"Have you?"

"Come over and see for yourself."

Burrows was a teacher (with a doctoral degree). He had been teaching in Texas, married a Mexican woman, and came to Victoria. He and his wife struggled in what he called an "emerging business" in Mexico—campgrounds. While his campground facilities were basic, they had a nice pastoral location, a talking parrot and a burro for the children to ride. A U.S. Army major and his family who had been stationed in Panama and had just been transferred to Washington were camped next to us. The major had a month's leave, and they had driven through Central America and Mexico in a rented camper. They gave us a number of good suggestions, including routes to take and places receptive to campers. We didn't realize it at the time, but this kind of networking among travelers would become the best source of information on what lay ahead—far better than that provided by travel guides or embassies. In the years to come, finding ourselves in remote corners of the world, such conversations with fellow travelers proved invaluable.

Mike and Krissie made friends with the Burrows' bilingual, twelve-year-old son, Russ Junior. The boy joined us on a drive into Victoria and showed us around town. He described what appeared to be mild discrimination against him in school because he had a North American father. The children bought candy at Artesinas Mexicanes, and the Sierra Madres turned purple as the sun set behind them. Back at the campground that evening, Lynette and I lay on a blanket under a starry sky and listened to backpackers softly strumming their guitars and singing. Maybe Burrows had gotten away from the rat race.

Climbing through twisted layers of sedimentary rock, we crossed the Sierra Madres and entered the Tropic of Cancer, then dropped into the desert to the west. The road turned south and goats, cattle, burros, pigs and chickens all grazed, rooted and scratched to find something edible in the sparsely vegetated land. Starving dogs with ribs bursting through tightly stretched skin seemed to outnumber people in the towns. Krissie and Mike worked on their school lessons, and we climbed again toward mile-high San Luis Potosi. We stopped to talk to several horsemen—handsome vaqueros who were quite interested in our camper. Gold teeth accented their smiles as they posed for photos. Colonial San Luis Potosi provided a pleasant diversion with its plazas, churches, cobblestone streets and glazed tile sidewalks. The children sampled *queso de tuna*, a locally made candy, and we became lost driving around the city and gave a ride to two men who volunteered to show us the way back to our road.

Life was better up on the Mexican plateau. Prosperous villas were surrounded by cultivated fields of corn and agave. We registered at a campground north of Queretaro and that evening drove into the charming colonial city where Emperor Maximilian was imprisoned in the Iglesia de La Cruz and later shot by a firing squad on the Hill of the Bells. Queretaro was wonderfully ablaze with Christmas lights, and signs proclaiming "!Feliz Ano Nuevo!" explained the carnival atmosphere. Bands played in the streets while people danced and drank. We joined in on the dancing and games, finally deciding it was impossible to throw those little plastic rings over the bottle necks. Later Lynette contrasted this evening with New Year's Eve one year before when we sat with friends in a sailboat, quietly anchored in a cove off a dark islet in the Florida keys.

Tula—the capital city of the Toltec empire! By the middle of the twelfth century, these truculent people ruled all of Central Mexico. Their ideas and customs influenced later cultures, including the Mayan, and especially the Aztec. The ancient city's impressive ruins stand on a hill overlooking present day Tula, a dusty village covered by chalky powder, detritus from a nearby cement processing plant. No one guarded the ruins, and we were the only visitors. We climbed around and over the pyramids and inspected the fifteen-foot high basalt warrior statues atop the temple of the great warrior god, Quetzalcoatl.

If Tula was impressive, our next stop, Teotihuacan or "the place where the gods are created," was breathtaking. Two thousand years ago, two hundred thousand people lived in this city. The Street of the Dead bisects these magnificent, sprawling ruins, and two enormous pyramids—Temple of the Sun and Temple of the Moon—flank the complex of ancient buildings. I stood with goose bumps at the top of the Temple of the Sun, gazing across the ruined "Abode of the Gods" to the Temple of the Moon and imagining thousands in ritual ceremony.

Two volcanoes, Popocatepetl at 17,887 feet and Ixtaccihuatl at 17,343 feet, dominated the view to the south of Mexico City and were the first snow-capped mountains the children had ever seen. We drove past the bullring at Texcoco, continuing on a bad, unpaved road that permitted slow progress toward our destination of Cocoyoc, a hacienda, originally built by Cortez, which had been beautifully renovated and turned into a first-class hotel. A friend had a financial interest in Cocoyoc, and we were his guests. We joined Rick and his girl friend, Karen, that evening for a late dinner at the hacienda.

After a breakfast of fresh fruit, we drove to the resort town of Cuernavaca. The camper seemed to lose power on the road's many hills and treacherous curves. Pink, blue and yellow pastel houses with red tiled roofs reflected the morning sun as we neared the city. Unfortunately, the Cuernavaca Volkswagen dealer was too busy to look at our problem. Much mountain driving awaited us over the next several months, and the power loss nagged me as we shopped for fruit at Cuernavaca's colorful market. I felt better when the camper's performance improved on the return to Cocoyoc.

An ancient aqueduct carried water through the hacienda's spacious courtyards, watering the brilliantly flowering shrubbery and trees and maintaining fresh water in the swimming pool. Cocoyoc offered tennis courts, a golf course and stables for the amusement of its guests, most of whom were Mexican. Orioles, doves, kiskadees, and warblers flitted about as we ate sandwiches next to the pool that afternoon. We swam, and I found a silver ring in the pool and gave it to Lynette when no one claimed it. Later, Mike and Krissie rode horses, and Lynette and I played tennis. For dinner, we joined a young Chilean couple, both medical students, and drank plenty of Mexican wine.

I had called the Volkswagen dealer in Mexico City and made an appointment to have the camper serviced, but, upon our arrival, they had no record of our appointment and were too busy to take the car. After I offered him a 50 peso tip, Luis, the service manager, remembered my appointment. We left the camper and visited the Olympic Stadium, University of Mexico, the fabulous Museum of Archeology and rode a train through the zoo at Chapultepec Park. The Museum of Modern Art boasted a wonderful exhibit of Velasco's turn of the century scenes of Mexican villages. In the warm afternoon sun we walked Mexico City's broad, tree lined boulevards emanating from the Zocalo (central plaza) and snacked in a sidewalk cafe.

We returned to pick up the camper late in the day, but they had not been able to fix the problem. The service manager told us to take it and return the next morning. We had driven only a mile in horrible traffic when the engine lost almost all its power. We literally crawled back to the Volkswagen dealer with much of the city honking at us. We found the service manager, and, for a price, he agreed to stay and work on the car. Late that night he declared the problem fixed, so we drove through the mountains back to Cocoyoc. The nighttime views of Mexico City to the east and

Cuernavaca to the west were small consolation for the difficult, twisting drive. Worse, on several occasions, the camper did not seem to be performing properly. When we arrived at Cocoyoc, I looked at my watch and discovered that its battery was dead.

In the morning, we washed and cleaned the camper, packed our things, and began the drive south to Oaxaca through a lush, agricultural valley with sugar cane, corn, and vegetables. Livestock grazed and scarlet tanagers were easy to spot in the trees. We began climbing and twisting through the mountains as the terrain changed dramatically. Thousands of years of wind and water had eroded deep canyons through the sedimentary rock, revealing vivid white, red, and brown layers, and the morning sun brought out the brilliance of these colors. Organ and pitaya cacti comprised the most obvious vegetation. Each poor village had a fine church of which the people were justifiably proud. Many of the towns had basketball courts in their schoolyards, but the children usually were playing soccer rather than basketball. We drove through Izucar de Matamoras where Zapata fought his land revolution in 1910 and Huatatuapan de Leon where we refreshed ourselves with beer and soft drinks.

We averaged no more than 15 miles per hour on the difficult, gravel road to Oaxaca. Often two cars could hardly pass safely. Guard rails were non-existent, even on dangerous curves with precipitous drops from the road's edge. Small white crosses and shrines frequently marked locations where motorists had met their Maker. Lynette talked constantly, telling us sometimes funny little stories, and then reminded us that it helped to have a good sense of humor on this road. Several times we experienced brief, intermittent power-loss problems in the mountains. Ten rough hours after leaving Cocoyoc, we arrived at a small campground on a hill overlooking Oaxaca. My notes say it "had good facilities and many beautiful flowers." In the campground's small gift shop, we bought an Aztec doll for Krissie, a colorful tin elephant Christmas tree ornament for Mike, and some bead necklaces. Then we chatted with a German couple also camping there, drank a bottle of wine, and watched the sun set behind the mountains.

On the way to the large, colorful Saturday Indian market in Oaxaca, Mike recited, "Al mercado, al mercado, comprar un puerco gordo!" To market, to market, to buy a fat pig! We didn't buy any pigs, but we did find some great fruit at Oaxaca's huge market. Vendors sold fresh fruits, vegetables, meats, bread, herbs and just about everything else from cheap plastic goods to expertly hand-woven fabrics, serapes, blankets and hand-crafted pottery. I even found a battery for my watch. Indian women wore colorful serapes and skirts, but seemed wary of tourists and certainly did not want their pictures taken. We ate ham sandwiches and fruit for lunch in front of the Church of Santo Domingo. Much of the ceiling and interior walls were covered with gold, just a hint of the booty taken from the Indians by the

Spanish in the sixteenth century, all, I suppose, in the name of God and King.

They called themselves "cloud people," the Zapotecs and Mixtecs, builders and defenders of Monte Alban, their capital city which lay on the outskirts of modern Oaxaca. These were the only people who successfully repelled the terrible Aztec invaders from the north. We climbed the winding road to the top of the mountain on which rests the ruins of Monte Alban's pyramids, temples and tombs. Tomb Number Seven was discovered unmolested by thieves, and it surrendered untold wealth in gold and silver, suggesting that the riches of the cloud people were beyond imagination. My beard was progressing, and Krissie photograhed me posing in front of a pyramid. From a letter to my parents: "Lynette, Mike and I were fascinated by Monte Alban. Krissie preferred the campground swimming pool." Dark clouds floated down over the sierras, and before long, we experienced the first thunder storm of the trip. The shower didn't last long, and, even while the rain pummeled Monte Alban, the sun shone on the mountainside, and a vivid rainbow appeared next to the dark blue clouds.

On the way back to Oaxaca, we passed a road sign pointing the way to the town of Cinco Senores. Mike began singing, "Cinco senores toman-dan siestas..." Lynette and I looked at each other—the kid's Spanish was coming along! Back at the campground, Krissie made friends with two students from a college in Maine. They had come with their professor to study anthropology and tropical ecology in Merida, a city on the Yucatan Peninsula. Their bus broke down near Oaxaca, and they were waiting for a part to be flown in from Boston. While Lynette prepared supper, Mike and I took a much needed shower. We were lathering up in the community shower room when nine-year-old Mike, who always seemed to be a bit shy in public, loudly and unabashedly, started singing "Home on the Range."

After supper, we took a drive into the foothills of the nearby sierras. We found ourselves in the middle of a large garbage dump where people lived in shacks. The stench was terrible, and, if that wasn't enough to make us want to get out of there, these destitute beings didn't seem very happy having us visit them in our luxurious little camper. The maze of tracks through the dump was confusing, but we somehow found our way out and headed back to the campground. The disparity between the wealthy and poor is often so obvious in Latin America. Even the camping area was surrounded by a wall topped with broken glass bottles embedded in concrete, a precaution commonly used in Mexico to protect property.

We left Oaxaca in the early morning darkness in order to reach the border town of Tapachula that day, hoping to cross into Guatemala early the following morning. Lynette spotted the Southern Cross shining brilliantly just above the horizon. Men carried rifles while walking along the road. They told us they were hunters. We stopped while it was still dark in Santa Maria del Tule to see the Tule tree, with a circumference of 162 feet, which the Mexicans advertise as the world's largest. The enormous tree, a variety of cypress called ahuehuete, gave us no reason to dispute their claim. Dawn came in time for us to see two small crosses along the road marking the spot where Che Estrado Menocal, Mexico's greatest race car driver, and his companion were killed in a Pan-Am road race. The sun rose majestically, and black and white crested caracaras rode the morning thermals as we descended from the mountains to the Pacific coast and entered the state of Chiapas. Agriculture took on a tropical nature—bananas, papayas, mangos, and coconuts. We had been told about the topless women of Chiapas, and sure enough we saw some of them, bathing children and washing clothes in the Tehuantepec River. Mike and Krissie had a welcome break from their school work when we stopped to watch a large snake cross the road. A yellow butterfly flew in the window and landed on Lynette's blouse of the same color. She picked it off and released it unharmed.

Near Tapachula, we asked permission to camp in the parking lot of a hotel, the Camino Real. For the equivalent of a dollar, the manager was happy to accommodate us. We swam in the hotel's pool and chatted with a Tapachulan family on holiday. From my notes: *Children are children, and Mike and Krissie seem to make friends almost everywhere we stop. Here they joined some other kids swimming. Later Mike played soccer with the boys, scoring 2 or 3 goals. We wanted to spend our Mexican pesos before crossing the border, so we ate in the hotel rather than cooking in the camper.*

The Mestizo race, a mixing of Spanish and Indian blood, predominates in Mexico. Well over half the population of Guatemala, on the other hand, is pure Indian. In the mountain areas, almost everyone is Indian. These Mayan descendants wear colorful garments of woven wool. Women braid ribbons in their hair and walk barefoot along the roads carrying jugs of water or baskets of laundry perfectly balanced on their heads and infants slung across their backs. Men also wear skirts and carry heavy loads of wood on their backs.

After spending two hours satisfying customs and immigration requirements, we entered Guatemala and drove off into the rain forest. In the lowlands, homes were constructed of sticks and thatched roofs. Young men worked in fields of coffee, bananas, cotton and sugar cane and carried machetes with unconcealed machismo. The road began its climb to the highlands through El Tapon, a deep canyon carved by the Selegua River, containing numerous waterfalls cascading hundreds of feet. Thick jungle gradually gave way to rolling hills heavily farmed with corn and wheat. Steep hillsides were terraced and crops were planted in strips following the contours of the land, practices which permitted more efficient use of the land

and prevented its erosion. At higher elevations, cooler temperatures prevailed, and homes were constructed of adobe brick and thatched roofs. By the roadside, a pretty little girl and her bashful younger brother sold ornaments and figurines cleverly fashioned from wheat stalks.

Clear and blue Lake Atitlan nestles beautifully in a bowl surrounded by three stately volcanoes. The picturesque village of Panajacel lies lakeside with its white sand beach. Two Volkswagen campers with Canadian license plates were parked on the beach. We set up camp near them and changed for a swim. When we emerged from the cold water, a beautiful girl and her mother were selling fruit from baskets they carried on their heads. The colors and designs of their dresses were different from those we had seen before. Indians from each region, we knew by now, had their unique dress and customs. We bought bananas, pineapples, and another fruit called zapote. After watching the setting sun playfully highlight the volcanoes, we walked into town with our neighbors, four French Canadians from Quebec. Along the way, we talked about their climb of one of the volcanoes and the spectacular views it afforded, and then we visited a lovely colonial church. Shops were open, one of them selling fish and fresh water crabs caught in the lake. The bank was guarded by two young soldiers with machine guns. We tried on some colorful, locally crafted shirts and, then, on our return to the beach, saw a black, opossum-like, creature waddle across the road. A full moon lit the panorama, and the images of three volcanoes reflected perfectly in serene Lake Atitlan.

The next day, we drove south toward Guatemala City via Antigua, a colonial town with historic buildings, cobblestone streets, and a population of ten thousand. At one time, Antigua had been the capital of Guatemala and, with a population of sixty thousand, it had been the cultural center of Central America. The city, over the years, had been devastated several times by earthquakes and now was in the process of having many of its Spanish buildings, arcades, patios and streets restored. Two volcanoes, Fuego and Agua (Fire and Water) towered over the old city. In the evening, residents gathered in Plaza Real and strolled along streets lined with flowering shrubbery. We explored the ruins of the Convent of Santa Clara and visited several churches and the Cathedral. Lynette suggested we return to Antiqua some day to study Spanish.

Guatemala City, the modern, present day capital, perches in the mountains a mile above sea level. Earthquakes had destroyed the city early in the century, and today it boasts little of historical interest. Near the city, we discovered Las Hamacas, a country hotel that permitted camping. Our campsite was surrounded by tropical flowers and shaded by rubber, banana and citrus trees. The owner's horses, geese and macaws kept the children busy for a while, then we swam in their warm pool, fed by geothermal springs, and fished in a nearby stream. Later, we ate an excellent steak dinner in the hotel restaurant, nothing more than a thatched roof hut. That evening I got involved in a rough game of water polo. The owner of the hotel, a burly outgoing man, had asked me to play, and the two of us almost came to blows during the game. He thought I was playing too rough. This surprised me, because I was trying to limit my aggressiveness to match that of the other players and didn't think I was playing any rougher than they were. I was bigger than most of them, however, and had scored several goals, probably, it occurred to me, the real reason for his complaint. Nevertheless, I apologized and tried to smooth things over without much success. Rather than making the situation worse, I quit playing. The incident left me feeling somewhat discomfited, and I was anxious to leave the next morning.

A little boy and an old man who appeared to have leprosy came to us begging while we waited an hour for our papers to be cleared by customs at the El Salvador border crossing. A soldier politely asked them to leave us alone and explained that the old man was the boy's grandfather. We descended from the mountains through the coastal rain forest and the coffee plantations at Santa Tecla. Further south, volcanoes, some of them smoking, dominated the landscape. The El Salvadoran section of the Pan American Highway bisected fincas, or farms, scattered throughout the jungle. Ox carts with solid wooden wheels transported coffee, cotton, bananas and tobacco. Barefoot men and women wore shirts and dresses of solid colors—pink, blue, purple, yellow, red and orange. At Los Chorros, a river cut through a canyon and plunged more than a hundred feet over a cliff. Naked children and their mothers bathed in the pool below the falls. The day was hot, so we joined them. Pink and yellow butterflies flitted above our heads while we swam, and colorful tropical birds called loudly from the surrounding jungle.

A drive to the volcano called El Boqueron left us depressed. We had never before seen such poverty. People lived on top of one another in shelters made of cardboard. Filthy, open sewers ran next to the shacks. Nobody smiled, and many appeared to be starving. The poverty in Mexico had been different—those people had a culture, a style, a history and appeared to be happy. These people seemed miserable, without pride or hope. The long, slow drive to the rim of the volcano took us past unsmiling field hands working coffee plantations. Two young boys waved us to a stop and volunteered to guide us to the volcano's summit. We agreed, and they quickly hopped into the camper. One lad had a grotesquely deformed face and mangled hands. Lynette opened a stick of chewing gum for him and slid it into his mouth. It felt good to see him smile. Clouds obscured our view into the caldera; nevertheless, we gave the boys a few coins and thanked them for being our guides.

After continuing south past La Libertad with its volcanic, black sand beaches and through the capital city of San Salvador, we camped in the village of Apulo on the beach of Lake Llopango, a crater lake in an extinct volcano. We bathed in the lake and ate a late dinner. Several native women grilled fresh fish taken from the lake and made pancakes from batter containing cheese and pork. The food was good, and Mike had a second helping of fish. Later, what promised to be a serene night on a lovely lake turned out differently—dogs barking, roosters crowing and a truckload of drunken boys shouting and singing.

The Pan American Highway crosses only a small appendage of Honduras. Our uneventful drive through the country passed women selling colorful vases from roadside stands and took less than a day.

My notes recount only two items: *His card read, "Gringo Jim Watkins, U.S. Navy, Retired." Gringo Jim's Texaco station, located in Choluteca, Honduras, is a landmark for motorists traveling through Central America. Enough people along the way have extolled the colorful personality of Gringo Jim to build this character into a legend that shouldn't be missed. We stopped to gas up, but, to our disappointment, Gringo Jim had gone fishing.*

A warning sign with the single word "Pelegroso" adorned a barrier across the road. The advertised danger referred to the fact that a section was missing from the bridge. We could see the problem and drove off the road down to the creek. Women doing laundry in the stream promised that the water wasn't very deep, so we plunged ahead and made a smooth crossing. This was our first, and one of the easiest, of our many fords or *wadi* crossings.

All our literature said that we only needed our passports—no visas—to enter Nicaragua. The officious border guard staring me down did not agree. He insisted that we had to drive back to Choluteca, Honduras, for visas. The 40 mile drive each way would have been inconvenient enough, but we had no idea how long the wait to have visas issued would be.

"We are only passing through Nicaragua on our way to Costa Rica. Isn't there an alternative?"

"Perhaps a transit visa, but they are difficult."

A couple of dollars was all the incentive he needed to go through the trouble to issue us transit visas. Critics may decry my complicity in this little charade, but I have a defense. It's simple: throughout the world, border officials have the power to let you pass or keep you out. A family in a Volkswagen camper can do nothing to change the system. This was only the first of many bribes we have been required to offer over the years to drive a camper from one third world country to another.

A line of volcanoes stretches between the Honduran border and Nicaraqua's capital city of Managua. Some of the volcanoes are active, the largest of which, Momotombo, dominates the northwestern shore of Lake

Managua. Dark, handsome Nicaraguans worked the fertile fields containing cotton, corn, sugar, coffee and bananas. Near beautiful, colonial Leon we narrowly avoided being rammed by an out-of-control motorist. I slammed the brakes, Mike slammed his head against the dashboard, and Lynette and Kristen flew off the rear seat onto the floor. Luckily, none of us was hurt— the idiot never even slowed up. A campground near Managua featured a friendly caretaker, monkeys and birds but few other campers. From my notes: "Happily there's a clean bathroom with a shower."

Volcanic ash enriches soil for beautiful farms, but, of course, the flip side to geothermal activity is its fury. Only a year had passed since the center of Managua was leveled by a terrible earthquake. We remembered Roberto Clemente, the great Pittsburgh Pirate outfielder who died in a plane crash bringing supplies to the city. Saddened by the devastation, we nevertheless found Managua on the rebound. Construction crews erected new buildings. Shoppers filed in and out of fully stocked stores. Colorful wares filled the stalls of a vibrant fruit market. People worked. Life went on.

Clouds darkened the sky just as we left Managua and drove along Lake Nicaragua. Volcanic cones rose dramatically from several islands in the lake. Winds whipped up whitecaps. Ages ago, the huge lake was cut off from the ocean by a volcanic eruption. Salt water organisms, including sharks, swordfish and tarpons were trapped and, as the water lost its salinity over many years, adapted to living in the fresh water. The sun returned, and we took in the verdant meadows lining the highway and cattle ranches stretching to the border with Costa Rica. A Brahman bull with a huge shoulder hump and pendulous dewlap posed proudly and fearlessly while I took his picture. He enjoyed his own pasture while hundreds of prospective mates shared another.

We arrived at the Costa Rican border during siesta. While waiting for the offices to reopen, we chatted with a Bolivian and his American wife. He had been living in New York since he was a boy. Now they were returning to his home, driving a large camper. Our paths crossed again in the high Peruvian Andes. I remember thinking the vehicle seemed out of place and wondering how he managed to drive that big rig over the rough terrain we had traversed.

We crossed into Costa Rica, and, wherever sugar, bananas and coffee didn't grow, cattle grazed in lush pastures. People lived in wood frame houses rather than huts and shacks and seemed much more affluent than those in the other countries we came through. We saw signs advertising a trailer park and thought it might be a good place to spend the night. Following the signs along a gravel road produced only an unpainted barn, so we turned around. We were about to drive off when a man walked out from a grove of trees and, in English, asked if he could help us. We explained that we were looking for a place to camp for the night. He welcomed us to stay there, emphasizing that a zoo and a restaurant were both nearby for our enjoyment.

The restaurant was spotlessly new and served delicious ice cream. Mike insisted that any place with such good ice cream had to be worth spending the night, so we drove back across the river to look for a camp site. We found a clearing next to the river, about a quarter mile from the main road. There were no other campers. Flowers bloomed in profusion, and birds sang gaily. We washed our clothes and then ourselves in the cool, clear rapids. I strung a clothes line between two trees to hang our laundry. The span was too long for the sagging wet clothes, so I searched for a pole to prop up the rope. A dead branch hung from a tree on the river bank. I reached for it and pulled mightily. Suddenly there was a low-pitched, roaring sound. It became louder and more intense, and I could only imagine screaming, charging lions. Then I saw them—howler monkeys! Wild and nobly untrainable, their howls may be heard from a mile away. I had invaded their territory when I tried to pull down a piece of their tree world. I released the branch; they soon became relatively calm, and we watched them swinging from tree to tree along and across the river.

Near the old barn was a hill overlooking the campsite. A short walk up the hill led to a small zoo with a good representation of the local fauna. We followed an overgrown path winding through a woods past cages, pens and pits containing tapirs, deer, peccaries, tropical birds, snakes, jaguars, alligators and howler monkeys.

That evening we ate in the restaurant. The menu was continental, the food was good, and the waitress filled in the blanks on our interesting but rather mysterious campground. We were staying on a farm owned by a Swiss couple. They had come to Costa Rica years ago, the husband as manager of the local manufacturing plant of a large European company. He retired recently and took up farming on a small scale. His wife loved animals and developed the zoo as a hobby. They started the restaurant for their two children so they would have a business of their own. We slept well that night, enjoying a place we might have missed had Mike not ordered an ice cream cone.

San Jose offered a number of tourist sights, including (even back in 1974) a McDonald's restaurant where we enjoyed lunch—Big Macs and milkshakes—what a treat! We went to the Panamanian consulate for visas and then drove to the top of Irazu, a live volcano with lava boiling in the crater. On the way, we stopped in the four hundred-year old city of Cartago, once the capital of the country, and visited La Negrita, the patron saint of Costa Rica, enshrined in Our Lady of the Angels Basilica. The little black, doll-like figure has survived earthquakes and thefts with miraculous reappearances. Before leaving Cartago, we stopped for gas, and, while one attendant tried to distract me with the oil dipstick, the other began pumping gas with the equivalent of more than four dollars already registering on the meter. I ordered him to stop pumping, and, when he did not, pulled the nozzle from the tank, dropped it, put the gas cap back on, called him a crook, and then drove off without paying a centimo.

The weather turned bad. Visibility at nearly twelve thousand feet was poor. Occasionally the sun's rays filtered through the mist and danced upon lush farmlands or, where the terrain had not yet been cleared, the thick rain forest. On clear days, both oceans were visible from this road, but that day we could see only the clouds below us. The mountain driving combined with the poor engine performance we were experiencing gave us concern about our gas supply. We conserved fuel during our long descent through the mountains to the town of San Isidro by coasting for twenty-four miles. We gassed up in San Isidro and continued toward Palmar Sur and the border with Panama, descending eleven thousand feet in eighty serpentine miles. The children occupied themselves in the back of the camper playing *Hangman* while the jungle thickened. Colorful birds filled the rain forest canopy, and snakes and iguanas crossed the road. We reached the border town of Paso Canoas and cleared customs smoothly, but only after the officials had thoroughly searched our camper.

A practically impenetrable stretch of rain forest called the Darien Jungle left a two hundred mile gap in the Pan American Highway beginning about thirty miles south of Panama City. Travelers wanting to continue south to Colombia were required to ship their vehicles from Panama City to a port in Colombia, either Cartagena or Buenaventura. A drive across El Puente del Mundo, the bridge spanning the Panama Canal, brought us to the docks where the shipping schedules could be checked out. We chose a ship, the Santa Cruz, scheduled to leave in the next few days for the Pacific port city of Buenaventura. The few passenger cabins on the Santa Cruz were already occupied, so we would have to fly to Bogota, then to Cali, and then hire a cab to Buenaventura in time for the Santa Cruz's arrival. We contracted with a shipping agent who assigned a man to guide us through the necessary paperwork. Riccardo had learned English working in the Officers' Mess of the Canal Zone. He drove with us, hand carrying and capably processing our papers through countless rubber stamp wielding officials at the Port Authority, Panama Customs, Colombian Consulate, Panamanian Ministry of Finance and other offices whose functions I never did comprehend. In those days, the Canal Zone was still administered by the United States, an arrangement that had become increasingly controversial among Panamanians. Riccardo, critical of his countrymen who thought Panama should administer the canal, wondered why anyone would consider delivering a shipping channel of such worldwide importance into the hands of "unpredictable radicals."

Later we toured modern Panama City, visited the ruins of Old Panama (destroyed three hundred years ago by the pirate, Henry Morgan), and bought some molas at a cultural center of the San Blas Indians. We camped in a parking area of La Siesta Hotel where we were offered the privileges of swimming in their pool and gambling in their casino. After a refreshing swim, we all watched the action in the casino with our noses pressed against the window because children were not permitted inside. Anyway, our strict budget contained no accounts for gambling. Back at the camper, we ate soup and liverwurst sandwiches for supper. In my opinion, a liverwurst sandwich without mustard and raw onions is not worthy of the name, so I included plenty of both in my sandwich. That evening, when mosquitoes violently attacked Lynette and the children but not me, we concluded that the awful, intense smell of onions emanating from every pore of my body created a wall of protection that the little buggers had no interest in penetrating.

In the morning, we dropped the camper at Pier 18 where it was loaded onto the *Santa Cruz*, watched a few boats go through the Miras Flores Locks, and then caught a cab for the airport. The driver gave us the name of his sister's husband in Bogota, and added, "He is a very successful hombre."

"What is his business?" I asked.

"Money."

"Money?"

"Yes, you must call him. He will assure you the very best rate for your American dollars."

Quite sure I had no interest in the Colombian black market, I forewent additional questions on the subject.

At the airport we boarded a Braniff jet with a colorful paint job designed by Alexander Calder. The children thought it was a "cool plane," and Lynette told them that riding in a jet designed by Picasso would have been "cooler." In Bogota, we registered at our budget hotel, the Presidente, and set off to see the city. Charming colonial buildings were scattered among modern skyscrapers. Vintage automobiles—DeSotos, Studebakers, Packards, and Kaisers filled the streets. Mike called our attention to a statue of George Washington in the center of a large plaza. Back at the hotel, Lynette ordered a club sandwich from room service. We all laughed hysterically while I photographed her trying to bite into this king-sized snack that included seven slices of bread with layers of ham, cheese, bacon, egg, turkey and steak.

We had to kill a few days until the camper arrived in Buenaventura, and Bogota turned out to be a splendid place to do so. Along the narrow colonial streets we felt the ubiquitous presence of Simon Bolivar: in the Plaza Bolivar where the National Cathedral is located, around the corner where his mistress lived, and down the *cuadro* where the revolution was launched. We visited national museums of art, history and archeology (where the mummies fascinated the children) as well as the Museo del Oro with its wonderful pre-Columbian collection of intricately designed gold figures. Lynette bought a small emerald ring which, back at the hotel, led to a discussion of values when the children questioned the inconsistency of our being so frugal with common everyday trip expenses like food and gasoline and so extravagant with the purchase of an emerald ring.

I don't remember how dinner that evening tracked with our discussion of values, but we ate at the Gran Vatel, an elegant mansion that had been the home of former Colombian President Alfonso Lopez. Local customs dictated that fashionable diners show up at fine restaurants between nine and ten o'clock. Having hungry young children dictated otherwise, and we arrived shortly after seven. Hardly anyone was there, so we had the formally dressed *maitre d'hotel*, the head waiter and a table waiter virtually to ourselves. They couldn't do enough for us, responding to our every request, "Con mucho gusto!" After dinner, the *maitre d'* took us on a tour of the mansion. A photo of Vice President Hubert Humphrey was hanging in one room. I started to explain that we too were from Minnesota when, in mid-sentence, he excused himself and walked away. It was now nine o'clock and apparently someone important had come into the restaurant. We never saw him again. Later, in front of the restaurant, I hailed a cab while Lynette was explaining the meaning of "fickle" to the children.

From Bogota we flew to Cali. Ours was the only airplane parked at the large, new, open air concrete airport. A cab took us to a cheap hotel, the Arici, where I had made reservations. You can imagine Lynette's and the children's accusations regarding my parsimoniousness when we learned that only cold water ran in this throwback to the 1930s with its art deco rounded corners and chrome accents. Luckily the hotel had a swimming pool to amuse them while I left to arrange for liability insurance on the camper. Two insurance companies turned me down, claiming they didn't handle insurance on foreign vehicles. Then I met a young American, a recent graduate from Gettysburg College who had married a Colombian woman and had come to Cali to live. With a little effort, he persuaded his company to issue us insurance. We chatted over coffee about his life as an expatriot, and then he drove me back to the hotel with an emphatic warning to be careful of thieves in Colombia. Early the next morning we hired a cab for the three hour drive to Buenaventura. The route descended through the mountains into the dense tropical rain forest where people of African ancestry wearing little or no clothing lived in thatched stick huts on stilts.

We arrived in the hot, humid and dirty port city late in the morning in time to see the *Santa Cruz* docking. Our intent was to get our camper and get out of town. The rude manager of the shipping agency offered us little help, merely telling us to wait at the dock until the camper was unloaded and then drive through customs. The dock area bustled with fork lifts speeding in every direction and cranes busily unloading cargo. Other people also waited for their vehicles including a retired U.S. Air Force couple traveling in a Winnebago motor home, a urologist, Dr. Graham (who coincidentally was from Lynette's home town of Winnetka), traveling with his son in a Land Rover, a Peruvian couple, a Morman missionary on his way to Ecuador, an English couple with an infant, and several Canadians. A man approached and tried to persuade me to give him my passport and other documents. He wanted to expedite our paperwork, but I hesitated to turn things over to someone I didn't know. The Peruvian standing nearby explained that the man was in a hurry to get our paperwork started because it was Saturday, and, at noon, everyone stopped working for the weekend. It was now eleven o'clock. They had my attention, and I eagerly gave the man my papers and followed him running from office to office.

With our vehicles unloaded and our papers in order, we only needed to clear customs when, at 11:45, the dock manager left his office. That seemed to be a signal to the workers who all quit working and walked behind him toward the exit gate. The man with our papers told the dock manager it was important to the people waiting for their vehicles to clear customs that day. The dock manager insisted he had no intention of paying anyone overtime. Both the captain and purser of the *Santa Cruz* intervened on our behalf but to no avail. The authorities impounded our camper and the other vehicles in the enclosed area for the weekend. We were permitted to leave the area, but not with our cars.

Reluctantly accepting our fate, we spent the afternoon re-packing and cleaning the camper. Ed Brazil, the retired Air Force sergeant major, walked over and invited us to have supper with him and his wife, Joy, in their large, comfortable rig. They explained that the Winnebago was their home, and, after traveling around North America and Europe in it, they intended to see South America. After supper the six of us chatted until there was a knock at the door. It was the purser from the *Santa Cruz*. He wore a big smile and carried a carton of wine for us and soft drinks for the children. Fried was a Swede with a great sense of humor and a wealth of sea tales, all of which he G-edited for the children. Our party broke up late; we could still hear the throbbing beat of African music blaring from shacks outside the compound, but sleep did not come easily anyway that steamy, hot night in the yard of the Port Authority.

After breakfast, we walked to the *Santa Cruz* with the Brazils. The night before, Fried had invited the children to come aboard for a tour of the ship before it left for Guayaquil. The crew laughed and joked with Krissie and Mike even as they were preparing for the ship's departure. The steward, a likeable Australian, presented the Brazils and us with boxes full of groceries for the weekend. Later, we stood on the pier and waved as the *Santa Cruz* eased away from its dock without the assistance of the tugboats standing by. Lynette and I then washed the camper while Ed and Mike filled the

Brazils rig with fresh water and Joy and Krissie played cards and painted each other's toenails.

Security was non-existent at the Port Authority. A large pipe ran from the docks through the compound and into the city, passing through the compound's fence behind a fire station. Where the pipe passed through the fence, barbed wire had been wrapped around the opening. Someone with a pair of wirecutters had eliminated that obstacle long ago, and people filed in and out of the compound, day and night, merely by walking on the pipe. We had been warned to be alert for thieves. Boys loitered around the vehicles. They were curious, and we tried to be friendly, but we suspected they were waiting for us to turn our backs. I laid my glasses on the edge of our icebox and looked the other way for a moment. When I turned back, they were gone. One boy was especially friendly. He introduced us to his mother and nine siblings. He said he had two fathers, one here and one in the United States who would one day send for him. To prepare for this he tried to learn English from anyone who would take the time to talk with him. He said that there were often men who came in on the boats and would help him with his English. I really liked the little guy and hoped he wasn't the one who had taken my glasses.

Joy and Lynette wanted to walk to the nearby market for some fruit. Ed and the children remained behind to guard the vehicles while I accompanied the women into town. We walked down streets strewn with garbage. Buildings stood crumbling, boats rested partially submerged in mudflats, and rusted machinery lay uselessly in unexplainable locations. Pounding African music throbbed from several directions and poor shoeless people with big, calloused feet glared at us in our conspicuousness. Occasionally laughter rang out above the hot music. Near the market, boys stood in their dugout canoes with one foot on the gunwale and paddled around the harbor. We bought papayas and plantanos (a rubbery fruit that looked like a banana but had to be cooked to be eaten), and wonderful, sweet pineapples with cores so tender they too could be eaten.

Night approached, and the rats became bold, venturing increasingly closer to the campers, hoping, I suppose, to find crumbs we dropped during the day. Mike and I amused ourselves for an hour before bedtime throwing stones at them each time they crept out of the shadows.

During the night Lynette wakened me by poking her elbow in my ribs. She said a man had been peeking in the window of the camper and left when he saw she had spotted him. I wasn't too concerned—Lynette's imagination goes into overdrive at night, especially when we're camping. I went back to sleep, and soon she poked me again and said she could see him sneaking back. This time I got a good look at him and the brown uniform he wore. I put my shoes on and jumped out of the camper, but he was gone. I ran around the corner of the compound to the fire station and told the men on duty there about the prowler. They brought large flashlights and helped me look for the man. When we returned, a guard in a brown uniform was sitting in front of the fire station. I knew he was the same man and accused him accordingly. He, of course, denied it. The firemen seemed to believe me and said they would keep their eye on him. I went back to sleep, but Lynette remained awake the rest of the night.

Clearing customs Monday morning went quickly. Dr. Graham said he would call Lynette's parents when he returned to Winnetka and tell them we were doing well. Then we went back to the compound to find the Brazils.

"When are you coming back to the States, Ed?" I inquired.

"When we get tired of South America. Maybe in a year or so."

"Will you write or look us up?"

"Maybe we should drive out to Minnesota. Never been there."

"That would be great! We have an extra bedroom and would be delighted to have you."

"Never mind the extra bedroom. Do you have a flat driveway?"

We all laughed and said goodbye.

Lynette strummed her ukulele, and our spirits soared as the camper climbed through the rain forest and we sang our way back toward Cali. We drove through Cali and continued south past the prosperous farms and ranches of the fertile Cauca valley, arriving late in the afternoon in the lovely colonial city of Popoyan. Lynette guided us on an enjoyable walking tour of the old town; we picked up groceries along the way, and then camped in the courtyard of an old convent that had been converted to a hotel. That evening the hotel's night guard informed us that the road south between Popoyan and Pasto had been closed for the past week, having been wiped out by a "derrumba." Our Spanish dictionary enlightened us: a landslide had closed the road. He added that the slide had been mostly cleared, and, fortunately, the road was scheduled to reopen tomorrow.

Five miles south of Popoyan the paved road ended. We drove a few more miles on a very rough, muddy road until two soldiers with rifles stopped us. Traffic was proceeding one lane at a time. After a 45 minute wait, we carefully descended into the area where the landslide had covered the road. Our tires spun their way through mud and rocks, and the car slid in and out of deep ruts carved by heavy trucks. Somehow the little camper churned through even the most difficult areas, and we emerged on solid gravel to the cheering of dozens of men who worked along the road to clear it.

We climbed further into the mountains, and the road turned from mud to dust. Several times the camper lost power. On one especially steep pitch, it lost power completely—the car would not proceed, even though the motor was running. And then the motor died. I had no idea what to do, and the owner's manual provided little help. The car had been performing fairly well until we began climbing. With some effort pushing and pulling, we turned the vehicle around. Coasting downhill, I was able to start the engine. After a mile, the motor seemed to be running well, so I turned around and tried driving up hill again, making it back to about the same place where we stalled before, and then lost power. Before the motor died, I turned around and ran the car down the hill as fast as I could safely go, operating on some naive theory that I would "blow out" the dirt or whatever else was sapping the power. I turned around again and this time progressed several hundred yards beyond our previous best mark before the power gave out. So I decided to turn around again and run downhill several miles and really "blow out" the engine, whatever that meant. But here there was little room to turn around. We had no power, so whatever way we coasted backwards, we had to get far enough around on the first swing to be able to push the car forward downhill. To the right of the road was a precipitous cliff; to the left rose a high bank. I opted for the bank. Unfortunately there wasn't enough clearance, and the camper became stuck with its rear bumber embedded in the bank.

It started to rain. I glanced at my watch—1:15 p.m. Soon I would have to think about hitching a ride to find a safe place for the family to spend the night. Then I heard a whine that became increasingly louder as a truck climbed up the hill toward us. I flagged down the driver and asked how far it was to where the road went downhill instead of up. He said about 10 minutes and agreed to pull us to the top. Incredibly, our nylon washline held while the truck jerked and the rope strained with each gear shift he made. At the top, the trucker told us to go ahead so he could pull us again if we stalled. The gravel road to Pasto was long and winding, but mostly downhill, and the motor performed much better. We thanked the trucker profusely, continued on a paved road from Pasto and spent the night camped in the parking lot of a hotel next to the border with Ecuador.

Lynette and the children had been upbeat during the day's trials, encouraging the car and me at each hill and cheering each time we crested the top. All the while we admired the Colombian scenery—picturesque fertile valleys with terraced crops flanked by high mountains with breathtaking canyons. Handsome, industrious Indians worked the fields with their oxen and crude tools and lived in homes with mud walls and tiled roofs. We went to sleep that night having made the decision to try to reach Quito the next day and hoping that city's Volkswagen service department would be up to solving our motor problems.

We cleared customs at Tulcan in about an hour, bought groceries including bread and smoked cheese, and set out for the next town, Ibarra, on a very narrow road with spectacular views. Driving was exciting but enervating. Usually two cars could not pass one another, and we tooted our horn as we approached each curve. Precipitous cliffs fell from the road's guardrail-less edge. Often large chunks of the road had broken away and dropped into the canyons below. The terrain turned to desert, and one interesting town, Chota, was populated only by black descendants of former slaves. On the dusty climb out of the desert, the camper again lost power and crept slowly, barely making the top of a hill.

The Indian market at Otovalo provided a welcome respite from the tedious driving. Men dressed in white pants and bright red and blue panchos and women wearing embroidered blouses, skirts and shawls sold their wares including panchos, shawls and colorfully woven blankets. We continued south on the Ecuadorian altiplano. Near Calderon, more than two miles above sea level, we crossed the equator, and Mike snapped a picture of Lynette standing in the northern hemisphere and me in the southern, kissing across the imaginary line. With the camper coughing and gasping, we somehow made it to Quito that afternoon, drove directly to the VW dealer and made an appointment to bring the car in the next morning. Then we went to a travel agent and signed on for a trip to the Galapagos Islands. We had planned on driving from Quito to Guayaquil and then flying to the Galapagos, but getting the camper running properly had suddenly moved to the top of our priority list. Conveniently, the VW service manager had agreed to an arrangement where, after fixing the engine problems, they would store the camper until we returned from our tour of the Galapagos.

The travel agent recommended the parking area of the Quito Intercontinental Hotel for camping. We made arrangements with the hotel manager and found a large motor home already occupying one of the sites. The Bardwicks, professors on sabbatical from the University of Michigan who were spending the year touring Latin America with their three children, greeted us and invited us to their camper for cocktails. In seven months they had progressed only as far as Ecuador, traveling at a far more leisurely pace than ours. The family used Quito as their center of operations while they explored Ecuador, especially enjoying their visits to Indian markets. We chatted about Indians, business, education and children, getting to know one another, and then threw some steaks on the grill.

John Bardwick's field was physics, Judy's psychology. After dinner, John excused himself to make a call to the States. He wanted to check on the status of an idea he had been trying to sell to General Motors for the past year, a concept that would save the energy that was lost in the form of heat when a car braked and then use it to propel the car, thereby reducing fuel consumption. We never learned the upshot of his inventiveness.

Judy's demeanor differed from my picture of a contemplative psychologist sitting in silence while her patients rambled on. Rather than leaning back pensively, she sat on the edge of her chair, jumping into the conversation at every opportunity. I asked her, "Judy, why are you here? I mean, what great book or new theory of behavior will come out of this sabbatical?"

"Nothing."

"Nothing? Don't you feel like you have to be productive, take some erudite discovery back to Ann Arbor?"

"No, not really. I do feel a little guilty about it, but I'm just having a good time." I poured us all another glass of wine.

More than six hundred years ago, Quito in the north and Cusco in the south were the twin capitals of the Inca empire. Quito lies at an elevation of 9,000 feet, nestled among snow-capped mountains more than twice that high. We walked the old streets lined with charming colonial buildings, visiting the monastery and convent of San Francisco, a small zoo with monkeys, llamas, macaws and tortoises and Calle Morales, a quaint arcade with government sponsored Ecuadorian craft shops. Krissie bought an Indian doll, and Lynette bought handmade dresses for Krissie and her best friend, Julie. Mike bought a Panama hat, and he and I each bought a hand woven rug and carnations for Krissie and Lynette. Late that afternoon, we dropped the camper off at the VW dealer and checked into the Savoy Hotel near the airport. Our Galapagos flight left at 6:30 the next morning, so we had a light dinner of omelette and beer and went to bed early.

You know you're flying when you are in a DC-6. The airplane took off to the south, flying low and slow as it lifted out of the snug valley in which Quito lay. Soon the pilot banked the plane and began a sharp right turn to the west. We pressed our noses to the cabin windows as he guided the DC-6 through a narrow gap between two volcanoes whose rugged, snow-capped peaks rose far higher than our altitude. Spectacular glaciers and crevasses stretched out below and seemed only at an arm's length from us. Then, astonishingly, the two mountains abruptly turned green as they sloped far below to the west, revealing the tropical rain forest that reached to the coast.

Variously known as the Islas Encantadas, the Archipelago de Colon, and the Darwin Islands, the Galapagos lie six hundred miles off the coast of Ecuador. A representative from the tour company met us in the airport lobby of steamy, coastal Guayaquil where we boarded another plane for the three hour flight over the Pacific Ocean. We landed and climbed aboard open air busses that transported us to our ship. We found our cabins, ate a buffet lunch and, within an hour of landing, steamed off to the small island of Daphne Chica. The Galapagos began immediately to live up to their reputation: nearing the island we identified two species of frigate birds, red-billed tropic birds, Audubon's shearwaters, swallow-tailed gulls and oyster catchers.

The Galapagos, relatively young geologically, are of volcanic origin. They have not existed long enough for a complete complement of plants and animals to arrive by natural means, so there is limited competition among species. The conditions are perfect for rapid evolution to take place. For example, the islands support fourteen species of finches that have evolved from a common ancestor. Each species developed specialties enabling it to go after different sources of food that until then went unexploited. One finch has a thick beak for cracking seeds; another a thin beak for probing lava pores for algae; and another, the woodpecker finch, has developed the ability to grasp twigs and cactus spines in its beak to pry ants and grubs from decaying logs. The ecological balance in the islands is extremely delicate. If true woodpeckers arrived on the islands, they probably would drive the less efficient woodpecker finch to extinction.

On North Seymour Island, swallow-tailed gulls incubated their eggs on precarious cliff-side nests. As we walked a trail, a mockingbird landed on Krissie's shoulder. One of four species evolving from a common ancestor, this specimen had a short, stubby beak. Later we saw the Hood Island mockingbird with its long beak useful for penetrating and sucking the fluids out of booby eggs. North Seymour does not have turtles. The prickly pear cactus on this island grows close to the ground and sports stiff spines, protecting the plant's flesh from iguanas. On islands with large turtles, prickly pear cactus grows more tree-like. Since the pads of these plants are not accessible to iguanas, the spines are soft.

On a rock along the trail, two six inch lava lizards lined up sideways to each other (they think they look bigger that way) and began doing pushups, a territorial warning. Soon we saw marine iguanas, relatively small and black on North Seymour, for the first time. Near the water's edge, red Sally Lightfoot crabs scampered over the black lava rocks. Nature protects some species with camouflage. Not so this crab whose only protection is its bright red color. Rather than hiding the crab, red warns potential enemies this animal could be dangerous. The ship's biologist instructed us to remain on the trails—for good reason. What appeared to be three or four sticks haphazardly lying on the ground might just as well be the nest of a blue-footed booby.

On the west side of the island, winds drove the surf hard against the cliffs. Many sea lions rode the surf while others sunned on lava rocks. Mothers dutifully nursed their young. One dominant bull rules a sea lion colony. All females and young are members of his family. When young males become sexually mature, the bull evicts them. He remains king until one of the other bulls wanders over from a nearby bachelor colony and successfully challenges him. Great demands are made on a bull in charge of a harem. He must service the females sexually and guard them from would-be suitors. He cannot remain at his physical peak very long, and his reign usually lasts no more than a few hours to a month.

Our trail led into a nesting colony of magnificent frigate birds. Males are black with red throats, females black with white breasts. During mating season, as a courtship display, the male blows up his red throat patch to a large balloon-like pouch. These birds often rely on other species to do their fishing for them. We watched one female chase a blue-footed booby around the sky until it dropped its catch. The frigate bird swooped down, caught the falling fish in mid-air and flew back to her nest.

Small boats took us from North Seymour to the nearby small sand island of Loberia. We walked around and through a sea lion colony, observing the way of life. Since our box lunches did not contain fish, the animals showed no interest in us while we ate on the beach. However, their curiosity eventually got the better of them, I suppose, when they joined us for a swim. Initially we were alarmed seeing those large, sleek bodies darting by under the water. After we became convinced they meant no harm, we relaxed, paddled around and enjoyed the show.

During the day I noticed a woman sketching the animals. She seemed to be traveling alone, so at the captain's cocktail party that evening, I asked her to join us for dinner. Elaine Barr's husband had worked with the State Department, and they had lived and traveled over much of the world. Now recently widowed, she still enjoyed traveling, and, while we took photographs to remember our experiences, she sketched.

During the night, the ship sailed nearly one hundred miles to Hood Island. Motorboats dropped us near the shore, and then we waded onto the beach among a colony of fur seals. Conical-billed ground finches foraged for seeds in the sand. Long-beaked Hood Island mockingbirds waited for blue-footed boobies to leave their nests unguarded. Hood is the only island where mockingbirds have evolved the ability to eat eggs, and here, predictably, boobies have learned to scare the mockingbirds away from their nests. On other islands, where mockingbirds have not evolved long, pointed, egg-sucking beaks, boobies allow mockingbirds to walk up to and even perch on their nests. On Hood, iguanas and lava lizards grow bigger than on other islands. Male marine iguanas paraded fearlessly across our trail, displaying their bright red and green breeding coloration. Like many other animals on the Galapagos, these iguanas have virtually no enemies (their taste apparently not appealing to hawks, sharks and other natural predators), which accounts for their lack of inhibitions.

Waved albatrosses nest only every other year and nowhere else in the world but on Hood Island. The birds spend their life away from the nest at sea, roaming as far as the Indian Ocean. Luckily, three of them still remained from the past nesting season. We walked within a few feet of them. Magnificent gliders with eight-foot wingspans, these birds are virtually helpless while on land where they laboriously stumble about. Unable to run fast enough to launch themselves into flight, they locate their nests near cliffs from which they can fall into an effortless glide. If cats or other predators gained a foothold on Hood Island as they have elsewhere in the archipelago, this wonderful large bird, defenseless on land, would most likely become an extinct species.

Blue-footed and masked boobies also nest on Hood Island. The larger, heavier masked boobies, like the albatrosses, are almost helpless on land. They, too, nest near cliffs in order to use the wind to assist them in take-off. Masked boobies usually lay two eggs, but the first chick hatched kills the second chick when it hatches. We wondered if, perhaps one day, nature will relieve this species of the burden of laying a second egg not useful to its procreation.

Blue-footed boobies are marvelous fishermen. These sharp-eyed seabirds glide fifty to one hundred feet above the water, to forage for fish far below. From the shore we watched them diving. A gliding bird would suddenly tip its head forward, fold its wings, and plunge like a bullet into water that, at times, was only two feet deep. The bird would disappear for a moment and then reappear at the surface, shaking off water and often holding a fish in its beak. One of the ship's biologists revealed the secret of these incredible gymnastics: upon entering the water, the bird arches its tail and reverses direction, catching the fish on its return to the water's surface.

On Floreana Island we identified white-cheeked pintails, flamingos, a whimbrel and more finches. Along the rocky coast a blow hole shot a jet spray of water fifty feet into the air. We motored off shore to Devil's Crown, a sunken volcano with only about fifty feet of the rim rising above the water. Two young great blue herons sat on a nest in a cactus plant growing on the rim while lovely red-billed tropic birds gracefully sailed above the crater, trailing their long white tail plumage. We snorkeled in the sunken crater and spotted starfish, sea urchins, anemones, sea cucumbers, and countless colorful fish among the coral. Sea lions joined the party, darting in and out among the divers.

Post Office Bay, on the other side of Floreana, retained a tradition dating back to the nineteenth century. Near the beach lay several gaily painted barrels. For many years sailors dropped letters in a barrel and collected any other letters addressed to ports of call on their schedule. The system worked well enough that people still used it. A woman from our ship dropped a letter in one of the barrels. Lynette had been watching her, thinking she knew her from somewhere. It turned out that she had had the same feeling. Over that barrel, Lynette and Angie remembered almost simultaneously they had been high school classmates. Returning to the ship, our guide explained the derivation of the Islas Encantadas, the enchanted or bewitched islands. A Spanish colonial ship became embroiled in the churning waters produced by the confluence of the Humboldt and El Nino currents. The ship's sailors were confused and thought the islands themselves were moving. The captain also was perplexed and referred to the "Islas Encantadas" in the ship's log.

During the night, our ship sailed to James Island. On the beach the next morning, ghost crabs disappeared before our eyes. Camouflaged to blend with the sand, you see their shadows before seeing the crabs. They quickly dig into the sand, and then their shadows disappear. A salt water lagoon lay only a few yards inland from the beach. Flamingos and black-necked stilts foraged in the shallows. A Galapagos hawk soared overhead, and we walked within several feet of a Galapagos warbler, a vegetarian tree-finch, and a vermillion flycatcher. The hawk landed on driftwood about a hundred yards down the beach. I walked slowly toward it with my camera. Incredibly, I approached within three feet of the bird, snapped several pictures, and walked away while the hawk remained perched on the driftwood.

Rain seldom falls on the Galapagos, and vegetation has evolved interesting strategies to deal with these climatic conditions. Some plants conserve water by turning the edges of their leaves to the sun and allowing only the edges to follow the sun across the sky, thereby minimizing moisture lost to evaporation. Other plants grow small hairs on their leaves and stems. The fuzz shades the plant, and catches and retains some of the evaporating water.

Along the rugged coast, receding tides leave tidal pools in hollows and depressions of the lava rocks. Close inspection of these pools reveals a teeming ecological niche. In about a half hour's search, we identified sea urchins, sponges, mollusks, octopuses, two species of starfish, sea slugs, hermit crabs and anemones. Life may be as brief as the changing tides if animals are trapped in small pools that dry in the sun before the sea returns.

In the case of the Galapagos praying mantis, nature evolved a bizarre relationship between the sexes. The act of mating, while insuring the survival of the species, brings to an abrupt end the life of one of the progenitors. Even as the male jumps the female and begins copulating, she turns around and begins chewing off his head, a curious expression of appreciation for his efforts. We found several praying mantises along an inland trail. One of the biologists turned over a rock, deftly caught a scorpion, showed us its poison gland and stabber, and explained how it drops its tail over its head, waiting for prey. Scorpions in turn are prey to lava lizards which are able to catch and eat them with impunity.

Years ago Galapagos ground doves were so trusting they could easily be caught by hand. Pirates and whalers, sometimes for food but often for fun, killed them by the thousands. The doves we saw were more wary of humans, fluttering away if we approached too close. Goat and burro droppings covered James Island, betraying even greater ecological catastrophies inflicted on these islands by humans. The introduction of new species, in every case, became a problem when the animals escaped and became established in the wild. Feral goats, pigs, dogs, cats and rats have all hurt the delicate ecological balance of the islands. Probably the greatest harm had been done by goats. While we were studying the ecology of the islands,

I must say the captain of the ship made his small contribution to the solution of this problem. He and several crew members took their rifles into the island's interior, and periodically we heard shots echoing through the hills. For the remainder of the trip, "cabrito" appeared as an addition to lunch and dinner menus.

After lunch, we swam and snorkeled in a beautiful grotto. A yellow-crowned night-heron watched us from its perch atop a natural bridge crossing the grotto. Marine iguanas sunned themselves on black lava rocks. Soon playful fur seals joined our swimming party. Fortunately they were now protected and were making a comeback from the dangerously low numbers they had been hunted to by sealers who prized their fur.

English pirates had frequented Buccaneer Cove on James Island's west side for turtles and fresh water, which was a scarcity on the islands. The giant turtles, some weighing more than four hundred pounds, have the ability to live for a year without food or water. Pirates often loaded one thousand or more at a time in their holds as a supply of fresh meat. Only two or three hundred of the animals now remained on the island. We didn't see any turtles on James, but we did see the high, tree-like prickly pear cactus, which bore evidence that the turtles once roamed the island in great numbers.

We sailed out of the cove. Ruddy terns flew above, and feral goats walked expertly along cliff ledges. Several hammerhead sharks swam near the island, and soon dolphins raced beside us, eventually confidently crisscrossing the bow of the speeding ship. Storm petrels winged their way out to sea. In the distance, we saw the largest island of the archipelago, Isabella, and, beyond, the large volcano on Ferdinana which had erupted as recently as the previous December.

After enjoying a good breakfast of scrambled eggs and bacon, we visited the Charles Darwin Research Station on Santa Cruz Island. Before humans came to the islands, fifteen different races of turtles thrived. Now six of those races were extinct or technically extinct (one race still had one male specimen living). The remaining saddleback turtles from Hood Island (thirteen females and one male) had been brought to the research station for a captive breeding program. Forty-three offspring from these captives were now being raised safely in the Santa Cruz rearing pens. Offspring of turtles from other islands with population problems also were being reared in research station pens. Estimates of one-time turtle populations on the islands range as high as ten million; now probably no more than ten thousand lived. Many species of Galapagos plant and animal life are found nowhere else. The director of the research station told us that their efforts concentrated on local animals which were endangered or in critical situations—hawks, flamingos, penguins (Galapagos penguins spend their lives within a few miles of the equator), flightless cormorants, fur seals, sea lions

41

and tortoises.

Among the islands of the Galapagos, Santa Cruz has the only significant human population. We walked from the research station through the small, sleepy town of Santa Cruz to nearby Angermeyer Point. Here Karl Angermeyer lived with his wife and an assortment of tame iguanas. We arrived just in time to watch Karl call the lizards to their lunch of shrimp and rice. Fifty yards farther down the point lived Karl's brother, Gus, in a cave. His cavernous utopia was complete with candles, incense and taped Ecuadorian folk music. Guests could take their seating choice on a reed mat or a whale vertabra. A bed made of sealskin and driftwood was the only other furniture to be seen. Cobwebs and quotes from Kahlil Gibran's *The Prophet* adorned the walls. Skeletons of sharks, turtles, sloths and sea lions were suspended from the ceiling. I was admiring a fascinating shell collection when I heard Gus, in German, introduce himself to a man.

"I speak only English," replied the man.

"I am sorry," apologized Gus in English. "When will the time come when all men speak the same language?"

"Never," answered the American. "At least not in our lifetime."

"Oh, but it will, my friend," corrected Gus. "One day we will all speak the language of the heart!"

The island of South Plaza was the ship's final stop. We climbed to the cliffs on the south side of the island. Swallow-tailed gulls, Audubon's shearwaters, masked boobies and red-billed tropic birds passed by as if in review. South Plaza was one of the most heavily visited islands, and the sea lions, consequently, had become quite irritable. We walked gingerly around the colony, and were especially wary of the bachelor bulls. Later, waiting for the motor launch that would take us back to the ship, I sat on a rock. A curious land iguana crawled between my outstretched legs, stopped and stared up at me. I reached for my camera, the iguana seemed to smile, and I snapped one of my favorite photos.

On the ship that evening, we enjoyed our last Islas Encantada dinner. Eleven people sat at our table. Much to his wife's dismay, one man, Fred, had been teaching Mike and Krissie to wiggle their ears. (Fred made a lasting impression on the children. Back home, Mike named his pet iguana Fred, and, years later, I've seen both Krissie and Mike attempting to pass along their ear-wiggling skills to our grandchildren.) On the ship biologist's quiz, ten-year-old Mike scored higher than most of the adults. He promptly announced he wanted to study biology and some day return to the Galapagos as a guide. (Today Mike has a biology degree, but he has not yet returned to the Galapagos.) Lynette and Angie Levinstein made plans to get together at their next New Trier High School reunion. And Elaine Barr presented us with sketches of Krissie and Mike she had secretly drawn the past few days.

Back in Quito, we picked up our camper and drove to a restaurant specializing in typically Ecuadorian dishes. Along the way, to our chagrin, the car began backfiring. After dinner, we drove back to the VW dealer and awakened the guard. From my notes: *Watchdogs bark like hell as I blow my horn. He comes out to open gate and shows me buzzer by gate I could have pushed to awaken him.* We camped in their parking lot to make sure we were first in line when they opened in the morning. Near noon the car was returned to us, allegedly fixed. Indeed, it did seem to be performing better as we drove off. In the meantime, I had developed a case of hiccups, or "hippos" as they were called in Ecuador. I tried all the remedies anyone could think of—holding my breath, eating a teaspoon of sugar, drinking water—to no avail. Whether it was stress from the car or whatever, I had the hippos on and off, mostly on, for the next three days.

The road led south through Ecuador's central highlands, often at elevations over eleven thousand feet. Hardy Indian farmers wearing bright red panchos lived in haystack-like houses in this starkly beautiful high country where the people saw few tourists and appeared quite shy. We stopped for lunch and watched as a curious little girl wearing a colorful red sweater and striped skirt sidled closer to the camper. When I smiled and walked a few steps toward her, she turned and scampered down the hill away from the road. We sat and waited. In a few minutes she peeked over a stone wall on the roadside. Then she ventured a bit closer, put a finger in her mouth and smiled, and I snapped a picture of the pretty little highlander.

Latacunga nestles in the shadow of snow covered Mount Cotopaxi, the world's highest active volcano. We bought fruit and vegetables at the nearby primitive Indian market in Sasquisili and then descended into the rain forests of the coastal lowlands, looking for a place to camp for the night. The area was sparsely populated, so, seeing a small sign with the words "Finca San Oswaldo," we pulled into the driveway. Finca means farm, and we later learned this farm belonged to Oswaldo Velasco. We asked Senior Velasco permission to park in his driveway for the night, and he cheerfully accommodated us. He lived there with his wife and their four friendly and curious children. The Velascos owned thirty hectares (about seventy-five acres) of land on which they ran thirty head of cattle and some chickens and grew coffee, bananas and sugar cane. We cooked dinner in the camper and, later, Senior Velasco walked through a hard rain, knocked on our door, and invited us into his home. We demurred, he insisted, and so we followed him through the rain to his house. Inside we learned that another family was spending the night with them. Their friends, the Olivos, lived in the town of Valencia, about 25 miles down the road. Ruben Olivo was a young merchant who ran his own general store with plenty of help from his wife, son and daughter. While we were getting acquainted, our host disappeared. He returned a few minutes later with a jug of sugar cane whisky and a bottle of

43

naranja (orange) brandy.

They asked me what I thought of the whisky after sampling it. Finding it difficult to get my breath, I could only whisper, "Muy fuerte!" They laughed and poured me another. Not wanting to be outdone, I pardoned myself, ran through the rain to the camper, and sped back with a bottle of Chilean wine we had been saving for a special occasion. We talked long into the night while the children enjoyed themselves comparing and trading Spanish and English comic books. Later the rain stopped, and we carried our sleeping kiddies out to the camper. We went to bed smelling the earthy odors of the farm, thankful we had stumbled upon these folks.

For breakfast we "took coffee" with the Velascos and the Olivos while the children drank boiled fresh cow's milk. We waved good-bye to the Velascos and followed the Olivos' truck to their store in Valencia where we bought groceries and other provisions. People were poor in Valencia—the Olivos were wealthy by their standards. We toured their home, an apartment with a kitchen, living room and two bedrooms above the store and noticed they owned a new car in addition to their truck. I watched operations in the store for a time, finding it interesting that, while it was obvious that Ruben's customers respected him, he treated them in a firm, almost condescending manner that would have been inappropriate for a local merchant back home.

We continued west through a valley flanked by snow-covered volcanoes and past cane and banana fincas to Quevedo, then on to Santo Domingo. This town with its cowboys on horseback, mud streets, bars with swinging doors and brothels was reminiscent of the old American West. Colorado Indians hold their market in Santo Domingo and live in a village nearby. We asked a soldier directions to the village, and he volunteered to take us there. The Spanish called them "Los Colorados," or "the red ones," because they color their hair with a flaming red dye derived from the seeds of the achiote plant. Our soldier guide introduced us to the tribe's chief who gave us a tour of the village, including their ceremonial center, school, central meeting place and a hospital run by a medicine man who showed us herbs for curing headaches, stomach disorders and rheumatism. Inhabitants of the village wrapped colorful striped skirts around their waists, above which they wore nothing. They painted black stripes across their chest and around their legs, and the men coifed themselves with a thick red paste. Buildings were simply constructed of sticks and thatched roofs. We watched women crushing cane and then visited the chief's functional one room home. The people spoke little Spanish, but, fortunately, our guide was an able translator.

Beautiful, colonial Riobamba hosts nine Saturday markets, certainly enough to satisfy anyone's haggling needs. We drove south through the mountains, carefully fording many mudslides, to Machachi, then south again past smoking Cotopaxi, arriving at Riobamba in time to find a hotel that permitted us to camp in their parking lot. In rural areas we felt comfortable finding a picturesque place to camp near the road, but in populated areas we looked for situations that offered more security. Hotels often satisfied that need for a small fee or an agreement to eat in their restaurant. We ate that evening in the restaurant of the Hotel Riobamba.

By now the four of us had become adept at haggling in the markets. We had learned that the best bargains were made early in the morning, while prices got higher as the day wore on. In Riobamba Lynette bought a dress from a woman who lowered her "precio ultimo" three times. Each time we walked away she called us back, shaking her head at our intransigence. We bought bread, cheese and a pineapple to take with us for lunch and started the five hour drive to Cuenca, the historic Spanish town built on the ruins of ancient Tomebamba where Inca Huayna Capac learned of the arrival of the conquistadores. We twisted and climbed, often through clouds, on the dangerous, unpaved road. Frequently the camper only narrowly escaped the grasp of a muddy rut. On several occasions Lynette took over the wheel while I pushed, the spinning tires showering me with mud. Enervated from a tough driving day, we checked into the small Hotel El Dorado near Cuenca and took much needed showers. The hotel's inexpensive restaurant, El Fogon, offered a mixed grill of steaks, pork chops and sausage. Carlos the waiter highlighted Cuenca's points of interest on our little map, and, in the morning, we followed his directions, walking the streets of the charming, colonial town. Lynette bought a hand-painted wooden spoon and Mike bought a bank covered with Ecuadorian five centimo coins for his growing foreign coin collection. The Museo Municipal exhibited some of the oldest Pre-Columbian art in South America, a few pieces dating back to 5000 BC. Cuenca's oldest buildings flanked a river running through the center of town where women washed clothes in the clear water, laying them on the grassy banks to dry in the sun.

Farther south, the road followed a mountain river cutting through spectacular scenery and leading to the remote market town of Gualaceo. It was Sunday, and the Indian market was in full swing, the week's social focus for everyone within walking distance of the village. On the other side of town we found a country inn called Hosteria Gualaceo. A hard right turn off the road and a short climb brought us to a parking lot in back of the inn. A bull-like, tough looking guy walked out of what appeared to be the door to the dining room, hesitated a step or two, frowned, and then smiled broadly.

"Minnesota!" he exclaimed as he walked up with his thick right arm extended. "What are you doing way down here?"

"Trying to get away from the winter." I started to tell him I was surprised he spoke English.

"Of course I do; I grew up in New Hampshire. The name's Sam

Jameson."

"Darwin Wile." I introduced the rest of the family and then, "Do you mind if we park here for the night? Be glad to pay you."

"Certainly not. And you can forget the paying. You can buy me a beer later."

Born in Poland, Sam came to New Hampshire with his parents at the age of three. In his early twenties, he signed a contract to come to Ecuador to work in the gold mines. He worked hard, was well paid and saved most of it.

"Wasn't anything to spend it on in the camp. I did spend a little though," he said with a long ago smile. "And I always had a bottle of whisky under my bed," he chuckled.

Young Sam bought some land, and built this inn with "my bare hands." I wasn't very surprised, since I had already decided those hands could build this inn or do anything else they wanted. Somewhere along the line Sam married a Spanish woman and raised a family. Now, "on the shady side of sixty," he's considering selling the inn and retiring. Sitting on 18 hectares (about 40 acres) and with a few cows and goats, a lot of chickens, some ducks and turkeys, and two Galapagos turtles (the acquisition of which Sam would not talk about), his little country inn was self sufficient. He must have done well over the years, for now he owned two other hotels in Cuenca run by his daughter and French son-in-law. Another daughter lived in the United States with her American husband. Sam said that he returned to the States every few years to see his family. Occasionally, he visited his sister in California who professed an inability to understand why he wants to live in Ecuador.

"She won't even come down to see why," he said, shaking his head in disbelief. "They live on the peninsula. Her husband fights the traffic going into the city every day, and, when he comes home at night, he eats dinner, turns on the TV and falls asleep. She thinks I'm crazy. She and her husband are the ones who've lost their marbles." I looked around at Sam's alternative to his sister's way of life, and had to agree with him.

Near the inn a clear mountain stream ran under an Incan bridge that, with large intricately interlocking stones, had been built to last. We drove the camper to the edge of the creek and watched a nun and some children playing tag. The village of Chordelac was located only a kilometer downstream. We could see the large blue and white church perched on a hill that had been built by the people from the small town below. I didn't feel very well, so I lay on the soft grass under a tree and took a nap. When I awakened, Lynette and the children had washed the camper. We returned to Hosteria Gualaceo and, still feeling poorly, I skipped dinner and went to bed. Lynette and the children enjoyed what they later told me was a delicious grilled steak dinner at the inn's restaurant.

In the morning I felt fine, and, having had plenty of sleep, was up and about before the others. Soon Sam joined me on the inn's porch where we sipped *jugo de naranja* (orange juice). He told me stories from the gold mining days and described the challenges he faced as an outsider building a business. After a bit the children were up. They went with a young Indian girl to milk the cows and were rewarded with fresh milk for breakfast. Lynette and I ate fried eggs with Sam, said our farewells, and we were on our way.

A stop sign hung from a gate lowered across the road at a military checkpoint twenty miles north of the Peruvian border. A friendly soldier told us the border closed at 6:00 p.m., only ten minutes from now, and suggested we spend the night camped behind the guardhouse. The children and I went birdwatching, finding kiskadee and vermillion fly catchers, while, in deference to my still sensitive digestive system, Lynette prepared a bland dinner of macaroni and cheese, peanut butter crackers and, for dessert, canned pears. After dinner the guards joined us for coffee, having little to keep them busy with the border closed.

About three o'clock in the morning Lynette poked her elbow in my ribs.

"Wake up!"

"What's up?"

"There's a truck trying to sneak by the guards," she whispered.

"Where?" I asked with little interest.

"Over there. It's moving inch by inch."

"I still can't see it."

"Out there! It has a white top. You must be able to see it!"

"Lynette, that's the guards' outhouse."

"Well, it looked like it was moving."

"Go back to sleep."

Mile after mile of slowly drifting sand dunes and wind-sculpted sandstone outcroppings flank the Pan American Highway on its journey through the desert of northern Peru. To the east lie the Andean foothills that eons ago were twisted, bended and folded by tremendous underground pressures. The road winds in and out of deep canyons carved by ancient torrential floods from the Andes. Vegetation consists only of small shrubbery and low cactus. Indians built their often roofless houses with pieces of driftwood. Occasionally we crossed oases where rivers from the Andes snaked their way across the desert on their way to the Pacific. A belt of green followed each river where irrigation had converted many square miles of arid desert into fertile farmland. Even rice grew in those erstwhile deserts. A sign along the road described what the Peruvian government considered a major challenge: to divert Andean water naturally flowing east to the rain forest instead to the dry, potentially productive land to the west where a large percentage of the population lived.

47

We drove all day toward a village called Cabo Blanco. One of our guidebooks made a sketchy, mysterious reference to a fishing club possibly being located in Cabo Blanco. If such a club truly existed, we hoped to camp there and perhaps do some fishing. The road led down from a high overlook to a village by the sea where we watched Indians in small boats tending their fishing nets. On a hill in the distance we could see a building that looked like it might be the club. The architecture appeared fifties-ish—an orange brick, one story structure with rounded corners. Closer inspection of the exterior revealed a few broken windows and a generally run-down condition. The inside, on the other hand, was clean and well cared for, but dated. A large fireplace dominated one wall, and over it stretched the biggest marlin I had ever seen. A huge tuna adorned a second wall, and numerous photographs of fishermen standing proudly beside their trophies covered other walls. Then I saw the smiling man behind the desk.

"Welcome to the Cabo Blanco Hotel! May I help you?"

"This is a hotel? Is anyone staying here?"

"One other couple. They are on their honeymoon."

When I asked him to explain the mystery of the hotel, he handed me a newspaper article; the story unfolded:

In the early fifties, world record black marlin and big eye tuna were being caught in the waters off Cabo Blanco. Wealthy sportsmen, many from the United States, built an exclusive fishing club here to join in on the fun. Alfred Glassel, Jr., caught the first black marlin weighing more than one thousand pounds, the very same thirteen or fourteen-foot long monster hanging over the fireplace. Glassel subsequently caught at least four more fish weighing more than a thousand pounds, including a 1,560 pounder which, forty years later, still holds the world record. The fish hanging on the other wall weighed 435 pounds, was caught by R.V.A. Lee, and still holds the world record for Pacific big eye tuna. We recognized many of the sportsmen captured in the photographs, including Ted Williams, Barry Goldwater and Ernest Hemingway. Each of them stood beside a fish considerably taller than himself. Record sized fish continued to be caught near Cabo Blanco during the fifties, but, as the decade ran out, so did the fish. By the early sixties, few game fish were being caught. The sportsmen left for greener pastures and took the money needed to run the club with them.

Now the club was run as a modest hotel open to the public. But all the memories remained: the pictures, the names, the stuffed fish, the lobby's blonde 1950s vintage furniture and, next to an old record player, a selection of platters from that era including recording artists like Dick Hayman, Doris Day, Carmen Cavallaro, Mantovani, Billy May, Dick Contino and David Carroll and his orchestra. The desk clerk gave us permission to camp in the parking lot, and, below the hotel, we had the beautiful white sand beach to ourselves. Lynette and I body surfed and then watched our children chasing crabs and frigate birds chasing pelicans.

After an excellent fish dinner in the hotel's restaurant, we put the children to bed in the camper and returned to the patio overlooking the ocean. The evening sky was clear and the breeze balmy. Late into the night we sipped wine and talked about Cabo Blanco. Why did the fish leave? Was it overfished or did the currents change? We were a bit sad, thinking about this small, forgotten cape on the coast of Peru that, twenty years ago, was one of the world's hottest fishing spots. The Firestones and DuPonts pictured inside the hotel undoubtedly sat with their cocktails in these very chairs, discussing the day's catch. The warm glow of wine fought off the cool evening air, and I could almost see the "Splendid Splinter" laughing and walking through the lobby door out onto the club's patio with his arm around "The Old Man of the Sea's" shoulder, martinis in their hands. We tried to figure out a way to revive Cabo Blanco and then went to bed deciding that, without the fish, it could not be done.

The Pan American Highway continued south through the desert towns of Talara, Sullana, Piura, Olmos and Chiclayo. Several naval destroyers were anchored in the harbor at Chiclayo. An officer told us that their duty was to patrol the territorial fishing waters of Peru that recently had been extended from two hundred miles to six hundred miles from the shore, much to the chagrin of fishermen from other nations. We camped at a highway patrol station near Chiclayo. Lynette and Krissie prepared supper while Mike and I kicked a soccer ball. An all white tom turkey interrupted our little football game, strolling past us in full display.

Peruvian truckdrivers took a creative backseat to no one when decorating their vehicles. Gaily painted designs adorned their rigs, and they obviously put great thought into naming the trucks which sported appelations such as *King of the Road, Virgin of Piura, Heaven's Destiny, Old But Rich, St. Judas My Protector, He Who Wants Is Able* and, my favorite, *Anywhere Is My Destination.* Later, on a washed out road high in the Andes, we had a chance to meet some of these roadway philosophers.

Near Trujillo we camped at Chanchan, the ruins of the imperial city of the Chimu kingdom covering 11 square miles. Chanchan was a good example of what treasure hunting thieves can do to unprotected archeological sites. The ruins had been pored over, dug up and trampled; even so, they were quite impressive. The Incas had been unable to defeat the Chimus militarily. They conquered Chanchan only by diverting its water supply, the life blood of the desert city. While exploring the ruins, we met Jennifer and Eric Walker, a young couple traveling around South America by bus. Several years ago Eric had lived in Trujillo as an American Field Service foreign exchange student. He returned to the University of Colorado and majored in South American studies. The Walkers were also heading south, so we invited them to ride along with us the next day.

The road south hugged the coast, taking us through Huanchacho, a fishing village where natives use boats made from tortora reeds. We sat on the beach and watched the fishermen expertly flipping fish from their nets into the boats. Driving further south, the Walkers rode with the children in the rear of the camper, playing Crazy 8s, Kings' Corners and Casino. Near the village of Buenos Aires, we camped on the beach. A small thatched roof restaurant served delicious grilled fish for supper. Later we walked the beach and watched the skies turn purple as the sun set over the Pacific.

The Moche pyramids, Huaca del Sol and Huaca dela Luna, are the largest pre-Columbian human made structures in South America. We followed an unpaved track from the main road and found it flooded in places. While trying to circumvent one low spot, we became stuck in the sand. Eric and I pounded rocks into the sand around the tires, while Jennifer and Lynette gathered sugar cane stalks which they spread in front of the camper. Lynette drove while the three of us pushed the van back to the track. On firm ground again, we then continued on to the massive pyramids. We explored the area, finding old pottery shards partially buried in the sand, and then carried our lunch to the top of Huaca del Sol where we pondered the world that was and, with my binoculars, eyeballed the best route back to the highway. In the afternoon, near Casma, we visited the ruins of Sechim. Huge stone monoliths depicting gory battle scenes stood next to a large temple, and skeletons and pottery filled the many tombs. The ruins had been recently discovered and dated back to 1500 BC Fortunatly, the Peruvian government arrived here before the treasure hunters. The site was under the control of archeologists whom we watched piecing together the thirty five hundred-year old story.

In the town of Huarmey, the Walkers registered in a small hotel where the owner gave us permission to camp in the parking lot. The sun was low, so we hurried to the beach for a cold but invigorating swim. Lima lay only a day's drive to the south, and this was to be our last evening with Jennifer and Eric. The children drifted off to sleep on a blanket while we chatted the stars across the heavens.

We stopped at the well preserved Chimu fortification at Paramonga. Lynette felt a bit nauseated and remained in the camper while the rest of us climbed to the top of the ancient bastion. We became concerned upon returning to the car and finding her gone. I called her name several times, frantically looking about for her. Then I saw her waving from the top of the fort. She later said she just didn't want to miss anything.

As the road approached Lima, the towns became less primitive. We crossed a twelve-mile long sand dune with spectacular views of the coast, and our excitement mounted as we neared the country's capital. When the Incas ruled Peru, Cusco was their capital. A mountaintop capital far from the ocean was impractical for the sea-faring Spaniards, so Francisco Pizarro built Lima, a city of which he presumably would be proud today. In the center of Plaza des Armes, across from the Hilton Hotel, the old conquistador charges on his furious steed toward a gushing fountain. Likewise, the huge equestrian statue of Jose de San Martin, the liberator of Peru, dominates beautiful Plaza San Martin. We dropped off the Walkers downtown so they could look for a hotel. Then we went to the suburbs, thinking we would more likely be able to find a safe place to camp in opulent San Isidro or Mira Flores.

The weather was perfect, and bronzed bodies covered the magnificent white beaches at Mira Flores. From the cliff above the coast, we watched the surfers riding waves that carried them more than a hundred yards. We bought fudgesicles from a street vendor and then drove to the Lima Golf Club in San Isidro. The manager of the club, Senior Barreto, was retired military and very much a gentleman. He welcomed us to camp in their parking lot for a few nights, emphasizing he wanted us to have good memories of his country. He encouraged us to use their locker room facilities and their restaurant and then introduced us to the superintendent, the night watchman and the women's locker room attendant, Maria. This woman combined the best of her two races, the pride and noble bearing of the Castillians and the angular beauty of her Indian ancestors. She took Kristen by the hand and led her to the locker room where she washed and powdered her little feet. Thus began an incredible friendship.

We cooked dinner, and a curious cat led her four kittens past the camper to see what we were having. Later Senior Barreto brought us a large platter of pastries and ice cream. What a welcome to Lima!

From my notes: *Lying in bed, Lynette and I discuss taking a camper around Europe next year. Before going to sleep, for the first time since we left Minnesota, I thought seriously about my job.*

In the morning we washed and cleaned the camper, took our clothes to a laundromat, shopped for groceries and bought a bottle of wine for our host. Then we drove into the city to take one of Lynette's patented walking tours. Armor clad Francisco Pizarro looked invincible, mounted monumentally in the Plaza des Armes. Across the street in the Cathedral, however, one could see what he really looked like. Lying in a glass case for public viewing, the naked, shriveled mummy that was Francisco Pizarro looked like anything but a fierce conquistadore. When we learned that his entrails were in a nearby vase, carefully maintained at a controlled temperature and humidity, Krissie said, "Ickie, yuk!" and Lynette said that this was going too far. The changing of the guards at the national palace was impressive, although Lynette thought they were less crisp than their counterparts at Buckingham. The Museum of Archeology and Anthropology featured scale models of the ruins at Chanchan, Sechim and Machu Pichu and an exhibit of beautiful and sophisticated early Peruvian art. We met the Walkers for dinner at Las Trece Monedas (The Thirteen Coins), a two hundred fifty-year old colonial mansion with three hundred-year old goblets, antique paintings, and marvelous continental food. While Krissie, retaining her antipathy for anything fancier than a hamburger, ordered fried chicken, Mike was developing a rather sophisticated palate—he ordered *canard a l'orange*.

We shopped at a National Heritage Center of Peruvian artisans. Mike bought a carved gourd for his teacher and a llama rug for himself. Krissie bought a stuffed llama, and Lynette bought dresses and purses for her friends. I bought a hand woven, blue and red wool tie with llamas in the design. That evening we saw our first professional soccer game—Peru defeated Czechoslovakia. In a conversation back at the Golf Club, an Argentinian volunteered his opinions about the political situation in various Andean countries. He thought the government of Chile was quite stable but that Bolivia offered a different story. He also warned us that road conditions in the Andes become treacherous during the rainy season. I resolved to go to the United States Embassy to check on politics and to the Peruvian Automobile Club to check on weather conditions.

During the next few days we attended to a number of administrative chores. At the United States Embassy an official told us that Chile and Argentina appeared safe for independent travelers. A few bearded, backpacking hippies had reported some harassment from border officials, but nothing that would likely affect us. Bolivia had just experienced what he characterized as a mini-revolt. He said it was still too early to tell how that situation might affect travelers. Letters from several friends and my mother awaited us at the American Express office. While I waited in line to cash a traveler's check at the Bank of London, a young American told me he had just been robbed for the second time in the past month. A thief on a motorcycle sped by and tore away his shoulder bag and almost his shoulder. I had the feeling I was talking to an unusual guy. He said he had no job but plenty of money. He lived both in Paris and New York and now was on a five year trip around the world sponsored by "a friend." I was about to ask him to elaborate when my turn came at the teller's window. By the time I received my money, the world traveler had disappeared.

A man at the Peruvian Automobile Club said there were three possible routes from Lima through the mountains to Cusco—conditions were bad on all three unpaved roads. Heavy rain had produced many landslides and washouts. As of now, the routes were open, but the auto club recommended the road through Arequipa, one that would take us 800 miles out of our way. Their second choice was the inland road through Huancayo, but it was one way only, changing directions on alternate days. The remaining route was the shortest and most spectacular. It was, however, the most susceptible to mudslides and washouts. Also, being very remote, the availability of gasoline and mechanical service was doubtful. Lynette and I looked at each other, wondering whether Machu Pichu and the Sacred Valley of the Incas were worth the trouble. Later we arranged our visas at the Bolivian consulate where an official told us the revolt was under control and that tourists should expect no problems. A quick check at the Chilean consulate verified that visas were not required. We also learned that Chile had a strict curfew in force that prohibited anyone being on the streets between 2:00 and 6:00 a.m.

On the day before our departure from the Lima Golf Club, Krissie gave Maria a flower and some candy she had bought. They had become very close during our stay in San Isidro. Amazingly, the two of them sat together and talked for hours, neither speaking the other's language. Perhaps this was what Gus Angermeyer meant by the "language of the heart." This erect, matronly woman with the proud, high cheekbones and her little friend said their tearful goodbyes that afternoon when Maria left for the day. In the evening we said goodbye to the nightwatchman whom Lynette affectionately called "our little friend." This nice old man seemingly never slept. During the day he was the club's groundskeeper and at night he walked around the clubhouse with his transistor radio hanging from his shoulder. We showered in the club's lavish facilities, put the children to bed, and enjoyed a prolonged evening stroll through the club's lovely gardens.

Not without some trepidation, we decided to take the third route to Cusco. Despite the auto club's warnings, it just seemed the most interesting. The Pan American Highway cut through stark desert moonscapes on its paved and straight route from Lima to Nazca. From Nazca, we planned to branch east over what promised to be the roughest, remotest, most dangerous and best part of the trip.

The ruins of Pachacamac lie south of Lima. Here also the Incan empire imposed its language and laws on a conquered people. Later, Francisco Pizarro's brother, Hernando, looted and destroyed the city. After visiting the ruins, we rejoined the highway as it began a gradual climb to Nazca. Just as our road emerged from a tunnel, we spotted a white Volkswagen camper with California license plates parked off the left shoulder. We tooted our horn and waved at the couple sitting on the step of the open sliding doorway, eating lunch. Soon we arrived in Nazca, the center of the great culture of the same name that flourished between 500 and 1000 AD and left enormous cosmological symbols and images along the coastal desert. I stopped in front of the tourist hotel and went in to ask permission to camp in their parking area. Returning to the car, I found the other camper parked behind us and Lynette talking with the occupants. Karl was German, and Dori Swiss, and, like many Europeans, they spoke several languages effortlessly. They lived in San Francisco and planned to spend a year traveling in South America.

We became better acquainted over dinner that evening. Karl was a chef and a merchant seaman who had sailed over much of the world. Dori had toured Asia and Europe as a single woman. Two years before, she and Karl met in San Francisco and fell in love. They also were headed to Cusco, and, so, after dinner, we walked the several blocks to the police station to check on road conditions in the mountains. The police encouraged us somewhat, reporting the road to Cusco open. We decided to tackle the drive across the Andes together, figuring we could help one another if we encountered problems.

We put the children to bed and joined our new friends on the hotel patio for a beer. An older man and his wife asked if they might sit with us. They lived in Lima and had been vacationing in southern Chile, hunting and fishing in the mountains and lakes. The man dominated our conversation, criticizing intolerant Chileans, dogmatic Peruvians and the profligacy of the United States space program. Neither did he have much good to say about the Germans, Russians or Chinese. Dori later wondered how the Swiss escaped his condemnation. We went to bed anxious to begin our adventure the next morning and thankful for having companions.

Happy Valentine's Day! The children made a valentine box, and Krissie instructed us to be sure to have our valentines finished and in the box by lunchtime. We had ascended only about thirty miles through a desert canyon when our right rear tire blew out. I was incredulous; these steel-belted radials had less than twenty thousand miles on them! Admittedly, they were tough miles, but the ads for these tires guarantee forty thousand miles. Already the decision to travel together was vindicated; Karl's spare tire provided security we would not have had by ourselves. We continued climbing. The soil began to support thin grass. A few cattle and an occasional Indian hut appeared. We crossed a ridge and saw snow capped mountains in the east and a herd of rare vicunas (wild relatives of the llama, alpaca and camel). The unpaved road, full of ruts, became muddy in places. Shepherds tended herds of llamas and alpacas. Lunchtime came, and we drew valentines out of the box. Lynette made one for me with a drawing of a heart containing an eye, a gopher, and the letter U. Mike easily broke the code: "I go for you, Valentine!" I reciprocated with "Over the Andes, high in Peru, I need a Valentine, do you?" Mike's valentine to his sister explained, "Wiener dogs are too long; rabbits are too short; you're just right!" Little Krissie offered more conventional greetings such as, "Be mine, Valentine!"

With each mile the road became worse—muddy ruts, washouts, and deep water-filled holes. Karl's car bogged down and became stuck. Eventually two truck drivers came along and helped us push him free. My turn, and the truckers warned me to keep moving through the treacherous stretch. They laughed and cheered as I skidded and careened through the mud, steering with my right hand and, out of the driver's window, raising my clenched left fist in victory. The altiplano provided wonderful vistas surrounded by the rugged Andean peaks, but the driving was laboriously slow. In ten hours of driving, we had come only 155 miles. We came to a small town and needed gas. *Corriente* (translated "running") flowed from the only gas pump in the village. It had an octane rating of 66. Having no alternative, we filled up.

Only a few hardy Indians dared making a living at this elevation. They lived in primitive stone and mud houses, tending their llamas and scratching out a meager existence from the rocky soil. Bird-life, on the other hand, abounded. High above treeline, multitudes of andean flickers nevertheless were content foraging on the ground. Gulls, terns, ducks, large black coots, sandpipers and plovers inhabited the waterways. The road skirted a carotene-hued alpine lake where a flock of two dozen flamingos waded, heads inverted, seining aquatic life from the bottom. The most evident mammals were strange creatures with long, rabbit-like ears and a bushy, squirrel-like tail. Lynette called them "squabbits." Later we learned they were vizcachas, relatives of the chinchilla and one of the highest dwelling mammals in the world. As evening approached, the temperature dropped. We crossed a fifteen thousand-foot pass and soon pulled off the road for the night. Snow began falling. We had driven from the hot desert at sea level to the wintry altiplano at over fifteen thousand feet elevation in one day. None of us felt well. Krissie went to sleep without eating. The rest of us ate a little stew. Lynette shivered and suggested we may be camping next to the highest and most remote road in the world.

We wakened early and found our campers covered with ice. Headaches reminded each of us to go slow until we acclimated to the high elevation. Soon the sun rose, and, as the ice melted and the coffee boiled, we all began to feel better. After a light breakfast, we had only driven a few miles when the road became rough and narrow, winding and descending into a canyon through which flowed the raging Pachachaca River. We rounded a bend and suddenly encountered a truck parked in the middle of the road. After sliding to a stop just in the nick of time, we found the driver of the rig lying on his back trying to repair his brakes. The gap between the truck and the wall to the inside the road was too narrow for the campers to pass. The distance from the truck to the cliff edge on the outside of the road seemed to be wide enough to pass. Karl and I grabbed our shovels and leveled the ruts to the outside of the truck so we could remain as close to it as possible as we passed. Then we slowly edged our campers along the precipice above the Pachachaca (needless to say, the women and children watched from the sidelines), clearing the truck with only a few inches to spare.

Progress through the mountains remained slow. We came upon a section of the road where water pouring over the mountainside had washed about fifty feet of the gravel road into the river below. Four trucks and two busses were stopped in front of us and about the same number of vehicles were waiting to come through from the other side of the washout. The road had been closed for twelve hours, during which time, with picks and shovels, the truck drivers had been hand carving a passageway deeper into the side of the mountain. Karl and I joined in to help, and, within an hour, they were ready to let the first vehicle, a bus, try to drive across what there was of a new road. Water continued pouring across the road, and Karl and I doubted that we had dug back into the mountain far enough. Incredibly, several women and children remained aboard the bus as it started across the breach. About halfway across the newly dug roadway, the siding gave way under the weight of the bus. The right rear wheel slipped over the edge, and the driver and others quickly evacuated the bus. Only the bus's body resting on a more firm area of the road surface prevented it from tumbling over the side into the raging river fifty feet below.

We all carried rocks to buttress the weak outer edge of the road. When our self-appointed foreman determined that the support was adequate, we tied a chain between the bus and a truck on the other side. The truck pulled backwards while the bus driver inched his way across with no further mishaps. Then we began digging further back into the mountain. The digging dislodged large boulders that rolled or slid down onto the road. While some men broke up the boulders with picks, others of us wrapped rope around the still large pieces and dragged them over the cliff. By now more trucks had arrived. With little leadership and about fifty men using only hand equipment, the roadway amazingly began to take shape.

Three trucks made their way across, each further weakening the home made road. The truck in line before us then made a terrible mistake, and for some reason, stopped halfway across. He was not far enough to the left and began to slip over the edge. The same technique previously used on the bus served to pull the truck to safety on the other side. Four more hours had passed, and now reinforcements began to arrive on horseback. Twenty more men armed with picks and shovels pitched in to repair the badly deteriorated roadway we had constructed. After several hours, it was my turn. I became hung up on the huge ruts created by the trucks, but there were plenty of men to push our little VW across. Karl followed me with no problem, and, after saying goodbye to our fellow highway builders, we were on our way. A few hundred yards further along, a large waterfall poured onto the road. This would probably be tomorrow's washout, but, in the meantime, it served the purpose of washing a lot of accumulated mud from our campers. Many more washouts awaited us, but, after stopping at each one to scout the depth and flow of the water, we forded them handily.

We found low octane gas in the village of Chalhuanca, but only after asking several people where gas was sold. It turned out the "gas station" was a dozen fifty-five gallon drums stored in a shed behind some guy's house. Karl and I had to siphon the gas into five gallon containers and carry them out to the campers. Driving out of town, we passed the two truckers who had helped push Karl out of the mud several days before. We tooted our horns as we drove by, and they gave us a smile and a clenched fist salute.

"Stop!" Lynette shrieked, suddenly.

I immediately did just that, if for no other reason than to inquire why she felt it necessary to arrest the beating of my heart.

"What is it?" As the camper slid over loose gravel, hurtling children and camping equipment in all directions. Then I saw it, crawling across the road—a tarantula half again the size of my fist. The creature posed long enough for our camera session and then went on its way. Nearby a path led away from the road. It was not much more than a footpath, but the clearing was wide enough for the campers. The afternoon sun was getting low in the western sky, so we pulled the campers off the road and followed the path about a quarter mile until it came to a river. A hundred yards upstream we stopped by a rope footbridge suspended high above the torrent. By now the skies were putting on a colorful show while the sun beautifully backlit the peaks of the Andes. Enjoying the views of majestic granite cliffs rising thousands of feet above and raging rapids hundreds of feet below, we parked for the night, unknowingly, in the path leading between the mountainside fields, where Indians grew their corn and potatoes, and their mud and grass homes further down the valley. A few Indians crossed the swinging bridge on their way home from the fields. Warily curious and friendly, they stopped to chat, wondering what we were doing there. They did not speak Spanish, but we got by with sign language and smiles. Later a soft rain began falling and continued all night. We slept well there after several difficult and exciting days. In the morning, while we ate breakfast, the same people, less wary, stopped for more conversation on their way back to the fields.

In the town of Abancay we shopped in the market for fruit under a clear, deep blue sky and siphoned more gas into our five gallon containers. Now only a day from Cusco, we followed the mighty, raging Apurimac River, descending to 6,000 feet elevation, with spectacular views all along the way. A footbridge stretched high across the Apurimac near the location of Thornton Wilder's *The Bridge of San Luis Rey*, a perfect place for lunch. We arrived in Cusco at dinner time, four hard, wonderful days after leaving Nazca. For a small price, the Hotel Cusco allowed us to use their showers. We enjoyed a delicious steak dinner at a small restaurant on the old Plaza Des Armes and later spent the evening leisurely visiting local shops. While the light vanished, the soft wail of wooden flutes drifted down from the hills and the town's inhabitants slowly deserted the streets. How amazing that, in 1530, this small town was the largest city in the western hemisphere! We parked the campers under some trees on the Plaza and put the children to bed. Then Karl and I opened a couple bottles of Peruvian red wine and the four of us drank the stars to bed.

Following the Urubamba River, a one hour drive through a valley of beautifully terraced farmland brought us to the market town of Pisac. Traditionally dressed Indians sold antiquities, panchos, blankets and jewelry. A man rang a bell in the open window of the church belfry as we parked the camper. Lynette bought a silver necklace with a tiny llama bell and Krissie bought a rag doll dressed like the local Indian women. Mike and I snapped some photos while Dori and Karl bought bread, cheese and fruit for lunch. Returning to Cusco, we stopped at the Incan ritual baths at Tambomachay and the huge fortress and parade grounds of Sacsahuaman. The Incas had built this impressive citadel for the defense of Cusco on a hill overlooking the city. Stones weighing as much as three hundred tons somehow were transported from quarries far below and fitted together perfectly like pieces of a gigantic jig-saw puzzle. The great fort has withstood plunder and earthquakes for more than half a millenium, not unlike the time tested foundations of the houses in the city it was built to protect. Most of Cusco's wooden buildings have been destroyed repeatedly by earthquakes, but not their mortarless, fitted stone foundations upon which new houses are rebuilt after each disaster.

We explored Sacsahuaman, feeling the mood that must have pervaded the Inca spectators watching their mighty warriors parade and their swift athletes play ball games. In the warm afternoon, we sat atop the imperial temple, eating lunch and watching the sun's rays bounce off the orange tiled roofs of Cusco. Mike and Krissie ran off to a nearby stream to catch polliwogs while the four of us set up camp outside the fortress walls. Karl ran out of white gas for their stove, so I gave him what was left of ours.

To our great relief, Cusco had a Volkswagon dealer. Karl remained with the cars while they adjusted the timing, changed the oil, and replaced a shock absorber for his vehicle and a spare tire for mine. The rest of us walked to the train station to buy tickets to Machu Pichu, to the bank for money, and to the Peruvian Automobile Club for information on the roads to Bolivia. The very helpful Senior Guillermo Lastarrio Escobedo, manager of the club, showed us potential trouble spots on our maps between Cusco and Puno, our next destination on the north shore of Lake Titicaca. He expressed confidence that the political unrest in Bolivia had been brought under control and told us where we could buy white gas after we had looked all over town for it with no success. Then he invited us to camp in the parking lot of the International Club, of which he was the president. In the late afternoon, we took some wine and cheese to the Plaza des Armes to celebrate a successful administrative day during which we serviced our cars and answered some important questions. Krissie and Mike joined some other children playing soccer. Later, we discovered that, in the Sacred Valley of the Incas, the sun doesn't set gradually. It slowly falls in the western sky and then plummets behind the cordillera with darkness immediately descending. Wine and sweaters kept us warm while Karl told us about life aboard ship and described the many ports they visited. Dori worked at the Swiss government's tourist office in San Francisco. It was difficult for them being separated for months at a time. Karl wanted to open a restaurant, get married, and settle down. We cooked some soup and then returned to the club for the night. Our train was scheduled to leave for Machu Pichu at 7:00 a.m.

The Indian market was in full swing upon our early arrival at the train station. With the exception of a few backpackers, an English couple and the six of us, most of the tourists on the train were Peruvian. The train left promptly, switchbacking up a mountain outside Cusco, then entering a lovely valley of farms. Willows and tall poplars lined the railway bed, reminding Lynette of rural Italy. The train then entered a deep canyon through which raced the powerful Urubamba River. A Peruvian sitting several seats from us retrieved a wooden flute from his backpack and began playing the Andean tune Simon and Garfunkel had popularized in the U.S., *El Condor Pasa*. The left side of the train offered spectacular views of the charging river. Magnificent snow-capped peaks could be seen from the right windows, rising abruptly from the gorge. The train stopped in a village. Indian vendors approached the train windows, selling fruit and delicious corn kernels, called "choclos," the size of large strawberries.

Only twenty kilometers from Machu Pichu, the train blew its whistle and slowed to a stop. Looking out of our window, we could see another train stopped in front of us. The other train pulled about a dozen cattle cars, all of them crammed full of Indians. Somebody explained that the fare was only a few cents on "the Indian Train." A rumor that the Indian train had derailed flew through our car. Karl and I disembarked and quickly learned what the problem really was—a landslide completely covering the tracks. A familiar scene unfolded as workers arrived on horseback with their picks and shovels. This time they also had dynamite. Soon they were shoveling and, when needed, blasting large boulders off the tracks. There seemed to be more than enough workers, so I grabbed my binoculars to see what birds might be seen. The English woman joined me with her binoculars, and we managed to find a number of hummingbirds and parrots.

After a four hour delay, the train was on its way again. The mountains became more precipitous and the river more narrow and vicious. Rain began to fall as we arrived at the Machu Pichu station. Small busses transported us to the top of the mountain on which the ruined city perched. We explored the temples and tombs and admired the remarkably precise interlocking stonework of the buildings. The views from the top of the mountain around which curled the Riobamba were magnificent. Clouds rolled up and over the mountain, and now we had a downpour on our hands. Karl found an old building with a roof but not before we were soaking wet. When the rain let up, we ran for the bus and returned to a small restaurant near the train station where we ordered hot potato soup. About 11:30 p.m., our train pulled into the Cusco station five hours behind schedule.

We spent another day in Cusco before leaving for the shores of Lake Titicaca. While having lunch at a small restaurant off the Plaza, we met a Seventh Day Adventist missionary, an engineer who had built many build-ings erected by the Adventists for Indians in Peru. He recently finished building a school for the Uros Indians on Lake Titicaca and encouraged us to take a look at it. He also warned us that a bridge had been washed away about sixty miles south of Cusco.

A very wet detour slowly led us across many drainages, circumventing the main stream that the erstwhile bridge had crossed. We continued south on the fifteen thousand feet high, cold, but beautiful, altiplano. Two snow-capped cordilleras stretched north and south, one to the east and one to the west of us, often a mile or more higher than the altiplano on which we drove. Friendly Indians waved when we passed, the women and children tending livestock and the men working the fields. Incan ruins dotted the countryside. The river draining the vast plain in many places overflowed its banks. Avocets and plovers foraged the mud; flamingos, herons, gallinules and ducks fed in the backwaters; hawks and gulls flew overhead. Livestock included sheep, goats, pigs, cattle, horses, burros and thousands of alpacas and llamas. We forded many streams and washouts along the way. A bus was mired down in a field about a quarter mile off the road, and men, women and children all pulled on a rope as the bus slowly inched through the mud. Once we stopped by the road to watch about two dozen gaily cos-tumed Indians, some playing flutes and drums while others danced. They offered us some of their substantial supply of beer and told us they were cel-ebrating a fiesta in honor of one of the local volcanoes.

From a hill overlooking Puno, we first saw Lake Titicaca, the highest navigable lake in the world at more than 12,000 feet. Inca legend teaches the first of their race emerged from this lake many years ago. Snow-capped volcanoes surrounded the large body of water. I flew over marvelous Titicaca three years before traveling from Lima to Sao Paulo on a business trip and vowed then that one day I would return to see it from the ground.

We drove into Puno, looking for a place to spend the night. A twelve-year-old boy named Victor walked up to our parked campers and announced he would be our guide in Puno. First he found us a place to camp, the parking area of the local tourist hotel. Then he showed us around town, pointing out a number of interesting and historically significant build-ings. He helped us arrange a trip to see the village of the Uros Indians and talked about his family life. He incidentally mentioned he enjoyed singing. When none of us reacted to this assertion, he waited until there was a pause in the conversation.

"Singing pleases me very much."

This was a little too obvious to ignore, so I asked Victor to sing something for us.

"What kind of song do you wish to hear?"

"What is your favorite song?"

"I like to sing about the Indians," confessed the handsome young Mestizo. "There is one song the Indians sing about the tortora plant," he added, pointing to the green reeds growing along the shore of Lake Titicaca.

"Let's hear it!"

In a clear, ringing voice, young Victor sang a lovely song in the Uros language. He then translated the words into Spanish for us. We were impressed with Victor's singing and with his selection although I only remember the first few lines:

"Tortora, Tortora,
Plant of the water.
Perhaps you have eyes for crying,
Perhaps you have a heart for feeling."

We returned to the tourist hotel where Victor and Mike played soccer with Victor's friends. We took much needed showers, ate dinner in the hotel restaurant, and played cards in the lobby before going to sleep with a steady patter of raindrops on the camper roof.

Victor had helped us arrange transportation from Puno's port to the floating islands of the Uros Indians. The six of us climbed into a small motor boat which threaded its way through tortora reeds for an hour and a half. Along the way Indians in reed boats tended their fishing nets. Coots and ducks skittered out of our way. The Uros build the islands on which they live by constantly piling dried tortora reeds on top of beds of older reeds. Many of these people never set foot on dry land. They have no chief or formal leaders, practicing true communal living with everyone being equal. I asked one man how long his people had lived there. He replied, "Since the beginning of time."

The economy of the Uros people is based on the small herring-like fish they catch in their nets. The fish are dried in the sun and then eaten or traded with mainlanders for other food and supplies. Tortora reeds dry in the sun for two or three months before being used to build houses, boats, or added island surface. Two men work four days to build a boat which typically lasts two or three months before becoming waterlogged. When walking on the islands, you can feel the reeds give with each step, indeed, leaving an impression that you are always floating. Large black ibises which are bred and raised by the islanders for food scamper from hut to hut, unable to fly away with their clipped wings. The local teacher gave us a tour of the only non-reed building in the village—his metal Quonset-hut style school built by the Adventist missionary we met in Cusco. I remember thinking these people had a very difficult life.

From my notes: *As we left the islands I wondered what caused the ancestors of these poor people at "the beginning of time" to choose such a seemingly unnecessarily hard life out on the lake. Perhaps they were driven from the mainland by more powerful opponents.*

Karl's camper had a flat tire when we returned. We fixed it, bought groceries, and headed south on the picturesque west side of the lake, driving through fields terraced by Indian farmers. Fields not planted were abloom with colorful poppies. A fox loped ahead of us along the gravel road, and, when we approached too closely, he bolted away over a hill and out of sight.

Again from my notes: *Seeing the fox, I find myself thinking of my boyhood in Pennsylvania, of working traplines along the Swatara Creek and hunting whitetail deer in the Blue Mountains and fishing in the Susquehanna River. This is good—my severance from the hectic life must be nearly complete when, for the first time in a long while, I can think about important memories from an earlier life.*

Near the Peru-Bolivia border at Yunguyo, we forded countless flooded streams and washouts of the road. By now Karl and I were pretty good at finding the most solid sub-surfaces and keeping the vehicles moving. The customs and immigration offices closed just before we reached the border. We spent the last of our Peruvian money in a small general store in Yunguyo and then drove to the military checkpoint at the frontier. We camped on a flower-filled hill overlooking Titicaca and its surrounding volcanoes. The evening was cool, but soup, grilled cheese sandwiches and a glass or two of wine warmed us up. The only damper to a wonderful day occurred when we left Yungayo and the "Check Engine" light on Karl's dashboard ignited. We checked the car as best we could and found nothing wrong. We would see how it ran in the morning.

Karl's car would not start, so we jumped it. Back in Yungayo we waited at the immigration office until 9:10 when an official sleepily walked downstairs and, without a word, stamped our passports. We entered Bolivia and continued south. In the morning light, Titicaca's waters changed colors— pinks, blues, purples, greens and yellows. Mount Ancohuma, the western hemisphere's second highest, rose majestically over twenty-one thousand feet on the eastern horizon. Terraced crops and flowering meadows climbed the hills to the west. Our enjoyment of the gorgeous scenery, however, was tempered by the poor performance of Karl's car. The engine had little power, forcing us to drive slowly. Once I pulled him to the top of a hill. Several times his engine just quit, and we hooked up the jumper cables. We drove into the picturesque red-roofed town of Copacabana nestled on Titicaca's shore and drank coffee. South of Copacabana, the lake constricted like an hour glass, the eastern and western shores separated by only a half mile of water. Two small wooden barges with outboard motors slowly ferried our campers across the Strait of Tiquina. On the east side we stopped for lunch and chatted with a half dozen sailors from the Bolivian Navy. While the country has no coastal exposure to an ocean, it retains a small navy to patrol Lake Titicaca.

Karl's camper continued having problems as we drove south toward La Paz along the snow-capped cordillera that joins Lake Titicaca with Bolivia's capital city. Late in the day his car stopped abruptly in El Alto, a busy suburb perched on the altiplano two thousand feet above La Paz. Carnival had started, and the local people were celebrating. Traffic became more congested as we hooked up the jumper cables and endured frustrated, honking revelers and an exasperated, gesticulating policeman. We filled up at a gas station and then, after dark, coasted down into La Paz, which at more than twelve thousand feet elevation, is the world's highest capital. Twice during the descent into the city, we jumped Karl's car. The sounds, costumes and excitement of Carnival surrounded us. Curious Indians in gay, often outlandish costumes interrupted their dancing in the streets to see what our problem was. Eventually we limped into a pension parking lot near the city's center. Karl seemed exhausted and a bit depressed from the day's problems. I felt empathy, remembering our similar problems in southern Colombia. We found a nice Italian restaurant to cheer up the old boy. After all, it was Carnival. As I recall, he became so cheery, he paid for the wine!

The Bolivian Automobile Club was located in a lovely neighborhood bursting with colorful, flowering vegetation. We arrived at the club in the morning and found another camper with Dutch registration in the parking area. The club manager eagerly gave us permission to join the other campers. We were becoming acquainted with the Dutch couple when the sound of a baby crying emanated from their camper. The Dutch woman retrieved the infant whom she said was five weeks old, and we made a suitable fuss over him. Later, in the privacy of our camper, Lynette remarked skeptically that the baby was too big for being born only five weeks ago.

That evening we all ate dinner at the auto club. By now the Dutch couple felt more comfortable and confided in us, telling the real story. Their five week old baby was, in fact, five months old. He was born into an Indian family in the Bolivian Orient where the Dutch couple was traveling at the time. His mother had died in childbirth. The family was large, and his father, concerned about his ability to support another child, asked a local official to find a home for the baby. The couple happened to be in the village and, hearing about the baby, quickly decided to take him. The official falsified the papers, creating the appearance that the Dutch woman gave birth to the child in that village. The couple brought the child to La Paz where they acquired a Dutch passport for him, and they planned on returning with the baby to Holland in two or three weeks.

We put the children to bed and talked late into the night about Bolivia. With no middle class, no sea port, no manufacturing base and the bulk of the population comprised of Indians living a subsistence existence, the plight of the people seemed hopeless. Land reform had accomplished nothing. In Santa Cruz and some other rain forest villages the Dutch had traveled through, the campesinos (peasants) militantly protested the government's raising of prices by blocking the roads. The couple were social workers in Holland, but they had no desire to do similar work in Bolivia, feeling depressed by what they considered to be a futile situation. In the morning I asked the manager of the auto club if we were likely to run into any political problems driving south to Argentina. He replied in the negative, "Everybody now thinks of Carnival, not of politics."

Commercial La Paz closed down for the week of Carnival, a non-stop party. During the day costumed people danced on the sidewalks. Youngsters lined the streets, throwing water balloons, buckets of water, and spraying hoses at cars driving by. Teenagers packed in the back of pickup trucks, wearing t-shirts sporting their school's name, barraged each other with water balloons while passing on the street. We joined in on the festivities, dancing in the streets and trying to avoid the balloons. Later we drove to El Valle de la Luna (Moon Valley) where harshly eroded formations blanket the terrain, creating a moon-like impression. One area contained hundreds of phallic symbols, boulders resting atop columns, the boulder having protected its column from erosion by wind and rain. At the present rate of erosion, Moon Valley promised to be worn smooth in a couple thousand years. We returned to the auto club and, encouraged by the music of Carnival in the background and having watched water being thrown around all day, Karl and I washed our dirty campers while Dori and Lynette washed our dirty clothes.

Like all the other businesses, the La Paz Volkswagon dealer was closed for Carnival. Karl and I tinkered with his engine most of the day, trying with no success to find his problem. That evening we dined in a restaurant with a view of snow-capped Illimani, another twenty-one thousand-foot volcano. The dinner was good, and so was the Bolivian wine that accompanied it and beer that followed it. Karl, normally a listener, was now well-loosened and dominated the conversation. He told us his story of coming to America. Ten years ago he worked as a cook in Sweden. Speaking little English, he took a chance and came to New York on a tourist visa. Not long after his arrival, he went to the United States Immigration Department to apply for an immigration visa. They told him he had to be employed to obtain an immigration visa. Knowing the Hotel Statler needed a cook, he went there to apply for the job. The hotel told him he needed a social security card before they could hire him. He left the Statler and, not knowing what a social security card was, stopped a man on the corner of Broadway and 42nd Street.

"Excuse, Sir. What is the social security card?"

The man tried to explain the social security system to Karl, but the young chef understood little of what he said. Aware he was making little progress, the man took his social security card from his wallet and showed it to Karl.

"Where I get it?"

So the man showed Karl the way to the Social Security Administration office. There they told him he needed a sponsor to get a social security card. It was true Karl needed work on his English, but this young man, who had been making it on his own in the cold world ever since he left home in his early teens, knew a thing or two about getting by. He hesitated only a few seconds and identified the Hotel Statler as his sponsor. He took his new social security card to the hotel, was hired immediately, and then successfully applied for his immigration visa.

The final day of Carnival arrived. We drove into the heart of the city to photograph the revelers who were in the streets at full strength. We closed our windows to discourage the water bombardiers from wasting too many balloons on us. We were driving up the narrow street leading to El Alto when Karl spotted a store selling balloons. I stopped the camper immediately and looked at Karl.

"Carnival has another day to go; let's have some fun."

"I'll get the balloons."

The girls said, "No!;" the children said, "Yes!"

Four to two, the "ayes" had it. We bought a package of 100 balloons, drove back to the auto club and filled them with water.

We adopted what we thought was an brilliant strategy. We drove down the street. When kids were on Karl's side, he kept his window closed while I opened my window and lobbed bombs over the camper at the kids. We reversed the operation when kids were on my side of the camper. This masterplan worked beautifully for a time. However, one group of ten boys wised up to us. They split up, five to a side, and waited for us. We made several passes but were unable to open our windows without three or four balloons being fired at us before we got off a shot. Their accuracy with a moving target was remarkable. The only way we could possibly win this battle would be to stop the camper and charge them. We reassured each other we could whip them with our superior fire power. Upon further reflection, we realized that would necessitate changing our level of involvement; that is, we would end up getting wet. Cooler heads prevailed, and we drove away with our tails between our legs.

That evening we walked to a park beside a river that flowed through La Paz. Refreshment stands sold soft drinks, beer and roast pork sandwiches.

We picked a stand tended by an Indian lady and her exceptionally pretty daughter. While we waited, the woman cut slices from a huge pork roast, lay them in fresh rolls, and added tomatoes, onions, and hot sauce. Carnival would soon be over.

The next morning Karl took his camper to the VW dealer while the rest of us attended to administrative details at the Swiss embassy, the United States Consulate, Bolivian Immigration, and a supermarket that had little food and no bread for sale. One of us spotted a small restaurant advertising "Hamburgers" in its window, and, since lunchtime was upon and us none of us had seen a hamburger in months, we found an empty table and enthusiastically placed five orders for their specialty. The waiter brought our big, beautiful burgers. For some inexplicable reason, Lynette turned her burger over and lifted the bun. La Cucaracha! Looking her right in the eye was a big, juicy cockroach spread eagle on her big, juicy hamburger!! I showed the disgusting morsel to the manager who did not seem nearly as surprised or apologetic as I expected him to be. We left the restaurant without paying and returned to the auto club to fix our own lunch—grilled cheese sandwiches.

We drove to the VW dealer to pick up Karl and his camper. Karl paid his bill, but the camper lost its power before he and Dori had driven out of the VW dealer's parking lot. They obviously had not fixed the problem.

Having to wait for Carnival's end to leave La Paz had put us well behind our schedule. A few days before, Lynette and I decided to scotch our plans to go to Chile and instead head straight for Argentina when we left La Paz. The time had come for us to part from our friends with whom we had experienced so much fun, companionship and adventure. Karl and Dori had more time than we did, and they were ensconced in a safe haven where they could wait for their car to be fixed properly. Regretfully, we said our good-byes. They knew where we planned to be the next few days, and we hoped they would catch up with us. I knew, however, our pace was a bit fast for my German friend and suspected we would not see them again on this trip. We were sad to leave.

Oruro had been hit hard by the rains and, having no paved streets, was almost impassible without a four wheel drive vehicle. By the time we found our way through and out of the city, it was almost dark. We forded a number of bad washouts south of Oruro, and the rain worsened. We saw no places we felt comfortable pulling over for the night. On the other hand, the road was very bad and it seemed unwise to continue without the benefit of daylight. We weren't sure we were even on the right road. In the distance we saw a Land Rover and sped up to ask directions. After verifying our route, the driver told us he and his family had been on a holiday in La Paz and were returning to their home at a government mining camp about sixty miles to the southeast. They invited us to come with them for the night, but it was quite far out of our way. On this road, sixty miles was a four hour drive. They understood and suggested we stay with a friend who was general manager of a mining camp in Machacamarca, a small town thirty miles south on our road. He wrote us a letter of introduction, and we followed them another fifteen miles to where they forked left. We forded one more tricky river and arrived in Machacamarca an hour later. The guard at the mining camp gate waved us through after reading our letter. Señor Julio Rosa, the general manager, was watching a movie when his caretaker showed him our letter. He came outside to greet us and welcomed us to sleep in his home. His family lived in La Paz, and he said there was plenty of room. We declined, asking only to be permitted to park in his driveway where we could safely sleep in our camper.

"Of course. As you wish," he graciously complied and returned to his movie.

We cooked a quick supper and, as Mike would say, crashed.

We had just finished stowing our sleeping bags when Señor Rosa's caretaker knocked on our door to inform us breakfast was ready. This was much more hospitality than we expected. The table was set formally and included fresh fruit, eggs, bacon and hot rolls. We thoroughly enjoyed our first sit down breakfast in a long time. After breakfast Julio asked me to join him in his office. We chatted for an hour about some of his relatives living in the United States and many of the social problems in Bolivia. He criticized the government, not with the fervor of a revolutionary, but with the quiet resignation of a man who believed the situation is hopeless and is ready to flee.

"One of our biggest problems," observed Julio, "is the Indian." Three out of four of our people are Indians. They are not productive. They want nothing better for themselves or for the country."

"Why do you suppose they are not more ambitious?"

"Perhaps it is the altiplano," he replied. "Life is difficult here. We need a dictator who is not interested in lining his own pockets, but in making things better. If he could force the people to work, to become educated, to want more, then perhaps things would improve."

"Why can't such a man be found?"

"Who knows? Now nobody wants to be president. They have to bribe a man to become president, promising him much wealth and, in a few years, wealth in exile."

"Of course, that perpetuates dishonesty in the presidency."

"Yes, I know."

Señor Rosa asked one of the mining camp's mechanics to check our car. He found a slowly leaking tire and fixed it. Bread had not been available in La Paz the past few days, apparently due to a shortage of wheat. We thanked Julio profusely for his hospitality, and, as a departure gift, he gave us a bag of rolls freshly baked that morning in the camp's bakery.

The rays of the morning sun slanted onto ruggedly eroded hills guarding the altiplano, reflecting a palette of blues, greens, grays, reds and browns. In the distance a pair of Andean condors soared on the morning thermals. Near Potosi, hideous tailings, remnants of a mountain that long ago had been mined for silver ore, lay exposed. The silver ran out, and the city died. Then tin was discovered on the same mountain, and Potosi again rose to prominence. We filled our gas tank, and, driving from the station up a hill, the car's engine lost power. Where was Karl when we needed him? After a minute the power returned. We found a pension where we could camp for the night. Peasant revolts seemed to be on everybody's mind. The manager of the little hotel wanted to talk politics, and he expressed sentiments similar to those of Julio Rosa—Bolivia needed a dictator interested in helping the people rather than becoming rich.

"Perhaps Brazil is the answer," he suggested.

"In what way?"

"People say Brazil wants our natural resources. One day they may draw a new frontier on their maps," he explained, "and we will be able to do nothing about it. Perhaps it should happen."

Fording flooded tributaries and washouts no longer was a problem. The wet, relatively flat altiplano gradually changed into a desert carved with deeply eroded arroyos. The road became a twisting, turning nightmare. We averaged less than fifteen miles per hour. Gas was supposedly available in two villages. We asked for gas in the first town. "No hay." There is none. In the second village we were told, "Hay poquito." There is very little. We waited an hour before buying two twenty liter containers of sixty-five octane gas—about eleven gallons and enough to take us to the Argentinian border.

The engine pinged loudly as we pushed south through the Bolivian desert. At Iscoyochi the road branched, the left fork leading to Tarija and the west fork climbing the central cordillero to the border town of Villazon. The road narrowed, becoming even more difficult and slow. We could average no more than ten miles per hour. I honked the horn approaching each curve, turning precariously within inches of precipitous cliffs. The twisting and turning and breaking and accelerating left us all feeling not too chipper. At 5:00 in the afternoon the border still lay twenty miles away, and the customs and immigration offices were scheduled to close in an hour.

We continued climbing slowly and then suddenly were on the altiplano with its gently rolling hills and relatively straight road. Our spirits soared with a renewed hope we would spend the night in the auto club parking lot on the Argentinian side of the border. We arrived in Villazon at 5:30. I ran to the customs office while Lynette and the children changed money. We returned to the camper, started it, but the car would not advance. Then the motor quit running and I could not restart it. I pushed it, and it began rolling downhill to the International Bridge. I left it stalled in front of the immigration office and finished our Bolivian paperwork by 5:50. With Lynette steering, I pushed the VW across the bridge. A synpathetic Argentinian official helped me complete our customs and immigration paperwork before the offices closed. With the paperwork finished, I walked across the street to the auto club to arrange for a tow truck to pull our VW up the hill from the border to a service garage. I heard a horn toot and turned around. Lynette waved and drove the camper into the automobile club, smugly smiling, I suppose, at her cleverness in starting the engine. We camped that night in the parking area of the Automobile Club of Argentina, incredulous we had made it. Lynette laughed and said she wished she had taken a photograph of me pushing the camper across the Puente Internacional.

A flat right front tire greeted us in the morning. The auto club mechanic repaired it before we finished breakfast, and we soon were on our way. Argentinian villages appeared more prosperous than those in Bolivia—with larger houses, extensive electrical and communications lines and automobiles. Usually the most important building in the town was a school rather than a church. After a few hours we descended from the altiplano through rugged mountains with scalloped, multi-colored rock layers, following a dry riverbed to the town of San Salvador de Jujuy where we picked up a paved road for the first time since we left Nazca. The mountains faded off to the west, and the terrain to the east was flat. Las pampas—vast grassland plains with farms and ranches—not totally unlike Kansas or Nebraska in the fifties before freeways, fast food and motel chains dominated the rural landscape. Lynette wondered aloud where all the gauchos were.

"They've had a change in their career path," I offered.

"How's that?"

"Haven't you noticed all the truck drivers? Apparently they're paid more to punch the pedal to the metal than to punch cows."

We arrived in colonial San Miquel de Tucuman late in the afternoon and joined about a dozen Argentinian families camped in a park in the town's center. One of our tires was almost flat, so we had it fixed. All day we anticipated eating a steak dinner. Argentinian beef was reputed to be, if not the most tender, the sweetest and best tasting in the world. Our camper neighbors directed us to the best restaurant in town where we scanned the menus brought by the waiter.

"We'll all have steak," I told him.

"Lo siento mucho, Señor. No hay."

"What do you mean, there is no steak. It's right here on the menu!"

The patient waiter explained. The Argentinian government had a new policy. Beef could be served only during the second half of the month. Today was March 3rd. We had come to Argentina during the beefless half of the month! The waiter supposed the policy was designed to save the country's beef for export. Can you imagine our disappointment? It wasn't the waiter's fault, so we ordered chicken, a compromise only Krissie was happy about. A large owl flew across the road in front of us on the way back to the campground.

In Cordoba we cashed a traveler's check in a hotel. The clerk remarked that we had come to Cordoba at the wrong time. He explained that the provincial governor and the local police were having a disagreement over who was running the city. I asked him why Peron didn't settle the argument, and he shrugged his shoulders. We drove further into the colonial city and encountered barracades and armed soldiers at many intersections. Lynette reminded me that several months ago American executives had been kidnapped and shot in this very city. Disappointed with not being able to see more of Cordoba, the religious and intellectual center of Argentina, we found our way out of the city and headed southeast toward Buenos Aires and, we hoped, a more stable atmosphere.

Late in the afternoon, about half way to Buenos Aires and in the middle of nowhere, we saw a motel. Lynette suggested we stay there and shower rather than dropping in on the capital in our present condition. I concurred since I wanted to shave my three month old itchy beard and preferred using hot water. Much to our surprise and delight, a restaurant next door not only had steak on the menu, but they were willing to serve it. Lynette said it was the best steak she ever had. I asked the waiter how the restaurant had obtained permission to serve beef during the first half of the month. He had no idea what I was talking about. I started to explain about our experience in Tucuman, but, feeling somewhat sheepish, I dropped it.

After dinner, Mike and I watched a soccer game on the fuzzy black and white TV in the lobby while the girls showered. Then Mike showered after which I did the same and shaved. I kissed the children goodnight and later snuggled Lynette. None of them noticed I had shaved. Krissie was the first up in the morning. She jumped into bed with Lynette and me and loudly announced, "Hey! You shaved!"

Our first stop in the port city of Santa Maria de Buenos Aires was the tourist office where we learned there was no place to camp within an hour of the city's center. We found a budget hotel within walking distance of Plaza San Martin and its equestrian statue of the national hero, Plaza Nueve de Julio and Plaza Cinco de Mayo, the city's three most important centers of interest. Buenos Aires is a city to be walked. Cafes and restaurants with continental menus line broad boulevards and wide avenues, while statues of historic figures grace beautiful plazas, all of this creating a distinctly European atmosphere. We spent our first afternoon in B.A. on one of Lynette's walking tours, leisurely becoming familiar with the city—the historic Cabildo (town hall), the Casa Rosada (pink government palace), the Cathedral with Jose de San Martin's mausoleum. After dinner we sat in a sidewalk cafe on the world's widest avenue, Avenida Nueve de Julio, drinking coffee and hot chocolate, watching the people walk by and talking about the many adventures our little family had experienced in the past few months.

Changing money turned out to be a time consuming operation in Buenos Aires. Tremendous volatility of the Argentinian peso created very interesting situations. The exchange rate with the dollar fluctuated as much as twenty per cent, depending on the time of day and with whom you were talking. With the rates varying so much, it paid to shop around. I was a regular visitor to the many casas de cambio (exchange houses) on Plaza Cinco de Mayo while Lynette and the children shopped on famous Calle Florida.

We picked up our mail at the U.S. Embassy. Included was a large envelope adressed to the children from their school back in Minnesota. They found a real treat inside the envelope—letters and valentines from their classmates.

Portenos (residents of Buenos Aires) eat four times each day. In addition to the normal three meals, Portenos have afternoon tea which usually includes not just tea but cakes and sweets as well. We preferred having our afternoon tea in one especially elegant confiteria (confectionery) with dark mahogany woodwork, mirrored walls, marble floors and large crystal chandeliers.

Mike and I were pretty shaggy after three months of camping. One morning we found a barber shop, an old fashioned affair with mahogany furniture and large mirrors, one where women are seldom found and then only when they bring in their little boy for a haircut. Mike and I sat in chairs next to each other, saying little. We looked at each other and smiled. There's something good about a father and son getting a haircut together. Mike's smile vanished, however, when the barber whipped out a straight razor, sharpened it and shaved the boy's neck.

Mike and Krissie experienced their first subway ride on the way to Palermo Park, which contained a rose garden, the Hipodromo Argentino (race track), zoological gardens, a tennis club, fencing club and the Buenos Aires Zoo. We admired the zoo's marvelous collection of South American mammals, birds (the penguin collection fascinated Lynette) and other animals and ate hot dogs for lunch.

From my notes: *Lynette and I drank coffee on a park bench while the kiddies rode on a carousel playing gaucho music. Wispy clouds raced across the warm, blue sky, and leaves skittered across the grass. How much I love this family!*

One evening, sitting in a sidewalk cafe on Avenida Nueve de Julio, I had a strange feeling of safety and belonging. Unlike Cordoba, soldiers did not walk the streets of Buenos Aires. People smiled and waved at one other. Friends hugged and kissed each other's cheeks. This easily could have been Paris.

We drove to B.A.'s busy port to book passage on the ferry crossing the bay of the Rio de la Plata from Argentina to Colonia, Uruguay, arriving at the pier in time to watch the ferry docking. The handsome, trim young captain stood on the bridge, tanned and erect, giving orders with very formal hand signals. Members of the crew expertly tossed weighted ties ashore. An officious man kept the people on shore behind an imaginary line, as he loudly explained, for their own safety. Lynette said all this drama played an important role, relieving the boredom of twice daily round trip voyages between Colonia and Buenos Aires. The captain and his crew, as she would have predicted, went through the exact same motions in Colonia after the three hour trip from Argentina to Uruguay.

Gas in Uruguay cost four times as much as in the United States. A gas station attendent quickly reminded us, when I gasped at the price, that at least there was no gas shortage in Uruguay. No surprise at those prices! That there was little demand for gas became apparent as we drove on. Beautifully paved, tree lined roads were virtually unused by gasoline powered vehicles. Most people either walked or rode bicycles. Only occasionally did an old car or motor scooter drive by.

We arrived in Montevideo after dark, drove directly to the Plaza Independencia situated in the city's center and ordered a steak dinner at a restaurant full of happy Uruguayans. Upon finishing eating, we had no obvious place to go for the night, so we set up camp right there in the Plaza Independencia under the equestrian statue of Uruguay's national hero, General Jose Artigas. The children went to bed, and Lynette and I strolled hand-in-hand around the Plaza—a moment of perfect peace.

La Carreta, Montevideo's signature monument of Uruguayan pioneers and their oxen, resides in Batlle Park. Lynette fixed ham and eggs while the children and I skipped stones across the pool below the famous sculpture. During breakfast she remembered that she forgot to congratulate me yesterday for not getting seasick crossing the bay, a reference to one of my many weaknesses I preferred forgetting. We went sightseeing in the Ciudad Vieja (Old City) and walked along the beach at Playa Pacitos and then visited a leather factory where Lynette surprised us all, including herself, by buying two coats, one of suede and the other of nutria. She needed a winter and a fall coat anyway, she reminded me.

Affluent farms dotted the rolling Uruguayan countryside. We stopped for gas in the departmental capital of the country's cattle and sheep raising area, Treinta y Tres, named after the thirty three patriots who followed Juan Antonio Lavalleja in the uprising against Brazillian domination. Now it became evident why we saw no gauchos in Argentina: they were all in Uruguay. Cowboys in typical gaucho costumes—pantalunes, sombrero, pancho, spurs—rode their horses along fence lines, driving cattle. We stopped and talked with three of them who were as curious about us as we were about them. They posed proudly for our cameras, and then one of them gave Mike a lesson on throwing bolas. With one toss he immobilized a heifer, the balls and thongs wrapping around her legs.

Surprisingly, the Brazilian border was still open at ten o'clock that evening. Brazilians speak Portuguese, but we knew only a few words. English speaking people don't often enter Brazil from the south, so, when the officious official rattled off a series of questions we didn't understand, I asked him if we could conduct our business in Spanish. The impatient official told me to speak Spanish. I told him I was doing exactly that. His Spanish wasn't so good either, and, moreover, he was not a little drunk. One doesn't win arguments with border officials or drunks; that is, unless one is prepared to wait until their replacements come, which I wasn't. So, with a smile, I endured his abusive references to my stupidity. A man from the immigration office came to our rescue, apologizing for the drunken customs official's behavior, checked our papers cursorily and sent us on our way.

The young attendant at a nearby gas station welcomed our camping in their parking area for the night. He had lived in Chicago for a year but, missing his friends, recently returned home to Brazil. Now he seldom spoke English and appreciated the opportunity to chat with us. He was a soccer player but looked big enough to play linebacker for the Minnesota Vikings.

We had just finished washing the camper the next morning when Mauro Ernani, the gas station attendant, showed up. Most of the stores were closed on Sundays, but he took us to a Casa de Cambio that was open and then to a friend who allowed us to shop in his closed grocery store.

Big beautiful Brazil! Modern highways, clean gas stations and fertile farmland greeted us. Brazil has geographic size and diversity, a large population and abundant natural resources. At the time, their economy was booming. While some people still traveled in oxcarts, commercial trucks filled the highways. Little poverty was apparent in the countryside. White stuccoed farm houses with red tiled roofs shone brightly in the green fields.

From my notes: *The government is a military dictatorship. They argue we are too quick to criticize this form of government and that democracy would quickly usher in anarchy or a communistic dictatorship. Admittedly the leaders do not seem to be lining their pockets at the expense of the people. But they do seem more interested in racking up great economic numbers than in making life better for the people. Freedom is permitted as long as it does not interfere with the government's programs.*

Porto Alegre with its lovely tree lined streets, parks and modern buildings perched on a hill above the Guaiba River. We enjoyed our lunch in a pleasant park and continued north along the coastal highway where the terrain changed dramatically. Forested mountains with monolithic granite outcropings often rose directly out of the ocean. A lush, tropical undergrowth vegetated the forest floor. Fresh water lakes occasionally lay between the mountains and the ocean, giving the impression the mountains were long ago scooped from the lake beds.

Possibly the sweetest, most succulent and delicious pineapples in the world are the small variety grown in the state of Rio Grande de Sul. We stopped at a roadside stand about half way between Porto Alegre and Curitiba and bought pineapples, corn and bananas, then spent the night in the parking area of a nearby modern gas station. We cooked corn and sausages for supper and enjoyed pineapple for dessert. We showered in the facilities normally used by male truckers but off limits to them while Lynette and Krissie took theirs, and then chatted (to the extent we could since they didn't speak English) with the attendants and a group of truckers who were also spending the night there.

At Curitiba we turned west for Foz do Iguacu or Iguacu Falls. The hilly terrain became more rain forested. We stopped for lunch and found the car difficult to restart. The rainy season was upon us, and while mornings and evenings were clear, heavy showers fell off and on during the afternoon. Wonderful bright rainbows, with blues and greens predominating the spectrum, appeared over lush green hills. Early that evening we arrived in Foz do Iguacu, a town fifteen miles from the magnificent waterfalls of the same name. The VW's motor had been running suspiciously all afternoon. I parked the car on a hill, diagonal to the curb, and asked Lynette to keep the motor running while I ran into a store for something. When I returned the motor had stopped and I could not restart it. With no little irritation, I foolishly blamed Lynette for letting the car die and impulsively called her a "spacehead." In the heat of the battles of life I have said many things I later regretted, but this peccadillo takes the cake. To this day, Lynette or the children resurrect the "spacehead" incident whenever any of them wants to prove a point concerning my short temper or any of my many other character flaws. In my ledger, the bill has been paid. Not so with them.

A few local fellows helped me push the camper back from the curb, so we could coast downhill. When I disengaged the clutch, the car started easily enough. I was encouraged—we could make it to the VW dealer in Sao Paulo as long as we could find hills to park on. The car ran without incident to the falls, and the parking area of a hilltop hotel above the falls provided a good campsite. That evening a pleasant breeze discouraged the mosquitoes and the roar of Iguacu Falls covered the uproar of a riotous party in the hotel.

In the midst of a virgin rain forest, the Iguacu River cascades over a two hundred thirty-five-foot escarpment in a series of cataracts stretching along a two and one half mile arc. Cloudy mists rose through tropical verdure from the gorge below. The jungle surrounded us as we walked down a trail leading to the falls. Lush vegetation with festoons of orchids lined the path. Colorful butterflies flitted about everywhere. Large spiders waited for hapless insects in huge webs, while the rising sun's rays reflected off the dew on the intricately woven patterns. Once we carefully stepped around a large, coiled black snake. The roar of the falls became louder and then deafening as we rounded a corner and came face to face with *Garganta do Diablo*, the Devil's Throat. A concrete pathway followed the brink of one tier of the falls and led deep into the *Garganta* where, surrounded by tiers of the roaring cascade above and below, we stood deafened, awe-struck and a bit frightened.

Downstream from the falls, the Iguacu River divides Brazil on the east from Argentina on the west. Above the falls, where the Parana and Paraguay rivers join and become the Iguacu, three countries—Brazil, Argentina and Paraguay—meet. We walked to the bridge crossing the Parana River to Paraguay. The waiting lines at immigration and customs were quite long, so we departed for Sao Paulo.

From my notes: *Lynette and I seldom quarrel at home, and, when it happens, we save our words for when the children are out of earshot. Living in close quarters tends to make things tense, but, until now, we have had no real quarrels. Maybe it was because the trip is drawing to an end, or perhaps because of the difficulties with the camper, in any case, the conditions were ripe for a good old fashioned spat. We drove most of the day, stopping for gas late in the afternoon. The car would not start. Two local fellows pushed us, and the engine started. I was tired of driving and asked Lynette to take over. The engine immediately stalled. I was furious, said more than a few things I now regret including "get out of the way so I can drive." Her embarassment and resentment were obvious. The fellows, amused at my outburst, pushed us again, and though the motor kept running, we both stewed driving off into the evening.*

Now I was concerned about making it all the way to the VW dealer in Sao Paulo. I had been driving all day and was tired, but knew that was a feeble reason for losing my temper, especially in front of the children. I was upset, mostly at myself. Sao Paulo was 120 miles away, and my objective was to get close enough to the city to drive into a VW dealer early the next morning. Then a tire went flat—at the bottom of a hill. I asked Lynette to keep the car running while I change the tire. The engine stalled again.

From my notes: *At this point I'm ready to trade her and the car in.* I changed the tire, and a truck driver stopped and got us started with jumper cables. We drove a few more miles to a gas station, had the tire fixed, and spent the night in the parking area—at the top of a small hill.

With a push downhill the car started and continued running all the way to Sao Paulo, the industrious commercial heart of Brazil. We drove directly to a VW dealer and explained the car's problems. They wanted a couple of days to service it properly. I made a few phone calls, and we took a cab downtown to meet the incomparable Mauricio Dantas, a business friend I had met several years before. Mauricio was bigger than life, literally and figuratively. The former olympic weight lifter from Belo Horizonte had owned a computer service bureau, sold it and was now running for Congress. Mauricio spent the day with us, showing us Sao Paulo, a city that is, mostly, all business. Serious, hard working "Paulistas" bustled on the city's sidewalks. Later, Mauricio dined with us at a Bahian restaurant where we joined a group of his congenial but boisterous friends for dinner. We talked about his weightlifting days, mostly for Mike's benefit, and, since Mauricio was an enthusiastic supporter of the government, politics. Krissie and Mike fell asleep in Mauricio's car on the drive back to the VW dealer where we camped in the secured parking area.

Lynette and the children busied themselves the next morning in the downtown area. Krissie and Mike were fascinated by the ubiquitous stilt-walking human billboards. Mauricio accompanied me, explaining he was too embarrassed by my "ludicrous attempts to speak Portuguese" to leave me alone, while I visited a number of shipping companies, checking the schedules out of Rio de Janeiro. In mid-afternoon the car was ready, so we bade *adieu* to Mauricio and departed for Rio. We spent what was to be our last night camping in South America in the parking area of a gas station half way between Sao Paulo and Rio.

With an early start we were in good spirits. After all, the car's engine was performing better than it had since Mexico. We hadn't gone far, however, when a tire blew out. I put on the spare. Fifty miles further and another tire blew out—we had no spare! I carried the wheel with the blown out tire more than a mile to a gas station, leaving Lynette and the children waiting in the car. They found a used tire and tube which were close to the right size, put them on the wheel, and drove me back to the car. Twenty-five miles down the road this tire went flat. Another gas station patched the leak and inflated the tire. We slowly limped into beautiful Rio, registered at a hotel near Ipanema Beach, went swimming, had dinner at a good charisciuro, returned to the hotel and crashed.

I went to the shipping company while Lynette and the kiddies went to the beach. The shipper's representative accompanied me, talking non-stop and stopping every few minutes for a beer, while we visited all the necessary offices to arrange the shipment of the camper from Rio to New York. This car now had 21,000 very rough miles on it. The camper's engine had been abused by low octane gas and its body by high risk roads. The cost to ship the car back home was probably more than the van was worth, but selling it was not an alternative. We had given the American Automobile

Association a letter of credit that guaranteed to all the countries we drove through that we would not sell it. I signed all the required papers to ship the van the following day.

Rio rivals any other city in the world for beauty. Pao de Acucar (Sugarloaf Mountain) looms majestically over lovely Guanabara Bay. Across the city, Corcovado with its colossal eighty-foot statue of Christ mirrors Sugarloaf. Avenida Beira-Mar follows a serpentine line along a series of crescent shaped, white sand beaches—Flamengo, Botafogo, Copacabana, Ipanema and Leblon. Mosaic tiled sidewalks flank broad, tree-lined Avenida Rio Branco. The Circuit of Gavea skirts Lagoa (lagoon) Rodrigo de Freitas with its Jockey Club, race track and botanical gardens. Polo fields and golf courses flank Avenida Niemeyer. We drove around the city, taking in these sights, then to Barra de Tijuca, a wonderful tropical forest with birds, orchids, butterflies and waterfalls.

In the morning we turned our camper over to the shipper and arranged with a travel agent the remainder of our schedule, flying home with planned layovers in Brasilia, the country's capital; Manaus, in the heart of the Amazon basin; and Tobago, a birders' paradise. Then to the beach where we body surfed and Mike and I, to the consternation of many of the other bathers, put on our baseball gloves and passed a hardball back and forth. Later, while Mike and Krissie played in the sand and frigate birds and boobies soared and swooped overhead, Lynette and I watched the carefree Cariocas (residents of Rio) strolling by. Bikinis were *de rigueur* for women and men on Rio beaches. Vendors walked by with large, aluminum coolers strapped to their backs yelling, "Le-mo-na-da." Boys and girls played paddleball and flew screaming thunderbird kites. Children romped in playgrounds and young adults played soccer in parks next to the beaches. These people were having a lot of fun, and, just think, Carnival was over! We had fun too the next few days, going to the beach, walking around town, loafing, and going to a soccer game at Maracana stadium where a quarter of a million people can sit to watch a game. Sipping cafezinho at a sidewalk cafe in the Lapa district late one afternoon, I said I was having a hard time getting used to hotel living. Lynette agreed, saying she preferred the confines of our camper.

Brazil's population is concentrated along the Atlantic coast. In 1960, after years of planning and building, President Juscelino Kubitschek moved the federal capital to Brasilia, located on the nation's central plateau. Official propaganda advertises the move was made to encourage westward expansion. Some locals, however, thought the move silly and Kubitschek superstitious. The president, according to some, believed in an old religious vision: if the capital were built where Brasilia stands today, it would lead the country to world domination. The old story specified, however, that the great city would stand by a lake. Everything about the location of Brasilia matched the description of the envisioned city except for the absence of a lake. Kubitschek was not deterred. He built a large lake so all the details of the prophecy matched.

Our flight from Brasilia to Manaus advanced a day, so, disappointed, we saw Brasilia and architect Oscar Niemeyer's famed ultra modern buildings only from a distance, flying into and out of the airport. On the flight from Rio to Brasilia, we met and chatted with a columnist named Branco who wrote for *The Globe* in Rio. At the Brasilia airport he gave Lynette and the children little gifts, key chains with scenes of the capital.

Flying low over the rain forest into Manaus, we saw "the wedding of the waters." Manaus sits one thousand miles from the Atlantic at the confluence of the Rio Negro and the mighty Amazon. The Amazon is cooler, faster and lighter weight than the Negro, and, for several miles downstream from Manaus, a line of demarcation separates the dark, black waters of the Negro from the chocolaty brown Amazon until they gradually blend into one.

Manaus was a splendid city a hundred years ago when it supplied the world with natural rubber. That ended when cheaper sources of rubber became available. The city decayed and almost died. Two developments in the fifties and sixties helped revive Manaus. It became an important source of cacao, and the Brazilian government, recognizing Manaus' importance in opening the Amazon region to its true commercial potential, established the city as a free port, granting tax incentives to industry for moving into the area.

Scaffolding surrounded the famed Opera House built by rubber barons in the nineteenth century. The building was being renovated and was off limits to visitors, but much of its earlier splendor remained visible. We walked the streets, getting a feel for the small city, and then visited the thriving floating market by the wharfs where we arranged for a guided river trip the next morning.

A young English couple joined us on the small boat. He had a job in Rio, working for the British government in educational TV. Our guide was only eighteen, but spoke English well and had a good knowledge of the area's natural history. Our boat left from its dock on the Rio Negro, motored past the floating market and out into the Amazon where we saw up close and personal the violent whirlpools and eddies caused by the impact of the two rivers' currents, a championship battle with the stubborn Rio Negro refusing to yield until miles downstream where the mighty Amazon ultimately prevailed. The flow of the Amazon was incredible—greater than the next eight largest rivers combined. For sheer bulk, the Amazon makes the Nile look like a brook; the Mississippi trench compares to that of the Amazon as the bore of a 22 caliber rifle compares to the cannon of a battleship! The Amazon/Orinaco system drains a basin larger than the area of the lower forty-eight states. In the Amazon's environs are some of the world's deadliest animals and most primitive humans. Draining the world's largest and most biologically diverse rain forest, the Amazon is truly one of the Earth's great natural wonders.

Through a maze of floating islands that had been torn loose from the shores upstream, our boat threaded its way to a large permanent island where we walked barefoot through deep mud, saw rubber trees being tapped, and sucked the white, slimy sweet coating from cocoa beans. Back on the boat, our guide caught two pirhanas. He lifted the retractable upper lip of one of the vicious little carnivores, showing us its serrated teeth. Then he held one fish next to the other and, ravenously, it bit chunks out of the other's back.

We tied up near a small island and had a delicious lunch of local food—fish, rice, eggs, and vegetables. Along the Amazon, we saw villages with houses that were built on stilts in order to accommodate the river's thirty-five-foot variations in depth. Kids swam and men fished from the banks. Then we sailed up a tributary of the Amazon where we saw fresh water porpoises, many birds, snakes and butterflies and caught huge catfish. We paddled dugout canoes into the wilderness and saw many flowers, including huge water lillies with pads large enough to walk on. Back on the Rio Negro we went swimming only after the guide assured us pirhanas inhabit more shallow waters. Not being completely convinced, we waited for him to take the first plunge.

We returned to Manaus late in the day. Driving back to the Amazonas Hotel, our driver stopped. He asked us all to get out of the van. Somehow a five-foot boa constrictor had gotten loose in the rear of the van. Twenty minutes passed before the snake was safely ensconced in its cage.

Our flight was scheduled to leave for Tobago at 6:00 a.m. I wakened the others at 4:30, dressed, carried the luggage to the lobby, and walked three blocks to find a cab. On the way to the airport, I remembered my watch was still on Rio time, one hour ahead of Manaus. My popularity plummeted when I broke the news to my sleepy companions. Things got only worse at the airport when we learned the flight had been delayed an hour. Soon the airline announced an additional delay of four hours. Then just before departure time, the airline announced the flight was postponed until 5:30 the next morning. We were warned to be at the airport by 3:30 a.m., and I was warned to set my watch to the correct time.

We arrived at the airport on time, only to learn at 5:00 the flight had been canceled. Why didn't they call us at the hotel? We slept for a couple hours and then went to the Cruziero airline office. Our only alternative, other than waiting a week, was the flight to Belem at the mouth of the Amazon scheduled to leave at 5:30 the next morning. From there we could connect to Paramaribo (Surinam), Georgetown (Guyana), and then on to Barbados. We decided to cancel our airline reservations to Tobago and instead spend a few days in Barbados before returning to Minnesota.

After our arrival at the airport on time the next morning, the flight was postponed an hour (6:30). We boarded the plane, and, at 6:28, we were told to get off the plane and go to a waiting room. I'm sure any minute we'll be told the flight is canceled and to return to the hotel. A half hour later we reboarded the plane, and it took off. We spent the last few days of our South American adventure enjoying the white sand beaches and Caribbean charm of Barbados. It was the beginning of April, and "the ice was not yet out," as the locals say, on the Minnesota lakes.

Minneapolis, Minnesota, April, 1974

Most people, including me, find it difficult to leave their jobs behind when taking a vacation. It's different, however, when you leave for an extended period of time, especially if it's an intensive trip, one that demands your complete attention. Then you find yourself forgetting the job. I spent little time in South America thinking about my job back in Minnesota. But there was never any doubt that I would return and resume working at the newspaper. I had made a commitment to do so.

I returned to Minneapolis on the date the newspaper's owner and I had agreed upon before I left. I have only a sketchy recollection of the conversations and sequence of events, but they went something like this:

I called my boss, told him I was back in town, and I would see him at work the next morning. He hesitated, then asked me to meet him for breakfast instead of coming to the newspaper building. I agreed, thinking this sounded a bit ominous. We met in the morning, and he told me he had replaced me. I asked him how he could do that when I was on a leave of absence. He said business was bad in the first quarter and he thought someone was needed in my position. He professed offense that I hadn't called him the whole time I was gone. I reminded him that I had suggested we set up times when I would call, but he told me not to call because it was too expensive and I couldn't do anything from South America anyway. He said he still thought I should have called. He was willing to hire me back in a lesser position. I declined the offer which I considered demeaning, and we parted with some frigidity.

I couldn't believe it. I thought the guy loved me. After all, he was the one who persuaded me to take a leave of absence rather than quitting. Had I known this was going to happen, we would have done everything differently—taken more time in South America, gone to Chile, sold our house instead of renting it so we could have continued our travels in Europe, Africa, or wherever we chose. It was also embarrassing. Instead of my making the decision to quit as I had originally intended, he was dumping me!

During the next few days I received several calls from people working at the newspaper suggesting I had gotten a bad deal. I assured them that was not the case, that I had no complaints. After the third such call, I telephoned the owner and told him I was getting calls from people who seemed disgruntled about the situation. I suggested he might want a letter from me stating I had no complaints about the way I was treated. He said he would appreciate my doing that, which I did. About one year later this man gave me a glowing recommendation when he was contacted by a company I went to work for—one of the best companies in the history of American business, and one at which I made a small fortune.

Chapter Three
Getting Serious: A European Holiday

Do not go gentle into that good night.
Rage, rage against the dying of the light.
Dylan Thomas

We four, Christmas, 1974; Estepona, Spain

PREPARATIONS

Europe was the most logical next destination on our camping tour of the world. Volkswagen offered a program that seemed tailor made for us: we could order a camper from a dealer in the United States, pick it up in Europe, drive it around the continent for up to a year, and then they would pay to ship it back to the U.S. The camper we drove to South America had seen better days, to say the least, so we took advantage of Volkswagen's program. We traded in the old, white camper after it arrived in New York and ordered a new rig—bright yellow—and made arrangements to pick it up in Luxembourg, since Icelandic Air offered the cheapest round-trip flight to Europe, originating in New York, stopping for twenty-four hours in Reykjavik and terminating in Luxembourg.

The American Automobile Association (AAA) published detailed touring maps and guides for all the countries in Great Britain and Europe, including passport and visa requirements, currency exchange information, customs regulations, weather information, language tips, historical background and descriptions of important cities and attractions. Camping and backpacking were common ways of traveling in Europe, and commercial campgrounds were ubiquitous and often open year round. Several comprehensive campground guides were published and available in bookstores. AAA also published a *Motoring In Europe* guide that included a planning map, itinerary planner and suggested itineraries, mileage and driving time between most cities, car ferry schedules and costs, driving regulations, and much other information helpful to motorists driving through Europe.

With the abundant availability of reference material on European travel, we quickly planned an itinerary, concentrating on northern Europe in the summer and migrating to the continent's southern environs in the fall and winter. (Quick inspection of a globe reveals that the latitude of "southern" Europe when compared to the United States isn't really very far south. We spent some very cold winter nights in southern Europe.) In the seventies, independent travel in the Soviet Union and eastern Europe was a bureaucratic nightmare, so we essentially eliminated most of those countries from our itinerary.

Beyond spending six to eight months touring Europe, our plans were uncertain. We talked about continuing on through Africa and Asia, but didn't make any specific plans to do so. I do remember all of us leaving the country with an ebullient attitude. None of us really had been especially anxious to quit traveling and settle back into our conventional life in Minnesota. All of the reasons to leave in the first place were still valid. In addition, now there was no concern about the unknown. South America had been a marvelous experience. We had met all the challenges and answered all our concerns—we were now veteran vagabonds, bona fide continental drifters. I didn't even mind my dad calling us "hippies."

After learning my services were no longer required at the newspaper, we remained in Minneapolis only about two months, long enough to update our travel plans for the children's teachers, our parents, our friends (including those who were paying our bills and boarding our cat, etc.), and to sell our house and store our furniture. We flew to Chicago to visit Lynette's family and then to Pennsylvania to see my family. My parents drove us from Harrisburg to New York and saw us off at Icelandic Air's terminal at Kennedy Airport.

Luxembourg City, Luxembourg, June 17, 1974

A twenty-four hour stopover in Iceland's small capital city of Reykjavik provided a nice break in our long trans-Atlantic flight. Iceland, land of Viking explorers—Eric "the Red" Thorvaldsson, who discovered and colonized Greenland, and his son, Leif "the Lucky" Ericsson, who sailed beyond to

North America! We did a bit of exploring ourselves, renting a car and touring the treeless tundra of the nearby rural area. Along the coast, clear blue coves were filling up with eiders and other sea birds returning north to their breeding grounds. Bubbling hot springs lay scattered around the countryside, and, following local customs, we bathed in one of those natural tubs, our nakedness mostly hidden by steam.

From my notes: *We bought wool hats and smoked cod in the duty free shop and slept on a very hard bed.*

The Grand Duchy of Luxembourg, a small, teardrop-shaped country nestled among Belgium, France and Germany, has a rich history, much of it having been tied to the fortunes of its larger neighbors. Luxembourg City is perched on a massive limestone outcropping rising above the Alzette River. A large fortress complete with turrets, spires and high stone walls dominates the city center. The nighttime illumination of the fortifications and bridges spanning the Alzette is unforgettable.

From the airport we went directly to the Volkswagen dealer to pick up our camper which was orange instead of the bright yellow we had expected. We drove through a rain storm into the small capital city, stopping for lunch at a cafe next to the railroad station. We changed money, bought liability insurance for the next eight months, visited the National Museum and the Citadel, and, that evening, drove across the Pont Adolphe one hundred fifty feet above the Alzette gorge on the way out of town. We camped in a woods outside the city, went to bed early, tired from the flight and a bit discouraged that our first day in Europe had been rained out.

Our spirits rose with the morning sun. We drove east to Grevenmacher and then north through the Moselle River valley. Vinyards cascaded down the slopes on either side of the river, and we stopped in Echternach, where we walked the narrow medieval streets and bought groceries, including wine, salami and bread for lunch. Mike was fascinated by the dungeons and torture chambers in the castle at Beaufort, which we gazed on while sitting on a hill and eating our lunch. Later, on the road to Clervaux which led through the Ardennes Forest, we passed several more medieval castles.

We set up camp in the parking area below the feudal castle of Clervaux, once the seat of the Counts of Clervaux, ancestors of the Roosevelts.

From my notes: *Lynette is more relaxed than I've seen her since South America.* Mike and I were playing catch in the parking lot when a camper from Denmark pulled in beside ours. The Danish couple, in English, asked what we were doing. Mike thought it odd they could speak English so well and not recognize a game of "catch" for what it is. We shared our wine with them after dinner, talked about our respective plans, and they invited us to their home when we came to Denmark. Driving that day, we had been surprised at the number of campers on the road, many of them appearing to be on fishing holidays. In time, a Dutch couple also pulled their camper in with ours, and, when I discovered I forgot to bring a corkscrew, loaned us theirs.

Driving from one country to another in western Europe involves nothing more than reading the signs telling you such a transition has been made—no border bureaucrats! Belgium appeared very clean. Women swept the sidewalks and streets in front of their homes daily. In rural areas, barns were attached to houses, and white lace curtains and window boxes filled with blooming geraniums were *de rigueur* on every house. Poppies smothered the rolling meadows. We drove through the thick Ardennes forest where thousands of soldiers were killed in 1944 during the Battle of the Bulge, then to Bastogne where, when the Germans surrounded the 101st Airborne and asked them to surrender, General McAuliffe sent them the elegant reply, "Nuts!" We shopped for groceries in Bastogne in the European way, not in a large supermarket, but stopping first at the butcher shop, then the bakery, then the greengrocer. Every shop was an experience in itself with elaborately painted signs advertising each business and friendly, cheerful proprietors wishing you *Bonjour*! In Bastogne's "Nuts" Museum, we saw photographs of the town's public square filled with tanks and soldiers only thirty years before—the same lovely and peaceful square where we shopped for groceries and sat on park benches under the trees to eat our sandwiches. Later we stopped at the Chateau de la Roche where the children fed a curious horse which walked up to our parked camper. We admired the citadel in Dinant where we bought gingerbread, the *chateaux* on the Meuse River, and the baroque churches, pink houses and eleventh-century citadel at Namur.

In 1815, more than fifty thousand men died at Waterloo in less than twenty-four hours, and the sun set on the French Empire. If you add the deaths resulting from the two world wars, you can see that the fields of Belgium have been bloody indeed.

From my notes: *It staggers the imagination, the number of those who have died fighting in this small country. Still, the roar of low flying fighter jets is never long absent—one would think by now they would have had enough of it all.*

We toured Wellington's headquarters and the battlefield and camped on a hill where Napoleon overlooked the field of battle. Jays, magpies, flickers and jackdaws landed near our camper looking for handouts. A curious boy named Jean rode his bicycle over to Mike and me while we played "catch." We let him join in, and it wasn't long before he began to get the hang of it.

We pulled into a campground near Brussels about noon. Showers felt good after a few days of "free-camping." Lynette and Krissie did our laundry, while Mike and I took a walk in a nearby woods. Recently he had been asking questions lately that demanded some explanation—women's menstrual cycles, marriage, etc. Mike's interest in biology simplified discussions about the facts of life. Flowers bloomed in the undergrowth and along the trail, giving us an opportunity to talk about internal and external fertilization and cross pollination in plants. One thing led to another. I resolved to follow up in a few days to see if we had covered enough for the time being.

An Australian couple with two children camped next to us. The "bloke's" mouth curled on one side when he smiled, and I thought he looked like Richard Harris. He had quit his job over a year ago and toured the Australian continent with his family. They were now spending a year camping around Europe, intending to go to Russia next. The four children amused themselves in a playground while we four adults got acquainted over a beer in a nearby cafe. We exchanged a few American coins for some of their novel Australian coins decorated with lyrebirds, kangaroos and platypuses.

Old Brussels retains its medieval past. Brick buildings with ornamental ironwork line the narrow streets. Mike and I bought the girls tulips in the flower market at The Grand Place, a large public square with fabulous gold-trimmed and gabled Guild Houses, sidewalk cafes and the enormous Gothic spired Hotel de Ville (City Hall). We visited the remarkable thirteenth-century Cathedrale St.-Michel, a Gothic beauty with wonderful sixteenth-century stained glass windows. We remembered that, as a young man, Lynette's father had lived in Brussels, running the European office of a Chicago advertising agency. We visited the residential hotel where he stayed as well as his old office, then called one of his old friends and colleagues, Willie Engler, and met him for lunch. What a gay life he must have led before the storm clouds of World War II sent him back to the United States!

Our route headed north through Antwerp, the Flemish cultural center and home to many important Renaissance painters, and then to Holland. Continuing north, we visited Van Gogh's birthplace and Bouvigne Castle near Breda, Kinderdijk and its picturesque windmills near Rotterdam, Gouda's cheese market, and the tall, narrow, gabled houses along Utrecht's picturesque canals and watergates. In Hilversum, with its opulent sixteenth-century homes, we camped near Soestdijk, the Royal Palace of Queen Juliana. We walked around the quaint little town of Lage Vuursche and treated ourselves to ice cream bars. Lynette and I sat on a bench and drank coffee, and the children fed bread to several brazen swans. Krissie bought us all bubble gum and Mike bought us licorice.

From my notes: *We again settle into our life as travelers with little talk of home. Scenes in Holland usually include bikers, fishermen with long poles, and, everywhere—flowers. Reclaiming land from the sea is an entirely understandable national priority—Holland is very crowded. Lynette tells the children the story of Anne Frank. It's difficult to visualize these countries ravaged by war—now it's so peaceful.*

Five hundred bridges connect seventy islands formed by fifty miles of tree-lined canals in Amsterdam. One of our first stops was the Heineken Brewery where we enjoyed free samples. Because of their introduction to the story of Anne Frank, the children were anxious to see the house where the girl and her family had hidden from the Nazis from 1942 to 1944. My favorite stop was the Rijksmuseum with its incomparable collection of works by Dutch artists, including the seventeenth-century masters—Frans Hals, Jan Vermeer and, of course, Rembrandt. How exciting to see *Nightwatch*, Rembrandt's monumental masterpiece! We bought our lunch in a downtown market and ate it sitting on a bank beside a canal. Lynette found a Delft plate and some tiles she couldn't live without.

We visited fishing villages like Monnickendam, shopped for wooden shoes at Vollendam (where Mike bought a smoked eel and ate it), and watched cheese being made in Edam. Sailboats plied the Zeider Zee while mute swans and their cygnets, herons, and storks foraged along the shore. Near Hoorn, we parked on top of a dike and set up camp. Mike found his fishing rod and tried his luck, but a half dozen swans insisted on interrupting his casts. That night the strong, unpleasant odor of smoked eel pervaded the camper.

A stiff morning breeze blew in from the sea, and windmills cranked all around us. We watched a farmer attach sails to the arms of one mill and start it up. Then we drove to Alkmaar where seventeenth-century buildings surround the Waagplein (public square) which hosts a large cheese market. From here our route turned south along the North Sea, through Haarlem and the center of the Netherlands' bulb-growing industry. We watched Grand Prix cars race through Zandwoort and found a campground in a national park on the beach at Bloemendaal aan Zee. The four of us played "hide and seek" among the sand dunes, frequently flushing grouse from the thick, low vegetation. Gulls, avocets, and other shorebirds waded and probed the mud flats for food in a saltwater inlet near the campground, and a falcon hovered above. Mike and Krissie found an orange and black caterpillar with long hairs on its back and erected a miniature obstacle course for it with rocks, sticks and tiny sand berms. The campground was busy, and Mike and I had to wait for showers. We sat on a bench wrapped in our towels. At the sinks in front of us, naked men bent over to dry their feet, their bare butts mere inches from our faces. I looked at Mike, and he stifled a laugh.

We continued south through aristocratic, cosmopolitan Den Haag (The Hague) and charming Delft (where Lynette decided their famous blue porcelain was cheaper in Amsterdam). We then retraced our route from Rotterdam to Antwerp in Belgium. The road turned west to Ghent, a wonderful city with narrow streets, medieval houses, guild halls and a very smelly river. We camped in the parking area of a private club in the resort city of Knokke. The June weather was a bit dismal, but not even a thick fog could conceal the large beach homes, casinos, opulent hotels and other signs of affluence. A cool, comfortable breeze blew in from the English Channel, and, in our pajamas, we drank coffee and hot chocolate with marshmallows while Lynette read *Little Women* to us.

A short diversion inland took us to Brugge, a medieval city that, perhaps more than any other, creates the illusion of being transported back to the thirteenth or fourteenth century. Horses tow boats along the canals. Narrow cobblestone streets run between beautifully preserved old buildings and fine old residences. Marvelous examples of Romanesque, Gothic, Renaissance and Baroque architecture surround the old public square where we ate lunch in an ancient tavern.

A quick drive back to the coast took us through the fishing and resort city of Oostende and then into France, to Dunkerque (Dunkirk). We cooked supper on the very beach where, thirty-four years ago, the Germans had pushed the out-manned English and Belgian troops. With their backs against the wall, the British and Belgians could retreat no further and were in danger of being captured. We tried to imagine the scene. Churchill had rallied virtually every private boat in England, enlisting them to cross the Channel and assist in a dramatic and successful evacuation effort. Fortunately, the British and Belgian troops lived to fight another day. After supper, we continued south to Calais, checked out Rodin's impressive sculpture, *Six Burghers of Calais*, and set up camp in the parking area of the "hoverport."

Hovercraft, large ferries that skim across the water on a cushion of air, must be seen to be believed. They claim two main advantages over conventional car ferries in crossing the English Channel—speed and stability in rough seas. The latter advantage was enough for me. I never met an ocean swell I liked. Hovercraft departures were "flights" rather than sailings, and "stewardesses" saw to your comfort. Our flight departed early in the morning, braving a steady rain through which we could barely see the fabled white cliffs of Dover, and arrived in Folkestone about forty-five minutes later. We ordered coffee at the hoverport snackbar, hoping the rain would stop. I struck up a conversation with a somewhat taciturn man attending a nearby newsstand.

"What's the weather forecast?"

"More rain. What else?"

I wasn't certain whether he expected nothing but rain or another annoying question.

"What's the best newspaper to buy?"

"Doesn't matter. They're all for the EEC (European Economic Community)."

"Is that bad?"

"Not for the big guys. Bad for us little guys. Newspapers are all monopolies. They should be nationalized. I'm a socialist. All big business should be nationalized."

"But wouldn't everything then be a monopoly?"

"Yeah, my kind of monopoly."

I didn't feel like I was getting anywhere, nor did I think he really was enjoying our conversation. I suppressed the urge to ask him the obvious— if the newspapers were monopolies, how come he had so many of them for sale?

Great Britain packs a dazzling amount of history and culture into a relatively small package. The Celts, Norsemen, Romans, Jutes, Angles, Saxons, Danes and Normans all left their mark on the British Isles. Anyone who didn't major in history planning to spend more than a week in Great Britain would be wise to carry along a copy of H.G. Wells' *The Outline of History* or some comparable tome on European history. There's just too much to remember, and so much of that relates directly and indirectly to other countries on the continent.

Canterbury is the ecclesiastical center of England. Here, in the sixth century, Rome sent Augustine to convert the English people. Here also, in the twelfth century, Henry II's knights murdered Archbishop Thomas a Becket, and, in the fourteenth century, Geoffrey Chaucer's pilgrims journeyed. We walked the medieval streets and visited the enormous cathedral with its 235-foot bell tower visible for miles. Then, near Gravesend, we toured Charles Dickens' home at Gad's Hill. Across the street we stopped for gas. I asked the proprietor if it would be safe to spend the night camped in the parking area of his gas station. He said, of course it was and then closed the station and invited us to join him at the pub next door for a beer. Derek's oldest child, a son, was a professional ballet dancer. The next oldest, his daughter, was an actress, and his youngest, a boy, was trying to decide between being a biologist and taking over his dad's gas station. Derek asked us a score of questions. He had traveled in South America and the Middle East and was knowledgeable about many parts of the world. He thought Americans generally were too formal. That surprised me, for I might have described us as less formal than the English. From my notes: *"Derek is handsome, friendly, a real charmer. A good man, and, I suspect, a ladies' man."*

Having kissed each other across the equator in Ecuador, Lynette and I felt compelled to strike the same pose across the Prime Meridian in Greenwich. We parked our camper on the Meridian and reset our car compass, although now I can't remember how or if we allowed for the discrepancy between magnetic and true north. We also synchronized our watches with the Greenwich time magnetic clock. Greenwich's National Maritime

Museum includes numerous galleries of naval and commercial ships and multitudes of naval instruments depicting the maritime history of England. The museum also houses the Old Royal Observatory where seventeenth- and eighteenth-century astronomers, among other duties, provided astronomical and navigational information to Britain's imperialistic sailors. We cooked our supper and parked for the night at Greenwich Pier where both *Cutty Sark*, the last of the tea clipper ships, and *Gipsy Moth IV*, the small boat in which Sir Francis Chichester sailed around the world, are docked.

From my notes: *It has rained almost continually the past three days.*

London, June 28, 1974

The rain stopped on my birthday. We checked in at the large Crystal Palace campground across the Thames from London and took advantage of the sunshine by doing our laundry and washing the camper. Then we rode a double decker bus into London and attended to some administrative chores—booked passage on a car ferry from Newcastle to Bergen, Norway, for the end of July, picked up our mail at American Express, serviced the VW, changed money and checked on visa requirements for several eastern European countries. From the bus we could see Parliament, Westminster Abbey, and London and Tower bridges. Back at the campground, the three cutie pies prepared my birthday feast—a bottle of pinot noir, grilled steak, mushrooms fried in butter and wine, canned creamed corn and gingerbread and apple sauce for dessert. In London, they had gone to a department store to shop for my birthday gifts while I was at the VW dealer. Mike gave me a deck of cards adorned with a photo of the palace guards and a tourist book on Loch Ness and its monster; Krissie gave me two carpet remnants for the floor in the front of the camper which a salesman gave her when Lynette was checking out oriental rugs; and Lynette presented me with two beautiful crystal wine glasses which have since accompanied us on all of our epic trips. (Deferring to our strict budget, she pointed out they were "seconds.")

Lynette thought the colorful antique market on Portobello Road was a "hoot." With bright red lipstick and a bored expression, a young woman absently tended her porcelain stocked stall wearing a mink wrap and a flapper dress. An organ grinder shuffled along the street with a hyperactive monkey and a loquacious parrot. A huge man with long hair and a beard wore baggy black trousers and a patched sport coat and showed his antique jewelry with tattooed hands. Lynette couldn't resist his charm and bought a small ring.

Driving in London is not for the fainthearted. Keeping to the left is bad enough, but you also have to remember to look right rather than left at an intersection, to keep to the left when you turn right, and to watch for cars passing on the right. If all of that doesn't make you want to take a bus or a cab, the omnipresent, confusing "roundabout" intersections certainly will. We caught a matinee performance of *Sherlock Holmes* and drove back to the Crystal Palace Campground resolving to take the bus into the city from now on.

Rarely did we see anyone from the United States camping in Europe, so we were surprised to find a California family of four in a small camper like ours parked at the London campground. Krissie and their little girl struck up a friendship which led to all of us getting acquainted. The burly father had lost a leg in Viet Nam, and more than that, the family seemed generally down on their luck. The father said they were running out of funds and thought they would work odd jobs on their way to Greece where they planned to pick oranges and to save some money.

The next few days we did all the things tourists do in London: watched the changing of the guards at Buckingham Palace, toured the eleventh-century Gothic Westminster Abbey where kings and queens are crowned and many of Great Britain's most important figures lie buried—Disraeli, Dickens, Burns, Darwin, Gladstone, Eliot, Kipling—to name a few, walked down Whitehall to Number 10 Downing Street, admired Parliament Square with its statues of Churchill and Lincoln and its three hundred fifteen-foot Victorian Gothic clock tower, Big Ben. We ate fish and chips for lunch near the Tower Bridge and then chatted with Beefeaters at the Tower of London, where Catherine of Aragon, Anne Boleyn, Sir Walter Raleigh, Princess Elizabeth and many other historical figures had been imprisoned, and where some of them lost their heads. We toured the Tower's armor museum and Jewel House where the Crown Jewels are displayed. Outside the Tower, fat ravens strutted on the lawn and would be knights held a jousting tournament. A man entertained an audience while he wrapped his partner in chains and collected coins in exchange for seeing his partner, like Houdini, extricate himself from his steel entanglement. On another day, we walked through Hyde Park to Kensington Gardens and picnicked under Admiral Horatio Nelson's column in Trafalgar Square. At St. James Square, we watched an old lady feeding peanuts to pigeons. When Mike tried to feed them, he was overwhelmed by the birds.

In the morning we restocked our pantry and left for the Victorian town of Windsor on the Thames. We drove by Ascot and Eton and then toured Windsor Castle. Here the children were sure their Grammy Kathleen was the model for a more than life-sized statue of Queen Victoria. (I remembered the way Grammy Kathleen treated Lynette and me during our courtship and decided they weren't far off the mark.) Across the street from the castle, a corner shop sold fine bone china, including names such as Wedgewood, Royal Worcester and Coalport. A craftswoman in the shop demonstrated to a small crowd how flowers were hand painted and mounted on the pottery. Krissie and Mike, mesmerized, watched her for an hour while Lynette and I roamed the shop. When we left, she gave each of the children a flower, painted and signed. We drove to Runnymede where, in 1215, King John signed the Magna Carta and then northwest through the English countryside where we camped at a gas station about ten miles from Oxford. In a field nearby, Mike and I kicked a soccer ball and then worked on his running. Krissie came over and said she too wanted to learn how to run. Lynette laughed, too polite to say it, but undoubtedly wondering who was going to teach me, an old interior lineman, how to run.

Lynette led us on a tour of venerable Oxford University. We walked down High Street, lined with stone buildings dating from the fifteenth through the seventeenth centuries, and then watched students punting on the Thames. Driving north, we stopped to see Churchill's birthplace at Blenheim Palace. Our route continued through the pleasant English countryside where quaint stone houses with thatched or tiled roofs were scattered among gently rolling hills. Hedgerows lined checkered fields where sheep and cattle grazed. We entered Stratford-Upon-Avon a bit unprepared for how touristy the bard's birthplace had become. We walked around town rather quickly, inspecting the buildings associated with Shakespeare and touring John Harvard's mother's home and Anne Hathaway's cottage.

Leaving Stratford, we turned back south toward the picturesque villages of the Cotswolds. Old houses and shops lined the lovely streets of Chipping Campden and Broadway. Thatched-roof houses, barns and fences were all constructed of honey-colored, yellow-gray stones quarried from the surrounding Cotswold Hills. We camped in a roadside pullover and continued our tour of the Cotswolds the next day—Moreton-In-Marsh, Stow-On-the-Wold, Bibury, Cirencester, Malmsbury—admiring the charm of the villages through the rain and trying to stay dry in numerous antique and art shops. Near Bibury the rain paused, so we fixed lunch by the rushing River Coin. Afterwards we played soccer—Mike and Lynette against Krissie and me. That evening, near the old market town of Malmsbury, we set up camp in the parking area of an old church. A cemetery next to the church was filled with gravestones from the seventeenth century. Inside the church, we found brass rubbings from the fifteenth century.

From the Cotswold region we climbed onto the Salisbury Plain. Near the present day village of Amesbury, four thousand years ago, unknown ancient clans constructed an imposing circle of monoliths, today called Stonehenge, probably as a center of religion and culture. We were about two weeks late for the summer solstice vigil of modern day Druids. That didn't prevent Mike and me from walking among the large stones, trying to feel some ancient force. Lynette and Krissie stood to the side, laughing skeptically, and snapped our picture while we pondered one of the old slabs.

The fourteenth-century Gothic spire of Salisbury's cathedral is the tallest in England, a landmark that may be seen from miles away. Rows of half-timbered houses, shops and inns line the streets of the charming town. We bought bread and cheese and, at nearby Old Sarum, fixed lunch by the ruins of an old Norman castle.

In England, towns with names ending in "cester" or "chester" usually have Roman roots. Dorchester is no exception. Stone age inhabitants of the area that is now Dorchester fashioned circles of stone, probably for ceremonial reasons, called the Maumbury Rings. Centuries later Roman gladiators performed in a huge amphitheater built over these rings. We inspected the rings and then drove to Maiden Castle, built by the Celts and England's largest prehistoric fortress. We visited Thomas Hardy's cottage, and, feeling it was time, checked into a campground with showers. After dinner, we walked by a creek where, from under some streamside rocks, Mike and Krissie gathered an assortment of snails for our perusal.

The secluded village of Cerne Abbas provided an interesting morning's diversion. We arrived amid the gaiety of the first day of their Festival of Flowers, Art and Music, the streets bustling with people. We joined the festivities, admired a row of quaint Tudor houses and visited a fourteenth-century church and the ruins of a tenth-century abbey. On Giant Hill, outside of town, the carved in chalk 180-foot Cerne Giant required some explaining to the children. Reputed to have been created as a fertility symbol during the Roman occupation, the giant wields a huge club and an enormous... well, he was a fertility symbol. Try explaining this bit of primitive graffiti to a nine-year-old boy and a six-year-old girl!

Our afternoon drive took us along the coast under red cliffs and through the small fishing village of Lyme Regis from where five of Sir Francis Drake's ships sailed to engage the Spanish Armada. We drove through Exeter with its medieval walls and fourteenth-century cathedral and, near the small village of Shaldon, set up camp on a hill with a fine view of the sea and Teignmouth beyond. A nesting colony of herring gulls noisily clung to red cliffs that dropped precipitously to the surf crashing below. After supper, we walked down the hill to the sea, past tidal pools teeming with small aquatic life, into the village. We bought popsicles for dessert and watched boys dancing a jig and wearing folk costumes with white shirts, colorful vests, knickers and bells on their ankles.

From my notes: *Lynette wondered if I could imagine American teenagers doing such a thing. Probably not.*

While we waited to board a ferry, a tree sparrow flew in the open door of our camper and slammed into the closed passenger side window. I tried unsuccessfully to revive it. The ferry crossed the Dart estuary to the historic port of Dartmouth. In 1190, crusaders, led by Richard the Lion-Hearted, sailed across the English Channel from Dartmouth on their way to the Holy Land. In 1944, American troops sailed from Dartmouth to take part in the Normandy invasion. Hilltop castles silently guard both points of the estuary.

We ate lunch below the walls of Dartmouth Castle and admired the town's seventeenth-century waterfront houses.

The bleak, desolate upland moors of Dartmoor National Park bring to mind Arthur Conan Doyle's *Hounds of the Baskervilles*. Peat bogs litter the heather-covered moors, and mist-shrouded granite outcroppings called "tors" rise darkly and obstinately out of the plateau. The few hardy inhabitants of the moors live in stone houses with thatched roofs. Sheep graze on sparse vegetation. Trout fill the rivers and wild ponies roam the hills. The children insisted on not leaving until we found some wild ponies, which we did.

We left the park and crossed from Devon into Cornwall's Bodmin Moor, setting up camp in the village parking lot of Bodmin. Three local girls—Pauline, Jacqueline, and Nicole—introduced themselves to Krissie. One thing led to another, and all of us were soon playing soccer with me as goalie for both teams. I noticed two official looking men leave a stately granite mansion adjacent to the park and walk toward our camper. Lynette and I excused ourselves from the game to ask the gentlemen if there was a problem. It turned out their visit was quite innocent. They had never seen a camper like ours and were curious about how it was rigged. We gave them a tour of the van, chatted about the World Cup soccer competition and, during our conversation, learned that the one man was governor of Cornwall and the other, his butler. The next morning the butler returned and invited us to breakfast and encouraged us to use the bathroom and shower facilities in the governor's home.

From a letter to my parents: *From the Lima Golf Club to the Governor's mansion. It could be argued we're traveling first class! Mostly, however, we camp in wayside rests, parking lots or gas stations, usually places with rest rooms and water. When we need a shower, we find a campground. Our days are more leisurely here than in South America. We find more time for relaxation and exercise, running and playing soccer (Mike and Lynette against Krissie and me) each day. Our biggest problem is lack of sunshine—it rained every day until yesterday.*

Cornwall's hedgerows often grow so high they obscure any view of the surrounding countryside. We grew weary trying to see over and around these famous features and were happy to return to the open views along the coastal roads. From twelfth-century Restormel Castle's fine drawbridge, we threw stones into a moat and flushed frogs from their sunny rock perches. Henry VIII built twin castles at St. Mawes and Pendennis to guard the Fal Estuary. We set up camp below the citadel of St. Mawes and walked into the village. I talked politics and English history with an old fisherman while Lynette rented a rowboat for us to take into the estuary to fish the next morning. Late in the day the clouds dissipated and that evening the children did schoolwork while Lynette and I returned to our reading of Tolkien's *The Hobbit* and *Fellowship of the Ring*.

We arose early but the fish did not reward our diligence. Lynette suspected something was amiss when we saw no other fishermen. Nevertheless, a red sky fit for an artist, the estuary's fresh air and numerous birds greeted us, so we had no regrets. After the obligatory minimum two hour rental, we returned the rowboat and headed south toward Penzance, Lynette singing a medley from Gilbert and Sullivan's *The Pirates of Penzance*. We ferried our car across the Fal Estuary and, at low tide, walked across a causeway to tour a fine old castle, St. Michael's Mount. We shopped in Penzance where I embarrassed everybody when I knocked over a table in an antique store. Later I sheepishly bought everyone an ice cream cone, and Krissie observed, "Mom, you always tell Mike and me to be careful in a store. I think Dad is worse than we are." We drove to St. Ives to visit a museum that was once a school attended by both Oliver Cromwell and Samuel Pepys and climbed a long hill outside of town to see the ruins of the two thousand-year old village of Chysauster. We camped by a tidal stream running through a field where horses grazed. Krissie and I fed snacks to the horses while Mike and Lynette fished.

The road northeast followed the rugged Cornish coastline through Newquay and Wadebridge to legendary Tintagel. Here King Arthur was born, and the ruins of his thirteenth-century castle lie near rocky cliffs rising from the sea. A cold mist blew in from the sea and shrouded the ancient fortress, making it easy for me to visualize the buildings in their unruined glory and imagine chivalrous knights and their ladies—all of it somehow enabling the plausibility of the legend. We shivered through a lunch of bread and cheese at Tintagel and then continued driving to Exmoor National Park with its mysterious upland moors and precipitous cliffs plummeting to the sea. Deer, wild ponies and sheep grazed among the hedgerows and granite outcroppings, and farmers wrung a hard-earned living from the wind swept hills. We walked the charming narrow streets of the harbor town of Lynmouth until it began raining and then drove to the small village of Lynton where we camped on a cliff four hundred feet above the crashing sea. After supper the rain turned to mist, so we walked into town where, in a small penny arcade, the children lost a few coins in slot machines while Lynette and I watched a serious game of chess in the town hall next door.

From my notes: *Unlike South America, we're meeting no friends, only acquaintances, and we feel more like tourists than guests. Not as dramatic or adventuresome. However, it's interesting and educational and very easy—campgrounds, laundry facilities etc.*

The woods scattered over the beautiful moor easily could have been those described in *The Hobbit*. We shopped for groceries in Minehead,

95

admired the thirteenth-century Cistercian ruins of a gatehouse, dormitory and refectory at Cleeve Abbey and visited Dunster Castle. Historic Glastonbury claims to have hosted Joseph of Arimathea and the Chalice of the Last Supper, and Arthur and Guinevere are supposed to be buried somewhere in the ruins of Glastonbury Abbey. We did some antiquing in Glastonbury and continued on to medieval Wells where we visited the twelfth-century Cathedral of St. Andrew and antiqued some more. Leaving the town, we saw a large, imposing brownstone home sitting on the edge of a forest. A sign displayed prominently by the driveway dissuaded curious tourists from trespassing: "Barwell Castle—Built in the nineteenth century and has no historic or other interest. Kindly remember that this Englishman's castle is his home and do not intrude." We stopped at a campground on the moor with a lovely view of Wells in the distance.

Nine species of wrens inhabit North America. Only one, the winter wren, may be found outside of that continent. While the girls showered, Mike and I grabbed our binoculars and went for a walk, coming upon a twelfth-century church. A flock of redpolls flitted among the trees next to the old church while doves cooed and fed on the ground. In the graveyard next door, a song thrush cracked a snail in its beak. Then from a nearby shrub came a familiar song—that of the winter wren. Mike spotted it first, skulking low in the bush. We froze, and the longer we remained still, the more active the bird became. Back at the campground, Krissie had met a cute ten-year-old Canadian girl named Wendy. The two of them played hopscotch. Mike and I kicked around a soccer ball, and soon several boys joined us.

The best grilled cheese sandwiches, in my opinion, contain the extra sharp white cheese made in Cheddar, England. One need not go to Cheddar to buy this cheese, but, as long as we were passing through, I made sure we had a good supply of it. From Worlebury Hill near Weston-Super-Mare we looked across the Bristol Channel to the Welsh coast, then continued through Bristol and across the channel to Wales. The eleventh-century Norman ruins of Chepstow Castle stand guard on a formidable cliff overlooking the Wye River. Parked by the tranquil Wye for lunch (cheddar cheese sandwiches), we watched a great black-backed gull work its way down the river and then circle over us, looking, I suppose, for a handout. Our route proceeded up the gorgeous Wye River Valley, past Wordsworth's thirteenth-century Tintern Abbey, twelfth-century Abergavenny Castle, and fourteenth-century Tretower Castle. Near Brecon, we joined two campers parked in a pullover. Both families were from Oxford and made no secret of their antipathy for the students, characterizing them as spoiled rich kids. Beyond that, they possessed a positive attitude. There were enough of us for a pretty good soccer game, and enough beer for a pretty good party that evening.

From my notes: *In Abergavenny, we stopped at a bakery for bread.*

Lynette saw a beautiful black currant bun and bought it for breakfast. In the morning she cut it into four pieces and noticed there were no currants. Cutting it into still smaller pieces, she didn't do much better. In all, she found only three currants. "This isn't a black currant bun," she said. "This is a three currant bun. Count 'em! Three currants!"

Brecon, Wales, July 13, 1974

"Happy Anniversary!" exclaimed the card made by Krissie and Mike and given to us while eating breakfast at a cafe in Brecon. We walked the medieval town's narrow streets, poking around a few antique shops, and then drove through the lonely moorlands of Brecon Beacons National Park to ancient Carmarthen where, alledgedly, King Arthur's magician, Merlin, cast the following spell: "When Merlin's Oak shall tumble down, then shall fall Carmarthen Town." To forestall such an unhappy event, somebody encased a bit of the rotting stump of a tree in a block of concrete and put it on display on Priory Street. The town had a rather crumbling aspect, and Mike wondered whether Merlin's prophecy was in the process of being fulfulled.

In Llanstephan we found the approximate point where, in 1853, an artist named William Pitt had painted a scene depicting residents in a street near the town's castle with a seascape in the background. I snapped a picture so we could compare the contemporary version of that scene with the original painting hanging in our home.

Dylan Thomas lived and wrote in Laugharne for sixteen years. A man trimmed weeds in the graveyard where the poet lay buried. The man's young son fed the trimmings to a gray mare and her colt. We stood by the simple white cross and the man walked to our side.

"It ain't much, is it now?"

I shook my head and smiled. The locals called him "Dylan." We walked to his home. A boy raked the garden.

"That's Dylan's house, Sir. You can go inside."

The door was unlocked. Furniture, photographs and letters remained apparently as he left them. It bothered me some that no one guarded the home, but maybe they didn't have to. When we left, I waved at the boy and thanked him. He stopped raking, shaded his eyes, and asked,

"Did ya like it, Sir?"

"We liked it."

We found a campsite near Dylan's home. Lynette remarked that our view overlooked the same picturesque tidal flats he saw from his house. We walked into the town and ate fish and chips for supper at a small restaurant on the sea.

Krissie asked, "Why does everyone love Dylan so much?"

We thought a moment, and Lynette answered, "Because he spoke with his heart." I remembered Gus Angermeyer and smiled.

I must admit that I had never heard Ireland calling. In fact, I had a generally negative image of the Emerald Isle and little interest in going there. However, the blood of Lynette's maternal ancestors ran thick in her, and she said, "We're this close—we're going!" So we ate breakfast by the sea near Pendine, stopped at Llawhaden Castle where Mike bought a Welsh flag, and then boarded a car ferry in Fishguard to cross the Irish Sea for Rosslare. About midway on the voyage, sunny Wales gave way to a steady Irish downpour. We arrived in late afternoon and set up camp near a half dozen tents on the beach at Rosslare Harbor.

Rain continued steadily through the night and the next morning, not doing much to improve my mean image of Ireland. Nor did the drunks on the streets of Wexford. Our route took us through New Ross, the ancestral home of the Kennedys. Here Krissie and Mike released a bottle into the River Nore with a note addressed to their grandfather in Pennsylvania. In Kilkenny, Lynette recited,

"There were once two cats from Kilkenny.
Each thought there was one cat too many.
So they fought and they fit,
And they scratched and they bit
'til instead of two cats, there weren't any."

And we toured thirteenth-century Kilkenny Castle. We made our way across the country singing Irish songs and stopping to see Cashel's magnificent castle with its high cross and round tower, Cahir Castle, Blarney Castle near Cork, and Killarney's thirteenth-century Dunloe Castle and fourteenth-century Ross Castle. We camped on a farm near Killarney, excited because it was located near a good trout stream. Mike Wile began fishing seriously at the age of three and, to this day, is an inveterate fisherman. He and I assembled our rods and set off into rain, mosquitoes, deep mud and cow patties, threading our way through barbed wire fences and thorny shrubbery. We fished for two hours and caught nothing. I was miserable. Mike loved it and didn't want to leave.

From my notes: *The Irish drink, but they're friendly and kind. They have fair skin, blue eyes, and black or red hair. Old, red-faced men walk the streets with canes, wearing tweed coats and Ben Hogan hats. You know you're in Ireland just looking at the signs on the shops—O'Conner's, O'Leary's, McGuire's, Paddy's. Very few tourists. Areas untouched by the dirt, grime and pollution of progress. Milk delivered by old men on carts pulled by donkeys. Peat bricks dug from bogs and used for heating homes. Beautiful countryside with mountains and limestone outcroppings, charging streams—occasionally being fished, moors and bogs, fields of grazing sheep, and fertile farms. Wonderful ruins, many with round towers where early families ran to escape marauding Norsemen, and pre-historic stone megaliths with written symbols.* I guess I was beginning to like Ireland.

The Ring of Kerry offered us spectacular views of the ocean. We stopped at the fishing village of Killorglin, Tralee on the Dingle Peninsula (where *Ryan's Daughter* was filmed), and the lovely village of Adare and then drove through Limerick to fourteenth-century Bunratty Castle, Lynette's favorite. The restored castle and adjacent Folk Park recreate an earlier Irish life—farm houses and craft shops with farmers, fishermen, basket weavers and blacksmiths dressed in period costumes. Our route continued northwest through the town of Ennis and the beautiful Irish countryside, where stone walls defined the fields and stone houses had thatched roofs, to Lahinch where we camped next to the clubhouse of the town's nine hole golf course. The nice caretaker let us use the club's showers. After supper, we walked into Lahinch. A small carnival and penny arcade entertained the children while Lynette and I sat on a bench playing cribbage. Later, sleep came easily with the surf pounding against the cliffs below the golf course—the same cliffs not far from which the Spanish Armada met its defeat in the sixteenth century.

The Cliffs of Moher rise seven hundred feet above the ocean, a dramatic sight any time of the year, but even more so in the summer when tens of thousands of sea birds nest on the cliffs' countless ledges. Atlantic puffins, razorbills, guillemots, kittiwakes, fulmars and gulls—incubating eggs, resting in great rafts on the swells, soaring past the cliffs in review, foraging the sea for fish, screaming at each other—all of this one of nature's great marvels. We trained our binoculars on individual birds, becoming increasingly better at separating and identifying them by species. Krissie's favorite spotting was a black and white puffin standing on a cliff ledge with half a dozen fish hanging from its colorful red and yellow beak.

Rare wildflowers flourish on the barren, Burren-limestone hills. We drove north through Lisdoonvarna and Ballyvaughan, past ancient dolmens and stone forts. And, for the first time since we came to Ireland, the sun appeared. Now Irish beauty reigned supreme—Galway Bay, emerald green rolling hills, the River Shannon. The monastic city of Clonmacnoise dates back to the sixth century. It thrived for a thousand years as a religious and intellectual center. Many of Ireland's kings and saints lie buried at Clonmacnoise, and the remains of eight churches, a cathedral, two round towers, and at least three important high crosses still may be seen. I'll never forget eating our lunch of fresh bread, cheese and wine in the warm August sun. While we sat on a grassy hill overlooking the meandering River Shannon, there was the one thousand-year old, sixty feet high, O'Rourke's Tower framed by the clear, blue sky. We fished and camped near Mullingar that evening, and I wrote to my parents, "Western Ireland may be the prettiest countryside I've ever seen."

Lynette and the children sang our way into Dublin—

> *In Dublin's fair city, where the girls are so pretty,*
> *It was there that I first met sweet Molly Malone.*
> *She wheeled her wheelbarrow,*
> *through the streets broad and narrow,*
> *Singing "cockles and mussels, alive, alive-o."*

Dublin's port of Dun Laoghaire had a small campground, and from that base we shopped for groceries, collected our mail from American Express, booked passage on a car ferry for Holyhead, Wales, and explored the city. Historic and literary Dublin sits astride the Liffey River. Two thousand years old; invaded by the Vikings, Normans and English; home to James Joyce, Oscar Wilde, George Bernard Shaw, Edmund Burke, Thomas Moore, Sean O'Casey and Samuel Beckett; the capital of the Republic of Ireland may be at its best in its friendly pubs. Lynette led us on a walking tour—Dublin Castle, National Gallery of Ireland, St. Patrick's Cathedral and Trinity College where the eighth-century *Book of Kells* is displayed in the college library. We toured the Guiness Brewery, antiqued along the Liffey, and birded St. Stephen's Green. Near supper time, we heard singing in a pub, so we found a table and ordered Irish stew. Everybody drank Guiness, so I tried one and wondered what the fuss was about. I tried another, and still another, and they began to taste very good.

I took my prescribed Dramamine, and, fortunately, relatively calm waters accompanied our return voyage across the Irish Sea. Krissie and Mike played a game they called "one finger hockey," flicking a red ball back and forth across a table on the upper deck while Lynette and I looked for sea birds. The ferry sailed into Holyhead Bay past seals sunning themselves on rocky beaches. We drove through the Isle of Anglesey's lovely countryside interspersed with ancient rock outcropings and then through Snowdonia National Park's wild mountains. The park lies in Caernarvenshire, coal country, the land that inspired Richard Llewellyn's *How Green Was My Valley,* and slag tailings marred some of the park's scenery. In Colwyn Bay the children watched a marionette theater, and we camped on the beach.

Back in England, I had a headache, so, while I slept it off, Lynette for the first time drove our camper up the M-6 Motorway through the charming Cumbrian countryside to the Lake District, land of the "romantics"— Wordsworth, Tennyson and Coleridge among others. We stopped in the old market town of Kendal for groceries, explored prehistoric rock formations near Ambleside, rode a steamboat from the resort town of Windemere to Bowness and back, visited Wordsworth's grave in the Grasmere village churchyard and then snacked on wonderful gingerbread, and camped near Keswick on a hill with a splendid view of Derwent Water. Several other campers also parked there. Mike and Krissie joined some English children playing "hide and seek" in the woods, and Lynette and I talked with a couple of Scottish birdwatchers.

Carlisle, with its attractive red brick houses and buildings, lies near England's border with Scotland. The city's eleventh-century castle and city walls are reminders of the bloody past between England and Scotland. Nearby, the remnants of Hadrian's Wall, built by the Romans in the second century as a defense against hostile tribes, mark the northern frontier of the Roman Empire. We wondered about the strategic value of the stone wall. It wasn't more than three feet high and seemed to afford little protection against an army of charging warriors. I think we were anxious to get to the Highlands and don't remember taking time to stop in industrial Glasgow. In Stirling, we explored a fine medieval castle and a fort/museum with a magnificent kilt collection, and then drove to Callander, the heart of romantic Scotland where Rob Roy (Robert MacGregor) traipsed around the surrounding area and Sir Walter Scott later immortalized the likable outlaw. Scott also wrote about nearby Loch Katrine, the subject body of water in Lady of the Lake. Our Highland road wound its way north and west past crystal blue lochs, across rushing streams, and through picturesque villages like Lochearnhead (at the head of Loch Earn), Crianlarich and Tyndrum. We crossed the River Orchy in Bridge of Orchy, followed the swollen stream out of town for a few miles, and pulled over for the night beside Lake Orchy. A fisherman and his beautiful son were doing pretty well, so Mike fetched his rod and quickly caught three trout.

The wind blew steadily over the Highlands, and rain came intermittently. Lynette sang a medley of Sottish songs, and Mike and Krissie became more thrilled as we followed the River Ness and neared the lake where they intended to spot "Nessie," the Loch Ness Monster. We shopped for groceries in Fort William and became soaked in a rain storm. Then we crossed the narrow end of Loch Ness at Fort Augustus and, keeping our eyes peeled for Nessie, drove slowly along the northwest shore of the lake, through the village of Invermoriston, to Drumnadrochit. On a hill above the tiny village was a farm that offered camping facilities. When we registered for the night, I asked the farmer why he kept both Aberdeen Angus and Highland cattle. He explained the latter were for sentiment while the former were "damn good beef cows." Cows mooed and horses neighed as we drove through the farmer's field to our assigned camping spot.

The weather had cleared a bit, and the sun actually shone warmly as we walked to the ruins of Urquhart Castle perched on a cliff above Loch Ness. Mike and I scanned the lake with our binoculars, looking for any sign of the legendary monster. The surrounding scenery sparkled with the afternoon sun's slanting rays glistening off the emerald green hills and deep blue lake. Krissie and Lynette soon grew tired of the search and instead worked on their cartwheels. Later, I tried to capture the spirit of the moment by snapping a photo of Kristen climbing over a stone wall in front of Loch Ness, giving her best impersonation of Nessie, while Mike feigned fright and ran away.

While Lynette and Krissie fixed breakfast, Mike and I did a little bird-watching, managing to find a treecreeper, a flock of linnets and a golden eagle. The children explored the farm while Lynette and I spent much of the morning poring over maps and tour books, trying to plan our last few days in Scotland before taking the car ferry across the North Sea to Norway.

From my notes: *Images of Scotland—kilts, plaids, Highlands, Lowlands, bagpipes, heather, thistle, red grouse, castles, firths, lochs, Highland cattle, shortbread, trout, people rather cold and unfriendly. Many of the people in the north say they believe Nessie exists. Actually, they think there's a large herd of the beasts living in the loch.*

We walked to Urquhart Castle once again to look for Nessie and then drove to Inverness where we saw a pipe-and-drum band and Highland dancers perform. Shops sold beautiful woolen products, including many plaids. Lynette and Krissie looked for wool sweaters and antiqued while Mike and I watched oyster catchers foraging in Moray Firth. We ate lunch and then walked on the beach at Nairn, tried in vain to hook a salmon in the River Lossie near Elgin and camped in a pullover near Keith.

Touring castles in Huntley and Kildrummy occupied much of our morning as we returned to the Highlands, driving along raging rivers, through evergreen filled glens, and over treeless hills covered with purplish pink heather. We visited Balmoral Castle, the sometimes residence of the royal family and, near Braemar, pulled into a parking area beside the River Dee where several other campers apparently had had the same idea. Mike decided we should climb a mountain, and it didn't take much coaxing to get the girls to join us. The higher we climbed, the more of the mountain we could see. As we climbed each pitch and reached each of a series of benches, we realized there were more. I became concerned about Krissie, but she kept on "truckin." Mike went ahead, and, after he had been out of sight for about an hour, I walked ahead of the girls to find him. When I reached the summit, he was sitting on a pile of rocks looking at his watch.

"How long do you think I've been waiting?"

"Twenty minutes?"

"No, eighteen."

Soon Krissie and Lynette appeared over the final ledge and both of them ran the last twenty-five yards. Later, back at the camper, Lynette and I watched Mike and Krissie catching minnows in a plastic pail. I glanced at the mountainside across the River Dee and saw several deer silhouetted against the sky. We grabbed our binoculars and counted seventy-three red deer browsing on the ground cover.

Curlews guarded their nests hidden in the heather on both sides of our road through the Highland moors. We stopped to see Glamis Castle where Princess Margaret was born in 1930, walked the centuries old streets of Dundee and ate lunch at a pullover on a cliff above the Firth of Tay. At Kinross, from Loch Leven's shore, we saw the fifteenth-century castle where Mary Queen of Scots was imprisoned in 1567. In St. Andrews, we walked along the Old Course, five hundred years old, marveled at the twelfth-century yellow stone cathedral, and carefully picked our way along a rugged promontory jutting into the sea, to St. Andrews Castle. That evening, at a campground near Edinburgh, my notes report, *The shower felt marvelous, and Lynette's spaghetti tasted great!*

Since the eleventh century, the old walled city of Edinburgh has occupied the lowland hills overlooking the Firth of Forth. The city boasts of such literary and intellectual giants as James Boswell, Robert Burns, Sir Walter Scott, David Hume and Adam Smith. Historic Edinburgh Castle, dating back at least to the eleventh century, dominates the city. Lynette led us on a cobblestone street walking tour down the Royal Mile to Holyroodhouse Palace, the onetime home of Bonnie Prince Charlie and Mary Queen of Scots, and to the Scott Monument, a high Gothic spire ornamented with characters from the author's works, and to St. Giles High Kirk, where John Knox, one of the leaders of the Protestant Reformation, preached his blistering sermons. In one antique shop Lynette bought an eighteenth-century walnut coal box with brass hinges and a nineteenth-century brass candlestick. The proprietress gave Krissie a pin and Mike a tiny brass slipper. At another shop, the proprietor was singing when we walked in. While Lynette and I browsed, he performed finger and rope tricks for the children. We didn't buy anything, but he nevertheless gave the children some old coins for their collections. At a nearby nature preserve, we camped on a beach with many birds—gulls, oyster catchers, curlews, and redshanks.

We drove to North Berwick, ate lunch on the beach, did some antiquing, and toured fourteenth-century Tantallon Castle. Perched on a sheer cliff one hundred feet above the Firth of Forth and protected by a moat on its landward side, the castle was thought to be invincible until Oliver Cromwell's army destroyed it in 1651. The cliff would still be daunting to anyone with a mind to take the castle, but it didn't seem to bother the thousands of gray and white fulmars soaring elegantly by and nesting on its ledges and in its crevices.

Berwick-Upon-Tweed today is in England, but, in the past three hundred years, the walled town has changed hands more than a dozen times. We drove across the seventeenth-century bridge spanning the Tweed and continued south along the sea, past Holy Island, to beautifully preserved and frequently filmed Bamburgh Castle. A nearby campground was convenient and offered the added attraction of being located next to a bird sanctuary. Off the coast, we could see the Farne Islands. Arctic terns plunged into the sea for fish; snipes called *teek-a, teek-a, teek-a* from the marsh; sand martins foraged on the wing for insects; and greenfinches and goldfinches whistled and twittered from deciduous trees. Mike and I had a run and washed the camper while Krissie and Lynette became acquainted with a German family. Later, over a glass of sherry, we learned the woman's maiden name was Wile. That night it rained, and Mike announced we had been in Great Britain five weeks and only four days had been without any rain.

Many castles and fortifications remain from the centuries of border wars between England and Scotland. We saw castles in Alnwick, Dunstanburgh and Warkworth and then drove to Hexham to see another section of Hadrian's Wall. In Newcastle Upon Tyne, we booked passage on a car ferry for the twenty-four hour crossing of the North Sea to Norway and then set up camp on the beach at Tynemouth. The next morning our camper received its five thousand mile servicing at the VW dealer in Whitley Bay while we shopped for groceries (much cheaper in England than Norway), did our laundry, and organized our maps and travel literature for Scandinavia. That afternoon I popped some Dramamine just before we drove onto the ferry. The kids were very excited—this would be their first overnight trip on a boat, and they had their very own cabin.

Our ship steamed down the Tyne River and out into the North Sea. Lynette and the kiddies went below to check out our nice, comfortable cabins. I remained on the deck hopeful the fresh sea breeze combined with Dramamine would keep my stomach settled. It was already evident the much ballyhooed ship stabilizers did little to keep the boat stable on the North Sea swells. Sea birds danced in and hovered above the ship's wake, but I felt uncomfortable enough to have no interest in birds. Once Mike and Krissie grabbed me by the hand to come see an alcid they had spotted following the boat. I verified their sighting and retreated to my deck chair. Our plan had been to enjoy our cruise across the North Sea—have dinner on the high deck, put the children to bed, have a drink or two in the lounge and dance to the music of the ship's combo. At dinner, I could eat only a few bites and felt pretty bad, so I went to bed and instead Lynette took the children to the lounge. I was ill all night, often violently so, and into the morning.

From my notes: *I took a shower this morning and got the dry heaves. Now I'm sitting on the top deck with a cold, wet wind slapping my face, riding it out and wishing it were over. Finally, land. Oh blessed relief!*

The ferry left the open sea, entered the fjord leading to Bergen, and immediately I felt better. Gabled wooden houses, brightly painted yellow, orange, red or green, clung to the sheer rocky cliffs rising out of the calm waters of the fjord. Bergenhaus, a twelfth-century fort, stands guard at the entrance to Bergan Harbor. Bryggen Wharf once serviced ships of the

Hanseatic League, an association of merchants that flourished in northern Europe during the sixteenth and seventeenth centuries. German merchants then lived in the old gabled, white-framed wooden houses near the wharf, never associating socially with the Norwegian community. We walked through old buildings with period interiors in Gamle Bergen Park; visited Mariakirken, a splendid Norman church built in the twelfth century and the town's oldest building; and, on Troldhaugen (Hill of Trolls), paid our respects at the home and grave of Edvard Grieg, the Norwegian composer, who, in writing the music for the Peer Gynt Suites, wonderfully captured the mysterious character of the Norwegian landscape. We shopped in Fisketorget, the fishmarket where fishermen wore slickers and vendors sold fish, fruit, vegetables and flowers at appallingly high prices. Near the village of Fana, we found a camping spot by a small river in the mountains. It drizzled all night and was only dark for an hour or two.

Silvery ribbons of water plunged over granite cliffs that rose more than a thousand feet directly and precipitously from the deep blue Hardangerfjord which wouned its majestic way north and east into the green Norwegian interior. Our road clung to the cliffsides and wound its way around jutting promontories and through dark tunnels. Sod-roofed farms and livestock occupied hillsides. Newly mown hay hung on wooden frames drying in sun warmed fields even as snow patches remained on shaded conifer forest floors. Commercial fishermen tended their nets in the fjord while recreational fishermen cast their lines from the shore. We gathered a few apples and pears hanging from trees along an isolated stretch of road and hoped the children wouldn't consider it stealing. Fishermen waved from the pier at Norheimsund and a hydrofoil ferry pulled into its berth at Kvanndal. At Eide, the fjord narrowed and ended, and our road climbed along a series of charging whitewater rivers interrupted by placid blue lakes and crossed cold Skjelingsvatn Pass where we camped for the night and threw snowballs at one another. I awakened at two o'clock in the morning and nudged Lynette—it was light outside!

In the morning, we descended from the highlands and ferried across Sognefjord, the king of Norway's fjords, from Vangsness to Balestrand, a fishing and climbing center situated under snow-capped peaks. We lunched under the warm sun beside a waterfall cascading into Sognefjord. A breeze interrupted our party, showering us with a cold mist.

Our route branched along the narrow, canyon-like, blue-green Lustrafjord and then climbed to 1440-meter Sognefjell Pass and presented us with wonderful views of the rugged, snow-capped peaks in the Jotunheimen (giants' home) range. We descended to Lom, a rough frontier-like town with an eleventh-century wooden stave church. The pulpit was high, and I could visualize the preacher looking down into the eyes of his congregation and filling them with the fear of the Lord. We camped for the night beside blue-green Lake Otta near the village of Garmo. After dinner, we walked into town, and Mike bought Krissie an ice cream cone. That evening, Lynette and I gave the kiddies their first bridge lesson—counting points. It was the first of August, and the sun shone all day. Lynette promised August would be the month of good weather.

Never out of sight of lakes, rivers and mountains, we drove south through the lovely agricultural valley of Gudbrandsdahl. I was impressed by the seeming equality of everyone's lot. They all were in the same boat—no rich and no poor. Their homes all looked alike, and they all wore the same clothes and ate the same food. I thought this must be what democratic socialism is all about. Hoping to get a conversation going, I remarked to Lynette that neither wealth nor poverty was apparent in Norway and that people were athletically lean, often blonde, and were more striking than attractive; and that they appeared to be rather cold, unsmiling and unfriendly and didn't seem to enjoy themselves very much. Generally, Lynette eschews generalizations, and, in true form, was noncommittal about those I had just uttered.

"Don't you agree?"

"With what?"

"My characterization of Norwegians as homogeneous and aloof."

"How many Norwegians do you know?"

"Not many."

"How many?"

"None."

"I think there's a campground in Ringelu. Maybe we should stop there for the night."

There was a campground in Ringelu, and we did stop there for the night. In fact, we stopped early in the afternoon and took advantage of the sun to do our laundry, air the sleeping bags, and wash and clean the camper. The children built a dam in a stream, and I found an interesting shorebird I was unable to identify.

Lillehammer sits at the head of Mjosa, Norway's largest lake. We saw the paddleboat Skibladner crossing the lake and visited four thousand-year old rock sculptures. In Hamar, I bought a current *Time* magazine that was full of Watergate and talk of impeaching Richard Nixon. We camped by a river where Lynette laughed and said she hoped no one was watching as I tried with great difficulty to find a level spot for the camper. Mike caught a fish, and we saw a snipe. Later, the children were surprisingly fascinated by our president's predicament, and we spent the evening talking about the political process and Nixon's difficulties.

From a letter to my parents: *We find the news a bit depressing. Nixon is just about finished. Problems in the rest of the world aren't much better—the Middle East, Greece and Turkey, and now Uganda has invaded Tanzania. Oh well, on to Sweden.*

Oslo is a relatively small capital city and easy to walk around. The fourteenth-century Akershus Slott, or castle, was erected to defend the harbor but found other use as headquarters for the Germans during the Nazi occupation. We saw the Fram, the ship that carried Fridtjof Nanse on his 1893-96 expedition to the North Pole and Roald Amundsen to Antarctica when he first reached the South Pole in 1911, and the Kon-Tiki, the raft in which Thor Heyerdahl sailed more than five thousand miles from South America to Polynesia in 1947. The Vikingskipshuset museum features three tenth-century Norse ships found in burial mounds along the Oslofjord. We visited the Holmenkollen where many international skiing competitions have been held, the contemporary Radhuset (city hall) where works of many of Norway's leading artists are displayed, and the Nasjonalgalleriet. Much of the city's art and sculpture takes on an unattractively heavy, bigger than life socialist worker theme. We ate our lunch in Frognerparken where Gustaf Vigeland's stone, bronze and iron sculptures of animals and naked humans of varying ages, sexes, and physiques fill the park. At Karl Johans Gate, Mike bought a Norwegian flag and Krissie an ice cream cone. Oslo's municipal campground boasted hot showers and an international clientele. A boy from Carleton College in Northfield, Minnesota, greeted us at the gate and later enlisted some of his backpacking buddies for a soccer game which Mike and I joined. After dinner and a shower, we drank a few beers with a couple from South Africa.

Fredrikstad's Old Town retains many of the features of a fortified seventeenth-century town—including a moat, ramparts, drawbridge and sortie gates. We walked the old streets, ate our lunch while sitting on the Kongsten Redoubt walls and then headed south on the Highway of the Ancients, Norway's most important archeological area, stopping to see three and four thousand-year old rock carvings, stone circles and monoliths along the way. In the border town of Halden we changed money and climbed the ramparts of Fredriksten Fort from which we had excellent views of Idde Fjord and the Swedish borderlands. We crossed into Sweden and worked our way south along the sea, through picturesque fishing villages like Stromstad where we bought groceries and Tjarno on the Koster Islands, beyond which we camped at a nature preserve. The best we could determine from Swedish newspapers was that Nixon admitted he had lied about the tapes.

A few scrubby conifers managed to survive the blustery coastal winds and clung to the rocky coast where heather in full bloom otherwise covered the ground. Sites rich in archeological importance seemed more numerous than contemporary settlements. Ancient monoliths punctuated the areas lying among barrows and burial mounds. Near Grebbested, red pictographs depicting life in the bronze age adorned granite outcroppings. The rugged, lovely coastal drive took us to the quaint town of Lysekil where we boarded a ferry, drove across a small island and boarded another ferry to Orust Island. An old seaman on the ferry lived on Orust in the village of Ellos and spoke a half dozen languages. When he realized we were Americans, he wanted to know what we thought of Richard Nixon. Like many Europeans we spoke with, he generally liked Nixon and doubted he did anything worse than their political leaders routinely do. Europeans generally were incredulous that we would consider impeaching a president for what they considered to be "all politicians do it" kind of offenses. When asked why they liked Nixon, these people invariably responded that he had resumed relations with China. Near Halleviksstrand, we camped on a beach with many granite outcroppings. After eating a sumptuous dinner of hot dogs, tomato soup and apples, we checked out aquatic life in the many tidal pools and then, with a peaceful world all around us, waded in the sea.

Goteburg is a charming city with tree-lined streets, canals, a busy harbor protected by a fort, fine old buildings, and an important university. However, if you asked any of the four of us today what we remembered about Goteburg, the response certainly would not be one of those tourist attractions but rather a certain club. We hadn't showered since Oslo, so when we found the municipal campground, we registered and paid our fee. Then we learned there was no hot water, so we asked for a refund. The attendant returned our money but warned us their's was the only campground in Goteburg. In our subsequent search for a place to stay, we came upon a private sunbathing club. I introduced us to the manager and explained our predicament. He laughed and said, of course, we could spend the night in their parking area and use their facilities. And using their facilities was our most memorable experience in Goteburg. After entering the club, men walked to the left and women to the right, then everyone stripped in his or her locker room. The facilities included saunas, cold pools, showers, and an enclosed outdoor sunning area. A warm sun shone late into the evening, and Mike and I stretched out on lounge chairs and wondered how the girls were enjoying all this naked freedom. Later, in the camper, we all had a good laugh. Krissie was embarrassed but said she enjoyed it. Lynette couldn't imagine sunbathing with her friends in the nude. Then we remembered the four of us swimming nude while camped on a remote island in Minnesota's Boundary Waters.

The English language newspapers in the Goteburg municipal library were full of news about Watergate. Nixon admitted he had been withholding information. The magazine, *Time*, was also very troubling. In addition to reporting on Nixon's increasingly imminent demise, *Time* informed us the world economy was in the tank, Greece and Turkey wanted to blow each other up over Cyprus, and cholera was "reaching epidemic proportions" in Portugal. All the bad news seemed to affect us in one way or another (We intended to travel to Portugal, Greece and Turkey, if not Cyprus.), and

Lynette and I left the library a bit depressed.

Our route continued south along the Swedish coast through medieval Halmstad, the resort town of Bastad where we ate lunch on the grass in a seaside city park, the quaint fishing village of Torekov, and Bejbystrand where we played miniature golf and camped on the public beach. In the morning we drove into the picturesque eleventh-century seaport of Helsingborg. From an old fort, the Karnan, the Danish coast could be seen across the Oresund Channel. We walked down a pleasant mall, bought some groceries and stopped at a newsstand. The Swedish language head-lines said it all, "Nixon Resigns!"

From my notes: *I'm glad it's over, but what a tragedy. He should have been honest—he was a Quaker! Almost worse, he should have known they would get him if he lied. They hate him. Kennedy and Johnson, and probably Eisenhower and Truman, did things just as bad. But they never went after those guys with such vehemence. They wanted Nixon bad. Why? Because of Alger Hiss? Had to be more than that. Setback for conservatism? I doubt it. Conservatives never considered Nixon one of their own. Ford is probably clean, but this is a setback for the country. Things will not be the same. Lynette feels sorry for his wife and family, the shame. Mike is ambivalent. Krissie is happy it's over, "Now you won't read the paper so much, Daddy."*

Our car ferry crossed the straits from Helsingborg, Sweden, to Helsingor (Elsinore), Denmark. Helsingor was an important medieval trad-ing port, and enormous, impregnable Kronborg Castle was built to protect the town from the Swedes. In the fifteenth century, the castle, with its com-manding position on the Oresund narrows, became the town's most prof-itable venture for the next four hundred years by extracting levies from mer-chant ships passing through the Oresund. Today, Helsingor remains an important commercial center, but the city is probably better known for its fic-ticious past—Kronborg was the setting for Shakespeare's Hamlet. Half-tim-bered houses in the city's old town preserve the Shakespearian flavor. We walked the streets of the town and, from Kronborg's walls, could see the castle's strategic position and the undeniable persuasiveness of its can-nons—pay the toll or get blasted out of the water. We went for a swim at the nearby old fishing village of Hornbaek and camped on the beach. After din-ner we discussed our initial impressions—the Danes seemed more pros-perous and more friendly than their Scandanavian cousins in Norway and Sweden. Villages had nice homes, and the countryside was clean and beautiful. And prices were much lower than the rest of Scandanavia. Lynette said she thought we would like Denmark.

From Hornbaek we drove south and west past the Danish royal fami-ly's eighteenth-century palace at Fredensborg and the large, moated seventeenth-century Frederiksborg Castle at Hillerod, and then to Kobenhavn (Copenhagen). Our route into one of the world's most beautiful cities threaded opulent suburbs and followed wide, attractive boulevards past wonderful parks with impressive bronze statues and gardens. In the old town, copper spires pierced the sky, and Dutch Renaissance buildings lined old streets. We walked along the Langelinie harbor promenade to the Lille Havfrue (Little Mermaid), a photogenic bronze statue inspired by a Hans Christian Andersen fairytale, and the symbol of Copenhagen. We watched the changing of the guard at the Queen's palace, Amalienborg, and toured Frederiks Kirke, a marble church with a ninety-eight-foot high dome. We paid our respects at the graves of Hans Christian Andersen and the philosopher, Soren Kierkegaard, in the Assistens Kirkegaard graveyard and, later in the afternoon, registered at the Charlottenlund municipal campgrounds and admired the fish in the nearby Danmark's Akvarium.

The next morning, the children reminded us this was to be their day, so we first drove to the Borsen, a sevententh-century tower comprised of four dragons standing on their heads, their tails twisting and forming a one hundred eighty-foot spire and then to the *piecè de résistance*, one hundred thirty-year old Tivoli, the city's wonderful gardens where children and even adults are entertained in numerous, unforgettable ways. Mike and Krissie enjoyed the playgrounds and rode the roller coaster. We walked through the gardens, past ponds and statues, sat on a bench eating ice cream cones, and watched wrestling matches, parades and concerts, including a children's band, with marvelous young drummers, playing the *Marseillaise*. We attended a variety show, a puppet ballet and a pantomime and ate lunch and dinner in gay cafes. In the evening, the buildings and trees in the park were brilliantly lit, and fireworks burst in the sky.

From my notes: *M and K slept on the drive back to the campground. L and I decided this had been one of the best days our family has ever had.*

After a steady rain all night, the morning sun rose into a cloudless sky. Back in Copenhagen, Lynette gave us one of her patented walking tours, visiting the turn of the century Raadhuset (Town Hall) built in the Italian Renaissance style, the seventeenth-century Rundetarn or Round Tower, and Christianborg, the seat of the Danish Parliament. We arranged for a visa at the Czechoslovakian embassy and picked up our mail at American Express. Shopping occupied the remainder of the morning—Lynette bought Krissie a Danish doll for Christmas, Mike bought several Scandinavian flags for his collection, I bought a belt for Mike, and Krissie tried to buy an old coin for her brother but the shopkeeper gave it to her instead (eminently understandable, she was very cute). That afternoon we drove south to Koge with its sixteenth-century half-timbered houses, stopping along the way to visit Vallo, a palace with a magnificent tulip garden, and, west of Koge, camped in a gas station parking area.

We meandered west through the pleasant Danish countryside and saw castles at Haslev and Gisselfeld and visited the Holmegaard glassworks near Naestved where they demonstrated glass blowing by hand. We arrived in Korsor just in time to catch the ferry for the one-hour passage to Funen Island. We landed at Nyborg, drove past sixteenth-century Holckenhavn Castle and twelfth-century Nyborg Castle, and then west to Odense, a small city with fairytale streets and authentically old half-timbered houses, tracing its roots to the ninth century. We visited the houses where Hans Christian Andersen was born and where he spent his early years, both now marvelous museums. The first displayed original manuscripts, letters to friends and girlfriends and original drawings by Andersen and a woman who also illustrated his books. The second contained Andersen memorabilia, furniture and murals of scenes with Andersen. Together, the museums instilled an appreciation and understanding of Hans Christian Andersen, the rather queerly imaginative and homely lad who endured many misfortunes, including the death of his father when he was eleven. He ultimately became a national treasure, having achieved success writing *The Ugly Duckling* (ironically), several novels and many fairy tales. That evening, camped in a pullover west of Odense, Lynette read *The Ugly Duckling* to us.

Crossing to Jutland, Denmark's long peninsula jutting far into the North Sea, we stopped in Kolding to see Koldinghus, a thirteenth-century castle, and continued southwest through the lovely, rural Danish scenery to the medieval town of Ribe with its half-timbered houses, cobblestone streets and gas lamps. Lynette supervised the children with their schoolwork, which somehow led to a discussion of the difference between fact and opinion, as we drove south through Tonder and into Germany. We spent little more time than was necessary to drive through Hamburg, a modern city rebuilt since its almost total destruction in World War II. I considered the perils of driving in London and Hamburg a tossup until I remembered, at least we were now on the right side. We continued south through the picturesque German countryside with cattle grazing and storks foraging in fields and past moated castles and earthy smelling villages that were no more than eight or ten farm houses with barns attached, grouped closely together near the road while their fields radiated in all directions. I wondered whether this arrangement stemmed from earlier times as protection from raiders. The charming, small medieval city of Celle featured sixteenth-and seventeenth-century half-timbered houses as well as a modern, twentieth-century gas station in the parking area of which we camped.

Wolfsburg, also destroyed during the war, now appeared modern, clean and affluent with wide streets and a large Volkswagen factory that assembled Golfs and Passats. We joined a two-hour factory tour with a movie, and the children were fascinated. We shopped for groceries and other supplies and then drove to the East German border, only a kilometer from the city center. The road, like most others on German maps of those times, ended at the border. Fences topped and flanked by barbed wire marked the Iron Curtain, and, on the East German side, armed soldiers guarded pens with dogs that looked like German shepherds. The west side of the fence, on the other hand, was absolutely unguarded, creating an almost comical picture.

Wolfsburg's municipal campground was a good one, situated on a lake, with a playground, a laundry facility and other modern conveniences. Lynette and the children changed for a swim, and I prepared to wash the camper. Adrian, a friendly but garrulous Brit camping next to us with his family would have none of my washing the car. Each time I put the sponge in the bucket, he pulled me over to his Volkswagen to show me some clever adaptation he had devised or to engage me in some other activity that was mutually exclusive with washing my car. He had two children, an eight-year-old girl and a five-year-old boy, who was a carbon copy of his father. Adrian was a Volkswagen mechanic back in England, and, when he saw the handle mechanism wasn't working properly on our sliding door, insisted on fixing it. His wife, Claudette, was aware of Adrian's obtuseness regarding my car washing intentions.

"For Pete's sake, Adrian. Leave the poor man alone."

"Nonsense, Claudette. His door needs fixing." Sometime during the hour or more Adrian worked on the camper door, my bucket of water became cold and unsoapy, so I gave up on washing the camper.

Adrian, Claudette, Lynette and I sat on a blanket, playing cards and drinking a bottle of wine while watching our four children in the playground. We talked about diving, skiing, photography and all the other things Adrian was interested in, and he poked fun at America's relative lack of history. He presented himself as a somewhat knowledgeable naturalist and insisted there were wolves and wild boars in the nearby woods. I excused myself and returned to our camper for another bottle of wine. I knew we were in for a long evening, but that was OK. After all, our camper door was working great.

Lynette's maiden name was Orwig. The village of Orwigsburg, Pennsylvania, had been first settled by her great, great, great, great grandfather Gottfried. Actually, Gottfried's surname was Urbecht until someone simplified it when he arrived in America. Lynette's dad said Gottfried grew up in Braunschweig, Germany, an old city only about ten miles from Wolfsburg, and he asked us to make some inquiries. Charming half-timbered houses lined the streets defining Braunschweig's town square where Der Lowe (The Lion), stood in front of the twelfth-century castle, Burg Dankwarderode. This oldest free-standing statue in Germany was put there by Henry the Lion, Duke of Bavaria, as a monument to himself. We thought the Rathaus (City Hall) was the logical place to see if any records existed containing Gottfried's name, but it was Friday afternoon and for some reason the city offices were closed. The afternoon was beastly hot, and we used the Rathaus bathrooms to spash cold water on ourselves. We returned to the camper to find the temperature inside registering 112 degrees.

We drove south, hoping to escape the lowland heat in the Harz Mountains and set up camp in the resort town of Bad Harzburg's municipal park. Lynette and I sat on a park bench, watching Krissie and Mike playing miniature golf. Older adults and young children waded in a nearby pool being filled by a continually running fountain. A sign on the fountain, in clear view, said *Keine Trinkvasser*. I translated to myself, certain I was being told that here was "Clean Drinking Water," and, being hot and thirsty, walked to the fountain and helped myself. When I returned to the bench, Lynette was a bit agitated.

"Are you sure that water was good to drink?"

"The sign clearly says 'Clean Drinking Water'."

"Those people wading in the pond looked at you in a peculiar way. Maybe you should look up the word *Keine*.

I walked to the camper and retrieved Langenscheidt's *Universal Dictionary* of German and English words. A number of negative translations followed the word *keine* on page 385, the most memorable of which was "by no means." I felt ill and was still wondering, days later, when the symptoms of some terrible bacteriological intestinal problem would appear. They didn't.

Thanks to the Brothers Grimm and others, folklore from this enchanting area of Germany is known throughout the world. The Pied Piper lured the rats from Hameln (Hamelin), Hansel and Gretel spread bread crumbs in the Reinhardswald (Reinhards Forest), Sleeping Beauty slept deeply in Sababurg Castle and Siegfried roamed the Odenwald. We stopped in Goslar where a walk through the town exposed us to a rich variety of architectural styles—Gothic, Renaissance, Baroque and Romanesque, and in Duderstadt with its Gothic churches and thousand-year old half-timbered houses. Gottingen featured a fourteenth-century rathaus and a flower market in the center of which was a Goose Girl Fountain. From the Trendelburg environs, the Brothers Grimm immortalized tales of the Reinhardsvald that had been passed along verbally for centuries including *Hansel and Gretel, Red Riding Hood* and the *Frog Prince*. We toured thirteenth-century Trindelburg Castle and Sleeping Beauty's castle at Sababurg. We camped in the parking area of a farm implement repair shop, on the edge of the forest where jays and black redstarts fed on crumbs we threw on the ground, and buzzards soared overhead. The proprietor joined us for coffee and told us that descendants of the Grimm brothers lived in nearby Lippoldsburg, and that some of them were still writing folklore of the region. That evening, Lynette read an article in *Time* in which the newspaper columnist we met in Brazil, Carlos Branco, was quoted and described as one of South America's most respected political writers. I wrote him a letter specifying no reply was expected, telling him how pleased we were to read the article and updating him on our travels.

The Romans founded the ancient city of Cologne in 32 BC. The Koln Dom (Cologne Cathedral) is probably the world's largest Gothic edifice. I tried without success to find a vantage point where I could photograph the entire building. Much of the cathedral has been rebuilt and restored, especially after the destruction of World War II, but the Dom's foundations date back to the thirteenth century, and a second-century Roman mosaic was discovered during recent restoration work. We walked around Koln's modern streets, looking for birthday gifts for Mike, and, south of the city, registered at a campground on the Rhine. Lynette and Krissie opted for the showers while Mike and I walked to the river to look for birds, and it was somewhat disconcerting to see the stream flowing north. Mike was very excited about turning ten years old the next day, and Krissie was even more so.

From a letter to my parents: *Mike's excitement about his birthday tomorrow is only exceeded by Krissie's excitement about Mike's birthday tomorrow, if you can figure that out. He's got the day all planned and intends to hold me to a promise not to drive more than seventy miles.*

Krissie couldn't contain her enthusiasm and gave Mike his card a day early—a "wiener dog" with the message, "Have an especially long birthday!"

Koblenz, Germany, August 19, 1974

Happy Birthday, Mike! He requested ham sandwiches for lunch. Lynette wrote "Happy Birthday, Mike!" with M&Ms on a marble cake. He was so excited. After eating lunch, we gave him his gifts—a Swiss Army pocket knife, a bag of candy, a large bottle of Coke, and a jar of mayonnaise. He was ecstatic. Lynette quietly asked me how a kid could get so excited about a Coke and a jar of mayonnaise. We drove south up the Rhine to Boppard, a wine-producing town with old Roman walls, and told Mike he could pick a restaurant for our dinner. Since our budget allowed us to eat dinner out only infrequently, Lynette and I tried to steer him to a rather up-scale restaurant we fancied with a lot of German atmosphere. Instead Mike chose an inexpensive, unatmospheric eatery that advertised hamburgers. He loved it. That night we camped in a park next to the river. While the kiddies skipped stones on the Rhine, Lynette and I sat on a bench and watched the river traffic—mostly tugs with barges and brightly lit tourist boats. Freight trains whistled from tracks running along the river's opposite side and friendly

Germans strolled along the walk in front of us. Mike walked up to the bench, thanked and hugged each of us, and said this was the best day of the trip.

Boats, trains and our VW camper followed the Rhine south. Fairy tale castles were perched on cliffs overlooking the river and vineyards cascaded down slopes flanking the river. Villages with charming streets of half-timbered houses were happily preparing for their traditional September wine festivals. Oberwesel's Gothic architecture was of interest, as were Rudesheim's turreted and gabled old houses. We stopped to see Bromserburg and Ehrenfels castles, and then left the Rhine at Bingen and followed its tributary, the Nahe, to Bad Kreuznach; the romantic, medieval Town of Roses and Nightingales. Lynette's paternal grandmother was born in the nearby hamlet of Roxheim. Apparently the village was too small to have a rathaus, and we gave up any hope of finding a record of Katherine Brack when we could find no one who spoke English. At home, Lynette regularly polishes the small brass tea kettle her grandmother carried to America from Roxheim when she was a girl, and, while eating lunch in the village, she said that it felt good to be in the town where her grandmother had lived regardless of our lack of success in finding any of her records. I thought of Adrian's accusing us of having no history. We drove through Worms where, in 1521, Martin Luther was indicted by the Diet of Worms, and, today, the city has erected a monument honoring Luther and justifiably boasts of their fine, eleventh-century Romanesque cathedral. On the autobahen near Heidelberg we pulled into a gas station layby for the night. Lynette and Mike whipped Krissie and me in soccer, 8-5.

From my notes: *Somehow Lynette persuaded me to wear nylon underwear on this trip, claiming it dries much faster than the cotton alternative. Today, in Heidelberg, she went entirely too far, however, when the water at the laundromat was too hot and turned our clothes pink. It's bad enough wearing nylon underwear, but pink nylon underwear is too much!* (When we returned to the States, I foreswore nylon underwear and promise I have never worn it since.)

We walked up the hill to the impressive thirteenth-century Heidelberg Castle with its enormous wine cask, the Heidelberg Tun, and through the old section of town, and then the amazing fourteenth-century medieval university. University students have gathered for centuries at the Rother Ochsen (Red Ox), immortalized in *The Student Prince*. We stopped there for an obligatory beer or two and then popped in on a distant relative who owned a gift shop. Sleeping in gas station parking areas had become routine, and that night we were lucky to find an especially agreeable one just east of Heidelberg on the lovely Neckar River.

The Neckar Valley scenery unrolled charmingly before us—lush green meadows, stone arch bridges spanning the peaceful river, ripe vineyards and deep forests, quaint villages with delicate church spires and brown and white half-timbered houses, and enchanting fairy-tale castles. Neckarsteinach alone features four castles, and Hirschhorn, Zwingenberg and Neckarzimmern have one each. We continued east through Mosbach and Heilbronn, visited Neuenstein Schloss (Castle) at Ohringen, then entered the Swabian Forest and stopped at Schwabisch Hall, an especially attractive and romantic town with old buildings and bridges, a rococo rathaus and a fortress. We camped at a nearby roadside Restplatz.

Medieval Dinkelsbuhl, on the Wornitz River, is arguably the prettiest town in Germany. Preserved intact from its past, the town is surrounded by a moat and a wall complete with gates and towers. Fifteenth-century St. George's Cathedral is especially interesting as are the old streets lined with half-timbered houses. Mike and Krissie thought the town's famous ginger-bread was deserving of its reputation. We drove south to Aalen and west to Stuttgart where we found a fine municipal campground. Lynette and I aired out our sleeping bags and did some hand laundry. Krissie and Mike washed the camper and cleaned the inside for twenty-five cents each and did a good job. Lynette and I finished first and watched the kiddies finish their job while having a beer with a German couple camping next to us. A couple from Oak Park, Illinois, joined us. They had attended a church youth conference and were touring in a rented camper. Soon we had a good soccer game going, and a German boy, with whom Mike had become acquainted, gave us all a lesson in ball handling.

Stuttgart rebuilt after the war's destruction, and modern buildings and shopping malls greet the visitor. We walked through the large, pleasant Hohenpark Killesberg with its gardens, sculptures and fountains and watched old men playing chess on huge open air boards with life sized pieces they moved by rolling them on their edges. We visited the sixteenth-century Altes Schloss (Old Palace), ate lunch at the zoo, inspected an architectural project on which Walter Gropius, Ludwig Mies van der Rohe and Charles-Edouard Le Corbusier collaborated back in the 1920s, and posted a few letters.

Some of Germany's most interesting towns and beautiful scenery may be found in the Schwarzwald or Black Forest region that features mountain lakes and healthy spas, lush vineyards and orchards, picturesque farms, spell-binding folklore, fairy-tale castles and charming villages. Many women in the small villages of the Schwarzwald wore traditional costumes. We drove west into the Black Forest through Nagold, with its half-timbered houses and thousand-year old Remigiuskirche, to one of Lynette's favorite German towns, the mountain resort of Freudenstadt where we camped in the police station parking area. We strolled through the narrow streets and around the large central Platz with its rathaus, elegant shops and restaurants.

From a letter to my parents: *Thankfully it was Saturday afternoon when the expensive boutiques closed or Lynette might have succumbed to the bedecked and beckoning mannequins. After wearing jeans, sweatshirts and worse for the past year, she found the idea of a new wardrobe tempting.*

From Freudenstadt our route turned north through Schwarzwald ski resorts to Germany's most famous spa, ancient Baden Baden, which has attracted international attention since before the Roman occupation. Then we drove south along the Rhine and crossed the river at medieval Strasbourg. After nearly three months touring Europe, Lynette was now at her happiest—we were at last in France. She majored in French and felt an affinity here not experienced elsewhere in Europe. With great enthusiasm, we set out on her walking tour—the eleventh-century Romanesque/Gothic Cathedral of Notre Dame with its 470-foot spire and allegorical clock; the Chateau des Rohan palace turned museum with works by Giotto, El Greco, Rubens and Rembrandt; and La Petite France, the old town characterized by high-gabled gingerbread houses, narrow streets and canals with small locks and gates used by pleasure and tourist craft. Boys practiced paddling their kayaks up sluiceways, rolling and turning in the roiling water. We bought ice cream cones, and I wondered whether the French reputation for being unfriendly was undeserved—the residents of Strasbourg were very friendly—and contrasted them with Germans who, with the exception of the old people in the spa towns, seemed not as friendly. South of Strasbourg we found a campground on a lake where the children swam. A backpacker from Boston saw the U.S.A. designation on the rear of our camper and introduced himself. He had developed a somewhat interesting lifestyle—working in Thule, Greenland, seventy-two hours per week for six month stretches at wages much higher than he could earn in the States, saving his money, then traveling for six months—not a bad way for a young single guy to live for a few years.

South of Strasbourg, in the town of Selestat, we looked in vain for storks. An article in National Geographic reported storks congregate in this area every August before migrating to Africa for the winter. It was August 26, and we thought perhaps they had already left. Lynette didn't feel well, so we stopped at a campground in the medieval Alsatian city of Colmar. I fixed cheese sandwiches for lunch, but Lynnie had no appetite. She went to bed and slept all afternoon while the kiddies and I walked to town where we did the laundry and shopped for groceries. We walked narrow cobblestone streets lined with old half-timbered houses sporting carved wood facades. We ate ice cream cones, and Mike found an Austrian coin for his collection. Krissie said, "Maybe Mom's homesick."

"Why do you say that?"

"Remember when we left Minnesota for South America and I threw up?"

"Of course I do."

"Well, I was homesick. I think Mom's just homesick." When we returned to the camper, I reported Krissie's diagnosis to Lynette. She smiled and said, "It doesn't feel like homesick. It feels like amoebic dysentery."

Near Colmar, in the old walled town of Turckheim, a stork sat on the huge nest it had built on someone's chimney. Our route wound its way over the Vosges mountains, then ran west across rolling farmland through Luneville, where we stopped for lunch, and Nancy, with its large Place Stanislas containing the Hotel de Ville (City Hall), the Grand Hotel and an Arc de Triomphe. The closer we approached Paris, the more chipper Lynette became. We crossed the Marne River at St. Dizier and camped in a gas station parking area.

Mike paid me five centimes as a reward for being the first to see the Eiffel Tower. Paris! More than two thousand years old and, today, in Lynette's and my eyes, the world's most beautiful and exciting city. Long ago, the Parisii, a minor Gallic tribe, occupied a prehistoric settlement confined to an island in the Seine, the Ile de la Cite. In the third century, the Romans brought Christianity to Paris, and the Franks captured the town in the sixth century. Notre Dame, the Sorbonne, and the Louvre were erected in the twelfth and thirteenth centuries. The cultural, political and commercial importance of Paris continued to grow. During the seventeenth and eighteenth centuries, marvelous palaces and gardens were built, streets were widened, and wonderful buildings were constructed—the Church of the Madeleine, the Pantheon and the Ecole Militaire. In the late eighteenth century, Paris was the intellectual and political center of the French Revolution. Then, with the dawn of the nineteenth century, came Napoleon, and much of Paris became what it is today. L' Empereur erected prodigious monuments, exceptional bridges, grand boulevards and immense squares.

Early in the afternoon, we drove onto the Boulevard Périphérique, crossed the Seine, and circled the city to its west side where the huge, crowded municipal campground was located in the Bois de Boulogne, the vast forested park that was once the hunting grounds of kings. We registered, found our assigned spot and ate our lunch while watching other campers go by—hippie backpackers, a caravan of Hell's Angels look-alikes on their motorcycles, fat men in warm-up suits, and women in pajamas or house coats. Then we drove into the city center to American Express. At the information counter I asked a man if he spoke English.

"Yes, a little," he replied. I explained that we wanted to exchange money and pick up our mail. In flawless, virtually unaccented English, he told us exactly what to do. (Travelers in Europe learn quickly that the phrase, "Yes, a little," used in response to an inquiry about the subject's English fluency, really means, "Yes, I speak English very well, most likely better than you do.")

We introduced Mike and Krissie to Paris while walking from the lovely, enormous Place de la Concorde with its Egyptian obelisk, fountains and monuments to the Place de l'Etoile, dominated by the Arc de Triomphe which was erected by Napoleon to commemorate his victories and through which the victorious Allied soldiers marched after the liberation of Paris in World War II. Connecting the two squares is the amazing Avenue des Champs-Elysées, with its shaded parks, sidewalk cafes and fashionable shops. We took the Metro (subway) to the Ile de la Cité where we saw the stunning Cathédrale de Notre Dame de Paris and then walked to the Rive Gauche (Left Bank) and shopped in a flea market. Mike announced that Paris was his favorite city and bought a small metal replica of the Eiffel Tower.

The next morning we parked on Avenue Foch near the Arc de Triomphe and walked down the Champs-Elysées to the Place de la Concorde. We fed ourselves and the pigeons in the Jardin des Tuileries and stopped at the U.S. Embassy to have pages added to our passports. We spent as much time as the children could stand (about 2 hours) in the Palais du Louvre's Museum of Paintings. I tried with little success to impress upon them the incredible privilege of seeing the Mona Lisa, the Winged Victory and Venus de Milo in one building. Then we walked down the Rue de la Paix to the Place Vendome at the center of which stands a fantastic monument to Napolean's unbridled arrogance, a 144-foot high column, accented with a spiraling band made from melted cannons he captured in the Battle of Austerlitz. A short ride on the Metro took us back to our camper in which we took a longer ride to the suburb of Chatou where old friends from Minnesota now lived. They had invited us for dinner.

Russ managed the European offices of the accounting firm he worked for, while Rosemary managed the large house in Chatou where they had lived the past few years. Their three children, Cindy, Jeff and Scott, attended American schools. All of them spoke French, especially Rosemary. We picked up a bunch of flowers on the drive to Chatou. It was Rosemary's birthday, so the children bought her a box of chocolates and made birthday cards for her. After an evening of splendid wining and dining and bringing us all up to date on each other, Lynette and the children were escorted to their rooms upstairs. I wasn't yet ready to forsake our little camper, so I slept in the driveway on the small, comfortable bed to which I had become so accustomed the past few months.

Jeff and Mike were about the same age. Lynette and I took the two boys to Paris with us while Krissie remained in Chatou with Rosemary, twelve-year-old Cindy and four-year-old Scott. I photographed the boys weighing themselves on a scale with Notre Dame as a backdrop, talking to a bookseller on a quay of the Seine, and crossing the Pont Neuf (New Bridge), the oldest bridge in Paris. We toured the Conciergerie where prisoners had awaited their fate during the French Revolution, walked through the Latin Quarter, visited the Sorbonne and the seventeenth-century Luxembourg Palace, and stopped at a cafe on Boulevard du Montparnasse. The boys had a great time, and Lynette and I did too.

Russ worked the next day, but the rest of us went into the city in the camper. We drove up to Montmartre (Mount of the Martyrs), the highest point in the city, where we parked in front of the Basilique du Sacre-Coeur and I snapped a picture of the five children eating sandwiches on the roof of the camper. By now Krissie had permanently attached herself to Cindy who didn't seem to mind the attention. We visited shops and ate ice cream cones while watching artists painting under a sunny blue sky. That evening, Rosemary and Russ hosted a small cocktail party that included, in addition to Lynette and me, two other American couples, both with the names Barbara and Jack, after which we all drove into Paris for dinner at the *tres gai Pot de Terre*. We sat at a very large and old country table, and soon several French couples joined us. Waiters brought an astonishing variety of pates, including pate de foie gras. Three men played guitars, and we all sang along. After dinner our waiter poured a bottle of cognac into a single large snifter which we passed around the table, each taking our turn.

Russ left for a partners' meeting in Brittany, the four girls busied themselves somehow, and I took the three boys fishing in the country. Scott, a very funny and likable boy, grew tired of not catching any fish, so we played "hide and seek." Jeff and Mike eventually grew weary of their lack of success and said they wanted to climb the Tour Eiffel, so we drove into Paris and paid for the privilege of walking up 750 steps. I suppose on a clear day we could have seen forever from the tower's lookout, but it had started raining and we couldn't even see the ground below. Little Scott held my hand very tightly, and I sensed we were higher than he wanted to be.

"Are you glad we came, Scott?"

"Yes," he nodded.

"You seem sad, Scott."

"I want to go down now, Mr. Wile." Jeff and Mike wanted to take the train home. It stopped near Jeff's home in Chatou, and times were different then, so I said OK. Scott stuck his house key in the camper ignition slot and blew a fuse, so he and I found a Volkswagen dealer, bought some spare fuses and drove back to Chatou where we found Mike and Jeff, who, in just a few days, had become fast friends, playing jarts in the yard.

Krissie did not want to leave Cindy; Mike wanted to stay with Jeff; Lynette and Rosemary cried on each other's shoulders; and I wanted to take Scott with me. (Russ didn't enter the picture—he was in Brittany.) With a tug at our hearts, we found our way back to the Boulevard Périphérique, drove around the city and then south toward Dijon. Somewhere south of the city, Mike told us Rosemary had packed groceries in the camper and told him not to tell us until we were well away from Paris. We drove only about forty miles further and stopped in Fontainebleau to see the magnificent twelfth-century palace. The natural beauty of the area surrounding Fontainebleau has provided inspiration for many artists. The afternoon had worn on, and we needed a place to camp for the night, so we chose a roadside pullover with a view Lynette was certain might easily have tempted Corot.

Continuing southeast toward Dijon, we stopped to see a chateau at Ancy-le-Franc and at the hillside town of Montbard, birthplace of the eighteenth-century French naturalist, George Louis Buffon. Rolling meadows and stone farmhouses characterized the pleasant Burgundy countryside. Near Sombernon, we camped by a lake and in the morning drove into lovely old Dijon with its fifteenth- and sixteenth-century wooden houses where we admired the Palais des Ducs de Bourgogne and the Hotel de Ville and bought two jars of the world's best mustard and a bottle of cassis liqueur. The day was clear, beautiful and pleasantly warm. We moved along toward Geneva and stopped for lunch beside a picturesque river. Orange-finned trout foraged for insects in the clear eddies below churning rapids. My back was killing me—I had been unable to stand straight for the past two days. Lynette and the children waded in the stream while I lay on the sun-warmed grass. When I got up to leave, the pain miraculously had gone.

For a hundred and fifty miles the Jura Mountains define the boundary between France and Switzerland. Our road climbed a green valley between lofty peaks and past rampaging streams and quiet blue lakes. Suddenly beautiful Switzerland lay before us—the city of Genève (Geneva) and Lac Leman (Lake Geneva) stretching out in the valley below, Mont Blanc and the snow covered Swiss Alps beyond. The camper switchbacked down the mountain, and, near the bottom, a cool breeze blew from the lake to the east. Lynette smiled and observed, "There's a tinge of autumn in the air."

American Express was our first stop in Geneva. We changed money and collected our mail. The officious clerk performing those duties was very short with the people in front of us, and Lynette whispered, "He must be having a bad day." A black woman behind us whispered in English with a heavy French accent, "Every day is bad for him. He is very frustrated, if you know what I mean." We inspected some antique stores in the old town, visited the twelfth-century Cathedrale St-Pierre and the sixteenth-century Hotel de Ville, saw the statue of Jean-Jacques Rousseau on an island in the Rhone, and walked to the Quai du Mont-Blanc from where paddle steamers depart for excursions of Lac Leman. Across the bay, Geneva's famous Jet d'Eau spouted lake water four hundred feet into the clear, deep blue sky. The kids played on a huge steel slide, and Lynette bought several small Swiss Army knives for gifts.

From my notes: *The people don't seem very friendly, but they couldn't have picked a cleaner, nicer place to live.*

We found a very nice campground on the lake and pulled into a slot beside a yellow VW camper owned by an American couple. Al was a psychologist on sabbatical from Michigan State and, we soon learned, was a friend of Judy Bardwick (South America). We compared notes on Judy and Eastern Europe over a glass or two of wine and then enjoyed a dinner of salad and Lynette's incomparable spaghetti. Later Mike and I looked for birds along the lake and found great crested grebes, black terns, coal tits and a nuthatch. That night we heard a distant freight train's eerie whistle echoing from the steep mountain walls.

Al gave us the names of friends for us to contact in Vienna, then we bade him and his wife goodbye. We walked around Geneva again, visiting the university, the walled old city and the lakeside quays. The drive north, past ribbon-like waterfalls pouring from high cliffs and terraced vineyards and colorful chalets sitting precariously on the steep mountainside, afforded marvelous views of the Alps across Lac Leman. The lovely university town of Lausanne sat perched several hundred feet above Lac Leman. Edward Gibbon, Voltaire and Charles Dickens all studied there. We continued along Lac Leman under the snow-covered peaks of the Pleiades and through the delightful towns of Vevey, where Nestle located its headquarters and Henry James located *Daisy Miller*, and Montreux, the latter with its thirteenth-century Chateau de Chillon erected on a rock outcropping from the lake. This wonderfully preserved, turreted medieval castle provided the location for Byron's *The Prisoner of Chillon* as well as our camping spot that night. The Alps rose directly and steeply from the lake. Great crested grebes fished off shore, and Mike joined several Swiss locals fishing from the castle's pier.

Devils played ninepins on Zanfleuron Glacier thereby providing a name for the nearby resort village of Les Diablerets. We ate lunch on the Col du Pillon pass and assessed the difficulty of the ski runs, and Lynette wrote letters in the camper while the children and I hiked a mountain trail through meadows filled with magnificent wildflowers. Flowers also filled window boxes of the colorful chalets dotting the hills around Gstaad where we watched a parade of antique cars. We continued on to Gruyeres, a medieval walled village perched precariously on a rocky crag and dominated by a twelfth-century castle. We toured a fromagerie and watched cheese being made. A slide show explained the whole process, and Lynette wondered why it was that Little Miss Muffet ate her curds and whey when the people who made Gruyere cheese fed their whey to the swine.

From a letter to my parents: *This trip is not without its instructive moments—so far we have seen glass blown, pottery baked, Volkswagens assembled, beer brewed and cheese processed.*

We bought a substantial supply of cheese and a bottle of wine and drove to a ski hill above the town to set up camp, and more beautiful views a campsite never offered. The green valley fell away below and white-topped mountains provided a backdrop in all directions. Chalets clung to mountain slopes and cows with large, painted bells grazed in mountain meadows. Krissie and Mike played a game in a nearby meadow while Lynette and I enjoyed a glass of wine.

From my notes: *We heard a whooshing noise from above, looked up, and were astonished to see guys tethered to sail kites, gliding over our heads.*

In this way, we were introduced to the sport of hang gliding. We followed the gliders with our binoculars and could see them landing on a target far below. Presently the sun dropped behind the mountains, the sky darkened quickly, and the air grew cool. The ringing of bells now came clearly from all directions, betraying every step of the grazing cows, the sounds traveling unhindered in the evening air. Lynette and I talked about home—where we might choose to live, the kind of house we wanted, what my next job might be, and agreed that all of that could wait. Several times I wakened that night and heard a clear chorus of bells ringing.

Our route took us north through Bulle, a principle market for Gruyère cheeses with a fine thirteenth-century castle, and Fribourg, which markets fine chocolate and boasts a fine thirteenth-century cathedral, to medieval and wonderful Bern, the capital of Switzerland. Bisected by the River Aare, the small city sports turreted buildings, arcaded walkways, decorated fountains, and a sixteenth-century Clock Tower in which, each hour, quaint characters reinact a play. We visited the U.S. Embassy to learn Henry Kissinger's latest assessment of Greece's and Turkey's war of words over Cyprus and then walked across a high bridge to the Tierpark (zoo) and through a forest to the Barengraben (bear pit). People threw carrots and other vegetables to the bears, and, in return, the animals performed, standing on their hind legs and spinning first one way then the other and lying on their backs with their feet extended in the air. Lynette extracted our lunch from Mike's backpack, and we sat in the sun on a bench overlooking the bear pit, admiring the view of the mighty Jungfrau dominating the Bernese Oberland. Mike had been studying our European bird book and, to our surprise, knew every duck and goose species in the zoo. Later, we registered at the municipal campground on the banks of the Aare and decided it was the nicest of our trip so far. Spacious, clean and uncrowded, it featured a good restaurant and a store with reasonable prices. The bathrooms and showers were unisex, but that was all right after we understood the routine.

Hand washing our laundry and sleeping bags occupied the morning. Krissie and Mike earned some pocket money by washing the camper. I took the car to the VW dealer for its 10,000 kilometer service, and then Lynette led us on a walking tour of the Nydegg (old town) including the charming fifteenth-century rathaus (town hall), the Munster (a beautiful fifteenth-century Gothic cathedral), and a series of fountains with colorful names like

Bagpiper, Samson, Justice, and Marksman. Back at the campground, we all went swimming in the rushing, copper-blue Aare River. Lynette struck up a conversation with a French-Moroccan woman and her English husband whose children were swimming with ours. That evening we polished off a bottle of good wine and a block of Gruyere cheese while the woman submitted good naturedly to our onslaught of questions about such exotic places as Casablanca, Meknes and Marrakech.

Interlaken, founded in the twelfth century by Augustinian monks, lies on a mountain meadow between Thuner See (Lake Thun) and Brienzer See (Lake Brienz), hence its name. The town had a special meaning for us, being the home of Dori Gertsch, our friend from South America. (The following year, Dori and Karl returned to Interlaken to be married.) We thought about contacting Dori's parents, but there were too many listings under Gertsch. We drove south and east through the old city of Thun with the icy, sculpted surfaces of the distant, majestic Jungfrau reflecting the sun's rays through the hazy morning air. Vineyards and chalets dotted the steep hills falling into blue-green Lake Thune. In Interlaken, later in the morning, the sun shone brilliantly from a clear blue sky. We joined the tourists walking the promenade and watched a man from Germany buy a very expensive Rolex watch. Mike bought a replica of a Swiss cable car. Lynette bought brightly painted wooden clocks for gifts, and I bought tickets on the switchback railroad that climbed to Jungfraujoch, Europe's highest train station at twelve thousand feet. We camped on the shore of Lake Thun where two ravens soared and croaked above us while we swam and bathed with the ducks and swans, and Lynette snapped a picture of me hunkered on a lakeside rock, shaving. An older English couple, retired farmers from Jersey, pulled into our little camping area. We chatted over wine, and I was enchanted by the woman's wit. At one point during our conversation, she expressed perplexity by the actions of some French boys.

"When they drove away from stop signs, it sounded as if they were starting with their brakes on."

Remembering growing up in Smalltown, U.S.A., in the '50s, I explained to her the concept of "peeling rubber."

"Why on Earth would they ever want to do that?"

"It's their way of showing their masculinity, that's machismo!"

"It's a better way of having to buy new tires; that's stupido!"

Our train left early in the morning, slowly winding its way up the lush, beautiful Lauterbrunnen Valley with its colorful chalets and ribbon waterfalls and then climbing a series of switchbacks through charming villages—Vengen where climbers wore knickers, boots and backpacks, and Kleine Scheidegg where people wore traditional costumes and men blew alpine horns so long the bell end rested on the ground—toward Jungfraujoch. Rugged, snow capped peaks surrounded us. We entered a five mile long tunnel and stopped briefly at a station where we could get off the train and look through large holes carved out of the rock wall and offering spectacular views of miles of blue iced glaciers rising to peaks and falling off below. Another tunnel entered cold, underground Jungfraujoch Station which included a restaurant and a scientific laboratory, carved into the side of the mountain.

Outside the sun was warm, and we climbed part way up the south face of the Monch Jungfrau and ate lunch on a granite outcropping. Fifteen mile long Aletschglacier stretched out spectacularly below us. I considered yodeling and remembered a high school classmate, Eva Ziats. She sang country songs and told us yodeling was easy if you remembered the phrase, "Ohhh—De—Old—La—dee—Ohhh!" We let loose with some pretty terrible yodels and were startled when the echoes sounded better, almost nice. After a couple hours on the mountain, our feet were wet and our faces burned. The train ride down the mountain presented us with wonderful views of the major peaks—Eiger, Schreckhorn, Finsteraarhorn and Wetterhorn. Women and children waved from picturesque, rustic farms. The train stopped in Grindelwald, where we bought ice cream cones and the *International Herald-Tribune*, and returned to Interlaken late in the afternoon. We drove only about ten miles along Brienzer See to the small wood carving center of Brienz and set up camp in the municipal parking lot. Another camper with California license plates was already parked there. The couple (Wayne and Grace) and their two children (Glen and Susan) had lived in Malibu and were on their way to Russia and then Australia. We spent the evening chatting while the four children had a race, on their knees, blowing cigarette butts along the path and across a finish line. At some point we learned Wayne and Grace actually had grown up in Norristown, Pennsylvania, and, incredibly, she had just baked a shoo-fly pie. That evening I enjoyed my favorite dessert.

The fifteenth-century, legendary Swiss patriot, William Tell, shot an apple from his son's head with a crossbow in the village of Altdorf. We drove east over seven thousand-foot Sustenpass and descended into picturesque Altdorf where an enormous statue of Tell commemorates his daring deed which ultimately resulted, according to the legend, in freeing Switzerland from Austria. We continued north to the resort town of Brunnen and then followed the beautiful Vierwaldstatter See lakeshore west into the charming, small city of Luzern. The town's medieval flavor is retained in its fourteenth-century town wall with nine towers, its lovely old Weinmarkt square with a remarkable gothic fountain, and the old Hofkirche with its twin Gothic towers. The Kapellbrucke and the Muhlenbrucke, two covered wooden foot-bridges with historical murals on their ceilings, span the River Reuss and date from the fourteenth century. The highlight of the city, however, at least as far as our children were concerned, was Lowendenkmal, the Lion of

Lucerne, a twelve-hundred square-foot sculpture carved into a sandstone cliff. Mike needed new shoes, and picked out a pair that, for some reason, he called "desert boots." He walked out of the store wearing his desert boots and a big smile on his face.

The municipal campground on Lake Lucerne contained more Americans than we had seen anywhere else since leaving home, six bus-loads of backpackers from John Wesley College. We talked to a man from California traveling by himself in a big, fancy rig. He said he liked to lure young girls into his camper, telling them he was looking for a traveling companion. I considered telling the police. A U.S. Air Force couple on leave from his station in Germany camped next to us on one side, and on the other were the Australians we met in Belgium who had now returned from Russia and had nothing good to say about that experience. Mike and I got out our baseball gloves, and Krissie skipped rope while Lynette tried to remove some stains from a rug in the camper.

Our route north took us through the medieval walled, lakeside town of Zug to Zurich where Lynette led us on a walking tour of the old town and its quays, and we ate lunch in a cafe on the Lake Zurich promenade. From Zurich, we drove east through the quaint resort town of Rapperswil with its fine castle and on to the peaceful, fairy tale principality of Liechtenstein, nestled between Switzerland and Austria. The tiny country's capital, the medieval village of Vaduz, sits on the Rhine. Benevolent Prince Franz Josef ruled the principality from the official residence of the Princes of Liechtenstein, a thirteenth-century schloss (castle) perched on a cliff a hundred yards above the town. We spent the night below the castle in a roadside pullover. Soon two other campers joined us, one driven by a couple from the United States who gave us a bag of plums.

Mountains surround medieval Feldkirch, an attractive Austrian border town featuring Schloss Schattenburg, a twelfth-century Gothic castle. We drove east through the jagged snow-capped peaks and past the placid blue lakes of the Austrian Tyrol, over the scenic Arlberg Pass and through famous ski resort villages—Stuben, St. Anton, Landeck—turning north at Imst, over the Fern Pass and found a camping place by a clear mountain lake with large trout. We fished unsuccessfully and then kicked a soccer ball around with an Australian couple who pulled in to camp beside us.

At the German border, an officious guard asked me for my "green book." I showed him my "green card" which is our proof of insurance. He insisted on seeing our green book, and I repeatedly told him we had no green book. Another guard explained that his colleague wanted to see our registration papers. It dawned on me we had never been given registration papers, so we called the dealership in Luxembourg where we picked up the camper. They had our registration papers there and explained to the border guard that they mistakenly had not given them to us. We arranged to have the papers sent to Salzburg, and, with the dealer's explanation, the guard let us pass.

We drove into the Bavarian Alps and Germany's picturesque winter sports center, Garmisch, nestled below the rugged Zugspitze, the country's highest mountain. South of Garmisch, we stopped in the lovely Bavarian alpine village of Mittenwald, crossed back into Austria, and found a campground near Innsburck, the capital of the Tyrol. The next morning we hand washed our laundry and hung it to dry just before the rain came. After a mail run to American Express, Lynette gave us her walking tour of the old town, stopping at Maria Theresa's palace, the fourteenth-century Gothic Stadtturm (City Tower), and the Goldenes Dachl, a copper-roofed fifteenth-century royal residence. The rain intensified, so, with wet laundry hung and strewn throughout the camper, we set out for Kitzbuhel, driving among reportedly beautiful mountains that were mostly hidden from our view by thick clouds. The rain continued unabated, so we set up camp in the parking lot of the Kitzbuhel train station. Lynette and I read while the children caught up on their school work.

Sometime during the night the rain stopped, and a clear Tyrolean blue sky accompanied us on the way to Salzburg. We crossed briefly into Germany again, stopping to see the Eagle's Nest, Adolph Hitler's mountaintop getaway above the lovely alpine village of Berchtesgaden. We re-entered Austria and drove through the scenic rural countryside flanked by snow-capped peaks to enchanting Salzburg. An eleventh-century fortress, Festung Hohensalzburg, stood guard on a hill above the city. It was Sunday, and many residents wore traditional costumes to church. We walked along the narrow, cobblestone streets, visiting Mozart's Geburtshaus (birthplace), the tremendous early seventeenth-century Dom (cathedral), the seventeenth-century Lustschloss (Pleasure Castle) with its many unusual fountains, the Dwarf's Garden of small stone caricatures at Schloss Mirabell, and listened to the Glockenspiel's bells fill the air with melodies. Krissie and Mike watched a Mozart opera at the Marionette theater. On Motzart Platz, cabdrivers tended their carriages while matched pairs of horses munched the contents of their feedbags.

At a city park Lynette and I watched the children play on a wooden merry-go-round. Some other kids soon joined them. While Mike ran and pushed the ride around, a bigger boy ran behind him and whopped him on the butt. Mike ignored him. The ride slowed down, and Mike got off and pushed again. The same boy ran behind him and whopped him again. Mike turned around, pushed the kid away, and told him to cut it out. Fortunately the kid backed off. Until then, I had never seen an ounce of aggression in Mike. I felt good that, when pushed, he was not afraid to defend himself. We talked about it later. I told him he had handled the situation very well. In addition, I suggested that if a bigger kid started a fight, he should make sure he got the first punch in. If that punch scares or hurts the kid, press your advantage in whatever way is appropriate. If the punch doesn't faze him, run like hell and hope he isn't as fast as he is big.

We camped on a hillside farm overlooking the city where we had delicious wiener schnitzel in the campground restaurant. Across the valley, rain clouds infiltrated the mountain peaks. The next morning was fresh and clear, and quite cold. The view of Salzburg with its alpine backdrop was exquisite. We could see the snow lines had worked their way further down the mountainsides. September was flying by. We drove into Salzburg to pick up our "green book" of registration papers sent from Luxembourg and then set off for Munchen (Munich).

Munich, Germany, September 24, 1974

From my notes: *Our hundredth day in Europe was a good one.*

For some reason I can't remember, although it was still September, Oktoberfest was in full swing. We parked in front of the famous Frauenkirche, an enormous Gothic church with twin onion-domed towers and walked to Marienplatz, the old city's center, and, in the bell tower of the nineteenth-century "new" Rathaus, watched the famous Glockenspiel's wonderful mechanical figures and bells announce the time. We shopped on Sendlinger Strasse and admired the Sendlingertor, one of the city's medieval tower gates. We visited Alte Pinakothek, Munich's art museum of European masterpieces, and Residenz, a fortress complex that housed Bavaria's rulers. Later, at the Hofbrauhaus, we listened to a brass band while drinking beer and eating sausages and pretzels, and then bought several Hofbrauhaus mugs. The focal point of Oktoberfest was a large meadow in the city's south called the Theresienwiese. We followed the crowds and the noise and found ourselves surrounded by Oktoberfest, walking the midway and popping in and out of the lively and colorful beer tents. We watched Louenbrau horses pulling beer barrel laden wagons. The children enjoyed the carnival rides and wanted to try the bumber cars. Krissie began crying after being bumped the first few times, and the attendant stopped the cars so I could carry her off the floor. Lynette thought it best that we wind down the excitement, so we finished the day by visiting the fantastic Olympic Park, where the 1972 summer olympic games were contested, and Tierpark Hellabrunn, Munich's famous zoo.

Lynette and I weren't sure about ourselves but were certain the children were not ready for Dachau. We circled east of the memorial and drove north through the lovely Bavarian countryside, where village churches sported onion dome steeples, to Regensburg. Picturesque farms and vineyards dotted the rolling hills. The rural peacefulness was periodically interrupted, however, by military jets screaming overhead, I supposed because we were within a few miles of the German Democratic Republic. We ate lunch at a roadside picnic table and ten fighter jets roared out of the clouds, descended almost to the treetops lining a nearby field, circled widely, and then sped away into the clouds.

From a letter to my parents: *Ancient second-century Roman walls and gates attest to Regensburg's long history.* We admired the city's red-tiled roofs and towers from across the Danube which was, as Johann Strauss's waltz promised, both beautiful and blue. The stone arched Steinerne Brucke, stretching one thousand feet across the Danube, is Germany's oldest bridge, dating from the twelfth century. We visited a fine thirteenth-century Gothic cathedral, several old churches, a seventh-century Benedictine monastery and the house where the astronomer Johann Kepler died. The emission control unit light was flashing on our dashboard, so I stopped at the local VW dealer to have it checked. They determined that we needed a part which they didn't stock and suggested we stop at the much larger VW dealer in Nurnberg (Nuremburg). The service manager let us camp in the parking area and use their facilities. The night turned cold, and I scraped ice off the windows in the morning.

Nurnberg dates back to the eleventh century. A medieval wall with 128 towers and four gates still intact surrounds the Altstadt, the old city. Tall, narrow half-timbered houses preserve old Nurnberg's charm. We proceeded straight to the VW dealer who, like the shop in Regensburg, did not have the part in stock. They ordered the part from Wolfsburg that day (Thursday) and said they should receive it the following Monday. The municipal campground was large and up to date, but now the weather was cold, and few campers were staying there. Nevertheless, Nurnberg offered much of interest to the visitor, and, despite the cold, I figured this was as good a place as any to have to spend unplanned extra time. Over the next few days, we visited the house where Albrecht Durer lived and painted; the Germanisches National museum with its displays of old musical instruments, folk costumes and antiquities and its galleries presenting many different periods of German art and a great exhibit of Durer's works; a natural history museum where Mike especially liked the Neanderthal and Cro-Magnon skulls and the half-million-year old jaw bone from Heidelberg Man; the eleventh-century Kaiserburg Castle; various churches dating from the thirteenth through the sixteenth centuries; and a fourteenth-century Gothic hospital that spanned the Pegnitz River. We explored narrow walkways and courtyards where craftsmen hid their shops and walked to the Hangman's Bridge and the Hauptmarkt with its Schoner Brunnen, a lovely fourteenth-century golden Gothic fountain ornamented with biblical heroes.

We shopped for groceries and supplies. Lynette and Krissie did our laundry and aired the sleeping bags while Mikey and I went birdwatching and found blackbirds, great blue and crested tits, turtle doves, crested larks, treecreepers, nuthatches and a great spotted woodpecker. In the evenings, the children did schoolwork while Lynette and I read. We listened to the Pitt-USC football game and to Gerald Ford's address in which he invited citizens to send suggestions for defeating inflation, his "Whip Inflation Now" (WIN) campaign. Each of us sent a letter to the president; Mike urged everyone to shop in quantity and Krissie suggested that people should watch less television. On Monday morning we walked in the woods and then drove to the Volkswagen shop. Just as we feared, the part had not arrived. We returned Tuesday morning—again no part. The children did more schoolwork and now were far ahead of their schedule, Lynette needlepointed on a pillow, and I washed and waxed the camper. Later we all jumped rope with a clothesline, and, that evening, we played Password.

The part arrived early Wednesday morning, and, before noon, with the emission control warning no longer flashing, we left for Richard Wagner's hometown of Bayreuth, where we visited the Festival Theater designed by the composer, an eighteenth-century opera house, and a medieval castle. We continued east and crossed the depressing Czechoslovakian border, complete with barbed wire fences, guard towers and soldiers armed with automatic weapons. At Cheb, political slogans were plastered on light posts and in shop windows, and Russian and Czech flags lined the streets. The countryside east of Cheb was scenic and charming with peasants in the fields and women wearing babushkas, but the farms seemed backward with only manual labor and horses, no tractors. Karlovy Vary (Carlsbad) lies in the wooded Bohemian hills and has been a fashionable spa resort since the fourteenth century. Here, in 1898, Marie Curie discovered radium. The setting was lovely, but we found the city run down and, after visiting a porcelain and glassware factory, we found the local campground closed and continued driving to Prague where the municipal campground was also closed. We talked with two policemen at a gas station who suggested camping was permitted in a nearby hillside city park that they described as safe. In the twilight, we looked at the old town center below. Rather than skyscrapers, old steeples and towers defined the city skyline. We put on our coats and watched for a half hour as night fell and the twinkling city lights came on, one by one.

Once the capital of the Holy Roman Empire, Prague has straddled the Vltava River for more than a thousand years. Today thirteen bridges span the river, including the Gothic, fourteenth-century Karluv Most (Charles Bridge) ornamented with thirty religious statues. Mala Strana (Old Town) retains its medieval character and features the beautiful baroque St. Nicholas Cathedral and Hradcany Castle, Prague's venerated landmark whose complex includes a ninth-century Slav fortress, a twelfth-century Romanesque castle, and a fourteenth-century Gothic palace. Staromestske Sal (Old Townhall) and its clock, considered a medieval masterpiece, sit on Mala Strana Square where seventeenth-century Bohemian lords were beheaded for advocating religious liberty. Tynsky Kostel, a fine Gothic church, features a twelfth-century courtyard and a pair of fourteenth-century Renaissance gables. Baroque buildings and palaces line Narodni, the boulevard connecting Old Town Square with Wenceslas Square.

Few people walked the streets of Prague. We changed money at the official exchange rate of ten korunas to the U.S. dollar despite black market operatives surrepticiously offering us much better rates, as high as thirty to one. Having been forewarned and fearful of being set up, we assiduously avoided dealing with them. Wonderfully beautiful buildings slipped further into decay. Many shops and grocery stores displayed virtually no merchandise. Where consumer goods were available, people waited in lines as they did at gas stations. We went to a government operated crystal and ceramics shop that accepted only hard currency, but the limited selection was of questionable quality and very expensive. Political signs and flags with a red star were displayed everywhere, reminding the people, I suppose, how good their lives were. No western newspapers or books were in evidence, although the local Communist newspaper, I think it was called *The Daily Worker*, was sold in a few shops.

From my notes: *Nothing seems very pleasant; everything appears rather drab. Few people smile. They are not unfriendly and seem even curious, but are reluctant to talk in public places.*

We stopped for lunch at a small restaurant where people ate standing at tall tables with no chairs. We ordered open faced sandwiches that came with delicious potato salad. Lynette tried to engage the waitress in a simple conversation, but her replies were only perfunctory. A man standing at the table next to us watched the exchange, shook his head and then smiled at us.

Late in the afternoon we drove to the city's outskirts and found a very good campground open for business, with tennis courts, a restaurant and hot showers. We parked in an apple orchard next to a young couple, the Bradleys, from Chicago. Duane Bradley was employed by the International Atomic Energy Commission and was assigned to their office in Vienna for two years. His mother-in-law was from Poland, had joined them on this camping trip, and was returning to Vienna for a visit with him and his wife. It was that time of year, and ripe red apples filled the trees. Krissie and Mike picked a sack for us and one for our neighbors. We five adults, over a bottle or two of passably good Czechoslovakian red table wine, chatted about experiences in Eastern Europe, and the Bradleys gave us their phone number and address in Vienna.

Nighttime temperatures in southern Bohemia now dropped below freezing, unseasonably cold for autumn. While our sleeping bags accommodated those temperatures, sitting in the camper in the evening before going to bed and then getting up in the morning were very uncomfortable.

Our Coleman stove helped, so we often cracked the car's windows and kept the cooker flame on. The cold evenings made us all irritable, and, apparently, especially me. Lynette said I was being hypercritical of the children and told me to back off. From my notes: *I am resolved to let them be for a change.* The early arrival of winter weather encouraged us to skip the eastern province of Slovakia and Hungary and instead head south to Vienna and, hopefully, to warmer weather in southern Yugoslavia and Greece.

A number of castles nestled in the lovely Bohemian hills south of Prague. We toured thirteenth-century Zbraslav built by Wenceslas II, the medieval Konopiste where Archduke Ferdinand resided before his assassination sparked World War I, the Renaissance Pruhonice with its wonderful botanical gardens, and the marvelous thirteenth-century Cesky Sternberk. By now we realized most Czechoslovakian campgrounds had closed for the season, including one on a lake near Tabor where we parked for the night anyway. The thermometer inside the camper registered thirty degrees the next morning, but things improved after I fired up the Coleman stove for coffee and hot chocolate.

The sun rose and warmed the world, and half a dozen members of the world's smallest grebe species, appropriately named "little grebe," bobbed about on the choppy lake and dived for breakfast. We drove off east to Pelhrimov and south to Telc, an interesting town with baroque buildings and a large arcaded square that the Czech government was admirably restoring to its former beauty. We continued south past lovely lakes and forests and through the picturesque Moravian wine country. Groups of peasants dug potatoes by hand. Deer nipped on shrubbery and pheasants foraged for seeds in the fields. Buildings in quaint rural villages were painted brightly with pastel colors and folk art. Mike and I saw a kestrel and a green woodpecker when we pulled off the road for lunch.

In Znojomo, near the Austrian border, blatant politicking resumed—the ubiquitous Czech and Russian flags, loudspeakers, and boring signs with hammers and sickles. The border was more of the same—high fences with towers manned by guards with automatic weapons, rolls of barbed wire, forests cleared and fields mowed within running distance of the fence. We waited while the border officials checked the stamps in our passports to verify that we hadn't forged anything and that indeed we were where we said we had been. It would have been so silly had it not been so annoying. I considered snapping a photo of the "iron curtain" and decided that was a bad idea. While waiting for the officials to return our passports, I heard a warbler singing and retrieved my binoculars from the camper. I looked into the tree where the birdsong originated and saw a whitethroat flitting about. I sensed someone behind me, turned around, and a guard grunted something in Czech and motioned with his rifle that I put the binoculars back in the camper. Lynette wondered if birdwatching rattled him so much, what would he have done had I really gotten subversive and taken a photo of the guard towers?

Late in the afternoon on a cold, overcast day we registered at the Vienna Municipal campground and parked next to a couple from Oregon, the Matsons, who were touring Europe after recently retiring. The six of us huddled together in our camper, trying to stay warm, while the former teachers taught us two dice games, Kaput and Yahtze. They also had just arrived, so we made plans to tour Wien (Vienna) together the next day.

Vienna is surpassed in beauty by few cities. It features lovely parks and gardens, wonderful museums filled with European masterpieces, a marvelous Gothic cathedral, historic palaces and castles, excellent shops and cosmopolitan restaurants, and an array of impressive buildings including the neoclassical Parliament, nineteenth-century Staatsoper (Opera House), Palace of Justice and the Rathaus. Haydn, Mozart, Beethoven, Brahms, and Johann and Richard Strauss all lived in Wien at one time or another. We parked on the Ringstrasse, the two and one-half mile long boulevard encircling Vienna's inner city. Lynette's walking tour began on Karntnerstrasse and Grabenstrasse, Vienna's answers to New York's Fifth Avenue and Chicago's Michigan Avenue. We strolled along the Danube Canal and then descended stairs leading to the ruins of a Roman settlement under medieval Hoher Markt Square, and, near noon, rushed to the Uhrenmuseum (Clock Museum) and watched Viennese historical figures march across the face of the Ankeruhr when it struck twelve o'clock. Then we snacked at a nearby konditorei that had come highly recommended to the Matsons and visited Figarohaus where Mozart lived when he composed *The Marriage of Figaro*. We toured the Hofburg complex, Emperor Franz Joseph's imperial palace, including the Albertina museum which contains a great Durer collection and works by Michelangelo, Raphael, Titian and Rembrandt, and attended a rehearsal of the Spanische Reitschule, the Spanish Riding School with its famous Lipizzaner horses. We visited the home of Johann Strauss; drove to the Prater on the Danube, once a hunting reserve and now an amusement park, where we rode the giant ferris wheel; and then spent another cold evening at the campground playing Kaput and Yahtze. Before going to bed, I updated our expense register and found our average daily expenditures since we arrived in Europe was, for the first time, below our budget of fifteen dollars per day.

The United States Embassy in Vienna now officially discouraged any independent travel in Greece since our government had not supported the Greeks in the most recent flare-up of their on-going dispute with Turkey over Cyprus. We obtained visas at the Yugoslavian embassy even as we digested this disappointing bit of news and then spent the day in Vienna conducting business—changing money, picking up mail, doing laundry, shopping for groceries and gifts—attending an antique auction at the Dorotheum, and stopping for pastries at a konditorei.

Visiting Maria Theresa's enormous, elegant palace, Schloss Schonbrunn, was a good choice on a cold, rainy morning. Few tourists were around, and we had a guide to ourselves. She oriented the tour to Krissie and Mike, and they both obviously enjoyed the attention. Afterwards, I gave her a tip and then Mike, surprisingly did the same—fifty groshen or about forty cents. Later, even in the big city of Vienna, Duane Bradley recognized our camper, flagged us down and invited us to their apartment for dinner. When we arrived that evening, he had prepared what he called a "Care Package" of American goodies from his employer's commissary, including peanut butter and cereal for the children. His mother-in-law prepared a delicious Polish dish she called "galumkas" or "pigs in a blanket," pork and rice wrapped in cabbage leaves. Mike and Krissie seemed very comfortable with all us adults, in fact, to the extent that, after they went to bed, we wondered if they had not behaved a bit too casually. We decided not, and Lynette attributed their informal behavior at the Bradleys to our very familiar lifestyle in the tiny camper.

Cold rain continued through the night and into the morning. The Matsons joined us at the Hofburg for a performance of the Lipizzaner horses, and afterward, on the Kartnerstrasse, I bought a hand painted ceramic bracelet and ring for Lynette. We then took leave of Vienna, and of our friends from Oregon, and drove south through Strauss' Wiener Wald (Vienna Woods) and past the twelfth-century Cistercian Abbey of Heiligenkreuz. About thirty miles south of Vienna, we spent a cold night in the parking lot of an autobahn gas station and found ourselves hoping Yugoslavia would be sunny and warm.

We made an easy border crossing into Yugoslavia and drove south through the picturesque countryside of Slovenia and northern Croatia. Fresh snow capped the nearby mountain range. It was harvest time; leaves had turned color and hay had been mown, and, late in the afternoon, peasants returned from the fields in carts pulled by cows, oxen, and horses. Women wearing babushkas and colorful folk dresses did much of the field work with hand tools. In the Drava Valley, the red tile-roofed town of Maribor spread below us with its twelfth-century cathedral and fifteenth-century castle. Further south lay Ptuji, one of Yugoslavia's oldest towns, with its medieval castle. A campground north of Zagreb was closed for the season; nevertheless we parked there. The day had been fairly warm and clear, but now, in the late afternoon, the temperature plunged with the sun. I made hot tomato soup and grilled cheese sandwiches while Lynette supervised the children with their school work. After supper, the still burning stove kept the camper tolerably warm, and we played a few games of Yahtze. Lynette suggested we skip Belgrade and forsake the cold highlands for the hopefully warmer Adriatic Sea coast, and we all agreed.

We drove through Varazdin and Zagreb and then left the Belgrade high-way at Okucani, heading south for Banja Luka where we saw our first mosque, the sixteenth-century Dzamija Ferhadija. Our road wound its way through primitive mountain villages and spectacular canyons, following the River Vrbas to Jajce, a small town with sixteenth-century fortifications, a Turkish mosque, fourth-century Roman ruins, and thickly polluted air emanating from a disgusting pulp factory. Late in the afternoon we found a campground open near Sarajevo and subjected ourselves to much needed and appreciated hot showers. Later, in the middle of the night, I was wakened by a jostling and much laughter. Our little bed had been invaded by the two children looking for a warmer place to sleep.

Old Sarajevo retains much of the influence of its occupation by Ottoman Turks during the fifteenth through the nineteenth centuries. The city sits astride the River Miljacka and is surrounded by mountains. We headed straight for the Bascarsija, the oriental market or souk with its shops selling Persian, Egyptian, Indian and Arabian rugs as well as brass, leather, copper and silver products. Lynette bought a brass coffee set, a nutcracker, and a doll for Krissie. The children bought halva, a candy made from burnt sugar. Moslems prayed at mosques, including the Ali Pasha and Emporer Suleiman's, both dating from the sixteenth century, and the beautiful fifteenth-century Begova Dzamija with its 155-foot minaret. We walked along the river past its many bridges, including the Princip Bridge where Archduke Ferdinand and his wife were assassinated by Gavrilo Princip on June 14, 1914, setting events in motion that led to World War I. Back at the campground, Mike and I washed and cleaned the camper and then tossed a baseball.

Driving in the morning's hard rain made quick work of our clean camper. Vineyards thrived in the lovely Neretva Valley which sometimes constricted to dramatic canyon-like proportions. Our route led us into the old Bosnian city of Mostar with its noteworthy sixteenth-century Turkish mosque. Even more impressive was the town's Mostarski Most, a gorgeous stone bridge constructed in 1566 and fortified with towers on both ends, its single arch spanning more than 150 feet across the River Neretva. This famous, graceful landmark had been serving the people more than four hundred years when our family drove through Mostar. Tragically, it was to remain only another twenty years and then was destroyed in the Serbian-Bosnian civil war. We continued driving in the rain southwest through the interesting hillside sixteenth-century town of Pocitelj with its ruins of an Ottoman castle and, as we neared the Adriatic, past olive groves and vineyards. At Neum we registered at a campground, and, while the temperature was not as cold, the rain continued.

The beautiful Adriatic coastline was as we had imagined—vineyards and olive groves running down hillsides to the sea, low scrubby groundcover where the land was not cultivated, tall slender cedars, and picturesque islands off shore. We drove about thirty-five miles south toward Dubrovnik and, when the rain became worse and the fog obscured the visibility, stopped at another campground and parked beside the sea. Despite the cold rain, we swam in the warm Adriatic. Later we read and did school work and then played Yahtze. Krissie won a running tally of five games, and, when Mike came in last, he was very upset and began to act like I often did when I lost—kind of like a jerk. I said, "Come on, Mike. It's no big deal."

Things didn't get any better, and, in sympathy, Krissie said, "Losing is the worst thing."

"There are many things worse than losing," Lynette corrected.

"Not when you're playing games, there aren't," persisted Kristen.

Through letters between my parents and me, we learned my mother had accepted our invitation to travel with us for a few weeks. She had never been out of the United States, and I thought she was very brave to come alone. I knew that she was terrified of flying all the way to Rome by herself. That night I wrote her a letter in which I said we would call when we reached Split to make specific plans. I enclosed a note from Krissie in which she wrote, "Try to bring just one big suitcase. If you have any room in your suitcase we want cookies and fudge."

Founded in the seventh century, Dubrovnik is surrounded by medieval battlements and armed gates. Palaces, churches, monasteries, bell towers and Venetian-style buildings line the old, narrow cobblestone streets. The city was delightful, but we saw more tourists here than we had seen since leaving Munich, and many of them were Americans. We changed money and picked up mail at American Express where an agent told us they were unaware of U.S. travelers experiencing problems in Greece. We returned to our campground in the rain, again interested in crossing Macedonia and into Greece.

The capricious sun graced us with its presence the next few days. We took advantage of the warmth and fresh air by doing our laundry and washing and cleaning the camper. Mike had some luck fishing, while the rest of us inspected tidal pools and found snails, shrimp, and hermit crabs. Fishing boats tended their nets beyond the surf on the blue-green Adriatic, and peasant women walked the beach selling eggs, cheese, vegetables and pomegranates from their baskets. We read and played on the beach and sampled the local food (mixed grill) near the campground. Now our clothes and sleeping bags were clean and dry, and so were we, and our spirits soared.

We followed the Dalmatian coastal plain north toward Split. Scattered offshore were picturesque islands, including Korcula, the legendary birthplace of Marco Polo. The popular Makarska Riviera stretched twenty-five miles along the Adriatic where olive groves, vineyards and stands of slender cedars connected the impressive, pine for rested Biokovo mountains with the sea. The ancient city of Split achieved preeminence in the fourth century when the Roman emperor, Diocletian, chose to live there. We toured Dicklecianova Palaca (Diocletian's Palace) which included the Temple of Jupiter, the Emperor's Mausoleum, and a four thousand-year old black sphinx from Egypt. The fortified palace walls and towers were erected much later in the Middle Ages. Graceful arcades connect buildings combining Romanesque, Gothic, Renaissance and Baroque architectural styles, and featuring marble columns and statues. We picked up our mail, including letters from the kiddies' friends, called my mother and made arrangements to meet her in Rome, and found a place to camp on the sea where Mike and I attempted to identify immature gulls, a very confusing enterprise. Not only does their plumage differ according to the species, but it also varies with their age. Some gulls change their appearance each year and do not gain their more recognizable adult plumage until their fifth year.

To our delight, the sun appeared for the third consecutive morning, and warmed the amphitheater's carved limestone steps on which Lynette and I sat drinking our coffee. Below us, the children hammed it up on what was left of the stage. The fourth, fifth and sixth century ruins of the ancient Roman port of Salona covered several square miles. In the burial grounds of early Christians, Latin inscriptions were still legible on the tombs. Many homes, columns, and aqueducts remained almost unchanged in the more than fifteen hundred years since they had been used.

One of the conditions Krissie insisted upon, if we expected her to leave her friends and travel for a year or two, was that, despite our limited space in the camper, she could bring "Bear" along. Bear was her tattered and well worn stuffed companion and best friend with whom she had spent many of her waking and all of her sleeping hours for the past six years. Without describing in detail "her" seriously deteriorated physical condition, it's enough to say that Bear certainly had seen better days. That morning, we arrived at the ruins of Salona quite early and left the car alone in the parking area. While exploring the ancient city, Lynette noticed me climbing to vantage points where I could see the car and asked, "What are you looking for?"

"I just feel uncomfortable leaving the car unguarded."

"Why is that?" Mike wanted to know.

"Well, if a thief broke into the car, he could steal everything we have."

"That's the best thing about Bear," Krissie offered. "Nobody would want her."

Dubrovnik, Yugoslavia, October 20, 1974

Our odometer indicated we had driven 10,012 miles since picking up the camper in Luxembourg. Because we had decided to visit Greece despite the warnings from the U.S. State Department, we retraced our way south and returned to the same campground on the sea near Dubrovnik where we parked beside Dee and Ian Christensen and their two young children, Sally and Rod. The parents were school teachers from Australia who had worked in London for a couple years and now were returning home in a Land Rover with a tent. Their intention was to drive the classic trans-Asian route through Greece and Turkey, across Persia, India, Burma, Thailand and Malasia, and then ship to Darwin from Singapore. (Their itinerary became indelibly etched on my mind.) After comparing each other's travel plans, we decided to drive in tandem through Greece. We didn't anticipate any danger, but, nevertheless, like a flock of shorebirds, we agreed that there's safety in numbers.

Dee and Lynette wanted to revisit Dubrovnik, which we did, after which we drove south along the coast and then came inland, hugging the shoreline of the Boka Kopturska Fjord. It seemed each island in the fjord had its own church. We stopped for lunch and Mike and Krissie spotted a kingfisher. They led us all to the spot where they had seen it. The bird soon returned in all its glory—with an orange breast and an iridescent turquoise-blue stripe running down its back—chattering up and down the rocky coast, and diving for fish in the shallow water. An old stone wall ran around the seaside town of Kotor and then up over the mountain, as far as we could see. Back on the Adriatic, picturesque 2,400-year old Budva was surrounded by a medieval, fortified wall. Further south, a causeway joined the fifteenth-century island town of Sveti Stefan, with its walled fortifications and narrow streets, to the Montenegro coast.

The rain began as soon as we left the Adriatic and drove into the Montenegro highlands. Gypsies camped by the roadside in tents with open fires. We stopped near Titograd and set up our own camp in the rain. I tuned into Voice of America's five o'clock news to learn the latest from Greece. The children had a good laugh when the program was introduced with its customary *Yankee Doodle Dandy* music. The rain continued through the night and into the morning. We changed money in Titograd and filled up with gas. One of the attendants tried to distract me while the other began pumping gas with money already on the meter, a practice, I learned, that was not restricted to Mexico. I threatened to call the police, but none of us spoke the other's language, so I called them a few names, paid the bill and left.

The rain continued all day as we slowly wound our way around the mountains, through beautiful, narrow canyons with waterfalls plunging over sheer cliffs, and fording flooded roadways and washouts. There were no campgrounds, and we stopped for the night in a muddy pulloff near Kosovska Mitrovica. Setting up their tent was out of the question, so Ian and Dee slept in the Land Rover, and Sally and Rod slept with the four of us.

138

During the night, our camper settled inextricably into the mud. Ian tied a heavy rope between the Land Rover and the VW and easily pulled us out. We felt much closer to Greece when we entered Macedonia, the land of Phillip and Alexander. The weather was marginally better, and, when the sun periodically poked through the clouds, the fall colors were stunning. In Skopje, we visited a large mosque and, in the Turkish section, ate a lunch of delicious little sausages. We drove to the wonderful third- and fourth-century Roman ruins at Stobi. Several flocks of skylarks foraged in the grass among the ruins, and Mike and I flushed a little owl, a species that typically inhabits ruins. That afternoon we drove all the way to the border, and, with the permission of the friendly officials, camped in the parking area of Greek customs.

There was not a cloud in the sky our first morning in Greece, an auspicious welcome, according to Lynette. Soldiers in traditional costumes ceremoniously hoisted the Greek flag. We drove southeast under a warm sun to the ruins of ancient Pella, the ancient capital of Macedonia and birthplace of Alexander the Great. Archeologists continued work on the excavations which had uncovered important buildings and memorable mosaics from the Hellenic era. In the village, we bought fruit, cheese, wine and wonderful bread fresh from the oven, baked by very friendly women in traditional dresses. In spite of all the warnings by the U.S. State Department to the contrary, the Greeks were incredibly friendly.

From a letter to my parents: *People are so friendly. If you pull over to the roadside to consult a map, a truck driver will stop or a pedestrian will ask if he or she can help. Folks laugh a lot and generally seem happy, if sometimes poor.*

Thessaloniki was named after the sister of Alexander the Great. We drove into the city, stopping at a travel agency to buy ferry tickets from Greece to Italy. The agent asked me how we were enjoying Greece. Hardly waiting for my answer, he issued a commentary on the political problems between Greece and the U.S. He stressed that Greeks were angry with our government, not the American people, because, after all, there were many family ties between the two countries. Thessaloniki's municipal campground was open and very nice. We washed the muddy camper, swam in the sea, and showered. We met a Dutch artist from Surinam and two American hippie couples who were broke and planned to make money by picking oranges. We all sat around chatting over a drink or two, and, after the Christensens and we put our children to bed, our gathering turned into a party.

Our time in Greece may have been the most relaxing of our lives. Over the next few days we did our laundry and some other chores, including pulling Kristen's loose tooth with a pliers, but mostly we read, swam, collected sea shells and looked at the birds foraging in olive groves and along the sea. One day we ate watermelon for lunch on a beach otherwise deserted except for a French couple sunning in the nude. Another time I watched an attractive woman in a shop smiling and looking at Mike. Suddenly, much to his embarrassment, she leaned down and kissed him on the cheek. We ate wonderful Greek food in a local restaurant where, instead of giving us menus, the waiter walked us through the kitchen and showed us what was being offered.

Happy, friendly people waved at us on our drive south past picturesque farms, olive groves and orchards of orange trees. Near Mount Olympus, the mythological abode of the gods, we stopped in a village and bought wine, cheese and hot bread for lunch. I told the proprietress of the bakery that the bread smelled wonderful, and she gave each of us a fresh hot roll to sample. Later we bought a watermelon and groceries at an open market in Volos and visited ancient Lolkos, the legendary home of Jason the Argonaut, where lie the ruins of three Mycenaean palaces. We continued along the coast to Lamia, through Thermopylae where Xerxes led the Persians to victory over the Athenians and Spartans, then south across spectacular mountain passes to Delphi.

With Mount Parnassus as a backdrop, Delphi overlooked the Gulf of Corinth and the Peloponnesus beyond—Delphi, where rulers and commoners alike consulted the sometimes omniscient but often enigmatic, Oracle. One story is told that, when asked by a general to predict the outcome of an imminent battle, the Oracle offered the puzzling reply, "The Greeks the Romans will defeat." We admired the fourth-century Temple of Apollo and its Greek inscriptions, the Temple of Athena with its columns of multi-colored marble, and a bronze statue of the Charioteer. Mike snapped a photo of Lynette and me sitting in box seats at the stadium. Later, the Christensens and we drove back over an apparently seldom used gravel road and set up camp on a south-facing hill overlooking the picturesque tiled-roof village of Itea. We watched the sun set into the Peloponnesus, warmed by it and a bottle of uzo, bitter but good Greek wine. I set up the Coleman outside and, for supper, we all had another bottle of uzo, home fries with peppers and onions and scrambled eggs with feta cheese and tomatoes. Not bad.

The drive to Athens took us through Arakhova, where Lynette bought an old copper pitcher, and Thivai (Thebes) which dates from the second millenium BC. This ancient city-state fought in the Persian Wars, the Athenian wars, the Peloponnesian Wars and was defeated by Philip of Macedon and later virtually destroyed by his son, Alexander the Great. In the Athenian suburb of Voula, we found a very good campground on the beautiful Apollo coast called Camping Athens. We played a game of soccer and, on our last night with our Australian friends, found a restaurant with great local food.

Founded over five thousand years ago, Athens became the early center of western intellectual and cultural history. Aristotle, Plato, Socrates,

Sophocles, Euripides, Aeschylus, Aristophanes, Pericles, Heroditus, Thucydides—Athenians all, whose ideas and works are still studied and celebrated. Some of the most important and impressive ruins of ancient Greece comprise the Acropolis, a limestone outcropping rising above the city. We walked through the Propylaea, the temple gateway entrance to the Acropolis, to the Temple of Athena with its Ionic columns and then explored the beautiful, twenty-four hundred-year old Parthenon, considered to be a world architectural treasure. I photographed Lynette standing among six stone maidens supporting the portico of the Erectheion, the temple dedicated to Athena and Poseidon. We walked to the Agora, the old marketplace and center of Athenian life, and down its concourse lined with Doric and Ionic columns. We saw the twenty-five hundred-year old Temple of Zeus and the second-century Arch of Hadrian. We visited museums and Byzantine churches with wonderful mosaic ceiling and wall panels, and, eating on the run, tried delicious little wooden skewers of lamb meat and other street vendor offerings. It was a holiday, Greek National Day (celebrating their refusal to join Italy in 1940), and we watched a parade in which President Karamanlis (Henry Kissinger's nemisis in the current standoff between the countries) waved to us from his limousine.

The next day was mostly administrative in nature. We bought travelers' checks and changed money, picked up a telegram from my mother confirming her November 19th arrival in Rome on a Pan-Am flight, and, for some reason my notes don't explain, bought gasoline coupons to use in Italy. We met many friendly Greeks and a nice old Russian couple who had emigrated to Australia after the revolution. In a park, Mike found little worms that, when touched, curl into balls and roll away in the wind. We shopped at a flea market. Lynette and Krissie bought rings, Mike bought a shirt, and I bought metal shish kebob skewers with replicas of ancient Greek coins for handles. Lynette also bought Halloween candy to put in the children's pouches, little cloth bags we each had hanging in the camper in case any of us wanted to buy treats for anyone else.

Krissie and Lynette picked up chest colds somewhere, so we stayed at the campground for a day where they could lie on the beach in the sun, a prescription, they assured Mike and me, that, along with their antibiotics, was certain to cure their infirmities. Mike and I did the laundry, went grocery shopping, and tried identifying the many shells and other marine life on the beach. The next morning, the girls felt better, so we went to the Ethnikon Archaeologikon Mouseion with its great collections from the Greek classical period and the Minoan period in Crete (2000 B.C.). In the gift shop, a brochure advertised a four day cruise to Crete, Mikonos, Santorini (Thira) and Rhodes, and we noted that the final departure of the season was to be the next day. The museum had whetted our appetite to see the islands, especially Crete, and we had been operating below our budget for some time, so we went to American Express and signed on. The moon would be full that evening, and we wanted to see it rise over the Acropolis, so we killed some time at the flea market and then ate at a good local restaurant. During dinner, a south wind blew clouds in from the sea, obscuring any view of the full moon. Nevertheless, we drove back to Camping Athens excited about leaving in the morning on our Aegean cruise.

Early in the morning the wind blew stiffly, and the sea appeared very choppy. On the drive to Piraeus, the port servicing Athens, I stopped for Dramamine, tossed down a double dose, and then dropped the camper at an indoor garage that Spirotiki Lines recommended. Our ship, the M.T.S. Jason, left port, and the wind continued unabated. I found a deck chair in the sun where I entered a Dramamine induced sleep for most of the day. When we sailed past Cape Sounion, Lynette and the children wakened me to see the white marble Temple of Poseidon, an event I only dimly recollect. They wakened me again to see the white buildings, churches and windmills of Mikonos gleaming in the sun, but the rough seas prevented us from landing at the picturesque island's small dock.

In the third century BC, Rhodes celebrated a victory over the Persians by erecting one of the seven wonders of the ancient world, The Colossus of Rhodes, a 98-foot high statue of Apollo straddling the entrance to the harbor. It lasted only about a hundred years before it was destroyed by an earthquake. In its place are two much smaller columns topped by a male and a female deer. After docking, we hired a cab to see ruins of the Greek Acropolis, including temples, a stadium and a theater, and ruins of a fortified medieval city surrounded by walls topped with parapets and towers. The day was pleasantly warm, and the vegetation was semi-tropical. We visited a porcelain factory.

From a letter to my parents: *I spent the Christmas money you gave me on six hand painted blue and white tiles which, when combined, form a scene with a deer. I hope they make it home without breaking.*

Back at the Jason, the four of us dressed for dinner as best we could with only camping clothes. We had our own assigned table, and, during the cocktail hour, a band played. People were dancing, so Lynette and I joined them. When we returned to the table, the children were uneasy. It turned out, they were embarrassed. Incredibly, they had never seen us dancing before! We had a good laugh, but were unable to persuade them either to dance together or with us.

Kriti (Crete) is the legendary birthplace of Zeus, the documented birthplace of El Greco, and the center of the Minoan civilization that dominated the eastern Mediterranean three to five thousand years ago. Our boat landed at Iraklion (Heraklion), the island's largest city dating from the ninth century. Nearby sits ancient Knossos, the capital of the Minoan kingdom. Here King Minos, who, according to Thucydides, organized the world's first navy, held court, and here, according to legend, Theseus slew the Minotaur. Palaces, including the Royal Palace with its Throne of Minos, and other buildings have been reconstructed, and beautiful frescoes, pottery and jewelry all help the visitor to visualize the ancient city and how its citizens lived. The Minoans built sophisticated drainage systems including flush toilets, kept records in a script called Linear A, developed a system of weights and measures, entertained themselves with bull fights and theaters, stored grain and olive oil to assure continuous supplies, and traded olive oil and perfumes for ivory, lapis lazuli and glass. In Iraklion, the Archaeologikon Mouseion displays frescoes, pottery, statuary, weapons, and household items from Knossos, much of it five thousand years old. A thought kept returning to me as we toured Knossos and admired its buildings, palaces and other relics: While the Minoan civilization was in full flower—building cities, sailing the seas, writing thoughts and records—Europe and much of the rest of the world still lived in caves, mired in the stone age.

The rough seas continued unabated, and we were disappointed that the Jason was unable to land at Santorini. The crew did their best to make it up to us, though, donning colorful costumes and performing wonderful folk dances. That evening the Greek dinner was exceptional, the dance music was delightful, and, fortunately, the children lost when they tried gambling with the ship's one armed bandits.

Back in our camper, we headed for the wonderful, warm Peloponnesus, stopping at Eleusis, where the Greeks believed that Pluto abducted Persephone, and the Romans built a temple by a grotto thought to be the entrance to Hades, and then at Korinthos (Corinth) on the strategic isthmus between the Peloponnesus and mainland Greece. We crossed the narrow canal connecting the Gulf of Korinthos with the Aegean Sea and picked up a hitchhiking backpacker, a lacrosse player who was traveling for a year on a leave of absence from the University of Maryland, and gave him a lift to the Acrocorinth where we visited the Temple of Aphrodite and a Byzantine fortress. On nearby Arhea Korinthos, we explored the ruins of the Agora and Temple of Apollo and toured the Roman ruins where the Apostle Paul preached to the Corinthians.

As the sun set on the Minoan Culture, the mainland Mycenaean culture rose to dominance in the fifteenth and fourteenth centuries BC, thriving through the defeat of Troy in about 1200 BC. Mikinai (Mycenae), Homer's legendary town of gold, built by Perseus with the aid of the Cyclops, became the historic capital of ancient Greece. King Agamemnon, the leader of the siege of Troy, ruled Greece from Mikinai and was assassinated here by his wife, Clytemnaestra, and her lover, Aegisthus. Mikinai was Heinrich Schliemann's first great discovery, late in the nineteenth century. Considered by some to be the "father of archeology," Schliemann believed Homer to be an historian as well as a poet and used passages from his works as clues in discovering Mikinai and, later, Troy. We walked along Cyclopean walls and entered the ancient city through the Gate of Lions with its two lions carved in stone. We climbed the Acropolis, flushing foraging larks along the way, visited the remains of a palace dating back to 1400 BC, and explored the Circle of Tombs, including the huge tombs of Agamemnon and Clytemnaestra in which Schliemann found vast quantities of gold treasure.

Further south, in Argos, we visited the Temple of Hera and Mycenaean Tirins, the legendary birthplace of Hercules, and then drove to the sea through Nafplion, setting up camp on the beach next to an English couple and their son. I had been concerned about getting stuck in the sand and gunned the car through an especially soft area to an island of much firmer sand. I asked the Brit if he liked my technique, and he said he would reserve judgement until he saw how it would work returning to the road backwards. We four adults became acquainted over tea while the children collected shells and built a castle of sand and bamboo. Later we all walked to the village of Tolon for groceries, then returned for a swim, and cooked our suppers on the beach. Two Italians driving on the beach became stuck, and asked us for a push. After we extricated them, they opened a couple bottles of Italian wine, and we sat around the fire and put it away.

From a letter to my parents: *Most of the tourists have gone home, but here the sun is shining and the surf is still warm. The birds are on their way back south, the Greeks are exceptionally friendly, and the four of us are happy and glad to be here.*

Driving west over the mountains, with great fanfare I pointed out our odometer was about to turn 11,111.1 miles. Mike thought it would be even more exciting when it registered 12345.6 miles. At Tripolis, we turned south through Tegea, stopping to see the fourth-century BC Temple of Athena, to historic Sparta. Beautiful Helen was married to Menelaus, brother of Agamemnon and great warrior-king of Sparta. Paris, the son of the king of Ilium, Priam, wooed Helen and carried her off to Troy, precipitating the Trojan War. Few ruins of ancient Sparta remain from the heroic era between the sixth and fourth centuries BC when this warrior society ruled the Peloponnesus and the Spartans led the Greeks in repelling the Persian invasion. The Spartans erected few monuments and no walls, instead trusting their defense to their heroic warriors. Near the city, however, lies Mistras, a whole mountainside full of Byzantine religious ruins including fourteenth- and fifteenth-century convents, one of which is still occupied, churches, and monasteries and a thirteenth-century Crusader fortress. While we walked on gravel paths among the ruins, Krissie and Mike found a nearly buried human jawbone. We showed it to a guard at the museum, and he said it was not important, that such discoveries were quite common.

Turning west and winding our way through rugged mountains, some with green terraced hillsides and scrubby trees and others moor-like with rocks and thick ground cover, we then descended through exciting, narrow canyons into a verdant valley that led to Kalamata on the sea. The city boasts a thirteenth-century Crusader castle, a fourteenth-century Byzantine church, and a convent known for weaving fine silks. The area around Kalamata features orange orchards, olive groves and fine beaches. The municipal campground was closed for the season, but we pulled in nevertheless and took cold showers.

Epano Eglianos is the largest and best preserved Mycenaean palace in Greece. From here, the Homeric hero, King Nestor, ruled ancient Pylos with great wisdom. The attractive village of Pilos sits on a picturesque bay and is overlooked by a Crusader castle. We crossed the peninsula from Kalamata, had a look at the castle, descended into Pilos and parked by the small harbor. Shops surrounded the town square where a man was in the process of carving a roasted pig on a spit. We bought fresh bread and butter and a big chunk of hot pork and then converted it all into delicious sandwiches dripping with butter, and we ate our lunch on the sunny dock. An Australian couple joined us and said they were camped by a tavern a couple hundred yards down the beach. They accompanied us on a short drive down the coast to visit Paleaokastro, an impressive thirteenth-century Venetian castle in the village of Methoni, and then we joined them camping on the beach where Lynette threw the rest of our pork into a great stew. The Aussies were into the second year of their plan to travel for four years. Their next stop was Kalamata where they planned to pick oranges for a while and save their money.

Driving north along the Ionian coast, we pulled over for lunch on the beach. An old man riding a horse stopped to talk with us. His English was fair, and he invited us to the cave where he lived with his goats. We enjoyed the little diversion, getting a first-hand look at this recluse's secluded home, and, near the cave, spotting an owl in the bargain. At Pirgos, we drove east, with a vivid, complete rainbow arching over the southern hills, to Olympia, where the son of Zeus, Hercules, decreed that, in celebration of his victory over Augeas, the men of Greece should assemble every four years to compete in athletic contests. For a thousand years the Olympic games reigned as the most important event in the Hellenic world. The marvelous ruins of ancient Olympia still remain on Holy Altis.

One couple from Australia and another from New Zealand had the campground to themselves until we arrived. The camping area lay beside a vineyard and in the middle of an orange grove. Pomegranates grew by the campground office. The proprietor welcomed us and sold us wine that came from his own vineyard and fresh raspberries from his garden. Krissie and I took a walk and came across an ewe trying to suckle two lambs who weren't sure whether they wanted to eat or play. They teased each other and jumped in the air, all four feet leaving the ground at once. We did our laundry and, after hanging it on a line, drove into the village of Olympia for groceries, and had a great dinner of local food.

What a morning! Cereal with fresh raspberries and then the magnificent ruins of ancient Olympia all to ourselves! The glorious Temple of Zeus with its enormous fluted pillars was simply awe inspiring. I sat in the stadium, silently, imagining runners and discus throwers, and the cheering throngs of people. We visited the gymnasium and the museum containing Paleolithic relics more than five thousand years old as well as sculpture and weapons from Hellenic times. Back at the campground, the children made a mosaic of our camper from small pieces of limestone, and Lynette said that for once they had learned something in a museum.

Lovely weather continued as we followed the Ionic coastline north to Gastorini and then drove on a peninsula to Loutra Kilinis, a small spa resort that was closed for the season.

From my notes: *This area may be the most beautiful I have seen in Greece. The wonderful white sand beach is deserted except for another couple in a Volkswagen camper. We saw the same car several days ago while crossing the mountains from Kalamata to Pilos.*

I invited the pair to join us for a glass of wine and learned they were French-speaking Swiss. While we became acquainted, Mike and Krissie built a sand castle complete with a switch-backing road leading up to the walls. The sun sank lower in the southwest, and we could see ferries leaving Zakinthos and even, in the distance, Ithaki or Ithaka, King Odysseus' island home from which he set sail for Troy and returned years later to rescue his wife, Penelope, from unscrupulous suitors demanding she marry one of them. I asked Jules, "Where will you go after Greece?"

"To Italy, and then on to Africa?"

"Africa! Where? How will you get there?"

"We will ship from Sicilia across the Mediterranean to Tunisia. Then we will drive across the Sahara."

"You're going to drive across the Sahara Desert? Are there roads?"

"In some places. But mostly there are tracks. I have done it before." And for the next hour or two my friend answered questions and regaled us with stories about the desert. I was fascinated. It never occurred to me that it was possible to drive a car across the Sahara. I think I was certain, even that night, that one day I would drive my car across the mysterious Sahara.

The middle of November was upon us, and whether we had a premonition of cold weather or common sense dictated, we thought it would be a good idea to stay put for another day and enjoy the warm sunshine. We walked on the beach talking about the events of Greek history and their significance—the Minoan culture, the Mycenaeans, and the Classical Period—and reflected on how, because of reports of political turmoil, we had almost missed Greece, the highlight of the trip. Other than some occasional, rather passionate criticism of Henry Kissinger, we had encountered no political problems. Stonechats and wheatears foraged on the ground and flew to perches on scrubby trees. We did schoolwork, read and planned our travels in Italy.

The next morning we drove north and east along the sea to Patrai, the historic capital of the Peloponnesus, where we visited a thirteenth-century Crusader fortress and a ninth-century monastery. We shopped for groceries, bought pastries at a great bakery, and booked passage on the ferry across the Gulf of Corinth before registering at the very good municipal campground.

A fifteenth-century castle overlooked the harbor at Rion from where our ferry departed. We headed north through Mesolongion, where Lord Byron died after helping Greece fight for its independence from Turkey, saw a Sardinian warbler at the ruins of Stratos, then admired a medieval fortress and fine old stone arch bridge at Arta, and visited Dodoni, the site of the oldest oracle in Greece where, from 2000 BC to 400 AD, rulers and commoners alike consulted Zeus, the king of the gods. In Ioannina, we visited a mosque with the tomb of Ali Pasha, the Lion of Albania, and toured an extensive and excellent cave system which the children thought was "cool" and Lynette thought was "cold" as well as "oppressive and claustrophobic." Our young, friendly guide gave us the now tiresome pitch that he was angry with Kissinger, not with us or the American people. We bought ground beef, onions and potatoes for dinner and a container of cheap, but good, table wine from a huge cask and found a primitive campground where we shared our wine with two French-Canadian backpackers.

Our ferry departed from Igoumenitsa, made a port of call at Kerkira (Corfu), and took most of the day to make a calm crossing of the Adriatic to Brindisi, Italy, the terminus of the ancient Via Appia (Appian Way) which extended from Rome. We camped at the port and, in the morning, since my mother was scheduled to arrive in Rome in a few days, we drove north along the sea to the port city of Bari, where we stopped only long enough to see the twelfth-century Basilica of St. Nicholas, and then, on the modern Autostrade, drove quickly through the Apennines, across the Italian peninsula, descending past ominous Mt. Vesuvius into crowded, lively and colorful Napoli (Naples). Wonderful palaces, buildings, churches and monasteries highlight the large city, the commercial and cultural center of southern Italy. Crazy drivers, flowers, fish markets and prostitutes were ubiquitous. At the municipal campground, we pulled in beside and had a fine reunion with the Matsons, our friends from Oregon who, in Vienna, had taught us how to play Kaput and Yahtzee.

We drove south past Vesuvius and over the mountains of the Sorrentine Peninsula to Amalfi, the quaint old port town clinging to a cliff above the Gulf of Salerno. The Amalfi Drive winds its way along the south coast of the peninsula, past white-washed, sun-bleached towns perched on mountainsides, and terraced vineyards and olive groves. Beautiful views of the peninsula and the blue-green sea appear around every hairpin turn. In picturesque Positano, we waited patiently while a long, solemn funeral cortege slowly marched down the town's only through street. The Isle of Capri waited off the tip of the peninsula, but we opted instead for lovely Sorrento, sitting on a natural terrace above the Bay of Naples. We walked around the town, talked to wonderfully friendly Italians, drank wine and soft drinks at a sidewalk cafe on the old square, and Lynette bought herself a box decorated with the typical wooden inlay work of Sorrento. The local campground had a playground, and I photographed Krissie hanging upside down from a monkey bar, with five teeth missing from the broad smile on her face. We met a family from Georgia, also camping. He was a teacher traveling from one air base to another, offering statistics courses to U.S. Air Force officers who were working on business administration programs. His beautiful wife was stepmother to their children. Lynette said she looked as young as her daughter. We returned to Sorrento's charming town square that evening and enjoyed a marvelous pasta dinner, after which we drank hot chocolate and coffee at the same sidewalk cafe and watched the happy people walk by.

On August 24, 79 AD, long dormant Mount Vesuvius erupted. Lying at the foot of the volcano, the village of Pompei, along with many of its citizens, was buried under a hail of stones, cinders, and ash. The excavated ancient city reveals life as it was nineteen centuries ago. Shops, theaters, temples, public baths, a city forum, an amphitheater and many other public buildings have been uncovered, as have magnificent houses with frescoes, paintings and mosaic tiled floors. Lead pipes transported water for drains, drinking fountains and sewage systems. We toured the fascinating city, restored so authentically that we could easily imagine life in those times. All the while, supposedly inactive Vesuvius loomed above us. Late in the afternoon we drove the motorway almost to Rome and camped in one of the service areas. The children were very enthusiastic about Grammy's joining us. We played Yahtzee and were very happy. Afterwards, we lay in bed, and Krissie said, "I can't wait for Grammy!" Mike added, "Me too. I'm ecstatic!"

Camping Roma became our base of operations for the next several days. Many of the campers spoke English, and Mike and Krissie had no trouble finding playmates. We washed and cleaned the camper, did our laundry, stocked up on groceries at a modern supermarket, and found a hotel nearby for Grammy. A little Australian boy threw a rock and hit Mike on the head. His mother told the kid to apologize to Mike, but he ignored her. The father called him, and the kid once again ignored his parent. The father then said, "I'll expect you to come!" and the boy simply walked away from him. Mike rubbed his head, looked at me and declared, "He's lucky he doesn't have you guys for parents."

After a quick breakfast, we headed for Leonardo Da Vinci Airport to meet Grammy Helen. Her baggage took its time, and we could see her waiting behind a glass divider wall. Krissie and Mike sneaked through the customs gate, but Lynette and I were stopped by a guard when we tried to do the same. After a happy reunion, we took Grammy out for lunch, where, as the kiddies had hoped, she extracted cookies and fudge from her carry-on bag, and then took her to her hotel for a few hours sleep. Late in the afternoon, we showed Grammy our campground and then went out for an authentic Italian spaghetti dinner. The reader will surely get to know Grammy during the next few weeks. For starters, however, no one has ever accused her either of being reticent or of pulling any punches. Walking to the restaurant, in almost painfully graphic detail, she brought us up to date on all my relatives. Along the way, we passed a small grocery store with a stack of fresh bread displayed on the sidewalk. Two dogs sat below the bread, sniffing and hoping that someone might take pity on them. Also, of course, the inevitable few flies meandered about on several bread crusts. Grammy stopped, appalled, and shook her head.

"These people don't know the meaning of the word 'sanitation!'"

Krissie looked up at her, perplexed, and said, "Neither do I, Grammy."

That the god Mars sired two sons, Romulus and Remus, who were nursed to maturity by a wolf and went on to found the city of Rome is speculative, at best, but there is little doubt that the Eternal City has sat on the banks of the Tiber for close to 3,000 years. By the end of the second century AD, the Roman empire controlled most of the known world. The city declined and then again ascended the ladder of greatness as the center of Christianity in the West and then as a birthplace of the fifteenth-century Renaissance. Today, Rome still retains much of its past glory—its magnificent ruins from the times of the Empire, the incomparable Vatican, and the masterpieces of Leonardo da Vinci, Michelangelo, Raphael, Titian and many others. With its palaces, monuments, churches, boulevards, parks, fountains and shops, Rome's beauty surpasses that of most other cities.

Driving in any major city is not for the faint of heart, but, in Rome, it's insane. We took a bus into the city center, deciding to start our tour of Roma in Vatican City, the Roman Catholic independent state under the rule of the Pope and the College of Cardinals. This holy center of Roman Catholicism, head of one of the world's most influential institutions, encompasses little more than a hundred acres. The Via della Conciliazione leads to Bernini's lovely Piazza San Pietro. The great square is flanked by two curving Doric colonnades, topped by statues of saints and martyrs, that culminate at the head of the square in front of the magnificent Basilica di San Pietro.

From my notes: *St. Peter's Basilica is the most astounding, awe-inspir-*

ing human creation I have ever seen.

The fifteenth-century church is the largest in Christianity, with standing room for one hundred thousand people, and is adorned with heavenly inspired art including Michelangelo's *La Pieta* and Bernini's hundred-foot high bronze canopy covering the high altar. Michelangelo changed Bramante's original architectural plans and built the church's enormous dome. We toured museums in the Vatican Palace, one featuring Raphael's mosaics and frescoes and another the Hall of Sculptures.

From my notes: *And then, we walked into the quiet thunder of the Cappella Sistina. I stopped and marveled at the walls adorned with frescoes by Botticelli, Rosselli and Ghirlandaio, depicting the lives of Christ and Moses. At the far end of the chapel, Michelangelo's panoramic "Last Judgement" unfolds. Looking up, I walked slowly as the "piece de resistance" on which the master, Michelangelo, lying on his back on scaffolding, painstakingly worked for four years, unfolded—the epic presentation of the creation and the fall of man, lavishly and profusely painted across the vaulted ceiling. There I felt and understood inspiration as never before.* And, now, as I reflect upon the experience, never since.

A quiet and beautiful old nun attended us in the tourist shop where we bought a few cards and such. I asked her how much the tickets were for the Papal Audience and was mortified when she smiled, shook her head, and said, "Nothing, Signore." We sat with thousands of others, waiting in the Vatican's new auditorium for the Pope to appear. Groups of nuns, children and tourists competed with one another singing, some accompanied by guitars or harmonicas, while others sang *a cappella*. As each group finished, the others applauded. It was fascinating, almost a Roman Catholic version of a huge, old fashioned revival meeting. For a moment, I expected Elmer Gantry to materialize. There was a commotion in the rear of the hall. The applause gained momentum, and sporadic cheers swelled to a roar. Then we could see him: Giovanni Battista Montini, Pope Paul VI, dressed in white, carried high on a golden litter and acknowledging the flock's spontaneous exuberance with both hands raised above his holy head.

From the Vatican, we went to a small, quiet Italian restaurant. With all the walking, Grammy had held up fairly well, but I could see she had slowed down the past few years more than I had realized. The next day we photographed each other at the Fountain of Trevi, where Gram threw a coin in the pool thereby assuring herself she would one day return to Rome, walked to the Colonnade of Marcus Aurelius, and had good pizza for lunch. We visited Rome's oldest building, the Pantheon, where Victor Emmanuel II, the Italian king who reunified the country, and Raphael, among others, are buried and then, in Piazza Venezia, the enormous Victor Emanuel monument. A marble elephant carried a 2,500-year old Egyptian obelisk in the

Piazza della Minerva. It began raining, and Grammy was tired, so we took her back to her hotel and returned to the campground where we ate popcorn and drank wine with the Matsons while the kiddies did their schoolwork.

Grammy was still not at her best. I left Lynette and the children with her at the hotel and took the camper to a VW dealer for its twelve thousand mile servicing. By the evening, Gram was approaching her old self, so we ate pasta at a good little restaurant and planned our assault on Roma the next day.

The bus dropped us at the Piazza Venezia. We walked through the Fori Imperiali, including the Forum of Caesar, Forum of Trajan with impressive Colonna Traiana (Trajan's Column), Forum of Augustus, and the Foro Romano. The Roman Forum was the city's center of public life and contains many temples including the Temple of Julius Caesar, the Curia where the Roman Senate met, the Arch of Titus, the Arch of Septimus Severus under which we ate our sandwiches, and the Tomb of Romulus guarded by statues of lions. At Piazza di San Pietro in Vincoli (St. Peter in Chains), I was very moved by the power in Michelangelo's statue of Moses. Now Gram was back to one hundred per cent and wanted to see everything. We sat on the steps of the Colosseo (Colosseum), trying to visualize fifty thousand spectators roaring their approval or disapproval of the gladiatorial performances, and walked under the magnificent Arch of Constantine. We visited marvelous museums—the Museo Nazionale Romano and Museo Capitolino.

The next morning, Lynette marched us off to Rome's immense flea market. Then I somehow summoned the fortitude to drive into the city, stopping at Palatine Hill where the city spread out wonderfully below us, past Mura Aurelie, the old wall encircling the Seven Hills of Rome, and the Piramide di Caio Cestio, a two thousand-year old sixty-foot high pyramid. We ate lunch in the botanical gardens of the Villa Borghese and parked by the Baths of Caracalla where Shelley composed Prometheus Unbound, disappointed we had missed the summer outdoor opera season. We stopped at a sidewalk cafe and also in a few shops on the Via Veneto. At the Piazza di Spagna, we photographed colorful flowers and walked up the Spanish Steps. Then we descended into the dark, damp Catacombs where Christians met and worshipped in secret during the Roman persecutions of the second century and where many of them were buried, including San Sebastian.

From Grammy's notes: *Thirty feet underground, smelly and damp, I hated it! Caskets, tombs, skulls and skeletons—ugh!*

The Galleria Colonna featured paintings by Tintoretto, Botticelli and Rubens, and the Appian Way was flanked by cypress trees, statues and monuments reflecting Rome's glorious past. We crossed Rome's oldest bridge, Ponte Fabricio, spanning the Tiber and stopped on Tiberine Island at the Teatro di Marcello. We found a small trattoria near the campground and enjoyed excellent lasagna for dinner. Another diner, a very funny and effusive Italian, sitting at a table next to us, engaged us all in conversation. Soon we invited him to join us, which he gladly did. He was a plant ecologist and sometimes actor and loved to tell stories, gesticulating with both hands and imitating jet helicopters or four wheel drive vehicles with graphic mouth noises. He mesmerized the children and kept the rest of us laughing.

Leaving Rome, we drove north and east through the medieval town of Spoleto with its Ponte della Torri, an enormous fourteenth-century viaduct. Vineyards and olive groves dotted the hills, picturesque old villages featured very narrow cobblestone streets and high, yellow-brown stucco houses with window boxes full of colorful flowers, and sheep grazed in green meadows blooming with autumn wildflowers. A shepherdess and her dog tended a flock of sheep, and she smiled and waved to us. Grammy became excited upon seeing several castles along the way, her first ever.

St. Francis grew up in twelfth-century Assisi and spent his youth battling the Perugians and then a near fatal illness before he converted to a life of penitence, prayer, and poverty. He established the Franciscan Order in 1210, and his devoted follower, St. Clare, founded the Order of Poor Clares two years later. Since then, the charming and quiet, peaceful town on the side of Mount Subasio has changed little. Late in the afternoon, a cold rain began, so we found Gram a hotel and a campground for us a couple miles away. The Aussies, with the unrepentant little brat who hit Mike with a stone in Rome, pulled in beside us. Maybe it was the rain or being parked next to them, but that night I was feeling a bit guilty about my unemployment, and thought I might be growing tired of the trip.

From my notes: *The uncertainty of getting a job and where it will be. The knowledge that it has been almost a year since I've worked— not the ethic I was raised on. Even the abundance of campers in Europe—not special like in South America. It's all getting to me.*

The dark skies and my dark mood were gone in the morning, vanished as the morning sun warmed up Assisi and us. We picked up Grammy and visited the Basilica di San Francesco, with the tomb of St. Francis and Giotto's frescoes depicting scenes from St. Francis' life, and the Church of St. Clare. We drove up a twisting, gravel road to Rocca Medioevale, a fourteenth-century castle, and Gram was certain one of the precipitous cliffs falling from the roadside would claim us. We twisted our way northeast across rugged mountains, past lovely farms and the medieval village of Gubbio, to the walled town of Fano on the Adriatic Sea and then north to Pesaro, the home of operatic composer, Gioacchino Rossini.

San Marino advertises itself as the oldest and smallest republic in the world. Surrounded by Italy and with a population at the time of less than five thousand, San Marino offered us a step back into medieval times. Perched on the western slope of Monte Titano, the capital city, also called San Marino, preserves the past with its stone ramparts and narrow streets and stone houses with red tile roofs. We arrived in the evening, found a hotel for Gram, and set up camp in the municipal parking lot. In the morning, we explored the old fort, visited the fourteenth-century Church of San Francesco, and shopped. Lynette bought a tray and Mike a flag while the fog descended upon the mountain. Then the rains came, so we left for Venice.

We drove east to the Adriatic and Rimini where, emulating Julius Caesar, we crossed the Rubicon. Then we continued north along the sea, through Ravenna, the one time capital of the Western Roman Empire, crossed the River Po delta, and arrived in Venice, Marco Polo's birthplace, late in the afternoon. We found a hotel for Gram and, for a bit extra, received permission to camp in their parking lot. We all used Gram's shower and then walked to a restaurant where we each ordered a different pizza and shared them. The weather had turned bitterly cold, so we sat in the lovely lobby of Gram's hotel and read. Krissie stayed with Grammy for the night when the three of us returned to the camper.

Venice, Italy, November 28, 1974

Happy Thanksgiving, indeed! Turkey was to be found nowhere in Venice. We took a street bus into the city, a water bus past the grand palaces and homes on the Grand Canal, and, that evening, eventually settled for pasta. We began our tour of Venezia, one of the world's truly unique cities, in the majestically proportioned Piazza San Marco. Trendy shops and expensive cafes line the enormous square's elegant arcades. We visited a museum and the ninth-century Basilico di San Marco, the immense Byzantine church rich in rare marble, works of art, mosaics and gold. We admired the Pala d' Oro, a tenth-century gold and enamel altarpiece studded with precious gems, and watched workers restoring several of the basilica's mosaics, and then talked with them when they dismounted their scaffolding. One man gave Krissie and Mike a handful of little gold mosaic squares.

We visited the pink and white marble Pallazo Ducale (Doge's Palace), then had great pizza for lunch, fed crumbs to San Marcos' pigeons and took a cold canal ride in a gondola. Shops lined the Ponte di Rialto which spanned the Grand Canal, and, in a glass shop, Lynette bought a colorful snail for Mike and a dish for Gram. At another glass shop Gram bought a glass fish for Mike, a turtle for Krissie, and a branchful of birds for herself. The handsome, friendly artisan flirted with Gram and told us he was a karate expert.

From Gram's notes: *The man was very nice, and we chatted with him for about an hour. He has many post cards from his customers from all over the world hanging on a wall. He gave me a necklace, and I promised to send him a postcard from the Pennsylvania Dutch country.*

Lynette photographed me in front of the Ponte di Sospiri (Bridge of Sighs) across which, the story goes, sighing convicts walked to their executions. We found a small trattoria, with three little old men playing violins and singing Italian love songs for the patrons, and gave thanks, after all, over a pretty good meal of pasta. Back at the hotel, we drank chianti with a friendly merchant seaman from Portovenere, a small town near Pisa, who had sailed the world. Krissie slept with her Gram again.

Winter had certainly arrived, even in southern Europe. We drove directly south through historic medieval cities like Padova (Padua) and Ferrara, where Gram especially liked the fourteenth-century Castello Estense with its stone walls and moat and the Palazzo dei Diamanti (Palace of Diamonds) built with diamond-faceted marble blocks. South of Bologna, for the third time since arriving in Italy, we crossed the Apeninnes, passing scenic mountain villages, castles and waterfalls, and driving through numerous tunnels.

Firenze (Florence) claims more than two thousand years of history, but never was its importance greater than when it became a cradle of the Renaissance. The list of Renaissance greats associated with Florence is staggering—Leonardo da Vinci, Michelangelo, Boccaccio, Machiavelli, Dante and Donatelli, naming a few. The wealthy and powerful Medici family, especially the Medici known as "Lorenzo the Magnificent," single handedly sponsored an atmosphere that landed Florence at the top of the art world where, in addition to Michelangelo and Leonardo da Vinci, masters like Ghiberti, Raphael, Botticelli, Giotto, Della Robia, and Ghirlandaio all toiled. Late in the day we arrived in Florence, registered Gram in the Hotel Milano, and found a campground a few miles outside the city. After dinner, my hands nearly froze doing the dishes.

From Gram's notes: *We eat a lot of pears and apples. Italian pears are especially delicious. Now we are in Florence, La Citta del Fiore— The City of Flowers.*

Red, green and white marble adorn the exterior of the Gothic style Duomo di Santa Maria del Fiore, the world's second largest church, while Michelangelo's *Descent from the Cross* and many other priceless works of art adorn the interior.

Gram's assessment in her notes: *The outside of the Duomo is impressive, with its great size and beautiful marble. However, I don't think the inside is very pretty; it doesn't compare with St. Peter's.*

We marveled, nevertheless, at the Duomo, as well as Giotto's fifteenth-century Campanile or bell tower, and the Battistero (Baptistery) with its "Gate to Paradise," Ghiberti's famous fourteenth-century bronze doors.

Over the next few days, we meandered along the city's charming streets for hours, picking up mail at American Express, changing money, stopping at cafes, and shopping. We followed the Arno to the Ponte Vecchio (Old Bridge), the charming fourteenth-century pedestrian bridge, covered with a red tile roof and lined on both sides with shops. Lynette bought a purse for herself and a wallet for Krissie. Late in the afternoon we drove to Fiesole, a town with an eleventh-century cathedral, a two thousand-year old Roman theater, and an exquisite view of Florence.

The Galleria Delgli Uffizi houses one of the finest art collections of the world. We spent several hours viewing the galleries of the Italian Renaissance which included masterpieces by Botticelli, Leonardo da Vinci, Caravaggio and many others. We walked to the huge Piazza della Signoria square, dominated by the fourteenth-century Palazzo Vecchio (Old Palace), now the city hall, and then to the Accademia where Gram was fond of Michelangelo's sculptures, especially the stupendous *David*. We saw the Medici tombs sculpted by Michelangelo at the Church of San Lorenzo, walked to the Piazzale Michelangelo with its great view of Florence and the Arno Valley, and visited the master's home. One evening, intending to return to the campground, we discovered at the end of the line we had taken the wrong bus and had to retrace our route. Grammy scolded me for not paying attention while Krissie and Mike laughed and egged her on.

From Firenze, we followed the Arno drainage west to Pisa and were all surprised at how much the 179-foot white marble, Torre Pendente really does lean.

From Gram's notes: *Every time I looked up at it I felt dizzy and off balance.*

I shot the compulsory photo of Mike standing beside the tower with his arm extended, as if holding it up. We continued to the sea and followed the Italian Riviera north past Puccini's house near Viareggio, through the port city of La Spezia where, it seemed, every ship in the Italian navy was moored, then to medieval Portovenere on the sea. (We found a nice hotel for Gram with a beautiful view of the picturesque harbor, and we camped on the beach below her hotel window.)

From Mother's notes: *Tonight we are outside the walled town of Portovenere. I am in a room on the second floor, and my glass doors open to a balcony overlooking the kids in the camper parked on the beach below and the Mediterranean beyond. Imagine me! Sleeping on the Italian Riviera! We walked into town—the streets aren't wide enough to accommodate cars. Krissie and I walked the length of the town, then up to the second and third levels and back down. Oh boy! I couldn't live in one of these towns on the side of a mountain—my legs couldn't make it. But it is so pretty—like Assisi or San Marino except not touristy. This is the home town of the nice Italian man we met in the lobby of my hotel in Venice. Because of his recommendation, we went out of our way to come here, and we aren't sorry we took his advice.*

Continuing north, the road edged its way along seaside cliffs, past terraced vineyards and stone walled fortresses, then descended to the sea, winding through beautiful coastal towns—the artists' haven and fishing town of Portofino and the trendy resorts of Rapallo and Santa Margherita Ligure—into Genoa, Italy's leading seaport and the home of Christopher Columbus and Nicolo Paganini. We stopped in Albisola to look at shops carrying the ceramics for which the town was famous, and then in Alassio, the center of an area which produces flowers for the European market. Gram checked into the Hotel Ligure, and we camped next to her on the beach.

From her notes: *The weather is much warmer here, and we are very happy about that.*

The sun reflected off the placid sea in the resort town of San Remo, and, by the time we crossed the border, France's Mediterranean playground, the Cote d' Azur (Blue Coast), was pleasantly warm. We drove through the resort towns of Menton and picturesque Roquebrune-Cap-Martin, the latter sitting below the medieval village of Roquebrune with the oldest castle in France, built in the tenth century to repel plundering Saracens. We entered the tiny principality of Monaco, admiring the yachts anchored in the harbor of La Condamine and the ramparts and narrow streets of Monaco-Ville, the old town, above which sits Prince Ranier's awesome palace. We visited Monte-Carlo with its gardens and parks and the glitzy Casino, mostly, just to say we did.

We continued along the Cote d' Azur, past castles and fishing villages and through resorts like Beaulieu-sur-Mer and, Renoir's favorite, Cagnes-sur-Mer. In Nice, we walked along the sea front on the lovely, flower lined Promenade des Anglais. We changed money, but a French postal strike assured us of receiving no mail. Gram registered at the Hotel Riviera in Antibes, and we found a plush campground nearby with, not only hot water, but heated shower rooms as well. I cooked us a delicious supper of pork sausages, fried potatoes and onions. We played games and then drove Gram the two miles to her hotel for the night.

From my notes: *French Riviera more modern than Italian, the coastal towns larger, a bit less serene and pretty.*

With perfect weather, this was a good day to clean up everything. Early in the morning I was in the middle of doing the laundry when I heard a familiar voice from over my shoulder, "My son, the washer woman." Grammy had also risen early, gone out to buy a baguette, and walked the two miles to the campground. I finished the laundry, and Mike and I washed the camper while the three girls went shopping at the campground supermarket. I saw a familiar camper pulling into the campground and realized it was the Australian family with Yuri, the incorrigible kid. Later, while they were playing, Yuri hit Krissie with a stick. His mother told him not to do it again, and, in character, he walked away and ignored her. I called Mike and Krissie over and told them, since the kid's parents are ineffective, belt the kid the next time he does anything violent. The next morning the kid threw a stone at Mike who rewarded him for his action with a slap on the fanny. The kid ran screaming to his mother who, to her credit, wasn't any more upset with Mike for spanking him than she was with Yuri's behavior.

From Gram's notes: *I talked with a Jewish lady from Holland at the campground. She said she had been in the concentration camp at Auschwitz for eighteen months and showed me a number tattooed on her arm. Her parents, brothers and sister were put to death in the ovens there. She said they travel all over, even to the U.S., but not to Germany. There are too many memories there.*

Palm trees lined the Boulevard de la Croisette and yachts filled the harbor in Cannes. Seaside resort towns like St. Raphael and Frejus boasted Roman ruins as well as casinos, villas, palaces and beaches. In the former, we stopped at the Rhone Cemetery to pay our respects to 861 American soldiers. Lynette steered us into St. Tropez to see the artists' colony, and I secretly hoped for a glimpse of Brigette Bardot. Our road strayed from the sea through scenic villages and flat rural countryside with shepherds tending their flocks to Aix-en-Provence, where we saw Cezanne's studio, and Van Gogh's Arles, where we saw aqueducts, an amphitheater and other Roman ruins. On the drive, Gram gave me a rundown on all our relatives, many of whom either I didn't remember or never knew and one of whom, Great Grandmother Ely, was suspected by other family members of being Jewish. All of this was interesting to me but lethally boring to the others. We camped in the parking lot of Mon Auberge, Gram's hotel in the village of Lunel. Krissie slept with Gram.

In Montpellier we bought groceries at the open air Sunday market, not Gram's favorite.

From her notes: *Fish and meat stands with the most awful scenes of skinned animals—rabbits, grouse, pheasants, squabs.* Mike, on the other hand, was fascinated by the variety of fish displayed.

Medieval fortifications rise out of the marshes at Aigues-Mortes from where was launched the seventh crusade. Further south at Meze, oyster traps filled the salty shallows of a coastal inlet, and road side stands offered the mollusks for sale. In Beziers, with great views of the surrounding countryside, we ate lunch in the parking area of the thirteenth-century hilltop

Cathedral of St. Nagaire. We stopped in Narbonne to see the twelfth-century Archbishop's Palace, the tenth-century Gothic Cathedral of St. Just, and a paleo-Christian cemetery at the Basilica of St. Paul. Nearing Perpignan and the border with Spain, the architecture revealed a Spanish influence. In Salses, we watched a rugby match and visited a Moorish fort that looked like it should have been sitting in the Sahara. Then in Perpignan, we registered Grammy at the Hotel Les Balares and us at a campground nearby. Mike and Krissie voted for a change in menu when I cooked beans and sausage for supper.

While waiting for the border officials to process our papers, I looked at the snow-capped Pyrenees and wondered what an astonishing sight it must have been for the peasants in their fields to see Hannibal and his elephants crossing those mountains. We crossed the mountains in the opposite direction, stopping in Figueres to see the eighteenth-century San Fernando Castle and in Girona to see a fourteenth-century cathedral. Our road descended to the sea at the Costa Brava and continued south along the Costa Dorada to Barcelona where we registered at the municipal campground and Gram checked into the Monte-Carlo, a small elegant hotel on the Ramblas, a wide promenade around the old city.

From her notes: *The Ramblas features tropical birds, flowers and shrubbery. Very pretty! Happy people stroll on the promenade day and night.*

We instantly liked Barcelona with its parks, gardens, fountains and wide, tree lined boulevards.

From Mother's notes: *Barcelona is a beautiful city, my favorite so far. Wonderful buildings. People have their wash hanging out windows and on balconies. Every morning women wash their doorsteps with hot water and soap, and everyone has flowers on their balconies and porches.*

Lynette began our walking tour at the Plaza de Cataluna in the city center. We visited the fourteenth-century Gothic Cathedral and the sixteenth-century Renaissance Palacio de los Virreyes de Cataluna (Palace of the Viceroys of Catalonia). Christopher Columbus came to Barcelona to persuade Queen Isabella to finance his explorations across the Atlantic Ocean. We paid the explorer tribute at his statue and at a replica of his ship, the Santa Maria, and then visited the Templo Expiatorio de la Sagrada Familia, an enormous and controversial monument with four lacelike towers. It was designed by Antonio Gaudi in 1891 and still was not completed. We drove to Tibidabo, a mountain affording good views of the city and the sea, and, to the delight of Mike and Krissie, an amusement park. On another mountain to Barcelona's south, Montjuich, we walked through a park, past the Palacio Nacional and the bullfighting stadium, to the famous Barcelona Fountains and then shopped for souvenirs in the Pueblo Espanol (Spanish Village) where period craft workers produced their wares and dancers performed. Back at the campground, we renewed our acquaintance with several couples we had met at various other European campgrounds.

A couple from Michigan joined us to take the bus into the city where we met Grammy at her hotel, then checked her reservations on Pan Am, changed money, picked up our mail, and had hotdogs and Cokes for lunch in Plaza Cataluna. Gram bought a purse at a Christmas bazaar near the Cathedral, and I bought a sack of terrific ginger cookies. We had an early dinner at a local restaurant across the street from Gram's hotel and then boarded a bus at Plaza Cataluna. We got off the bus at the enormous Plaza de Espana, intending to transfer to the bus going to the campground. However, I couldn't find the stop for our bus. Some of them stopped in a tunnel under the square, others across the square. I scanned the other side of the plaza with my binoculars and saw our bus. I grabbed the children's hands, and we ran across several concrete islands, leaping over steel guardrails along the way. Lynette became hung up on a guardrail and, either because she was too tired or laughing too much or both, could not extricate herself. By now, all four of us were laughing uncontrollably at her predicament. Krissie and Mike helped me lift their mother off the guardrail, and we turned around just in time to see our bus leaving.

Perched high in the rugged mountains northwest of Barcelona, Montserrat was the scene for Wagner's opera, *Parsifal*. Founded eleven hundred years ago and still the home of several hundred Benedictine monks, the Monastery houses the Black Virgin of Montserrat, object of thousands of pilgrimages each year.

From Gram's notes: *We climbed perilous roads to Montserrat Monastery. The mountain is jagged and looks as tho it were carved into many figures and shapes. We were up in the clouds and it was beautiful, but I was scared stiff.*

The weather cleared, and the mountains gave way to mesas dotting the dry terrain. A policeman pulled me over for passing in a no passing zone. I tried to convince him he was wrong, but he nevertheless charged me four hundred pesetas. We stopped a few miles west of Lerida at a lonely hotel, newly converted from a farmhouse by the government. In Mother's words: *Tonight I am in a beautiful Spanish hotel and only 135 pesetas ($2.43). I've never seen any like this except in the movies. It is the Hotel La Cruzanzanos.*

We watched the sun set behind a mesa, and pink, orange, blue and purple waves of light filled the western sky. Grammy said, "That's one of the most beautiful sights I've seen." Krissie said, "Me too, Grammy."

The drive west across the Spanish plains could have been in Arizona or New Mexico with scenes reminiscent of the Painted Desert. We stopped in Zaragoza, the birthplace of Francisco Goya, to see an eleventh-century Moorish castle and a baroque, blue tiled basilica with cupolas. Villages with adobe brick construction blended into the hillsides, betrayed only by smoke curling from chimneys. Old castles of all sizes guarded archaic boundaries, and shepherds and their dogs guarded their sheep. We parked along the road near a small grove of trees, and, while Lynette fixed lunch and the children kicked a soccer ball, Gram and I watched long-tailed tits foraging, flitting from limb to limb. We continued through Guadalajara and Alcala de Henares (where Catherine of Aragon, King Ferdinand I, and Cervantes were all born) to the Spanish capital, Madrid. We registered at a campground just east of the city, and Gram checked into a cabin at the campground which, in her notes, she described succinctly, "Pretty awful." Our friends the Matsons greeted us. They had been there for four days and planned to stay until Christmas. When Krissie saw them, she ran to Mrs. Matson and jumped into her arms. The girls walked to an open market next to the campground for groceries while Mike and I set up our campsite. Gene Matson brought some fish to us he had caught and cleaned, and we decided to drink a beer while waiting for the girls to return. That night, Mike slept with Gram in her cabin.

The Matsons had rehearsed taking public transportation into Madrid the past several days, so, on a cold morning, we happily let them show us the way as we boarded a bus for the Metro station, then transferred for the train ride into the city, emerging from the station in Plaza Canovas del Castillo where impressive Neptune's Fountain gushed in the center of the plaza. Gram registered at the Hotel Trianon, near the Museo del Prado and next door to the American Express office where we changed money and picked up our mail. Then we toured the Prado, Spain's fabulous art museum which displays one of the world's best collections, including masterpieces by Goya, Rubens, El Greco, Velasquez, Murillo, Titian, Raphael, Van Dyck, Corregio, Fra Angelico, Tintoretto and others. Afterwards, we walked to Plaza Puerta del Sol (Sun's Door) and met the Matsons for lunch, and later Lynette gave us a walking tour of Madrid's Old Town with its narrow streets and attractive seventeenth-century buildings, including the picturesque, arcaded Plaza Mayor where vendors sold Christmas trees and ornaments.

Most shops and public buildings close for siesta in mid-afternoon. Gram seemed a bit unhappy for the first time since she arrived and wanted to go back to her hotel. We complied and then returned to the campground, joining the Matsons on an excursion to the market where, from large casks, we sampled and bought several liters of cheap but good table wine.

From Gram's notes: *I rested a while and then walked across the street for supper. It was horrible. You haven't much choice, all nice restaurants are closed until 9:00 p.m. In Spain, everyone takes a siesta.*

Gram was her old self the next morning when we arrived at her hotel. We shopped until the stores closed at noon and bought nothing except hot dogs and soft drinks which we carried to Plaza de Espana where we ate lunch and admired the statues of Don Quixote and Sancho Panza astride their steeds. In the Parque de la Montana, palm trees rustled in the wind, and a hilltop vantage point provided us a lookout over Madrid and, forty miles to the northwest, the snow-capped Sierra de Guadarrama beyond. We visited the three thousand-year old Egyptian temple of Debod (from Aswan) and then, while the children played in the warm sun, sat on a bench talking and waiting for the Palacio Real (Royal Palace) to reopen after siesta.

In Gram's words: *The gardens around the palace were beautiful. This is the first palace I have toured. We went through 100 rooms (there were 1200). The palace was built by the Bourbons in the eighteenth century and is beautifully decorated and lavishly furnished. It has a grand marble staircase leading up through its eight floors. The throne room is scarlet and gold and contains 800 valuable tapestries. We saw arms and armor; tapestries, paintings and frescoes; silverware, china and crystal; diamonds and other precious jewels; and silks and items of gold.* Grammy picked a Bavarian restaurant, the Edelweiss, for dinner and thought the food was delicious.

The next morning, we bade adieu to the Matsons, drove into the city to pick up Gram, and went to the very crowded and colorful Sunday morning flea market at El Rastro. In Grammy's words: *I bought a deck of cards and several wallets for gifts. There were thousands of people there and it was push, push, push.* Later, at the Parque del Retiro, we sat on benches in the warm sun, eating our lunch and admiring the rose garden, fountains and statues.

Windmills dot the high, dry countryside between Madrid and Toledo where Cervante's Don Quixote rode on his quixotic quest for the lovely Dulcinea. The moat-like River Tagus hugs the base of yellow-brown Toledo's medieval town walls. We entered the city through the Puerto del Sol, a massive gate penetrating the town's immense stone wall, and walked the narrow, twisting streets. Artisans made and sold their Moorish-influenced Damascene products, metal objects decorated with inlaid enamels. We stopped in their shops and bought gifts such as thimbles, scissors, and serving spoons. Fortunately, we had little room in the camper or our budget for the large, expensive swords Mike found especially attractive. We visited the thirteenth-century Gothic cathedral (which features hundreds of stained glass windows, paintings by El Greco, Goya and Velazquez, and a black Madonna and Child. El Alcazar, a splendid fortress overlooking the city was built in the fourteenth century by Charles V. After exploring it, we toured the

El Greco Museum, the fourteenth-century Santo Tome church which displayed El Greco's masterpiece, *The Burial of Count Orgaz,* and the medieval Castle of San Servando. Then we crossed the Tagus on the picturesque, stone arch Bridge of St. Martin and climbed a hill overlooking Toledo where Gram registered at the Los Cigarrales, and, since the municipal campground was closed for the winter, we spent a cold night parked in her hotel parking lot.

Ice covered the camper by morning. When I lit our Coleman stove, thick, black smoke spumed from the flame and covered the interior, including us. Concluding something was wrong with the cooking gas we had last purchased, I turned it off, and we ate a cold breakfast with the motor running and the heater on.

Continuing south, the drive took us past many castles, including the marvelously preserved, fifteenth-century Castillo de Guadamur, and many bucolic scenes—donkeys pulling carts on the roadside and cattle and sheep grazing in fields dotted with whitewashed windmills. Our route took us through the attractive city of Ciudad Real, then on to historic Moorish Cordoba. Gram registered at the Parador Nacionale de la Arruzafa.

From her notes: *It is beautiful and lavish, with terraced gardens, swimming pool, tennis courts, etc.,—like a country club. I have a large bedroom, large bath, sitting room, and spacious balcony. They are at a very nice campground nearby.*

The four of us spent what was left of the morning cleaning smoke stains from the camper and our clothes. Gram stayed at her hotel.

From her notes: *I stood on my balcony looking out over the town and down to the gardens and kidney shaped swimming pool. Birds sang and flew all around. I ate a leisurely breakfast and then took a walk through the gardens. Groves of olive, orange, lemon and tangerine trees! Flowers in abundance—geraniums, roses, cactus, bougainvillea, wisteria, and fabulous shrubbery.*

In the afternoon, we all drove into Cordoba's old town and walked the quaint alleys called *las callejas.* Picturesque white houses with red tiled roofs, courtyards, fountains and flower filled balconies lined the narrow streets. Graceful seventeenth-century arcades surrounded Plaza Corredera, and a sixteenth-century fountain gushed in the center of Plaza Potro. We crossed the old Puente Romano (Roman Bridge) spanning the Guadalquivir, and threw some of our popcorn to the fish, and visited the Mezquita, an enormous eighth-century mosque that was converted to a cathedral in the thirteenth century. Wonderful arches, gates, courtyards, fountains and domes continue to preserve the building's Moorish flavor. We admired the ruined Alcazar fort and the city's medieval gates and watched artisans turning fine wooden table legs on lathes driven by foot pedals.

Christmas was only a week away, so we returned to the city the next morning to shop for a couple hours before driving south to Granada.

Castles, windmills and sheep punctuated the picturesque Spanish countryside, and once we saw a Gypsy family in a colorful, horse-pulled wagon. Espejo featured a fortress, Castro del Rio, which was surrounded by orchards bursting with ripe fruit. Baena boasted an ancient wall with a fine tower and a Moorish castle. The children decorated stockings for Christmas and sang carols. Once, when they stopped singing, Grammy gave us her rendition of *Granada*. We stopped along the roadside, and, while the girls fixed lunch, Mike and I went bird-watching, climbed down a hill to a river and saw a fox. Through the haze, the distant snow-capped peaks of the Sierra Nevada slowly assumed more definition. Late in the afternoon, we drove into the city to one of the world's architectural treasures, the Alhambra, just to see it. Touring it would come later. Gram checked in at the Hotel Atenas, and we registered at the municipal campground where we met two very nice young couples, one from Vancouver (Maureen and Rob) and one from Australia (Gail and Ian).

Lynette began our walking tour of historic Granada at Capilla Real (Royal Chapel), the sixteenth-century Gothic church containing the mausoleum of Ferdinand and Isabella. She took us through Albaicin, the Moslem old quarter with its narrow streets, crowded plazas, and remains of Moorish battlements, and then we visited Santa Maria de la Encarnacion, the sixteenth-century Renaissance cathedral with an impressive dome and colored marble exterior.

We crossed the Rio Darro and drove to the Alhambra, the thirteenth-century Moorish palace of Al Ahamar. Rarely can words adequately describe indescribable beauty. Washington Irving had the unique genius to do so, and, in his *Tales of the Alhambra*, accomplished the impossible, creating in words an altogether splendid description of the Alhambra's incomparable beauty. All of that said, I have to tell you, my mother, who barely finished tenth grade, described the Alhambra in her notes creditably:

We drove up the mountain to the Alhambra, the Moorish citadel which overlooks the city. Construction of the first palace here was begun in 1238. It is surrounded by walls fortified with 13 towers. The complex is entered thru the Puerta de las Grandadas or Gate of the Pomegranates. Inside, we visited the Alcazaba, an 11th-century Moorish citadel of which only the outer walls, towers and ramparts remain. The Palacio Arabe has many intricately carved ceilings, arches, columns and fountains. We entered the palace thru a courtyard, the Patio de los Arrayanes, with a marble colonnade and a pool with goldfish. The Patio de los Leones is surrounded by 124 white marble columns and paved with colored tiles, and contains the fountain of the Lions, an alabaster basin supported by 12 white marble lions. The patio walls are of blue and gold tiles. Also here is the Palacio de Carlos V, begun in 1526, it was never finished. It has a courtyard in the center. The park in the complex has pools, orange trees, myrtle, hedges and flowers. After lunch, we went to the Generalife, a summer retreat of Moorish kings. It is beautiful, serene, and relaxing. It is a maze of terraces, grottoes, fountains and pools. From here is an excellent view of the city, and on the opposite mountain (Sacromonte or Sacred Mountain) we could see the caves where Gypsies have lived since the sixteenth century.

While strolling through the gardens of the Generalife, we met the Aussie and Canadian couples from the campground. Ian and Gail's camper had been broken into the previous night, and their keys and money had been stolen. Maureen and Rob said they saw a suspicious man looking around our camper, and Gail and Maureen said they saw a guy looking in a high window when they were in the bathroom. With that bit of disturbing news, none of us was in a hurry to return to the campground. Instead, we drove up the Camino del Sacromonte to see the Gypsies. In a little bar/cafe, a man played flamenco music on a guitar. The waiter told us that, later in the evening, the place would be full of people dancing the traditional *zambra*.

After eating dinner in the camper, Lynette and Gram went to the campground bathroom together. They came back and said that a guy had walked into a stall Lynette was using. I went to the women's building and found a tall, thin boy, apparently in his late teens, loitering in the back of the building. He told me he worked there and was emptying wastebaskets. I asked him to come with me. Lynette identified him as the guy in question, and, when I called the other two couples, Gail and Maureen did the same. While we discussed what we should do, the culprit walked into the men's building and locked the door. I ran around the back of the building and caught him when he lept from the window. Rob, Ian and I held him, and, while we led him to the campground office to call the police, incredibly, he broke away from the three of us and ran out the gate and away from the campground. He was a very fast runner, and, after a few hundred yards, we lost him. All of us decided it would be prudent to leave the campground and travel together.

I walked across the street to check Gram out of her hotel. I told the clerk our story, but he still insisted I pay for her room. I told him I wouldn't pay and that he should call the police. He picked up the phone, thought better of it, and told me to forget it. The three campers headed south in tandem and found another campground near Motril.

From Motril, our three camper caravan followed the Costa del Sol (Sun Coast) past fields of sugar cane and banana trees and hills with herds of grazing goats. Perched on a knoll overlooking the white houses of Salobrena, the ruins of a castle no longer provided protection for the picturesque village. We continued through the quaint beach town of Nerja to cosmopolitan Malaga, Picasso's birthplace, where we stopped to secure Grammy's arrangements to fly home from Casablanca. The Aussies and Canadians continued on to Estepona where we intended to meet them in a day or two. Gram took us to dinner that evening at Antonio Martine, a popular local restaurant with a commanding view of the harbor. Lynette and I tried the paella, Krissie and Gram ordered the more familiar wiener schnitzel, and Mike, who enjoyed eating fish as much as catching them, courageously selected a mixed plate of fried fish including sardines and squid. A pile of curly, deep fried curiosities, looking a bit like small, thin onion rings, also lay on the plate. The waiter explained these delicacies were unborn baby squid. While Krissie and Lynette squirmed, I tried to keep the conversation positive.

"Mike, do the babies taste like the adults?"

"No, Dad, but they're very good. Would you like to try them?"

"No, thank you. What do they taste like?"

"Kind of lemony. You can tell when you come to the eyes; they're crunchy."

We picked Grammy up at the Hotel Maestranja and walked through a park which Gram remembered as ...*a vast one, with fountains and ponds, lovely trees, purple and red bougainvillea, and date palms.* Our route followed the Gold Coast south and west through old Andalusian fishing villages which have become picturesque artist havens and tourist destinations. We walked the narrow shopping streets of Torremolinos, ate lunch on Fuengirola's beach, and admired Marbella's "beautiful sea." Gram checked into the Hotel Caracas, and then we registered at the Estepona campground on the beach where our friends from Granada greeted us, saying they had saved us a campsite next to them. Grammy stayed with the children and Maureen and Rob, while Ian, Gail, Lynette and I walked on the beach, scattering sanderlings and ringed plovers, and talking about Australia. That evening we drank cheap Spanish table wine.

From my notes: *Maureen's a bit drunk, but still vivacious. Rob, who is 23 and just received his bachelor's degree in public transportation, and I talk about business school.*

Estepona, Spain, December 22, 1974

The next few days we spent relaxing on the beach, waiting for Christmas. Siskins and goldfinches flitted about the campground conifers. Lynette gave Mike and me haircuts. Krissie made friends with a beautiful little redhead from Nova Scotia, and they spent a whole afternoon building a wall of sand and stones. Mike played beach soccer with her three brothers, and Lynette and I met her parents while doing our laundry. In town, we boys bought poinsettias for our wives and Gram, and Lynette ordered several roasted chickens for our Christmas dinner to which she invited our young neighbors. With a hatchet, I hacked off a large tree branch, hacking off the tip of my thumb in the process, and, with twine, rigged it among our campers as the community Christmas tree. The children cut snowflakes and ornaments, including a star for the top, out of foil wrappers they had been saving from chocolate bars, and hung them.

After dinner one evening, while the children studied in the camper, Lynette and I walked slowly along the beach, sipping coffee. A clear, star-studded, night sky covered the Mediterranean. I broke the silence.

"Things don't look so good back home."

"What do you mean?"

"The economy. It's getting worse."

"So what?"

"Maybe we should go home."

"Why?"

"I'm concerned about being able to get a job. When the economy's bad, people don't hire."

"So let's take another year and do Africa and Asia. Probably then the economy will be better, and it will be easier to find a job."

What she said made sense, but I was losing it. I had not held down a job for over a year. Maybe at heart I was not a true drifter. I wanted to go home and get productive again, whatever that meant. The two of us talked more about it over the next few days. In the end, we decided to go to Morocco and get a flavor for North Africa and the Sahara, then return to Europe and fly home. Looking back, I often wish we had continued drifting for another year or two, but, at the time, I couldn't do it. Our lives certainly would have been different had we done so. I guess I was the only one in the family not ready to go on.

On the day before Christmas, we walked into town for our final Christmas shopping and then wrapped our gifts. The owner of the campground walked by each camper, wishing everyone "Felices Navidades," and generously gave every adult a bottle of champagne. Lynette hosted our party on Christmas Eve, serving popcorn, potato chips, roast chicken, corn on the cob, and plenty of wine. We sang carols, got fairly smashed (even Lynette), and had a blast. At one point, a French Canadian and I got into an argument on a subject I knew nothing about—Quebec separatism—had another drink and agreed to disagree, then, with an arm around each other's shoulders, joined the caroling.

Christmas Day of 1974 was crystal clear in Estepona. Despite our hangovers, we could see the Rock of Gibraltar thirty miles away and the coast of Africa beyond. We waited for Gram to arrive from her hotel and then opened presents—my favorite being from Lynette, a copy of Washington Irving's *Tales of the Alhambra*.

Late in the afternoon we took leave of our friends and drove south to Algeciras. Gram's notes commented, *Lovely countryside and oceanfront, and The Rock getting closer all the time. It looks just like Prudential says it does.* Grammy registered at the Hotel Reina Christina, and we set up camp in her parking lot where the five of us had a supper and watched the lights of Gibraltar greet the darkness.

The day was overcast, but, thankfully, the seas were calm for the one and a half hour crossing of the Straits of Gibraltar. After our arrival in Spain's African enclave of Cueta, Spanish and Moroccan customs cleared us relatively quickly, and before long we were seeing camels. On the drive south along the Mediterranean, storks hunted for frogs and snakes in the marshes, shorebirds foraged on the beach, and wintering shovelers filled saltwater inlets.

Our route turned west through the former Spanish Moroccan capital of Tetouan, and, while crossing the rugged Rif mountains, took us past Moorish villages with colorful mosques where men wore striped robes and women with shawls covering their faces wore colorful costumes and wide brimmed hats. We descended to the Atlantic fishing town of Larache, turned south and, near Souk-el-Arba-du-Rharb, stayed the night at a small but pleasant hotel/campground complex where we were required to endure English hunters returning late in the afternoon from their endeavors. How proud they were of their prowess in killing with shotguns dozens of snipes, small birds with bodies not much more than five inches long.

On the drive south, along the Atlantic, the surf pounded against the rocks and sprayed a hundred feet into the air, and *casbahs*, or walled fortresses, guarded the coast from perches on high cliffs. Many women worked in the fields, others carried babies on their backs and water jugs on their heads. People sat or walked along the road, some of them waved and others tried to hitch rides.

From Mother's notes: *When we stopped in towns, children flocked to the camper begging. One sweet little boy turned nasty and spit at Lynette through the window when she said no and closed the door. Ugh!*

Morocco's capital of Rabat featured Roman ruins, medieval walls and Islamic mosques. We continued south through Mohammedia to Casa Blanca where Gram registered in a hotel in the Centre Ville, and the municipal campground was quite nice. We confirmed Gram's tickets home and picked out a French restaurant where we would celebrate Krissie's eighth birthday the next day.

Happy Birthday, Kristen! She was so excited, she wakened us at 5:00 a.m. From my notes: *Krissie looks so grown up in her new blue and yel-*

low knit dress. After she opened her gifts, we picked up Gram and took Lynette's walking tour of exotic, old Casa Blanca with its narrow streets and Moorish architecture. We joined the people of the desert, shopping in the souk and enjoying the spicy aromas of the open air market. Gram watched with amusement as we bargained so seriously, sometimes only over pennies. Back at her hotel, with Lynette's help, Grammy itemized for customs declarations all the gifts she had bought. After she finished packing, we went to Krissie's French restaurant to celebrate her birthday.

From Krissie's notes: *Saturday, Dec. 28, 1974. It was my Birthday! I got a braclet from Mike. I got a purse from Juile (her best friend from Minnesota), and a dress from Grammy K. and Grandad W. We drove in town. I got a birthday cake! It had eight candles. We picked up Gram. We walked around. I bought a lolly pop! Man it was good. We went out for dinner. I had an omlette. We had cake and a double ice cream cone for desert.*

Lynette made breakfast in the camper, parked at the airport, while I went to Pan Am to check Mother's bag and choose her seat. Tears filled all our eyes when Gram boarded her plane.

From Mother's notes written the night before: *I'm anxious to go home tomorrow, but I do hate leaving all of them. It's been a wonderful six weeks, and the time seems to have flown by. This has been an experience I never dreamed I would ever realize!* And, from her notes written on the plane: *We ate breakfast in the camper, and then it was time for our goodbyes. They were wet ones. I hated to leave.*

Dramatically silhouetted against the pale blue sky, camels grazed in the sparsely vegetated desert south of Casa Blanca. Picturesque oases occasionally appeared. The high Atlas mountains provided a scenic backdrop fifty miles in the distance. The earth turned red as we neared Marrakech, and so did the buildings, constructed of bricks from that same clay. We all missed Gram, but I had other thoughts. I was so happy that she had been brave enough to travel so far by herself. Confident and rather matriarchal at home, she was wide-eyed and innocent abroad. For the first time in my life, I saw her as the girl she left behind when she quit school and went to work on her sixteenth birthday. She always enjoyed reading about exotic places, and now, incredibly to her, she had seen some of them in person. My thoughts then are now vindicated, almost twenty-five years later. Today, when she still talks about our drifting through southern Europe and Morocco in a camper, the girl returns, and she counts the experience as one of the highlights of her life. Mine too.

The hot desert sun heated water that ran through black hoses switchbacking across the bath house roofs in the Marrakech campground, providing daytime hot water showers. Hippies from California, Canada, Australia,

Holland, and Germany filled the campground. We didn't smoke dope, but in many other ways, we felt right at home. We had read Michener's *The Drifters*, and the book didn't seem all that alien to us. Istanbul, Kathmandu and, of course, Marrakech were primary destinations, almost Meccas, for the hippie drifters in the 1960s and 1970s. The more foreign the culture, the more comfortable drifters felt. And old, red walled Marrakech, situated at the foot of the Atlas Mountains, was positively exotic. Berber tribesmen, Arab merchants and craftsmen, and Moslem black Africans converge daily on Djemaa El Fna, the old town's huge central square. Dancers, snake-charmers, fire-eaters, musicians and acrobats provide constant entertainment, story-tellers spin their age old tales, and water sellers carry skins of water that they spray into elaborate brass and copper cups, quenching parched throats for a few cents a drink.

Snow fell the night before in the high Atlas, creating a breathtaking contrast between the white peaks and the red town. We walked from the campground into Djemaa El Fna where a host of aromas, most of them pleasant, wafted through the open air of the market. We wandered around the square, snapping photos of the performers as unobtrusively as possible. Can you imagine the mesmerized looks on the children's faces while they watched a cobra rising from a basket, hypnotized by the charmer's waving flute, or their astonishment when a tall, slender African, wearing only a loincloth, inhaled fire from a torch and blew it out of his mouth and nostrils? An enormous market, or *souk*, surrounded the square, and we had been warned not to enter the confusing labyrinth of shops without a guide. An eleven-year-old boy, irresistibly handsome, approached us.

"Mister! You want to go to market? See wool souk? Tin, silver, gold souks?"

"Stop, I have no money."

"I no want money. I only want to speak English with you."

Later we learned that, in addition to his native Arabic dialect and English, he spoke French, German, Italian and a little Spanish. We agreed to be guided through the various souks, but I resolved to remember our route and not be dependent upon this boy. He led us into the warren of shops, and, at each turn, I stopped to imprint one or another landmark. Alas, after three or four turns, I was hopelessly lost. Mysterious music and veiled-faced women drifted through the narrow streets. Our young guide took us to each souk or collection of shops specializing in wool or other fabrics, rugs, furniture, jewelry, etc. In the wool souk, we watched wool being spun, dyed and then woven on looms into rugs. Artisans crafted tin, silver, and gold into jewelry and clay into pottery. A man propelled a lathe with a bow, masterfully turning a table leg with a knife sharp chisel. In shops, the bargaining attained levels of seduction we had not seen before:

"Very cheap, I show you. Only two hundred dirhams."

"I can't afford it."

"What will you pay?" What is your last price? Speak to me your serious price."

"Fifty dirhams."

"What is your last price above fifty dirhams?" At this point our little guide begins arguing with the vendor, ostensibly for our benefit.

"I tell him you have little money. He will come down his price."

And it goes on. Mike and I bought Berber knives and the girls a few pieces of inexpensive jewelry. Later, a man offered us the "student price" rather than the "capitalist price" he normally charged Californians and Germans while persuading us to let the children ride on his camels, and then hugged and kissed us all when we agreed. Back at the campground, a Berber man made the rounds selling wool blankets hand woven by his wife and daughters. He pointed to the Atlas Mountains and said he lives there with his family of seven children. We traded old clothes, which he greatly preferred to money, for a blanket.

Krissie's version of the day's events: *Monday, Dec. 30, 1974. We walked in town. It was 2 miles. A little boy came up to us and gave us a tour of the Berber market. We saw some men weeve rugs and blankets. Mike bought a nife. We saw a mosk. We got to ride a camel. I got on a baby one too. When we were sitting in the camper a man sold us a blanket. We traded some of my cloths. We saw a snake charmer.*

An arm of the Atlas range protruded toward the Atlantic, requiring us to negotiate a tricky, cliff-hugging, gravel road without guard rails and to cross the cold seven thousand-foot Tizi-n-Test pass before descending to Agadir's warm, sandy beaches. Along the way, we visited a mule market at Tahanaoute and stopped for lunch near the pass. Colonies of burrowing, squirrel-like ground mammals with large, flat tails lived in the meadows surrounding our luncheon pullover. Lynette predictably christened them "squeavers." In the lowlands south of the pass, adults wore indigo robes and children's heads were shaved except for a pigtail. As the rocks and soil changed color from red to brown to gray, so did the villages built of the same material, blending into the landscape and often betrayed only by the shadows they threw. Prickly pear cactus enclosures fenced in livestock. Donkeys and camels grazed on sparse vegetation, and goats climbed low branched cypress and olive trees to eat the leaves—a most unusual sight.

We sat several days in Agadir's very nice campground with hundreds of other campers who fled Europe to spend January on the sunny beach. The town was modern and uninteresting, having been rebuilt after an earthquake destroyed it fifteen years before. We relaxed—swimming, reading, shelling, looking for birds and cleaning the camper. From Krissie's notes: *It was new years day! I found some girls to play with. I played "May I" with my friends.* Lynette bargained with the same man for two days over a blouse and eventually bought it.

We headed east and a bit north, back across the High Atlas and through the colorful desert. Near Taliouine, a boy tended his tree climbing goats. We set up camp in a pullover near Ouarzazate and, with three local boys, traded a few old clothes for stones—calcite, gypsum, topaz, amethyst and cobalt. Later we walked out into the desert and found our own stones in a dry *wadi* or riverbed. We continued north through spectacular desert and mountain scenery, past oases like Ait-Benhaddou and Tiffoultout, each of which had a casbah. Poor but friendly Berbers had their distinct style of colorful dress and camels pulled single bladed plows. We saw groves of date palms and a fine casbah in the Dades Valley and an impressive gorge near Tineghir.

Late in the afternoon we arrived at Erfoud on the edge of the Sahara and found a small campground surrounded by a walled enclosure in which we were the only guests. A young man came to our camper and offered his services to guide us into the desert the next day. During our negotiations, he noticed our Coleman stove and insisted that he preferred it to money. We explained it didn't work very well. He said, never mind, he could fix it. We had a deal—our stove for his services. Then the campground guard, an old veiled woman wearing silver necklaces, bangles and rings and blue tattoos on her forehead and hands, invited us to her mud brick home for tea. It had been a long day, and the children were already in bed, so we politely declined her overture. Soon she returned with tea service for five and an armful of colorful bead necklaces. She obviously was in a trading mood, eventually talking us out of a towel, my ski hat, and two pairs of stockings.

Off to the Sahara! Or, at least, to its edge. Atmospheric conditions must have been perfect for mirages that morning. Lakes appeared and, as we approached them, disappeared. In the distance, I saw a heavily laden caravan of camels. We drew closer, and, magically, the vision turned into a young goatherd walking with his small flock. Tent dwelling nomadic tribes-people, hardy Berbers, tended their animals and ignored us. Stones packed into the sand gave the desert's surface an almost asphalt like firmness that allowed easy driving. Far away the flat horizon took on a waviness. We were approaching the Grand Erg Occidental, the Great Western Sand Desert. Small at first, the dunes became enormous, fifteen hundred feet high. The wind sculpted intricate patterns and contours in the slowly drifting, beautifully colored orange sand dunes, nature once again displaying, as she so often does, unparalleled artistry. Near the Merzuga oasis, I shot a photo of Mike and Krissie laughing and running down a dune, their long straw colored hair blowing behind. Our guide took us to a nomadic village where people lived in wool tents and grass houses, and to a briny lake, pink with carotene pigmented greater flamingos, and then to an area rich in fossils, large and small, left from three or four hundred million years ago when the Sahara was submerged by the sea.

From Krissie's notes: *We got a giude to take us to the desert. I beet evreone onto a sandoon. We saw people that were like Jipsees. They were called nomads.* And from my notes: *I am fascinated by this immense other world. Nowhere have I ever seen anything remotely like it. Now I know, one day I will have to return to the Sahara.*

We threw some clothes into the deal when we dropped our guide off in Erfoud. He had been a bargain. We filled up with gas in Ksar el Souk and found a small campground in Midelt.

The imperial city of Meknes retains its rich market town flavor with an extensive and colorful souk and buildings and gated walls dating back to the thirteenth and fourteenth centuries. We walked through the large, elaborately decorated Bab Monsour gate into the magnificent Dar el Kebira palace complex and then to the old medina where street vendors sold us skewers of lamb and vegetables for lunch. We continued on to Fez, arriving late in the afternoon at the busy campground which, surprisingly, offered plug in electricity for our small space heater. Mike and Krissie kicked around a soccer ball with two young Australian friends they had played with in Marrakech while Lynette prepared a delicious stew for supper.

More than a thousand years ago, the Arabs swept across North Africa and founded Fez, and, today, life in the old town has not much changed. One of the world's largest souks comprises a multitude of covered bazaars in which operate an endless variety of artisans, markets offering everything from food to rugs, jewelry shops and ethnic restaurants. Exotic music and aromas drift through the labyrinth of twisting, narrow streets, and muezzins call from numerous mosques. After entering old walled Fez through one of its impressive city gates elaborately decorated with blue tiles, we strolled around Fez el Bali, the Old Town. We saw the remarkable El Kairouyyin and other ancient mosques, the amazing Dar El Makhzen (Sultan's Palace) with its golden gates, and the Medrassa (colleges) of the oldest university in the world.

The difficult, unpaved road to Tetouan, twisting through the Rif mountains, took much of the morning to drive and assured us of not making the early afternoon ferry from Cueta. Space was available on the 8:30 p.m. boat, so we took it and then slept in the parking area of customs in the port of Algeciras, Spain. In the morning we drove only a few miles to Tarifa and stopped at a terrific campground on a hillside with a ruined tower, a sandy beach full of shells, and a marvelous view of North Africa. A dozen or so cats prowled the campground, and the children adopted two kittens whom they named Charlie and Elizabeth. Charlie, especially, had a lot of character, and it was tempting to take him along with us, but he seemed happy and well fed. In the warm late afternoon sun, we drank wine with an English couple we had met in Yugoslavia and watched the ships filing through the Straits of Gibraltar out to the Atlantic.

Phoenicians founded Cadiz three thousand years ago. Over the years since, the colony succombed to the Carthaginians, Romans, Visigoths and Moors, and then became part of Christian Spain in 1262. We toured the old city with its Moorish watchtowers and thirteenth-century Catedral Vieja and then headed north through vineyard surrounded Jerez de la Frontera, from which comes the name for the fortified wine we know as sherry. We stopped to watch two bulls fighting in a pasture and then drove to picturesque Sevilla (Seville), the home of ballad-singing Gypsies, matador-fighting bulls, and whirling flamenco dancers, not to mention Don Juan and Figaro. We visited charming neighborhoods, or *los barrios*, such as Macarena with its Roman walls, Calle de la Feria with its flea market, and especially Barrio de Santa Cruz with its maze of narrow streets and balconied houses. We toured the thirteenth-century, twelve-sided Torre del Oro (Tower of Gold) and then walked across one of the tiled bridges to beautiful Plaza de Espana and visited the fifteenth-century Gothic Catedral de Santa Maria de la Sede, the third largest in the world, in which lie the remains of Christopher Columbus.

South of Sevilla, near Torre de la Higuara, herons, ducks and waders filled the marshes of the Guadalquivir River delta. Further west, in Huelva, we admired the 115-foot statue of Christopher Columbus, and, in La Rabida, from where the discoverer departed on his voyage to the New World, we visited the fifteenth-century Iglesia de San Jorge (Church of Saint George) in front of which he recruited his crew. From Krissie's notes: *We saw the church where Christafer Columbus signed up his men to take the boat to Amarica. We had dulishish cheese fondu.*

A ferry transported us across the Guadiana River into Portugal, and we drove west along the rocky coast through the fashionable resort town of Monte Gordo to Olhao, a photogenic town with a North African flavor. We registered at a very nice campground, and, while eating dinner in the campground restaurant, met the Dutch owner who had been an exchange student at Lynette's alma mater, DePauw, when she was there. Even though they had not known each other, they of course had mutual acquaintances and had a gay time playing "remember when..."

A flat tire greeted us the next morning, Sunday, and the local service stations were closed, so we spent another day reading and sunning on Olhao's sandy beach. We had our tire fixed first thing Monday morning and drove west with the surf pounding the rocky coast and lapping the lovely white sand beaches of the Algarve, Portugal's most southern province. On the way, fishermen and their boats filled the scenic harbor in Portimao and Henry the Navigator's statue filled the square in Lagos. Whitewashed villages with red tile roofs dotted the picturesque and somewhat primitive countryside. People rode in carts with large, solid wooden wheels which were pulled by horses with red collars. Lynette thought it a bit reminiscent of Ireland. When we counted, there were more people driving motor scooters than cars.

Charming Lisbon, the City On Seven Hills, has been around for thousands of years, at least since the Phoenicians, and the broad Tagus River estuary, from where Vasco de Gama set sail for India, has always provided the city with an avenue to the sea. Colorful floral plantings filled iron balconies on the pastel colored, tile-facaded houses lining Lisbon's narrow, tile-inlaid streets. We strolled through the ancient Barrio Alto with its interesting sixteenth-century Igreja Sao Roque (Church of St. Roque), and then around the Alfama (Old Town), dating from the sixteenth-century Moorish occupation, where the twelfth-century Cathedral of Lisbon looks down on the Tagus. We climbed Lisbon's highest hill to the Castelo de San Jorge, originally built by the Visigoths fifteen hundred years ago. The castle dominates the city and offers splendid views of the old town and the Tagus estuary, and behind its walls we found lovely gardens and aviaries with elegant white peacocks, swans, doves and many smaller birds. We admired the large equestrian statue of Jose I on impressive Terreiro do Paco (Black Horse Square) and, while we inspected the shops on the Chiado, the city's Champs Elysees, the rains came.

We knew our adventure was winding to a close. Winter clasped the Iberian Peninsula firmly in its grip, and, as a cold rain doggedly hounded us on our drive north, we pressed onward, more interested in going home than weathering the storm. We made almost perfunctory stops in Obidos with its fine Moorish castle and city walls, in Alcobaca, the scene of the romantic tragedy of Dom Pedro and Ines, and in Batalha with its Santa Maria Monastery dating back to the fourteenth century, and then camped near Coimbra's sixteenth-century Holy Cross Monastery where we saw a number of wintering red kites. The rain continued through the night and the following day. We crossed the Estrelha Mountains, drove through Guarda, an ancient town with Paleolithic ruins, and then back into Spain. We stopped briefly in Ciudad Rodrigo, a town featuring ruins of a Roman bridge and aqueduct, a twelfth-century Romanesque cathedral, and a fourteenth-century fortified castle, and then continued to beautiful Salamanca, the golden walled city designated in its entirety as a national monument. After registering at the municipal campground, we walked to the porticoed Plaza Mayor with its impressive baroque buildings and visited the twelfth-century Catedral Vieja, or Old Cathedral, and the sixteenth-century Catedral Nueva—you guessed it, New Cathedral.

In the morning, we pressed on, north and east, through Valladolid, the city of Phillip II's birth, Ferdinand and Isabella's marriage, and Columbus' death, and through medieval Palencia. Despite the gray rain, the snow cov-

174

ered Cordillera Cantabrica provided an impressive backdrop in the north for the quaint rural landscape. We continued to Santillana del Mar, the quaint seaside village surrounding the sixth-century Monastery of Santa Juliana, and planned to tour the famous Caves of Altimira to see the Paleolithic rock paintings of animal figures. It was such a disappointment to find them closed for restoration. We found a virtually deserted but nice campground, however, and spent the evening drinking wine and talking with the couple who owned it. They laughed at our Spanish and said we sounded like we were from Mexico.

The Basque country, Spain and France, January 18, 1975, Odometer—18,123 miles.

The rain continued, and so did we, following the coast of the Bay of Biscay, through the Basque country. We drove through old Bilbao and the resort towns of Zarauz and San Sebastian and the medieval, walled border town of Fuenterrabia, then crossed into France where Krissie was impressed that "the policemen wore flat hats." The rain stopped, and a few patches of blue appeared. We rolled through Ravel's birthplace, St. Jean-de-Luz, and the pretty Basque seaside resorts of Biarritz and Bayonne, then continued north past vineyards and *chateaux* of the picturesque Bordeaux countryside, and found a very good campground open on the Dordogne River near Libourne.

For some reason, my notes stop here. I suppose I was no longer in the drifting mode, probably thinking about getting a job and wondering where we would live. I remember we drove through the chateau country in the Loire Valley, stopping at wine caves and *chateaux* along the way, and spent a few days in Paris with our friends from Minnesota. Within two weeks we flew to New York and then took a train to my parents' home in Pennsylvania. We bunked with them for a couple weeks and then with Lynette's parents in Winnetka for a similar period while I looked for a job.

I don't remember now my thoughts then about the year and a half of drifting we had just finished. I do remember being surprised when, right after he told me I was hired, my new boss asked, "You aren't thinking of taking any more of those long trips, are you?"

I had to think, because I knew, like a bird that had just completed its long migration, even though I had absolutely no intention of going anywhere, one day the irresistible urge would return. After a few seconds of consideration, I smiled and answered, "No, I'm not thinking about it. And I'll commit to not thinking about it for the next five years."

That was good enough for him.

In retrospect, that year and a half was magical. Our little family was closer than it would ever be again, and I have to tell you our family is still very close. Lynette and I would do a lot more drifting in the next twenty five years. There would be marvelous experiences and wonderful times I'll always cherish. But never again would we regain that singular magic of the four of us living in a little Volkswagen camper—cooking, sleeping, teaching, studying, learning—and loving every minute of it.

INTERREGNUM #1
Call It A Mid-life Crisis

In 1954, Frank Smith, with the financial help of the adventurer/broadcaster, Lowell Thomas, founded Capital Cities Communications which would become one of the great companies in the history of American business. In 1957, "Cap Cities" offered its stock to the public for $5.75 a share. When the company acquired American Broadcasting Companies (ABC) in 1986, a transaction many compared metaphorically to "the minnow swallowing the whale," one of those original shares had grown in value to more than $5,000. At the time of the Capital Cities/ABC merger with Walt Disney Company in 1996, that same share was worth more than $10,000, an increase of nearly two thousand times the original investment.

I joined Capital Cities in 1975 after returning from our camper trip through Europe. For two years, I ran one of the company's weekly newspapers in Arlington, Texas. Then, for ten years, I ran one of their daily newspapers in Belleville, Illinois. I owe my modest financial success to this company, and, more important, I owe my business ethic to the men who ran the company with uncompromisingly high standards.

This remarkable company's philosophy of doing business was very simple: Hire intelligent people; explain to them what their job is; make sure they know how to do it; then get out of the way and let them do it. Once a year the operating heads of each Cap Cities property gathered at a corporate meeting to review the past year's results and the budgets for the next year. Tom Murphy, the CEO, wisely recycled the same basic speech every year which stated the above hiring philosophy, reminded us to run our property as if we owned it, assured us that no one would ever be fired for making a mistake, but emphatically admonished us that there would be no second chances for improbity.

Life was certainly good. Tom Murphy called the operators who ran the company's properties "The Crown Princes" of Capital Cities and, without exaggeration, said we had "one of the world's best jobs." For ten years, I ran a newspaper, one of the largest companies in southern Illinois, with no interference from my boss, and made more money than I ever thought I would, probably more than I was worth. Lynette and I had enjoyed twenty-two years together. Mike was in college and Krissie in high school, and both were developing into people who made us proud to be their parents. We lived in a beautiful house and had many good friends. How could anything be better? After ten years, all of a sudden, I found myself asking that question too often.

Call it a mid-life crisis, or whatever. But I thought I knew what was bothering me. I was climbing the same mountain every year, and it just wasn't fun anymore. I was bored! What was worse, it didn't look like anything was going to change. And that began to drive me a little crazy. And pretty soon

I began to drive Lynette a little crazy.

"What's the matter with you?"

"I don't know."

"You've got everything anyone could want."

"I know. But I'm bored."

"Well, what are you going to do about it?"

And conversations in some variation of the above exchange took place almost every day. Then one day Lynette said, "You're just going through your mid-life crisis."

Why not? I was forty-five. Certainly other guys and, I suppose women too, near my age experience similar questions about their careers. Some have been "pushed aside," "bumped upstairs" or even fired. Others feel they're "tired of the rat race" or see someone else getting the promotion they're convinced should have been theirs. Whatever the case, it seems to me that many of us just get tired of what we're doing. At least, that's what happened to me. I'd spent ten years in the same job that had become very easy and very boring, and prospects for a change just didn't look very good.

Coming to terms with the idea of leaving Cap Cities was not easy. Lynette thought I was more than a little wacky to be thinking about quitting a company that had given me my own property to run and then left me alone to run it the way I wanted.

"What more could you want?"

"I don't know."

"What are you going to do?"

"I don't know."

"How are you going to figure it out?"

"I'm going skiing."

We had a little condo in Jackson Hole, Wyoming. A few days by myself out there, away from employees, customers, lawyers and telephones seemed like a good prescription for some clear thinking. I grabbed George Gilder's *The Spirit of Enterprise*, a book I had been wanting to read, and winged my way to the erstwhile trapping digs of Davy Jackson.

Jackson Hole, Wyoming, February, 1985

The skiing was marvelous—no lift lines, powder on Rendezvous Bowl, and warm sun at the top of the mountain. Each evening, after enjoying a supper of pasta or ribs and a beer at the Mangy Moose, I walked back to the condo and picked up Gilder's book which, intellectually, was just what I needed. I thought George was trying to tell me something—show me a way out of my boredom. He said enterprise was alive and well, not only in Japan, but also in the good old U.S. of A. I knew I was a pretty good "mechanic" and could keep a company running pretty well. That, as I learned at Cap Cities, was easy: Look for more revenue, don't spend money you shouldn't, get good people and let them do their jobs. Nothing to it. Prosaic after a while. But George was talking about something different: Coming up with a new idea! Bringing it to the marketplace! Creating jobs! Now that sounded like fun!

Then the phone rang. Little did I know that my entrepreneurial fantasy was about to be shattered.

"Hello?"

"It's me."

That would be my friend, Mark.

"What's up?"

"I just wanted to see how you're doin'." Mark cares about things like that.

"I'm fine. Good skiing, good food, and a blazing fire. What else is there?"

"Are you finding any answers?"

"I don't know. Maybe I'm just tired of being a mechanic. I've been reading this book about entrepreneurs. Maybe I should do something entrepreneurial."

Silence...more silence.

"Hello?...Mark?...You there?"

"I'm here. I'm thinkin'."

"What are you thinking?"

"Forget it."

"Forget what? What's wrong with this conversation?"

"Forget bein' an entrepreneur."

"Why?"

"The world needs mechanics. Some people are good at startin' things. Some people are good at keepin' em goin'. Stick with the girl you brought to the dance."

That's Mark. Nothing glossy. Most of the time he couldn't make up his mind what restaurant to go to or what to eat after he got there. But when this old boy acted with certainty, you could bet he was on to something. And he sure knew the difference between a mechanic and an entrepreneur. I guessed, at the time, whatever I wound up doing, in one way or another, I would stick with the girl I brought to the dance.

So then I had another thought. Why do anything right away? It might be time to get some living done, time for some drifting. There were still many places to see, especially the four As—Africa, Alaska, Asia and Australia. Then, after a year or two of drifting, instead of deciding what I wanted to do and, like we always have done, moving where the job takes us, why not do the reverse? Why not take some time to decide where we really wanted to live, move there, and then decide what to do to make a living.

I returned from Jackson Hole with an answer for Lynette. She neither understood it nor liked it. I began the long process of trying to persuade her for the second time to sell her beautiful home and leave her friends. For me, the decision was already made. It was just a question of when. A year before, the idea of leaving one of the world's great companies would have been too alien for me. Now I had become comfortable with the idea.

Less than two years later, at the end of 1986, I left the company. Early in 1986, one of the few jobs in the company in which I had any interest became open. It was given to someone else, and I was given a consolation prize, being responsible for a group of newspapers in addition to my own. Of course the people who ran this wonderful company made the decision they thought was best. It wouldn't have been my choice, however, but, by then, I had other things on my mind.

I bought a brand new 1985, brown Volkswagen camper in, what I thought was, silent anticipation of our next trip. Over a year remained before I would announce my departure from the company. While many of our friends knew about our previous travels in Volkswagen campers, the implication of my buying this one escaped everybody; that is, everybody except Lynette's friend and confidante, Barbara. At a party, she waited until I was alone and then walked over to me smiling.

"Darwin, what is it with the Volkswagen camper?"

"I like Volkswagen campers, Barbara. What else is there?"

"You're out of here, aren't you?"

"What do you mean?"

"I smell an odyssey. Where are you going this time? Africa? Asia?" Being Barbara, she was tenacious and smoked out the truth. I asked her to keep it confidential, and, true to her word, she never told a soul except her husband, Ed. However, in exchange for her confidence, she did extract a commitment to keep them informed of our plans.

"Who knows... Ed and I might want to join you somewhere along the way."

Chapter Four
The Call of the Wild: Alaska

Let us probe the silent places, let us seek what luck betide us;
Let us journey to a lonely land I know.
There's a whisper on the night-wind, there's a star agleam to guide us,
And the Wild is calling, calling... let us go.
From: *The Call of the Wild,* **by Robert W. Service**

Krissie, Thompson Pass near Valdez

PREPARATIONS

The Iranians hated Americans and the Soviets and Afghans were killing each other, making crossing Asia a very complicated affair. That would have to wait. We thought distant Australia might tie in well with an Asian trip someday, and therefore put the land down under out of our consideration for the time being. That left Africa and Alaska. We decided to take a year and do them both, Alaska during the North American spring and summer, saving the Sahara and equatorial Africa for the fall and winter. Over the years we had traveled and camped in much of the United States, but we had never seen western Canada, the Yukon, and America's last frontier, Alaska—our largest state with the most lakes, greatest number of islands, longest shoreline, the world's largest glaciers, and North America's largest mammals and highest mountain.

I was anxious to sail among the many islands of the Inside

Passageway, gaze upon the stark beauty of the Alaska and Brooks ranges, follow countless species of birds that had flown thousands of miles over oceans and mountains to reach their nesting grounds in the Arctic tundra, and marvel at countless caribou migrating in enormous herds. I wanted to visit Eskimos and Athapascans in their native environments. I wanted to see the contemporary pioneers John McPhee talked about in *Coming Into the Country*. Who were these people who chose to live with such difficulty and why did they do it? How did they differ from the rest of us who chose the familiar, the comfortable, the traditional? But mostly, I think I was feeling just a bit of what Robert Service felt when he wrote *The Call of the Wild*.

Alaska and Africa. Why not? Adventure, scenery, cultural diversity, and wildlife awaited us in those two lands a world apart. The decision was made. Drive to Alaska and back, ship our camper to Africa, and all the while be thinking about where, after we finished traveling, to settle down. For nearly two years before leaving Cap Cities, I spent my spare time planning the trip. I read everything I could find about independent travel in Alaska and Africa. Lynette slowly became accepting and even enthusiastic about our plans, but it was difficult for her. She had been uprooted before, but this time we were leaving our college age children behind. Selling our house, placing our pets with friends, disposing of many memorable things at a garage sale, and putting our furniture in storage wasn't much easier.

Health care is always an issue on these trips, especially when time will be spent in remote areas and/or in tropical countries. We underwent physical examinations, brought our recommended immunizations up to date, and assembled a functional first aid kit which included antibiotics, a variety of medicines, malaria prophylactics, syringes, needles and sutures, and a complete first aid manual. We hoped to be prepared in the event of an accident or emergency. However, we readily agreed that, if either of us became seriously ill, whatever the cost, we would scuttle the trip and fly to a hospital in Europe or the U.S.

In 1985, Volkswagen no longer enjoyed the distinction of having the cheapest camper on the market. However, the manufacturer had improved the unit, enhancing the engine's power, installing a two burner gas stove, and replacing the icebox with a bona fide refrigerator. The newer version was quite comfortable, especially considering it only had to accommodate two rather than four people.

We led a festive social life the two weeks or so before we left, attending parties and farewell dinners with friends. Our party clothes were in storage, so we had to wear our traveling clothes to these functions, showing up very casually, like we had just emerged from the bush. Our being underdressed wasn't a problem for Mark who thrived on casual. We met him and his wife, Carol, and another couple across the Mississippi River in St. Louis for dinner at Favazza's, a casual Italian restaurant on "The Hill." About the same time I left my job, Mark, who was younger than I by a few years, sold his company. He had been investigating several possibilities that would permit him to offer his services gratis for a year or so, and, coincidentally, had learned only in the past few days he was going to be working as a United Nations volunteer in Geneva.

"Any regrets?" Mark probed.

"About what?"

"Leavin' the job."

"No, not really. I'm doing exactly what I want. There's only one problem."

"What's that?"

"I don't know what to tell people when they ask me what I do. Like, on visa applications. They have a space for your occupation. Technically I'm retired, but I feel too young to be retired. It's embarrassing."

As a young man, Mark was a pretty good boxer, advancing with some distinction in the national Golden Gloves competition. Boxing metaphors infiltrated his everyday speech. For example, in business, he didn't "compete," he "duked it out."

"Whaddaya mean 'embarrassing'? I tell everyone I'm retired. I love it. Let 'em think we're retired. We'll fool around for a couple years just doin' what we want. Just long enough to let 'em forget about us. Kind of like our own version of 'rope-a-dope.' Then we'll be just like Ali! We'll come out of retirement and be even better!"

Lynette grew up as a suburban girl. She pictured a married life similar to that her parents led—me commuting to "The Loop" on the Chicago-Northwestern, her packing groceries and the kids in a station wagon, and us playing bridge on our neighbors' screened porch on Saturday nights. I grew up quite differently, hunting, fishing, trapping and camping in the central Pennsylvania countryside. Aside from our year and a half drifting in the early seventies, we had spent most of our married life as suburbanites. Our vacations, on the other hand, were usually spent in the out-of-doors. The arrangement worked well. We had joined our good friends and neighbors, Janet and Dick for dinner at Cunetto's, also on "The Hill." Dick was a hardworking attorney and wondered aloud how I could toss my career aside and drop out. Lynette smiled and offered, "I've seen it coming for years."

"What do you mean? How did you see it coming? I didn't know I was going to drop out until two years ago."

"Because you're all alike."

"Who are all alike?"

"Boys! You all become men and then, sooner or later, you want to go back from where you came! You never were a suburbanite."

For the past couple of years, since we had decided to uproot ourselves, we had been checking out potential places to live. I wondered if we would ever find a place on which we could agree. One evening I offered a brilliant proposal to solve our dilemma.

"Lynette, this marriage is a partnership, and where we live should be a joint decision."

"What a revelation."

"How about I come up with ten places that are acceptable to me? You choose any one of those places, and that's where we'll live."

"How about I give you ten places and then you choose?"

"Sure, you'll pick ten suburbs of Chicago."

"O.K., give me your ten picks."

"Jackson Hole, Tucson, Sedona, Santa Fe, Mendocino (California), Colorado Springs, Anchorage, Bar Harbor (Maine), Hanover (New Hampshire), and Victoria (British Columbia). Not necessarily in that order."

"Interesting. I'll think about it."

As long as winter was likely to embrace the Inside Passageway for a few more weeks, we decided to begin our Alaskan adventure with a diversion to the Southwest to see if we wanted to settle somewhere out there when our year was finished.

Only a few days remained before our departure. Spring had arrived in southern Illinois. Magnolias and forsythia were blooming in the woods behind our house, and dogwoods and redbuds weren't far behind. Crocuses and daffodils colored the lawn, and the tulip buds were loosening. Worm-eating migrants were just beginning to appear as the leaves on the oaks, hickories and sycamores began to unfurl. Lynette and I taped and tied boxes and did our last minute packing. My pal, Albert, and I snuck away with our binoculars whenever we could to see what birds were coming through. One afternoon we added an albino robin, mostly white with an orange breast, to our short list of local albino spottings which previously had included a cardinal, a red-tailed hawk, and a house sparrow. Lynette, with some help from me, brought the house to a spotless condition, and my notes accusingly state, "She means to get the house cleaner when we leave than it ever was while we lived here."

On our final day, the movers left late in the afternoon. My notes don't include how we felt about leaving. I suppose we were ready to get on with the rest of our life.

Interstate 70, between St. Louis and Kansas City, March 30, 1987

So here we were, on our way to Alaska... via Arizona! We stopped somewhere east of Kansas City for a fast food supper at the Golden Arches and continued west to Lawrence where we spent the night in our camper parked in a service area on the Kansas Turnpike. We arose early, and I was shaving when a truck driver walked into the men's room and bid me a good morning with, "Oh shit! One of those mornings."

"At least it ain't snowin'," I observed in the vernacular of the highways. The road to the west had been closed twice in the past couple of days when blizzards blew through. The morning was beautiful and deserved better than this sourpuss had to offer. Besides, this was the first day of the rest of my life, and I thought it was pretty great.

Driving west, Lynette pointed out an abrupt line in the distance where the green of winter wheat gave way to the white of snow. We stopped at a roadside rest and learned this was the land of the anti-slavery guerrillas known as Jayhawks. I was ecstatic about being on our way, but Lynette seemed mildly depressed and wasn't talking much. Listening to Gilbert and Sullivan makes me dizzy, but Lynette likes their operettas. I put on a G&S tape to try to cheer her up. We crossed the rolling hills of western Kansas and eastern Colorado toward the Rockies, and, just as the snow-capped peaks came into view, left I-70 and headed southwest to Colorado Springs where we found a run down but clean campground open. The next day we drove four hundred miles to Durango and registered at a campground which had just opened that day and at which we were the only ones staying. Were we pushing the season a bit?

The owner had designated a portion of his farm for camping. In the reception room, a stack of quarterfold magazines on Colorado camping had a sign encouraging me to "Take One, Free," so I did. I gave it to Lynette, and took my binoculars to a field next to the camping area to look for spring migrants. A black goat nursed two very young kids and a stallion sprinted across the pasture. I heard Lynette laughing and returned to see what was so funny. She pointed to a picture of the husband and wife co-publishers of the camping magazine. The man, Hilton Peaster, had escorted her to the New Trier High School Junior Prom.

Pinyon pines, junipers and large spruces replaced desert cacti along the road winding its way upward to the Mesa Verde cliff dwellings, the ancient home of the Anasazi who had lived on the mesas until the twelfth and thirteenth centuries when, for some reason, most likely defensibility, they moved down to the cliffs. Lynette said the walk back to the cliff housing would have been quite difficult had the Anasazi not gone to so much trouble building such a nice road. Later we stopped at Four Corners, the location where corners of Colorado, New Mexico, Utah and Arizona converge, the only such point in the U.S. A man asked his wife to take a picture of him with his foot covering the unique point which was marked with a plaque on the ground. He raised his right hand with four fingers erect. He laughed good naturedly when I told him the surveyors had made a mistake and the point in reality was over that red rock cliff a half mile to the north.

We entered Arizona and the Navajo Reservation. A sign along the highway advertised dinosaur tracks. A boy and his grandmother sold her hand made jewelry at a roadside stand. Other women in traditional garb tended sheep and goats. I asked the woman where we could see dinosaur tracks, and she offered the services of her grandson as a guide. The boy motioned for us to follow him and pointed to an adobe village lying at the foot of a cliff a couple of miles away.

"That village is our home."

"Is that where your grandmother makes her jewelry?" I asked.

"Yes. We get our water from a spring. And we have toilets."

He had been through this before. We returned after a fifteen minute walk through the desert where the boy showed us many tyrannosaurus and dilophosaurus tracks, seventy million years old. The boy had done his homework and was expert on dinosaurs, especially these two species. It was obvious to us that this fine boy loved his job, his grandmother and his people.

'How much do I owe you for your guide services?

"How much am I worth?"

"A lot more than I can afford to pay."

Mount Humphreys and the other San Francisco peaks soon appeared in the west, rising abruptly from the desert floor. We camped in Flagstaff and the next morning drove on to Sedona through spectacular Oak Creek Canyon with its ancient red wall cliffs painstakingly carved by cottonwood lined Oak Creek during many millennia past. Arizona's scenery is unsurpassed. Since Sedona was one of the ten choices I offered Lynette, we drove through the town's lovely subdivisions, all with wonderful views of red rock formations framed by clear blue skies, and checked the prices on houses for sale. We ate lunch outside on a restaurant deck thrust over a ravine filled with willows and cottonwoods. Four kestrels were doing their spring thing, diving and looping and displaying, shining orange and blue in the bright sunlight, demonstrating phenomenal aerial gymnastics to anybody caring to look. We walked through the shops and galleries of Tlaquepaque and then left for Phoenix via the copper mining ghost town of Jerome and then Prescott. We crossed the Prescott Valley and picked up I-17 south toward Phoenix.

Geographic names in the American West, including Arizona, take first prize for originality and descriptiveness. Driving south on I-17, signs advised us of the approach to Horse Thief Basin, Bloody Basin Road (Lynette said that one was probably named after a guy like me who was always looking at a map while he was driving.), Dead Man Wash, and the seeming redundancy, Table Mesa. Lynette explained the derivation of that one when "some dude told his pardnur to look at that mesa yonder whut looks like a table." The desert was coming alive with yellow, orange and purple flowers, and the late afternoon sun highlighted the cholla.

After seeing a sign for the Maricopa County Shooting Range and Camp Ground, we exited at the Carefree Highway and for only three dollars had a picturesque desert camping place with hot showers.

"Why is this place so cheap, Lynnie?"

"Maybe they expect you to run around and let them shoot at you."

A cactus wren's low-pitched rattle pierced the cool morning air as we took a brisk walk around the perimeter of the campground. Lynette spotted a Bendire's thrasher and a curve-billed thrasher foraging in the sagebrush, offering an unusual opportunity to compare these similar desert species next to one another. A small group of pickup trucks with camper inserts on the back was parked near us. Most of the occupants were men and appeared to be shooters. We walked by one truck where three guys fried bacon and eggs over an open fire.

"Smells good! Can you put a couple more on?'

"Sure can. How y'all want em?"

Who says shooters can't be good guys?

On the drive to Carefree we chose a tape of Strauss waltzes to accompany the array of colorful hot air balloons taking advantage of the morning thermals. A verdin sat on a shrub whistling while we drank coffee at one of Carefree's outdoor cafes. Further south, in Scottsdale, we toured a number of western art galleries and then continued south, stopping at a roadside rest for lunch. I opened a bottle of wine while Lynette retrieved a bagette and a chunk of Gruyere. At a campground in Tucson, we washed the Kansas winter and Colorado dust off our camper and did our laundry.

From my notes: *Hope Lynette likes Tucson. Unfortunately she has a cold—nothing looks good when you're not feeling well.* She did like Tucson after touring the city, looking at some subdivisions in the foothills, and watching skiers on Mount Lemon.

We camped at Molino Basin where Lynette rustled up some soup with noodles and ring bologna added for substance while I was out chasing a painted redstart. We wrote letters to the children and shared thoughts about Lynette's dad who had recently passed away. She said one of her fondest memories was when we arrived for our last visit before he died, six-foot three-inch Mike bent over his much shorter grandfather, hugged him, and Grandad Woots looked up and said, "How are you, Mike, old boy?"

During the night, coyotes paid us a visit and serenaded us just outside the camper. We spotted a pair of Lewis' woodpeckers on our morning walk, and I reported them to the Tucson Audubon Club since, it seemed to me, they were out of their expected range. The woman who answered the phone said they had been seen off and on all winter and thanked me for letting them know they were still there. We drove to Tanque Verde Ranch east of Tucson to see the "dudes" and then to the University of Arizona campus. We ate dinner at a fine restaurant in the old town and then set up camp at Catalina State Park, north of the city. The park bathrooms lay an inconvenient quarter of a mile from our camp site. Upon awakening in the morning,

Lynette complained, "It's a long way to the bathroom."

"But it's a nice walk."

"Not when you have to go, it isn't."

I joined her on the bathroom trek and was rewarded along the way by seeing about a half dozen vermilion flycatchers attracted, possibly, by Lynette's shirt of the same color, and by hearing the trilling songs of numerous Lucy's warblers.

Lynette and I decided to take off a few pounds. She was reading a book called *Fit For Life* that made a pretty good case for becoming a vegetarian. We were getting close to California and, I suppose, becoming a vegetarian sounded pretty much like a California thing to do. Around noon we drove into a roadside rest.

"What's for lunch?" I wanted to know.

"Sandwiches."

"What kind?"

"Vegetable."

"Vegetable? What's in a vegetable sandwich?"

"Lettuce, cucumbers, tomatoes, avocado, and sprouts."

"No meat? Who ever heard of a sandwich without meat?"

"Give it a try."

The sandwich, of course, was excellent. That day I became a vegetarian and remain so today.

The afternoon turned hot, and Lynette said, "I could go for a Dairy Queen."

"What does the guy in the book say about eating Dairy Queens on this diet?"

"I haven't gotten to that chapter, but I think he thinks they're good for you."

We entered California on I-10, and the contrast occurred to me—our driving to California in our nice little camper compared to the Okies in Steinbeck's *Grapes of Wrath*. We stopped for the night at a marvelous, if primitive, almost deserted campground in the hills of Joshua Tree National Monument. We hadn't enjoyed a shower for several days, so I hung up the water bag of our portable shower. It was late in the afternoon, and the sun didn't have enough time to work its magic on the transparent plastic bag. I strapped up the shower in the unoccupied women's wash room. Then I heard Lynette screaming and squealing while she showered with water from which the chill had hardly been removed.

As dusk gathered, a camper near us set up a sophisticated looking telescope. I asked him if there was anything special to be seen tonight. He replied that every clear night is special to an astronomer. I learned that he was a druggist from Modesto, and that he had taken up astronomy as a serious hobby. He was really setting up for an early morning view of Saturn and invited me to join him. I arose at 4:30 a.m., but we had to wait a bit for the moon to set before we could see the planet. This guy, Dennis, turned out to be very interesting. He played saxophone in a classical quartet, was quite an expert on Civil War history and ran a pharmacy for a living. He planned to get married soon and said the only thing wrong with life was that there wasn't enough time to do everything he wanted. Later in the morning, Dennis, Lynette and I hiked to Cottonwood Springs where we saw an old abandoned mine along the trail and the Salton Sea in the distance. Dennis was familiar with Tucson, liked the city, and said he had recently heard the symphony perform Mahler's 5th and that they were "really good."

Lynette treated for lunch at an opulent restaurant, the name of which escapes me, in Palm Springs. We crossed the desert and drove north through Bakersfield to Sequoia National Park. I assumed California's nickname of The Golden State referred in some way to the 1849 gold rush. The true derivation of the nickname could just as easily be the state's vast mountain meadows spectacularly ablaze with springtime golden poppies. We marveled at the giant sequoias, many of them having been quite tall over two thousand years ago when Aristotle was teaching young Alexander of Macedonia.

We continued north through the magnificent Sierra Nevadas into the Yosemite Valley where we camped and where every turn of the road brought another heroic Bierstadt vista. I always thought his paintings were overdramatized—not so. You have to see Yosemite Falls, Half Dome and the rest of the vista up the valley in person. The clouds, mist, sunlight and shadows create dramas that Bierstadt in no way exaggerated. We saw several herds of deer while walking to Lower Yosemite Falls and admired formidable looking El Capitan. Along the road a car had stopped, and the driver was feeding a coyote. Another car had to slide to an abrupt stop to avoid hitting the animal. I walked up to the first car.

"Respectfully, Sir, feeding the animals is dangerous to everyone, especially the animals."

"Well, we won't feed them anymore," he responded seriously and credibly.

Heading north for Lake Tahoe, we drove through old gold mining towns with colorful names like Chinese Camp and Angels Camp, the latter the setting for Mark Twain's *The Celebrated Jumping Frog of Calaveras County*.

Lynette's great, great, great uncle, Isaiah Hoover, soldiered for the Union Army in California during the Civil War. In his diary, he described a large, beautiful lake he called "Lake Bigler," a body of water we could never find on contemporary maps. Lynette's dad concluded Uncle Isaiah had to be talking about Lake Tahoe. Uncle Isaiah had little formal education, but he described his experiences with lyric enthusiasm. From his diary, his thoughts about Lake Bigler/Tahoe:

Camp No. 12, July 27, 1862, At Lake Bigler in the mountains. The sun rose and I felt much better. The first thing that I don in the morning was to step to the shore of that majestic body of watter and you bet it looked grand. One broad sheet of watter as far as the eye could carry with her blewe crested waves rolling to and froe. This lake is betwixt the two summits and it reminds me of past days. And what a beautiful viewe for the artist. I think it is the most beautiful viewe that ever my eye rested on. I think it caps them all. This lake is from 15 to 20 miles wide and forty miles long and the circumference is 300 miles and the depth is not knowing for they have sounded in several places and have found no bottom. Yet they have went down over 400 feet they told me and no bottom. As for me I think the bottom is hell. Out there is some of the finest fish that ever swum in watter but that is all the good it don us as we had plenty of hooks and lines. But no bite him John! The lake is magnificent. All around her shore the tall pines border her. To the north there is snow peaks looming up and to the west. So take this all into consideration it presents a grand viewe. Thus I close.

The next day he wrote: *The sun was fast sinking in the west it was a very beautiful site to look at. The lake and the clouds seemed to meet and the reflection on the clouds looked as tho they had been bathed in blood. There was several little sail boats that looked like white specks on the dark blowe watters.*

Lynette insisted I defer to Uncle Isaiah and call the lake "Bigler," and that I pay her a nickel every time I said, "Lake Tahoe." We were the only campers spending the night in the snow covered state park campground on the west shore of Lake Bigler. That evening I nosed out Lynette for the Lake Bigler cribbage championship.

We drove along the lake to Squaw Valley, spotting two white headed woodpeckers on the way. A sign advertised "Nevada Weddings—$39," and a small wedding party celebrated at a scenic pullout overlooking the lake. We drove through the Comstock Lode country, stopping in Carson City, Virginia City and Reno, and then drove back into California, crossed the Donner Pass and descended through the golden poppy strewn foothills of the Sierras to the bluebonnet covered hills of Napa Valley. We read about a campground near Lake Berryessa. I asked a kid on a bike directions to the lake. He told us to drive to "Spanish Fly" and take a right. He meant "Spanish Flats." At the campground, while I was washing bugs off the front of our van, I heard one guy call to another, "Hey Getsy!" That was the first I had heard that name since I was a boy. Gordon "Getsy" Smeal was a friend who never seemed to have his heart in it at school. But was he ever good in the "woods!" Whether it was catching frogs, fish or shooting marbles, Getsy was without equal. I thought about the popularity of nicknames when we were kids—"Getsy" and his brother, "Hot" Smeal, "Skinch" McGraw, "Smoke" Barge, "Red" Boyer, "Had" Stare, "Heavy" Reider, "Butch" Griffith, "Junior" Fusselman, "Sag" Espenshade and the Pfautz brothers— "Fearless," "Fearful" and "Scareful," to name a few. I didn't remember our kids' friends having such colorful nicknames and wondered why.

We tasted wine at half a dozen Napa Valley wineries and toured Beringer. Fritz was the older Beringer brother, and, as was the custom in old Germany at the time, inherited the family business. Jacob, the younger Beringer brother, learned the trade working as an apprentice in a German winery, came to America and ran a winery in New York State, and when he heard this winery in Napa was for sale, borrowed $14,000 from Fritz and bought it.

You can bet we were half blitzed by the time we got around to fixing a picnic lunch in mid-afternoon. We had been in touch with Dori and Karl, our pals from South America, and had made plans to have dinner with them in Sonoma. I had seen them a year and a half ago at their home in San Francisco, but Lynette had not seen them since we left them in Peru thirteen years before. Karl made reservations at a restaurant owned by an old shipmate of his. We had a wonderful time, talking long into the night. We reminisced about South America, and it seemed Karl might be getting the wanderlust again. Over the years I have felt closer perhaps to Karl and Dori than many other friends we've known better, probably because of the unique adventures we shared.

We wound our way north along the California coast, stopping for lunch in Mendocino. A few years before, we had searched the Maine Coast in vain for Cabot Cove, the television setting of *Murder She Wrote,* only to learn the picturesque little harbor was a continent away in Mendocino. Several dozen brants swam just outside the breakwater and presented our first glimpse of the western race of this species. We continued north, stopping for the night in a wonderful redwood forest thirty miles south of Eureka and knowing we had less than a week to our ferry departure from Vancouver Island.

A curtain of fog and rain greeted us as we crossed into Oregon and remained with us up the coast until we turned east and found the sun in Eugene. We met friends for lunch in Albany and continued north through Portland. The weather worsened as we drove north through Washington, and we camped in the rain at Potlatch State Park.

Wintering ducks filled Port Townsend's harbor, and gray clouds filled the sky, but, at least, the rain had abated. We ate breakfast in a short order restaurant with a bunch of overage hippies, and Lynette, a celtic harp aficionado, bought a Patrick Ball tape. Then we drove to Port Angeles, caught the Vancouver Island ferry, and enjoyed a smooth crossing to Rudyard Kipling's favorite city in the world, Victoria. Harlequin ducks bobbed along the shore of the outer harbor, while fishing boats and pleasure craft bobbed in the Inner Harbor. The city enjoys a year round mild climate and exudes English charm—from the turreted Parliament Buildings and the ivy-covered Empress Hotel to the beautiful ever flowering gardens, tearooms, double-decker buses and horse-drawn carriages. In the parks, large, intricately carved and brightly painted totem poles are reminders of vanishing native cultures of the Northwest.

The municipal campground on the harbor offered terrific views of the city and of lumbermen in hobnail boots walking across large rafts of logs floating in the harbor. The sun shone warmly, and we strolled through Beacon Hill Park, enjoying the flower beds and cricket games. We explored the shops and had tea in the Empress Hotel, ate dinner in a small Italian restaurant, and then strolled again around the Inner Harbor, getting a feel for the city and admiring the lights of the Parliament Buildings.

Butchart Gardens is arguably the finest botanical facility of its kind in the western hemisphere. Tulips, daffodils and azaleas bloomed in colorful profusion. Spectacular tuberous begonias burst with enormous blossoms in a fabulous array of colors—from white to pink, red to orange and yellow to bronze. We strolled through the English Rose Garden, the Japanese and Italian gardens and the magnificent Sunken Garden, and we had "tea" in the Greenhouse before turning our attentions north again.

Route 1 wound its way through the clean, quaint, island towns along the scenic eastern shore of Vancouver Island. A clear, beautiful day afforded marvelous views past forested islands and across the Strait of Georgia to mainland British Columbia with its snow-covered mountains and twisting fjords. We crossed the Cowichan River at Duncan and just had to drive by the Glass Castle, a house built with thousands of bottles stacked on their sides. Fishing and logging provided the economic backbone of communities like Ladysmith, Nanaimo and Campbell River, while towns like Parksville and Qualicum Beach thrived as summer resorts and centers of outdoor tourism. At Port McNeill, we saw the Vanishing River plunge underground into a maze of caves and disappear, and, at Port Hardy, we parked under a lonely Douglas fir in the municipal campground. A bald eagle sat near the top of the fir, watching thirty Nimpkish Indian boys playing soccer in the park next to us.

While taking a morning shower, I met R.V. ("My name's Rollie, but call me RV.") Wagner. He and his wife were traveling with several other couples from Oklahoma. RV worked for Arco and was proud of the company's role in the North Slope oil development.

"Why are you going to Alaska, RV?"

"Ah'm anxious to get into some real fly fishin'."

"Living in Oklahoma, I'd bet you're a bass fisherman back home."

"Ah shure am. What do y'all do fur a livin'?"

"I'm a newspaperman."

Later in the morning, RV said he supposed I would be writing about our travels and asked me to mail him any articles I wrote.

"I will for sure if I ever write anything, but it may be some time before it happens."

The Scottish influence on the town was evident by the names on the retail shop signs. Friendly locals chatted on the streets in the warm morning sun. We bought a small electric heater for the camper, two ceramic cereal bowls to replace our plastic bowls, and filled our propane tank. At the ferry dock, we waited in line to load our vehicles, and it was evident we were departing for Alaska. Men wore jeans, sweaters or flannel shirts, wool hats, hiking boots and beards. Women wore sweaters, corduroys, boots and bandanas covering their long hair, tied behind. A rugged looking couple sat in a pickup truck in front of us. She had the face of a woman in her twenties, but it was heavily creased, creating the impression she was older and had led a tough life. Lynette frowned.

"It's obviously the way he treats her. A woman shouldn't have to live in such a harsh environment."

"Maybe you'll look like that in a year."

"Try two weeks."

We boarded the *Queen of Prince Rupert* and soon were crossing the open waters of Queen Charlotte Sound. RV's wife didn't feel well, so Lynette gave her a few motion sickness pills. The Coast Mountains rose directly from the sea and penetrated the clouds hanging over the mainland. People excitedly rushed to the windows to cheer on a half dozen dolphins racing the boat. We entered Fitz Hugh Sound; the Passageway narrowed and the mountains closed in on us. From the ship's railing, Lynette and I were watching a dozen bald eagles working the shore line through our binoculars when I sensed that someone had joined us. A tall, blond young man smiled into his binoculars and said, "I see you're bird watchers. I'm a bit of one myself."

Dave had lived in Prince Rupert for five years and had just put his house up for sale. He was a steam engineer for a pulp company, and his wife was an optician. He had told his boss he was ready to move on to something else and was returning from Vancouver where he had a job interview with a company that converted industrial and municipal waste into energy. They and twenty-eight fishing families lived on an island with no roads or schools. In "his and her" boats, they commuted to the mainland where they kept two cars to drive to work. I thought he might be the only North American I know who didn't have a TV. That night, after Lynette turned in, Dave and I bought each other a couple of beers in the ship's lounge.

Prince Rupert's *Queen* sailed into the harbor past cranes transferring coal and grain from railroad cars to a large ship, the *China Fortune*. We registered at the municipal campground perched above the mouth of the Skeena River and spent the afternoon in the campground laundramat. I had loaned Dave several tapes of bird songs to take home and copy. His wife, Myrna, had left town for a few days, so, when he returned the tapes, he spent the evening with us. We enjoyed tomato soup, grilled cheddar cheese sandwiches, Vivaldi and wine for supper and cribbage and wine after.

In the morning, Lynette conducted her walking tour of the town. We visited the terraced Sunken Gardens behind the attractive courthouse, the art deco city hall and a park with two interesting and colorful Haida totem poles flanking a statue of the town's founder named Hays who died on the Titanic. He had gone to Europe to raise funds for the completion of a railroad from Rupert to the interior. Down by the docks people wore knee-high Wellingtons (rubber boots), eagles soared above the blue waters and two ravens were busy building a nest.

Dave picked us up at the docks shortly after noon in his aluminum runabout. He manuvered us through the colorful fishing fleet and across the deep water harbor into a cove where prehistoric Indians had carved figures into rocks. The best was a replica of a person over five feet tall called "Man Who Fell From Heaven." Dave guessed the carvings were over two thousand years old. Lynette packed us a lunch which we munched on while we explored life in the tidal pools, and Dave had brought fruit cake and coffee which we put away while motoring in and out of coves and around small islands, birding. I saw my first ever yellow-billed loon, a fairly uncommon bird, and we identified a number of gulls, common and Pacific loons, red-necked grebes, guillemots, goldeneyes, buffleheads and pelagic cormorants. That evening Dave joined us for dinner at Smile's, a local favorite specializing in fish (halibut) and chips.

After a long wait at U.S. Customs, we drove aboard the *Taku*, one of the huge blue and gold ferries in the Alaskan Marine Highway fleet. The five and one-half hour voyage to Ketchikan was uneventful. I stood by the ship's railing following gulls and small alcids with my binoculars, trying to distinguish among the latter as they bobbed on the water's surface and dived with the approach of the ship. Two women joined me.

"Have you seen any whales?" one of them asked.

"No, I haven't. But I'm really looking for birds more than for whales."

"Oh, my mother is a bird watcher. Did you see all those eagles along the shore shortly after we left Prince Rupert?"

Before she finished her question, two glorious bald eagles soared across the bow of the ferry, and we all gasped. Both women taught French at a high school in Saskatoon and were off to Juneau for spring break. One grew up in France, the other was born there but grew up in Canada, and they spoke both French and English without an accent.

Ketchikan, Alaska, April, 21, 1987

The ship steamed past Misty Fjords National Monument and then dramatically threaded its way through the narrow strait between Gravina and Revillagigedo islands before arriving at Ketchikan, Alaska's southernmost and North America's wettest community with more than 150 inches of precipitation each year. Ketchikan was as I had imagined—colorful wooden buildings with tin roofs, mountains rising steeply only three or four blocks from the sea, a deep blue water harbor, and intermittent rain falling from always churning clouds.

We drove off the ship and stopped to see the Totem Bight where numerous magnificent totem poles are on display and a tribal lodge house floats during high tide and rests in the mud at low tide. Continuing downtown, we quickly concluded that Ketchikan's float planes far outnumbered its automobiles. Lynette's walking tour led us past *The Raven Stealing the Sun* and other totem poles featuring eagles, wolves, bears, whales and ravens. The tour also included the colorful Thomas Basin waterfront with its multitudes of fishing boats, Creek Street where former bordellos perching upon stilts and jutting over Kechikan Creek have been restored and converted to shops, and the Deer Mountain Hatchery and salmon ladder. Stores sold little of interest for tourists and outsiders, catering mostly to the much more practical needs of locals. We stopped at a small grocery store to buy milk for breakfast. I asked the proprietor, "If you only had one night to spend in Ketchikan, where would you choose to eat?"

"There are three places worth mentioning, but with only one night, I would pick The Narrows. Try the halibut or the shrimp. They're both excellent."

We took his advice. The attractive old establishment, cantilevered over the Tongass Narrows, presented a fine view. The owner told us she had bought the restaurant about a year ago and wasn't certain it was a good decision. Her first husband had been killed in a fight, and she was about to divorce his replacement. Worse, I looked around and saw only two other tables occupied. The food was very good, and so was the friendly piano player, Bob Arden, who asked us to say hello to some people at a restaurant where he used to play in Anchorage.

Ketchikan's municipal campground, built by the Civilian Conservation Corps, sat on the edge of scenic Ward Lake. I had just slipped out of consciousness when the sound of Lynette's voice prodded me awake, "Are there bears here?"

The next morning we discovered our camping neighbor was Howard Lentz, RV Wagner's brother-in-law.

"So you're married to RV's sister? Where is she?"

"She's at home. She don't go for this roughin' it."

"She's in Oklahoma?"

'Nah. We live in Spokane, actually. Spokane's kind of a backward place that's goin' nowhere. But that's all right, cause I fit right in."

Lynette and I walked the perimeter of Ward Lake. Sitka spruce, hemlock and alders comprised the forest, and yellow lilies lined the shore. Common mergansers and a red-throated loon swam in the lake, diving for fish. Eerie, flute-like notes emanated from the conifers, the chillingly beautiful song of varied thrushes. Pine siskins sang their trills and twitters, and Steller's jays called, "Scraaatch, scraatch scraaatch!" Lynette sat on a rock, and a beaver paddled up to her, chewing on a branch it carried.

We drove into town the next morning and passed a pulp mill, a cannery and four or five dozen brightly colored bush planes, and then stopped at Helen's Tea Room, an establishment specializing in fudge and chocolate pie. Business seemed slow, but Helen didn't care, since she expected it to pick up in the summer when the cruise boats began coming, and, besides, she enjoyed the off season better because "I have more time to talk with my customers." A woman sitting next to us wore a U.S. Forest Service uniform and asked us how long we would be in town. She and her husband had tried to homestead in British Columbia in the seventies, but the Canadian government insisted that they renounce their U.S. citizenship. Officials told them they had grown tired of "undesirables," a reference to kids from the U.S. trying to escape the draft during the Vietnam era. The couple eventually gave up their quest, moved to Hyder, a small settlement in Misty Fjords National Monument, and, three years ago, they again moved to Ketchikan.

"Why did you leave Hyder?"

"Oh, there was a shoot-out."

"A shoot-out?"

"Yes... My husband was the ringleader of a group of townspeople trying to get rid of drug trafficking. More outsiders were coming in to work at the copper and gold mines, and they were bringing in drugs. The problem had gotten out of control. There was no local law enforcement. We were under Ketchikan's jurisdiction, and the police only came up there once or twice a year."

"So they formed a modern day vigilance committee."

"Yeah... Kind of."

"What happened?"

"Well... they burned our house down and one of them shot my husband through the neck. As he was falling, he shot back and killed the man. He was indicted for first degree murder, because he had a gun with him. The prosecutor said he should have run away and let them burn the house down. The judge disagreed. He said you can't run away from a 357 magnum. He let him off on self defense."

Several fishing families lived on Herring Bay. A fisherman was working on some nets. I waved and held up my binoculars.

"OK if we walk out to the point and check out the birds?"

"Sure, go ahead."

"We won't disturb anything."

"Ain't nothin' you could disturb out there."

We had some time to kill before our ferry left, so Lynette led us into an opal shop on Creek Street where the chatty Australian owner gave us a lesson on opals. He was anxious for the cruise season to begin and said we were lucky, this was the first sunny weather they had seen in three weeks. Bob Arden, the piano player from The Narrows restaurant, walked by outside the shop. We excused ourselves and joined him on a stroll to Thomas Basin where we inspected the fleet of fishing boats. Most of them sported names of women. Wives and girlfriends, I suppose—June Rose, Katy D., Jodi, Marcie K., and even Princess Diana. We followed Bob's advice and spent our last hour in town visiting the Totem Heritage Center, an interesting museum containing information about native people of the Southeast Alaska and British Columbia coast and featuring Tlingit (Klink-it), Haida and Tsimshian art.

Our ferry, the *Aurora*, stopped in Hollis, not much more than a ghost town. A guy steered a small fishing boat with a Johnson outboard motor to the pier and waited for his wife and daughter. They loaded a couple of dozen boxes of groceries onto the little boat, then chugged across the bay and disappeared into the darkness. I talked with a young man also standing by the ship's railing. He was on his way back to Petersburg where he worked long hours in a cannery and saved his money so he could travel for months at a time. Killer whales and porpoises raced and played tag with the boat, and deer swam across the Wrangell Narrows. Once, when the fog acquired pea soup density, the ship anchored for two hours in the Narrows, waiting for better visibility. There were no cabins available on the ferry, so we took our sleeping bags from the camper to the ship's solarium where, in the open air, we slept well on recliner chairs.

A high school track team disembarked at Petersburg, and, since the ferry would be in port a few hours, so did we. The small town was settled by Norwegians and retains its Scandinavian heritage. Quaint and traditional hand-painted floral designs adorned brightly painted wooden houses. Equally colorful fishing boats bobbed in the harbor. Lynette and I walked out of town on a boardwalk, also decorated with floral designs, and, for the first time, encountered muskeg, a boggy, spongy soil formed by the accumulation of spagnum moss, leaves and other decaying vegetation. We admired world record salmon in a museum and wondered about a very curious admonition on a sign by St. Peter's Episcopal Church—"Thou Shalt Not Park Here!"

The *Aurora* stopped briefly in Kake, a Tlingit village with the world's tallest totem pole, and then continued north through Chatham Strait and around Baronof Island to historic Sitka, once the capital of Russian America. Lynette's walking tour included Castle Hill, the site of Alexander Baronof's headquarters, and the mid-nineteenth-century Russian Bishop's House. Isabelle Miller gave us a personal tour through the historical museum that was named after her and gave us a copy of her biography from the local newspaper. We visited the Sitka National Historical Park where, in 1804, the Battle of Sitka was fought between the Tlingits and the fur hunters of the Russian-American Company. There is a marvelous cultural center and twenty-eight Tlingit and Haida totem poles. Late in the afternoon, for a five dollar fee, we arranged to spend the night camped in the parking lot servicing the fishing fleet.

The coffee was hot at the new Sitka McDonald's the next morning. I walked out on the deck to scope the various sea duck species diving in the foamy water below the restaurant. A man approached me, offered a cheerful "Good Morning!" pointed to our little VW camper and, got right to the point.

"How much did that rig cost?"

I came up with a ball park figure close enough to satisfy him.

"Where you from?"

"Wyoming. How about you?"

"Montana. Been here twenty-five years.'

"You like it here?"

"I like it everywhere, but the kids won't leave." He pointed across Sitka Sound to the mountains. "Just go out there a little ways and you're in wilderness."

"What do you do for a living out here?"

"I drive our fishing boat while my sons do all the work. They're up in Juneau picking up a new forty footer. Costs $80,000." He shook his head in resignation.

Lynette and I hiked the six mile Gavin Hill Trail, crossing muskeg and bisecting a hemlock forest. She hummed and sang all the way. I smiled. We held hands and had little to say. After returning to the town, we resumed her walking tour from the day before. The name Baronof was ubiquitous—Baronof Street, Baronof Island, Baronof Realty, Baronof Elementary School, and one restaurant even offered a Baronof Burger. We visited the Sheldon Jackson Museum with its native artifacts including ceremonial masks, skins, utensils, sleds, tools and kayaks. James Michener had spent the previous year here writing *Alaska.*

I was feeling a bit under the weather. Lynette spotted Helga's Bed and Breakfast just outside of town and decided what I needed was a night of pampering. "I'll treat with my mad money." She picked a room with a large window and balcony overlooking the bay. In gusting winds, kittiwakes, mew and herring gulls, and bald eagles fished skillfully for herring just off the shore. When a gull or kittiwake caught a fish, the other birds dived bombed and attacked it, often intimidating the bird and forcing it to drop its catch. When an eagle caught a fish, the others left it alone.

Helga and her husband, Joe Garrison, fell in love in Germany in the early sixties when Joe was stationed there with the U.S. Army. They returned to Alaska where Joe worked in the logging camps. Now he was a charter boat fisherman. He seemed very knowledgeable about Alaskan political issues and was the epitome of the rugged individualist. The B&B was immaculate. I slept long and hard and felt fine in the morning and had no trouble getting into the hearty, delicious breakfast Helga served—egg souffle, bacon, spinach, toast, jam and coffee. Two other guests, men who worked out of Fairbanks for the Department of Transportation, joined us in the dining room. They were engineers and had been in Ketchikan, inspecting the road system which one of them said was essentially a bridge hung on the side of a mountain. One of the DOT men seemed a bit more aggressive and talkative than the other. Trying to get a conversation going, I observed that Alaska was enormous and wondered how people from different parts of the state viewed one another.

"If you live south of Fairbanks, you don't live in Alaska," asserted the rather abrasive engineer.

"What about Anchorage," I prodded.

"The best thing I can say about 'Los Anchorage' is that it's the closest city to Alaska," he continued.

The conversation turned to Alaska's "dividend program." By now I was growing weary of the one engineer's self righteousness. He was down on the state passing out oil dividends to Alaskan citizens.

"The state should keep the money."

"Why? Isn't it a financial windfall for the residents of Alaska?" I asked.

"Most of it just goes into drugs. The people don't need the money."

"I don't know," countered Joe. "My kids' state dividends are all in the bank earning interest for their education."

Whether he thought he was being ganged up on or what, I don't know, but the seething DOT fellow stood up and huffily strode off, not offering a word of leave. The other DOT fellow, a wiry, handsome guy with dark hair and eyes and a beard, shook his head and told Joe not to worry about it. We all talked for another hour about Alaska and Sitka. The more reasonable DOT guy told us he had been taking advantage of land lotteries and other programs for years and now owned several parcels of land around Fairbanks with rental cabins sitting on them. He lived in one of the cabins which had no utility services or running water. Solar panels provided him with basic electricity, and he carried water from a nearby stream.

Lynette and Helga decided to do laundry. Helga's one teenage daughter tended to ducklings she was raising to replace ones that had been preyed upon by eagles and gulls. The other daughter worked on Joe's boat. Rather than working like the others, I was looking at several double-crested cormorants. I had never before seen the bright silver temples that were characteristic of the breeding plumage in the western race of that species.

On board the ferry *LeConte*, plying its way from Sitka to Juneau, I stood on deck with my binoculars, and the sun shone off and on all day. The fresh air was invigorating, and, especially when we passed Admiralty Island National Monument, the scenery was spectacular. Here brown bears out-number humans and high peaks fall away through conifer forests, alpine lakes and mountain meadows to coastal rain forests. Bald eagles perched in conifers and glided along the shore line and across Chatham Strait in such profusion that the bird's threatened status in the lower forty-eight seemed simultaneously incredible and inexcusable. Seals, sea lions and whales made sudden appearances on the surface of the sea, acted as if they were plying the same route as our ship, and then just as suddenly dis-appeared. Two guys from Juneau joined me at the ship's railing. One chain-drank Ranier beer and the other sucked enthusiastically on a large contain-er of vodka and orange juice. I looked at my watch—9:30 a.m. I could hear Willie Nelson singing a line from *Sunday Morning Coming Down*, "The beer I had for breakfast was so good I had one more for dessert." They skipped lunch, and, early in the afternoon, they stretched out on two deck chairs for a couple of hours, snoring. After their nap, they resumed their liquid diet.

Two other guys I met on deck were from Chile. One said he had been in the food business in Naples, Florida, the other had been painting houses in Boston. They were on their way to Juneau, looking for jobs in the fishing industry. The housepainter was somewhat familiar with the birds we were seeing.

"Why did you fellows leave Chile?"

"It is very difficult to make a living in Chile unless you have your own business," explained the painter. "Wages are very low. There is no middle class, only the rich and the poor. The government is bankrupting the coun-try with their theories they adopt from the Chicago School of Economics. Chile is not Chicago. Chile is not America."

"Was it better under Allende?"

They looked at each other, smiled and both shook their heads.

"No, it was much worse," answered the other man.

"Will you go back to Chile?"

"We want to go back," replied the painter, "but I do not think we will. It is too difficult to make a living."

Lynette spent much of the day talking with a young Tlingit man and his old chief whom he had been accompanying to Angoon, a village on Admiralty Island. The old one had been in the hospital in Sitka and now, according to his young escort, was coming home to die. The young Tlingit told Lynette he lived between two worlds, being married to a Caucasian who worked in filming and who had been living in Unalaska for the past year doing a TV documentary. The old chief slowly and elegantly regaled Lynette with stories about his people. She told me later she couldn't get enough of him.

The *LeConte* stopped at Angoon long enough for the two Tlingits and their magnificent black and white malamute to disembark. Never was a village located in a more beautiful setting. People gathered around the pier to welcome the old man home. He turned toward us, grimly waved and then smiled at Lynette, sending a bit of his spirit with her.

During a brief stop at Tenakee Springs, we walked from one end of the village to the other, passing small, colorful homes erected on stilts and cantilevered over the sea. The ship returned to its course north. Between eight thirty and nine o'clock, the sun set behind rugged snow-capped peaks, leaving sky waves of deep pinks, reds, and blues. Lynette said the scene looked like she imagined the North Polar sky might look with the sun tracking the horizon during summer solstice. Perfectly calm water reflected the early evening sky, mountains and the rest of the world. We made another brief stop that evening at the Tlingit fishing village of Hoonah and then arrived in Juneau at one a.m. We disembarked and set up camp for the night in the ferry terminal parking lot. I happily removed my seasickness patch.

Dick Newell owned and operated a heating and air conditioning business in Buffalo, N.Y. After retiring, he and his wife, Jean, sold their house and bought a large motor home in which they were traveling with their little poodle, Annie, and in which they spent the night parked next to us. After getting acquainted, we all joined Lynette on her walking tour which began at the Alaska State Capitol. We visited the State Office Building with its hundred-year old totem pole, the Alaska State Museum with its fine exhibits of native artifacts, and the large, Victorian hilltop mansion of Judge James Wickersham. That afternoon we drove in tandem to a campground just outside of town, got settled into our slots, and then joined the Newells for cocktails in their rig where we learned that the next day was Jean's birthday.

Early in the morning we drove into town and found a bakery. Lynette ordered a chocolate cake with chocolate frosting and pink roses. We returned an hour later to pick up the cake, and Lynette was disappointed that "Happy Birthday, Jean" was written in red rather than pink to match the flowers.

"Sir, is there any chance you can erase this and write it in pink?"

"Erase it? Lady, I really don't think I can do that and guarantee anything. How about putting red tips on the rose petals?"

"O.K. But can't you write over the red script with pink frosting?"

The baker shook his head and smiled and then, as she had suggested, very cleverly and successfully overwrote the message in pink. Lynette walked out of the shop with a smile.

Impressive Mendenhall Glacier was one of the trip's highlights, an enormous river of light-refracted blue ice, twelve miles long and a mile and a half wide. We met the Newells at the visitor center where a funny fellow who sold us a package of fudge described the glacier as "ab-soo-lute-ly awe-some!" A trail led us over the terminal moraine and onto the glacier. We followed a lateral moraine and enjoyed spectacular views of the Juneau icefield. The Newell's little dog, Annie, ran on the trail and reminded me of the story of John Muir's little dog, Stikine, who saved the naturalist's life when he became hopelessly lost on a glacier.

That evening we celebrated Jean's birthday with the much decorated chocolate cake. A young Australian couple, Paul and Mim, whom the Newells had previously met, joined us. Both of them were teachers traveling in the States on a leave of absence. Mim was seven months pregnant, and they would soon leave for home where she wanted to have the baby. We talked about Australia and Jean's favorite subject, wildflowers. The ferry south left sometime in the middle of the night. Dick and Jean drove the Aussies to the terminal to catch it and then spent the rest of the night in the terminal parking lot.

The morning was totally sunny, a rare sight in Juneau. We met Dick and Jean in town and strolled through the shopping district. In one store, I saw Lynette admiring a ceramic vase and later returned to the shop and bought it for her birthday the following week. We visited the fine, late nineteenth-century St. Nicholas Russian Orthodox Church and then returned to the campground where I washed the camper and looked for birds. That evening, Jean read a collection of Robert Service poems, and we drank wine.

Alaska's capital is inaccessible from the outside by highway. It can only be reached by air or sea. Juneau's only real road, the Glacier Highway, stretches six miles south of town to Thane and forty-three miles north to Echo Cove. We drove twenty-three miles north of town to the Shrine of St. Terese, a picturesque stone chapel on a small island connected to the mainland by a causeway with a gravel road. It was Juneau's answer to France's Mont St. Michel. A group of teachers were having a retreat at the shrine and happened to be studying tidal pools when we arrived. We walked down a trail to a lovely cove filled with marbled murrelets bobbing in the choppy sea. A bald eagle guarded its nest at the top of a dead conifer. Orange-crowned warblers flitted about and sang in the brush lining Peterson Creek, and we found a chimney and other remnants of a trapper's cabin. We hiked eight miles to see Herbert Glacier, and, along the way, saw red-breasted sapsuckers, blue grouse, varied and hermit thrushes, mergansers on a rushing river, lots of winter wrens, a rufous hummingbird, and plenty of bear signs. Lynette, who was certain a bear lurked behind every tree, talked non-stop all the way to announce our presence. A wonderful waterfall plunged into a lake at the glacier's foot, and the glacier itself threatened to take my breath away.

Later, with Jean and Dick, we looked across a picturesque bay dotted with islands. The Chilicut Mountain Range provided a wonderfully dramatic backdrop to the scene. While we ate pizza and drank beer, a steady stream of geese, scoters and sea ducks settled into the bay for the evening.

Early in the morning we waited for McDonald's to open. A bearded drunk who was a Vincent van Gogh look alike walked by with a newspaper. I asked him where he got the paper since I hadn't seen any newsstands. He sold it to me for a dime. While eating breakfast, Lynette read that the local birding club planned an outing that day. We drove to the Mendenhall wetlands in time to find the group assembling. Walking over to the apparent leader, I asked, "Any room for some outsiders?"

"The more the merrier," came the smiling, enthusiastic response from Mary Lou, the club's president. She introduced us to her husband, a naturalist who worked for the state of Alaska, and the others. Lynette and I wore only hiking boots while the others all wore high rubber Wellingtons, much better footwear for the marshy habitat through which the bird walk would take us. I chided Bill Cole, a friendly and chivalrous chap, for carrying Lynette across some of the streams and not offering to carry me. Lynette came to his defense, "Just keep slogging. How else will you learn whether or not your boots are water proof?" During the walk, I noticed a woman looking puzzled every time I mentioned Lynette's name. It turned out she too was named Lynette and was married to Bill Cole.

Black-bellied plovers, western and least sandpipers, and greater yellowlegs foraged in the flats, their long beaks probing the mud like sewing machine needles. Mergansers, wigeons, shovelers, scaup, and scoters segregated themselves in the deeper water. Two eagles tumbled precipitously from the sky, locked in a courtship embrace, pulling out of their suicidal free fall only a few yards from impact. Arctic terns, having just completed their incredibly long, half a world migration from Antarctica, circled wide above and scanned the wetlands with beaks pointed down, looking for aquatic prey. Every so often, the strikingly handsome blue-gray and white, black-capped predators would stop in mid-flight and dive toward the water's surface, sometimes pulling out if success seemed doubtful, other times plunging into and disappearing under the water, then emerging with a fish wriggling in its beak.

Late in the morning, we started back toward the road to avoid being trapped by the incoming tide. Flocks of horned larks foraged for insects and seeds along the shore. Bill and Lynette Cole introduced us to their good friends, Roger and Betty Stephan. The two couples were very friendly to us on the walk, and the Coles suggested the six of us have a late lunch at their house. We accepted but returned to the campground first to shower and change from our wet and muddy clothes.

Bill was a physician with a family practice, and Roger worked for the state. The Coles lived with their son and daughter in a log home built by an Indian woman after the turn of the century. Totem poles and prehistoric carvings flanked their fireplace in which gold nuggets and an assortment of other minerals were embedded. Bill and Lynette had lived in Ethiopia for a couple of years.

"Would you ever leave Alaska, Bill?"

"Only if we could go back to Africa."

The Coles' house sat on a hillside overlooking a bay. Hoary redpolls attended their feeder just outside the living room window, and crossbills foraged in the tops of conifers below the cabin providing an unusual perspective of a species ordinarily seen only high above the observer. We spent the afternoon talking about Alaska, Africa and birds. Later, we migrated to Roger and Betty's house where another couple joined us for dinner. Martha and Bud had grown up in Boston. He had been stationed in Juneau with the U.S. Coast Guard. They liked Alaska so much they stayed.

"How long have you been here?"

"Twenty-five very enjoyable years," responded Bud with a broad grin.

"Do you ever miss Boston?"

"Never!" Bud emphasized.

"Only the Boston Symphony," corrected Martha.

Back at the campground I scrubbed the mud from our boots. Dick put them in their motorhome bathroom with the heater turned high, and they were soft and dry in the morning.

We dropped our laundry off at the Mendenhall Mall and hiked six miles on the West Glacier Trail. Rain fell steadily while we walked between enormous ice peaks and bottomless crevasses. Clouds moved up the valley and hid the trail above and below us. We felt our way back to the laundromat and returned to the campground to dry out.

Juneau, Alaska, May 4, 1987

Mikey comes today! (Mike was twenty-three years old and six feet, three inches tall, and his mother still called him "Mikey.") Mike had just finished his first year of graduate school at Michigan and was going to join us for a couple weeks. Lynette and I drove to the ferry terminal to meet him. As he came down the gangplank, Lynette wiped a tear from her eye and said, "Look at Mikey. He's so tall and handsome."

"He sure is. And he's growing a beard."

We took him to the glacier and then on a tour of Juneau where we ate lunch in the old Juneau Hotel, the inside of which looked like a set for a Western. Later we drove north on the Glacier Highway to see the views and to look for birds. We camped on a lake with an eagle's nest and old boat launch. Mike tried his luck fishing in the rain and caught three Dolly Varden on his first four casts. After a while the Newells pulled their motorhome in beside our camper, and we all had chili for supper.

Mikey went fishing early, caught a large Dolly Varden and fixed it for breakfast. Peterson Creek ran into a serene five or six acre lake and then cascaded over a rocky fall into the ocean. I tried my hand with a fly rod, walking along the rocky shore where the stream flowed into the sea, and was not as successful as Mike. Rain fell steadily. Less than 30 yards away, across the creek's mouth, two eagles perched above me in a Sitka spruce. Alcids fished in the ocean, diving and reappearing on the surface at irregular intervals and in unexpected locations. Two marbled murrelets broke away from a dozen other murrelets and swam toward the shore, affording me excellent views. The birds were midway between their splendid gray and white winter plumage and their relatively lackluster breeding garb, a plumage phenomenon somewhat different from most other species whose breeding appearance outshines their more prosaic non-breeding plumage. I wasn't very offended when Dick asked Mike rather than me to give him casting lessons on his spinning rod.

Later in the morning, while Mike and I continued fishing, Lynette drove into town with the Newells. She and Jean had lunch at the Baronof Hotel and Dick continued his forty years of perfect attendence in Rotary by joining the Juneau Rotary Club for lunch. Mike and I fixed lunch in the camper and then, when the sun emerged from the clouds, found some birds he had never seen before ("Life-birds")—Townsend's warblers, orange-crowned warblers, white-winged crossbills, and blue grouse. Later, we drove to Fritz Cove so Mike could see Arctic terns and then we met Dick at the campground.

From my notes: *So good to be with Mike. We walked to the campground store, and he brought back a six pack of Labatt's. Tomorrow the boat leaves for Haines and Skagway.*

The ferry *Taku* caught up with us again. A tractor cab off-loaded ten or twelve trailers from the ship before we were permitted to drive aboard. We ferried north to Haines via the Lynn Canal, a spectacular natural fjord flanked on both sides by dramatic mountains rising directly from the sea. Haines is situated amid sensational scenery near the point of the Chilkat Peninsula. Each year one of nature's great marvels occurs when thousands of bald eagles winter in the Chilkat Preserve, feeding on the salmon at the mouth of the Chilkat River.

Gold was discovered in Bonanza Creek in the Klondike in 1896, precipitating one of history's greatest goldrushes. Thirty thousand men and a few women, carrying supplies for a year, braved the perilous, freezing trip from Skagway over either of the equally treacherous Chilkoot and White passes and then down raging rivers to the Klondike. Before the turn of the century Skagway was Alaska's largest city with more than 20,000 people. Now the population was less than one thousand. Upon our arrival in Skagway, clouds obliterated much of the area's beautiful scenery. We registered at the small municipal campground, and, on the attendant's recommendation, walked to the Prospector Inn for dinner. Later the clouds broke up, and we began to see that, indeed, Skagway's setting was unsurpassed in beauty.

"Skagway" comes from a Tlingit word which means "Home of the North Wind." While the deep blue fjord ended at Skagway, the mountains did not, and the town sat in a natural wind tunnel. A cold early morning breeze blew off the icy Arctic waters and whistled past our camper, carrying a perfumy aroma from a stand of unidentified, aspen-like deciduous trees with leaves beginning to unfurl. I set up my tripod in the main street of town and snapped a delayed photograph of the Newells and the three of us with the onion domed Golden North Hotel and Sweet Tooth Saloon in the background. Two pickup trucks patiently waited until we had taken our photo to drive by. Mike had left his sleeping bag on the ship and didn't discover his mistake until after it sailed. We ate breakfast at the Golden North, and I mentioned the problem to the waitress.

"Well, let's just give Gary a call."

"Who's Gary?" I wondered.

"He works for Alaska Marine Highways. He's a friend."

Fortunately, someone had noticed the bag and brought it to the terminal. We waited until 10:00 when it opened, and Gary gave Mike his sleeping bag. In one of the shops, I saw a copy of the *Skagway News* dated July 8, 1898, which described on its front page the shooting of a local desperado, Soapy Smith, by Frank Reid. Soapy's gang regularly relieved miners returning from the gold fields of their burdens. A group of citizens met at the Golden North to decide what to do about Soapy. The group adjourned their meeting at the hotel and re-convened at the Juneau Dock. Smith evidently heard about the meeting, walked down to the dock, and jammed his rifle in Reid's stomach. Frank drew his 38 and both men pulled their triggers simultaneously. Smith died immediately and Reid was taken to the doctor fatally wounded. After reading that account, we just had to go to the Gold Rush Cemetery, and, sure enough, the graves of Soapy Smith and Frank Reid were both there.

Our camper laboriously climbed the Klondike Highway over the White Pass, just like the miners of the 1890s, only we weren't walking. The highway was built in 1942 by the U.S. Army in order to lay a gas pipeline from Skagway to Whitehorse. Snow melted first from the great rock outcroppings, creating a starkly dramatic black and white landscape. Trucks carrying zinc and lead concentrates in large caldron like containers barreled menacingly at us down the gravel road. We passed an abandoned cabin and the old Yukon Railway built in 1900, then crossed White Pass and re-entered British Columbia. A chatty Royal Canadian Mounted Police customs official fired off five or six friendly questions. Not to be outdone, I asked the Mountie, "What's the marge of Lake Lebarge?"

"Well, I don't exactly know... It's Robert Service... It's the marge, eh?"

We pulled over for lunch by frozen Tutshi Lake. The sun shone, but the wind was howling, and the landscape was frozen, reinforcing Lynette's image of the area—"Everything I've heard about the Yukon is true!" (Technically, we were still in B.C.) Mountains surrounded and towered over us, and water pipits scrambled over lakeside rocks, combing the beach for early insects. We entered Yukon Territory and stopped for gas at Carcross, a settlement that shortened its name from the original, Caribou Crossing. Further north, we drove across the Carcross Desert, a large dry lake bottom of shifting sand deposited by retreating glaciers. Sandy soil and strong winds create an unfavorable environment for most vegetation, and not much more than stunted lodgepole pines and kinnikinnick survive. (The latter is a low evergreen ground cover, the leaves of which are sometimes used to make tea.) Beautiful mountain lakes flanked the road, including Emerald Lake where white sediment on the lake's bottom amazingly reflected the colors of the rainbow.

Our route joined the Alaska Highway and then ran through Whitehorse, capital of the Yukon Territory. Gold prospectors who successfully crossed the mountains from Skagway floated on anything available from Whitehorse more than one thousand miles down the Yukon River to Dawson City. We visited a turn of the century log church and the *SS Klondike*, the retired river steamer moored on the banks of the Yukon River. For several decades during the first half of the century, the grand old sternwheeler plied the Yukon between Whitehorse and Dawson City, hauling cargo and passengers alike.

> The Northern Lights have seen queer sights,
> But the queerest they ever did see
> Was that night on the marge of Lake Labarge
> I cremated Sam McGee.

From: *The Cremation of Sam McGee*, by Robert W. Service

Scenic Lake Labarge wasn't any more so than many of the other wonderful lakes in the great northwest, but how could anyone read those lines above and not drive a few miles out of the way to see Robert Service's setting for his frozen pal's happy ending? We returned to the Alaska Highway and followed the Takhini and then the Dezadeash rivers to Haines Junction, where we set up camp in the Shakwak Valley at the foot of the towering Kluane Range.

In the morning, as we were finishing breakfast, a chunky guy pulling a small trailer behind a pickup truck slowed to a stop and waved at us.

"Hullo! Where'd you come from?"

"Whitehorse and Skagway."

"Oh. We're goin' down the Alcan. Heard there were some pretty bad road problems down that way. You hear anythin' about it?"

We couldn't provide him with any fresh information about the Alcan, but Lynette had a fresh pot of coffee brewed and poured a cup for the man and his wife. They had spent the past two years in Alaska and now were headed for Seattle with all their worldly possessions. They intended to sell their truck and trailer, buy a boat, and sail to Mexico.

"Why are you leaving Alaska?"

"Alaska's a fine place to live, but we're awful tired of the long, cold, dark winters."

He had a point. We wished them well, they reciprocated, and then we set off in opposite directions. Snow began falling as we left the campsite and drove higher into the foothlls. South of Sheep Mountain the snow let up long enough for us to spot a herd of white, or Dall, sheep. An eagle circled slowly over the herd, reminding us that sometimes newborn sheep are taken by eagles. We skirted the mountain, and then the snow resumed falling.

"For Pete's sake, Darwin, the next time you bring me to the Yukon, make sure it's August!"

The Alaska Highway followed the west shore of Kluane Lake north. The sky cleared, and the sun's warm rays glistened lustrously off the deep blue lake. To the west lay Kluane National Park and the rugged St. Elias Mountains which now emerged from the clouds, bringing into view enormous glaciers and icefields as well as magnificent Mt. Logan, North America's second highest peak at 19,516 feet. We stopped for lunch at the small lakeside settlement of Destruction Bay which received its name in the aftermath of a raging storm that destroyed the town's buildings. Lynette and Mike tried a few casts with no luck, and I lay on the shore, basking in the sun, and recollecting an interesting morning during which we had driven through snow, sleet, hail and rain.

Entering its namesake state and under a clear sky, the Alaska Highway headed northwest along the Tetlin National Wildlife Refuge to Tok, a trading center for area Athabaskan villages and a major crossroads. Tok also advertised itself as the center for breeding and training of sled dogs. Tok's Sourdough Campground was pleasantly located in the woods. At the edge of the campground, with a prospective mate watching, a male sharp-tailed grouse, with quivering wings, inflated its reddish-violet air sacs and fanned its tail, performing a regally formal courtship display. He strutted and pranced in circles and, every so often, bowed in the direction of the object of his affections. Mike and I watched a flock of Bohemian waxwings moving through the conifers, and then a snowshoe hare watched Mike and me pitching his tent.

The morning presented us with a wonderful day. Lynette sang, "Blue skies, smiling at me...," and we broke our fast with delicious thick sourdough flapjacks served with maple syrup and strong, black coffee at the small campground cafe. Then we continued north toward Fairbanks. Stands of aspen and Sitka spruce alternated along the highway, and utility poles leaned precariously, apparently sinking into the muskeg. We stopped to photograph two moose browsing next to a lake. The majestic Alaska Range paralleled us to the west, and the peak of Mt. Hayes rose through a smoke ring-like cloud almost to 14,000 feet. We crossed the Delta River, and so did the Alaska Pipeline, giving us our first view of the ecologically controversial engineering marvel. The highway passed Eielson Air Force Base and then North Pole where, at Mike's insistence, we drove down Santa Claus Lane, visited Santa Claus House, and paid our respects at the gigantic statue of our favorite jolly old elf.

Fairbanks sits astride the Chena River just east of its confluence with the Tanana River. The city typically endures annual temperature fluctuations of 150 degrees, from -60 in winter to +90 in summer. Lynette led us on her downtown walking tour and took us to lunch at a restaurant/saloon next to the Chena Pump House National Historic Site from where Chena River water was pumped to the dredging operations at Cripple Creek. We walked off our lunch at Creamer's Field, a 2,000 acre migratory waterfowl refuge where we successfully identified solitary sandpipers, sandhill cranes, fox sparrows, orange-crowned warblers and mosquitoes. An Aussie woman was birding by herself and eagerly joined us, lamenting that the friends she was traveling with weren't high on birdwatching. Next we toured the University of Alaska campus and and then got down to some serious visiting.

A bunch of the boys were whooping it up in the Malamute Saloon;
The kid that handles the music box was hitting a jag-time tune;
Back of the bar, in a solo game, sat Dangerous Dan McGrew,
And watching his luck was his light-o'-love, the lady that's known as Lou.
From: *The Shooting of Dan McGrew*, by Robert W. Service

Seven miles west of Fairbanks lay the old gold mining camp of Ester where the Malemute Saloon was the central attraction of the Cripple Creek Resort. The complex of old wooden buildings also included the Bunkhouse Hotel, the Firehouse Theater, and the Bunkhouse Mess Hall. I read the rest of Service's poem on the short drive to Ester to get us all in the mood—we had some beer bets to pay off and thought the Malemute Saloon would be an appropriate place to retire our debts. Mike owed me for being the first to see Dall sheep and for finding him, on one of our ferry legs, a northern fulmar ("life-bird" for him). I owed him for finding Bohemian waxwings ("life-bird" for me) at the Tok campground. When we arrived at the saloon, a bunch of boys and just as many girls, as far as I know none of them named Lou, indeed were whoooping it up. Lynette was tolerant as Mike and I did some whooping of our own, and before long she too joined in singing various jag-time tunes accompanied by a kid handling a music-box.

At 9:30 p.m. the sun still hung fairly high in the western sky. Its soft pink light blanketed the Alaska Range as we drove south toward Denali National Park. A haze concealed Mt. McKinley, 100 miles away. Suddenly the haze evaporated, and "The Great One" emerged, putting everything else into its perspective. North America's highest peak rose 20,320 feet from sea level, and a cloudless blue sky outlined the majestic white massif. None of the other mountains we had been seeing since leaving the "Lower 48" prepared us for this dramatic mountainscape. We found an isolated spot not far from the road and set up camp. As the sun sank lower and then disappeared, we watched the changing colors play against the vista, and I thought of another verse from Service's *The Shooting of Dan McGrew:*

> *Were you ever out in the Great Alone, when the*
> *moon was awful clear,*
> *And the icy mountains hemmed you in with a*
> *silence you most could hear;*
> *With only the howl of a timber wolf, and you*
> *camped there in the cold...*

We passed Skinny Dick's Halfway Inn and Nenana, a small settlement at the confluence of the Tenana and Nenana rivers where, each year, a lottery attracts participants from all over the state trying to guess the exact minute of ice breakup on the Tanana River. When a log tripod sitting on the frozen river is dislodged by the melting and surging ice, a line stretched to the shore trips a clock thereby recording the official time of breakup. The tall tripod leaned inconspicuously against a small log cabin designated "City Hall," tucked away for the summer. Our route continued south through Anderson and Healy, and bogs, ponds and small creeks flanked the road. Place names were either derived from Indian words—Nenana, Tatlanika, Chena—or from events of the white man's era—Fortune Creek, Hard Luck Creek, Wooden Canoe Lake.

With some of the world's most dramatic scenery surrounding us, we rode through Denali National Park looking for wildlife. Caribou grazed along the Park Road. Once Mike spotted a red fox picking its way across the tundra. Willow ptarmigans with reddish bodies and white heads, in the process of changing from winter to breeding plumage, perched in the low shrubbery or on rocks, eating buds and insects. We climbed Primrose Ridge and saw Arctic ground squirrels and Arctic marmots. Flocks of Lapland longspurs foraged for insects and seeds on the tundra. Golden hued grizzlies meandered across mountain meadows, searching for small mammals.

We crossed the Alaska Range at Broad Pass, elevation 2,300 feet, where the wide mountain valley was surrounded by high peaks. The sun's slanting afternoon rays reflected brightly off the white mountains, sculpting them by smoothing the sloping hills and accentuating the craggy peaks. The panoramic vista was shiny white interrupted only by a few patches of green spruce stands and a few black rock outcroppings on the rugged mountain peaks.

From my notes: *Like being on top of the world. Lynette thought it looked like the North Pole. Mike wondered if this was where "Never Cry Wolf" was filmed.* Magnificent McKinley dominated the panorama. Mighty glaciers—Ruth, Takositna, Kahiltna—fingered their way toward the Susitna River Valley. We followed the raging Chulitna River, stopping for lunch at an overlook near a high bridge. Later, a bull moose foraged on aquatic vegetation in Kashwitna Lake. The placid waters reflected Mt. McKinley, and we set up camp on the lakeshore and watched a beaver swimming toward its lodge. Mike caught a couple of fish in Little Willow Creek, and the sun's rays performed miracles in the sky just before setting at 10:30 p.m.

Anchorage, Alaska, May 11, 1987

Happy birthday, Lynette! We drove through the pioneer town of Talkeetna from where many of the climbing expeditions of McKinley originate and then through the fertile Matanuska Valley. We stopped to admire the Knik Glacier and crossed the Knik Arm of Cook Inlet, arriving in Anchorage in time for Mike and me to get haircuts. I asked the barber, "Where are you from?"

"A place you never heard of... Townsend, Montana."

"Wanna bet? You know a guy named Jepsom? He's a newspaper broker."

"How do you know him?"

"I used to be in the newspaper business. I even spent a day in Townsend visiting him."

"Well, I'll be damned. It's a small world."

Lynette wanted a night in a hotel for her birthday, so we registered at the Captain Cook. After dinner in the hotel restaurant, the three of us had a party with cake and ice cream in our room. Mike gave his mother a scrimshaw necklace made from caribou horn and a scrimshaw handled ulu, an Eskimo cutting instrument. I gave her the blue and white ceramic vase I had bought in Juneau.

"Hey, Dad. Come here a minute."

Mike was looking through my spotting scope from our eleventh floor hotel window at the beach far below.

"What's up?"

"I think those large shorebirds are Hudsonian godwits."

And, sure enough, they were. Their dark chestnut breasts and black tails could be discerned even at that distance, confirming Mike's call. Another life bird for us both. I owed the man a well-deserved beer.

We left for Seward in the morning and drove south on the east side of the Cook Inlet's Turnagain Arm, named so by Captain Cook when he saw that that bay was just another in a series of dead ends he had encountered while looking for a sea passage across North America. At low tide, the Turnagain Arm virtually empties, leaving only a sea of mud and dangerous quicksand. When the tide returns, often it is in the form of a bore tide, a wall of water abruptly filling the bay. People fished for smelt with dip nets, and glaciers flowed from the Chugach Mountains. Explorer Glacier was a text-book example of glacial geology with its medial morraines forming eskers, long narrow ridges of deposited gravel. Huge blue icebergs floated in Portage Glacier's terminal lake. The town of Portage was virtually a ghost town with remnants of homes among tree stumps being all that remained of the community that was destroyed in Alaska's devasting 1964 earthquake.

At the mouth of the Placer River, a male Barrow's goldeneye courted a mate, rocking to and fro, then cocking and stretching his head up and forward, and then rolling from side to side. Our road climbed into the Kenai Mountains. Mike wanted to fish for grayling, so we parked the camper and hiked several miles toward Grayling Lake. On the trail we met a bearded guy wearing waders and a holstered pistol and carrying his fishing rod. He told us he was returning to the parking area because deep snow and overflowing streams had rendered the trail impassable. We turned back toward the camper, and Lynette remarked, "I feel like Captain Cook!"

Seward's importance is that its harbor remains ice free. The scenic, historic city sits at the head of Resurrection Bay and is surrounded by mountains and enormous icefields. We set up camp on a beach near town where we had an unfettered view across Resurrection Bay with high, snow covered mountains rising from the far side, and then we walked into town and chartered a boat to look for sea birds the next day.

Large tidal fluctuations required that, rather than stairs, ramps with angle irons lead from the dock to the boats. Monty and his wife, Florita, welcomed us aboard their boat. His card read, "Monty Richardson, Skipper." He said he was an Irish lord by birth, but that he had grown up in Oklahoma and come to Seward thirty-one years ago because of economic problems and because he liked the out-of-doors. He and Florita were both retired teachers who spent the winter driving around the Lower 48 in their motor home. We followed the rugged, glacially carved shoreline of Kenai Fjords National Park. Porpoises soon joined us and playfully raced beside the boat.

"Why do they do that, Monty?"

"Some people like to think they're social animals. Others think it's because the boat stirs up food."

"What do you think?"

"I prefer the latter theory myself."

Sea lions sunned on offshore rocks and huge rafts of common murres and kittiwakes rode the swells. Mike and I scanned through the thousands of birds swimming in and flying over the rich waters and added four new species to our life lists—fork-tailed storm-petrel, Kittlitz's murrelet, tufted puffin and horned puffin. Monty pointed out bunkers and gun emplacements on the shore and said they were built during World War II to protect Seward, a warm water port the military feared was coveted by the Japanese.

After showering at the Harbormaster's Building, we set off for Homer, picking up the Sterling Highway at Tern Lake Junction and following the Kenai River through Sterling and Soldotna to Cook Inlet where, across the sea, Redoubt and Iliamna volcanoes rose in the distance, the latter belching a spiraling column of steam. Moose browsed on willows along the road in the Isaac Walton League State Park. We stopped in Kenai and photographed the onion domed Holy Assumption Russian Orthodox Church, Alaska's oldest, and then followed the coastline into Kachemak Bay and picturesque Homer.

Scores of shorebirds, gulls and terns foraged along the Homer Spit. At the end of the narrow peninsula we found a good restaurant, the Chart House, specializing in sea food. Our waitress was from Minneapolis. She had entered the Alaskan land lottery and received a grant in the bush north of Fairbanks. She built a cabin in minus 40 degree weather, lived there for two years, and then decided she was too old for that kind of living. Sally moved to Homer where the climate is mild most of the year. After dinner, we set up camp on the beach at a spot with spectacular views of the glaciated Kenai Mountains rising across the deep blue waters of Kachemak Bay. Mike tried his hand at surf casting, while Lynette and I walked on the beach to the tip of the Spit where we saw eagles, eiders, fork-tailed storm-petrels and harbor porpoises.

The tide ebbed fully early in the morning, and a family dug for clams on the otherwise deserted beach. Mike and I climbed to the top of the bluffs overlooking Homer Spit to look for woodpeckers in the spruce forest.

"Whoa!" Mike cautioned. I looked to my left, and he was standing frozen, staring into a moose's face not more than six feet away. "What should we do?" he asked in a quiet, controlled way.

"Let's just keep talking in a calm manner and slowly walk away." I took a step backwards, turned around and was staring into the face of a smaller moose, again not more than six feet away. "Mike, it may be that we have managed to walk between a mother and her offspring."

"Now what should we do?"

"Let's just assume this is their territory. I think it's very important we get out of here in a way that doesn't make Momma uncomfortable." We continued talking as calmly as possible and backed off slowly to our left. The two moose resumed their browsing, and Mike and I found another area to look for woodpeckers.

It was soon time for Mikey to return to the lower forty-eight. We spent the night on a beach near Ninilchik, a village of Indian and Russian heritage situated on the Cook Inlet. The three of us walked upstream along a river that emptied into the Inlet. We came upon a wonderful lake. Sandpipers prodded mud flats along the shoreline, and ducks bobbed in the mildly choppy waters. A single trumpeter swan floated regally in a small, calm bay, and a moose swam across the lake where it was widest. From my notes: *We're going to miss Mikey.*

Back in Anchorage, we confirmed Mike's flight reservation and visited the Alaska Zoo. Then we picnicked in Earthquake Park, on a bluff overlooking the point where the Turnagain Arm branches from Cook Inlet. Early the next morning, we saw the old boy off at the airport, a rather sad parting for all.

Housekeeping chores occupied a few days in Anchorage—replenishing our groceries and supplies, cleaning the camper and having it serviced, filling our propane tank, picking up mail, doing laundry, arranging for a flight to the Priboloffs, a ferry to Valdez, etc. We ran into the Newells and later joined them camping at a municipal park on the outskirts of town. One evening, while taking a shower, I met another camper who was vacationing with his family. Steve McCall was a U.S. Coast Guard officer stationed in Valdez, Alaska. He was a genial sort, and I was destined to meet this interesting man again later in our trip.

Lynette and I visited native craft shops and art galleries and walked leisurely around Anchorage which was now wonderfully abloom with spring flowers and sadly populated with drunken derelicts. At the terrific Anchorage Historical and Fine Arts Museum, I was knocked over by the paintings of Fred Machetanz, an Alaskan artist who documented traditional Eskimo life in his paintings. Our inquiries revealed that Machetanz was not only a living artist, but that he was exclusively represented by a nearby gallery, Artique, Ltd. Tennys Owens, the gallery owner, showed us several paintings by Machetanz and also made arrangements for us to meet the artist and his wife at their cabin near Palmer, Alaska, where many more of his paintings were hung. I should mention that, in the museum, one painting by Machetanz especially impressed me. *The Quest For Avuk* was a marvelous seascape depicting whale hunters in a boat. I noticed it had been donated to the museum by the Rasmussen family. I suspected this was the same family which owned the National Bank of Alaska, the Chairman of the Board of which was Ed Rasmussen, a classmate and friend at Harvard. I made a mental note to give Eddie a call.

Palmer lies in the lush Matanuska Valley between the Talkeetna Mountains to the north and Chugach Mountains to the south. Dairy and truck farms thrive in the fertile valley where vegetables grow to enormous sizes. We stopped at the town's visitor center where a sign unabashedly advertised the community as "Alaska's Best Kept Secret." Friendly faces greeted us at the Machetanz cabin, and the happy couple proudly showed us around the homestead with its views of High Ridge Lake and the Chugach Range.

Inside the house, Sara Machetanz explained the Norwegian system of building log cabins that was taught to her and Fred by other local settlers back in 1950. She offered us coffee and, before long, with some gentle prodding from Lynette and me, Sara and Fred told us their life story. After graduating from Ohio University, the young artist joined his uncle who was living in the Eskimo village of Unalakleet. He sketched, and later painted, the natives in their daily activities and, in doing so, created a historically accurate and culturally invaluable depiction of their traditional life. He met and courted Sara in Ohio and persuaded her to visit him in Unalakleet.

"What should I wear?"

"Why, anything you want!"

Sara showed up in Unalakleet in high heeled, patent leather shoes. She had only arrived when Fred said they had to get married right away because the preacher was leaving the village and wouldn't be back for the remainder of the summer. With some confusion, she consented. A few days later, the preacher returned.

We all laughed at the story's retelling. I asked Fred how, at the time, he explained to Sara the glaring inconsistency of his story with the reality of the preacher's unexpected presence.

"I told her it was the philosophy of the wild."

"The philosophy of the wild?"

"Yes. You never give a sucker an even break."

The couple walked us through Fred's gallery. Each painting had a story or an explanation, as well as a creative title most often composed by Sara. Several Eskimo and sourdough models Fred was particularly fond of showed up repeatedly in his works. Sketches from the Unalakleet days were pinned everywhere, and many authentic props hung from the cabin's ceilings and walls—canoes, spears, clothing, and a baby basket. Sara pointed to one of Fred's paintings with a woman wearing a basket and told us the Eskimo legend of the baby basket—if a woman wears a baby basket, she'll get pregnant.

"Even today, many Eskimo women avoid getting near the baby basket," Sara laughed.

"Does it really work?" Lynette wanted to know.

"It worked for me. After years of no luck, I wore the basket and finally had a son."

"Do you have grandchildren?"

"No," she replied with obvious disappointment. "I'm tempted to take the baby basket to my daughter-in-law in Anchorage."

All of Fred Machetanz's paintings were appealing. We promised the hospitable couple we would think about what we had seen and return before the summer's end.

We followed the Glenn Highway east along the Matunuska River past the mighty Matunuska Glacier flowing from the Chugach Mountains. Moose and caribou browsed on the willows in the drainages and sheep grazed on the mountain slopes. We drove twenty miles off the road to Lake Louise where we camped on the shore with no one within sight. On the lake, swans and shovelers performed elaborate courtship displays, the males stretching their necks and swaying their heads in ceremonial ritual. Vivaldi provided a soft background for our supper of rich lentil soup accompanied by red wine, and, according to my notes, "A nice time was had by all."

Many Alaskan towns assign themselves sobriquets by which they promote themselves: Even as Palmer is "Alaska's Best Kept Secret" and Valdez is the state's "Gateway to the Interior," the small town of Glenallen boastfully billed itself as "The Hub of Alaska." From Glenallen, we turned south on the Richardson Highway toward Valdez. The Alaskan pipeline paralled the road to the west, like a silver thread running through a velvety green background of spruce forest. Lynette checked out a roadhouse as a prospective place for her and Krissie to stay and declared it acceptable—"We'll have sourdough hotcakes for breakfast here." (Krissie would be spending two weeks with us during her summer break after her sophomore year at Northwestern. I had planned a few days birding in the Priboloffs during that time, and the girls were planning their own outing during my absence.) We admired the Worthington Glacier and then crossed Thompson Pass which recorded a world record 975 inches of snowfall in the winter of 1952/3. The elevation of the pass is only 2,771 feet, yet, this far north, it is above tree line. The road descended from the pass and followed the Lowe River through spectacular Keystone Canyon. Waterfalls cascaded from the cliffs and bore bromidic names like "Bridal Veil" and "Horsetail."

Near the town of Valdez, pronounced with a long "e," the road was freshly tarred, and, before I knew it was happening, the camper became splattered with the thick, inky substance. At the Bear Paw Campground next to the town's small boat harbor, a smiling woman waved and greeted us.

"Hi! How are you?"

"A better question would be," I responded, taking in her apparent condition of very late pregnancy, "How are you?"

"I'll make it. I see you got yourself tarred. Common occurrence here."

"Any suggestions on how to remove it?"

"Sure. The grocery store down the street keeps bug and tar remover stocked. It's one of their best sellers."

After getting settled, Lynette and I walked to the grocery store to stock up on supplies and to buy some of their bug and tar remover. I saw Steve McCall in the check out line looking quite different in his impressive commander's uniform than he did back at the Anchorage campground shower room in flip-flops with a towel wrapped around his waist. We chatted for a few minutes, and then he invited Lynette and me for a personalized tour of the Coast Guard facility the next day. We accepted enthusiastically and returned to the campground where we spent the afternoon applying bug and tar removal to our splattered camper. We showered and waved at a woman pulling into the campground. She was traveling alone. We had met her in Prince Rupert and recognized her immediately, especially because her camper sported an Illinois license plate with Lynette's initials (LJW).

"Hey! You made it!" she exclaimed, as if there had been a great deal of doubt. She joined us for a glass of wine and then for dinner—lentil soup and fresh bread from the local bakery. We listened to a Haydn symphony while she reminisced about her childhood in Granite City, Illinois, a town lying a few miles up the Mississippi River from Belleville where we had lived for ten years. Her plans were no more developed than to continue traveling around Alaska in her camper, and she impressed us as a very nice but very lonely woman.

Valdez, Alaska, May 21, 1987

Valdez is a port town surrounded by impressive snow-capped mountains rising from the sea. Old Valdez was destroyed in the 1964 earthquake, and the new town was moved four miles west to the port area. Valdez is eminently walkable, and we enjoyed the scenery as we strolled through the town, visiting the Pipeline Terminal of the Alyeska Pipeline Service Company and the Valdez Heritage Center with its exhibits featuring pioneers, goldseekers and local history. A travel agent helped us with our plans to visit the gold mining town of Nome and Eskimo Village of Kotzebue, both communities being accessible only by boat, airplane or dog sled.

After lunch we walked to the Coast Guard station to get what Steve called his "cook's tour." The Commander walked us through the station, explaining the function of the various state of the art equipment and introducing us to the people responsible for its operation.

From my notes: *This facility was built primarily as a part of the pipeline agreement. An average of three tankers each day enter or leave Prince William Sound, and, according to Steve's personnel, there has never been even a near mishap. Furthermore, they expressed such confidence in their systems that they assured me there would never be a major accident.*

Every commercial tanker, boat and barge as well as every passenger ship over a certain size is tracked on radar and maintained on constant radio contact. Other important responsibilities of the facility include providing local weather service and search and rescue missions.

"Steve, has there ever been an oil spill here?"

"None worth talking about. The only spills we've had are accidents with small fishing boats and other small private craft."

Steve was obviously very proud of his operation, and, it would appear, he had every right to be. Lynette and I thanked him profusely for his hospitality and then walked back to the campground through a steady rain.

Less than two years later, early in the morning of March 24, 1989, the Exxon Valdez, captained by Joseph Hazlewood, ran aground on Bligh Reef, spilling eleven million gallons of crude oil into the Prince William Sound ecosystem. I watched the TV in shock and sorrow. I was sad for the birds and for the mammals and fish of the sea. I was sad for the people from the Prince Wiliam Sound area who relied on the sea's bounty to make a living. And I was especially sad for Commander Steve McCall as I watched him try to answer reporters' accusing questions and to defend the system of which he was so proud.

We retraced our route thirty miles north on the Richardson Highway and then turned east on the Edgarton Highway, driving up the valley through which flows the mighty, charging Copper River. We pulled over to make lunch by Kenny Lake and saw our first Pacific loon boasting its rich purple breeding plumage. The Edgarton continued to Chitina where we filled our gas tank and entered Wrangell-Saint Elias National Park and Preserve. We turned onto the McCarthy Road which was nothing more than a narrow, one lane, rough gravel track that meandered in a generally easterly direction for sixty-three miles to the old mining town of McCarthy. Actually, the road was an abandoned railroad bed. Much of the route was a jaw-jarring experience tantamount to driving over a corrugated roof. A pair of Pacific loons performed courtship displays, and a bald eagle exploded into flight from a near-by tree when we stopped the camper by a lake. Two cinnamon colored grizzly bears suddenly emerged from the brush beside the road, rose on their hind legs to see who or what we were, and then, just as quickly, disappeared into the brush on the road's other side. Lynette was so excited at seeing the animals she forgot to snap a photo even though her camera was hanging around her neck. I laughed.

"You're funny, Lynette. You say you're terrified of bears, yet I think you are really very fond of them."

"I can't explain it, but you're right. I'll never forget how they stood on their hind feet and stared at us. But I sure am glad they didn't need a closer look."

218

Even more exciting than seeing the bears was the heart-stopping crossing of the Kuskulana River bridge. The old railroad bridge spans Kuskulana Canyon, six hundred feet across and 283 feet deep. The bridge has no guard rails and is scarcely wider than a car, and the driver must keep the vehicle's four wheels on two continuous planks. I crept across the bridge, looking out of the side window to make sure the left wheels remained in the center of the left plank while Lynette kept similar watch on the right side. All the while, we both could see the river's white rapids far below.

The road ended about a mile west of McCarthy on the banks of the Kennicott River, a torrent of glacial melt fed by the rapidly receding Kennicott Glacier. To go further, you had to hand-pull yourself across the rushing river in a small, two person cable tram. The first half of the cable car trip was downhill and didn't look too difficult. Pulling ourselves up the other side, on the other hand, appeared more challenging. Our tour book warned of the danger in trying to ford the stream, and, looking at the fearsome rapids, I concurred. We tried pulling ourselves across the river and back just to get the hang of it and found the exercise tiring and the spray from the rapids quite wet. You just don't have the strength to pull when you are sitting in the car that you do when you stand on the river bank and pull. Nevertheless, we successfully crossed the river.

We set up camp for the night in a parking area downstream. Nearby, in a wretched shack, lived CJ. We could tell only because a crudely made sign said, "CJ lives here" and that he or she or whatever CJ was, would, for a small fee, take you to the abandoned Kennecott mines, guide you fishing or on the hiking trails, or sell you gas. Or, for free, give you information about the area. We took a short walk before dinner to see what was up with CJ, but he or she wasn't home.

Mountains and glaciers surrounded the remote valley, and we knew we were in a world apart. The magic of Mozart and an oaky bottle of cabernet emphasized the specialness of our situation. Lynette said she wished Mike were still with us to experience this bit of Utopia.

After breakfast, we packed our lunch, a compass, mosquito repellent, camera and binoculars and left for our day hike. Two fellows began crossing in the tram from the other side when Lynette and I arrived at the river. I gave them a hand pulling the cable. Then Lynette and I sat in the tram, and one guy said, "Hang on, we'll give you a ride." And did they ever! Spray from the Kennecott's rapids barely dampened us as we flew across the river in a fraction of the time we required the night before.

We walked about a half mile, crossed a smaller branch of the river in a second cable tram, and then walked another half mile and entered what there was of McCarthy, population 7 to 20, depending upon which source you read. The settlement offered a few buildings, including the old McCarthy Lodge, a colorful bar and hotel in the process of being renovated, and the old railroad station which had been turned into a museum of sorts and featured photographs of McCarthy in its glory when the Kennecott mines were operating. Pictures taken in the '20s of the Kennecott Glacier revealed dramatically how rapidly the enormous river of ice was receding.

An abandoned railroad bed led four and a half miles along the glacier's lateral morraine to the old Kennecott mine buildings. Lynette and I pulled out our lunch and sat in the sun on two glacially deposited rocks. Colorful wildflowers poked their blossoms through the glacial debris. At least two of the Kennecott settlement's buildings had been renovated and appeared to be residences. Several fellows worked hard on the restoration of the Kennecott Lodge perched on a ridge above the railroad bed and just below our perch on the lateral morraine.

"When will you be open for business?"

"June fifteenth. Our grand opening won't be until July Fourth though."

"How much are you charging for a room?"

"$135 per person, including meals."

We returned to the camper about 2:30, had a glass of cold apple juice, drove the hundred or so miles back to the Richardson Highway and then another twenty miles to a campground near Copper Center.

Puffy white cumulus clouds hung low on the eastern horizon, but the sky otherwise was clear blue on a beautiful morning. Two eagles soared in the river valley below us. We filled up with gas in Glenallen and set a course northeast on the Tok Cut-off. The Wrangell Mountains stretched out to our south, and two trumpeter swans called a pond their own. We stopped at the Christochina Lodge for a breakfast of sourdough pancakes. We noticed three Indians had ordered the same and figured they knew what was best.

"You fellows know anything about bears?"

"What do you want to know? He's an expert!" The man in the middle pointed to a rugged guy on his right who looked like he had probably gone mano a mano with a grizzly or two in his lifetime. And like maybe he won once or twice. I told him about the two bears on the McCarthy road and asked whether it was unusual for bears in that area to have a cinnamon color.

"No. But they could have been cinnamon colored black bears. How big were they?"

I looked at Lynette, and we agreed on their size.

"About three to four hundred pounds."

"They were grizzlies. Cinnamon black bears are little. Not more than a hundred pounds."

The pancakes were terrific. We continued toward Tok. Caribou and moose browsed beside the road, and, near Metasta, in a deep blue lake, a common loon rolled over showing his white belly and preened his breast with one black leg sticking up at a seemingly impossible angle. We pulled over to see snow capped peaks reflected perfectly in the lake and then decided to hike the lake's periphery. Patches of ice held on to winter, but the light green emerging leaves of the poplars scattered among the spruce made it clear that spring was on its way. Two terns worked the lake, alternately hovering above their prey and plummeting, immersing themselves and sometimes flying away with a fish. Delicate little red-necked phalaropes swam among a small flock of Bonaparte's gulls, spinning one way, then another, as pretty and graceful as floating ballerinas. A male yellowlegs chased its mate up and down the shoreline, and a young eagle rode the thermals up the mountain slope. How wonderful I felt to be alive and in Alaska, the Great Land.

In Tok we camped at the same place where we had stayed with Mike several weeks before. The woman who ran the campground invited us to attend an after dinner slide presentation she had prepared about the Tok area. I found myself sitting beside a pretty girl about ten years old. The narrator was talking about Tok's gold mining era, and I leaned toward the girl and whispered.

"Don't you wish you could find some of that gold?"

"They would make me put it back."

"Why would they do that?"

"Because the land wasn't mine. I know a man that happened to. Where did you come here from?"

"Valdez. Where did you come from?"

"Fairbanks. We're moving."

"Where to?

"Illinois."

"Where in Illinois?"

"Belleville."

"That's where I'm from."

"Go on! You are not."

"Sure I am."

She later introduced us to her folks, and we learned her father was a nurse in the U.S. Air Force and was being transferred to Scott Air Force Base just east of Belleville. Small world. Back at the camper, I turned off the lights, and Lynette requested a 6:30 wake up call.

The next morning I showered and then, as she requested, wakened Lynette at the designated time by turning on a tape of Pavrotti singing *Nessun Dorma*. She scrunched down into her sleeping bag and, like Turandot, threatened to have my head. Enormous snow mosquitoes buzzed our heads but did not land on us as we walked to the campground restaurant. A man sat with his wife beside their motorhome with Florida license plates.

"Here comes the birdwatcher!"

"That's me!"

"What birds are you seeing here?"

In response, I probably went into more detail than the man required—Bohemian waxwings, a different race of fox sparows, the Myrtle race of yellow-rumped warblers, etc. Lynette, still not fully recovered from Luciano's arial awakening, scolded, "Drop it, Darwin! The man's just being polite. He doesn't need a symposium on Tok's ornithology."

Less than an hour later Lynette was her old pacific self again. A cup of black coffee and a short stack of sour dough pancakes was all she needed.

Twelve miles southeast of Tok, at Tetlin Junction, we turned northeast onto the Taylor Highway and drove through the contrasting colors offered by a mixed forest comprised of black spruce and birch. Dark knobs topped each spruce, often looking like silhouetted birds and thereby complicating things—you tended to ignore a bird sitting on a treetop until you've sped by too fast to identify it. We stopped at the Country Store in the settlement of Chicken. Locals call willow ptarmigans "chickens." The town was originally settled by miners who wanted to name it "Ptarmigan." However, the old boys couldn't spell "Ptarmigan" and settled for "Chicken" instead. At least, that's how folks at the Chicken Country Store explain the town's name to strangers.

Shortly after passing the Eagle Cut-off, we entered Canada's Yukon Territory and the road became known as The Top of the World Highway. It wound its way over the treeless tundra covering the rolling mountains, giving one precisely the impression of being on top of the world. For miles in all directions, there were no utility poles or wires, no buildings, no ATV tracks. With the single exception of the gravel road on which we traveled, nothing betrayed the hand of man. Later our route dropped down the mountain slopes and through thick forests into the beautiful Yukon River Valley, providing an excellent view of Dawson City and the Klondike River spilling into the mighty Yukon. We ferried across the Yukon, and I asked one of the crew members if the ferries on the Dempster Highway were running, and she said she thought they were.

On August 17, 1896, George Carmack, Skookum Jim and Taglish Charlie struck gold on Bonanza Creek, a tributary of the Klondike River. Less than a year later, Dawson had thirty thousand inhabitants. When we arrived, the town's population was less than a thousand. It was in old Dawson that Jack London first saw Buck, the St. Bernard/German Shepherd cross that became his star in *Call of the Wild*, and where Robert Service wrote his colorful poems of the North. Mines and dredges may be visited, and gold may still be found in the streams and hills near Dawson. Many historic buildings survive and remain in use—the Red Feather Saloon, Madame Tremblay's and the Flora Dora to name a few. We visited the cabins where Service and London lived and wrote, drank a few beers at the

Sourdough Saloon, and ate dinner at the Jack London Grill. And it was easy to imagine Jack sitting in the corner on one of those velvet Victorian chairs, legs crossed, pencil in hand, and a glass of beer and a pad of paper lying on the table before him. We stood in front of the Yukon Hotel, visualizing the gold rush tents lining the Yukon River, and walked the dusty streets that turned into quagmires when the rain fell.

From my notes: *This to Lynette—We think Jackson is a pretty good replica of the "Old West." This, my dear, is the "Old West."*

The guy parked next to us in the Dawson campground was a retired Bell Systems engineer. Now he was a self-described "wagonmaster for RV caravans." He had driven up from Lancaster, Pennsylvania, to scout for the next trip he was scheduled to lead—Alaska and the Yukon. He was surprised when I told him I was born in Lancaster and grew up near by.

Twenty six miles southeast of Dawson City, the Dempster Highway intersects with the Klondike Loop and runs 462 miles north across the Arctic Circle and into the Northwest Territories, ending at the Eskimo Village of Inuvik, "the place of man." The gravel road is one of the world's most remote, and we planned to make the adventurous drive all the way to Inuvik and back.

I had heard about a book called *Birds Along the Dempster* written by Robert Frisch, so, the next morning, Lynette and I walked into town to try to find it. A water truck drove by us spraying the Dawson streets in an attempt to control the dust. "Good luck!" was all Lynette could say. We checked with the local book stores, library, museum and a dentist who was the head of the local conservation society. Robert Frisch had died, and no one knew where to find a copy of the book. We did learn that Frisch's widow was a sometimes resident of Dawson and owned a home there, and that she sold copies of her husband's book. At that time, however, she was renting the home to someone else and lived instead in a cabin with her daughter near the seven mile marker on the Dempster.

From my notes: *After two years of anticipation, feels great finally to be on the Dempster!*

We drove to the seven mile marker and walked about a hundred yards off the road to Juliana Frisch's cabin. Unluckily, it was padlocked, but there were signs of someone's living there—freshly planted garden, laundry hanging, and a child's toys in the yard. We decided to wing the Dempster trip without the help of Frisch's book in finding the birds. We set out following the North Fork of the Klondike River as far as Tombstone Mountain where we set up camp for the night. A moose browsed by the river, willow ptarmigans foraged on tender buds, and Say's phoebes sang on their territories. Lynette and I explored the area, and suddenly I heard a gasp of surprise. She had been scanning a clearing with her binoculars when a rock ptarmigan popped into view, a life-bird for both of us.

Back at our camp site, another camper had joined us. He was a retired military guy, about my age, traveling by himself and trying to decide where to live—in the Yukon or in Alaska. He seemed to prefer the former because of its fewer inhabitants. He was reluctant to talk about himself, but, with careful prodding and after a glass or two of wine, we learned he wanted to live in a small cabin in the bush where there were no other people. He intended to carry his own water, have a canoe and a snow machine and live on a river so he could go to town two or three times a year. Why he wanted to live such a solitary life he never revealed.

We crossed the Ogilvie Mountains and followed the Blackstone River which flowed north, emptying into the Peel. The Peel in turn flowed into the Mackenzie which drained much of the Northwest Territories into the Beaufort Sea and the Arctic Ocean. The Continental Divide ran through the Mahoni Range just to our west. Only a few miles away the Porcupine River collected its many tributaries and joined the Yukon River which flowed into the Bering Sea and the Pacific Ocean. We stopped and hiked up a mountain, looking for tundra birds. Our trail petered out, so we bushwhacked through thick brush and "swam" across several snow fields, distributing our weight over our whole bodies rather than walking and sinking up to our crotches in snow. Our efforts were rewarded when we saw long-tailed jaegers and upland sandpipers, life-birds for us both. Coming down the mountain, we saw caribou grazing and a red fox paralleled our route only fifty yards away, far less wary than I would have expected. Later, we found a good campground at Engineer Creek.

On the Dempster, the scenery is always interesting and often spectacular. Along the way, we inspected cliffs for gyrfalcons, in vain I'm sorry to say. Nevertheless, waxwings, crossbills, ptarmigans, eagles, white crowned sparrows, Dall sheep and foxes were all easy to spot. Once we saw a sign: "Caution: Watch For Small Aircraft Using This Highway For A Runway."

"That's just ducky!" was Lynette's feeling on that possibility.

The town of Eagle Plains wasn't much more than a truck stop-bar-restaurant-campground. We took showers, drank a couple of beers, and, while we watched a hockey playoff game between Edmunton and Philadelphia, played cribbage on a giant board with bear teeth for pegs.

From my notes: *The bar had a fine pictoral display of the Dempster's two best known stories—the "Mad Trapper" and the "Lost Patrol."* The latter is a reference to the Fitzgerald Patrol of four men who set out from Fort McPherson for Dawson City on December 21, 1910. Their frozen bodies were found fifteen months later by Corporal W.J.D. Dempster of the Royal North-West Mounted Police. Unfortunately, I have no recollection of the story of the mad trapper.

I checked with a highway worker and the gas station attendant on the status of the Peel River ferry, one of two ferry crossings between Dawson and Inuvik. During winter, vehicles drive across the frozen rivers. In summer, traffic is ferried. For a few weeks during spring break-up, floating ice renders the crossings too dangerous. Both ferries were expected to resume operation any day. We ate a good dinner in the Eagle Plains restaurant, looking out over the whole world to the west, with no sign of the hand of man beyond the porch.

The Dempster led us past long-tailed jaegers mating on their nests. He stands on her back and deftly slides his long tail under her, and she turns her bottom up to facilitate the "cloacal kiss." Ptarmigans fought over territories and mates. Shortly after mile marker 250, a sign told us we had reached the Arctic Circle, a line describing a series of points around the Earth where, on the shortest day of the year, the sun reaches but does not rise above the horizon. I set up a camera on a tripod and, with the delay feature, snapped us kissing across the imaginary line. We crossed the Richardson Mountains, and, at mile marker 292, entered Canada's Northwest Territories.

At the Peel River crossing, we could see Fort McPherson on the opposite bank. The river raged, and the cable ferry was not operating. I walked up to a man, John, who appeared to know the score and started asking questions. John was waiting for Richard to arrive on the other side of the river so he could contact him by radio to see when they wanted to put the ferry in the water. John's job was to bring the cable across the swollen river. Richard arrived, and they began talking on the radio. Richard was very casual about the whole thing. He thought the ferry should not be operated for at least another three days. Ice was still blocking the Mackenzie and backed up to the Arctic Red River ferry. John shook his head.

"Richard doesn't want to do one ferry and not the other."

"Why not?"

"Too many people would overtax Fort McPherson's facilities. They are already quite limited in their facilities." He laughed. I didn't. Indian women sat nearby tanning ungulate hides. Their men dodged ice floes and motored back and forth across the Peel in small skiffs, I suppose, attending to their business. Lynette and I turned around and drove back to Eagle Plains. We scotched Inuvik.

The weather remained marvelous on the Dempster. More snow vanished each day, and the emerging tundra crept up the mountainsides, the polar light accenting its wonderful colors. Lynette and I climbed Sheep Mountain. We saw pipits, wheatears and Say's phoebes, but were unable to find Smith's longspurs. We lay down on the tundra, protected from the wind by the rock outcroppings surrounding us and warmed by the sun. Red lichens gaily splotched the rocks, and tiny alpine flowers shone their reds, blues, whites, lavenders and yellows. Lynette thought Nature had taken a great deal of care in designing such a beautiful palette for us. Back at the camper, she broke out a bottle of Lafitte Rothschild given to us by a friend, and I played Mozart's *Quintet for Clarinet and Strings*.

At mile marker seven we stopped again and walked into the woods to Juliana Frisch's cabin where this time somebody was at home. A black and white dog lay sleepily on the porch, and the front door was open. The dog got up and lazily walked up to us and licked my hand.

"Hello, Mrs. Frisch. Are you home?" I called. A young woman and her daughter appeared in the doorway, the latter pointing to the dog and being the first to speak.

"Rudy is my friend."

We introduced ourselves and explained the purpose of our visit. Juliana immediately warmed to us when she learned we were birdwatchers, and invited us into her sparsely furnished cabin. We talked for an hour, and I bought one of her late husband's books. She was from Minneapolis and met her husband fifteen years ago in the bush. He was a self taught naturalist and had contributed much to the knowledge about nesting birds in that part of the Yukon. One day, while conducting research in the mountains, his heart stopped. Juliana said she and her daughter loved living by themselves in the bush, but now that the girl was almost five, she had to consider moving back into Dawson for her schooling. The girl grabbed me by the hand and led me outside. She clasped my hand tightly and showed me the stream from which they carry their water. Then she took me into her woods and told me stories about her friends, the animals and birds who lived there.

Back in Dawson, we replenished our supplies and then drove along Bonanza Creek Road, the heart of the goldrush. From my notes: *Many mines are still active. Huge dredges mechanize the operations. The valley is depressing—they're raping the damn place! Apparently no obligation to clean up the tailings.* We re-crossed the Yukon River and re-traced our route over the Top of the World Highway to Jack Wade Junction where we took the gravel Taylor Highway sixty-five miles north to Eagle, Alaska.

Eagle is a small gold mining town of less than two hundred people on the banks of the Yukon and is accessible by road only in the summer. Most of the vehicles we saw were pickup trucks with rifles lying in racks mounted above the rear windows. One man shaved burled spruce logs in front of his house. Pelts and fish dried in the sun at Eagle Village, the Indian settlement. Eagle's public boat landing on the Yukon's banks was called Hajec Landing, and a sign there explained why:

"IN MEMORY OF JOE HAJEC (POLACK JOE) ONE OF THE LAST OF A TOUGH, INDEPENDENT BREED OF MEN THAT HAVE VANISHED ALONG WITH THE LAST FRONTIER. SHOT AND KILLED ALONG WITH HIS MINING PARTNER DEWAYNE BOWERSON ON 22 DEC 1977 WHILE WORKING HIS CLAIM ON THE SOUTH FORK OF THE 40 MILE."

We ordered lunch at a local eatery. The owner of the establishment waited on us. She brought our sandwiches, and I asked her, "Did they ever catch Polack Joe's killer?"

"There were two of them. They were both caught and put in jail."

"Why did they kill Joe and his partner? Were they just really bad guys?"

"Nah. They're both real nice guys. They're out now."

"The killers are out of jail now?"

"Yeh. It was just a mining dispute. They didn't spend much time behind bars."

Lynette spotted Michael David's grave. John McPhee wrote extensively and fondly about Eagle Village's young chief in *Coming Into the Country,* his 1977 book about "America's Last Great Wilderness—Alaska." David, in his short life, apparently epitomized the difficulty of bridging contrasting cultures. He understood the arguments of the outside but preferred the life of his heritage. He was killed in a tragic truck accident.

Mary Lynn Robbins was from Tennessee. She and her husband, Frank, owned the Village Store which sold gas, groceries, native crafts and some tourist items. And the birds she carved from wood—loons, ducks, and sandpipers. She was charming, and looked and talked as if she had been raised in southern society, and I could see her as a young girl making her debut in a chiffon dress at the country club cotillion.

"Did you meet McPhee when he was here?"

"We arrived just after he left."

"How accurately do you think he portrayed Eagle?"

"He wasn't here long enough. You have to live here for a long while before you're accepted. Some of the locals were mad at him for what he wrote. But anyone who wasn't here any longer than he was would have carried away the same impressions. I did meet him though. He came back once and came to the store to tell me my pigs were loose."

Mary said she likes the natives and that they did most of their business with her. Frank was away for six to eight weeks working their gold claim. They also owned a trap line which produced martens, minks and wolves. They had decided to put the line with its three cabins on the market for six thousand dollars.

"How many acres go with the trap line, Mary?"

"Acres? Why none. We don't own the land."

"You don't own the land? What do you own?"

"Just the trap line and the cabins."

"What's to prevent someone else from trapping the same area?"

"Nobody messes with someone else's trap line. You don't own the land, you just find a place nobody is using and start trapping."

She had spent several winters working the line with Frank. They checked it by dog sled and snow machine, a cold and lonely operation.

Checking their lines involved working in the dark, carrying water from holes chopped in the ice, and sleeping in the utilitarian one room cabins. They built their first cabin in three days in the dead of winter. She said it was a tough but rewarding life.

"Why did you come to Alaska, Mary?"

"Frank and I had a problem in Florida."

"A problem?"

"Yes. It was time for us to move on." Her eyes said, "Don't ask!" I didn't.

"How do you like living in Eagle?"

"We're here to stay."

Lynette and I opened our dinner menus at a small restaurant on the bank of the Yukon. The waitress/cook was from Wyoming via Fairbanks. This was her summer job. Her advertised specialty was chicken and homemade noodles, the latter too tempting for me to refuse.

"My mother used to make homemade noodles. Man were they good! Haven't had homemade noodles in years. She rolled out the dough and cut the noodles individually. That the way you do it?"

Lynette gave me one of those "Keep it up, Buddy!" kind of looks reserved for any man talking with a modicum of affection about his mother's cooking.

Four guys pulled up outside the restaurant in a truck with Montana tags, trailering a twenty-one-foot fishing boat with a canopy and a 145 horsepower Evinrude outboard. They sat at a table next to us. Soon we learned three of them intended to spend the next two months floating from Eagle to Circle, Alaska, fishing the Yukon and its tributaries. One of them was one of the meanest looking hombres I've ever run across. A greasy looking black leather hat covered his greasy looking black shoulder-length hair. A black beard gave him a sinister and frightful mien, and his black laser-like eyes seemed to pierce anything or anyone at which they were directed. I decided he was a tough customer, as hard as they came. Yet, when he finally talked, he was as friendly as pie and bent over backwards to be nice, seemingly to prove he wasn't as mean as he looked. Even so, I wasn't quite convinced. One of his buddies looked like a clean cut IBM engineer who merely hadn't gotten around to shaving the past few days. He was equally friendly and even poured coffee for us. The third wore long black hair and was missing most of his teeth. He could have been part Indian. Taciturn at first, he too warmed up a bit. The fourth was the one not joining them on the river trip. He was from Fairbanks and would meet them with the truck in Circle. I asked them about a hundred questions.

"You sure seem interested in our little adventure. We could make room for another guy." This from the IBM-er. Lynette looked at me.

"Don't even think about going with them!" She looked at their table.

"He would, you know. Don't encourage him."

We camped at the Bureau of Land Management campground. Rain fell for the first time since we left the coast. It continued all night and the next day on our drive back to Tok. Now, instead of dust, we had to contend with mud. Back at our now familiar campground in Tok, the proprietors treated us like guests rather than customers.

Wildflowers lit up the Matanuska Valley with lupine and poppies predominant in the roadside meadows. Phalaropes and a yellow-billed loon foraged in a lake. This loon is distinguished from its more numerous cousins, common and Pacific loons, by its upward curving lower mandible which tends to give the bird a generally snooty appearance. Moose cows kept close watch over their newly born calves. Some people say a cow moose with a calf is more dangerous than a sow grizzly with her cub. Can you imagine being a grad student with the assignment of proving that theory?

Mount Sanford rose from the valley floor to more than 16,000 feet elevation. We ordered dinner at the Ranch House Lodge near Glenallen. An Alaskan named John was talking to a friend at the next table which, like our's, had legs made from caribou antlers. John pointed to the antlers and told his friend, "This place reminds me of a bar in Jackson Hole, Wyoming. I can't remember the name of the place."

"The Million Dollar Cowboy Bar." I offered. "Sorry, but I couldn't help overhearing your conversation, and I spend a lot of time in Jackson Hole."

"That's OK. Yeah, that's the name."

John grew up on the upper East Side of Manhattan. A machinist by trade, he now spent most of his free time hunting and hiking. He was about forty years old, handsome with a heavy black mustache, and had been through several divorces and most of South America, the Middle East and Europe along the way. The previous week he had to kill a black bear that had climbed into his corral, hungry for fresh horse flesh. I posed the question to John which was more dangerous—a mother moose or a mother grizzly. Our waitress overheard my question and pointed out the window to her pickup truck. The passenger side of the cab looked like it had taken a broadside shot from a cannon.

"That, boys, was the work of an enraged mother moose."

"How did it happen?"

"Was driving up a road near my place. She was on one side and the baby was on the other side of the road. She went beserk when I drove between them."

We drove from the restaurant down a side road into a valley pockmarked with sloughs. Caribou grazed the meadows and beavers swam in the ponds. We spent the night in a small state park pullover next to a pretty lake with wigeons and phalaropes. A mother moose and her young calf fed on aquatic vegetation near the lake's edge. We watched the tender scene from a distance.

In Palmer, we met again with Fred and Sara Machetanz. They told more stories about their winters in Unalakleet when they had forged a close relationship with the natives. One or two of the natives turned out to be related to Fred through his uncle. Fred showed us a painting of a musher and his dog team he soon would finish. They agreed to hold it for us until we returned in the middle of June.

From Palmer, we followed Willow Creek up the Hatcher Pass Road and hiked the last few miles to the well preserved ghost town at the old Independence Mine. Then we drove into Anchorage and found a safe place to leave our camper during the few days we planned on being on Kodiak Island. Our flight from Anchorage followed the Cook Inlet south, affording dramatic views of the Aleutian Range on the right and the Kenai Peninsula on the left, and then made a short hop across a corner of the Gulf of Alaska to Kodiak Island.

Alaska's oldest European community, Kodiak, was founded in 1792 by Russian explorers and trappers of sea otters. Russian Orthodox churches with their onion domes were reminders of the days when Alexander Baranof administered the Russian territories from Kodiak. Lynette and I registered at the Sheffield Hotel and walked to the Visitor Center. A young woman helped us and, to Lynette's delight, gave us a copy of their recommended walking tour of the city. When the two of them were finished highlighting the major points of interest, I asked the woman, "Where's a good place to get a beer?"

"Oh, the Sheffield Hotel. Just walk..."

"Pardon me for interrupting you, but where do you and your friends go to have a beer?"

"That's easy," she laughed. "Solly's."

Baranof stored furs in a warehouse that today has been turned into a museum featuring collections of early native artifacts. We were the only visitors, and a docent gave us her exclusive attention. Lynette was especially interested in their display of Russian samovars, so the woman related fully, it seemed, her expertise on the subject. We visited the late eighteenth-century Russian Orthodox Church, several shops, and then found Solly's. Marie tended bar and two fishermen had the stools to themselves until Lynette and I joined them.

"Can you recommend a good seafood restaurant in town?"

They all looked at one another and agreed there were no restaurants offering fresh seafood in Kodiak. Lynette frowned and said, "That's odd. Kodiak is one of the largest seafood exporters in the world and you can't find a restaurant serving fresh seafood."

One of the fishermen suggested the Northland Ranch for a good meal and cheap rooms. Marie added, "By the way, the VFW makes a pretty good meal too."

At Miller Point we toured Fort Abercrombie, a Second World War fortification with a terrific view of the rugged coastline and offshore islands. Sea otters frolicked in Monashka Bay while an Aleutian tern hovered over them to see what was up. On the way back to town, we stopped at the VFW where a few men were eating and watching TV.

"Hi, fellows. Back in town a woman told us you can buy a pretty good meal here. Do you have to be a member to come in?"

A tall lean guy with a pencil thin mustache looked around from the TV.

"You sure do. But I can sign you in as my guests which it would be my pleasure to do."

"Thanks. We appreciate your hospitality."

"I suggest trying the western omelette. They're the best you'll ever eat."

We tried them, and they were.

The next day we drove south along Women's, Kalsin and Isthmus bays to Chiniak Point, stopping for lunch at the Northland Inn which we liked so much, we told them to expect us back for the night. We walked the trail to Cape Chiniak and saw Aleutian terns, red-faced cormorants, puffins and other sea birds, and a number of World War II bunkers strategically placed where they overlooked the beaches and rolling breakers below. A northern shrike hovered in the strong wind and then swooped precipitously, nabbed a vole and carried it away, presumably with the intention of storing it impaled on a thorn somewhere.

Back at the Northland Inn we joined Alma and Bill for a couple of beers. They were the parents of the woman who owned and operated the Northland Ranch. Their daughter and her husband missed the ferry from Homer, so the parents were filling in until they returned. Alma and Bill come to Alaska in their motor home in summer and spend winters sailing the Caribbean in their trawler. They told us about the time several years ago when they joined the Peace Corps and built outhouses and wells in Ghana.

"Do you feel like you accomplished anything as Peace Corps volunteers?"

"Nah," Bill answered. "Not as far as the Africans are concerned. It was interesting for us though. We learned a lot."

Charlie and Robin came in and joined the four of us. Charlie was a fisherman from Chatham, Massachusetts, and Robin was from Minnesota and had recently gone through a divorce from a guy in the Coast Guard.

"Why did you leave Chatham for Alaska, Charlie?"

"The fish were running out down at the Cape."

"Charlie, it's so foreign to me that a person would want to go out in the Bering Sea for six months at a time and fish. If I had to make a living that way, I'd starve. Why did you choose to be a fisherman?"

"For the money, I guess. I was a marine. I'm forty-five years old and have a college degree. I've got some banking experience, but this is the only thing I've ever done in which I've been successful. I own my own boat and make plenty of money. It's a good life for me."

Tricia was the cook at breakfast. Her mother had written a book on the history of Kodiak Island. She showed it to us proudly and said she had helped her mother when she published an updated edition. She wanted to write and also worked part-time at a local weekly newspaper.

Matt, our waiter, wore a Central Dauphin Rams sweatshirt. He was surprised I not only knew where the school was (near Harrisburg, Pennsylvania) but also knew the Rams' athletic director who was one of my best friends from high school. Matt had just finished his sophomore year at Juniata College.

"What did your friends think, Matt, when they found out you were coming up here to work?"

"They thought I was a little crazy at first. But then I told them I was going to look for gold, and they thought that was OK."

Back in Anchorage, huge cranes made by Mitsubishi dredged the harbor in the Port of Anchorage where Lynette and I waited for my parents to disembark from their cruise ship. They were celebrating their fiftieth wedding anniversary by cruising the Inside Passageway, and now they were joining us for a few days. More than anything else, they wanted to see Denali National Park. They arrived on time, checked into a hotel, and then we gave them a tour of Anchorage. In the morning, we left for Denali and, along the way, saw an abundance of wildlife, including a cow moose and calf, and much beautiful scenery, including great views of Mount McKinley. We rode a tour bus into the park and saw everything my parents hoped for—grizzly bears, caribou, wolves, Dall sheep, moose, foxes, ptarmigan and wonderful wild flowers. In the evening we took a wildlife drive in our camper and saw a moose dancing frantically, trying to get away from a cloud of voracious mosquitoes. Eventually, the tortured bull wisely ran to a large patch of snow where the mosquitoes left him alone. We also saw several northern hawk owls perched in black spruce trees. My mother was fascinated by these large, diurnal owls with the hawk-like tail, the first she had ever seen.

Krissie's visit with us overlapped that of my parents by one day. We picked her up at the Anchorage airport and then went to the zoo to see their blue bear, a color phase of the black bear which, along with the resident wolverine, fascinated my dad. We drove toward Portage and had a great dinner at a restaurant in Girdwood that Lynette had read about. She had also checked the tide tables for the Turnagain Arm and knew a bore tide was expected around nine o'clock. The wall of water showed up as predicted at nine, and, parked in a pullout, we all enthusiastically waited for it. To this day, Mother isn't sure that there isn't a bit of northern magic tied up in those bore tides. I'm inclined to agree with her.

We saw my parents off at the airport and then showed Krissie around Anchorage, including a visit to the Museum of History and Art. Then, on a hike in Chugach State Park, we saw bear tracks, harebells and wild roses, and a family of shrikes. Later we shopped with Krissie in the tourist stores where she bought porcupine quills and beads in a native shop to make earrings for her friends. I had called my friend, Ed Rasmussen, and he had invited us to his home for dinner. His wife, Cathy, was out of town, but two other couples joined us, and we had a great evening talking mostly about Alaskans and how they party all summer and rest up all winter.

I had signed up for a four day birding trip to the Priboloff Islands. During my absence, Krissie and Lynette took the camper on a four day loop that included driving from Anchorage to Portage, loading the camper onto a train to Whittier, ferrying across Prince William Sound to Valdez, and then driving back to Anchorage via Glenallen and Palmer. They reportedly had a great time, doing all the things mothers and daughters enjoy doing together. For myself, birding the Priboloffs was a special treat.

From a letter I wrote to Mike: *...I'll leave it to Krissie and Mom to tell you about their camper and ferry circumscription and, instead, give you a report on my trip to St. Paul Island, the Priboloffs.*

As you know, Beringia connected Asia and North America during the last glacial age. The Priboloffs rose like lofty mountain peaks somewhere near the southern edge of the land bridge. Most of the landscape today is volcanic with relatively recent activity leaving large lava flows on the island.

About 200 years ago, the Russians sailed to the Priboloffs with their Aleut slaves to harvest fur seal pelts. Although the islands today retain much of their Russian cultural heritage, now the seals are protected from anything but native subsistence hunting. Saints Peter and Paul Russian Orthodox Church and its pastor, Father George Pletnikoff (an Aleut) offer spiritual guidance for the natives who make up most of the population (less than 700) of the islands. The church is lovely, beautifully cared for, and contains many wonderful icons. Many of the names of the people, streets and landmarks on the islands are derived from their Russian past.

The islands have a reputation for dreary, rainy weather, so we were pleasantly surprised when our Turboprop Electra approached St. Paul Island and the cloud cover below vanished. (Back in the early '60s, these planes were the newest thing, replacing the old prop jobs and introducing the jet age into commercial transportation. If I remember correctly, there were a lot of mechanical problems with them, and perhaps even a few of them went down, a recollection that didn't escape me when we climbed aboard and I saw "Electra" painted on the fuselage.) St. Paul's runway was com-

posed of a red volcanic gravel called "scoria," the same material used for all roadbeds on the island. Kenn Kaufman, a first class birder I had met before, was on the plane leading a bird tour for VENT Nature Tours, a happy coincidence because he invited me to tag along with their group.

The island appeared to be tundra, but, technically, it was "semi-tundra" since there was no permafrost. There were no trees except one or two varieties of ground-hugging types that looked more like vines than trees. Wild flowers were in full bloom with the lupines, including a pink albino variety, dominating the landscape and Arctic poppies, louseworts, rock jasmine, spring beauty, lady ferns and many others adding to a marvelous pot pourri of colors.

The Aleut community was quite colorful also with its buildings painted various shades of blue, red, grey and yellow. The elimination of commercial fur sealing in 1984 threw the island's economy for a loop, but the town was trying to rekindle the economy by developing a fishing industry. We checked into the King Eider (I swear) Hotel which was located across the street from a baseball diamond where a game between the local volunteer firemen and a church team was in full swing, so to speak.

The Priboloffs are the breeding grounds for more than two-thirds of the world's population of northern fur seals, putting the resident number at over one million individuals. The five hundred pound and up breeding males, called "beachmasters" for obvious reasons, are the first to arrive on the islands each year to establish territories. Then come the pregnant females, congregating in harems of anywhere from twenty to fifty or more. After having their pups, they are usually impregnated again. Many of the bulls evidenced nasty battle scars. The younger, sexually immature males and older, battle weary bulls haul themselves out of the sea and congregate in "hauling grounds" farther down the beach where, at the risk of sounding a bit anthropomorphic, I suppose they either are awaiting their day in the reproduction arena or reminiscing about the battles and copulations of days gone by.

The birding was spectacular. Where else can you see thousands of nesting puffins (tufted and horned), common and thick-billed murres, black and red-legged kittiwakes, red-faced cormorants and three species of auklets (least, parakeet and crested)? Not to mention large numbers of rock sandpipers, snow buntings, Lapland longspurs, and red and red-necked phalaropes? Or such rarieties as a common sandpiper, a long-toed stint, and a McKay's bunting (apparently mating with a snow bunting)? And even curiosities such as light and dark phase fulmars, Eurasian wigeons,

Priboloff gray rosy finches, king eiders, and the Eurasian race of the green-winged teal?

Other interesting observations included copulating thick-billed murres and Arctic foxes stepping unsurely onto precariously narrow cliff ledges, trying to filch bird eggs. I think my fondest memory, however, is sitting near the edge of a cliff high above the Bering Sea watching kittiwakes flying by gracefully, one at a time, as if they were passing in review. Mikey, old boy, I wish you could have been there!

Lynette and Krissie met me at the airport, full of enthusiasm about their travels. Krissie was especially excited about having seen her first puffin, sitting on a floating chunk of ice near the magnificent glaciers that dropped into Prince William Sound.

The three of us had a great dinner in Anchorage at a restaurant called Simon and Seafort's. From my notes: *Lots of laughs. What a sense of humor Kris has developed. We put her on a plane late that night. Lynette and I were so sad to see our baby leave.*

In 1987, only vehicles with permits from the Alaska Department of Transportation were allowed to drive the Dalton Highway, commonly known as the "Haul Road," to Prudhoe Bay. I had arranged for a journalist's pass before we left Illinois. Now we were required to stop at the DOT in Fairbanks to have the permit registered. I asked the agent how I could obtain permission to drive onto the property of the oil companies to see their operations and observe what impact they have had on the wildlife. He referred me to Jo English of Arco's Public Affairs Office who in turn arranged for us to be given a tour by Kris Garlasco from their Office of Environmental Relations.

Thirty-nine miles north of Fairbanks, the Elliott Highway turned to gravel. After another forty-five miles, we left the Elliott and followed the Dalton Highway beside the Trans-Alaska Pipeline for 416 miles to Prudhoe Bay, the pipeline's northern terminus. Rain fell steadily. The Wildwood General Store was located about a hundred yards downhill from the highway in a muddy quagmire, but we needed gas, and it was only available here. We slid to a stop beside the only pump. I inserted the hose in our tank, but the pump didn't work. A kid who looked about six years old stood nearby and watched.

"Anybody around to give us a hand?" I asked, wiping water from my face.

"Sure. Me," came the squeaky-voiced answer.

"Yes, but I need some gas, and the pump doesn't work."

"I'll get it. Pull over to those drums." And the boy began hand pumping gas from a fifty-five gallon drum into a five gallon container, then poured it into the camper. I shook my head and looked at Lynette.

"Shades of the Peruvian Andes!" she smiled.

"What's your name?" I asked the boy as he pumped the second container full.

"Chad."

"Where do you go to school, Chad?"

"My mom teaches us."

"Do you have brothers and sisters?"

"Fourteen."

"Fourteen? Wow!"

"Well, really only four regular brothers and sisters. But there are nine adopted."

Chad collected our money and I slid and fishtailed our way back up to the highway, thankful for the apparently firm surface under the layer of mud. We continued up the Haul Road to the Yukon River. Signs along the way informed us of the colorful names of creeks, rivers and other landmarks—No Name Creek, Beaver Slide, Roller Coaster, Gobbler's Knob. Finger Rock was a rather accurate if somewhat obscene description of a Tor, or rock outcropping, near the top of one of the many passes we drove over. Lynette commented that "the Haul Road is more like the Dempster than the Dempster."

The Coldfoot Truck Stop lay fifty-seven miles north of the Arctic Circle and advertised itself as the furthest north truck stop in the world. We filled up with gas, washed some of the mud from the car, and went inside to have a couple of beers. Dick Mackey, an Iditerod winner, owned the place. I had brought an article from our newspaper along that had been written a year and a half ago about him and his truck stop. I wanted to show it to Mackey, but he was out of town.

In the foothills of the Brooks Range, the rain turned to snow and obscured much of what we had hoped to see. The snow became worse on the Chandalar Shelf and turned into a real blizzard as we fishtailed our way up toward the Continental Divide at Atigun Pass and I silently wondered whether we would make it without chains. Across the pass we began our gradual descent down the North Slope. Snow continued for another fifty miles, and golden plovers and jaegers roosted beside the road bed. The snow stopped, we began seeing caribou and then passed through a herd of thousands. Calving had just begun.

From my notes: *The pipeline museum in Valdez and the accompanying literature make the pipeline seem awesome, and it truly is. Yet, when you drive beside it for hundreds of miles, it almost begins to look like something out of a tinker toy box with all of its bends and seams.*

Arriving at the first human colony on Mars may not be more alien than arriving at the community of Prudhoe Bay. Building modules were set on stilts to prevent melting of the permafrost. There was a sameness to the modules, and there were no Chevron signs or Golden Arches to tell you where anything is. I stopped the camper and flagged down a guy driving an Arco truck.

"Welcome to Prudhoe Bay!"

"Thanks! I'm looking for a gas station and then a public telephone."

"I'll take you to a place where you can get gas. Then the best thing is for you to use my car phone. Who are you calling?"

"Kris Garlasco."

"No problem. She's a friend of mine. My name's Charlie. Charlie Hurst."

Charlie was from Atlanta. He worked in Prudhoe two weeks on, two weeks off, with a schedule of ten hour days, seven days a week. He spent his two weeks off in Anchorage. Our self-appointed guide and friend found us a gas station and then took us to see Kris Garlasco who dropped everything she was doing and gave us a tour of the "Unit."

The area was clean with no apparent industrial debris or waste. Waterfowl dabbled and bobbed in natural ponds beside the streets. Kris stressed the importance of maintaining the environment in its natural state as much as possible. She showed us where gravel had been dug from pits for use in the construction of roads and building pads. The pits filled up with fresh water during spring breakup and now provided the community with a supply of fresh water and habitat for fish and birds.

Kris gave us a tour of the oil fields. She explained that refining in Prudhoe was limited to their own use. Gas and water were separated from the oil with the later being pumped back into the ground to maintain well pressure. The oil was pumped from the drill sites to flow stations, and then through the pipeline to Valdez. Gas was used to fire their own power plants. The community had plants for water recycling and desalinization.

The port area was our next stop where breakup was just beginning in the Arctic Ocean. The lighting created a scene with floating ice floes that looked like one of Fred Machetanz's paintings called "Breakup."

"What's the ratio of men and women in Prudhoe, Kris?"

"Less than 10% are women."

"Where do you buy your groceries?"

"Groceries?" She laughed. "Nobody does any cooking up here. There's a 'sundries' store at the Grizzly Bear Inn. Other than that, I wouldn't even know where to go to buy a bottle of milk!"

The heart of the community was the Prudhoe Bay Operation Center which included their offices, recreation areas, living quarters, and dining room. The facilities and food were fabulous. Their's was a remote assignment in a harsh climate, and it seemed nothing was spared to provide the workers as much away from home comfort as possible. Arco even had two 727s on call to fly their people to and from Anchorage every day.

We used Arco's bathroom facilities and ate in their dining room, but we spent the night camped in the parking lot of the Deadhorse Hotel.

Prudhoe Bay, Alaska, June 28, 1987

Lynette shook me awake and whispered in my ear, "Happy Birthday, Darwin!" Mostly I lose the sense of time while traveling and don't even think about dates and time. I looked at the date on my watch, and, sure enough, it was my 47th birthday. We met Kris Garlasco for breakfast. She gave us directions to Kaparuk where we met Paul Hampton, a biologist Arco employed for environmental oversight of their activities. Paul was a good birder and spent the better part of the day taking us to some of his favorite habitats. We drove around the many lakes and ponds filled with nesting ducks, phalaropes, shorebirds, and king and spectacled eiders. We drove to Oliktok Point on the Beaufort Sea, and, on the pack ice, we saw ringed seals, a polar bear delicacy. We scoped the pack ice but saw no bears.

"Paul, from an environmental standpoint, how are these guys doing?"

"I'm in their employ, so my answers to that question, of course, must be considered suspect. But I have to tell you they really try. I can't say we don't have our differences, but there aren't many. Usually they listen to me and try to do the right thing."

It's a fact that, if you are driving on a gravel road and don't slow to a crawl when you pass an oncoming truck, you are very likely to incur damage to your windshield. Driving back to Prudhoe, a speeding truck approached us, and I was talking to Lynette about spectacled eiders or ringed seals or what a nice birthday I had had, and I forgot to slow down. A big spider like crack in our windshield was the result. The up side was that the rain had stopped, the sun shone brightly, and the sky was only blue as we climbed the North Slope toward the spectacular snow-capped Brooks Range. Yellow wagtails and northern wheatears flitted among the willows surrounding the roadside pullover where we ate lunch. Atigun Pass offered marvelous vistas of the dramatic alpine scenery, and a rainbow spread out below us.

The Dietrich River raced beside the road, and we found a wonderful place to camp. Lynette prepared dinner while I opened a birthday bottle of Piper Heidzick champagne given to us by a friend for just such an occasion. We had just finished dinner and were settling in when we heard the roar of heavy equipment. A road grader and a truck pulled into our campsite. The guy driving the grader left it parked no more than twenty yards from us and jumped into the truck with his colleague. Both of them smiled and waved as they drove away. Looking at an enormous yellow road grader was not what we had in mind for a view, so we decided to drive on. An hour south we found a serene lake filled with scaups, buffleheads, and grebes. Darting and hovering terns foraged for fish, and a moose with gigantic antlers fed on aquatic vegetation. Across the lake, the low sun turned the White Mountains pink. Now here was a campsite.

Dick Mackey had not yet returned when we stopped at the Coldfoot Truck Stop and filled our gas tank. Lynette and I sat on stools at the restaurant and ordered breakfast. A guy with a Notre Dame sweatshirt sat next to me and must have seen us driving the camper.

"See you're from Illinois. What part?"

"Southern. Where you from?"

"South of Chicago. Blue Island."

"Do you know Bob Damm?"

"Sure do. I know his brother, Dave, better though. I went to school with him."

F.M. Heffernan worked on the pipeline for Alyeska. His son sat next to him. The two of them were going to float the Kouyukuk River to Bettles. Another guy sitting next to Lynette left the Lower 48 and a job in commercial real estate to work a gold mine. He thought the life would be less stressful and help him lose a hundred pounds and quit smoking.

"How much have you lost?"

"About thirty." He lit up a smoke.

The guy who was driving the road grader came in and pulled up a stool.

"Are you the guys that were pulled over up the road?"

"We are."

"I sure hated to pull that grader over and ruin your view."

"No problem. We just moved on and found another place."

"Well, I was sure sorry."

The pancakes were so big Lynette and I shared a short stack. The waitress looked at me.

"You're not a small man. Are you sure that'll be enough for you?"

"Probably will be. If I want more, I'll order them. They're the biggest pancakes I've ever seen on a plate."

"That's the way these boys like them. After all, they're truck drivers." I asked her to give Dick Mackey the newspaper article I had been carrying for the past three or four months.

We stopped at the Yukon River bridge for lunch. Not much was left of a disassembled hovercraft that had been used to transport Haul Road trucks across the Yukon prior to the bridge being built. Cliff swallows came to the river's edge to collect mud for building their nests under the bridge. Yellow warblers sang in the willows. A guy and his dog floated by in a kayak with a sail. He appeared to be taking a picture of us with his telescopic lens while we followed him with our binoculars.

How many places in the world see temperatures vary 150 degrees or more in a year? The answer is, at least one—Fairbanks, Alaska, which typically sees temperatures fall to -60 degrees Fahrenheit in the winter and climb to 90 degrees in the summer. Lynette and I can vouch for the higher extreme, because that's what our camper thermometer registered when we set up camp in the Fairbanks campground. We spent the day preparing for our friends from Belleville, Barb and Ed Brennan, who, as they promised months before, were flying to Anchorage to join us for ten days. We washed and cleaned the camper, shopped for provisions in the air conditioned grocery store and did our laundry in the un-air conditioned laundromat. We slept in separate beds to escape the heat—Lynette "upstairs" in the camper's pop-top and I in the "downstairs" pullout bench seat.

Early in the morning, we left for Anchorage and enjoyed the spectacular views of Mount McKinley rising mightily into the clear blue sky. We were running a few hours ahead of schedule, so Lynette and I took a bus into Denali National Park to Igloo Creek, just to find Arctic warblers. We heard several of them singing in the willows and eventually saw the clandestine little skulkers when they perched high in the shrubbery.

We greeted the Brennans at the Anchorage airport as enthusiastically as can be expected at one o'clock a.m. After a few hours sleep, Lynette and I picked up fresh sweet rolls, then picked up Barb and Ed, and drove to Ship Creek where we had breakfast and watched bright red king salmon climbing the fish ladder. The Anchorage Museum was closed for the holiday weekend, so we deferred that visit and instead drove to Portage Glacier where we loaded the camper and ourselves onto the train for the short ride through a number of mountain tunnels to Whittier. There we boarded the same ferry Lynette and Krissie took on their trip from Whittier to Valdez.

Huge kittiwake colonies nested on cliffs and puffins and other alcids lept out of the sea to avoid the ferry's approach. Sea otters swam on their backs, admiring their catches. The ferry's route brought us within spitting distance of Columbia Glacier. The ship weaved its way through a maze of calved icebergs on which harbor seals slept in the afternoon sun. Further east in Prince William Sound, commercial fishing boats tended their miles of nets. Between exclamations over the scenery and wildlife, we had a lot of laughs as our friends brought us up to date on the hometown gossip.

The ship served salmon for dinner. I saw a plate of beautiful ginger cookies on an empty table. A waiter walked by.

"May we have some of those cookies for desert?"

"Sorry, Sir. They're for the ship's officers."

"Are you sure you can't find some of them for us?"

"I'll see what I can do."

It wasn't long before we had ginger cookies with our coffee. The plate on the empty table had disappeared.

On our last trip to Valdez, Lynette had found a B&B for the Brennans and made reservations. The pregnant attendant at the Bear Paw Campground now was a proud mother of a two day old son, twenty-four inches long and ten plus pounds. We had made reservations, so she saved our same space even though the campground was full.

Valdez, Alaska, July 4, 1987

Happy Independence Day! Ed wanted to go salmon fishing more than anything else. The pinks were running, and holiday fishermen and women were lined up along the shore and on the pier catching them. We rented the appropriate equipment and found a couple of empty places to fish. A guy to our right fished from a rock and caught six, his limit, very quickly. During that time Ed and I caught nothing while everyone else seemed to be successful. A Japanese man to my left caught three quickly, and his family cheered him on. Ed became frustrated and quit. The Japanese man, who didn't appear to be very skillful with his fishing rod, cast his line over mine into the hole where Ed had been fishing and promptly pulled in the biggest fish we saw all morning.

We headed north on the Richardson Highway over Thompson Pass to Copper Center where we had made a reservation at the Copper Center Lodge for the Brennans. Barb felt like a nap, but Lynette, Ed and I felt more like a beer. We left Barb at the lodge and drove down the highway a few miles to the Grizzly Bear Saloon. Two or three dozen motorcycles were parked outside the bar, and, when we went inside, only three stools were empty at the far left end of the bar. All the other stools and the tables were occupied by the Hell's Angels of Alaska. I tried to strike up a conversation with the Angel to my right. He was pretty unresponsive, and the more he resisted my charming questions like—"How many are in your club?", "How do you become a member?" etc.—the more determined I was to engage him in a friendly conversation. I could see another guy at the other end of the bar watching us. Soon he walked down to us, extended his hand, and introduced himself.

"Hi, I'm the president of Hell's Angels. Welcome to Alaska, and Happy Fourth of July!" That's all it took. Now they all wanted to talk with us. They even bought us a beer and asked us to join them in a toast to the birth of "the greatest country on Earth, the United States of America!" A ragtime pianist played on a tinny old upright, purportedly Alaska's oldest, and was terrific. We returned to the lodge and found Barb rejuvenated and then joined people of all ages and types at Copper Center's Independence Day Street Dance.

Later, still in a patriotic and celebratory mood, we mixed a large pitcher of vodka gimlets and took a drive on a rugged track into the bush. After midnight the light turned wonderful—pinks and oranges and yellows. On the deeply rutted road, we drove precariously along a cliff, and a cloud fell down the other side of the canyon. The track left the canyon and followed the high rolling contour of the tundra. Mount Wrangell shone pink in the distance, and the Klutina River was a winding thread of glass in the valley below. We parked the camper, poured four gimlets, and cranked up a Hank Williams, Jr., tape. I still have a vague memory of Eddie and me running across the damp, dimly lit tundra, trying not to spill our gimlets and splashing water up our bare legs. A pleasant, light rainfall began while we climbed a ridge singing "Whisky Bent and Hell Bound."

After a late breakfast of sourdough pancakes at the Copper Center Lodge, we headed west over the Denali Highway. Caribou grazed in the meadows, and, in a pond, a half dozen bufflehead hatchlings trailed behind their mother. Lynette, in an accurate description, said that, from a distance, they looked like swimming chickadees. In a stream, a mother moose and her calf fed on aquatic vegetation. We stopped to watch them, and she sent the calf up the far hillside to hide in the brush where, except for moving its ears, it remained perfectly still. She continued eating, submerging most of herself and then emerging above the surface of the creek with huge mouthsful of dripping vegetation. Mosquitoes swarmed around her head, and she wasted no time getting back under the water.

At Denali National Park, we saw grizzly bears, wolves and Dall sheep on our wildlife drives. Willow ptarmigan now were watching over their young. We ran the exciting rapids of the Nenana River gorge and saw cliffs with a volcanic layer of eighty million-year old basalt overlying sedimentary shale. Our raft rounded a bend in the river, and a bull moose with enormous antlers stared at us from the shore, only a few feet away.

On the way to Fairbanks, we stopped at Skinny Dick's Halfway Inn for a cup of the "free coffee" they advertised. Skinny Dick was truly deserving of his popular appelation. Hanging on the wall was what Dick described as "the largest interlocking moose antlers in Alaska."

"How much for the antlers, Dick?"

"I turned down $10,000. But I'd take $20,000."

We spent the night at the Cripple Creek Resort. After dinner, we "whooped" it up at the Malamute Saloon. A boy played "jag-time" tunes on the piano and a woman recited Robert Service verses. The Brennans were really getting into Alaska.

On the way back to Anchorage, we stopped in Eklutna and visited the Russian Orthodox Church. Father George from St. Paul Island on the Priboloffs had asked me to pass his regards along to Father Simeon in Eklutna, a request I dutifully fulfilled. Then we drove to Palmer to visit Fred and Sara Machetanz. The six of us drank margaritas while we listened to more stories about Unalakleet. Spending an interesting afternoon with Sara and Fred is a privilege and a pleasure not to be forgotten. We reviewed again the paintings Fred had for sale. Ed and I looked at each other, smiled and knew what we wanted to buy. Two of the paintings were rather a natural pair. "Language of the Snow" was a scene of an Eskimo father teaching his son how to read animal tracks in the snow. "New Boots" was a scene of a father lacing boots he had made on his son's feet.

"Which one do you want, Darwin?"

"You choose. I like them equally."

"Language" now hangs in the Brennan' home and "Boots" hangs in ours.

Our flight to Kotzebue was uneventful except for one noticeable bump. The pilot announced we had just crossed the Arctic Circle. In Kotzebue, each year after June 3rd, the sun doesn't set for thirty-six days. With a very friendly population of 2,100, it is the second largest Eskimo village in Alaska. We took Lynette's walking tour of the town, and Ed expressed at least some interest in buying the Yamaha dealership. (Transportation in Kotzebue was provided primarily by snow machines in the winter and ATVs in the summer.) Our Kotzebue excursion included a folk show with dances and blanket tosses. We took a bus to an Eskimo fishing camp six miles south of town, and I walked back so I could check out the birds. If you can believe it, we had dinner at a Chinese restaurant.

Ed and I decided to stay up the whole night which, as I said, was really day. About midnight, we grabbed a six pack and two chairs and made ourselves comfortable on the Nul-Luk-Vik Hotel's balcony overlooking the Chukchi Sea. The sun had slowly sunk in the west, but, instead of setting, began following the horizon north. Far in the distance, a couple miles away, we could see a small red sail. Through my binoculars we determined a wind surfer was on a fast tack toward our beach. We looked at each other trying to imagine who would be windsurfing far out in the Chukchi Sea at 2:00 in the morning. When our hero beached his board, Ed went to see who he was and learned the guy was a world-class wind surfing competitor who lived in Kotzebue.

The night, or day, as it were, wore on. The sun followed its phenomenal path along the western horizon to its northern most point and then tracked the eastern horizon south. Sometime early in the morning it began to rise from the eastern horizon. What a show!

Nome was our next stop. Gold on the beaches lured more than thirty thousand people to Nome in 1898. Today the population is less than ten percent of that number. Gold is still sought on the beaches of the Bering Sea and in the streams near Nome. We toured a gold mining operation and tried our luck at panning, managing to separate a few flakes of the shiny metal from a panful of creek gravel. A tour of the city could not ignore a plethora of bars and many drunks, most of them Eskimos. What is it in the genes of some native peoples—Eskimos, Indians, Aborigines—that makes them so vulnerable to alcohol?

Nome is the terminus of the annual Iditerod sled dog race. The last few miles of the Iditerod route follow the coast south of Nome. Small gold mining operations lined the beaches. The miners wait for storms to bring in fresh sand and gravel and then work their sluice boxes. Howard Farley, a veteran of the Iditerod, kept his dogs at his place on the beach. I asked him whether he joined his neighbors sluicing for gold.

"Dogs are my gold. I win every day."

I visited with Nancy McGuire, the owner and publisher of the Nome Nugget. The newspaper's office was located on the main street, and it appeared to have an independent and aggressive editorial policy. A black mongrel dog lay at Nancy's feet.

"What's your dog's name?"

"Walter Cronkite," she replied smiling.

Remaining true to the town's image, our hotel sported a large sign advertising its name, The Nugget Inn. The four of us found an empty table at the bar. The bartender, Marilyn, took our order. I asked her where she was from.

"St. Paul, Minnesota."

"How did you end up in Nome?"

"Ten years ago, my husband and I canoed into the wilderness from Selawik, a village east of Kotzebue just above the Arctic Circle. We had our traps and four dogs with us in the canoe. We built a small log cabin in the bush, and our supplies didn't arrive until four months after they were scheduled to be flown in. We almost starved to death! A pack of wolves took up residence around our cabin. We were afraid to go out to hunt or fish. The wolves knew we were in bad shape. Then the Indians told the BLM (Bureau of Land Management) we were on their sacred land and the BLM kicked us out. We burned down our cabin, came back to Nome and have been here ever since."

"Wow! What a story! You must like living in Nome?"

"We do. My husband works on a gold dredge in the summer. Twelve hours a day, seven days a week. You may have heard of him. He paddled a canoe from New Orleans to Nome. It's in the *Guiness Book of World Records!*"

A friendly state trooper, A.J. Charlton joined us.

"What are you guys doing up here?"

"Just seeing what's up at the top of the world."

I wanted to look for gyrfalcons, so Lynette came with me while A.J. drove Ed and Barb north to the village of Teller. Lynnie and I drove south along the Iditerod Trail to Safety Lagoon. Dwarf fireweed and wild sweetpeas lined the road, and bar-tailed godwits nested in the grassy meadows. Salmon hung from racks drying in the sun at fish camps, and we saw a beached walrus. Then we took a road inland toward Taylor and saw nesting gyrfalcons on a cliff. Back at the Nugget Inn, the Brennans told us a very rare white wagtail had been reported foraging on a sand spit near Teller. We were scheduled to leave for Anchorage in the morning.

Nome, Alaska, July 13, 1987

Happy Anniversary, Lynette and Darwin! The plan was to fly to Anchorage and be the Brennans' guest for our anniversary dinner at Simon and Seafort's before Barb and Ed left for St. Louis early the following morning. At the airport we were told the plane was late. That gave me an idea. I would try to arrange a flight to Teller to see the wagtail and take a later plane back to Anchorage. Our scheduled plane was going to be late anyway. After some inquiries, I found a mail plane making a run to Teller and Wales. The pilot said he could drop me off at Teller and pick me up on his return trip. I would have two hours to find the bird, and we would be back in Nome in time for me to catch the second plane to Anchorage. I could meet Lynette and the Brennans at the restaurant. Brilliant! Nobody else thought my idea was so great, but they all agreed to indulge my birding eccentricity.

The low altitude flight over the Seward Peninsula tundra was magnificent. At Teller, I helped a guy push start his truck in exchange for a ride from the landing strip to the sand spit several miles away where the bird had been reported. I checked every bird I could find on and near the sand spit. The wagtail was not there. Back in Anchorage, Barb, Lynette and Ed were all a bit surprised when, just as I said I would, I showed up at Simon and Seafort's in time for dinner.

"Did you guys think I was going to miss my own anniversary dinner? With Brennan picking up the tab?"

"The thought occured to me," Lynette smirked.

"Hey, Darwin! That was an expensive bird not to find."

"Thanks, Ed."

We spent the next few days in Anchorage getting ready for the rugged Alcan Highway drive south to the Lower 48. We shopped for groceries, and had the camper serviced at the VW dealer. I settled with Artique, Ltd. for the Machetanz painting, and Ed Rasmussen and I met for lunch again where we talked mainly about Alaska. His family had played a significant role in the great state's history, and he was proud of what they had done.

"Darwin, when you come to Alaska, you're not reading history, you're making it."

One evening, while Lynette finished the laundry, I fixed dinner—sauerkraut, fried potatoes and sausage. Later, we watched a softball game in progress at a park next to the campground while enjoying a mug of coffee. I could tell Lynette was pondering something important.

"I've been thinking."

"You wish we had brought along our baseball mitts."

"No. I've been thinking about where we should live."

"Have you concluded anything?"

"I think we should live in Jackson. If it turns out that it's too small, we can always move. But we both like Jackson, and we don't know whether we would like the other places we've talked about."

"You've sold me!"

"Instead of leaving for Africa right away, we can live in our condo while we look for a home. Then, hopefully, we could move in this fall, take our furniture out of storage, and leave for Africa after Christmas."

"I'm there!"

Now I was ready to get on with it. We drove to Tok to pick up the Alaska Highway. The woman at the Sourdough Campground greeted us.

"So you're back!"

"Yep. We're going home."

"I didn't think we were ever going to see you again."

"You didn't think we would leave without saying good-bye?"

We crossed into Yukon Territory, drove through Whitehorse and on to Watson Lake where we spent a hot night at a mosquito infested campground. This was after having our dinner interrupted at a lovely roadside pullover by a pickup truck full of drunken adults with young children. I wakened at 1:30 a.m., and, for the first time in the past two months, saw complete darkness.

Crossing into British Columbia, we continued south on the Cassiar Highway and camped on beautiful, turquoise Kinaskan Lake which turned almost black when a storm moved in and the wind whipped up whitecaps. With an unobstructed view from inside our camper, we saw the storm moving through the lake system. People throttled up their boats to get off the lake. The threat blew through, luckily, mostly wind, dark clouds and little rain. Later, I built a fire and roasted hot dogs.

At Prince George, we did our laundry, picked up supplies and cleaned the car. We camped in Purden Lake Provincial Park where, in the evening, we walked along the lake. Vegetation re-emerged in a small burn covered with pink and lavender fireweed. Two baby loons swam alone, then their mother surfaced behind them with a fish. She fed it to one of them, then sang her mournful song. Lynette wondered if she weren't trying to teach the fledglings that captivating call as well as how to catch their supper. Later we attended an outdoor astronomy talk by a guy from the Vancouver planetarium. He had long blond hair and wore a blue sweater with holes over a black sweatshirt and had a great rapport with children. After a long twilight, we looked through his seventeen inch telescope and saw Saturn and various nebulae. At Lynette's request, I built a campfire.

The Canadian Rockies had always been described to us in superlative terms, and we could see what all the fuss was about when the Yellowhead Highway entered the Rockies and Mount Terry Fox and Mount Robson came into view. Near a bridge crossing a canyon stream, black swifts, the first I had ever seen, swept into view foraging for insects. We crossed Red Pass and descended into Jasper, a small lovely town with a European flavor. A naturalist at the Jasper National Park Visitor Center gave me good leads for finding black-backed woodpeckers, olive-sided flycatchers and white-tailed ptarmagans, all birds I had never seen. Lynette and I saw the woodpeckers on an afternoon hike past mysterious Medicine Lake which rises and falls with no outlet apparent except during spring runoff when underground caves become full of water. On the trail, a young couple from Sudbury told us they had never before traveled but now were on their way to Queen Charlotte Island where they intended to help the Haida fight development of their sacred ancestral grounds.

"What are you looking at with your binoculars?" the fellow wanted to know.

"Mostly birds."

"I like birds. I'm now into *National Geographic* and all that. I like to watch their specials on TV." His girl friend gazed at him admiringly. In Malign Canyon's narrow, deep gorge, we saw mountain goats picking their way along cliff edges. Later, a brown black bear and a small herd of elk seemed very much at home walking through our campground.

The next day we hiked Portal Creek Trail and heard the pip-pip-pipping of olive-sided flycatchers. Then a male perched at the top of a conifer and sang the characteristic "Quick! Three beers!" The following day we hiked over the tundra to Wilcox Pass, admiring the spectacular glacial scenery. Delicate alpine forget-me-nots, blue with yellow, star-like centers, grew profusely along the trail. We reached the pass and rested, sitting on a large rock outcropping beside another couple with binoculars strapped around their necks. I asked them if they had seen any white-tailed ptarmigans. They hadn't. I looked over my shoulder. A mother white-tailed ptarmigan and her two chicks picked their way along a small stream only thirty yards away. The park naturalist's suggestions had delivered all three birds I inquired about.

The enormous Columbia Icefield straddles the Continental Divide, and its huge glaciers, hundreds of feet thick, feed three oceans, the Atlantic, Pacific and Arctic. We drove the Icefields Parkway through rugged terrain with marvelous scenery—snowcapped mountains, waterfalls, glaciers— and, as we crossed Sunwapta Pass, entered Banff National Park, Canada's oldest. In the town of Lake Louise, we enjoyed a free pancake breakfast at a grand opening of a shopping mall developed and owned by Cree Indians.

Storm clouds rolled in and fell over the cliffs as we climbed three and a half miles along Lake Louise through alternating rain-sunshine-hail-thunder to a teahouse. We hiked back to town and stopped at the bar of the venerable Chateau Louise for a beer. Bruce Harding joined us at our table. His friend, Jacqueline Dolan, was playing a Celtic harp and singing Irish songs. She took a break and sat with us. I looked at her dark hair and blue eyes.

"How did an Irish lass get a name like Jacqueline?"

She laughed. "My parents were good Catholics and were going to call me Jacinta, the name of one of the Fatima girls, but my sister couldn't pronounce Jacinta."

"Is there a saint named Jacqueline?"

"I don't know, but I'm working on that."

We hiked four miles up the Spray River drainage and sat below a wooden bridge on a limestone outcropping, cooling our feet in the water. A tail-bobbing pipit walked to the stream's edge where the sun's rays sparkled off the cascading water. Bighorn sheep grazed the highlands. We returned on the river's other side to the Banff Springs Hotel, drove up Sulphur Mountain for lunch, and then hiked to Lake Minnewanka and sat on a rock, enjoying the cool breeze coming off the lake. Back at the campground, I made a salad for dinner. The next morning a little boy about five or six years old came into the bathroom while I was shaving. He was carrying a pot, I suppose for water, and looked at me with lather all over my face. I said "hi," and he ran outside.

"There's a stranger in there." I could hear him declare.

"Well, what do you expect? This is a campground." Apparently from his sister. He came back inside.

"Are you the waterboy?"

"I have to do everything. I'm the waterboy and the watergirl."

"You don't look like a girl to me."

"I'm not a girl," he laughed. "Where are you camping?"

"Just across the street from the washroom. Where are you?"

"Down there," he pointed.

"Have fun."

He left with a full pail.

We continued south through Calgary and Waterton Lakes National Park, and into the United States and Glacier National Park. Under any other circumstances, such a drive would have been exciting. But, for me, our route had become prosaic. Since we had left Alaska, we were no longer meeting "drifters" and pioneers. Now we were meeting vacationers, and, as nice as they were, I was ready to return to Jackson Hole. Lynette had laid out a plan to establish roots there. I was ready to get on with that. And to begin preparing for our next odyssey—Africa.

Chapter Five
Drifting Darkly: Africa

Isak Dinesen, in her book, "Out Of Africa," wrote about her life in the Ngong Hills near Nairobi, Kenya. Once, when she returned to her home from an airplane ride with her friend, Denys Finch-Hatton, an old Kikuyu tribesman greeted her:

"Did you see God?"
"No, Ndwetti, we did not see God."
"Aha, then you were not up high enough."

Lynette, Johnny, and friends; Kenya

PREPARATIONS
Jackson Hole, Wyoming, September, 1987

Soon after returning to Jackson, Lynette and I found a log home for sale that seemed just right for us. The property was distinctly western. Surrounded by mountains, it sat on a willow lined stream and included two barns and a pasture for horses. We moved in and have lived here ever since. True to the plan Lynette laid out at the softball game in Anchorage, we spent the next few months decorating the house to her taste and enjoying autumn in Jackson.

Wonderfully warm sunny days and cool clear nights continued through most of November that year. Each day I looked across the Snake River through my binoculars and watched Munger Mountain. The aspen leaves turned golden and the elk slowly grazed their way down to the valley. In the mornings, I rode my bike under the Tetons, trying to whip my aging body into condition in anticipation of the strenuous demands certain to come from the sands of the Sahara and the mud of the Congo. In the afternooons, I sat on our deck, reading books like Lonely Planet's *Africa On a Shoestring* and Simon and Jan Glen's *The Sahara Handbook.* I studied maps, trying to find a route that would get us across the Sahara to Kenya without going through Chad or Sudan where people were killing each other in bloody civil wars.

Arrangements had to be made. Friends agreed to watch the house and pick up our mail while we were gone. A Chicago freight forwarder would handle the shipping of our camper from Newark to Le Havre, France. The American Automobile Association issued International Driver's licenses for Lynette and me and a *Carnet de Passage* for our camper. We contracted for insurance, updated our innoculations and medicine kit, and bought airline tickets to Paris where, at the appropriate embassies, we would arrange for necessary visas while the camper was being shipped.

Newark, New Jersey, January 13, 1988

Along with December came the snowy winter. We spent the holidays in Jackson, and then drove to Chicago to spend a few days with Lynette's mother and to Pennsylvania to see my parents. Then we drove the camper to the docks in Newark where, it seemed to Lynette, "Everybody speaks everything but English. Even the few people who speak English do it differently." I was told to take the camper to Tommy Carrs in the warehouse. There I was told Tommy was either "at the pen, at the office, or in the trailer."

"What does Tommy look like?"

"He's short, blond with a page boy, and very skinny."

When I finally found him, I had no trouble recognizing Tommy from that graphic description. "Taciturn" Tommy, Lynette's nickname for Mr. Carrs, was a man of few words. He slapped a sticker with our ship's name, "Starzynski," on the windshield and held out his hand for the car keys. Without a word, he drove the camper to a line of vehicles waiting to be loaded onto the ship. He pulled into a slot that was between a Volkswagen and a Mercedes-Benz and behind another Mercedes. I watched and hoped my camper was going to be all right. Lynette, evidently, had other concerns.

"Why is everyone shipping their VWs and Mercedes back to Europe?"

We returned our dock pass at the security gate, and snow began falling as we walked the mile or so to the bus stop. We transferred to a train at the Newark Station and took a cab from Pennsylvania Station in New York to the French Consulate to pick up our visas for France. Then we took a bus to Kennedy Airport, and, just as we had done with Krissie and Mike fourteen years before, flew first to Iceland and then to Luxembourg since Icelandair was still the most economical way to go. Later, in the Luxembourg railroad station, feeling like zombies we tried to stay awake, waiting for the train to Paris. Strong black coffee and a slice of apple streudel at a local *patisserie* helped only a bit. When the time came, we boarded our train and eventually arrived at Paris' Gare d' Est at 9:15 p.m. With no reservations we checked into the Hotel Europe, an old fashioned establishment with a stairway wrapped around an elevator cage with an open shaft. The room was somewhat the worse for wear, but it was clean, and we were tired. Besides, we thought nothing else might be available at that hour.

On violins, oboes, and cellos, young musicians played classical music for their breakfast at each of our Metro stops. It was a new day, and we had much to do. We booked a more permanent stay at a small charming hotel on the Ile St. Louis and then easily acquired visas at the Algerian embassy. The bureaucrats at the Niger embassy, on the other hand, seemed determined to keep us out of their country. Reluctantly, we agreed to leaving our passports with their consular office and picking them up the next afternoon. Back at the hotel room, we put our feet up, drank a bottle of wine, and called it a day.

Several members of a British rugby club were having breakfast at the hotel the next morning. We had a few laughs with them about their massive bodies fitting into the rather small French hotel beds, and then we set off walking down the boulevards of Strasbourg and St. Martin to Porte St. Martin. Outside the Centre Pompidou, bare-chested men threw darts into each other's big stomachs. Andean musicians, clowns, and African dancers performed for pocket change from their audiences. We toured the Museum of Modern Art, and especially enjoyed pieces by Picasso, Matisse, Derain and a number of other Fauves. From our table at the roof-top restaurant, we had marvelous views of Montmartre and Sacre Coeur and indeed the whole city. We walked through the Marais and visited Victor Hugo's home on the Place de Vosges; then passed through Place de la Bastille and followed Boulevard Bourdon across the Seine to Ile de la Cite. A choir practiced in Notre Dame, and the enchanting voices sent chills through me. We walked across the Pont Neuf to the Left Bank and drank coffee in a cafe. Later, we returned to our hotel for a glass of wine and some rest. We finished the day on the Place de Vosges, eating dinner at a little old restaurant with gray stone walls and dark oak beams. Oh, yes, our passports were returned with valid Niger visas.

For the next week we worked on visas. The problem was that visas had to be processed one at a time. You submitted your application, usually with your passport, and then waited for each consulate to turn it around. Usually it took at least twenty-four hours. Problems were compounded because most of the Africans, understandably, spoke French rather than English. Lynette's French was rusty, and she was saddled with the need to communicate with people who spoke a very non-Parisian French and who some-

251

times could be very rude and impatient.

Between visits to consulates or embassies, we enjoyed Paris. In the Orangerie, I watched Monet's water lillies come to life as we walked back and forth between two oval shaped rooms in which the great panels were displayed. Each time I entered a room, I saw more depth and detail unfolding in the master's murals. We wandered through the Louvre and then made reservations on the ferry from Marseilles to Algiers. One day we walked along Boulevard Emile Zola to the park below the Eiffel Tower and, joined by pigeons and jackdaws, ate our baguette and cheese lunch and drank our wine under a warm winter sun. After dinner one night, as we walked back to our hotel on the Ile St. Louis, Lynnie pointed to the sky. Even though the city's bright lights had obliterated the stars, we could still clearly see Jupiter almost cradled in a crescent moon. Another day we walked along the Seine, past the Louvre and Place de la Concorde, and I drank a beer and read the *International Herald-Tribune* while Lynette shopped at the Samaritaine. Each day we dealt with our visas, either picking them up at one country's consulate or making application at another. Central African Republic, Zaire, Tanzania and even Chad all issued us visas. We skipped over many of the countries we intended to visit, knowing that they issued visas to travelers at their borders. Theoretically, we now had all the visas we needed to travel between Algeria and Kenya. That, by any assessment, was a great start.

On the day before our camper's scheduled arrival, we caught a cab to the Gare St. Lazare and boarded the train for Le Havre. There we found a hotel across the street from the train station, made arrangements with the shipping agent to pick up the camper the next morning, had a pleasant aperitif at the hotel, and, after ten days of rich French food in gay Paris, enjoyed pasta at an Italian restaurant.

The following morning, we took a cab to the docks where we met George Renault, our shipping agent. He had spent three years in the U.S., working in restaurants in New York, Boston, and Nantucket, and he spoke English. Also, as a merchant seaman, he had sailed to Africa, Asia, and South America. The three of us watched our camper being unloaded. We inspected it and found the radio missing. George helped us file a claim and sent us on our way to Marseilles.

We camped south of Paris in a roadside rest stop, and, at 6:30 a.m., we began driving south in the dark. It was drizzly and windy—a typically wintry day in France. The sky lightened sometime after 8:00, and the rain continued falling. Nevertheless, we enjoyed the drive which took us past old stone farmhouses with red tiled roofs and through quaint villages with churches in their center. Castles, abbeys and chapels dated from the twelfth century. Lapwings and rooks foraged in unplowed fields, and red kites entertained us with their aerial acrobats. We spent the night at a campground on the outskirts of Marseilles. At a small restaurant nearby, a waitress, possibly unintentionally, shortchanged us by about twenty dollars when we paid our dinner tab, but she was hardly apologetic when I explained the mistake.

In the morning, we filled our propane and water tanks, treating the latter with iodine as we would now do for the remainder of the trip through Africa. Our strategy for remaining healthy in areas where food supplies were suspect was to keep control of our food preparation. Accordingly, in Marseilles, we stocked several months' supply of canned and dried groceries.

While waiting in line to board the ferry for Algiers, we had met two Parisian couples who were on a month's holiday and intended to drive their campers across the Sahara. The six of us had coffee together on the ship and discussed routes and other plans. They had driven our route before and knew where gas and water supplies were available. They suggested we buy *plaques de desemblage* in Algiers. We had no idea what they were talking about until Lynette wrestled with the translation and eventually determined that these plaques were "sand ladders," metal planks about four feet long that would be placed under a stuck vehicle's wheels to help get it out of soft sand. From my notes: *Lynette thinks the younger Parisian looks like Robert Redford. I'm just happy for smooth seas, thank Neptune!*

Algiers, Algeria, January 26, 1988

I spent about an hour and a half changing money, buying insurance, and clearing Algerian customs during which time Lynette became acquainted with a Dutch couple, Jan and Juul, who were driving a 1979 Toyota Land Cruiser. They planned on visiting a friend in Guinea Bissau on the African coast far west of where we planned to go. Our routes through the northern third of the Sahara coincided, however, so we decided to travel that portion together.

Lynette led us on a city tour of Algiers, where we visited the fishing port and then the Kasbah, the old native quarter and fortress. The city was sprawling and, on the surface, otherwise uninteresting, so we drove to the airport south of the city and set up camp in the parking area. Our French wine was good, and we spent the evening in enjoyable conversation. Jan was 46 years old, Juul 27. They lived with his twenty-year-old son in an apartment above her parents' house and planned to marry soon. They both spoke English fluently as well as German, French, Spanish and, of course, Dutch. Juul was a nurse and Jan a retired artillery officer. They would sell their Landcruiser in Guinea Bissau and fly back to Holland after their desert adventure.

Lynette was a different person now that another couple was traveling with us. She told them she was very nervous about the mysteriousness of the unknown, and that she was delighted they were going to be with us for a while. Juul confessed to feeling the same way. Jan laughed.

"Lynette and Juul... Don't let these people know you are nervous. I am nervous too. But they will never suspect it. For them, I will always be in charge."

Our route southeast from Algiers climbed and wound its way over the Atlas Mountains, passing through the picturesque town of Bou-Saada where we bought hot, fresh, delicious bread. South of the mountains, the terrain slowly but inexorably changed, mile by mile, to desert. Young goatherds and shepherds tended their flocks. One of them, a beautiful young girl, waved enthusiastically. Wagtails and wheatears foraged on the ground, and shrikes perched on top of desert shrubs.

From my notes: *I feel so good. The pièce de résistance of adventures has begun!* We followed a track from the road and found a spot to camp where we were hidden behind a hill. After dinner, J and J joined us for coffee and cookies. Then we set up our scope and took advantage of the cloudless nighttime sky to look at the stars and planets.

In Biskra we refueled and bought bread and then continued to El-Oued. Riding by the roadside, men straddled donkeys and wielded small switches which they used both to steer the animals and to accelerate them. We entered the Grand Erg Oriental, the Great Eastern Sand Desert, where enormous, wind-sculpted, drifting sand dunes flanked the road—beautiful and graceful creations of the kind only produced by nature. Camels roamed freely, and date palms grew in small oases. A boy sold desert foxes and sand roses (crystalized sandstone) along the road.

Jan enjoyed stopping in the small towns where he asked directions of the police or anyone else, shaking their hands enthusiastically. Once his Land Cruiser became stuck in the sand. We dug its wheels clear with shovels, stretched a rope between our cars, and carefully pulled it out of the soft sand onto a firm area. While shoveling, I found a sand rose and gave it to Lynette.

I could see a car in the rear view mirror speeding behind us, the driver blowing his horn and waving his arm outside the window. I flashed my lights at Jan, and we both stopped. The man smiled.

"I want to do business with you."

"What kind of business." Jan assumed the duty of our official spokesman, while I concealed a can of mace behind my back.

"Anything you like. Do you want to change money? My rate is much better than the official rate."

"We have already exchanged the little money we have."

"Fine. I will buy your spare tires, clothes or anything else you want to sell. Even your cars."

Jan assured him we had nothing to sell. After a brief, disappointed look, the man shook hands with each of us, wished us luck, assured us we were in Allah's care, and left with a wave and a smile. We camped in a hotel parking lot in Touggourt.

From my notes: *Shower not bad, but the water was smelly.*

Our route continued southwest through the caramel colored sands to Ouargla. Lynette read aloud from the *Sahara Handbook*, and took notes on driving on the sand, methods of extricating yourself when you get bogged down, and the routes we planned to follow. We stopped for lunch under a small grove of date palms and climbed a dune. A white-crowned black wheatear was sitting on the Land Cruiser when we returned from our walk.

The fascinating oasis of Ghardaia was really a cluster of five towns, each of which could be viewed as our road dropped into a valley. Ghardaia was populated mainly by Mozabites, a devout Moslem sect which has defined its own version of Islam for the past 900 years. People came to the town's marvelous market from miles around by camel, donkey, and horse, and, of course, on foot. Everything imaginable was sold there—from beautifully woven rugs to fresh fish and shrimp brought in from the sea. We wandered through the market with pleasant spicy aromas wafting through its aisles, and we bought bread and oranges.

We registered at Ghardaia's walled campground located next to a dry riverbed and found other campers from Germany and Poland who intended to cross the Sahara. Jan, Juul, Lynette and I walked around one of the towns, Beni Isguen. Boys played soccer on a dry riverbed. We followed the town wall up a long hill and were rewarded with a wonderful view of Ghardaia. A muzzein perched on the minaret of a mosque, calling the faithful to prayer. Men knelt on prayer rugs, facing Mecca, and intoned in Arabic, "There is only one God, and Allah is His prophet."

Back at the campground, Lynette and Juul fixed supper, while Jan and I followed a desert fox by the riverbed. Later, we drank wine, reviewed what we could remember about the North African campaign in World War II, and followed a star map around the clear night sky.

From my notes: *I feel so lucky to be here, and to be able to observe life so foreign to what we know.*

We took warm showers in the morning and didn't think much of them at the time, but they would be our last real showers for the next few weeks. Afterwards, we washed the camper and did our laundry by hand. Water was plentiful in Ghardaia, but that would not be the case soon again. We returned to the market and bought a back-up propane burner for cooking, a tire pump, and a strong rope. I looked for sand ladders without success. We stocked up with carrots, onions, potatoes, tomatoes and more canned food. Few women wore western clothes. Some wore a veil over their nose and mouth; others covered their faces and left only one eye showing.

Shortly after noon, we left town. There was only desert between Ghardaia and El-Golea, our next stop, 152 miles south. The wind was blowing, and there was limited visibility. Sand blew across the road. We stopped at a construction site just south of town, and the friendly workers gave me four wooden planks to use as sand ladders. We were all happy when the wind abated, and we could see our surroundings. The desert was always changing—sometimes sculpted dunes, other times rocky wastelands, and often honey colored sand, flat and vast, as far as you could see. A man sat beside the road in the middle of nowhere apparently waiting for nothing. A microwave tower wavered in the distance. Lynette wondered, "Is that KSAH?" It took a moment, and then I laughed.

The walled campground in the beautiful El-Golea oasis was truly international. In addition to our Dutch friends and ourselves, there were two Japanese bikers who met in Algiers accidentally and decided to ride together, five Germans driving three Mercedes and two Peugots and planning to sell them somewhere in Cameroon, and two Aussies on motorcycles. Next to us were two Italians playing John Denver tapes in a Land Rover. Lynette thought they were a bit too macho with their military shirts, knives on their belts, and scraggly beards. A very handsome boy from Boston showed up. He had hitchhiked around Europe for the past six months and planned to spend the next year in Africa, working his way down the west coast to South Africa and then north to East Africa and Egypt. There was also a camper from Germany with an older couple who planned to cross west to Agadir. He had a huge belly, and she remained in the camper playing her organ. A passing camel caravan stopped at the campground, and the two nomadic Tuareg leaders were incredulous of the sounds emanating from her camper. Juul, Lynette, Jan and I all pitched in preparing fresh vegetable soup for supper. We drank our last bottle of wine.

Our original plan was to circumscribe Lake Chad to the north and then drive south through Ndjamena to Bangui in Central African Republic. The consensus in the campground, however, was to go to Central African Republic via Niger, Nigeria and Cameroon rather than through Chad. That implied we had to go well out of our way to Niamey, Niger, to get visas for Nigeria and Cameroon.

Our Italian neighbors loved Lynette. "Ciao, Boys!" She waved to them as we pulled away from the campground, setting our course directly south. We filled our spare gas cans since two hundred forty-eight miles of remote desert lay between *El-Golea* and *In Salah,* the next oasis where fuel could be bought. Sand flanked the track on both sides with dunes sometimes closing in on us and other times backing off in the distance. There was little apparent vegetation, only an occasional clump of dry grass. The day was clear and beautiful with a moderate easterly wind. About forty miles south of El-Golea, the road forked. Here our Dutch friends were to head west to Timimoun, and we were to continue south to In Salah. Lynette and Juul embraced in a tearful farewell. "We see you," was all my friend Jan had to say.

Now we were truly in the middle of the Sahara—by ourselves. The track led up onto a plateau, and the terrain was flat and desolate as far as we could see. Occasionally, a herd of camels foraged on unseen vegetation, or a griffin or Egyptian vulture soared overhead looking for carrion.

The wind blew harder and began picking up sand. From my notes: *I remarked to Lynette, "There's no such thing as an uneventful day in the desert." I didn't realize how true that was.* The wind blew harder and the blowing sand became progressively worse, and, before long, we were in the middle of a true sand storm. I drove as far as I could, then stopped when the visibility dropped to zero. The wind howled and Lynette wept.

"Why are you crying, Lynnie?"

"I'm so frightened."

Beauty and everything else is certainly in the eye of the beholder. Lynette was afraid we were going to die. From my perspective, we were safely ensconced in our little camper with plenty of water and other supplies. After all, wasn't being in a sand storm part of the Saharan experience?

After a few hours the wind abated a bit, and I began driving slowly. Soon, through the blowing sand, I saw ghost-like images moving ahead of us. They disappeared and reappeared several times and then returned more clearly. They were the cars being driven by the five young Germans who intended to sell their vehicles in Cameroon. They stopped, and we pulled up among them.

"We're lost in this sand storm. Do you mind if we follow you to In Salah?"

"Certainly not," smiled one of the drivers. "We're lost too! But don't worry. We will find In Salah." Four guys drove four of the cars, and the fifth was driven by a woman.

"How much do you want for your Kombi?" asked one of the fellows in tortured English, surmising, I suppose, that we had seen enough of the desert.

"Don't trust these guys," interrupted another, laughing. "They are bandits. They will try to buy your car very cheap and sell it for much."

Now the wind abated, and decent visibility returned. For the next hundred miles we drove on *piste*, or hard packed sand. Five sedans and a VW camper raced across the desert, sometimes abreast, other times trailing one another. Often we saw each other one or two thousand yards off to the side, speeding across the flat, hard sand terrain, and kicking out a sandy cloud of dust to the rear. We stopped for a break.

"Why do you guys do this? For the money?"

"I do it for that!" responded Johann, pointing to the vast expanse of desert and then moving his flat hand in a gesture that expressed his enjoyment in racing a car across the vast desert piste.

About twenty miles north of In Salah we picked up a single lane, pot-holed asphalt road. The wind returned and the storm raged, drifting sand across the asphalt. One of the Germans got stuck, and we all wrapped towels around our heads and shoveled him out. On the outskirts of town, we pulled into a campground with a wall that offered some protection from the wind and sand. I pulled into a slot and turned off the motor. I heard a sob from Lynette, and then the tears came.

"I shouldn't have come with you."

I walked around the campground, talking to Dutch motorcyclists and campers from Austria, France and Holland. None of them planned on leaving for a few days. A VW camper from Austria rolled into the campground. Louis and Heidi were from Kitzbuhl and planned to leave in the morning. Louis was very confident.

"Do you have four wheel drive on your VW?" I asked.

"No. It is not important."

He had worked in Saudi Arabia and other desert countries and seemed to know his way around. Lynette seemed to feel better knowing we would be traveling with another couple for the next few days. That evening, Heidi and Louis walked up to our camper.

"Morgen!" Louis exclaimed.

"Morgen?" I looked at my watch.

"We have a special schnapps for to drink in the morning," Heidi explained. "We think it is better for dessert." We all laughed and drank our dessert.

Our next fuel stop was Tamanrasset, 408 miles to the south. For the first fifty miles we drove on asphalt, and then we were back on sand. When the sand was soft, we frequently became stuck, extricating ourselves in a variety of ways. Often we jacked up each wheel and inserted Louis's sand ladders under them. Then, once we got the car moving, we gunned the motor and kept it moving until we found a firm surface where we could safely stop. The obvious problem was walking back through the soft sand a quarter mile or more to retrieve four heavy ladders, and then returning to the car with them. Sometimes we towed each other out of trouble, and, other times, when the sand was soft, we let air out of our tires to provide more surface, and then pumped them up again when we returned to the firm piste. All of this was very hard work. Once while I was jacking up the car, I became exhausted and stopped. I looked up, and my very own angel, Lynette, stood there with a fresh orange. I ate it, almost immediately felt like a new man, and then, greatly refreshed, returned to my task.

It became very hot, but now there was little wind, and the scenery was wonderful. From my notes: *The desert is awesome. Certainly the sculpted dunes, the distant mountains, and the remote canyons are beautiful. But the desert is much more than that. It is sand storms, and mirages, and oases, and no water, and heat, and sand. It's magnificent in its enormity. It's vast. It goes on forever.*

We stopped for the night at a small campground near the oasis of Arak. When Lynette paid the attendant, he said we were the first Americans ever to stay there. A young Austrian on a motorcycle, Manfred, pulled into the campground an hour after we did and joined us. The five of us ate dinner together. Louis had spent four years during World War II as an officer in the German army's special mountain forces, much of it in Russia. He was wounded in the battle of Stalingrad and sent home. An expert skier and climber who had climbed many Himalayan peaks, Louis now worked as an engineer for a company that made steel pipes. Heidi spoke English well and translated my questions and Louis's answers. She was a professional photographer and felt a lot less comfortable talking about herself than she did talking about Louis. During the evening, we learned that, when he wasn't racing his motorcycle around the Sahara, Manfred was a cabinet maker.

For dinner, Heidi prepared a Tyrolean specialty for the five of us—smoked sausage. Louis found a bottle of Sicilian wine and later provided dessert—schnapps. We took a "Sahara shower," a trickle of cold water from a jerry can hanging in a hut made of dried grass, and went to bed. The drive to Tamanrasset was long, and we wanted to leave early in the morning to beat the heat.

A cloud of mist hung over the eastern mountains and changed colors as the sun climbed to the horizon. Lynette took a turn driving over the piste and found the experience thrilling. At lunchtime, we stopped by a solitary acacia tree. Cold canned apricot nectar tasted wonderful, and a splash of water on our heads felt even better. One of Louis's tires had developed a slow leak, so we changed it. Further along, a small troop of armed soldiers stopped us and asked to see our "travel permit." We showed the leader our passports, visas, carnets, and international driver's licenses, and with each document he shook his head. We had no idea what he wanted, but he refused to let us pass until we produced whatever it was. Then Louis figured it out. He said they were just shaking us down for a bribe.

"Watch me."

All of a sudden, Louis was again an officer in the German army. He threw his shoulders back, strutted up to the soldiers, snapped to attention and saluted. Startled, they saluted back.

"You good controller!" Louis barked at the surprised leader who took a step backwards and nodded his head.

"I commander! Four stars!" Louis held up four fingers and pointed at his shoulder. The leader continued nodding his head.

"I give you something for being good controller." Louis handed the man a bottle of wine.

"We go now!" The man took the bottle of wine in one hand, maintained his salute with the other and continued nodding as we returned to our cars and motorcycle, started the engines and left.

After a long day of driving, we arrived in Tamanrasset at about 5:30 p.m. We bought oranges, carrots, and potatoes and drove about ten miles into the desert to camp in a canyon in the foothills of the Hoggar Mountains.

A full moon rose over the Hoggars into a clear nighttime sky. Lynette made vegetable soup, and Manfred, Heidi, and Louis joined us for supper. I asked them if they had known anything about what was going on with the Jews during the war. Heidi was only a year older than we and too young to remember. Louis spent most of the war in Russia and was unaware of the treatment of Jews until 1943 when he was sent home after being wounded. At a railroad station, he saw and heard people being herded into box cars. He became angry when a guard would not tell him what was going on. That was the only time he was personally exposed to the situation. He later asked some of his fellow officers about the rumors, and none of them knew anything for sure. Then, in 1944, in Romania, an SS officer came to the village where Louis was stationed and ordered him to have the Jews rounded up. Louis told the SS man he had five minutes to get out of town or he would shoot him.

Now it was the sun's turn to rise over the Hoggars into a clear morning sky. In Tamanrasset, I arranged to have aluminum sand ladders made in exchange for a jacket I no longer needed. We bought tomatoes and fresh, hot bread. The Tuareg residents of the oasis were very friendly. Heidi bargained for jewelry, and the shop's proprietor told her, "We are honest people."

"I know. I can see it in your eyes," she replied.

We returned to our campsite and climbed to a mountain spring to wash ourselves, performing what Lynette called a "true Sahara shower." Then we scrubbed our clothes. A lanner (falcon) glided over our heads, searching for small mammals. Rock martins foraged for insects on the wing. Subalpine warblers, white-crowned black wheatears, chiffchaffs and shrikes perched in the shrubbery. A very relaxing afternoon.

After we enjoyed goulash for dinner, a Nigerian man speaking a lilting but difficult-to-understand English, approached us.

"I have a problem, my friends..." and he embarked on a long story which basically explained that he had nothing to eat. Heidi gave him a bowl of goulash which he ate silently, then thanked us profusely, and left.

In the morning, Lynette had another cry.

"Lynnie, we can go back if you want. With no hard feelings."

"No. Maybe I'll get better."

From my notes: *I'm so sorry this isn't as good for her as it is for me. It seems to be a love/hate thing with her. I'm concerned the latter will prevail. We'll see.*

An auberge of sorts called The Source was recommended to us by other campers. We tried their omelette for breakfast. The proprietor was surprised to see us.

"I haven't seen an American here for years. I think the last ones were from Idaho." Outside the restaurant was a spring water tap where we washed our hair and filled our campers' water tanks. Manfred wasn't feeling well, so Louis and Heidi accompanied him back to our campsite. They planned to remain in Tamanrasset for a few more days and then head east and north to Tunisia. We were heading south, and I knew it was critical that we find someone to travel with.

Lynette and I drove into Tamanrasset to see who was in the municipal campground. There we found the Germans who were driving the five cars and whom we had followed through the sand storm. I waved at their bearded leader, Stefan. We knew they were heading for Agadez, and so were we. This stretch of almost 520 miles was reputed to be the most difficult desert passage we would encounter. I explained to Stefan that Lynette was very frightened to travel alone and asked him if we could tag along with them. He hesitated for only a moment and then smiled and said, "Yes, of course." Lynette breathed an audible sigh of relief, and I guess I did too.

The Germans were leaving early the next morning. We returned to our campsite to tell Louis, Heidi, and Manfred that we would stay at the municipal campground that night to assure we wouldn't delay the scheduled departure south. Manfred was too ill to care much, but the four of us shared an emotional farewell. Then we stopped in town and bought groceries, including twenty-five cans of apricot nectar, the only juice we could find. That night, sleep came slowly for me. I was so exhilarated about the next 500 miles of adventure. The Sahara had gotten to me.

Stefan, the leader of the Germans, owned a used automobile dealership with a friend. He and Johann had crossed the desert five times before. Thom worked for a software company, and his girlfriend, Margot was an accountant. Jurgen was a surveyor. Driving with the Germans was an adventure in itself. They didn't have much of a system, only that the last car should keep track of the ones in front and make sure they were all there. Most of the time we were driving abreast, flying across the desert at what seemed like a hundred miles an hour but probably was only forty-five or fifty. During our turn to bring up the rear, I saw Johann disappear behind a hill to our left. I wasn't sure what to do. Rather than turning around and trying to find him, I continued on. Several miles later, the hill came to an end and Johann was nowhere to be seen. I began flashing my lights and trying to catch up with the others. They didn't see my lights, and I couldn't catch them. Twenty or thirty miles must have rolled by before Stefan and the others pulled to a stop. Johann was still missing. I told them the story. Stefan said we should wait here for a while. Still no sign of Johann. After a half hour, Stefan said, "Let's go. Don't worry, he'll show up." I wasn't so sure.

About 140 miles south of Tamanrasset we met three Tuareg men on foot. With sign language, we determined they were walking to Tamanrasset. They carried nothing, so we gave them water and food for a couple of days.

I began to have trouble downshifting from third to second gear. Sand seemed to have found its way into my gearbox. Sometimes the difficulty shifting forced me to slow down too much and sink into the soft sand. Several times I became stuck when I shouldn't have. Each of the others, except Stefan, had also gotten stuck at least once, but I felt terrible about slowing them down. We had traveled about 160 miles that day. Stefan thought it prudent to stop well before dark. Johann was still missing. We circled the cars as in an old west movie and built a small campfire in the center. Earlier that afternoon, Stefan had wrapped our beer cans in wet paper towels. The moisture evaporated, cooling the beer—a nice trick. After dinner, the night air cooled, and the sky was cloudless. I set up my spotting scope, and our friends were fascinated by the closer views the scope afforded of Jupiter, Venus and the moon. Later, I went to bed and lay awake, scared stiff about Johann.

The desert driving ranged from exciting to difficult to impossible. Sometimes the piste was hard and good and we flew along at forty-fifty-sixty and once even close to seventy miles per hour. Driving on *fesh-fesh* was a different story. *Fesh-fesh* is soft sand with a wafer-thin, slightly firmer layer on its surface. If you go too slowly, the vehicle easily sinks through the *fesh-fesh* and becomes stuck. If you keep moving, the car rides on the *fesh-fesh*. Inevitably, though, you must slow down to avoid hitting bumps or depressions at excessive speed, and that's when your vehicle sinks into the sand. All of us, except Stephan who was expert at this driving, became immobilized a number of times. Each time we helped one another with ropes, jacks, pumps and/or sand ladders—whatever was appropriate for the situation. While driving on *fesh-fesh*, we let air out of our tires to flatten them somewhat, enabling us, as Lynette saw it, to "float like a butterfly."

Later in the morning, we arrived at the fabled "Dunes of Laouni," miles of beautiful but treacherous sand dunes which were always shifting and therefore were totally unpredictable. We stopped to assess what might be our best route. I heard a car in the distance, and, a few minutes later, Johann caught up with us. We all cheered and embraced our no longer missing colleague. I was ecstatic and probably hugged him harder than anyone else did.

Johann told us his story. After becoming separated from us, he didn't realize he was on the wrong piste until, after many miles, it began heading east. He came upon an abandoned well drilling rig and remembered he had been at that very same place two years before. There were a few trees nearby which had made the drillers suspect a water source. They had drilled through solid rock but never reached water. Johann's choices now were to set a course directly west through the sand, hoping to reach the north-south piste we were following, or to backtrack almost a hundred miles to the point where the pistes diverged. Completing the triangle would be much shorter but he would have risked becoming lost again and running out of fuel and water in an area where it was highly unlikely other travelers would pass. He wisely chose the latter option and had been driving hard most of the past twenty-four hours to catch up with us. Stefan smiled knowingly. He had never lost confidence in his friend's survival instincts.

Later, we met five men making the eight day, thirty miles per day, walk in the desert wilderness from In-Guezzam to Tamanrasset. One of them was cut badly on his leg. We gave them food and water, and Johann cleaned and bandaged the injured man's wound. Lynette leaned toward me and whispered, "Johann has his own way of living, but he is my favorite of them all."

The dunes slowed us terribly. Finding firm sand and extricating each other required much time. At times the wind was blowing so hard that we were literally sand blasted as we dug each other out of a problem area. Our camper and we ourselves were now well impregnated with sand. Our little caravan was indefatigable, however, and we persisted, hoping to make the border with Niger before the customs and immigration offices closed for the day.

Children threw stones at our cars when, at 6:30 p.m., we arrived at the Algerian border town of In-Guezzam. Customs officials were still working and passed us through quickly. One of them said that Lynette and I were the first Americans he had ever seen at this border crossing. That evening Johann joined us to drink coffee in our camper. He had a supply of car radios he had brought along to sell, and, to replace our stolen radio, he found one that fit the hole in our dash board fairly well. He told us about his bouts with LSD and his brief married life. Recently, he had lived with his thirteen-year-old son in Togo for eighteen months, but now his wife wouldn't let him see the boy. He had also lived in Cameroon for a year with an African girlfriend who eventually left him.

"When it comes to Europeans, I'm a loner. I like the Africans. I take them for what they are."

"What were you thinking when you were lost in the desert back there?"

"You have a few liters of petrol, a few liters of water, but you are far away from anything. Any feeling of a security. You come to terms with yourself."

The crescent moon lay in the sky horizontally like a saucer. From my notes: *Tonight we are so exhausted. It was physically a very tough day. The wind blew the sand so hard it hurt. I have sand in my mouth, eyes, ears, nose and hair. I'm even becoming accustomed to this gritty existence. We're hoping to make the 120 miles to the village of Arlit by tomorrow night where, reportedly, we can buy cold beer!*

The next day was our roughest yet—very bad problems in the sand. Lynette and I did a lot better, though, becoming stuck only once. We careened over a bad hump we did not see until it was too late, and, trying to slow down at the last moment to avoid major damage to the car, we sank deeply into the sand. I looked under the car for damage and saw a large dent in the gas tank. Even Stefan and Johann were each stuck once—their first such experience of the trip. At one time, Jurgen and we were driving abreast, and, while I drove high on the side of a dune and found surprisingly firm sand, Jurgen opted for the valley between two dunes and became, seemingly, hopelessly stuck. It took all of our wits, strength, and hundreds of yards of slowly placing sand ladders in front of each other to create a road to get him out of trouble.

"Happiness is a good piste." Lynette was unamused by my somewhat racy attempt at humor. Twice we saw camel caravans plying their way across the desert. Once a group of women and children were walking in the wilderness, and we gave them cookies and water.

The terrain slowly changed. Technically, we were now in the Sahel, a transition zone between the desert and the sudan. In a letter to my parents, I called this part of Niger "the Africa Hollywood never found." Everything remained quite dry, but now there was more vegetation—some scrubby shrubbery and a few trees.

From that letter: *Life is difficult here for the people who scratch out a living somehow despite economic and hygenic obstacles that would have defeated most of us long ago. Since Tamanrasset, we have been traveling with young Germans who brought cars from Europe to sell at a handsome profit in West Africa. This has added an interesting dimension to our trip in that we are witnessing capitalism in its rawest form.*

In Arlit, street vendors sold snacks and drinks, children sat in the street with their teacher and did their lessons on small slates. We registered with the police and, at the White Horse Bar, we all ordered cold Flag beer, pronounced "Flack" by the Germans. African music blared. Stefan and Johann commissioned an agent who found buyers for the two Peugots. Negotiations proceeded in a friendly manner with lots of smiles, handshakes and tea. More wheeling and dealing was conducted for tires and other automotive spare parts that the Germans carried in their car trunks. The buyers took us to lunch at a second floor local restaurant where we enjoyed omelette, French fries and beer. When we had finished eating, a lot of cash abruptly changed hands. The mood changed just as abruptly. Now everyone was in a hurry. Johann grabbed Lynette's elbow and then mine and pulled us downstairs to our waiting vehicles.

"What's up, Johann?"

"News travels fast in Africa. We now have enough cash to make a dishonest person very happy. We must, as Clint Eastwood would say, get out of town."

The road to Agadez was fair, and we arrived there shortly after dark. We all registered at the Hotel de L'Air, and Lynette and I drew what the establishment called its "Honeymoon Suite." No doubt it was their best room, but it wasn't much. We showered under a cold water trickle, and it was marvelous. Then we met the Germans for beer on an upstairs veranda that overlooked a mosque and the city. We celebrated our friends' success in selling their cars, and Johann graciously bought all of our dinners. Afterwards, we walked the old town's narrow bustling streets weaving between mud-brick buildings and then stopped at a cafe for coffee. Jurgen was sad because he didn't sell his car, and he missed his girl friend.

From my notes: *I did not sleep well in the hotel—I'd rather be in the camper.*

Our group moved to a campground in the morning where we cleaned our cars and washed our clothes. A very important looking man wearing a purple *jelaba* came to look at our cars. He was especially interested in our camper, and was disappointed when I explained that we needed to keep it to continue our travels.

We walked into the Agadez market where Margot, while she waited, had pants made from fabric of a colorful African design. Children with terrible deformities begged in the streets. Later that afternoon, while drinking Flag on the veranda of the Hotel de L'Air, Johann explained that often parents would intentionally deform their children at birth so that they could beg for cash. The children themselves, he said, enjoyed the status of being so important, economically, to the family—"This is Africa. You have to take the bad with the good."

That evening, we sat around our campfire, eating dinner and then drinking coffee, and reminisced about our trip across the Sahara. Now everyone (except for me) was laughing about Johann's detour. I still felt a chill when talking about it. Jurgen was the target of some good natured ribbing over his homesickness. It was an evening of sincere friendship brought out by our collective overcoming of adversity. How special I felt. This had been an adventure and a world Lynette and I had dared to become a part of, if only for a couple of weeks. The Sahara was one of Earth's greatest natural wonders. And life here was as exotic as any we would ever see. It was a bittersweet moment. We were saying "good-bye." Our German friends had some more car selling to do, and we had to leave early in the morning for Niamey.

The drive south and west through the Sahel, a drought-prone region below the Sahara, changed almost by the hour. The variety of vegetation and number of trees increased steadily. People carved out a subsistence living. Small settlements were comprised of mud homes with woven mat roofs. Unarmed soldiers at military checkpoints gave our papers a perfunctory glance and then waved us along. In Birnin-Konni, a boy named Adam asked if we needed petrol. He led us to a back street where other boys converged on us with fifty liter cans of black market gas from Nigeria that they sold for half as much as the pump price. We filled up and I wondered whether the gas had been watered down. Adam smiled as another boy poured our gas and asked, "How do I get to America?" Lynette thought he looked like Cockroach on the Cosby show.

The terrain remained arid, but now occasionally we saw ponds and creeks. Black cattle sported long, curved white horns with black tips. After driving all day, we arrived in Niamey, Niger's capital, after dark. Fires blazed in 55 gallon drums, and people flooded the streets, shouting and waving their arms at us as we slowly drove through them. We never learned why they were antagonistic, and we were relieved when we finally found the campground.

In the morning, we went to the United States Embassy, possibly the most opulent building in Niamey, and were shocked to learn that Cameroon did not have an embassy in Niamey. Cynthia Akuetteh was very helpful, however, and gave us a letter that put us in a similar category to that of Peace Corps volunteers. She was confident that, when we arrived at the Cameroon border, they would give us a transit visa upon presentation of the letter. Next we went to the Nigerian embassy where we made application for visas and left our passports.

Our next stop was a pretty good supermarket where we saw John Ayer, a man we had met earlier in the day at the American embassy.

"Could you guys go for a cold drink?"

"You bet!" from Lynette.

"Follow me to my house. You'll love my wife. She's from Argentina."

John worked for a private company that had contracted with the U.S. State Department to beef up embassy security. They were in the process of installing concrete walls heavy enough to stop vans loaded with explosives. His next assignment after Niamey was Asuncion, Paraguay, where they would do the same thing for our embassy there. John's Argentinian wife naturally couldn't wait for their Paraguay assignment.

That afternoon we visited the National Museum which included exhibits of regional costumes and dwellings. Craftspeople and skilled artisans sold their products—rugs, jewelry, baskets and leather goods; and a zoo featured Niger's birds and mammals. Lynette bought a pad of original sketches from an artist. We enjoyed the museum, but the line of beggars and deformed children waiting outside the building, despite Johann's rationalization, left us sad and depressed.

266

We returned to the Nigerian embassy the next morning. The receptionist, a little guy with glasses and a squeaky voice, told us in his sing-song English, "My boss wants to see you."

His boss, in perfect British English, wanted to know,

"Why did you not obtain your visa in Washington?"

I tried to explain the distance between Wyoming and Washington, the original intention to go to Chad, etc.

"Why are you applying for seven days?"

"We thought we might spend some time in Kano and Maiduguri, perhaps get a better feel for your country."

"All right. But I will only give you six days."

As it was required, we registered with the Niamey police and then left the city, returning east on the same route we had traveled before. In the cities, there didn't seem to be enough to keep all the people busy. Men stood on street corners talking and deal making. People begged in the streets. In the rural areas, on the other hand, people were occupied tending livestock, pounding grain, and cultivating crops. Men carried wood and hay; and women fetched water from the village well, carrying jugs on their heads or hanging them from a yoke across their shoulders, while their children were strapped to their backs or scampered behind.

At a police check station on the outskirts of Birnin-Konni, a young man gesticulated wildly. I slowed up but saw no police.

"You are not a policeman."

"No. I am Adam. Adam. Remember me?"

He wore glasses and seemed older. For a small fee, Adam showed us where the campground was, filled our gas tank again, and arranged an exchange of money.

Leaving Niger was uneventful, but entering Nigeria was less so. The Nigerian customs agents were officious and unfriendly. Shamelessly, they asked us for wine and cigarettes. We complied so we could be on our way. About every ten miles we were required to stop at police checkpoints, but usually these guards were quite friendly and eagerly answered any questions we had.

Kano's history goes back a thousand years when it was a jumping off place for trade routes across the Sahara. The Kano Tourist Camp was situated next to the Central Hotel, the bar of which was a popular watering hole for expatriates. We registered at the campground where a roller flew among the trees and performed an aerial dance for a prospective mate. The attendants giggled when they saw me writing with my left hand, an affliction Africans do not have since they are taught to reserve their left hand for a specific hygenic purpose. We took a walk, bought a few gifts and then repaired to the bar. There sat Margot and Thom and a clean shaven Stefan. Jurgen had driven to Niamey to try to sell his car, and Johann had a date with a woman he had known from a previous visit in Kano. The five of us enjoyed a few drinks and dinner. On the way to the rest room, I was accosted by an attractive, articulate, and persistent prostitute.

"Take me to your room, and I will love you in a way you have never known before."

"Sorry, but I don't have a room. I'm staying in the campground next door."

"Oh, take me there instead. It will be much more exciting."

"No thank you. My wife is waiting for me with my friends." I pointed to our table.

"Let her wait. She will never know."

"You don't know my wife. No thanks again." I smiled dismissively and was relieved when she didn't try to follow me into the men's room.

As we drove east toward the Cameroon border, the car's engine began missing and otherwise acting up, and it caused me to wonder whether the black market gas we had bought in Niger was a bargain after all. The harmattand, a desert wind from the east, presented us with a very hazy sky. A red-billed hornbill sat in an acacia tree, and olive thrushes flitted about in the roadside shrubbery. We picked up a boy who had just been dismissed from the hospital in Maidugari and gave him a ride to Bama. At a police control point, we talked to Tams Ngeri, the man in charge of the post, and explained that, rather than a Cameroon visa, we had a letter from the American Embassy. He had spent four years at the University of Nebraska and said he would accompany us to the border to make sure we had no problems. We drove to the border patrol at Kumshe/Banki, and, wisely, instead of processing us out of Nigeria, Tams walked with us to the Cameroon post to see if our letter would suffice. The Cameroon officials were confused by the letter, not to mention my writing with my left hand, and said they did not have the authority to grant us a visa. They told us to return the next morning at 9:00. Tams explained, "They are very formal in Cameroon and do not have the latitude to make decisions as we do in Nigeria."

We camped at the Nigerian border station. Tams left and then returned with his friend, Ayuba. They brought a package of small cakes and ten bottles of Niger Beer. We opened a bottle of wine and proceeded to become better acquainted. Tams and Ayuba talked easily in response to our questions about the conflicts among Nigerian tribal cultures and the local implications of being educated in America. African music blared in the background, and the beat continued late into the night.

Nobody objected to our watching the military inspection in the morning. The drill was an amusing mixture of British formality and African indifference. We followed the instructions from the previous afternoon and walked across the border, but the Cameroon contingent had a new chief who had no interest in helping us. Tams thought we might have a better chance at the N'gala border crossing where one of his friends was "Chief of the Post." N'gala was at the northern tip of Cameroon, only a stone's throw from Chad. To get there we had to retrace our route west to Maiduguri and then east to N'gala, a distance of 150 miles. Tams insisted on staying with us, and, on the drive, he told us more about his life. Though his assignment was in Maiduguri, his family lived in Lagos, the coastal capital. He was the bread-winner, not only for his wife and two children, but for his extended family also—his mother and several brothers and sisters. As a young man, he had worked as a security guard at the Lagos port, then he worked at a bank. He applied for and received a government scholarship to the University of Nebraska where he maintained a 3.4 GPA in finance. He was now thirty-five and was assigned to Nigeria's immigration service.

For three hours we waited to talk with someone in Cameroon customs. Eventually, the Cameroon official in charge listened to our story politely but then abruptly told us there was nothing he could do. He said "the First Commissioner" was expected in the morning and suggested that we come back then to see if he would help us.

Tams was serious on the exterior, but he was very likable and had a lot of friends in N'gala. And he knew how to throw a party. We drove to the home of two of his friends, newlyweds, Mosha and Maryam. They were very receptive to Tams' plan for a party and graciously invited us to camp in their yard. Soon the people began arriving and continued doing so well into the night. We drank Niger Beer, talked about religion (Nigeria is mostly Christian in the south, Moslem here in the north), books and football, and listened to wonderful African music.

From my notes: *Great time had by all.* And a non-sequitur—*The simple meals Lynette makes taste so good here—dried soup with local veggies cut up and thrown in.*

Most of Tams' friends had been doubtful that we could get Cameroon visas at the border and thought we would have to drive the 1,200 miles to Lagos to get them. In the morning, we walked with Tams to the Cameroon post. Children in the street recited the Koran in a harmonious chant. The "First Commissioner" was very handsome and not at all officious. He was almost friendly.

"How long do you want to remain in Cameroon?"

"Just long enough to drive from here to N'gaoundere and then to Central African Republic."

"Nonsense. You certainly want to spend time in Waza National Park. The animals are marvelous. I shall give you one week."

Tams seemed sad. We had enjoyed our time together. I think he had left a part of himself in Nebraska, and we had been a connection to that loss. He shook my hand solemnly, and then Lynette's. Tears came to her eyes, and she threw her arms around him.

We had only driven a few miles when, south of Kousseri, the engine began sputtering and missing. I changed the fuel filter, and the car's performance improved immensely. The Cameroon countryside was lovely. We saw a couple of bikers who had stopped and joined them for lunch. Eric and Nellika were from Holland, and had biked to Spain, ferried to Morocco, and ridden through Algeria, Niger, Chad and into Cameroon. We gave them a lift to Waza where, after arranging for a guide the next day, we camped outside the park.

As far as we could tell, the four of us and our guide were the only humans in Waza that day. This was our first visit to an African reserve, and it certainly was a marvelous introduction to the big animals.

From a letter to my parents: *Hundreds of elephants of all ages splashed and sprayed themselves and each other in a small lake. Giraffes nibbled tree leaves; and gazelles, springboks and antelopes galloped across the plains. Jackals and baboons lazed in the morning sun. Hippos swam and snorted in a river. A female lion fed on her kill until we arrived and then circled our camper warily. I suppose she was sizing up what she feared was a competitor for her kill. The bird life was no less spectacular with saddlebill storks, African crowned cranes, vultures, hornbills, garganeys and many other species. Best of all, wonderful ostriches put on a rich show, as they ran across the plain with ungainly but swift strides.*

Driving south, we noticed the terrain becaming more mountainous and the vegetation more lush. Men wore western clothes, but women, often naked above the waist, wore traditional tribal garb. We drove all day and didn't arrive at N'gaoundere until 11:30 p.m. Night driving in Africa is dangerous. People and livestock walk along the road and are difficult to see, and trucks often park well out on the road. We were unable to find a camping place and instead registered at a very basic hotel.

The road was now a red gravel and quite rough. The climate and vegetation had become tropical as we neared the great African rain forest. We saw a hitchhiker and picked him up. Wilfried was from Austria and had backpacked all over the world. The three of us were together for the next several weeks. We crossed into Central African Republic, the former realm of the vile and heinous dictator, Jean-Bedel Bokassa, and spent the night camped on the grounds of a Swedish Baptist mission near Bouar. Two U.S. Lutheran missionaries were also there. These two men drove trucks on which they had painted colorful appelations which reminded us of the names given their trucks by drivers in South America—"God's Assistant" and "Elephant of the Piste." Two women also were staying at the mission. Anna was from Virginia and spoke French and Norwegian. Her friend, Kree (short for Kristina), was a bee specialist. I wasn't sure of their relationship with the mission.

"I hope this isn't too offensive for missionaries, but do you know where

I can buy some cold beer?"

"God damn it! I'm not a missionary!" Anna protested as Kree held her sides laughing. The women explained that they were Peace Corps workers and, despite having to reside in the mission, they had many disagreements with the Baptists and had little sympathy for their fundamentalism. Anna had come to Africa to help Kree teach the locals to raise bees. Kree was a year into her three year assignment. Suddenly, at 10:00, all the lights in the town went out—an energy saving measure of which we had been unaware. Lynette and I washed by candlelight under a shower that trickled cold water.

Clouds of fine red dust churned from the road and permeated every crevice, nook, and cranny of the camper. Women ululated and children waved as we drove through villages and tried to avoid chickens that seemed determined to run under our wheels. Near Bossembele, the Mbali River fell precipitously over the Chutes de Boali. Later in the spring, that river would swell to major proportions, and the falls would almost rival those at Victoria. Ross's turacos, large violet birds with crimson flight feathers and an orange face and bill, cackled from the trees overhanging the river. Wilfried continued to travel with us and made an interesting companion. He had spent two years backpacking in South America and had walked 150 miles through the Darien Jungle. He had also traveled through Asia, Australia, Europe and North America and, now, he was hitchhiking his way through Africa. His home was a village near Innsbruck where he was a textile engineer. He would work for two years and then travel for a year, and he never had a problem being rehired when he returned home.

We had to surrender our passports at a military checkpoint seven miles west of Bangui. The officious guard instructed us to retrieve them at the immigrations office in the city the following morning. Leaving our passports at an office and returning the following day to pick them up was reason enough for concern. I certainly didn't like the idea at all of leaving our passports with this guy and picking them up somewhere else. It seemed to us like more bureaucratic nonsense, but we had little choice in the matter.

The pleasant, tropical town of Bangui, the capital of Central African Republic, lies on the Ubangui River. The Catholic Mission was filled with visiting missionaries, so we drove to the Centre d'Accueil Touristiques (Tourist Welcome Center) on the M'Baiki road. Several trucks with fifteen to twenty people each had already set up camp there. These trucks were an African phenomenon that had sprung up in the past few years. Companies offering overland adventure travel would convert large trucks to vehicles with seats to accommodate passengers and storage for food and camping gear. People, usually young adults, paid them to experience the adventure of crossing Africa with a driver who had some familiarity with the terrain.

At the foot of the Grand Corniche, fishermen paddled their canoes to the Ubangui River bank. A few blocks away, merchants and artisans sold their wares at the Central Market. We visited the Boganda Museum with its collection of African musical instruments and, late in the morning, collected our passports at the Office of Immigration. We then presented our passports and visas to officials at Zaire's embassy and filled out the necessary entry papers. Back at the campground, we learned that the road from Zongo on the opposite bank of the Ubangui to Libenge was flooded. We would have to take the northern route through Bambari and cross the Ubangui at Mbaye.

The red gravel road to Bambari was very dusty but otherwise in fairly good condition. Most of the birds we had seen in North Africa were wintering European migrants. Now the much more colorful tropical species had become common. The white-throated bee-eater had a white face and breast with black stripes running across its throat and through its eyes, and a black cap. Its cinnamon-colored nape blended into its irridescent green back which merged into a blue rump and tail, the central feathers of which extended well beyond its outer tail feathers. The remarkably conspicuous paradise flycatcher had a black head with wide blue eye rings, a chestnut body and a tail which, on the males, was more than three times the length of its body.

Both Catholic missions in Bambari declined our requests to camp on their grounds. The Baptist Mission, on the other hand, welcomed us enthusiastically and would take no payment for their hospitality. The American missionary couple who ran the mission, the Elmers, had spent fourteen years in Africa. Their two sons were away at college, but their two teen-age daughters lived at home. Grandmother Elmer also lived with them. Though Mr. Elmer was gone for a few days visiting another town, Mrs. Elmer smiled and assured us, "We turn no one away."

"Of course we expect to pay to stay here."

"That is not necessary."

"Then we want to make a contribution to your mission."

From my notes: *Mrs. Elmer invited us to have supper with her and her daughters. Best tomato soup I've ever had, grilled cheese sandwiches, a piece of cake and good, cold water.*

The Elmers built the mission by hand and originally had hardly any furniture. They had kept their house in Grand Rapids over the years, mostly so their children had a place to call home. We talked about the mission and their work with the Africans. The Elmers had translated the Bible into Santo, the native language, and used it to train Africans whom they then employed as surrogate pastors to spread the Word. While the mission provided some social services for the Africans, its thrust was primarily religious. I directed a question to the girls.

"Are your African friends as close as your friends in the U.S.?"

"Tell the truth," Mrs. Elmer warned, smiling.

The girls explained that their African friends were different. Girls their age were getting married and having babies. Marriages were arranged by uncles. The Africans did not "date." If a girl did much more than have a polite conversation with a boy, she was considered "loose."

"How does the government feel about your being here, Mrs. Elmer?"

"They usually encourage our presence. There is so much work to do. The government thinks the country is underpopulated and has an official policy of discouraging birth control."

Early in the morning, I walked around the grounds, looking at the many singing birds. I stood beside a stream, and a gray-headed kingfisher chattered as it flashed by with its bright cobalt blue wings and tail and, striking rufous breast. I heard footsteps approaching me from behind and turned to see Grandmother Elmer.

"Good morning, Mrs. Elmer. You're an early riser."

"Yes I am, Mr. Wile. I see that you are a birdwatcher."

"I am. Do you enjoy the birds?"

"I do... There is one question I have wanted to ask you."

"What would that be?"

"Do you know if you are going to Heaven?"

I answered her warily, and tried, in a respectful way, to change the course of the conversation she had embarked upon.

"I wonder if the Lord can do anything about this red dust. We can't seem to prevent it from infiltrating our camper. Our clothes, food... everything is covered with red dust."

"Remember, Mr. Wile. The roads in Heaven are paved in gold."

"You're right, Mrs. Elmer, thanks for reminding me." I laughed, held her arm affectionately and walked with her back to the mission. Along the path, I remembered it was Sunday.

We arrived in Mbaye about noon and were surprised to find the customs and immigration offices open. Our paperwork was speedily processed, but the ferry across the Ubangui to Zaire was not operating. A friendly policeman told us the ferry operator probably was watching a soccer game in progress. The policeman walked with Lynette, Wilfried and me to the soccer field, and, sure enough, the ferry operator was there. He laughed good naturedly when I asked him if there was any chance we could get a ride across the river today and told me this was his day off. We watched the soccer game and then camped near the river with two overland trucks filled with kids from New Zealand and Australia. One of the boys had a bad case of malaria and was waiting to catch a bus to Bangui to be treated. We suggested to the English leader that they consider taking him to Bambari where the missionaries operate a pretty good hospital.

A number of the overlanders, some topless and others naked, went swimming in the Ubangui. It became obvious that, not only were these travelers swimming in streams which harbored dangerous parasites, but they were also drinking untreated water. I asked the driver about their seeming lack of concern over these matters which I considered to be serious.

"We tell them to swim only in rivers that are moving."

"Do you think it's OK to drink untreated water?"

"After you're in Africa for a while, your body acclimates."

Lynette and I drank a glass of wine near the river. A moustached warbler uttered its raspy call from the reeds and striped swallows foraged for insects above the river. A Senegal coucal perched in a tree. The muddy Ubangui rolled by. Through our binoculars, we could see children playing in the streets of Mbayi-Mbongo across the river in Zaire.

The ferry driver smiled and wished us a good morning. We entered Zaire with no difficulty and only a perfunctory inspection of our camper. One of the officials picked up my can of mace and was trying to determine what it was and how to operate it. He came dangerously close to spraying Wilfried, so I asked him to let me show him how to use it.

Zaire is mostly covered with a vast, dense jungle which is drained by long, wide and deep rivers. Wildlife is abundant and the tribal cultures are diverse and ancient. There are few roads in the interior, and those are often impassable. Traversing Zaire is not for the faint of heart. The old Belgian Congo undoubtedly offers at least as much adventure as the Sahara.

Fifteen miles south of the river crossing, we reached Gbadolite, the home of President Mobutu. This town was one of the few in the interior where, supposedly, the telephones worked. We tried to call our daughter, Kristen, without success. Also, the town was out of gas because "the river was too low." I pulled into the entrance of a European company's shipping and receiving area and explained our situation to the manager. He led us to a loading dock where we siphoned gas out of 55 gallon drums.

We drove all day on a very bad road. Shifting gears became difficult, and I was unable to put the car in reverse. Ahead of us, we had a long, difficult drive overland, or, if our timing was lucky, we might be able to catch the riverboat at Lisala and ride it up the Zaire River (Congo River) to Kisangani. Now we were in the jungle. The rain forest was so thick that you could not look into it more than a few feet from the roadside. We arrived in Lisala after dark and learned that the river boat had left only a few hours before, so we camped in the garden of the Protestant mission. We would try to catch the river boat the next day upstream in Bumba.

Lisala's Catholic Mission had a good Belgian mechanic and a garage. The mechanic had earned a good reputation for fixing motors and almost anything else, and he trained and employed local people. Wilfried walked down into the pit with one of the workers and discovered what our problem was. The spare tire was stored under the car, and we apparently had hit something which resulted in the tire being pushed against the gear shift mechanism and preventing it from working smoothly. Before long the bent wheel cover and brace were straightened, and we were on our way. Wilfried had just paid for his passage.

The eighty-five mile drive to the upriver port of Bumba took five hours. We arrived at 1:00 p.m. and drove to the dock. There we saw four vehicles and ten Europeans who had been waiting from five to ten days for the boat to arrive. Our timing was remarkably fortunate. We bought three tickets for us and one for the camper from the "Chef" of the harbor and then became acquainted with the other passengers—two brothers from Iceland (Anar and Bjorne), a woman from Spring Hill College in Alabama (Mary Donald), a couple from Germany, a couple from Holland, a woman from Italy, and a couple from Yorkshire, England (Karin and George).

When we joined the group by the dock, Anar was encircled by wide-eyed local children. He spoke mostly in Icelandic, and the kiddies couldn't understand a word he said (nor could we), but they sat mesmerized by his repertoire of sleight of hand tricks. The afternoon was hot, so George and I hopped in our camper to fetch beer from one of the town's bars. Later in the afternoon, the beer was gone and George nudged me in the ribs with his elbow.

"Darwin, old buddy, how are things, you bloody Yank?"

"I know. You want me to take you back for some more beer."

He looked at the others with a wrinkled brow, threw his thumb across his chest and pointed it at me. "Clever, that one!" Lynette stayed with our newfound traveling companions, and George and I took off for town.

George suggested we first have a beer on the bar's shady porch before taking a supply back to the others. It sounded like a good idea to me, so we found an unoccupied table. George obviously had been drinking beer all afternoon and was totally uninhibited in answering my questions. A rolled cigarette dangled from his lips, and he wore a sweat-stained bush hat. He was a burly man with deep set blue eyes and a beard that masked his features to the extent that his mood was only betrayed when he laughed. He looked like a killer, and, not surprisingly, had been a mercenary in Zimbabwe when it was Southern Rhodesia. George was forty years old, and, aside from his old Land Rover and a bit of cash, he was broke. He and Karin had both been married and divorced but had been together for seven years. Karin was a perky beauty with frizzy brown hair and slender legs running up to her short shorts. George bragged about her shamelessly—bordering on the maudlin, how wonderful and beautiful she was, and how understanding she was to put up with him and his crazy ideas! All of a sudden, I felt a sharp pain on my left shoulder and saw a set of keys ricochet onto the table between us. Simultaneously, I was startled by a shrieking howl from behind me. Then she was in front of me, picking up George's glass, throwing the beer on him and tossing the empty glass out into the street.

"Don't you EVER speak to me again!" She spun on her heel and ran away down the street. George and I were momentarily speechless. I looked around us, and the Africans were all laughing. George looked dumbfounded, and I wasn't sure what to say.

"George, is Karin angry?"

"Why, I don't know, Old Boy. Do you think she was?"

George and I returned to the dock with a supply of beer, but Karin was not there. George professed to having no idea why she had been so upset. He had the keys to their Land Rover, but, to his great dismay, Karin had all their travelers' checks. For the next several hours, he was frantic, unable to find Karin or anyone who knew of her whereabouts. Then, just minutes before the boat left, a smiling Karin returned and ran into George's arms. The ensuing display of loving tenderness was bizarre only in my eyes, I suppose, since the others had not witnessed Karin's outrage at the bar. Nevertheless, I was happy for my drinking buddy who, while embracing his lover, looked over her shoulder and winked at me. He rubbed his fingers against his thumb in a gesture that assured me that the travelers' checks were again readily accessible.

Life on the river boat, the *Muyanzi*, was unlike anything I have ever seen before or since. The boat was a steamer with five barges tethered around its perimeter. I cringed while I watched a rusty and rickety old crane loading our vehicles. Our camper was set on one of the barges, for some reason, apart from the other cars which were loaded on a barge on the opposite side of the boat. Thousands of people populated the boat and its barges. Transient shops traded African essentials—chickens, goats, crocodiles, and colorfully feathered birds. There was something for every palate—grubs the size of oranges, dried monkeys, manioc bread, fish, eels, snakes, rats, pineapples, bananas and nuts.

The *Muyanzi* labored upstream against the wide fast flowing Zaire River. Each village along the shore specialized in certain products to be traded. As the boat approached a settlement, villagers in dugout canoes called "piroques" brought goods to the boat, bartered with the traders on the boat, and then returned to the village laden with products from other villages. Boys and men paddled the piroques very skillfully in the dangerous fast moving currents. They stood while they paddled and timed their arrival at the boat perfectly so that people on board could grab a gunwale and help tether their canoe to a barge. An hour or so later, after completing the trading, the canoe would be released and the villagers simply rode the current back downstream to their homes.

African music and drums played non-stop. When they were not trading, people danced, told stories, ate, drank, and visited. Many of the traders remained on the boat for the full round trip, from Kinshasha (Leopoldville) to Kisangani (Stanleyville) and back again. Everybody was very friendly and as curious about us as we were about them. Men usually wore western clothes, while women dressed in more traditional tribal fashions with their hair styled in rigid spikes wrapped in black thread. Once the boat made a stop to put off stowaways. Another time we watched as a thief was thrown into the treacherous, crocodile infested river—a sentence of death and one well within the captain's power.

While adults and children slept all over the deck, even under our vehicle, Lynette and I slept in the comfort of our own bed. African music played long into the night. At five in the morning we awakened to "What A Friend We Have In Jesus." The weather was very hot and humid day and night. Lynette spent much of the days on board visiting with the others on the boat's opposite side while I guarded the camper. I sat on its hot roof wearing only shorts, and, to replace the fluid pouring from my pores, I drank quart bottles of beer or orange soda, whatever they happened to be selling at the moment. With my binoculars, I followed the colorful tropical birds flying along the shore and across the river. Once Karin came over to keep me company. She climbed up onto the roof and sat beside me.

"I feel like I owe you an explanation."

"No, not really. Just a lovers' quarrel."

She explained that George had asked her to make him a sandwich. She went to the Rover to accommodate him, and, when she returned with the sandwich, he was gone. She thought that he had just wanted to get rid of her so he could go to the bar without her. This infuriated her, and, after finding us and throwing the keys, she had made up her mind to leave George. She tried to cash the travelers' checks, but, without his signature, was unable to do so. She then stopped in a bar or two on her own. After a few beers and a few flirtatious comments from admiring men, she felt better. She decided to return to George when she saw the boat arriving.

"I'm still angry with George... But what can I do?... I love him."

"I know this, Karin. George was ecstatic when you returned."

"Was he, now? How nice!" She smiled prettily.

Wilfried relieved me on guard duty for the camper. I joined Lynette and the others as the boat headed closer to the shore and steamed along where the current wasn't as strong. A trumpeter hornbill stretched its wings on a limb, and a flock of gray parrots flew into the thick jungle. Occasionally a hut or two or even a small village came into view on the river bank. Children waved and looked longingly at the world floating past them.

Walking from barge to boat to barge was not without danger. There were, of course, no guard rails. The gaps between the vessels narrowed and widened with the tugging currents, and the water churned below. Once a pig fell into the breach, screamed and met an instant crushing death. A few of the African boys played a risky game. They jumped into the river from the bow of the front barge, drifted alongside, and then, before reaching the end of the second barge, grabbed a tethered piroque and allowed the current to throw them over the gunwale and into the canoe. The game was to see who would wait the longest before hauling himself back aboard. Bjorne dared Anar to give the game a try. The older brother declined. Bjorne flapped his elbows and squawked like a chicken, and then took the plunge himself. Anar shook his head.

"Our mother told me to care for him. He is her baby. If something happens to Bjorne, she will kill me."

Bjorne, however, was as agile as the Africans. He timed his moves perfectly and easily flipped himself into a canoe. Moments later he strutted proudly up to our group, smiling broadly.

After a few days on the boat, the novelty began to wear off. The heat made Lynette miserable. From my notes: *Hot, dirty, smelly, sweaty—this is enough! That paste they make from cassava root (manioc) smells awful! Scratches and sores become infected and won't heal. Worried about roads east of Kisangani—they become impassable in rainy season. Hope rain holds off for ten more days until we reach Tanzania and the dry Serengeti. Lynette says she's going home when we reach Nairobi. I hope not, but if she does, I'm leaning toward continuing on to South Africa by myself.*

Watching our cars being unloaded in Kisangani after six days of river travel was gut-wrenching. The crane operator and his ground crew seemed to have no idea of what they were doing. They took most of an afternoon unloading only two of our cars and then quit for the night. Our group met at the Hotel Olympia which permitted camping in its garden. Lynette and I suffered mosquitoes, a dripping cold water shower, and a smelly bed in our hotel room which had only torn screens on the windows while Wilfried slept in our camper on the boat. This would be a true test of the efficacy of our malaria medication.

The next morning we learned that the crane could not reach our barge. The Europeans and we rounded up several coils of heavy rope and a group of Africans, and we all pitched in to pull the barge closer to the shore by hand. Our car was lifted ashore safely, as was that of the Dutch couple. The last vehicle was owned by a German couple. As the crane lifted it off its barge, we could see that the camper was hanging improperly in the sling. The vehicle started slipping out of the sling as it swung across the open water and fell from the sling just as it reached over the dock. The camper crashed to the ground with a sickening thud. Closer inspection revealed that the car's frame had been broken. We felt so lucky our little VW camper was safe and sound.

That evening our group met for a farewell dinner at a Chinese restaurant in downtown Kisangani. With luck, many of us would meet again at the campground in Nairobi. Sadly, however, we would not see our pal, Wilfried, again. He was staying on in Kisangani for a few days and then planned to work his way south through Zaire rather than heading for east Africa.

From a letter to my parents: *...the drive from Kisangani to Goma on Zaire's eastern border with Rwanda via Nia Nia, Komanda, and Beni was unforgettable. The roads were tortuous and diabolical—the worst I've ever seen. When we weren't stuck in the mud, we were trying to average ten miles an hour, but often made only six or seven. Somehow we survived the rains, the hot days and nights, the unrelenting humidity, and the ravenous mosquitoes. The jungle crept to the edges of the road and seemed impenetrable. Along the way we saw pygmies, okapis (a beautiful forest animal, very rare, and related to the giraffe) and wonderful birds.*

It took all day to drive to Nia Nia on a road that was very bad. The skies were often dark, but the rain held off. The Catholic Mission in Nia Nia permitted us to camp in their garden for the night, and we enjoyed our first African hot shower. Wilfried had become disenchanted with the inhospitality of Catholic Missions, and Lynette thought it was "too bad that Wilfried isn't here to see a Catholic Mission that would have us."

On the road east from Nia Nia we sometimes traveled only two or three miles in an hour because of having to wind our way through and around deep ruts carved by heavy trucks. We stopped at the Station de Capture d'Epulu, a reserve for the endangered okapi, where there was a beautiful campground on the Epulu River. Pygmies populated the countryside. One old man sold me a bunch of twenty or thirty bananas and two pineapples for less than ten cents.

We continued on horrible roads, east to Komandan and south to Beni. Progress was so slow that we found ourselves driving at night and trying to find a safe place to camp. We descended a hill and, at the bottom, became stuck on a rudimentary bridge when our tire slid between two logs. I got out of the car and, as I began jacking up the wheel, I heard drums—boom-boom-boom-boom, boom-boom-boom-boom. They became louder and seemed closer. I looked around and, in the moonlight, could see dark faces emerging from the thick jungle. I worked the jack handle as fast as I could, slid a sand ladder under the tire, and then pulled off the bridge. When I returned to retrieve my sand ladder, the people who had gathered by the bridge backed away, seemingly as frightened as I was. Unable to find a place to camp, we continued driving to Beni and checked into the Hotel Beni in the middle of the night. The next morning, according to my notes, "we had a fine breakfast."

Two of our tires were badly worn, so we had to buy two new ones in Beni. While I took care of the car, Lynette stocked up on some groceries in the local market. Afterwards, she accompanied the wife of the auto shop manager to a fabric shop to buy material. Then she watched while a man made her an African-style dress on a pedal sewing machine. We continued south very slowly and camped at a Protestant Mission near Lubero. We gave two hitchhikers a ride, and they reported that the road to the south was very bad. During the night it rained hard and steadily for more than three hours. This was reason enough to became very worried.

Near Lubero, Zaire, March 3, 1988

From my notes: *Leave mission early. Incredibly muddy. Unbelievable problems. Two huge trucks stuck in ruts four feet deep. Difficult to walk let alone work. We dig new road to by-pass trucks. Bridge ruts with sand ladders and push camper across ladders. Tie rope to camper and about a dozen curious onlookers help pull us along newly dug road. Mud walls of ruts very tenuous as we pull our camper alongside the trucks. The camper leans closer and closer to a truck as mud wall gives way. We tie a second rope across the camper and another group of Africans pull it to the side of the road to keep camper from falling into the trucks. Very slow progress! Very nice people!*

We entered Zaire's incredibly beautiful Virunga National Park at Kayna-Bayonga. Lush green rain forests crept up the flanks of the Ruwenzori volcanoes and snow covered the mountain peaks. Hippos snorted and splashed in a river, and large herds of antelopes grazed by the road. Buffaloes leered threateningly from the plains. Marabou storks, Egyptian geese, wattled plovers and hamerkops foraged in ponds and marshes. Male baboons sucked their fingers while they watched females caring for their young. Still covered with mud from the aftermath of the first rains of the season, we camped at a wonderful lodge near Rwindi where we washed ourselves and then the camper. Lynette struck up a conversation with a brother and sister, Moslems from Goma, who were traveling together. He owned a small trucking company. I told him about the two trucks hopelessly mired in the mud.

"How do you make money in the rainy season. These roads become virtually impassable."

"Make money?" He laughed. "Now we stop doing business until the rains are finished. Now there is no money to be made."

The road south to Goma was dry and in fair condition. We picked up two hitchhikers, journalists from England, and treated them to coffee in Goma. Then we crossed the border into Rwanda where much of the forest land had long ago been converted to farms by Hutu tribespeople. The contrast with Zaire's rain forests was dramatic. Farmers with hand implements worked the treeless rolling green hills. In the capital city of Kigali, we changed money on the black market and then checked into the Hotel Diplomat, where we were assured that we would be able to make calls home to our familiy.

Our car's engine had continued to give us problems, and I had used all of the spare fuel filters I had brought along. The Kigali VW dealer, unfortunately, had no fuel filters. Our fuel pump was going bad. The power steering seal leaked, and steering had become a real workout. The mechanic didn't have these parts either but did the best he could and hoped his jury rigged repairs would last until we reached the much larger VW dealership in Nairobi. There, they assured us, the parts would be stocked.

Our road deteriorated significantly after crossing the border into Tanzania. At one point, a man tried to drive his recalcitrant cattle across the road, but they wanted none of it. We waited while he prodded and then beat the rump of the leader with a stick until the feckless animal bled from its flanks. In the end, the cow prevailed and continued down the same side of the road. In Lusahanga, we stopped at the police station where I asked an officer if we could spend the night parked in the adjacent garden. He agreed but obviously wanted something in return for the favor. I offered him two small reed chairs we had bought on the Zaire River boat, and he eagerly accepted them. Continuing north and east, we arrived at lovely Lake Victoria and then boarded a small ferry which transported us across an arm of the lake. During the passage, I talked with an Indian who was in the office supplies business in the nearby town of Mwanza. He directed us to a mission on the lake where we spent the night.

Lynette and I entered Tanzania's vast and spectacular Serengeti National Park from the remote west. Serengeti, combined with Kenya's Masai Mara National Reserve lying immediately to the north, must be considered one of the world's natural wonders. Now we really were in Africa! Giraffes browsed on branches of tall trees. Vast herds of buffaloes, zebras, dik diks, and gazelles grazed by the roadsides. An endless sea of wildebeests, or gnus, migrated across the endless grassy plains. Ferocious-looking wart hogs grazed peacefully, their tusks scraping the ground; and a pride of lions rolled playfully on a hill.

The park's roads were in poor condition and poorly marked, and we became lost several times. Lynette was trying to direct us to the Seronera Lodge where we hoped to be able to stay for a night or two. Eventually we arrived at the lodge in mid-afternoon. The place appeared deserted. I approached the clerk.

"We would like a room for two nights."

"I'm sorry. We have no rooms."

"No rooms? There's no one here. You have no rooms available?"

"Everyone is out on safari. They will all come back later."

"Look, my friend. My wife and I have been traveling for months. We have crossed the Sahara Desert. We have driven through the Zairian rain forest. We are very tired and need to rest and clean up. Isn't there something you can do to help us?"

"I shall see. Please, go and see the animals. Come back at 7:00 this evening, and perhaps there will be a room."

As the man suggested, Lynette and I spent the next couple of hours viewing the wildlife. The numbers of animals in the migrating herds were prodigious, especially the wildebeests. Birds were everywhere—including large species like bustards, secretary birds, and ostriches. We returned to the lodge at 7:00. The lobby was so full of people we could hardly make our way through the doorway and across the room. I waved at the clerk and caught his eye. He signaled me to wait ten more minutes. Then across the lobby I saw a man who looked very familiar. I grabbed Lynette's hand and weaved our way through the crowd to his side.

"Pardon me, Sir. Are you from St. Louis?"

"Yes. My name is Joe Glik."

"I thought it was you. Joe, your son, Bobby, is a friend of mine. The three of us had lunch together once. You may not remember me, but my name is Darwin Wile."

"Darwin! Of course I remember you. You look awful! What's happened to you?"

I laughed and introduced Lynette, and Joe introduced his daughter, Judy, with whom he was traveling. After I told them our story, Joe insisted we could sleep with them in their room if we were unable to get our own room. Fortunately for all of us, the room clerk was able to accommodate us. That evening the scenario seemed so remarkable as we drank beer and enjoyed dinner with Joe and Judy Glik in a far-off corner of the African Serengeti.

Our next stop was Ngorongoro Crater. Lonely Planet's *Africa On a Shoestring* suggests that if "Serengeti is spectacular, Ngorongoro is unreal." The crater of this extinct volcano is more than 2,000 feet deep and twelve miles in diameter. The bottom of the crater is an amazingly beautiful plain that supports a cross section of much of Africa's wildlife. We drove to the rim of the crater and were incredulous of what unfolded below us.

From my notes: *If I were an elephant, this is where I would want to be.* Instead of entering the crater, we drove to Crater Lodge and checked their upcoming reservations. Sure enough, as we had planned months before, the following week's listing contained the names of Barb and Ed Brennan and two other couples who were friends of ours from Belleville. We added our names to that week's reservations and then drove on to Gibb's Farm, a coffee plantation we had read about and wanted to visit.

In the settled areas of Tanzania, round huts with mud brick walls and thatched roofs housed farmers who worked the fields with only hand imple-ments. Away from the settlements, Masai tribesmen tended their cattle. The legendary warriors wore scant but colorful clothing. Lynette admired their tall and slender physiques and, after reading that their diet consisted mainly of milk and blood drained from the cattle they herded, she wondered if she too could possibly attain "tall slenderness" by learning to like such fare. Once we stopped at a particularly beautiful setting for lunch. Colorful birds sang from the trees and a small herd of elands grazed nearby. Secretly I had mixed beet juice with a small bowl of cottage cheese and then offered it to Lynnie, passing it off as a Masai delicacy. She wouldn't consider trying it. Another time when I stopped to identify a bird I had seen flying by the road, we were attacked and bitten by voracious, cross-winged tsetse flies. Fortunately, it was a variety that did not carry the parasites which cause sleeping sickness.

Gibb's Farm sat on a hill overlooking a lush green valley of coffee trees. To the south lay the imposing Manyara escarpment and to the west rose the Ngorongoro crater. We took a room at the farm, a small but immaculate whitewashed cabin, and laundered our clothes and cleaned the camper. We later had the privilege of talking with Margaret Gibbs. She was born in Tanzania of British parents. We described our trip across Zaire and emphasized the awful condition of the roads. She said that her first husband had driven across Zaire in the late '40s when the route boasted good roads and offered very nice places to stay. Such traveling amenities had certainly changed—unfortunate casualties accompanying the fall of colonialism.

Page and Edward were from the Chesapeake Bay area and were living on Gibb's farm for the winter. They were working on projects for which they had been retained. She was studying birdlife on the farm and had compiled records on more than 200 species. Edward's degrees were in engineering and art, and he was restoring some of the farm's paintings. Lynette and I walked with Page to a waterfall and saw paradise and blue flycatchers and mountain wagtails. In the evening, the three of us and Edward met for dinner, and we were joined by two fellows from New Zealand who had set up a wildlife safari business using Gibb's Farm as a center of operations. Lynette and I deferred to the others in selecting from the menu and consequently enjoyed their choices of English dishes subtly touched with African flavors.

Our friends, the Brennans, had planned their African itinerary around our tentative schedule and had given us a copy before we left home. Because we had arrived in East Africa about a week later than expected, we had thereby missed the Kenyan portion of their schedule. We doubted that they would expect us now, since we had missed them in Kenya, and we wanted to surprise them at Lake Manyara National Park. Just before noon, we registered at Manyara's lodge with its magnificent setting on the Rift Valley escarpment overlooking the park and valley 1,000 feet below. The Brennans were scheduled to arrive late in the afternoon with our other friends, Janet and Dick Boyle and Terry and Norm Kastner. Lynnie and I had lunch and then drove into the park where we saw elephants, hippos, giraffes, and many other mammals. Tree-climbing lions lay on acacia branches, basking in the afternoon sun. The park also boasted a splendid variety of birds. Thousands of flamingos foraged at one end of Lake Manyara, forming an incredible pink blanket stretching across the alkaline lake.

Lynette and I cleaned up in our room and then stationed ourselves in the bar to wait for our friends. They arrived and a very noisy, joyful, and tearful reunion ensued. We answered their many questions about our journey across the continent, and they brought us up to date on the gossip from home. I had the nagging feeling, however, that they didn't seem to be very surprised to see us.

"It almost seems like you guys expected to find us here. Didn't you give up on us after our non-show in Kenya?"

"Nah," scoffed Ed, "we knew you'd be right here in the bar."

"How the hell did you figure that out?"

"Elementary, my dear Darwin. We saw your camper parked behind the hotel."

I had parked the VW behind the hotel so that they wouldn't see it. I never expected their driver to show them the grounds before they checked in.

During our little reunion, I noticed a fellow who was sitting with his wife at a nearby table. They took a great deal of interest in our conversation, and he sported an unabashed broad grin. I nodded at them, and he returned the gesture. Soon our friends and we returned to our respective rooms to prepare for dinner. Lynette and I stepped inside the door to our room. Staring right at us from the railing on our balcony was a baboon who proceded to inflict upon himself one of the most complicated and, Lynette thought, disgusting sexual acts imaginable.

In the morning, I was the first of our group to arrive for breakfast. The grinning man from the previous evening walked up to my table and introduced himself. Bob Volpa and his wife, Gloria, were Californians who have been living in Cairo for the past four years. He was a communications engineer. Over the years, his company had also assigned him and Gloria to international stints in Borneo, Algiers, and Saudi Arabia. He had found our travel tales fascinating and wanted to hear more about our experiences. Bob and Gloria were planning on going to Ngorongoro, as was our group. He had heard us talking about our VW's motor problems, and suggested that Lynette and I drive to the crater with him and Gloria in their mini-bus. Eight people plus a guide/driver would make for a tight fit in the ubiquitous minibusses used by people on safari, so we took Bob up on his offer. After introducing everyone all around and swelling our group to ten, our two vehicles drove in tandem, the four of us in one and the six Bellevillians in another, first to Gibb's Farm for lunch and then into Ngorongoro Crater.

From Ngorongoro's rim, elephants looked like ants a half mile below. The winding descent to the grassy plain took forty minutes and took us past many animals, including marabou storks soaring on the thermals creeping up the crater's slopes. We then drove onto the crater's floor which covers more than 100 square miles. The magnificent ecosystem is permanent home to an enormous number of animal species which in one way or another depend upon each other for survival. Shallow alkaline Lake Magadi supports thousands of flamingos and other wading birds. Elephants may be found in wooded areas and on the crater's slopes. We saw lions on their kills, cheetahs testing the speed of antelopes, and an elephant with tusks so long that it seemed to require a heroic effort for him to keep them from dragging. Herds of gazelles and zebras grazed on the plains and always posted several alert sentries. We saw buffaloes, zebras, wildebeests, monkeys, baboons, hippos, and rhinos—many of them up close and personal. This was surely one of the world's most impressive sights and an experience none of us would soon forget.

That night at dinner we reviewed the day's experiences. It was Norm's birthday, and he was wishing for a Black Russian more than anything else. Our guide, Moses, was sufficiently resourceful and rose to the challenge of finding the necessary ingredients, foul tasting as they turned out to be, and the ten of us had a grand celebration.

Dick Boyle may be the only friend I have who consistently awakens and rises before me. We were both on the hotel's deck at daybreak looking for lammergeyers, the rare beardless vultures which reportedly may be seen occasionally soaring above the crater's rim. We didn't find lammergeyers but did see bateleurs, a raptor with a tail so short you can hardly see it. The time arrived for our friends to drive back to Nairobi for their return flight home. Our intent was to follow them, and Bob insisted that he and Gloria drive in back of us in case our VW broke down again. We had no problems, but Bob's van broke down not far from Arusha. The Volpas rode with us to Nairobi where we all registered at the Hilton and had a farewell dinner together.

After seeing everyone off at the airport, Lynette and I took our camper to Cooper Motors, Nairobi's huge Volkswagen dealer. They did not stock power steering seals or some of the other parts we needed, so the parts manager, Joseph Navoo, called Germany. He said the replacement parts would be flown from there in a day or two. We left the car there so that they might begin work on some of its problems, and we registered at the historic Norfolk Hotel where we ate dinner in the Lord Delemere Room. Lynnie was in a much better mood after having been with friends from home. We agreed that the physically most challenging aspects of the trip were behind us, and she decided to continue with me on the trip to South Africa.

Lynette awakened the next morning feeling ill. I left her for a few hours to take care of some administrative things, and, when I returned to the Norfolk, she was writhing in pain. The desk clerk helped me find a doctor who made house calls. He examined Lynette, diagnosed her problems as intestinal and said that they would probably go away soon. He gave her what he said was appropriate medication. I ate dinner alone while the poor flower rested.

Lynette was still feeling not well in the morning, so I went to breakfast by myself where I met an Englishman named Kevin who worked for General Electric. He had previously been in India and now lived in Kenya. I asked him why Kenya seemed relatively affluent and seemed to work better than other former European colonies. He attributed Kenya's apparent success relative to the others to three factors: First, during the colonial period, the Brits became Kenyans, while the French and Belgians usually came to Africa only for a two or three year period and then were replaced. Secondly, the Kikuyus were business-oriented and naturally shrewd and often welcomed British and Asian commercial presence. Thirdly, the system that the Brits installed was capitalistic and not the same as the corrupt socialistic forms prevalent in the other former colonies.

I made myself busy visiting the U.S. and Tanzanian embassies and then Cooper Motors where they worked on the VW's brakes, changed the shock absorbers, and apologized for the parts which still had not arrived. Lynette was feeling a bit better when I returned to the Norfolk.

The next few days were more of the same. I arranged for Zambian visas, tried not to get angry when the VW's parts still had not shown up, and one day went birding with the local bird club at the Nairobi Arboretum where I saw about a dozen new species including the Zambezi honeyguide, Klaaus' cuckoo and amethyst sunbird. After we had been in Nairobi a week, Cooper Motors pronounced our car sound. We drove to Ma Roche's campground, a well-known meeting place for campers in Nairobi, where we saw Danielle, the German whose camper had fallen from the sling in Kisangani. The insurance companies were making everything so difficult that he was ready to give up and go home. Nobody we talked to at the campground had seen George, Karin and the others.

Late the next day I discovered that the power steering fluid was again leaking badly. The new seal had not solved the problem. We returned to Cooper Motors just before closing, and the Pakistani service manager, Rashid, told us to follow him to his home where he and several of his friends tore apart the steering mechanism and worked on it until 12:30 a.m. It still leaked, so we gave up for the night. Rashid's wife, Selma, invited us to join them and one of their friends, Charlie, for a very late Indian dinner. Charlie, was a German Moslem who lived in Kampala with his Ugandan wife. He was staying with the Rashids and, during the meal, came up with the suggestion that we, rather than waiting for another part that might not work, drive the camper without the steering pump belt. Rashid and Charlie predicted the car would steer hard at low speeds but otherwise would perform fine. We all agreed on Charlie's solution, had a nightcap, and Lynette and I camped in the Rashid's driveway.

At breakfast, we made plans to join the Rashids and Charlie for dinner, and then Lynette and I returned to Ma Roche's Campground where we had a joyful reunion with Karin, George, Anar, and Bjorne. George and I spent much of the day working on his Land Rover with Karin and Lynette periodically monitoring our progress. We talked about trying to meet in South Africa and touring Botswana together. That evening we met the Rashids; their eleven-year-old son, Johnny, and Charlie at The Carnivore. This restaurant, as its name implies, specializes in meat especially the red varieties, including beef, lamb, and pork as well as a selection of native African specialties such as hartebeest. Rashid and Charlie talked candidly about their problems living in black Africa which they characterized as becoming worse. Whites, and Asians in particular, they said, were discriminated against. Admissions to schools were based on race rather than merit. Especially because they were concerned about Johnny's education, the Rashids were planning to emigrate to Canada. We talked about our plans to tour Masai Mara and Samburu game reserves, and, when we learned Johnny was disappointed that he would be leaving Africa without having seen either, we asked Rashid and Selma if he could come with us. Somewhat to our surprise—after all, they had only known us for two days—they agreed.

After eating breakfast with George and Karin, we picked Johnny up and drove in the rain to Masai Mara, viewing a great variety of animals along the way. Johnny was a bright kid with a terrific sense of humor and a budding entrepreneurial streak. In the park, we became stuck in the mud. I showed the boy the efficacy of sand ladders by jacking up the car, sliding the plaques under the wheels, and thereby extricating the VW from the mud's clutches. Johnny shook his head and muttered something in Urdu.

"What's that, Johnny?"

"This one thinks he could make a lot of money with these sand ladders."

In addition to speaking English and Urdu, Johnny also spoke Swahili. For the first time on our trip, we had no problems asking directions. The boy eagerly talked with Africans along the road, and, having him with us, I felt more confident and sensed that we were afforded more respect by the Africans. We drove along the Rift Valley escarpment and, that evening, camped on Lake Naivasha, a beautiful fresh water lake with great numbers of animals—fish, hippos, and birds, including a huge flock of pelicans. In the morning, our camper was surrounded by monkeys, sacred ibises, and marabou storks. We washed Masai Mara's mud off the car, and then the three of us hiked along the lake where we saw hoopoes, bee-eaters, anteater chats, glossy ibises, and a variety of shorebirds. The next day, we stopped at Nakuru National Park where, in addition to giraffes, waterbucks and rhinos, we saw thousands of flamingos in the shallow, alkaline lake. Along the way, Johnny wanted to know, "Do you enjoy telling jokes?"

"Certainly," Lynette responded, "but I like to hear others tell them too. Do you know any jokes, Johnny?"

"Yes I do. Perhaps we should take turns. I'll begin, my friend. Ummmm... take a bit of time to think of a good one."

At Thomson's Falls, we camped with a Swiss couple and their two children and built a large bonfire. Earlier, our young friend had bought himself a cake he just couldn't live without. After dinner, he shared two small pieces with the Swiss children and promptly ate the rest himself. He went to bed not feeling well, and, in the morning, when Lynette suggested we buy another cake, he just rolled his eyes and said, "No ways, my friend!"

The morning clouds dissipated, and Mt. Kenya popped out of the surrounding mountains, climbing somewhat unobtrusively above 17,000 feet. Samburu National Reserve combines scrub desert with forests and swamps lining the Ewaso Ngiro River. The arid areas support reticulated giraffes, gerenuks, Grevy's zebras, and oryxes while rhinos, elephants, buffaloes, cheetahs and lions favor the riparian habitats. Lynette thought she and Johnny deserved a treat, so we registered at the Samburu Lodge's tented camp and went to the ranger station to arrange for a guide. The ranger, Joseph, said he would engage a guide for us.

"This guide will meet you at 6:30 tomorrow morning."

"Will he be a good guide?" I wanted to know.

"He will be good enough."

Johnny wanted to buy a gift for his mother. We went to the lodge's shop where I observed him putting a bracelet in his pocket without paying for it. I told him to put it back and had a talk with him outside the shop. That evening we watched enormous crocodiles slither onto the riverbank to feed on carcasses of various animals thrown there by lodge staff members for the benefit of their guests.

As planned, we met our guide at 6:30. It was Joseph himself. The ranger showed us many mammals, including two female lions with four cubs, three months old. The birds, included a Verreaux's eagle owl. Then he led us to a leopard, the first we had seen in the wild. We observed the elegant cat from less than twenty yards away as the animal circled a tree and then lept onto a limb where he lay stretched along its length, and groomed himself, getting ready for his nap. When we returned to the lodge, I thanked Joseph for showing us so many animals and added, "As you promised, our guide was 'good enough'."

"When you asked if the guide was good, I did not want to say much.

But I know this land and the animals."

"That is so. When my friends come to Samburu, I will tell them to ask for Joseph."

Johnny gave a polished stone to Lynette to keep until he could give it to his mother. She mentioned the stone to me, and we weren't sure what to do. I asked him if he had paid for the stone. He said that he had, and I told him to come with me to the shop where I asked the shopkeeper if the boy had paid for the stone. He said "no."

"This one came in and asked me questions. He did not pay me."

I looked at Johnny.

"I paid the other one."

"That one will be back soon," smiled the clerk.

When the other attendant came back, he confirmed that Johnny had paid him. I felt wonderful that the boy had not stolen the stone and terrible that I had put him through this ordeal. I apologized to Johnny and then explained to him that stealing or lying creates difficult problems.

"Even friends can't trust a dishonest person, Johnny. I am sorry that I thought you did not pay, but you must accept part of the responsibility."

"Yes, I know this."

Farther south we camped on a hill near the Naro Moru River Lodge in the shadows of Mount Kenya. At 2:30 in the morning, I was awakened by Lynette's firm elbow thrust in my ribs.

"Darwin! There's a man outside the camper!"

I grabbed a mace cannister and looked out an unzipped window in the camper's poptop. Sure enough, there was. The man approached the camper and seemed to be reaching toward the top of it. I shouted, "Hey, you!" I waited a couple of minutes and then opened the sliding door. He was gone.

"Johnny! Come down here." The boy climbed down from the top bed. I pulled the windshield curtain down and drove the camper with the poptop still raised down the hill to the lodge. I told the guard what happened and that we wanted to park for the remainder of the night next to the guard-house. While we talked, another guard approached us, listened for a moment, and then explained.

"That was me. I was just doing my job inspecting the area. There are ten of us who patrol the area around the lodge."

"Why were you gone when I opened the door."

"I heard you shout and just thought you were having a bad dream."

Everybody had a good laugh, but I remained unconvinced about that guy's intentions.

Back in Nairobi, we found Karin, George and Bjorne. Anar was in the hospital, they said, with foot problems. The six of us enjoyed a farewell feast of chips and beer for lunch (Coke for Johnny). Karin and George were going to the American Embassy to try to get a tourist visa for the U.S. We wrote a letter which invited them to stay at our house. They took it along and hoped it might improve their chances of getting the visa. I didn't really expect to see the boys from Iceland again. Somehow, however, I believed that George and Karin would show up later—either in South Africa or perhaps one day in Wyoming.

We returned Johnny to his home where Selma served us a marvelous dinner and Rashid informed us that our waterpump had arrived from Germany. Lynette and I had grown very fond of Johnny, and I had a tear in my eye when he gave me his *Marlboro Safari Rally—Kenya* poster which still hangs above my work bench in Jackson Hole. After camping in their driveway, we bade "adieu" to Selma and Johnny and followed Rashid to Cooper Motors to pick up the waterpump. I felt better about leaving Nairobi now that we had the spare pump.

The Karen Blixen (Isak Dinesen) Museum in the Ngong Hills west of Nairobi was impressive and quite moving. It represented a different time in Africa. White Europeans came and carved out a new life in a sometimes hostile and always beautiful new land, and they saw cultures and wildlife in their purest forms. It could not last, and, with the end of colonialism, came African determination. Nevertheless, a bit of the past was preserved in the museum as were many momentoes of this very interesting and talented writer, painter, farmer, and storyteller. A certain irony of change wasn't lost on me as we drove to Ma Roche's campground through black clouds of diesel exhaust belched by passing lorries and buses. While we registered, a large overland truck pulled into the compound. It was one of the trucks we had seen in Bangui. The road to Goma had closed by the time these overlanders had come across Zaire, so they came through Uganda instead.

Princess Elizabeth had learned of her father's death in 1952 while she and Prince Phillip were staying at Treetops Lodge in Aberdare National Park. Spending a night at Treetops was one of Lynette's priorities for the trip. Aberdare was limited to four wheel drive vehicles, so we registered with a tour company, met them at the Outspan Hotel in Nyeri, and were taken with a tour group of loud and insensitive Americans to the famous lodge in the trees. These people tried to outdo one another patronizing and sometimes ridiculing the natives. After dinner at Treetops, instead of being quiet so that the guests could see more animals, they drank excessively and became even more boisterous and obnoxious. Lynette and I were mortified.

Treetops perches on posts among a grove of trees opposite a natural water hole. The area around the water hole is lit by floodlights so that, when animals come at night to drink, guests may watch from their rooms or from viewing platforms on the roof. Lynette and I remained awake most of the night. A steady parade of animals and birds came to drink—buffaloes, waterbucks, bushbucks, hyenas, warthogs, and a white-tailed mongoose.

Despite the horrid manners of our fellow countrymen, Lynette was very taken by the place, because of its history and also because of the way one wildlife drama or another unfolded under the lights all night long.

Mount Kilimanjaro rose through a clear sky to more than 19,000 feet and provided a splendid backdrop for Amboseli National Park, our next stop. Imagine the breathtaking drama of a herd of elephants parading in front of Africa's highest peak. Or the fabulous vision of a herd of giraffes galloping seemingly in slow motion across a dusty plain. Amboseli hosted an incredible variety of mammals and birds—elephants, lions, giraffes, cheetahs, impalas, oryxes, gerenuks, buffaloes and rhinos—and spectacular Kilimanjaro was a silent sentinel watching over everything. Lynette, for the first tme, said she wanted to come back to Africa—to climb Kilimanjaro.

We spent the night camped near the park lodge and then, in the morning, drove east, heading for Tsavo National Park. Our road entered the park at Chuyulu Gate and forded the Shetani Lava Flow near Mzima Springs. Tsavo accommodates the world's greatest concentration of elephants as well as many hippos, crocs, monkeys, rhinos, and birds. At times, groups of elephants numbering in the hundreds may be seen. Dramatic vistas unfolded as we rounded granite outcroppings or crested red hills that overlooked the park's semi-arid plains, and, in some ways, the unexpected appearance of impressive individual elephants in these grand natural settings was even more exciting than seeing the large herds of the animals.

The city of Nairobi is mostly a product of the colonial era. It had been nothing more than a watering hole where the Masai brought their cattle prior to the British construction of the Mombasa to Uganda railroad. Sultry Mombasa, on the other hand, has been an important Indian Ocean port for seven or eight hundred years. The Old Town is interesting with historic sixteenth-century Fort Jesus, the Old Harbour and its Arabian dhows, and the bazaar where products from both the African interior and the Arabian peninsula may be found. We explored the city and then ferried across Kilindini Harbour, driving along the white sand beaches south of town to Tiwi Beach and the attractive Twiga Campground.

Twiga was a throwback to the sixties and seventies and was filled with drifters. The aroma of marijuana permeated the campground as did a distinctive hippie aura. I loved it. A refreshing breeze wafted from the Indian Ocean, cooling an otherwise hot and steamy evening, and we drank beer at the bar with a group of Dutch and German drifters. We knew that Americans traveling in a camper in Africa were a rarity and likely to attract attention. Several times in the past few weeks we had heard references to another American traveling in a camper, and now, apparently, we had caught up with her. She and her Swiss companion pulled into the campground in a Chevy truck with a camper insert and New Jersey tags. They joined us for beers. We compared notes and learned they had taken basically the same route as we but had started last May when we were still in Alaska. They had been waiting in Mombasa for five weeks while they tried to get a permit to sell their vehicle. We went to bed a bit drunk and didn't realize until the next morning that the mesh in our top window had come loose. A host of mosquitoes had found the opening and joined us during the night.

From my notes: *Hope the malaria pills work!*

The white coral sand Indian Ocean beaches were beautiful, clean, and virtually deserted. We had a morning swim at Diani Beach, drove south to the border on a good tarmac road, and then reentered Tanzania where the road degenerated into a rough gravel affair and threaded its way through coconut and sisal plantations. Tanga was a small, sleepy port city with a quaint dhow and fishing boat anchorage. The Inn by the Sea sat on an isolated beach south of town and was run by an Indian/African named M.A. Karimjee and his brother-in-law, both nice fellows who, with little apparent success, were "trying to get the business going." They allowed us to camp inside their enclosure and swim on their beach in exchange for eating dinner in the hotel restaurant that evening. A little African man offered to wash our car for 100 shillings, about 65 cents. I asked Karimjee, "Should I give him a tip?"

"No, 100 shillings is very good for him. He only makes 1600 shillings each month, and he is very happy to do it for 100 shillings."

The man then offered to do our laundry for 150 shillings, about a dollar. After he finished, I paid him.

"Thank you, Sir. Please, Sir. Please, come with me. You and your wife."

"Where are we going?"

"Come to my home. My wife wants you to eat African food. This food, very good!"

Lynette and I went with him. He and his wife were poor but generous and hospitable, and very nice. And the food was very good. And, when we left, I gave him a tip. Then, as we had promised, we ate again at the hotel's fish fry on the beach.

Driving south over yet one more of Tanzania's abominable roads, a loud "thump-thump-thump" began. Under the car, I could see one of the tires wedged against the chassis. My immediate concern was a bent axle or broken spring. I took the tire off, and determined that the wheel was bent. I put the spare tire on, and the car ran well. After Dar Es Salaam, the road improved.

Mikumi National Park, a reserve we had never heard of before, proved to be an unexpected treat. Few people visited this out-of-the-way park, and the animals were quite accepting of human presence. Herds of zebras, gazelles, wildebeests, and hartebeests grazed on the open plain. Giraffes browsed in the tree tops, hippos splashed in pools, and elephants casually crossed the road only a few feet in front of our car. Here in the Uluguru Hills, the weather was cooler, and we spent a pleasant evening camped near the Mikumi Wildlife Lodge.

Mbeye lies in a fertile area surrounded by coffee, banana, tea, and cocoa plantations. A tire and wheel repair shop run by two Indians was the most modern and best equipped we had seen in Africa, better than Cooper Motors. They discovered one of our shock absorbers was broken, replaced it, and straightened the wheel I had removed. We arrived at the Malawi border just after the customs offices closed and set up camp there in the garden. We chatted with friendly locals and shared our cookies with a group of cute children. An attractive young couple from Malawi sat nearby. She nursed her baby and smiled lovingly at it. A little girl played with the father who obviously adored his family. This father taking such an active part in caring for his children prompted a discussion between Lynette and me. At times, during our drive through the many African villages we had seen, it seemed that women did most of the work—caring for the children, working the fields, preparing the meals. By contrast, the men did most of the talking—sitting in groups in the village centers gesticulating and discussing important matters. During the night, a hard rainstorm wakened us and left the countryside fresh.

The Malawi border authorities performed a rather perfunctory physical search of our camper. On the other hand, they were almost phobic in quizzing us about our literary tastes.

"What newspapers do you have?"

"None."

"What magazines do you have?"

"None."

"What books do you have?'

I showed him Lonely Planet's *Africa On a Shoestring*. He leafed through it, asking me to read captions below pictures that caught his eye. Eventually he waved us on, persuaded, I suppose, that we did not carry any subversive literature.

The country of Malawi is a land of great natural beauty—from its picturesque mountains to its great inland sea, 350 mile long Lake Nyasa (Lake Malawi). Several fine national parks contain an abundance of wildlife. In 1961, Dr. Hastings Banda had come to power and has ruled Malawi with an iron fist ever since. The people of Malawi had no political freedom and were very poor. Nevertheless, we were impressed by their beauty, friendliness, and apparent happiness. Children waved and smiled and, unlike many other places we had been, neither begged nor shouted at us. Men were exceedingly polite, and women curtsied.

Our car developed another troublesome noise. We stopped at a hotel in Mzuzu to change money and enjoyed a fine vegetable curry lunch. I asked the waiter if he could recommend a mechanic, and he introduced us to a man drinking a beer at the bar as the owner of Malawi Motors. The fellow was very accommodating. He actually called one of his mechanics to bring his tools to the hotel to fix our problem while we joined him for a beer or two. The mechanic found the noise to be caused by another defective shock absorber and proceeded to fix the problem.

Farther south on Lake Nyasa, we found a government-run rest house which rented cabins on a lovely beach. We cooked dinner on the porch of our cabin, only a few yards from the water, and a guard found us some cold beer (the best brew I had drunk since leaving Niger). After dinner, while the sun dropped in the west, the lovely lake slowly changed colors.

"Lynnie, what have you learned on the trip?"

"That's funny. I was just wondering what I would answer when someone back home asks me what I liked best about the trip. I think I have learned that, despite their best intentions, the missionaries and colonialists should have left these people alone."

"I felt very good seeing that couple with their children back at the border. They seemed so happy."

"Do you know why they were happy?"

"I'm not sure. Why?"

"Because they were from Malawi. There's something about this place that makes people happy."

Lynette was right. Certainly I was as happy as I had ever been sitting there on the shore of Lake Nyasa.

George and Karin had made the drive between Kenya and South Africa and had suggested we spend some time at Monkey Bay near Cape McLear on the southern end of Lake Malawi. Specifically, they recommended Mr. Stevens' Cabins, a popular gathering place of drifters. Woodland and striped kingfishers foraged along the lake's tributaries as we drove on a very rough road to Cape McLear. At one low spot the road was covered with water. Tracks of previous travelers went to the right of the water pool, so I followed them. We became mired in mud up to our axles.

A South African couple in a Land Rover soon came along and, seeing us stuck in the mud, they stayed left and drove through the water with no trouble. They stopped and tied a tow rope between our vehicles. When they tried to pull us out, they became stuck themselves. We lifted the Rover's right rear wheel out of the mud so that the car's front wheels could pull it out of trouble. Then I tried in vain to shovel enough mud away to be able to jack up the VW and slide sand ladders under the wheels.

Soon a pickup truck full of Africans arrived. They jumped from the truck, insisted Lynette and the South African woman should not help, and then they all pitched in. With the Land Rover pulling, we successfully pushed the VW out of a big mess. I shook hands and thanked each of these very nice guys individually. We were all covered with mud, and I had swallowed more than a few mouthfuls of road water. From my notes: *If this part of Nyasaland has bilharzia, now I do as well.*

Mr. Stevens' Cabins was owned by two brothers, George and Ernest Stevens, and was located on the lake at Cape McLear. We enjoyed an omelett and chips dinner at the Stevens brothers' restaurant. Later, in the beautiful, clear evening, fishermen paddled their canoes to the shore, and young people smoked pot quietly on the beach. Lynette and I sipped cold beers on the porch of our small cabin.

Two boys asked to wash our camper in the morning and gave it the best cleaning it had seen in months. Then they did our laundry in the lake. While they worked, Lynette and I took a swim after being assured hippos and crocodiles did not inhabit the lake's south end, and then we read in the warm sun. The boys next cleaned the inside of the car and even washed the floor mats. When they were finished, it looked like new. From my notes: *What a great car! In the immortal words of Eddie Murphy, "I should have it bronzed!"* Later, Lynette cried. She was sad not to be home for Easter.

While we relaxed on the beach, a young woman introduced herself to us. Mary was a Peace Corps volunteer from Seattle. She was teaching in Blantyre but had a business meeting in Lilongwe where she had heard we were driving the next morning. She asked to come along and joined us when we left early. We drove along the Mozambique border, past camps filled with refugees from the civil war, and stopped along the way to see hippos. Mary was nearing the end of her assignment, and I asked her, "What do you think you have accomplished for the Africans?"

"Not very much. If I've done anything, it's a PR kind of thing. I've helped the Africans to understand the U.S. and I've helped my friends understand what it's like in Malawi."

Malawi's new capital city was nicely planned with tree-lined boulevards and plush gardens filled with blooming flowers. We drove Mary to a guest house where her Peace Corps conference was to be held. We waved goodbye, and, as I turned the car around to leave, I backed into an angle iron embedded in concrete to protect a flag pole and badly dented the rear of the camper. After the camper had served us so well, I was not a little perturbed with myself for not taking greater care. We drove to the city golf club where we received permission to camp in their lovely garden. After a very good vegetarian dinner at the club, we sat in our camper and drank a bottle of wine. We talked about the African people. Then we talked about the trip, and I compared Africa to South America.

"Africa has been at least as interesting and educational as South America. The contact with the people has been even greater. But it hasn't been as magical as South America was."

"That's because it's a different time in our lives."

"Maybe. I'm not so sure."

"Certainly. We're fifteen years older now and have seen a lot more. Besides, the children were with us then, and we were carving new ground."

A friendly guard joined us, and we poured him a glass of wine. He offered us marijuana in return. He had been trained to be an accountant, but there were no jobs available in his profession. After a bit, he said he had to continue his rounds.

"Sleep well! You are very safe with me guarding."

We set the alarm for 4:15 a.m. We were to enter Zambia the next morning. Our intent was to arrive at the Zambian border before it opened. Throughout Africa people had warned us about travel in Zambia (colonial Northern Rhodesia). Insurgents, soldiers, and police all had guns. And they all used them. Shootings, rapes, and robberies were reported to be commonplace. Travelers were being slapped into jail or otherwise detained for little or no reason. But, in order to get to Victoria Falls and Zimbabwe, we had to traverse Zambia. Our plan became to minimize our time in this allegedly dangerous country. Camping was not permitted, so we would drive the 450 odd miles to the capital city of Lusaka the first day, spend the night in a hotel there, and drive the 300 miles to the Falls and Zimbabwe (colonial Southern Rhodesia) the second day.

The border opened, and we approached a uniformed official. Lynette handed him our passports. He looked at her passport and then at her.

"You were born in Chicago?"

"Yes, I was!" with a big, friendly smile.

"Your city has been in the news lately."

"Oh, really? What's been going on?"

"The crime rate has become very high. People are killing each other, and there are many rapes and robberies. Chicago must be a very bad place to live. I am sorry for you." Lynnie and I looked at one another and began laughing aloud. She looked at the puzzled guard, started to explain the irony to him, and then, thinking this thing was best left unexplained, she smiled and shrugged her shoulders while shaking his hand. This guy obviously preferred the relative safety of Zambia to Chicago.

We set off through the pleasant rolling countryside. Once we stopped to photograph a waterfall in a beautiful canyon. A soldier appeared out of nowhere and motioned for us to continue driving. Later, we stopped to pick up a hitchhiking policeman. He had nine children, and his wife, who was also in the police force was pregnant again. They had recently borrowed money from the government to buy a farm in the northern part of the country and had hired a manager to run the farm for them.

"Do you want your children to become police officers when they are old enough?"

"Oh, no. Police jobs are much too dangerous."

"Will they have trouble getting jobs?"

"No. They will live and work on my farm."

Despite the border official's preference of Zambia to Chicago, we thought it imprudent to spend the night camping and, instead, registered at a hotel in Lusaka.

Mosi-O-Tunya, or "smoke that thunders," is the African name for Victoria Falls, one of the world's natural wonders. In a thundering roar, the mighty Zambezi River pours over the brink, plunging three hundred feet and creating clouds of spray high enough to obscure views of the falls and wide enough to water a lush rain forest. The next day, on the Zambian side of the falls, we walked through a cloud of water, and the heavy spray prevented us from seeing anything. We visited the wonderful Livingstone Museum which, in addition to its Dr. David Livingstone memorabilia and an exciting witchcraft exhibit, displayed African art and culture including exhibits of crafts, musical instruments, costumes, and tools.

We crossed to the Zimbabwe side of the river where the spray and mist were not nearly as dense. We donned our raincoats and followed paths and approaches which afforded excellent views of the spectacular falls. I tried to imagine Livingstone's astonishment when he first saw these incredible cataracts in 1855 which he described in his notes as: "scenes so lovely must have been gazed upon by angels in their flight." That evening we ate dinner on the patio of the venerable Victoria Falls Hotel and camped at a caravan park in the nice town of Victoria Falls.

Hwange National Park, Zimbabwe's largest game reserve, accommodates an amazing variety of animals, including elephants, giraffes, lions, rhinos, zebras, cheetahs, jackals, buffaloes, wildebeest, impalas, hippos, and leopards. We saw gorgeous sable antelope and kudus for the first time and many birds as well, including shaft-tailed whydahs, and long-tailed and white-tailed shrikes. At lunch, we met two young birding couples from Malawi. They were Peace Corps volunteers and lived in Blantyre next door to our hitchhiking friend, Mary.

The camping facilities at Caravan Park in Bulawayo may have been the best in Africa. A Brit named Charlie introduced himself while Lynette and I were setting up camp there. He was an artist and had been traveling among the Bushmen with a Botswanian teacher while sketching their way of life. Charlie had obviously been smitten by the beautiful simplicity of these peaceful people. He showed us an illustration he had made of two Bushmen having a conversation. The men, according to Charlie, had been smiling and very cordial during their clicking dialogue. Afterwards, he asked one of the men what they had been discussing and was told they had been trying to resolve a property dispute. Charlie stressed how kind and nice these people were and expressed great sorrow that they were rapidly losing their isolation and their way of life.

"It will all be gone in ten years," Charlie predicted. I told him how Fred Machetanz had preserved the life of the Unalakleet Eskimos on canvas and suggested he might consider doing the same for the Bushmen.

"You obviously care deeply about these people, Charlie. Why don't you go back to Botswana and capture their way of life in your art?" He smiled and nodded.

"I have been thinking of doing just that. I will go back."

"Maybe I'll go with you, Charlie."

"Perhaps you really should," added Lynette.

During the thirteenth to the fifteenth centuries, one of the world's remarkable building civilizations flourished in the area where today are found the Great Zimbabwe Ruins. This complex of stone buildings covered several square miles and once accommodated a population greater than 10,000. I was impressed that the construction of many of the walls and buildings was more than a little similar to that of the Incan structures at Machu Pichu and other Peruvian sites. Stones fitted together snugly without the benefit of mortar. The thickness of the walls decreased as they rose higher from the foundations—a building strategy that served the Incans well in enabling their buildings to withstand many earthquakes over the years. Some of the Zimbabwe walls reached a height of thirty feet.

As we drove into Masvingo, the town nearest the Great Zimbabwe Ruins, the camper's alternator light flashed on. We toured the ancient structures and bought small vases and other handicrafts at the curio shop located there. Then we set up camp at the ruins, where resident monkeys had become quite tame and a bit of a nuisance, and I installed a new regulator and cleaned the alternator.

Fifty miles north of the South African border, we camped at the Lion and Elephant Caravan Park. The sun sank through a clear sky in the west, and a balmy breeze graced the evening. On the porch of a small restaurant, we were joined for dinner by a self-described "Rhodesian" couple named Clo and Edge, white farmers who had emigrated from South Africa 26 years before. They had built their farm from scratch and fought to keep it in the Rhodesian War.

"Were you ever afraid, Clo, when all the shooting was going on?"

"No. It's just not in me. I lost my son during the war, but I was never afraid."

"Will you folks be here ten years from now, Edge?"

"I love Rhodesia. We are not treated well by the government. But, if it doesn't get worse, we'll stay. Look, we can't take money out of the country. Nor can we leave the farm to our children. If we left, we'd lose everything."

"There's too much of us here," added Clo.

"What about Mugabe?"

"He's the best of a bad lot." Edge explained, "The workers are not loyal.

Taxes are very high. They take 70% of what we make."

Clo shook her head. "We've worked twenty-six years for what we have. Our children are gone, and we're getting old. If we had young children, we'd leave and start over. Now the schools teach children that everything about our way was bad, and everything about the new way is good. Everything that is black is positive. Everything that is white is negative. The black side was good during the war. The white side was bad."

Edge seemed quite evenhanded and had a good handle on both sides of the argument, and Clo impressed me as a stalwart pioneer woman.

"So, what does it all mean? Where does all that has happened leave us?" I wanted to know.

"I've thought about it for years." Edge mused. "There are no answers. Only life."

The sun set elegantly, and, only a few yards from our table, through the twilight, a magnificent golden brown eland with spiraling horns ruminated in the meadow.

We crossed into South Africa without incident, and the rainy sky cleared. The car's engine began making a loud noise, and, when we stopped for gas in Potgietersrus, I tightened a loose belt and filled our engine with coolant, and the noise stopped. We dined on hamburgers, chips, and milk shakes at Wimpy's and continued south through the cotton fields of the Transvaal. Nearing Pretoria, Lynette predictably burst into song: "We Are March-ing To Pre-tor-i-a, Pre-tor-i-a, Pre-tor-i-a." Late in the day, we arrived in Johannesburg and drove to the Bey Valley municipal campground.

From my notes: *Jo-Burg seems to be doing fine economically. The world's against them, but so far they seem not to have figured that out.*

After threatening to do so throughout most of Africa, the camper's waterpump breathed its last. Niko, the campground attendant, had formerly worked as an auto mechanic and volunteered to help me replace the defective part with the pump we had bought in Nairobi. Unfortunately, the pump was in a very tight position, and we spent most of a full day trying to remove it without success. We jacked the vehicle off the ground to expand the space around the pump, but a pipe prevented us from removing it from its screw shafts. Niko and I gave up for the day, and Lynette and I walked to a nearby kiosk for tea. We talked with a Hungarian couple who had fled Budapest twenty years before, opting for what they thought was going to be a free life in South Africa. Now they were gravely concerned about the inevitable advent of black rule.

"What will we do," he lamented, "I'm fifty-five. I can't go back to Hungary. It will be the same thing all over again."

The next day, I called the VW dealer, who was unable to fix the car at the campground and, instead, towed it to his service garage. After the waterpump was replaced, I returned to the caravan park where Lynette had just finished our laundry. The manager of the park engaged us in conversation. I told him the campground appeared to be well run, and he asked me to write him a letter stating that. He was trying to extend his retirement date two years and thought such a letter might help his cause. I saw nothing wrong with helping him, and wrote the letter as he requested. I gave the man the letter and told him Niko was a very nice young man and a credit to the organization. He responded, "Yes, he's a Christian."

Niko was very fond of Louis L'Amour books. He and a friend practiced quick draws with their revolvers in a local stone quarry. Niko even talked like a Louis L'Amour character: "My wife is a good woman." That evening, Lynette and I picked up Niko and his wife and daughter, Kim and Bantara, at their flat to take them out for dinner. The apartment seemed quite nice, but the young couple said they wanted to move to the loveldt, the country. They thought the neighborhood was deteriorating and feared for Bantara's education. Niko looked at the evening sky and wondered.

"It looks like it could rain. Should we bring umbrellas?"

"You know what Louis L'Amour would say, don't you, Niko?"

"I'm afraid I don't. What would he say?"

"Well, it's like the two young cowboys who were going into town after a long cattle drive. One asked the other if they should bring their guns. The other responded that it was better to have them and not need them than to need them and not have them. See, Niko, I've read a few Louis L'Amour books myself."

Later that evening, after eating pizza and ice cream, I relayed to Niko my conversation with his boss. His reply betrayed a distinct lack of respect for the man, "If he thinks so much of being a Christian, why doesn't he act like one himself? He has a good wife, but he does not treat her like a Christian should."

The next day we toured downtown Jo-burg and attended to a number of business issues. The used car manager at the VW dealer offered us about 12,000 rand for our camper which, after taxes, would net us only $3000. As it turned out, after paying to ship the car back to the U.S. and then getting it back to Wyoming, we probably should have taken the deal. But the offer didn't sound like much, and I really wasn't ready to sell the old girl who was nearing 100,000 miles on her odometer and who had carried us from as far north as Prudhoe Bay to nearly as far south as Capetown. How could I be so fickle as to sell her? In fact, I was considering having the VW painted white, gray and black, like a stylized Arctic tern, a sea bird which twice yearly migrates from pole to pole, and also installing a new engine in it. Instead of selling the car, I arranged to ship it from Capetown to Baltimore. Then we booked tickets on one of South Africa's famous luxury trains from Capetown to Jo-burg where we would connect to home. Lynette had her hair cut, and then the same woman cut mine. We shopped for gifts, bought a couple bottles of wine, and returned to the campground where we shared our cheese with a long-haired calico cat.

From Johannesburg, we continued south through Bloemfontein to Port Elizabeth on the Indian Ocean. We stopped to camp in Mountain Zebra National Park where the only significant population of the rare Cape mountain zebra exists. From a population that had declined to twenty-five, the animals now numbered more than two hundred. The climate was marvelous in the highlands, and we saw many birds and other animals including elands, springboks, kudus, hartebeests and wildebeests. Lynette said she could understand why the whites didn't want to leave. "Europe would be so confining after all of this." Over a camp fire and a bottle of wine, we discussed the very difficult situation faced by the people of South Africa. Most of the white South Africans we met went out of their way to be friendly and to show us that they had, in many ways, been the victims of a press that was largely ignorant of their situation.

From my notes: *Lynette and I reviewed the arguments. Blacks want to vote and determine their own destiny. But where else in Africa can the people vote? After the blacks take over, will there be autocratic rule like the rest of the continent? Or will democracy prevail? I doubt it. Where else in Africa do blacks have better clothing, food, shelter, health care, and education? Does the poor black in Zaire feel better because he's being screwed by blacks rather than whites? The answers aren't as easy as American newspaper editorial writers portray them. On the other hand, blacks in South Africa don't exhibit the happiness and friendliness we saw throughout the rest of the continent. Even if South African blacks are better off economically than their brothers to the north, perhaps being ruled by blacks under any system is better than being ruled by whites. As Edge said, "There are no answers. Only life."*

Addo Elephant National Park was set aside in 1931 to protect the last of the Eastern Cape elephants. Nearly two hundred of the rare elephants thrived on the park's unique vegetation. I stopped the camper to take a picture of a bull and baby elephant only a few yards from the road. The young elephant threatened to charge us, and Lynette and I laughed and remarked to each other how cute the little guy was. Suddenly the bull elephant fanned his ears, waved his trunk above his head, and roared a terrible scream. Then, with only that gesture as a warning, he tucked in his ears and trunk and charged us. I gunned the engine, and the car slipped and slid, fishtailing up a hill as we sped away and barely outran the speedy giant. Despite all the mechanical problems we had experienced since Algeria, our little camper performed like a champion in the Addo bush.

Port Elizabeth boasts an attractive setting on the Indian Ocean as well as fine beaches and a number of tourist attractions such as an oceanarium, a snake park and a tropical bird house. We toured the city and then camped on the beach at nearby Cape Recife. After an early morning swim in the Indian Ocean, we were enjoying a second cup of coffee when a fisherman approached and struck up a conversation.

"Where are you from?"

"The United States. Feel like a cup of coffee?"

"Don't mind if I do. How do you like South Africa?"

"The country is exceedingly beautiful, and we're enjoying our tour. How's the fishing?"

"Not much biting. It's my day off, so I thought I'd try my luck. This is a good country, much better than the press leads you to believe. The U.S. should not have imposed sanctions on us. Not doing much good. Japan trades with us. No offense, but the U.S. is going the way of England."

"How's that?"

"Oh, it still is a great power. But Japan is taking over. At least economically. They'll trade with anyone who can pay their bill."

"So what's going to happen here?"

"Who knows? What we've done to the blacks is wrong. It must change. But it must happen in a way that protects our rights. We have nowhere to go. The whole world is against us, but that only makes us more resolute. If we have to fight a war, we will. Whatever happens, happens."

We continued west along South Africa's lovely, sparsely populated, and naturally endowed, coastal Garden Route. We swam and collected shells in St. Francis Bay and looked at birds in the lagoon formed by the Seekoei and Swart rivers. In mid-afternoon, we stopped in Tsitsikama Forest and Coastal National Park, setting up camp on the beach. Lynette did the laundry and sent me off to look for birds. I found Cape doves near the road; dusky flycatchers, black-headed orioles and Knysna woodpeckers in the forest; and Cape gannets plunging into the sea. I returned to the campsite in time to help Lynnie hang the clothes. A Brit who had lived in Zambia for seventeen years walked up to us and introduced himself. He described the situation in Zambia as awful, full of corruption, and said he was on his way back to England. He said he had been interviewed by a *New York Times* reporter who was very sympathetic to the black cause and had very little interest in hearing and trying to understand his perspective. "All he did was lecture me about how wicked we were."

Nature preserves outnumbered towns along the Garden Route. Near Plettenberg Bay, we looked at birds and marine life in Robbeberg and Keurboomstrand nature reserves. Near Knysna, we explored Knysna Lagoon, Knysna Forest, and Groenvlei and Goukamma nature reserves. In Oudtshoorn, we saw ostriches being raised on farms. The birds' feathers were used for dusters and their skins for handbags and shoes. Their flesh was popular in many restaurants and homes. Each of their eggs was equivalent to a dozen hen's eggs.

Portuguese explorer, Bartholemew Diaz, landed in Mossel Bay in 1488, as did Vasco da Gama in 1497. Today, the popular resort town standing there is lovely, the climate mild and pleasant, and the swimming exceptional. Lynette and I found Mossel Bay depressing, however. Prominent signs proclaimed openly, "Whites Only," on the beaches, rest rooms, and other public facilities; and at the campground entrance. With a bottle of wine, we sat on a rock outcropping on the beach watching surfers. Along with our rather black mood brought on by the blatant and unabashed racial segregation, a fog rolled in from the sea and enveloped the bay area. All night long, from a lighthouse perched on a cliff above the campground, a fog horn belched its loud warning each and every minute. The hour was late for us, and for South Africa, when we eventually fell asleep.

The owner of the campground in Cape Town smiled, shook my hand and declared, "If I had known you were coming, I would have run up the American flag." We registered at his pristine facility and then drove into the city. Cape Town is a beautiful, colorful, and historic city in an incomparable setting. Leisurely, we visited the city's highlights, including the daily flower and produce markets, the Houses of Parliament, a seventeenth century castle, Greenmarket Square, and various museums and galleries. Lynette led her walking tour of the city during which we watched the Changing of the Guard at the Castle of Good Hope, snacked on chips and vinegar at Hout Bay Harbour, and visited the South African National Gallery. We attended to a number of business matters including confirming our train reservations to Jo-burg and finalizing our car's shipping arrangements, and then toured Groot Constancia, South Africa's oldest winery. Lynette chose a restaurant at a lovely old hotel on Beach Street for dinner where we shared a newspaper, Capetown's Argus. The lead story read: "The Minister of Law and Order, Mr. Adriaan Vlok, said today a mini-limpet mine was used in the attack on a block of flats and offices in Spin Street, one hundred meters from the Houses of Parliament... Politicians of all parties have expressed their shock at the blast, the sixth in South Africa in the past nine days." While we read the paper, I overheard a man and woman at the next table discussing the considerable dangers of living in or visiting New York.

Gorgeous scenery, picturesque villages, pristine harbors and numerous wildlife sanctuaries greet the traveler on the Cape of Good Hope peninsula. Coastal mountains dropped precipitously to the sea in some areas, while, in other places, white sand beaches stretched inland for hundreds of yards. As we approached the southern tip of the peninsula where the Indian and Atlantic oceans converge, Lynette pointed out, "Now, Darwin, I can truly say that I have followed you to the ends of the Earth." Ubiquitous troops of baboons roamed the Cape of Good Hope Nature Reserve, and we spotted rare and endangered bonteboks and mountain zebras. Numerous species of birds frequented the Cape's various habitats. I found an orange-breasted sunbird, and Lynette spotted a malechite kingfisher. Cormorants, gannets, and gulls by the thousands soared along high cliffs. A marvelous campground secluded on a pristine beach became visible in the distance. Lynette announced it would be her choice for the night. Nearer the entrance, a sign grew legible, "Non-whites Only." We saw not a soul in the campground. That experience put a damper on an otherwise wonderful afternoon.

Gordon's Bay had a campground as delightful as was the village. Lynette had read somewhere a vague reference to a small colony of nesting jackass penguins in the area. Otherwise, the nesting location of the birds, which derived their name from their braying-like vocalizations, was a well kept secret which Lynette was determined to uncover. She saw a stuffed penguin in a shop window and naturally assumed the shopkeeper knew something about the penguins. Lynette interrogated her, explaining that we were serious bird watchers and that we understood the necessity for not disturbing the birds, and could she please tell us where we could observe these penguins from a distance?

"Of course, we would do nothing to disturb the penguins," Lynette repeated.

"Why, I do believe they're nesting down at Betty's Bay," the careful woman offered.

"Beaty's Bay?" I repeated. "Where's that?"

"No, Darwin," Lynette interpreted, "Betty's Bay!"

Well, of course I knew where Betty's Bay was. We drove there first thing the next morning. We searched the rocks along the shore of Betty's Bay for an hour. Then Lynette spotted a penguin. Soon we saw a few more and eventually counted as many as fourteen birds tending nests there—the first penguins we had ever seen in the wild! We watched them waddle somewhat clumsily across the rocks and then jump into the sea. Incredibly, they underwent an immediate transformation from their ungainly land behavior into their sleek swimming mode.

"Lynette, great going! You deserve the 'Bird of the Week' award," I exclaimed sincerely.

"Baloney! I deserve the 'Bird of the Year' award for finding that bird!"

"You've got it. What a shame to call them jackass penguins. They're beautiful animals and deserve something better."

"I nominate the name, 'wandering penguin,'" Lynette offered. "Any bird that can swim this far from its home in the Antarctic should have a name of distinction!"

Our next stop was Stellenbosch and the picturesque wine country where we, according to my notes, *sampled entirely too much wine. South*

Africans know how to make good wine. In fact, these people know how to do everything well down here, except, that is, come up with a fair solution to their number one social problem.

Capetown, South Africa, April 26, 1988

We drank a bottle of wine and then had dinner with Ron and Hilda, the proprietors of a caravan park located high on a hill overlooking Cape Town. We had done our laundry and packed our camper for shipping. The next day we would ride the luxury train to Johannesburg and then fly home. There was no thought in either of us to continue traveling in a camper. Africa had been very difficult for Lynette. She was only there because I wanted to do it. There were times during the past few months when I thought she would leave me, and, to this day, I'm not sure why she didn't do so. As for me, I now realized that I had some unfulfilled expectations in my business career. I had figured out that I had quit one level below where I believed I was well qualified to operate. It left me with a feeling of having left something undone. I had no doubt I would continue my continental drifting some day. Australia and Asia remained. But now it was time for both of us to go home. Ron wondered about our plans.

"Well, Darwin. Where will you go next?"

"Back home to Wyoming."

"No, I mean after that. You won't quit now. Drifting's in your blood. Where will you go next?"

"I don't know. I'll think about it later."

INTERREGNUM #2
Call It Pretty Much A Mistake

Occasionally we make emotional decisions to do things that, intellectually, we know are wrong. After returning from Africa, I hadn't been back in Jackson Hole very long when I received a call from a man who asked me to run his company, a collection of business newspapers located in major cities across the country. From the start, I knew I wasn't dealing with the kind of people who ran Cap Cities, but I liked the business, and I thought doing this would satisfy some of my unfulfilled career objectives. So I took the job. For two years, I was left pretty much left alone. The fortunes of the company improved greatly, and I enjoyed accomplishing what I had set out to do. Then a series of events took place during which my greatest fears became a reality. There was no doubt that my association with the company had been a mistake. After the third year, unable to continue with them, I walked away, proud I had not compromised my values. On the plus side, I had satisfied my remaining business aspirations, and I did take with me not an inconsiderable pile of dough.

Jackson Hole, Wyoming, April 1993

Mike Wile now lived near Seattle with his wife, Lori, and their infant son, Zach. Lynette and I were free again and had decided to drive a camper around Australia, and I was in the middle of researching the project and making plans. Lynette and I were reading in bed one evening, and the telephone rang. It was Mikey.

"Dad, what's the latest on your Australia plans?"

"I'm in the middle of all that now reading books and magazines and trying to decide what we want to see and what route to take. The animal and plant life are like nowhere else on Earth, and I want to see it all."

"When are you planning on leaving?"

"Well, their spring, our fall, seems like the best time to be there. That timing is great for birds and wild flowers, and it's well beyond the wet season, making the Outback much more accessible. I'm thinking we'll probably leave here in August or September."

"This year or next?"

"This year."

"Oh, that's too bad."

"Why is that?"

"I thought if you did it next year, we might come along."

"How would you do that? What about your jobs?"

"Lori and I think we could both arrange for leaves of absence. If not, we would just quit our jobs. The problem is, Zach is too young now. By next August, he would be two and probably old enough to make the trip."

"Mike, if you guys are interested in going along, we'll go whenever you want. Talk it over and let us know. I can't think of anything better than having you go with us!"

　　After we hung up, I looked over at Lynette and smiled.

　　"What was that all about?"

　　"They want to go along. Next year though."

　　"What about their jobs?"

　　"He said they would just leave. One way or another."

　　"Isn't that just a little irresponsible?"

　　"You're kidding? After what we've done over the years?"

　　"Yes, I must admit he's come by it honestly."

Chapter Six
Drifting With Grandchildren: Australia

Oh! there once was a swagman camped in a Billabong,
Under the shade of a Coolabah tree;
And he sang as he looked at his old billy boiling,
"Who'll come a-waltzing Matilda with me?"
From: *Waltzing Matilda*, by Banjo Paterson

Mike on the Great Barrier Reef

PREPARATIONS

Mike and Lori succeeded in arranging four month leaves of absence from both their employers. We would tour Australia with two campers in tandem. Because their leaves were finite, we decided to rent two campers in Australia. Buying and then selling campers might take more time than Mike and Lori could afford. Renting campers also meant this would be the first, and only, time our continental drifting took place in a vehicle other than a VW camper. VW units simply were not available to rent in Australia.

For the next year after Mike's unexpected phone call, we all studied various books on independent travel in Australia. Lonely Planet's publications had become more thorough since our African odyssey, and the Australian Tourist Commission published a very helpful planning guide called *Destination Australia*. A large selection of field guides for Australian birds and flowers was also available. We read books about Australia including titles like *The Fatal Shore, A Town Like Alice,* and even *The Thornbirds.* All the while we compared notes on the phone, and our excitement mounted.

Krissie had married a young man from Jackson a couple of years before. They lived next door to us with baby Abigail in a barn that we had converted into a little house. They agreed to take care of our house; our dog, Kiska; and our horses. They would also pay our bills.

A few days before we left, some friends held a Bon Voyage party for Lynette and me. We sat on their deck under the magnificent Tetons and next to the pristine Snake River and drank gimlets. Our host had recently become a birdwatcher. Rufous, broad-tailed, and calliope hummingbirds squabbled over whose turn it was to visit his feeders. My pal, Phil, sat beside me and wondered if we were prepared to leave all this beauty surrounding us. I laughed. He wondered about primitive conditions in the Outback.

"You know me, Phillie, I'd rather be in a camper than in the Ritz-Carlton."

"Can you say the same for Lynette?"

"No, but she's really going to like Australia. I promised her I would be very sensitive on this trip."

"You already broke that promise."

"How's that?"

"If you were sensitive, you wouldn't be taking her to Australia in a camper."

Los Angeles, California, August 2, 1994

Mike and his family flew from Seattle to L.A. where they laid over for a few hours before flying directly to Sydney. Lynette and I flew to L.A. from Jackson Hole and, unable to make a same day connection on our airline, had to spend the night there. On their layover, we renewed our relationship with little Zach, our first grandchild, and finalized our plans to meet them the following day in Sydney. We watched them board, and Lynette turned to me, wiping a tear of happiness from her eye. "Isn't it understandable why grandparents become so excited?"

The next morning we watched boys fishing on the Santa Monica Pier and then drove north along the coast. At Malibu, I showed Lynette the beach where years before I had been watching a group of shorebirds foraging and saw an unusual looking specimen that turned out to be a bartailed godwit, a Eurasian bird rarely seen in the lower forty-eight. Later, we ate lunch at the Los Angeles Museum of Art. That evening, we boarded our plane for the long overnight flight to Sydney.

After two years of planning, the magical day had finally arrived (a day late because we crossed the International Date Line) and we descended into Sydney. We were thrilled to fly over the Harbor and the Opera House and then to see Mike, Lori and Zach waiting at the gate with smiles. Having gone through the drill the previous day themselves, they efficiently took us to Koala Camper Rental where "Jim" very methodically explained the interminable rules, regulations, and operations of the camper. Next, we set out for the campground where our companions had stayed the night before. The city's traffic was awful, and driving on the left didn't simplify things. After making a left turn, I forgot to stay left and slid over to the right, while Mikey made the turn properly. We became separated and didn't see each other again until we arrived at the campground, a lovely forested spot on a hill overlooking the city. We registered and set up camp. Then we took a walk around the campground, and Mike and Zach introduced us to some of Australia's colorful bird life—kookaburras, lorikeets, galahs, rosellas, and currawongs. Lori served dinner on a table between the campers, and I was as happy as any man could ever be.

We rose early the next morning and took a train into the city—Zach's first train ride. After crossing the enormous Sydney Harbour Bridge and visiting the Opera House, we bought tickets on the city bus tour which enabled us to get off and on busses at will, to stop wherever we wanted for as long as we wished. Sydney's people were cheerful and friendly, the temperature was pleasant, and, under clear blue skies, sailboats in the Harbor ran before the wind behind colorful spinnakers. In the marvelous botanical gardens, sacred ibises picked at insects in the grass, and we sat on large exposed roots under a gigantic eucalyptus tree and ate our lunch which we had bought at a kiosk. Lynette led us on a walking tour of The Rocks, an area settled when the "first fleet" of convicts and immigrants arrived. We drank a beer in a tavern were sailors where "recruited" and then visited the moored replica of the H.M.S. Bounty and the statue of its famous captain, William Bligh, who was governor of New South Wales early in the nineteenth century. At a market, Lynette suggested, "Why don't you pick something out for dinner?"

"OK Look at those beautiful Brussels sprouts."

"No. They smell too much to cook in a camper."

We both continued looking at displays of vegetables.

"Well, aren't you going to pick something out?"

"I did. Brussels sprouts."

"OK If you must."

The Sydney Zoo boasted a terrific selection of Australian marsupials and birds. Lori snapped photos of Zach playing with young koalas. At the spiny anteater display, Mike gave us a lesson on echidnas—egg-laying, burrowing, nocturnal mammals which rely on a long sticky tongue to capture ants and termites. Remarkably pleasant cool and sunny weather accompanied our days in Sydney. Once we ate a lunch of peanut butter and jelly sandwiches at a park on the Harbor, and Zach laughed heartily while Mike pushed him on a swing. Another day, Mike and I left the others to visit a state park where we saw sulphur-crested cockatoos and blue fairy-wrens. We stopped at a tavern where the cordial proprietor offered us samples of a variety of Aussie beers and then returned to the campground where, for dinner, Lynette had prepared a marvelous soup with fresh vegetables.

Australia is a land of fascinating flora and fauna, but it is also a land of remarkable scenery. In the Blue Mountains west of Sydney, our road snaked below a spectacular sandstone escarpment and wound through canyons with rushing creeks that cascaded over precipitous cliffs and formed silvery ribbons of misty waterfalls. Vistas stretched for miles over eucalyptus forests lying under the soft blue haze that gave the mountains their name and that was created by gaseous emissions from the sea of trees. We lunched at the Majestic Hotel, an opulent, early twentieth-century building that was used as a hospital for soldiers during World War II. The dining room offered a marvelous view of the valley and the Three Sisters beyond, so named when an Aborigine medicine man turned his daughters into three stone peaks to protect them from evil.

After buying a bag of apples at a farmer's roadside stand, we followed the Hawkesbury River and, later, set up camp at Cattai State Recreation Area. As far as we knew, we were the only people in the park. New birds greeted us everywhere we looked—ibises, shrikes, swallows, moorhens, and spoonbills. At the park playground, Zach played on a slide and a spring-loaded teeter-totter. Dusk approached, and the others returned to the campsite to prepare supper. I walked to a nearby pond to see if any different birds had flown in. A spotted dove cooed from a pile of branches and other vegetative debris. I scanned the field behind the debris with my binoculars and came across three kangaroos, two adults and one youngster, leisurely hopping down the hill toward our campsite. I quietly worked my way around them to the campers to tell the others. As darkness gathered, the five of us watched as the animals approached the campsite where they seemed to be enjoying the freshly mown grass, and where closer inspection revealed a Joey in its mother's pouch. A pair of kookaburras laughed from a gum tree. Zach was fascinated by the scene, and Lynette remarked how special this was seeing "roos" in the wild for the first time.

Early in the morning, frost covered the ground and a dozen wild gray kangaroos hopped and foraged around and between our campers. The shades were also raised on Zach's camper, and we could see the three of them pointing and laughing at our visitors. Later, two foxes crossed the road as we left Cattai. Our route followed a clear river that ran under sandstone cliffs. We forded the river on a small ferry and drove through picturesque mountain villages. In Cessnock, Mike and I were buying fresh bread at a bakery when I saw a jar full of large cookies. I pointed to the jar.

"Are they ginger cookies?" I asked the pretty young woman behind the counter.

"No, I'm afraid not. They're ..." and she called them a word which was unfamiliar to me and which I can't remember.

"Do you have any ginger cookies?"

"No, I don't, but try these instead. I think you'll like them." She dropped a half dozen in a sack, smiled, and handed them to me. I tried to pay for them, but she wouldn't have any of that. I'm ashamed that the thought occurred to me that they might be a bit stale. They weren't. They were fresh and contained a lot of butter and coconut—delicious! We walked across the street toward our parked campers. Mike looked at me and winked.

"I think she liked you."

In the Hunter Valley, we toured the wine country and visited a Lindemann's winery, sampled their good wine, and bought a bottle to accompany the bread and cheese which we ate for lunch in their lovely garden. A flock of red-rumped parrots had the same idea about a picnic spot and roosted in the red gum trees surrounding the area.

The climate changed dramatically as we followed the Hunter River from the cool dry mountains to the moist coast. A gravel road led us through Myall Lakes National Park, past sand dunes that separated waterfowl-filled fresh water lakes from the sea, and through banksia woodlands in which we spotted whistlers and Jacky Winters. We entered the coastal rain forest and found a campground in Forster where, according to my notes, *Rain poured on us all night, as hard as I have ever seen or heard it. Washing dishes in the campground kitchen, I managed to drop three glasses and watch them shatter into thousands of pieces on the tile floor.*

Australia, we were discovering, was a throwback to simpler times. Lynette compared life in the Aussie countryside to rural America in the fifties. Motels were small and offered none of the resorty frills commonly found in those along interstate highways in the U.S., and here the major highways contained only two lanes. Often ferries were the only way across rivers. People swam on the beach or in rivers and ponds rather than in concrete pools. Summer homes were small cabins or shacks rather than opulent second homes. And drive-in theaters were ubiquitous. All in all, Lynette and I agreed it had a very nice feeling.

Our road followed the coast north, through Port Macquarie, an early nineteenth-century convict settlement, and the heathlands of Hat Head National Park where we identified several species of honeyeaters. Miles and miles of banana and sugar cane plantations lined the highway. Of course, most of them had replaced valuable rain forest habitat. Near the Coff's Harbor campground, we took Zach to see the Big Banana, a much larger than life symbol of the area's banana belt economy. This example of

Australian kitsch would be repeated often in other towns, and we often saw giant replicas of items of local importance.

In turn, our road followed clean rivers, impressive sandstone cliffs, and lovely white sand beaches. Along the ocean, surfers rode large rollers to the beaches. At Cape Byron, we stood under a lighthouse looking for humpback whales, and I met a surfer my age who said he's "still learning after 35 years of surfing." Near our campground at Hastings Point, we walked along a cliff high above the ocean. Gannets plunged head first into the water and disappeared under the surf. More often than not, they emerged on the surface with a meal. Mike set up his spotting scope and, far in the distance, found long-winged shearwaters fluttering high and then gliding low over the water. For supper, I fried potatoes and onions and scrambled eggs.

From my notes: *Delicious, but I was the only one of us not looking for Tums afterwards. Later, Zach slept on a bench while the four of us played pool. Compared to Africa, this seems fairly plush, staying in campgrounds with showers almost every night.*

From New South Wales, we crossed to Queensland and followed the Brisbane River into the capital city of the same name. We toured the city, visiting the university, Victoria and Albert parks, and, on the river, the market and the botanical gardens. Then we continued north along Queensland's touristy Gold Coast, and Lynette said the area reminded her of "Atlantic City, Myrtle Beach and Fort Lauderdale rolled into one." Lori agreed and said she thought it was time we got away from the cities. Further north, the coast became rugged and scenic. We stopped in Noosa National Park where we hiked to Dolphin Point and Mike carried Zach in a backpack. Then we camped in nearby Noosa Heads. Meanwhile, Zach learned new words every day. I asked Lori what her favorite part of the trip was so far. She responded, "...having kangaroos share our campground and seeing Zach learn the word 'platypus'."

Lori's dad, Howard, was a golfer, so we made a necessary stop in the town of Howard to buy him a souvenir shirt from the Howard Golf Club. A bit further on, we drove through the town of Gin Gin near which we set up camp on Monauran Lake where we saw white-bellied sea eagles. On our evening wildlife drive, we spotted two species of kangaroos. Once, four roos were lined up beside the road and frozen in our headlights. I stopped our camper, and they hopped across the road and then toward us and stopped within five feet of our car to peer inside to see what was up. Zach exclaimed, "Kangaroo, Mommy!"

On the road to Rockhampton, near Miriam Vale, Lori spotted a new kingfisher species and Mike found our first emus—a father with some chicks. Emus are ratites, a group of flightless birds which also includes ostrich and cassowary. Among ratites it is typical for males to care for the offspring. In Rockhampton, we attended International Day at the University of Central Queensland, and sampled ethnic food from many of the booths. Our first taste of kangaroo! Mike and I played catch with a baseball on the school's rugby field, and we all ate dinner at a small bistro. We were settling into a routine that we all found very pleasing—free camping in the bush and, every second or third day, finding a commercial campground where we could shower, do our laundry, and shop for groceries. What a life!

Kangaroos were becoming a frequent sighting; and colorful and interesting new birds greeted us daily. South of Mackay, we stopped for lunch and then walked on a beach where we found sunbirds—brightly colored nectar-eating birds with long, slender down-curved bills, and rainbow bee-eaters which flashed gold, green, blue, black and yellow colors during their acrobatic flight. Later, at a campground near Mackay, while I was doing the dishes, two opossums climbed from the canopy of a nearby tree to its lower branches. They had apparently come to oversee my work. I was being careful not to scald myself with the extremely hot water, when a woman next to me smiled.

"Can't complain about the hot water, can you?"

"Only that it's too hot."

"That it is."

"What kind of opossums are those fellows supervising our dishwashing?"

"Why, they're bushy-tailed opossums. My name is Aileen Duthie, and the gentleman walking over here to check on me is my husband, Al."

The Duthies were from Adelaide where they owned a small vineyard. Unlike many Aussies we had talked with, the Duthies had traveled over much of the continent and now were on holiday, visiting Queensland. Soon Lynette came by, checking on me, and, before we knew it, we were all having a beer or two. Late in the evening we said good-bye, but not before the Duthies invited us to call them when we reached Adelaide.

The next morning, Lori and Lynette went shopping while Mike and I went birding while pushing Zach in front of us in a stroller. We saw a striated heron and a forest kingfisher and then noticed that Zach had fallen asleep. Mike picked the little guy up carefully and carried him back to his camper.

"Mike, you don't have to carry him. Couldn't we just push him back slowly in the stroller? I don't think he'll wake up."

"I don't want him to get a stiff neck, Dad."

While Zach napped, Mike and I struck up a conversation with an Aussie from Brisbane who had been assigned to an American Airborne unit in Viet Nam. He was with a friend who was actually his daughter's father-in-law, a Brit who now lived near Melbourne. They handed us each a beer.

"We never wanted for a beer, I'll say that for you Yanks," allowed the Aussie.

"What kind of beer did they supply?" I wondered.

"Budweiser. You don't call that beer, now do ya?" He laughed.

"I can't disagree with you."

"Sometimes they gave us Hamms. Now that was O.K., especially cause we only had to pay ten cents a can." He looked at his friend who had been mostly silent until now.

"Hey, Mate! You want another beer now?"

The Englishman wrinkled his brow, hesitated a moment, and responded, "I really suppose I ought to, eh?"

One of Australia's most popular birding destinations is the Townsville Town Common Environmental Park, a marvelous location for water birds. Mike and I found yellow-billed spoonbills, brown falcons, white-bellied cuckoo-shrikes, varied trillers, rose robins, kori bustards, sarus cranes, and a number of other species we had never seen before at the Townsville Commons. North of Townsville, the vegetation became increasingly luxuriant as we drove higher, winding our way into the mountainous rain forest. We stopped for lunch at a tea house in Paluma where, in the garden and on a walk through the rain forest, we saw many more birds for the first time— little eagles, brush-turkeys, red-kneed dotterels, grey-headed robins, little shrike-thrushes, chowchillas, Macleay's honeyeater, spotted catbirds, and Victoria's riflebirds.

We continued north through the rain forest to Mission Beach where we hoped to find a southern cassowary, a much rarer and more colorful ratite than its cousin, the emu. We drove to a forest recommended in one of our bird-finding guides and had no luck seeing the bird. The woman who owned our campground suggested we might find a cassowary just before dusk by taking a trail she knew that led up a mountain into the rain forest. We followed her advice, and Mike and I took turns carrying Zach up the mountain on our shoulders. We saw cassowary signs, but never the bird. The late afternoon got away from us, and it began to get dark, even darker in the dense forest. Several times we were unsure of which path to take back to the parking area. I was confident we would find our way back, but Lori and Mike were becoming a bit worried. My chief concern was Mike's footing as we descended the damp trail down the mountain with Zach on his shoulders. Lynette told them not to worry.

"Believe me, your dad has a guardian angel watching over him."

I had never heard her say anything like that before and wanted to ask her what she meant by that, but I didn't get around to it. Mike slipped once but fortunately regained his balance without falling. Another time Zach was whacked in the face with a branch but, bravely, did not cry. We arrived safely back at the camper, and I could sense everybody's relief when I promised we wouldn't enter any more rain forests late in the afternoon.

Lynette's birding skills are considerable, but her interest in the pasttime is usually marginal. Sometimes, however, if a bird is sufficiently special, she focuses on the quest and, so many times, while I have searched in vain, she has found the bird. The southern cassowary was big, colorful, and relatively rare. We all wanted to see the bird, even Lynette. We explored several rain forest trails near Mission Beach leading through ideal cassowary habitat, and, when we weren't busy removing leaches from our bodies, found several new species of birds including shining flycatchers. After several hours, I had all but given up on finding a cassowary. Mike, Lori, Zach and I were talking with another couple on the trail who seemed knowledgeable about birds. I asked them how to distinguish between two confusing species—yellow-spotted and graceful honeyeaters. As the woman was explaining that they could be separated only by voice and that both species were in this forest, I heard, "Darwin!" I turned around, and, twenty yards further along the trail, a cassowary was standing only a few feet from Lynette. We all trained our binoculars on the giant bird and had a good look. Lynette had done it again. Later, during our high-fiving and celebrating, she suggested, "Just call me 'Cassowary Kate'."

Thirty years ago, world record black marlin were being caught near Cabo Blanco, Peru. Now the big black marlins were being caught in the waters off Australia. Mike wanted a fishing trip along the Great Barrier Reef as a present for his thirtieth birthday which was the next day. Lynette and I agreed to spend the day ashore with Zach while his parents tried their luck fishing for black marlin. We drove into sleepy, tropical Cairns and arranged a day fishing trip for Mike's birthday and, for all of us, a reef diving trip the following day. Colonial Cairns sits on the Coral Sea coast below the Daintree mountains and the Atherton Tableland with the Great Barrier Reef lying only a few miles offshore. We shopped for groceries and a cake for Mikey, and made reservations for his birthday dinner at the seafood restaurant of his choice. On our way to the campground, Mike spotted two bush thick-knees and pointed them out to us.

Cairns, Queensland, Australia, August 19, 1994

Happy Birthday, Mikey!

While his parents were fishing, Zach and his grandparents walked to the Pier Marketplace where they bought his father an Aussie flag and a t-shirt with a picture of a black marlin leaping from the water. Unfortunately, it would be the only marlin he would end up snagging that day. Zach said he was hungry for a hamburger, so the three of us had lunch at a diner. The mini-skirted waitress asked Zach his name, and, after he told her, she played "Hit the Road, Jack!" on the juke box. She and several other employees came to our booth and sang along with the record, changing "Jack!" to "Zach!" each time the title phrase was repeated. Zach enjoyed the attention immensely, and, after finishing lunch, the three of us walked out of the diner singing "Hit the Road, Zach!"

Cairn's Esplanade offers a pleasant walk along the sea as well as excellent shorebird watching. Zach, Lynette and I strolled down the Esplanade with our binoculars hanging from our necks, stopping every few steps to scan the sandpipers foraging on the beach. A wiry, tanned old fellow sat on a stool looking at the birds through a spotting scope. He wore baggy shorts and a muscle shirt and had sun lotion smeared on his face. I smiled and pointed toward his scope.

"Seeing anything different?"

"No. Just the usual. I come down every day just to see what's coming through." He leaned down to Zach's level and chuckled at his plastic binoculars.

"What birds are you seeing?"

"Curlews and knots." The old birder's grin disappeared. Now, a bit perplexed, he turned to me, wrinkled his brow, and returned his gaze to Zach.

"What else are you seeing?"

"Godwits."

Now the man was dumbfounded, because those three species indeed dominated the vast numbers of birds on the beach. His mouth hanging open and his arms stretched to each side, palms up, he now looked toward me beseechingly.

"How old is the boy?"

"He's almost two. But he's had some help."

The sea was rough the next day, and, fully medicated, I stood far forward on the boat's bow, hoping the salt spray would keep my mind off the ship's malevolent yawing, pitching, and rolling. Not a minute too soon, we arrived at the piers that floated above the reef and from which we would make our dives. We spent much of the day in the water, swimming in pairs and marveling at the coral that came in many varieties—fans, mushrooms, staghorns—and colors—yellows, pinks, reds, chestnut with blue tips. Everywhere we looked, something new turned up. Nowhere in the world had I ever seen such a extraordinary display of coral. The reef's fish life was equally impressive, as were the giant clams, the enormous valves of which we assiduously avoided stepping or reaching into. That evening, back at our campground, we all agreed the Reef had to be considered one of the wonders of the natural world.

An old diesel train snaked its way from the coastal lowlands up to the old mountain town of Kuranda. People from miles around attended the town's Sunday market, and Lori and Lynette wanted to see what all the excitement was about. Zach was fascinated by the spectacular ride as the train labored its way into the rain forest, around horseshoe bends, over high bridges that spanned deep chasms, past scenic waterfalls, and through fifteen tunnels. At Kuranda, Lynette, Lori and Zach inspected every stall in the market while Mike and I slipped away to look for birds. The shoppers bought carvings and other crafts while Mike and I added a Pacific baza and a red-headed honeyeater to our life-lists.

We drove north on the Cape York Peninsula to the fishing village of Port Douglas. The countryside became increasingly primitive just as the climate became increasingly hot and humid. At Mossman Gorge, a trail led through the rain forest to a magnificent waterfall. Further north, we camped near the town of Daintree, next to the Daintree Rain Forest National Park. Late in the afternoon, we walked around the village of Daintree where we engaged a guide to take us up the Daintree River on a boat and then took a wildlife drive on which we saw feral pigs and stunningly beautiful emerald ground doves. That evening I wrote several letters and cards to friends, including one to my brother-in-law in which I agreed with his choice of Willie Wagtail, a ubiquitous and friendly black and white bird with a pretty song, as my Australian favorite.

From my notes: *The architecture in Australia is largely unremarkable and uninspired. The most interesting and attractive buildings are the trop-ical one-story, often on stilts, with a tin roof and a wrap-a-round porch, and the stone farm house.*

The small boat crept upstream on the nearly currentless Daintree River. Enormous strangler fig trees and bamboo lined the banks, and the thick jungle appeared impenetrable except where mangrove swamps allowed light to penetrate the forest canopy. An orange-footed scrubfowl scampered along the forest floor to its ten-foot high nest mound of dead leaves and vegetative debris in which the female lays her eggs. The male tends the eggs, inserting his beak into the mound to test the temperature, then uncovering the eggs when they are too warm and adding leaves when they are too cold. Irridescent kingfishers chattered along the banks, and the incredibly beautiful wompoo fruit-dove, with its purple breast, gold vent, green back and wings, and white head, roosted in the trees. Crocodiles slithered down the banks, inches away from our boat. The guide told us these carnivores were almost wiped out by the locals in the early eighties after a drunken woman decided to go skinny dipping late one night and never returned. Now they were protected and were regaining their former numbers. A green tree snake waited on a tree limb stretching over the river, and archer fish swam along the side of the boat. A beautiful white-bellied sea eagle perched fifteen feet above us and seemed unconcerned by our presence. We saw a number of other birds, including herons, storks, green pygmy-geese, gerygones, and nutmeg mannikins. Driving back to the campsite, we excitedly reviewed what we had seen on the trip. Mike could-n't contain his enthusiasm.

"I have to tell you guys... Next to the Barrier Reef, the Daintree River is my favorite part of the trip so far!"

"Me too, Daddy," agreed Zachary.

Atherton Tablelands, Queensland, Australia, August 23, 1994
Happy Birthday, Zach!
The Atherton Tablelands is another favorite area of birdwatchers. We found a campground there with good services, did our laundry, and I bathed Zach on his birthday. Later, Lori, Mike, and I did the dinner dishes. When we returned to the camper, Lynette was teaching Zach to blow out candles. When we celebrated the little guy's birthday, he successfully blew out both candles on his cake, and had little trouble opening his presents.

On an early morning walk through the rain forest, we followed a winding creek, and, while we didn't find a platypus, we did see wallabies, turtles, kangaroo rats, iguana-like water dragons, and a female sunbird building her nest which hung precariously from a single vine. After removing leaches from each other, we explored the Tablelands, visiting Tinaroo Falls, several enormous strangler fig trees and Mt. Hypipamee, a volcanic crater. Mike and I added many new bird species to our Australian list, including shining bronze-cuckoo, tropical scrubwren, and red-browed firetail. That evening, we set up camp at Malanda Falls where platypuses were reputed to inhabit a small creek, opened a bottle of cabernet, and discussed the trip. I asked Lynette, "What's your favorite bird so far?"

"Probably the emerald ground dove."

"Not the cassowary?"

"I loved seeing the cassowary, but ratites aren't really birds, are they? They can't even fly."

"You have a point."

"What I really want to see is a platypus. It's hard to imagine an egg-laying animal with a bill like a duck, webbed feet, and mammary glands."

Lynette shook me awake just before daybreak, the best time to see platypuses. She and I sneaked along the dark stream, and, before long, she spotted one of the sleek animals diving and surfacing in a backwater pool. She grabbed my arm and pointed excitedly, and we watched the marvelous creature going about its business for several minutes before returning to the campsite to awaken Mike and Lori. Lynette and I stayed with still sleeping Zach while they hurried to the creek and looked unsuccessfully for the animal. In the kids' camper, Lynette rested with her head on my chest, my arm around her shoulder.

"I'm so happy. I really wanted to see a platypus. Now I'm ready to head west."

From a letter to my parents: ... *We hiked the trails in the Atherton Tablelands. Lynette was determined to see a platypus and found one for us in a river running through the rain forest. We've seen an abundance of wildlife including kangaroos, wallabies, emus, a cassowary, and dingoes.*

Mike and I have identified close to 250 birds so far.

The Gulf Development Road left the eastern rain forest and led west across the Cape York Peninsula through towns which were not much of anything but which had big-sounding names—Mt. Surprise, Georgetown, and Paramount. Where the road was gravel, the washboard surface rattled our teeth. Where the surface was blacktop, there was only one lane or track. In the face of oncoming traffic, one drove with the left wheels on the gravel shoulder and the right wheels on the bitumen, or "bitch-you-min," as pronounced by the Aussies. Lynette, emulating Shelly from TV's Northern Exposure, called them "bitchin' roads." The good news, there was little oncoming traffic.

Now we were in the Outback where termites spent lifetimes building red, brown or gray mounds six feet high. Dry grass and a few gum trees were the only vegetation in sight. On one stretch of the drive, long black fingers of volcanic lava spread across the otherwise flat and dry terrain. Mirages shimmered in the distance. Despite the apparently barren nature of the countryside, wildlife thrived. Only a few yards from the road, a male emu foraged for seeds and insects, and his cute, striped chicks followed closely behind. Near Mt. Surprise, a half dozen black kites deferred to a wedge-tailed eagle feeding on a kangaroo carcass, probably a casualty of nocturnal traffic. In Georgetown, a flock of red-tailed black-cockatoos roosted in one of the town's few trees. And in Croyden, hundreds of galahs, pink and gray birds of the cockatoo genus, screamed their shrill "chi-chi-chi' from their perches in gum trees, on telephone wires and poles, and from anywhere else they could gain purchase.

After setting up camp in Croyden's small park, we repaired to the bar on the square and ordered beers all around and a glass of milk for Zach. The locals were having a gay time, some of them playing pool and others watching a rugby match on TV. Before long, we were invited into some of their conversations. When the boys at the bar learned Big Mikey had played rugby in school, they tried to recruit him for the local team. We felt right at home. I asked the woman tending bar for a refill. She put her hands on her hips, smiled and shook her head.

"I love you Yanks! I'm pourin' this one on the house."

I proffered a return of affection, "Well, we love you Aussies too!" And we all drank to one another. "By the way, what's with all the galahs outside? They've taken over the town!"

She looked at me puzzled. "Doesn't everybody have this many galahs?"

Our happy family of five sang *Waltzing Matilda* walking back to the campers. The moon had not yet risen, and the town's lights were few. Venus and Jupiter shone brightly in the dark sky, and Alpha and Beta Centauri pointed to the Southern Cross. Mikey and I ran into a shop and bought flowers for the girls who insisted we were *très galants.*

From my notes: *This is the Australia I've been waiting for. The locals look at you like—"What're ya doin' here, Mate?" Lynette likened their tough life in the Outback to life in the small frontier towns of Alaska—a good analogy.*

In the desert, any source of water attracts wildlife. Dawn arrived accompanied by a symphony of birdsong. I rubbed my eyes, raised one of the camper's shades and saw that, during the night, the park's water sprinklers had deposited several pools around the campsite. Birds bathed and drank in the fresh water and sang from perches in the trees, among them, five new species—diamond dove, white-winged triller, rufous-throated honeyeater, zebra finch, and apostlebird.

In Normanton, we stopped at the Purple Pub which, at that moment, other than us, was patronized only by Aborigines. From Normanton, the Matilda Highway ran north through the remote gulf savannah, the vast area which, in the wet season or "the wet," is drained by rivers like the Norman, Gilbert and Carron. At Maggieville, we turned west toward the Gulf of Carpentaria. The gulf's prawn-fishing fleet is based in Karumba, a small town at the mouth of the Norman River. The day was pleasant, sunny and mild, when we stopped for gas.

"What a beautiful day," I told the attendant. "Is it always this nice here?"

"Nice here?" she laughed. "You should be here in the summer! If you like 50 in the shade, it's nice."

Like most people in the world, Aussies think of temperature in degrees Celsius rather than Fahrenheit. I did an approximate mental conversion—F=9/5 C+32—and realized she was talking in excess of 120 degrees!

We arrived at the campground on Karumba Point where the owner invited us to attend a fish fry he and his wife were hosting that evening.

"It's pot luck, Mate. Bring whatever you want."

Lynette and Lori threw a major salad together while Zach, Mike, and I gave the campers a long overdue washing. Later, we joined about a dozen friendly Aussies at picnic tables while Donald fried fish on a grill. After dinner, pratincoles and marsh sandpipers foraged in the meadow, and avocets and dotterels poked along the shore. The sun took a long time to set while I stood with my binoculars, looking west over the gulf, thinking this was a perfect place to see the green flash. Donald walked to my side and pointed to my binoculars.

"Now, what are you lookin' for, Mate?"

"The green flash."

"The green flash? What's that, Mate?"

"You know. When the sun sets over the ocean, at the last second before it drops below the horizon, there's a green flash. You've seen it here, haven't you?"

"Haven't seen it. Never even heard of it. Is it a joke?"

I was beginning to wonder about that myself. I had been looking for the green flash for years. Atmospheric conditions must be perfect, apparently, for the phenomenon to occur. I had watched for the green flash all over the world, including half a dozen times in Key West where many of my friends say they have seen it, but always in vain. Perhaps it was a joke, a conspiracy of my friends. Donald and I concentrated on the horizon as the sun disappeared, neither of us seeing the green flash. It wasn't until several years afterward that my patience was rewarded. On a cliff high above the Oregon coast, Lynette and I sat on a bench in front of our cabin, drinking a glass of wine. The sun set under a bank of low clouds, and, rather than a quick flash, a warm, green glow spread over the horizon just as *el sol* disappeared. I have seen it once again since then.

The long road from Karumba south to Mt. Isa was almost all single track. At one stretch, we drove more than a hundred miles without seeing a house, a telephone pole or any other human structure. Lynette doubted that could be done anywhere in the "Lower 48" and suggested that much of Australia is what may be the world's only remaining large, unpopulated wilderness in a temperate climate. Along the way, we passed several "road trains"—trucks fifty yards long with enormous cabs and four or five trailers. They were big, scary and beautiful in a futuristic sort of way. In an American diner, you might hear a waitress talking about the big guy who just pulled up in an "18 wheeler." Road trains, if you can believe it, were "62 wheelers!" When we saw one coming, we stopped and pulled our campers as far off the single track onto the shoulder as possible. Even then, the van shook and the dishes rattled as the eddies of rushing air filled the vacuum behind the speeding monster.

Copper mining drives Mt. Isa's economy, and the town's giant mining complex appears to be its leading tourist attraction. Having spent enough time in mines over the years, I voted to forego visiting the copper mine and found no one dissenting from that view. Instead we checked out the birds on and near Lake Moondarra where we saw, among others, plumed whistling ducks and red-winged parrots. Then, while Mike and I registered at the Mt. Isa campground, Lori and Lynette looked through their list of community activities. Every Australian town of any size has a bowls club where members dress in white and roll wooden balls on manicured courts. The Mt. Isa campground offered guest passes to the local bowls club, so we gave it a try. The dinner was good, and the members were very accommodating. Only a few people were bowling, however, many more of them preferring to watch Australia dominating the Commonwealth Games on TV.

Like the Sahara, the Outback is vast. It changes from dry, flat grassy plains that fall away with the curvature of the earth to barren stretches of red rock and soil with little vegetation. Almost always, it's treeless as far as the eye can see. Sometimes we drove fifty miles without seeing another vehicle. When vehicles do pass in the Outback, the two drivers usually acknowledge one another by lifting their index finger from the steering wheel. It's a custom similarly practiced in Wyoming; I guess it's a cowboy thing. Wildlife is abundant, especially kangaroos. Ranches, or stations, encompass hundreds of thousands of acres or more, and, occasionally, cowboys on horseback may be seen going about their business. Every hundred miles or so, a roadhouse appears—Three Ways Roadhouse, Frewena Roadhouse, Barry Caves Roadhouse. The roadhouse is the social center for an enormous area surrounding it, where cowboys or truck drivers stop any time of day or night for a beer, doctors from the Royal Flying Doctor Service make their rounds, or friends meet for dinner. The roadhouse offers gasoline, motel rooms, television, camping facilities, and radio contact with the outside world. We stopped for the night at Barkly's Homestead Roadhouse where we drank a few beers and played a couple of games of pool. Again, the locals wanted to recruit big Mike for their rugby team. From my notes: *The night sky is so clear, so many stars. I truly feel at home.*

The Stuart Highway runs from Darwin to Adelaide, cutting through Australia's remote center via Alice Springs. We followed the Barkly Highway west to its intersection with the Stuart at Three Ways, then cut south through Tennant Creek, where we found gas and groceries, to Devil's Marbles Scenic Reserve. In this fascinating area large granite boulders, many of them round like marbles, lay strewn over the landscape and were sometimes perched precariously on even larger boulders. Just beyond the reserve parking area, beautiful spinifex pigeons with rich, reddish-brown bodies and red, white and gray faces held their long, thin crests erect while they foraged in the clumpy, sharp tipped grass from which they derived their names. A black-breasted buzzard soared high above our car, an Australian hobby hovered over a granite outcropping, and weebills tittered in the nearby mallee shrub. Only one other human was anywhere within sight, a lean, grizzled old Aussie squatting on his hunkers on the other side of the parking area. I walked over to him, a can of cold Coke in each hand. His clothes were well worn, and he seemed oblivious to the desert fly crawling from the juncture of his lips, up his cheek and over the bridge of his nose, to his eye brow. He could have been Banjo Paterson's swagman, for all of me.

"How about a cold drink, Mate?"

"Don't mind if I do."

· "You live here?"

"Nope, just passin' through." His means of passage was not apparent.

"How about these marbles? Wouldn't you like to see the Devil shootin' a game with these babies?"

He laughed. "The Aborigines have a better name for the marbles. They call them Eggs of the Rainbow Serpent."

I thought about it for a moment, and was inclined to agree with him. We chatted for a few more minutes.

"Thank you for the Coke, Mate. I'll see you." He walked away, and disappeared behind the rock formations. We didn't see him again.

We drove about a dozen miles further south and camped at the Wycliffe Wells Road House. After taking a shower the next morning, I walked over to a sink to shave. A man shaving at the next sink pointed at my right foot.

"Say, Mate, you've got a spider on your ankle."

"So I do." I leaned down and flicked the arachnid from my ankle to the floor. The man and I took a closer look.

"Is it venomous?" I didn't know anything about Australian spiders.

"I believe it is. Do you see that red area on its back?"

"I do."

"It's a red-backed spider. They're very poisonous."

"I suppose I'd better step on it."

"I would."

I returned from taking a shower and saw five birds flying toward our camper. At the last moment, four of them veered away, but one of them flew into the van's open window. Mike and I approached the car slowly and found a white-plumed honeyeater trapped between the front window and the dashboard. We weren't sure how to approach the bird without frightening it, and, then, Mike had an idea. He broke a twig from a tree, slowly reached through the side window, and held it near the bird's feet. The honeyeater climbed onto the twig, Mike brought the twig and the perched bird back through the open window, and the bird flew away safely.

"By the way, Mike, do you know what a red-backed spider is?"

"Sure I do."

"I had one on my ankle when I came out of the shower."

"You're kidding. Those things are deadly!"

The first European structure in Alice Springs was the Old Telegraph Station built in 1872. For years, Alice was a desert shanty town that serviced the mining and cattle industries. Now it has all the modern conveniences of any other Australian town plus the advantage of its remarkable setting. We looked down on Alice from Anzac Hill and then walked around the town's shopping district and admired a variety of Aboriginal art and crafts. Lynette and Lori bought several pieces of pottery, and Mike and I tried very hard to get an audible response when we blew into a didgeridoo. In the evening, we drove to the restored Old Telegraph Station three miles outside of Alice. It was in the town's lovely original site on the Todd River. Red kangaroos scampered among the red rocks and hundreds of pink galahs perched in the ghost gums on the banks of the dry river. We walked a trail and saw several new birds, including red-capped and hooded robins and white-backed swallows.

After receiving our permits to drive west into the Aboriginal Lands, we spent the next few days hiking and birding at various stops along the Glen Helen Gorge Road. At Simpson's Gap National Park, we saw rock wallabies hopping on the rocky slopes above the trail. Zach pointed and laughed when two of them paired off and began boxing. Further west, on a trail along the deep, narrow Standley Chasm, Mike found tiny dusky grasswrens. Later, we hiked at Ellery Creek Big Hole Nature Park with its enormous red gums and native figs and found yellow-rumped thornbills. We hiked into Serpentine Gorge and then into spectacular Ormiston Gorge where white gum trees contrasted against the orange rock background. At the campground in Ormiston Gorge, we found exquisite pink cockatoos and western bowerbirds, the latter a species in which the males exhibit the remarkable behavior of constructing bowers of grasses and twigs interspersed with colorful, eye-catching items like ribbons to attract females. These males proudly displayed their pink nape crests, as they engaged in their elaborate courtship rituals.

At Glen Helen Gorge, we set up camp and then walked to the Mt. Sonder Safari Lodge for a beer or two. The lodge's patio offered a splendid view overlooking a marshy valley with dramatic red cliffs rising in the background. Lori and Lynette thought it quite surprising to see a marsh in the middle of the dessert. Like any water source in the desert, the marsh attracted an abundance of wildlife, and various mammals and birds visited the marsh while the five of us talked about many things. Mike and I heard a new song and walked to the marsh's edge where we saw a male clamorous reed-warbler, clinging to the tip of a cattail and singing its heart out.

We spent all of one day driving through very remote Aboriginal territory on rough, gravel roads.

From my notes: *The astonishing beauty of white bark gums contrasting against the reddish brown dry river bottoms. One must see it to understand. Wallace Stegner said you have to like brown to like the American west. In Australia, you must have progressed far beyond the enjoyment of suburban green to appreciate the stunning beauty of a dry river bottom.* At an Aborigine settlement, we bought enough gas to take us to King's Canyon where we camped. That evening, two dingoes, one of them jet black, slowly and gingerly approached the campground. Several campers coaxed them closer and fed them. From my notes: *Why do they do it? If one of the dingoes bites a kid, they'll kill the animal. Why don't they have signs that prohibit feeding of the animals? Probably still wouldn't do any good. There are signs in Yellowstone, but people still feed the coyotes and other animals. Why do people want to feed wild animals? Why do they want to make them tame? Is it a need of humans to control their environment?*

Mike carried Zach in a backpack during our early morning hike through King's Canyon. We had almost finished the hike and were walking down a hill only a few hundred yards from the parking area when Mike slipped on scree and strained the ligaments in his right knee. Zach was fine, and I carried him the rest of the way while Mike limped back in considerable pain. Lori drove while Mike propped his leg up, and we continued all the way to Ayers Rock in Uluru National Park. We arrived at the Ulara Tourist Resort in time to register at the campground, shop for groceries, and then drive to the Ayers Rock to enjoy tall frosties and cheese while watching the marvelous purplish-red monolith change colors as the sun set. It was supposed to be one of the nature's greatest shows. It wasn't to be this night, however, since, as the afternoon waned, the cloud cover increased and obscured the sunset. From my notes: *We'll try again tomorrow night.*

That evening we enjoyed an outdoor concert of traditional Australian music performed by Indigeny, a group with an outstanding didgeridoo player. Afterwards, Mike and Lori took a sleepy Zach to the camper while Lynette and I sat on a bench eating an ice cream cone. A couple from Norway struck up a conversation with us. After a bit the woman engaged in a long monologue, contrasting life in Norway to the U.S. and boasting about the superiority of their social services, including long maternity and paternity leaves, free health care and university education, etc. When I was sure she had finished, I asked her what the marginal tax rate was in Norway.

"Yes," she frowned. "There you have the bad news."

The weather pattern the next day was identical—clear all day until the late afternoon when clouds moved in and obscured the setting sun's supposedly spectacular illumination of Ayer's Rock. In the morning, Mike's leg was feeling almost a hundred percent, so we walked around the base of the Rock, a distance of six or seven miles. Little crows called from their roosts on white-wash covered ledges, and variegated fairy-wrens with blue heads and tails and black throats and white breasts sang their pretty trills from the brush. The many wonderful perspectives provided along the way confirmed our assessment that the Rock deserves a place among the other natural wonders of the world. The Aborigines consider Ayers Rock, or, Uluru, as it is known to them, to be sacred, and we complied with their wishes that the Rock not be climbed even though we could see a number of people doing so.

That afternoon we drove to The Olgas, known as Katajuta or "many heads" to the Aborigines. These large, purple-hued, dome-shaped peaks separated by narrow ravines lie about twenty miles west of Ayers Rock and are included in Uluru National Park. Mt. Olga, the largest of the domes, reaches to nearly 1,800 feet. We hiked a trail and, in addition to wallabies, saw crested bellbirds and white-browed babblers and then visited the Aboriginal Cultural Center where Lynette and Lori bought hand carved lizards, and Zach, Mike, and I saw mulga parrots in the garden.

The clouds remained well into the morning, and the temperature was unseasonably cool. The odds of having a clear western sky at sunset seemed low, so we gave up on seeing Ayers Rock in its perfect glory and began the drive back to Alice Springs. Pink cockatoos are especially handsome birds with a pink head, breast, and underwings and white back and upper wings. The males have an elegant, long white crest which, when extended, is magnificently accented with bright yellow and red stripes. One of these birds was foraging on the left roadside, and, as we drove near, he took off to the right and flew in front of our car. I slammed my brakes too late and saw the bird hit the passenger side of the windshield. After coming to a stop, I could see the bird lying on the road with its splendid crest fanned.

From my notes: *Mike and I walk back to the bird. I feel awful. We see him shake and quiver, then remain still. As we approach him, he suddenly flips over onto his other side. He sees us, struggles to his feet, gallantly lifts off the road and laboriously flies to a nearby tree. Thankfully, his wings are OK. He hangs his head for a moment, as if in prayer, then raises it and proudly fans his crest. I think he'll be fine. Later, I hit a Willie wagtail. He didn't fare as well as the cockatoo. Not a good day for the birds.*

Back at the Alice Springs campground, we boys washed the cars, and the girls did the laundry. Later, spiny-cheeked honeyeaters scolded us from the trees as Mike grilled steaks and I fried potatoes and onions at the campground's outdoor kitchen. An Aussie handled a similar assignment, grilling sausages and eggs for his wife and three young children. They had just sold their business, one that installed alarm systems in schools, and were taking a year off to see the country. We all ate together on picnic tables, and, at dusk, took a drive to the Old Telegraph Station to see the red kangaroos. The three women compared notes on life in Australia and America while the two young fathers slowly walked with their excited and enthusiastic children among the grazing roos. I sat on a rock by myself and, with damp eyes, remembered times in the early seventies when Lynette and I walked hand in hand with Krissie and Mike—all of us so excited and enthusiastic, during our drifting through South America and Europe.

From Alice, we re-entered the Tropic of Capricorn and retraced the route to Tennant Creek, then camped a few miles north at the Three Ways Roadhouse. After dinner, we drank a few beers with a Danish couple whose path we had crossed twice before on the trip. The temperature was balmy, and the sky mostly cloudy as, in unsurpassed beauty, the sun slowly dropped in the west, painting the puffy woolpacks varying hues of pink, red, and purple. Happily, the glorious sunset seemed to go on forever. At dusk, three road trains loaded with cattle pulled into the roadhouse parking area.

All night we could hear the animals lowing and the trucks groaning under their shifting weight, and I was glad to be a vegetarian.

The temperature and humidity increased noticeably the further north we drove. By the time we arrived in Katherine, Lynette was pretty uncomfortable. "If this keeps up, tomorrow we're registering at the air conditioned Darwin Hilton!"

From a letter to my parents: *The bush flies were awful, making it impossible to eat outside. They attack you unmercifully, trying to get moisture from your eyes, mouth, and nose.*

The Katherine Gorge National Park visitor center contained instructive natural history displays as well as interesting descriptions of the local Aboriginal culture. The rangers, on the other hand, were of little help, unable to answer our questions and to provide us with trail maps. Nevertheless, we ventured forth, Mike and I taking turns carrying Zach on our shoulders, and we hiked a trail overlooking the spectacular canyon carved by the Katherine River. Crimson finches chattered "che-che-che" from the pandanus lining the river while white-gaped honeyeaters whistled "whit-o-weee" from freshwater mangroves. Across the chasm, a brown goshawk raced along the brightly colored sandstone cliff that climbed straight up from the water's edge.

In the campground near the park, brown quails foraged for seeds and kangaroos grazed on the lawn, and, when Zach tried to approach a Joey, it ran to its mother and climbed into her pouch. That night, during dinner, Mike sported a big smile as Lori told us she was expecting our next grandchild. They hadn't yet chosen names, so, since the child technically began its life in Australia, we tossed around a few Aussie names like Alice, Kimberly, Sydney, Adelaide and, of course, Katherine. Then, in case it was a boy, we added Ian, Rod, Shark, Hobart, Sydney (again), and, of course, Darwin. As it turned out, seven months later, our little Aussie arrived and was named Alexandra Katherine.

Further north, as we approached Darwin, the terrain became tropical and the temperature soared, as did the height of the termite mounds along the road with their Gothic-looking spires rising ten feet or more from the ground. Just north of the small city of 70,000 people, we registered at a seaside campground. While the girls prepared dinner, the boys walked on the beach and spotted pied herons, common sandpipers and greenshanks. At dinner, I told the others a story about my best friend in grade school, Gary Sheeler, and me. In geography class, we studied about Gary, Indiana, and Darwin, Australia, and, each of us took an unprecedented academic interest in the city whose name we shared. In an ongoing argument over which city played a more important role in its country, Gary and I recited and compared statistics supporting each city's economic, cultural and strategic value.

"Did anyone ever win the argument?" Mike asked.

"In a sense, yes. This argument was taking place only five or six years after the war, and Gary was a major steel producing center in those days. I don't remember admitting it to Gary, but I think I always had the feeling that he had the better argument."

"Why am I not surprised at that?" Lynette wanted to know. "You know you're wrong, but you still make the argument. Some things never change."

"OK. Maybe he was right. But look at it now. If we revisited the debate today, I think Gary would be hard pressed to win his case."

"Yeh. That's irrelevant. I think you owe Gary Sheeler a letter of concession."

Darwin proved to be a very interesting city. The architecture was tropical, and the town, in many ways, looked like a set for a movie from the forties. The Museum of Arts and Sciences featured a Gallery of Aboriginal Man which included wonderful displays of Aboriginal art and culture. We visited the late nineteenth-century Hotel Darwin where I bought enough T-shirts to last a lifetime and Government House, Darwin's oldest building. The Botanical Gardens featured tropical plants and a rain forest, and East Point Reserve featured wallabies. We ate finger food at a market on the beach and, in the downtown Mall at Smith Street, drank beer at a great pub where we learned that Darwin boasted, far and away, the highest per capita beer consumption in the country.

While I lived on Earth, I had very special people around me.
There were always animals, birds and water creatures in abundance.
I felt that the sun and the moon and the stars were mine.
While I lived on Earth, I had everything I ever needed.
From: *The Dreamtime,* by Jean A. Ellis

Kakadu National Park is among the best in the world. Almost the entire South Alligator River drainage system lies within the park and includes nearly all the habitat types of Australia's Top End—coastal lowlands with their monsoon rain forests and estuarial mangroves, open eucalyptus woodlands, tropical wetlands and waterways, grasslands, freshwater mangroves, paperbark swamps, and billabongs (water holes). The high sandstone wall of the Arnhem Land Escarpment extends across Aboriginal Arnhem Land, dividing the Arnhem Land Plateau from the rest of the park below. A treasure chest of wildlife is supported in the park's extensive ecosystem. Species lists tally 25 amphibians, 130 reptiles (including fresh and saltwater crocodiles, monitors, pythons and frilled lizards), 60 freshwater fish (including archer fish, sharks and sawfish), 72 mammals (including echidnas, flying foxes and wallaroos), and 270 birds. Much of Kakadu belongs to the Aboriginal people who are spiritually linked with their traditional homeland. Aboriginal rock art peppers the escarpment and preserves cultural history, some of it tracing as far back as 20,000 years.

The Arnhem Highway stretches east from Darwin to Kakadu. We stopped at the Fogg Dam Conservation Reserve where we spotted jacanas and crakes and then stopped again where the highway crossed the South Alligator River and saw mud-skippers, fish capable of surviving on the muddy river banks. From atop the escarpment, wonderful views unfolded over Arnhem Land, including some of the dramatic scenery shot for the Crocodile Dundee film. At Ubirr, we walked a trail leading past rock over-hangs that sheltered ancient Aboriginal camps and protected the inhabitants' artwork. Some of the oldest paintings depicted a Tasmanian tiger, fish, turtles and other flood plain animals. Other animal paintings, "X-ray paintings," were fascinating in that they included the internal structure of the animals. Still other paintings represented parables—two sisters who were turned into crocodiles, and a man who rolled a boulder in front of his cave after his fish were stolen. Many Aborigines retain the beliefs their ancestors held thousands of years ago that their life substance is no different from that of other animals, plants and even inanimate objects. You are at one with Mother Earth, and, if you do not take care of Mother Earth, she will not take care of you. It occurred to us that these primitive people had a far better understanding of our place in the world than did much of contemporary society.

From my notes: *Aboriginal women teach their children not by telling them what to do or not to do, but by telling them stories from the Dreamtime, stories about their revered ancestors and spirits and how they lived their lives in a good way.*

A campground near the village of Jabiru served as our center from which to explore Kakadu. We toured archeological sites at Anbangbang Shelter which the Aboriginal people have been using for twenty thousand years. A trail led us past the rock art at Nourlangie Rock which included X-ray paintings of various animals and of Narmagon (Lightning Man) and his wife, Barginj, as well as other spiritual representations. We visited towering waterfalls below which partridge pigeons drank from pools, white-lined hon-eyeaters flitted among the trees, and a black-tailed treecreeper pecked in the bark furrows of a tree trunk. With our binoculars, we scoped billabongs containing thousands of magpie geese and jabirus and ubiquitous croco-diles. Dingoes, emus and wild horses (brumbies) roamed the plains. Termite mounds rose to twelve feet and weighed as much as six tons. Lynette was fascinated by the scenery and wildlife. Her assessment: "Kakadu is not unlike the Serengeti. The vistas are vast, the natural world still rules, and human civilization is incidental."

The Kakadu Highway led us southwest to the Pine Creek Road House where we stopped for gas. In the bathroom, a snake lay coiled in a corner. I found the proprietor and told him I wasn't familiar with Australian snakes and had no idea whether it was venomous. He said they were all venomous, grabbed a long handled rake, and promptly killed the reptile.

We followed the Great Northern Highway south to Katherine where we camped on the Katherine River. Lynette and I took a walk and saw thousands of flying foxes, large fruit-eating bats, hanging by their feet, upside down, in the trees lining the river. That evening, I was sitting outside the camper, writing my notes, when I sensed a large presence behind me. I turned around and saw, staring at me from only five feet away, two brolgas—gray cranes with red cheek patches. The 4½-foot tall birds apparently had become tame and begged food from campers.

From Katherine, the Victoria Highway led west through landscape dominated by urn shaped boab trees. We stopped for lunch at the Victoria River crossing where we saw freshwater crocs sunning on the mudflats, but the flies were so aggressive we ate in the campers. The road continued west to Kununurra following an escarpment that afforded stunning views along the way. Giant Gothic inspired termite mounds gave way to giant mushroom shaped termite mounds. Traffic was sparse.

From my notes: *A sixty-two wheeler running at sixty to seventy miles per hour on a single lane road can be frightening. How long does it take to stop one of those things? The driver pulled half off the road onto the gravel but didn't slow down.* Near Kununurra, we camped in the red sandstone hills of Hidden Valley National Park and found banded and bar-breasted honeyeaters and sandstone shrike-thrushes, all local specialties.

We entered the state of Kimberly and followed the Great Northern Highway west and south to Halls Creek. Zach rode with us and asked Lynette to "play Baldy" which, she soon determined, meant he wanted to hear our Vivaldi tape.

"A budding musician?" she wondered.

At Geikie Gorge National Park, we set up camp and arranged for a ranger boat trip on the Fitzroy River where it cuts through a scenic canyon's multicolored cliffs. While waiting for the boat, we saw a flock of cockatiels flying across the river and black-eared cuckoos and northern fantails in the woods near the dock. Just before the boat left, Zach began pointing at his back and screaming rather violently, "Hurt back! Hurt back!" The nearby town of Fitzroy Crossing was on the Royal Flying Doctor Service route. When we arrived at the small hospital, however, the flying doctor was not scheduled to be there for two days. Fortunately, a very capable nurse was on duty and examined the little fellow, and she could find nothing wrong. By now, Zach apparently felt much better. He had stopped crying and wanted to go back to the gorge to take the boat ride, which we did. As the ranger explained that the cliffs had been formed of coral reefs millions of years ago, Zach was unconcerned with both his back and the cliffs. His attention was riveted on the many freshwater crocodiles lining the shore, and on the sawfish and stingrays jumping in the river.

Broome was established as a pearling center in the late nineteenth century. Today the small town is the highlight of the Kimberly. After suffering the intense heat and ubiquitous flies of the north country, Broome's cooler daytime temperatures, balmy evening breezes, and lovely sand beaches were a welcome relief. Many of the town's early residents were pearlers from Malasia, Japan, and the Philipines, and their descendants have added a pleasant Asian air to the charming downtown's tropical and colonial atmosphere.

We showered at the campground and then walked across the street to a beach hotel where we sat on a wonderful, cool patio drinking Mai Tais and watching the sun set over the Indian Ocean. A bikini clad beauty led a string of camels down the beach, leaving us all, including Zach, fascinated, possibly for different reasons.

"You can have my vote to stay in Broome for a few days," I offered.

"Zach and I are with you," Lori agreed.

"Like a bird resisting a long migration, the urge has to get a lot stronger before I'm leaving," Mike added.

"I'm thinking about moving here permanently," Lynette concluded.

Early the next morning, Lynnie and I took a beach power walk through a proverbial pea soup fog. When we returned to the camper, water, fresh not salt, dripped from our hair and clothes. The fog lifted as we walked downtown where, in several jewelry shops, specialists educated us on pearls and then tried unsuccessfully to sell us necklaces and bracelets costing a fortune. Mike and I couldn't resist the local tattoo shop. I had decided to commemorate my encounter with the red-backed spider by tattooing its likeness on my right ankle. Later, Lynette was curious.

"How much does a tattoo cost?"

"A lot less than a pearl necklace."

"Are you suggesting I have a pearl necklace tattooed on my throat?"

"Now, that I would like to see."

Near the town, Gantheaume Point juts into the ocean. At low tide, dinosaur footprints are visible on the point. We waited for the tide to ebb and then walked onto the point to see the tracks. The ancient giant left an indelible impression not only in those seaside rocks, but also in Zach who, from that moment, acquired an intense interest in Jurassic period wildlife which he sustains today. Later in the afternoon, we returned to the campground, changed clothes, and went to the beach for a swim. Little Zach was thrilled by his introduction to waves, and Mike and I enjoyed some serious body surfing. That evening, Lynnie and I watched Zach while his parents went out on a date, and, after low tide, the three of us found marvelous shells on a deserted beach.

Lynette and I were in the middle of another early morning power walk when two buxom women walked out of the sea, remarkable in their nudity. "Helloooo," one smiled and waved.

"Have a nice swim?" I responded, trying, under the circumstances, to seem as nonchalant as possible.

"Lovely!" the other woman exclaimed.

"The sea snakes don't bother you?" Lynette and I had seen several five and six feet long, venomous sea snakes thrashing about in the surf only moments before, causing us to wonder about the wisdom of our having gone swimming the previous day.

"Oh, no. They're not dangerous this time of year."

I meant to verify her confidence in the snakes' seasonal innocuousness but never got around to it.

Up to a million shorebirds are concentrated on the beaches between Broome and Port Hedland, making the area one of the best ornithological spots in the world. Roebuck Bay, just south of Broome, annually supports shorebird concentrations numbering as many as 100,000 individuals. The Broome Bird Observatory at Fall Point provides birdwatching access to these hordes of avian waders. Tail-wagging Jacky Winters called, "jacky-jacky-winter-winter-winter," and black-chinned honeyeaters, with their striking gold, black and white coloring, greeted Mike and me at the observatory's parking area. We followed a trail to the water where countless shorebirds foraged, picking at the mudflats in a sewing machine-like staccato, and set up our spotting scopes. For those birders, like Mike and me, who have a passion for watching shorebirds, Roebuck Bay was the *pièce de résistance*. The numbers and variety of birds were simply staggering, and Mike and I found a number of species we had never seen before, including Mongolian and red-capped plovers, grey-tailed tattlers, and collared kingfishers.

Lynette and I, on our own that evening, found a marvelous restaurant on an otherwise deserted, beautiful white sandy beach. The place had a tropical, oriental feel to it, with corrugated metal siding and lattice trim and, in the garden, ancient Chinese war figures on horses. We sat under red and green Emu Export patio umbrellas, palm fronds quivering in the balmy breeze. The sun subsided into the sea, and a fiery orange sky followed it into the deep blue water. Nine camels, their riders in silhouette, walked along the beach, backlit by what photographers call the "sweet light." Lynette ordered snapper and pronounced it the best fish she had ever eaten. Later, a new moon followed Jupiter and Venus across the night sky, and we had the empty beach to ourselves.

On a remote stretch between Broome and Port Hedland, a large bird standing beside the road appeared to be injured. After stopping, Mike and I walked within two feet of the eighteen inch long bush thick-knee, a normally nocturnal bird. We inspected the dazed bird as well as possible and found it bleeding from a surface wound on the right side of its face, but, otherwise, seemingly all right. We decided the thick-knee had survived a glancing encounter with a vehicle and would probably recover.

Like beauty, most subjective analyses are in the eye of the beholder. Everyone sees things differently. Lori and Lynette sometimes became aggravated with Mike and me for spending too much time birding, especially since our being gone meant they always had a two-year old in tow and couldn't spend their free time doing anything but babysitting. From Mike's and my perspective, on the other hand, we were annoyed that the girls were trying to curtail what we boys already considered to be an inadequate amount of birding time. After all, Australia offered some of the world's most unique birding opportunities, and we didn't want to miss any of it. Mike and I had intended to take Zach along on our bird walks, but it proved impossible to hold the binoculars steady with a squirming two-year-old strapped to your back. (As I reviewed this section on Australia, I admit I was hard pressed to defend Mike's and my position. This recounting of our trip does seem a bit birdy.)

We drove south and west from Port Hedland, and the vegetation became greener and the wildflowers more profuse. Emus were numerous, and an occasional Kori bustard grazed in the meadows. In the west, enormous sheep stations had replaced the cattle stations of the northeast. The four to five-foot tall termite mounds took on a shape that was similar to the shepherds' huts. Many of them were covered with "whitewash," indicating that raptors used the mounds that were taller than the surrounding vegetation as lookouts to search for prey.

At Bullara, we drove north on the sparsely settled North West Cape Peninsula toward Exmouth and Cape Range National Park, and the weather turned pleasantly cooler. Lesser crested terns lined up on the beach where we had Exmouth's municipal campground almost to ourselves. White-winged fairy-wrens trilled from the saltbush as Mike and I washed and cleaned the campers. Then we walked around the town where Lynette beat me in a game of miniature golf. Later we drove out to the local golf club which was easy to find since it was marked by a gigantic white golf ball with big dimples teed up next to the clubhouse. The course was like none we had ever seen—red gravel fairways and greens of oiled sand. A sign declared greens fees to be three dollars.

A United States Navy communications station sat strategically at the tip of North West Cape, a carpet of purple wildflowers surrounding its tall communications towers. Whale sharks may be seen off the cape, but, we were disappointed to learn, not until March when the coral spawns occurred. However, we knew the coral reefs off Cape Range National Park were spectacular and brought our lunch and snorkeling gear along, planning to spend the day seeing what we could find in the underwater paradise.

The park's lovely white sand beach was exclusively ours, and we changed to our swim suits and donned our fins and masks. We snorkeled in pairs, taking turns on the reef while one pair splashed and played with Zach near the shore. The coral was almost as impressive as that of the Great Barrier Reef, and the fish, if anything, were even more interesting. Even Lynnie, who has a great respect for the unknown, relaxed and enjoyed the experience. That is, she did up until that sea snake showed up. We were peacefully exploring the reef when suddenly she wrapped her arms around my neck and pulled herself astride my back, choking me in the process and causing me to inhale two or three mouthfuls of saltwater. As I struggled for air, I could hear her shouting largely unintelligible screams. Once I did hear the word "snake" and then saw the cause of the crisis—a six-foot sea snake like the ones we saw in Broome was frantically snaking across the surface only a few yards away. It headed out to sea, as frightened, I'm sure, by our thrashing about as Lynette was of it. We swam and rode the surf back toward shore, and, as soon as we could stand, she made sure I understood. "That's enough! I'm finished!" And we were.

After the sea snake encounter, we stowed our gear and took a walk. The beach soon petered out near a rocky point which abruptly emerged from the sea. We searched the tidal pools on the outcropping and found anemones, starfish, and crabs, and, in the larger ones, giant clams. Off shore, sea turtles frolicked in the peak of their mating frenzy. On the drive back to the campground, we saw many kangaroos grazing, and, just before dark, a large goanna or monitor lizard warming itself on the road.

Like many places in Australia that have no access to fresh water, the campground at Coral Beach used a bore well. These wells are tapped by drilling a half mile or more into the earth to extract water that emerges at about 150 degrees, saturated with minerals. "Bore water" is satisfactory for washing and other purposes but must be desalinated for drinking. I personally preferred bathing in the ocean to using bore water. Lynette and I played a game of miniature golf that evening in which I evened our series, and then we took bore water showers.

"This water from Hell makes my skin itch," Lynette complained.

"Maybe the Aussies aren't marketing it right. They use essentially the same product in Baden-Baden and charge people a premium for the privilege."

From my notes: *Mike makes marvelous onion soup and great omelette for supper. The bush flies are really getting to me. They are the singular bad thing about this country.*

Further south, banana and other tropical fruit plantations drove the local economy. We walked Carnarvon's beach early in the morning and thought we could just as easily have been in one of Florida's beach towns in the fifties. We stopped for gas at the Overlander Roadhouse and drove north on the narrow Peron Peninsula with wonderful seacapes unfolding to the east and the west. We stopped for a walk on Shell Beach where Pacific gulls glided overhead, and a pied honeyeater sang, "tee-tittee-tee-tee" from a shrub. The beach was composed of a layer of compressed shells eight to ten meters thick, and, later, we saw, in the attractive little town of Denham, buildings with walls constructed of blocks that had been cut from the compressed shell formation.

Shark Bay surrounds Cape Peron and is a naturalist's paradise and a World Heritage Area. Manatee-like dugongs, moray eels, green sea turtles and bottlenosed dolphins all breed in the bay. Each day, a pod of dolphins swims into the shallow waters off the small, lovely settlement of Monkey Mia where rangers hand feed them small fish. Cormorants, pelicans, and gulls follow the dolphins, hoping for a free handout as well. Rangers willingly assist visitors standing in the shallow water, showing them how to hold the fish so the dolphin is able to swim up and take it. Lynette, Lori, and Zach each took a turn feeding a dolphin while Mike and I snapped pictures. One large female dolphin was easily identifiable with her white scars, remnants of severe sunburn she incurred when temporarily stranded on a sandbar. We camped on Monkey Mia's beach, and, after supper, took an evening walk on a path leading through the low vegetation growing in the sand. Laughing turtle doves and common bronzewings foraged for seeds along the path, and a thick-billed grasswren squeaked from the cane grass. All the while, welcome swallows flitted and darted just above our heads, devouring the insects we disturbed along the way.

Near Denham, the Nanga sheep station welcomes visitors and maintains a small campground as well as a small pub. The flies became very aggressive in the heat of the late afternoon, so we repaired to the pub to escape the annoying critters and ordered Swan Lager all around. We joined the few patrons watching a semi-final game of the exciting Australian rules football championship in which the West Coast Eagles were playing one of the Melbourne teams. Before long, Mike and I became Eagles fans, like everyone else at the Nanga sheep station, and were not disappointed as they blew away the Melbourne team. That evening, a cool wind blew away the flies. The full moon rose late, so we were treated to a fabulous, star-filled sky.

Stromatolites are reef-building microorganisms and with few exceptions are found only as fossils. We drove south along the coast to Hamelin Pool and explored one of the few areas where living rocks are still being formed by communities of stromatolites. Then we continued south to Kalbarri National Park where spring was in full bloom, and wonderful wildflowers covered the meadows—orange and yellow banksias, blue hibiscus, white grevillea, pussytails, pink milkmaids, and white, red and yellow featherflowers. A shingle back lizard crossed the road just before we pulled into a parking area. Southern scrub-robins whistled from the mallee along the trail that led us to a cliff edge looking down into the winding gorge of the Murchison River almost 500 feet below. Vividly stratified limestone and sandstone comprised the walls of the canyon, and, through binoculars, I could see red gums and coolabahs thriving on the banks of the river pools. We explored the park further and drove along the coast past the colorfully named Rainbow Valley, Grandstand Rock, and Layer Cake Gorge to Natural Bridge.

From Kilbarri, we drove south through rolling hills past tall thick stands of wildflowers that grew almost hedgerow-like along the road. Colors flew by—red, pink, orange, blue, purple, lavender, violet, yellow and white—and, when we took the time to stop, we could identify red pokers, honey myrtle, kangaroo paws, sheep's tails, and cat's feet. In Geraldton, we stayed in the best campground since Alice Springs and toured several buildings of historic interest. We walked the beach to a picturesque nineteenth-century red and white striped lighthouse where we sat on the beach and watched a beautiful sunset. Then I fixed everyone grilled cheese sandwiches for supper.

Continuing south, we stopped in the historic towns of Greenough with its eleven attractivly restored National Trust buildings and Dongara with its nineteenth-century flour mill and courthouse where we bought shortbread. Crops grew in the irrigated fields, and sheep grazed on grass far more plentiful than on the northern sheep stations. Young emus were much bigger birds by now but still remained with their fathers. I had caught a cold in the last few days and asked Lynette to take over the driving. We found a campground at Cervantes, and, while I slept off my cold, the others drove to nearby Nambung National Park. The park features the Pinnacles Desert with its limestone tomb-like structures which are, in reality, fossilized roots of ancient coastal plants.

Upon arriving in Perth's cool, green metropolitan area, we first registered at the campground in the wine country suburbs which would be our base of operations for the next week, and then took our campers to the rental agency to arrange the scheduled maintenance our contract required. In the late afternoon, we drove into town and quickly saw why everyone liked the place so much. Aside from its wonderful climate, the city was clean and well landscaped, included an interesting mix of the old and the new, and emphasized a creative use of public space in its splendid parks and gardens.

After dropping the campers off to be serviced, we took a bus downtown where Lynette led us on a walking tour. We visited the Government House, several cathedrals, the Old Post Office and Old Fire Station, the Citiplace pedestrian mall and a shopping plaza or two. Other points of interest included the Old Perth Boys' School, Parliament House, London Court, and His

Majesty's Theater, the handsomely restored home of the Western Australia Opera and Ballet companies. Sometime during the day, I called home and was sad to learn that a friend had passed away.

Rain poured hard on our campers that night, but, in the morning, the sun again shone, and we drove to Fremantle, Perth's port city cousin and the venue for the 1987 America's Cup race. We bought fruit and vegetables in the town's market and then toured the waterfront where an authentic replica of Captain Cook's Endeavor was docked. The ship was scheduled to sail for Sydney in two days where it would reside in the Maritime Museum. After a day of walking, we found an especially charming pub and took a load off our feet. The only thing anyone was talking about was the football championship game to be played the next day between the West Coast Eagles and the Melbourne Cats. By now, Mike and I were diehard Eagles fans, and the boys in the pub insisted on buying us a beer or two.

The Eagles creamed the Cats, and, everywhere we went in Perth, people were pretty excited about it. Mike, Zach, and I went birding in King's Park while Lori and Lynette shopped for gifts. The park perched on a high hill, overlooking the shining city astride the Swan River. Many flowers were approaching their peak—the best early bloomers being the deep red and black kangaroo's paws and, in the adjacent botanical gardens, the pink and white everlastings which dominated the thick understory of the forest. We spotted several new bird species including western gerygone, little wattlebird, and western spinebill. The girls joined us for lunch at the park tea room after which we attended an art exhibit and walked through the botanical gardens. We drove to Northbridge, an old section of Perth with a variety of popular restaurants, and then to a vineyard near the campground where we bought a couple of bottles of wine. That evening, Zach amused himself in the R.V. park's playground while the four of us talked and enjoyed a glass or two of wine.

Lake Joondalup, an important freshwater reserve for a variety of waterbirds, lies about a dozen miles north of Perth. The lake didn't disappoint us, and we found a number of new birds, including great crested grebes, Australasian shovelers, blue-billed ducks and a buff-banded rail. Most interesting were a pair of bizarre looking musk ducks, a blackish stiff-tailed species that swims semi-submerged. The male has a lobe of skin hanging from his bill which he inflates during his elaborate courtship display.

The three golfers in our group, Lynette, Mike and Lori, wanted to check out the Joondalup Country Club golf course. A flock of red-capped parrots screamed from a eucalyptus tree as we proceeded slowly up the club's entrance drive. We were careful to avoid any collisions with numerous resident kangaroos hopping about and grazing on the manicured lawn. This was no red gravel fairways and oiled sand greens course like the one in Exmouth, but rather a lush, beautifully designed, and landscaped affair any golfer would enjoy playing. We stopped long enough to admire what could be seen of the course from the clubhouse and to enjoy a *café au lait* on the patio. Then we drove to Yanchep National Park to see the wildflowers growing profusely in the banksia scrub and the small captive breeding population of koalas maintained by the park.

In the early morning, we washed the campers, did the laundry and attended to some other administrative duties. Lynette had caught a cold, most likely from me, and felt bad enough that she wanted to remain in bed. I did what I could for her and then joined the others on a wildflower outing to the Darling Range. This was the time of year for flowers, and they were splendid. The groupings in the small meadows and patches along streams and beside ponds looked like gardens arranged by Mother Nature herself. They made a persuasive case that, when it came to natural beauty, there was little humans could do to improve upon the works of nature.

Lynette was feeling a bit better when we returned to the campground late in the afternoon. We walked to a nearby vineyard, tasted a selection of wines, and brought several bottles back to the campground. Lynette forewent alcohol during our wine cocktail hour during which Mike and I prepared and cooked a marvelous vegetable soup for dinner. Later, while doing the dishes, I chatted with a group of Aussies from Sydney who were on a cross country wildflower/camping trip. One old boy wanted to know where we had been, and, after I told him, he asked where we were going from here.

"We're headed south and then back east."

"Are you going to Albany?"

"Sure we are."

"That's good. There's a family of 'whales' down there."

"How did you know my name was Wile?"

"I didn't."

"There's really a family of 'Wile's' in Albany?" This was interesting to me since Wile is a fairly unusual name.

"There is."

"How do you know about them? Who are they?"

"Well, everybody knows about the 'whales.' It's been in all the papers."

Hello world! I got it! In Aussie, whale=Wile. I explained what had been going on to the friendly fellow. He laughed and shook his head.

"Anyway, my name is Darwin Wile. What's yours?"

"Grady. Jack Grady."

"Well, it's nice to know you Jack."

"Same here... you bloody Yanks sure have an accent!"

We spent our last morning in Perth, touring the university area and leisurely walking the downtown. The billboards at His Majesty's Theater informed us that *The Magic Flute* had just closed, and *A Midsummer's*

Night Dream would open soon. One of the entrance doors was unlocked, and, when we peeked through it, a woman invited us inside and gave us her personal tour of the theater which had been newly restored in its Victorian era tradition.

After a pleasant lunch in King's Park, we followed the Swan River to Fremantle and then turned south to the coastal resort town of Rockingham. We set up camp on Point Peron where we looked for rock parrots unsuccessfully but did see white-browed scrubwrens scolding from the low shrubbery.

The next morning, a short boat ride brought us to Penguin Island where a nesting colony of fairy penguins, the world's smallest, thrives. Bridled terns circled near the dock and plunged into the surf for fish. On the beach, a sign warned us that the penguin nests were active and that the primary nesting area was off limits. We walked north on the beach, away from the nesting area, discussing ways in which we could possibly see any of the penguins. Suddenly Lynette stopped.

"I just saw something black run between those two rocks below the cliff."

We waited patiently for about a minute, and, sure enough, Lynnie had done it again. Several non-nesting penguins less than a foot tall inched into the clearing and watched to be sure we would come no closer.

Continuing south, we took a series of backcountry roads lined with paper bark gum trees through Mandurah, where several thousand black swans congregated in Peel Inlet, to the seaport of Bunbury where we camped on the beach. On a lovely evening, we drank wine and talked about Australia. I posed a question to everyone.

"There have been many aspects of this trip that I have especially enjoyed—the '50s feeling in the east, the vastness of the interior, the independent spirit of the Aussies. But, of all of this and everything else we have seen, each of you, what is your favorite experience or memory about the trip so far?"

Everyone thought for a minute.

"Mine has to be the Great Barrier Reef," Mike responded first.

"I can't get over the vastness of Australia," Lori added. "I'll never forget the beauty of the remoteness."

"Well, I thought the Reef was pretty awesome," Lynette chimed in. "But my favorite experience was finding my very own platypus."

"What about you, Dad?" Lori asked. "If you can only choose one experience, what would it be?"

I had been thinking about my answer. When Australia had drifted away from the rest of the world, evolution of the continent's life had taken an entirely separate road. The results we had been witnessing the past few months had fascinated me.

"More than anything else, the uniqueness of Australia's wildlife has impressed me."

"You know," Mike amended his response, "not to be sappy, but my favorite memory will be that I got to spend all this time with my family. Other than that, it's the Reef."

On an impeccably gorgeous morning, we started the beautiful drive to Cape Naturaliste, passing a variety of species of eucalyptus trees, including enormous tuarts which sported profiles similar to those of large oaks. In Busselton, we enjoyed "Devonshire tea" (scones, jam and cream, tea or coffee) on the patio of a tearoom that once had been a jailhouse. A beautiful pair of bright yellow and green regent parrots perched quietly in a tree above our table. While Zach dozed in a high chair, Lori and Lynette indulged themselves with a second cup of tea, and Mike and I indulged ourselves with a birdwalk through the garden on which we saw scarlet robins and inland thornbills.

Giant swells crash violently against high rocky cliffs, the dramatic result of the Indian and the Southern oceans merging off southwest Australia. Unsurpassed coastal scenery unfolds before the traveler. The area between Cape Naturaliste and Cape Leeuwin is among the most interesting and beautiful in Australia. Fine wineries welcome those who prefer a leisurely progression of tasting experiences; limestone caves populated by rare animal forms await adventurous spelunkers; extensive sand beaches accommodate swimmers and surfers; fine eucalyptus stands of marri and jarrah and well defined patches of banksia scrub, heathlands, and melaleuca offer opportunities to see unique vegetation; and, of course, a variety of ideal habititats support an abundance of birds.

Graceful red-tailed tropicbirds, with pinkish-white bodies and long, red central tail feathers streaming behind soared gracefully above Sugarloaf Rock near Cape Naturaliste. Sea lions sunned on the rocks, and, centered in our spotting scopes, a pod of whales breached and rolled off shore. Lynette couldn't resist the obvious.

"It looks like the 'Wile' family moved from Albany to Cape Naturaliste."

Only two or three minutes later, a woman walked over to where we were standing and nodded at my scope.

"Have you seen any Wiles?"

A square-tailed kite hunted over the heathlands bordering our campsite on a pristine beach near Yallingup. While Lori and Mike engaged in some serious spelunking, Lynette, Zach and I birded the scrubs behind the beach where we found a male golden whistler in the middle of his rich, melodious song, and southern emu-wrens flitting about the dense coastal thickets. By now Zach's vocabulary included an incredible number of birds, reptiles and marsupials, and his ability to identify many of them was not far behind. That evening, for the umpteenth time, he and I paged through our Field Guide to the Birds of Australia. The little guy pointed out scores of birds, including his favorites, Willie wagtails and frogmouths.

Wine tasting occupied most of the next day, so, for obvious reasons, we didn't drive very far, only to Prevelly Park, where we found our own little unspoiled beach. We saw few people, and Lynette declared the place her favorite. She had bought wine glasses and several bottles of wine for Lori and Mike at the Red Gate Winery. While red-winged fairy-wrens sang their melodic trills from the heath, we drank a bottle of cabernet, and then, at a small restaurant on the beach, a very thin person with a shaved head, an earring and a nose ring served us pizza. He, or she, wore a University of Michigan shirt where, we were told in a non-gender revealing voice, his or her father went to college.

Boranup State Forest featured tall karri trees with an understory of ferns and wonderfully flowering shrubbery. In Hamelin Bay, we saw Australian shelducks swimming, masked woodswallows foraging for insects over our heads, and the incredibly beautiful, dark blue and black, splendid fairy-wren flitting about in the nearby saltbush. We registered at a campground in Augusta and then walked to the Cape Leeuwin lighthouse, below which rock parrots scampered among the rocks.

From Augusta, we drove inland through Nannup and Pemberton to see the three hundred-year old Gloucester Tree, a two hundred feet tall giant karri, under which we ate lunch and were joined by a pair of purple crowned lorikeets and a chattering flock of spotted pardalotes. Marvelous scenery unfolded as we drove through rural sheep country and returned to the rugged coast and its precipitous cliffs. We stopped at a winery in Denmark and, in the pleasant town of Albany, after finding a campground, we visited a whaling museum and The Old Gaol. We felt especially honored when the Endeavor arrived in Princess Royal Harbor just before us and, later, the "whale" family made an appearance on our behalf in King George Sound. That evening, we drove to Torndirrup National Park where huge swells from the Southern Ocean slammed against the towering granite cliffs. Nowhere else is the overwhelming power of the ocean more dramatically evident than in several features that have been carved into the cliffs over the millenia: waves roar and explode as they surge through a deep crevice called The Gap; geyser-like spouts of water shoot high in the air as the foaming sea is forced through vents in the granite called The Blowholes; and the deafening boiling sea rushes in and then out under an immense granite arch called Natural Bridge. Zach and I were carefully peering into The Gap when vigilant Mike called to us. He had spotted, far out at sea, flesh-footed shearwaters in their graceful fluttering and gliding flight.

The oldest building in Albany was a farmhouse that had been converted to a tea room. After having Devonshire tea there for breakfast, we drove to the Stirling Range National Park, one of Australia's best wildflower reserves. The park's rich mixture of habitats, including forests, open wood-lands, mallee and heath tracts, marshy areas, and shallow saline lakes, sup-ports an incredible variety of flowers, more than 1000 species. With our wildflower field guide in hand, we identified a number of plants, including dryandra, grevillea, hakea, kangaroo paws, and several orchids.

As we approached the town of Ravensthorpe, I wondered to Lynette if it was more than a coincidence that there were so many dead ravens lying beside the road. She thought there had been an unusual number of mam-mal road kills and suggested ravens were feeding on them and falling victim to speeding traffic. Less than a minute after she offered that explanation, I saw a raven feeding on a road kill, did everything I could to avoid hitting it, but sadly saw it smash into our left front bumber as it tried to fly away from its meal.

From Ravensthorpe, we diverted south to see Fitzgerald River National Park, another marvelous wild flower reserve where Lynette found, among others, two beautiful, wonderfully red wild flowers—scarlet banksia and hot pokers, and Mike and I found, in the heathlands, two elusive and long sought after birds—tawny-crowned honeyeaters and brush bronzewings. With many roadside wildflowers blooming along the way, we then drove east to Esperance with its splendid beaches and imposing granite cliffs. A trav-el agent sold us tickets for our planned trip from Melbourne to Tasmania, and then, at the campsite, Mike and I "beefed," a term he used for lifting weights.

Esperance, Western Australia, October 12, 1994

From my notes: *At home, it's Columbus Day. Cook (as in Captain James) "discovered" Australia, Hawaii and a number of other Pacific Islands. Makes me wonder if anyone celebrates Cook Day.*

We drove north from Esperance toward the goldfields, through towns with charming names like Grasspatch and Salmon Gums, the latter named after the salmon like color of the eucalyptus (gum) trees growing there, and then past several large, mostly dry, salt lakes. An array of wildflowers con-tinued blooming along the road.

While gold is still being mined in the Kalgoorlie area, the goldfields are not nearly as productive as during their heyday a hundred years ago. We stopped first in the ghost town of Coolgardie where, on the mostly deserted main street, only a few miners with long, shaggy beards hung around an equally few commercial establishments. We toured an old house that had been converted to a small museum and that displayed pictures of the town during its thriving turn of the century era. One picture of Afghanistani camel drivers confused us—the camels were one-humped dromedaries, the kind used in northern Africa and Arabia. We thought Asians used two-humped or Bactrian camels. Later I learned that dromedaries are common in western Asia.

Unlike Coolgardie, Kalgoorlie has retained much of its former glory. Many of the turn of the century buildings are well preserved or restored, and the town appears to be prospering. Gold mining still drives the economy, and there are plenty of bars to service the scores of thirsty miners. We toured some of the interesting old buildings—the Town Hall with its stamped metal ceilings, the York Hotel with its intricate cupola and the large, century-old, pink post office. We drank a few beers at the Hotel York bar and then returned to the campground where I grilled skewers of potatoes, onions, zucchini, and lamb for dinner. A couple from Perth was cooking on the grill next to me. They had lived in Port Hedland for six years, and I silently wondered why anyone would live in Port Hedland, a drab industrial town in the far north.

The next morning, Lori walked to a public telephone outside of the campground office to call her parents. She had awakened with a headache and had taken an Advil after breakfast. The heat was oppressive—Mike and Zach were sitting in our camper chatting with Lynette and me when a man came running up to our open door.

"Come quick! Your wife has collapsed by the phone!"

The three of us ran to the telephone where a small crowd had gathered by now. Lori lay on the blacktop, her head cradled on the arm of the woman who had been cooking next to me the previous night. The woman's husband held Lori's hand, taking her pulse. We later learned they were assigned to Port Hedland by the Flying Doctor Service, she as a nurse and he as a midwife. He had just completed medical school and was now an intern. Lori, as it happened, has low blood pressure and had fainted while talking with her parents. The couple recommended we hold ice to her forehead and keep her still for a while. Later, we picked her up and took her to the hospital where they took blood tests, pronounced her OK for now, and told her to return in the morning to see a doctor.

Mike and Lori checked into a hotel room where she would be cooler and more comfortable. Lynette and I took Zach so she could rest. The three of us toured an open pit mine and then the house where Herbert Hoover lived when, as a young man, he worked in the Australian gold fields. Later, we visited a primitive gambling operation, called "2UP" and run by Aborigines. That evening, for dinner, we carried pizza and cheesecake, Lori's favorite foods, to the hotel.

Lori's blood tests confirmed she was pregnant. Aside from her blood pressure and iron being low, the doctor said she was fine. With that diagnosis, we drove south toward Norseman from where we would turn east and begin our formidable seven hundred mile journey across the flat, sparsely vegetated and uninhabited Nullarbor Plain.

Nullarbor is Latin for "no tree." We spent the night camped in the

Belladonia Road House, and, the next morning, drove off into the treeless, flat plain. In fact, one stretch of highway was perfectly straight, curveless, for ninety miles. Several stops along high cliffs offered us marvelous views of the endless sea and of breaching whales. Golden dingoes worked the sparse vegetation, searching for small mammals, and, on one cliffside stop, two peregrine falcons rode the strong winds, searching the edges of the precipice for smaller winged prey.

In eastern Australia, chambers of commerce promoted their areas with "The Big Banana" and the "Big Crab." Nullarbor kitsch included "The Big Whale," "The Big Kangaroo" and "The Big Galah." We crossed into South Australia and stopped for the day at Nullarbor Station, where, in the bar, we drank a few brewskis with some Aussies, and Mike again was the object of recruitment talk for the local rugby team. All afternoon, a strong south wind thrashed the Nullarbor. Just outside the bar, a pair of white-fronted honeyeaters hung on to a bottlebrush branch for dear life, sucking nectar out of the fuzzy red flowers while the wind threatened to blow them into the next shire. Mike and I had been looking for these birds for the past 1,200 miles and, unexpectedly, found them in the treeless heart of the Nullarbor.

Almost suddenly, the flat barrenness of the Nullarbor gave way to rolling hills and agriculture. Grain elevators interrupted the horizon, betraying the approach of a town and reminding us of a drive in the American midwest. We saw a flock of blue-winged parrots in a tree on Port Augusta's main street and, foraging on the mudflats outside of town, banded stilts, stunning birds with black wings, a white body with a red band across its breast, long pink legs and a slender black bill.

The Barossa Valley lies south of Port Augusta and was settled by Germans and Poles, industrious farmers who brought along their European traditions and values, including the fine art of wine making. Even though picturesque rolling farmland and lush vineyards had replaced the valley's natural vegetation, the result offered a very pleasant atmosphere as we visited a number of wineries, tasting many varieties and buying a few bottles. We camped in the garden of one of the vineyards and, after dinner, drove to a *bakerei* in the town of Lyndoch for dessert. *Bakereis* replaced tea houses in the Barossa Valley and, rather than Devonshire tea, they offered coffee and delicious *apfelstrudl* or Black Forest cake.

We found a campground on the beach north of Adelaide and then drove into the small city which, like Perth, has preserved large areas for parks and gardens. Many of Adelaide's colonial buildings are constructed of stone, while others with tin roofs and balconies emit a tropical Australian aura. The Botanic Gardens lie by the River Torrens which flows through the center of town and offers relaxation on its grassy banks and recreation for scores of scullers. We especially enjoyed the Art Gallery of South Australia which featured works by many of the country's finest painters.

Lynette and I took an early morning walk on the beach and admired a series of sleek thoroughbreds pulling sulkies as they passed us by on their morning beach workout. Lori telephoned a man who had been a friend of her grandfather, and who had taught him the opal business, and arranged to meet him for lunch. Lynnie, Zach and I explored Adelaide and the Botanical Gardens while Lori and Mike kept their lunch date and, later, joined us on a pleasant walking tour of the city.

We drove east from Adelaide in the morning, following the river past apple orchards in full bloom and through Torrens Gorge, and stopping in picturesque German settlements with lovely stone buildings. In Halinsdorf, we visited an exhibit with the works of Albert Namatjira, Australia's most famous Aboriginal artist who developed a unique and much admired landscape school. At an old mill that had been converted to an antique shop, Lynette bought a brass tea kettle and an old beer bottle for Mike. One stop Zach insisted upon featured a giant rocking horse. Continuing east, we entered the state of Victoria and spent the night camped near a town called Nhill.

Grampians National Park offers some of Australia's best mountain scenery, most abundant wildlife, and a wonderful array of wildflowers. The area is also a traditional homeland of the Aborigines and contains more than a hundred caves with primitive art. We registered at a campground in Halls Gap, the commercial center of the park. Yellow-rumped pardalotes sang triplets from the mallee, and yellow-tufted and crescent honeyeaters foraged in a tree next to our campers. Kangaroos grazed on the lawns, and kookaburras laughed in the old gum trees (sclerophylls). We had just settled in when I heard Lynette sing.

"Darrrrwinnnnn! Come over heerrrrre!"

Clinging to a high eucalyptus branch was a burly koala, champing on a fistful of leaves. Then Lori saw another koala, closer to the ground. At first, Zach had difficulty finding the animal. When, at last, he did, he became very excited.

"I like this place," he gushed, pronouncing place like the Australians, "plice."

"Me too," Mike laughed. "Just think—kangaroos, kookaburras and koalas in our back yard! Let's stay here for a while."

We followed a trail along Dairy Creek and spotted more koalas feeding in the forest canopy. While tiny striated thornbills called *tizz-tizz* from high in a sclerophyll tree, a varied sittella crept nuthatch-like down its trunk. Back at the campground, white-winged choughs whistled as they foraged in the parking area. A flock of long-billed corellas, gorgeous white parrots with a pink wash on their face and neck and a yellow wash on their underwing and undertail feathers, flew in a frenzy from tree to tree. That evening, gang-gang cockatoos, slate-gray birds with a scarlet head and crest, screeched like squeaky doors from their night roosts high in the campground trees.

Lori and Mike went on a date for dinner, and Lynette and I bathed little Zach.

The nights had become cool and the days clear and warm. Happily, we had left the annoying flies and mosquitoes behind. After doing our laundry, we hiked the trail to the Pinnacle, first past steep granite walls and then along high cliffs and marvelous formations of sandstone which had been geologically tilted and lifted. Our efforts were rewarded by the sight of magnificent wildflower displays, their composition evolving as we ascended, and, at the Pinnacle, spectacular views of the beautiful park.

The small commercial center of Halls Gap could have been the setting for a movie filmed where I grew up in the fifties. That evening, we walked from the campground across the street to a drive-in restaurant that specialized in pizza and ice cream. Whoever was feeding the jukebox played every song Bill Haley and The Comets ever recorded including *Rock Around the Clock* and *See Ya Later Alligator.* Later, in bed, Lynnie and I were puzzled over the source of a cacaphony of grunting and snorting coming from the trees outside the camper and, with relief, laughed aloud when we determined koalas were the culprits.

Tourist literature represents Old World influenced Melbourne as the financial, intellectual and cultural capital of Australia. The city boasts fine museums, a great university, a wonderful climate, lovely parks and gardens, attractive boulevards, and pleasant outdoor cafes. Melbourne may be one of the most livable cities in the world.

Cable cars raced by as Lynette led our Melbourne walking tour, through the nineteenth-century Royal Arcade, past the Edwardian Flinders Street Railroad Station and the statue of the explorer, Matthew Flinders, to bustling City Square. We visited St. Paul's Cathedral where I bought several wine glasses, the State Library and Museum of Victoria which featured natural history and science collections, and the Old Melbourne Gaol where, in 1880, the notorious outlaw, Ned Kelly, was hanged.

In 1934, the stone cottage in which Captain James Cook dwelled between his voyages was transported from Yorkshire, England, to Melbourne and reerected in Fitzroy Gardens. We followed the Avenue of Elms past Cook's Cottage and enjoyed a genteel lunch in the Gardens Tearoom. Later, song thrushes scratched the ground for seeds and grubs as we spent the afternoon exploring the Royal Botanical Gardens which, in addition to native trees, included large, specimen trees from around the world and, in the Gardens' old Tennyson Lawn section, four giant English elms more than 120 years old.

Late in the afternoon, at a travel office, we picked up our tickets to go to Tasmania the next day. Now it was only a week before Mike and his family would leave us and take a more direct route back to Sydney. Time was running short on their leaves of absence, and they wanted to save enough days for a tour of New Zealand. Lynette and I didn't want to think about their departure.

Most large groups touring Australia did so in a bus which carried tents and other camping gear for the passengers, a method of traveling which, if not first class, at least preserved privacy and individualism. However, group travel reached a low that evening when a large group of Germans drove into our campground in a huge truck, the rear of which had been modified to accommodate sleeping passengers in pigeon hole-like compartments. The arrangement seemed claustrophobic and impersonal and reminded me of the English convicts being shoehorned into small ships and transported like cattle to Australia.

If I were permitted to live any place in the world except the United States of America, I think I would choose the Hobart area of Tasmania. The island has an English flavor and, with a population of less than a half million people, enjoys a simpler, slower lifestyle. Tasmania's many mountains permit good skiing in the winter as well as excellent summer wilderness hiking. Rugged coasts and dense rain forests in the island's southwest have been subjected to minimal exploration. The state boasts an abundance of wildlife diversity, most of it indigenous, and an extensive national park system. Hobart, a small city of less than 185,000 people, nestles below Mt. Wellington, straddling the River Derwent, and enjoys a pleasant year-round climate with cool summers and mild winters and moderate precipitation. The small city offers good restaurants and a vibrant cultural atmosphere, including concerts by the Tasmanian Symphony orchestra and plays performed at the fine old Theater Royal. Crimes in Hobart are few and, those, mainly petty.

European greenfinchs chipped outside an open window as we checked into a bed and breakfast, an old mansion on a hill overlooking the mouth of the Derwent and Storm Bay. We walked to the clean, attractive waterfront, admired the boats moored at Constitution Dock, and then visited the Tasmanian Museum and Art Gallery which included exhibits on the island's unique wildlife and its extirpated Aboriginal culture. We inspected historic, mid-nineteenth-century sandstone and colonial brick buildings and browsed in the shops of the renovated old warehouses at Battery Point. We checked out Hampden Road's antique shops and Arthur's Circus, a circle of authentically restored mid-nineteenth-century cottages surrounding a village green. From a multitude of seafood restaurants, we chose the Drunken Admiral, an establishment with a salty decor, a loud but friendly clientele, and good food.

From 1830 to 1877, many of Australia's notorious offenders were housed in the Port Arthur Penal Settlement where they were treated with extreme cruelty. We all rode in our rented van from Hobart through the green rolling England-like countryside, with its herds of sheep and stone houses with thatched roofs, around Storm Bay and out the Tasman

Peninsula to Port Arthur. Mike spotted an echidna along the road. In the bay, black-faced shags perched on sea markers, holding their wings out to dry. Later, a pallid cuckoo whistled a mournful "tooo-tooo-tooo" as we toured the ruins of the convict settlement, the peaceful remnants making it difficult to envision the horrors that once were visited upon the residents. A yellow-throated honeyeater, a bird endemic to Tasmania, sang, "Pick-em-up!" from the courtyard, and Mike and I wondered if this species had learned that song a century and a half before while listening to and mimicking prison guards shouting orders to convicts and their fallen comrades.

The drive north through Tasmania's interior took us past lovely, pastoral sheep ranches and through charming towns with stone houses built during the convict era. While Lori, Lynette and Zach browsed through one village's shops, Mike and I walked across a picturesque stone arch bridge and then along a slow moving creek to look for birds. Suddenly, splashing and rolling in the stream, a platypus did everything it conceivably could to attract our attention. When the animal was certain we were aware of its antics, it dived beneath the surface and, while we searched the creek for the next half hour, did not reappear. Mike had seen his first platypus.

Mike and I made arrangements with a guide to take us trout fishing while our three companions planned to spend a day shopping and relaxing in the nice towns of Launceston and Devonport. Early in the morning, our guide, Ashley, took us on a long drive to a mountain lake. He had warned us fairly that it was too early in the spring to expect to catch much of anything, but Mike wanted to fish at least one day in Tasmania, so we signed up. Fishing has been a passion of Mike's since he was four. I don't get much out of it myself and do it mostly for his company. Just as the guide had cautioned, the fishing wasn't too good. Mike continued casting diligently, but I gave it up and instead talked with Ashley. He asked me where I was from.

"From the States."

"Yeah, I know. But where in the States?"

"Oh a little town in the west."

"Where in the west?"

"In the state of Wyoming. Just a little town. No reason you would have heard of it."

"What's its name?"

"Jackson. I live in Jackson Hole, Wyoming. Haven't heard of it, have you?"

"Heard of it? Ha! I was there only two or three years ago. Fished in the One-fly Contest. Do you know Jack Dennis?"

"Sure do. He's a neighbor. Great fly fisherman."

"I know. He's going to put on a fly fishing seminar in Melbourne next month. Then he's coming down here to fish with me."

Cradle Mountain National Park lies south of Devonport and includes great hiking trails with marvelous alpine scenery. Black currawongs greeted us noisily outside the Cradle Mountain Lodge where we stopped for lunch. We spent the afternoon hiking and then, near the village of Sheffield, registered at a bed and breakfast with comfortable cabins. An open forest wrapped around much of the farm on which the B&B was located. After dinner, Mike, Zach and I walked the forest edge and spotted flame and dusky robins, Tasmanian thornbills, yellow wattlebirds, and strong-billed and black-headed honeyeaters. We circled back toward the B&B past a stock pond where a platypus cruised and splashed on the water's surface, seemingly oblivious to our presence. Lori was the only one of us who had not yet seen a platypus, so I ran back to the cabin to fetch her and Lynette while the boys tried to keep an eye on the usually elusive animal. The cooperative platypus waited for the girls to arrive, splashed and performed for another minute or two, and then dived and disappeared. Our family, for some odd reason, celebrates half-birthdays, and that day was Lori's half birthday.

"Happy half-birthday, Lori," Mike declared after the platypus disappeared below the surface.

"Mommy, did you like your half-birthday present?"

Lori picked the little guy up, kissed him, smiled and replied, "Zach, it's the best half-birthday present I've ever had!"

That evening, we gave Lori her little half-birthday presents. With hers, Lynette included a verse—"Lori, Lori, she's no wuss; today she saw a platypus."

Back in Melbourne, the National Gallery of Victoria displayed good collections of seventeenth-century Dutch and Impressionist art, especially the Renoir exhibit. We enjoyed a very civilized lunch at the museum restaurant and then drove to Dandenong National Park to search for the very secretive superb lyrebird. Rain drizzled steadily all afternoon on the forest of huge mountain ash trees as we walked a trail, looking among the ferns comprising the understory for the bird's tell tale scratchings. Bird song resonated through the woods, and we saw many species, but not the lyrebird. The path led past a teahouse where we ordered Devonshire tea and Zach threw table crumbs to several rather bold crimson rosellas. We decided to try to find the lyrebird again the next morning and returned to the campground. That evening, Lynette seemed sad.

"What's the matter, Baby?"

"Nothing, really... They're leaving in three days."

"Does that make you sad?"

"Yes it does. This is the last time we'll ever be able to spend this much time with Mikey."

The morning walk through the rain forest was pleasant, but our search for the lyrebird was again unsuccessful. We drove 80 miles south of

Melbourne to Phillip Island to see the much trumpeted "Penguin Parade" on Summerland Beach.

From my notes: *What I dislike the most about Australia is the bush-flies. Running very close behind, however, is the Penguin Parade which, after the Great Barrier Reef and Ayers Rock, is Australia's third largest tourist attraction. At seven dollars each, 500,000 visitors make this a $3.5 million enterprise. Now this isn't big business, but, when the gift shop and restaurant concessions are included, along with all the other attendant lodging, fuel, and dining revenue brought to Phillip Island, it ain't peanuts either. About a thousand fairy penguins are each evening subjected to floodlights and busloads of gaping tourists with flash cameras as they battle their way through the surf and emerge on the beach to return to their burrows in the sand dunes. They come out of the water frightened and run back into the surf several times until they mount enough courage to cross the beach. If that's not enough, their dignity is further dismantled as people walk along floodlit boardwalks and gawk at the penguins' private comings and goings. The birds seem positively cowed by this human infliction.*

Watching birds is one thing. But here the activity is shamelessly commercialized by bringing in thousands of people who have little or no interest in birds or penguins otherwise. This goes far overboard, and I'm disgusted by the whole thing. We were all depressed when we left the beach. All of this having been said, I did enjoy seeing little penguins in such great numbers and especially enjoyed the spectacular side show of thousands of short-tailed shearwaters and gannets flying back from the sea to their nesting burrows in the sand dunes.

Phillip Island, Victoria, Australia, October 31, 1994

Happy Halloween! Mikey gave us all tiny pumpkins. Lynette and I powerwalked early on the beach. We met a man coming the other way who waved and then stopped to talk.

"Have you gone to the Penguin Parade?"

"Yes we have, last night," I replied.

"What did you think of it?"

"We were pretty disappointed."

"Oh, there'll be more of them in the next few weeks."

"It's not that, there were plenty of penguins last night. We were disappointed in the program. It's not what I would call 'low-impact ecotourism'." I went on to describe the indignities and harassment inflicted upon the birds.

This fellow was an official of the Penguin Parade, and he explained that the behavior of the birds running back into the surf was natural, that they're just afraid of predators when they first emerge from the sea. He also said that the lights don't bother them as long as they're turned on every night. He agreed that the behavior of the spectators was sometimes pretty awful but that they tried to control it with rangers.

"Maybe what you say is so, but I still feel sorry for the penguins."

"They don't seem to mind too much," he went on. "Their numbers increase every year. I hope they keep increasing and bring in more tourists. We need the money. Besides, we can't deny people seeing the penguins if they want to see them."

Australia's mainland stretches south of Philip Island to its southernmost point, Wilson's Promontory. During the last ice age, Australia was connected by land bridges to New Guinea and to Tasmania. Wilson's Promontory once was part of the land bridge to Tasmania. Today, the granite based peninsula supports many marsupials including kangaroos, wallabies, wombats, koalas and opossums, and more than 250 bird species have been recorded there. Yellow-tailed black-cockatoos wailed at us as we set up camp at Tidal River. We grabbed our binoculars and set out on our last bush walk together. The Lilly Pilly Gully Nature Trail led us through heathland where we saw orange-bellied parrots and rain forest where we picked up a few leeches. That evening, we had our last dinner together. We were all sad to be parting.

The next day, Lynette and I drove to The Lakes National Park, stopping at several nice coastal towns along the way. We camped at the settlement of Lakes Entrance. Another fellow and I were washing our campers next to one another when he excused himself.

"I'll just be gone for five minutes. The Cup, you know." Then I remembered the Melbourne Cup was being run today. The man returned after a bit.

"Did your horse win?"

"No."

"Do you follow the horses regularly?"

"No. I don't have much interest in horse racing. Only when the Cup is run."

"Sounds like the Kentucky Derby, I suppose. That day everyone's a fan."

From a letter to my parents: *While Lynette did the laundry, I walked along the Esplanade hoping to see fairy terns. I returned to the campground and became very sad when I saw only one camper instead of the two I had grown used to seeing together.*

That evening, I looked through my Australian bird book and found a number of the pages stuck together. During the trip, Zach frequently rode with Lynette and me. He liked to look at my bird book while we drove, sometimes doing so after eating a peanut butter and jelly sandwich. How I missed the little guy as I carefully separated the sticky pages.

After a morning walk on the beach, Lynette got her hair cut. Then we left the sea and drove through the foothills to the mountains, or "The Alps" as the Australians call them. The Alps they're not, but the drive was quite beautiful anyway. Once we were held up by a herd of sheep walking on the road. Two sheep dogs steered the animals along, responding to whistles and barked orders from a shepherd leisurely strolling behind the flock.

"If I were a rancher, I would want to raise sheep," Lynette mused.

"Why a sheep ranch?"

"You don't have to kill them. You just shear the wool."

The Australian gold rush created many of the area's alpine towns. Now some of those same towns which we drove through had been converted to ski economies. After setting up camp in a picturesque valley on the outskirts of Bright, we took an evening wildlife drive on the slopes of Mount Buffalo. Our hopes of spotting wombats and lyrebirds were unrewarded, but we did see a koala and a number of very dark colored wallabies.

We left early the next morning for Mount Buffalo National Park where we climbed a trail that led to a high waterfall cascading over a large concave slab of granite. Scratching sites provided evidence of the presence of lyrebirds, and once we saw a female running away into the woods. Later we stopped for Devonshire tea at the venerable, turn of the century Mount Buffalo Lodge. The lodge had been run by the government until the past couple of years when a young couple had taken it over and were trying, apparently with considerable success, to polish this gem from an earlier era. We took another hike and, on it, decided to splurge and spend the night in the lodge. This was Lynette's kind of place, refined and genteel. We returned from the hike and checked in. After a pleasant lunch in the lodge's chalet, I waited in the lobby for Lynette to come down from our room. A group of several people were talking nearby, and one of them was an older, soft-spoken lady whom I decided must have been a real head turner in her day. From their conversation which was impossible not to overhear, I concluded the woman was a birdwatcher. Soon Lynette came, and we set off on the day's third hike after which we returned to the lodge's smoking room and ran off a few games of billiards.

That evening, the *maitre d'* escorted us to a large table with two empty chairs. Six people already had been seated there, including the birdwatcher I had seen earlier in the afternoon. I cleverly positioned myself to sit in the empty chair beside her. After we introduced ourselves all around, I leaned toward my birdwatching neighbor, smiled and said rather softly, "Fate has been kind in bringing us together."

"Really? Why would Fate waste her time on us?" she smiled demurely.

"Because of our shared passion."

"Now, what might that be?"

"Why, the birds, of course."

"How in the world did you know I was a birdwatcher?"

Margaret and her friends had been enjoying annual holidays to the Mount Buffalo Lodge for many years. Her "hubby" remained at home in Melbourne because, "He doesn't care for the mountains." Like Americans, most Australians are quite informal and very friendly. We had a lovely time talking with our dinner mates who were more than a little interested in our impressions of their country now that we had seen so much of it. One older man, Tom, had been very quiet during most of the conversation. He seemed, however, to hang on Lynette's and my every word. When dinner was over, he walked around the table to shake our hands. In a very formal manner, he stated his piece.

"On behalf of Australia, I would like to thank you for what America did during the war." He then elaborated on the subject and related several of his personal experiences and explained that he and many of his fellow countrymen would not be around today had the United States not intervened in the Pacific war. This was all said, if formally and frankly, in a way that moved me very much. This was not the first time an Australian had told us of his appreciation for our support against the Japanese in World War II, but never before had it been said so eloquently. I often wondered why Australia had remained steadfast in its support for the United States, especially during our protracted conflicts in Korea and Viet Nam. Now I knew. That evening, Lynette and I took a wildlife drive and saw a wombat for the first time.

And down by Kosciusko, where the pine-clad ridges raise
Their torn and rugged battlements on high,
Where the air is clear as crystal, and the white stars fairly blaze
At midnight in the cold and frosty sky,
And where around the Overflow the reed-beds sweep and sway
To the breezes, and the rolling plains are wide,
The Man from Snowy River is a household word today
And the stockmen tell the story of his ride.

From: *The Man From Snowy River*, by Banjo Paterson

The Snowy Mountains, sometimes called "the roof of Australia," contain a number of peaks over 7,000 feet, including the continent's highest, Mt. Kosciusko. The popular Australian poet, Banjo Paterson, immortalized this area in his celebrated poem, *The Man From Snowy River*. The man behind the legend, Jack Riley, lies buried in the town of Corryong. We stopped to see his grave and then crossed the Murray River and entered Kosciusko National Park. Kangaroos and emus thrived in the lush valley meadows. One adult emu guarded seven small chicks, and we wondered whether it wasn't rather late in the year to see birds that young. We climbed through the rain and the clouds and drove through attractive villages with colorful names like Khancoban, Jindabyne, Tom Groggin, Geehi, and Thredbo, the last a popular ski resort. We crossed the Snowy River and then stopped for lunch on its banks. The clouds separated and, for a while, Mt. Kosciusko stood in clear view.

Our time in Australia was growing short. From the Snowy mountains, we headed north along the Murrumbidgee River to the capital city of Canberra. We stopped about twenty miles south of the capital to see the Cuppacumbalong Craft Center, a pioneer homestead where potters, weavers, painters, and woodworkers have their studios. Later we found a campground next to the Botanic Gardens in the Black Mountain Nature Reserve overlooking Canberra.

The Captain Cook Memorial Jet shoots a stream of water high into the air from Lake Burley Griffin, the large artificial lake fed by the Molonglo River around which the planned city was built in the 1950s. Australians are divided on their opinions of Canberra, and a city tour quickly helps you understand why. While the city is spacious and well-planned, there's an undeniable sterility and lack of warmth. Each of the many public buildings has its appeal, but it takes some patience to feel comfortable with them collectively.

We visited the Australian-American Memorial, a slender octagonal obelisk which commemorates American soldiers who, in World War II, assisted in Australia's defense. Our next stop, the Parliament House, featured a domed glass roof and a 250-foot flagpole with an enormous Aussie flag. Inside the building is an eloquent quote from Captain James Cook:

From what I have seen of the natives of New Holland (Australia) *they may appear to be the most wretched people upon Earth, but in reality they are far happier than we Europeans; being wholly unacquainted not only with the superfluous but the necessary conveniences so much sought after in Europe, they are happy in not knowing the use of them. They live in Tranquility which is not disturb'd by the Inequality of Condition. The Earth and sea of their own accord furnishes them with all things necessary for life, they covet not Magnificent Houses, Householdstuff Ec, they live in a warm and fine climate and enjoy a very wholesome air, so that they have very little need for Clothing and this they seem to be fully sensible of, for many to whome we gave Cloth Ec to, left it carelessly upon the Sea beach and in the woods as a thing they had no manner of use for. In short they seem'd to set no value upon any thing we gave them, nor would they ever part with any thing of their own for any one article we could offer them; this in my opinion argues that they think themselves provided with all the necessarys of Life and that they have no super-*

fluities. James Cook—*The Voyage of the Endeavour 1768-1771*

At the Australian War Memorial which is a marvelous museum as well as an impressive monument, we paid our respects to the Aussie soldiers who gave their lives from the late nineteenth century until the Vietnam War. Then we visited the Australian National Gallery which included a few works of several European masters but was much more interesting in its comprehensive and beautifully displayed collection of great Australian artists like Tom Roberts, Sidney Nolan, and Arthur Streeton.

A strong wind blew from the south, pushing and buffeting our northbound camper. The Big Merino (a giant likeness of one of the sheep grown in that region) welcomed us as we drove into Goulburn and checked into a partially sheltered campground. The winds howled all night and through the next morning when we resumed the drive to Sydney and swerved from lane to lane. We entered the rain forest at Albion National Park and, as we descended an escarpment to the coast, Lynette spotted two lyrebirds, a male and a female, scratching in the gravel along the roadside. We came to a stop downhill from the birds and then walked back up to where we enjoyed rare and excellent views of the pair.

After three and a half months, we were back in Sydney, and the route we had been highlighting on our Australian map now circumscribed the continent. We cleaned up the camper, turned it in to the rental company, and checked into the Harbor Rocks Hotel in the old Rocks section of the city. Flying foxes hung upside down in the fig tree outside the window of our room. While Lynette caught up on her gift shopping for friends back home, I sat in the garden of the Sydney Opera House reading in *U.S.A. Today* about the Republicans capturing the entire legislative branch of the federal government as well as that of many of the state governments. Writers had difficulty hiding their bias as they voiced great concern over "congressional gridlock" which they predicted would be the result of having a Democratic president and a Republican congress. It occurred to me that the condition liberals feared with what they called "gridlock," conservatives might hail as "inactive and unobtrusive government."

The sky was blue and the temperature mild as ferries and pleasure boats tooted their way around the harbor. We walked to the tea room where, in August, we sat with Zach, Lori, and Mike after our arrival. We ordered coffee and spent the remainder of the afternoon reminiscing about our Australian travels with the kiddies, and playing "remember when."

Melbourne's charm is its provincialism, its unabashed enthusiasm for all things Australian. Sydney, on the other hand, effuses a cosmopolitan air and does so without effort. Australia's heritage is deeply rooted in the city's culture, one that eschews affectation, and, therefore, to the extent that Sydney is sophisticated, the city comes by it honestly. For several days we leisurely absorbed Sydney's spirit, and visited shops, cafes, and parks, and rode the ferry from Circular Quay to the various mansion studded neighborhoods lining Sydney Harbor. We strolled through the Taronga Zoo, the Royal Botanic Gardens, the Art Gallery of New South Wales, and the Sydney Aquarium. And, on balmy evenings, we dined under the stars in the patios of harborside restaurants including an especially enjoyable Italian trattoria where the waiters sang popular arias.

Sydney, Australia, November 12, 1994

From my notes: *A double holiday for the Aussies as they celebrate their Armistice Day as well as the anniversary of the hanging of the notorious outlaw, Ned Kelly, and a travel day for Lynette and me as we sit in the airport waiting for our flight to Aukland and planning our next few weeks in New Zealand.*

New Zealand is a land of contrasts with beautifully desolate sandy beaches, high snow-capped mountains, enormous icy-blue glaciers, impenetrably dense rain forests, and rolling sheep-filled meadows. Our plan was to spend minimal time on North Island and instead concentrate our remaining month of travel on South Island. Renting a camper for such a short period of time was impractical. Instead, we rented a car and stayed in hotels. With only one day in Aukland, Lynette guided us on one of her walking tours which took in the *art nouveau* Civic Theater, Albert Park with its many statues and formal gardens, and interesting Parnell Village, an avenue of Victorian buildings housing antique shops, boutiques, and cafes. We toured the Aukland City Art Gallery which included works by the renown New Zealand artist, Frances Hodgkins, and climbed Pukekawa, an extinct volcano, to visit the War Memorial Museum which boasted a marvelous collection of Maori artifacts. During our walks around Aukland, we saw fourteen species of birds. These included mallards, rock doves, eastern rosellas, welcome swallows, song thrushes, silvereyes, chaffinches, house sparrows, starlings, mynas, white-backed magpies, red-crowned parakeets and southern black-backed and red-billed gulls. I thought it interesting that all but the last three of these species were introduced to New Zealand from Europe or Australia.

Lovely rolling green countryside, sheep country, unfolded before us on our drive south to Rotarua, a center of geothermal activity which was interesting but which, for residents of Jackson Hole, paled in comparison to Yellowstone. We explored the hot pools and geysers, near which we found several native birds including bellbirds and tuis, and then visited the much more interesting Maori Arts and Crafts Institute with its traditional buildings and cultural activities. We continued south to Taupo situated on New Zealand's largest lake of the same name where we found a nice motel on the lake and several new birds including a shining cuckoo, grey warblers, and fantails.

Our route continued south through Turangi, where we saw purple gallinule-like pukekos, and scenic Tongariro National Park with its ski resorts and three 9,000-foot plus volcanic peaks, Tongariro, Ngauruhoe and Ruapehu. Sheep grazed on rugged hillsides as we made our way through the beautiful pastoral countryside toward Wellington. New Zealand's seaside capital sits on the Cook Strait, the narrow, usually very rough, body of water separating the country's two largest islands. We spent the night in a bed and breakfast on a hill overlooking the city and, in the morning, caught a ferry to South Island. The weather improved greatly as we left Wellington, and during the crossing, scores of black petrels soared low across the relatively calm sea, that condition being one that earned my sincere gratitude. Majestic Australian gannets plunge-dived for fish, and delicate black-billed gulls foraged for aquatic insects as the boat threaded its way through the narrow, winding fjord-like Queen Charlotte Sound to the ferry terminal at Picton's beautiful harbor. We checked into a hotel, and I immediately crashed, thanks to the double dose of seasickness medication I had taken that morning.

Most of the bird species we had seen in New Zealand so far had been introduced over the years. The same was true for mammals. While the islands do have a few native birds, only two mammals are native, and they're both bats. New Zealand's vegetation is also largely exotic. Over beers that evening, Lynette and I tried to account for these phenomena. We concluded the geologic youth of the islands explained its limited natural diversity. Until 150 million years ago, give or take ten or twenty million years, Australia was part of the great African/South American/Antarctic land mass called Godwanaland. Until the portion that was Australia drifted away and became the island continent, flora and fauna was shared over the extent of the land mass. After Australia left Godwanaland, life on the island pursued separate evolutionary paths for scores of millions of years, hence the unique and diverse animal and plant life thriving on the island today. New Zealand, on the other hand, is the product of relatively recent volcanic activity, and life on the islands has not had time to evolve the biologic diversity found on older land masses like Australia.

We wound our way slowly in and out of the scenic fjord-like inlets and bays of Marlborough Sound. Lynette spotted a small seaside hotel tucked into one of the bays. We checked in and, hand in hand, took a long walk along the shore of a tidal estuary. The birdwatching was pretty good, but we didn't see a single mammal. New Zealand pigeons, large doves with metallic green heads and chests and snow white bellies, flapped their wings while feeding in fruit trees hanging onto the side of a cliff. On the beach, large flightless rails called wekas foraged among the kelp while a pair of iridescent green and blue New Zealand kingfishers chattered "kik-kik-kik-kik" as they flew low along the water's edge, searching for small aquatic animals.

The morning sky was clear and deep blue, but trucks, backhoes and plows slowed our progress through the mountains as they cleared mudslides and debris from the roads and rebuilt road bases where they had eroded during recent heavy rains. Ferret roadkills were common along the way, and we assumed that this introduced mammal must be abundant. Typically, when an aggressive predator like a ferret invades an area where it has no competition, it quickly and very successfully fills the previously unexploited biologic niche. Unfortunately, most of its prey have not had the time to develop defenses against the unique skills of the introduced animal, and the ecologic result is often disastrous for prey species.

Following the northern coastline, we stopped in the pleasant town of Nelson, then continued on through the picturesque fishing village of Mapua Port to the very nice seaside town of Motueka. We checked into a hotel and then drove to Abel Tasman National Park where we hiked a track following the coast. A large flock of South Island pied oystercatchers, black and white shorebirds with red eyes and legs and a long red bill, foraged on the tidal flats below the trail. Further along, Lynette and I heard a bellbird, stopped and, with our binoculars, searched a tree for it. A New Zealander guiding three hikers came from the other direction.

"What have you got?"

"A singing bellbird." We showed them where it was.

"Where are you from?"

"The U.S."

"But where?"

"Wyoming."

"Wyoming? That's where I want to go. I've heard a lot about Jackson Hole."

"That's where we live."

"Lucky you. I want to go skiing there. It's supposed to be a great hill. What's the name of that one chute everyone talks about?"

"Corbet's Couloir. I've never skied it."

"From what I've heard, that's smart!"

We followed the Motueka River south past farms with high fences constructed to impound imported deer. The route curved west toward the sea, taking us to the coastal town of Westport where we planned to meet Mike, Lori and Zach for a little reunion. They were just now finishing their tour of New Zealand and were about to return to the States. Our schedules were such that we planned to cross paths in Westport and enjoy one last evening together before they flew home. We checked into the hotel that was our designated rendezvous site and found them waiting in our room. After a happy reunion during which we compared notes on what had happened since we parted almost three weeks before, we walked to the beach where we sat on rocks in the warm late afternoon sun. Off shore, spotted shags in their handsome breeding plumage sat on piles drying their wings. They seemed to be entertained by white-fronted terns working the harbor area, hovering and plunge-diving for small fish. Then Lori called our attention to a colony of seals not far away, like us, lazing in and enjoying the warm sun.

Our room included a kitchenette. After Mike and I went out for a bag of groceries, Lynette cooked dinner, and Lori and Mike gave us their recommendations on where to be sure to go during our three remaining weeks in New Zealand. Of course, Mike also gave me a few tips for finding interesting birds. That night, little Zach slept with Lynnie and me.

The kiddies drove north in the morning to complete their clockwise tour of South Island, and Lynette and I continued south on our counter-clockwise route. At a shop in Punakaiki, I bought Lynette a bouquet of flowers. Milk was sold in glass bottles, and Lynette declared an empty one a vase, filled it with water, and carried the flowers with us in the car. We entered Paparoa National Park and walked along the beach to the Pancake Rocks, formations of limestone rock layers stacked high above the sea which reminded me of the ruins at Machu Pichu. Towering geysers of seawater shot high into the air through blowholes as we sat on the pancake-like stacks watching acrobatic members of a breeding colony of white-fronted terns circling the area and employing their deeply forked tails to stop abruptly in mid-air, turn sharply, or dive suddenly into the sea.

Further south, snow-capped mountains rose from the sea as we followed the scenic coast to Franz Josef Glacier. Tomtits, little black birds with a white forehead and breast, sang their high-pitched trills from exposed perches in the shrubbery as Lynette and I followed a trail through the rain forest flanked valley to the glacier's face. Along the way, we could hear the enormous river of ice creaking and groaning as it crept down the mountain slope, reportedly, at a rate of five feet per day.

The Truman Track wound its way through the rain forest to Monroe Beach where the surf crashed against the surrounding cliffs that sheltered the tiny, isolated white sand beach. I was looking for birds along the trail and moving a bit too slowly for Lynette who walked on ahead of me. I emerged from the rain forest onto the beach and saw a dark form moving behind a pile of driftwood. I stopped, trained my binoculars on the spot, and watched a solitary Fiordland crested penguin, with a yellow stripe running from its bill, above its eye and terminating in a crest behind, come into view and waddle its way across the beach and plunge into the surf. I could see Lynette several hundred yards to the north standing among the rocks, watching several more penguins crossing the beach only a few yards from where she stood. I joined her. Two more of these fascinating birds appeared at the forest edge where they nest and proceeded to waddle across the beach and dive into the raging surf. Lynette was smiling when I put my arm around her shoulder.

"Now this is the way to see penguins," she said. "They're hardly aware of our presence. We had to earn the privilege by hiking here. Our reward is seeing the birds going about their business, undisturbed by human intervention."

Later, we hiked to the face of the Fox Glacier. Back at the trailhead, keas, native olive-green mountain parrots with red and blue wings, foraged on the ground for insects in the parking area. We stopped for coffee and scones in a teahouse and then continued south along the coast to Haast. There we turned inland and, following the Haast River, climbed into the New Zealand Alps and admired a number of 12,000-foot-plus peaks. We crossed Haast Pass and descended to Makarora at the northern end of Lake Wanaka. A flock of redpolls twittered from a stand of alders, and black-fronted terns whistled in flight as they foraged for insects along the lake shore. We continued along the east shore to Wanaka, a pretty little town at the southern end of the lake. With snow-capped mountains creating a backdrop for the wonderful view across sparkling blue Lake Wanaka, this could have been Switzerland. New Zealand truly was a land of contrasts. In the past few hours, we had hiked through a rain forest to see penguins on a beach where the raging sea pounded surrounding cliffs, then we had threaded our way across the face of a glacier where we photographed parrots feeding, and, now, we were relaxing with a glass of wine on the deck of our alpine hotel overlooking a placid lake that reflected magnificent shimmering mountains.

Arrowtown was an old gold mining settlement with many of its original buildings now being used for retail shops. A steady rain fell, so we stopped there only briefly and continued driving to Queenstown. Further along, we watched a score of daredevils bungy jumping from the 143-foot Kawarau Suspension Bridge. I respectfully declined Lynette's offer to spring for the tab if I took the plunge. I've taken a few crazy risks during my lucky lifetime, but I generally eschew these situations when I have to rely on others for my safety.

The small year round resort city of Queenstown suffers from an abundance of tourism but undeniably enjoys a remarkable location, sitting at the edge of pristine glacial Lake Wakatipuin, and nestled at the foot of The Remarkables, a magnificent range of jagged peaks. We left our hotel early in the morning and hiked to Bob's Peak from where we had splendid panoramic views of Queenstown, Lake Wakatipu and The Remarkables. That afternoon, we toured the town and tended to administrative affairs such as confirming our airline reservations home, buying tickets to enchanting Stewart Island, and booking a cruise on Milford Sound.

Rain continued to fall the next day as we drove to Te Anau, the gateway to Fiordland National Park. Our reservations for the Milford Sound Cruise were for the following day, so we made the best of the bad weather by doing our laundry and visiting the town's tourist shops. The sun shone early the next morning while we drove to Milford Sound, a glacially carved canyon/fjord with walls rising as much as 4,000 feet from the 1,000-foot deep, ten mile long inlet from the sea. Annual rainfall averages 250-300 inches on Milford Sound, but, incredibly, the sky was clear when we arrived at the boat dock where crested grebes dived in the harbor and drab, slaty-gray robins foraged in the forest undergrowth. The cruise followed the fjord to its mouth at the Tasman Sea and then returned. Along the way, waterfalls plunged hundreds of feet and exploded upon impact with the sea. Mitre Peak, truly shaped like a bishop's hat, rose more than a mile directly from the sound below, dominating the view from either direction. Seals lay on rock piles and ledges, possibly enjoying the rare sunshine at least as much as we did. We saw a number of sea birds, but no penguins.

One of the most sought after birds in New Zealand is the tiny rifleman. Only three inches long, the nuthatch-like species is bright green with a white breast and eyestripe and a short tail. Mike told us he had seen them in the forest at Gunn Lake near Milford Sound, so we stopped there to look for them. We had been there only a few minutes when we heard "ki-ki-ki-ki-ki-ki" calls overhead and saw a pair of yellow-crowned parakeets landing in a tree. Lynette and I looked together for about an hour without seeing a rifle-man. We decided to split up and try our luck separately. After a while, Lynette spotted one of the birds foraging on a tree trunk in the thick forest. She didn't want to call aloud for fear of flushing the bird and tried to get my attention by waving and even throwing rocks. For an excruciatingly long time, I did not look her way, and she was sure I was going to miss the bird. When I eventually glanced at her, she was pretending to tear her hair out, and I knew something was up. I ran to her to find the wonderfully coopera-tive rifleman foraging on the same tree where she had been observing it for the past five minutes or more. Lynnie had done it again. I have long ago concluded, when there is a bird I especially want to see, my best bet is to persuade her to come along and help me find it. Back in Te Anau, I asked my Sweetie to come with me to the Fiordland National Park Visitor Center where I bought her a beautifully hand-painted, life-sized replica of a rifleman I had seen there the previous day.

Lynette detests flying in small aircraft, and I abhor sailing in rough seas. We had made reservations to spend a few days on Stewart Island which, unfortunately, lies about twenty miles off the southern tip of South Island. Even more unfortunate, these two islands are separated by the Foveaux Strait, a notorious and diabolically rough body of water. Lynette chose to make the one hour crossing on the daily catamaran ferry; I chose Southern Air's twenty minute, single-prop flight. At the Invercargill ferry terminal, Lynette and I each ordered a stout. Then I drove to the airport and had another. Each of our means of transport was quite bumpy; nevertheless, we both arrived safely.

Though much smaller than North and South islands (only forty miles separate its longest and its widest points) Stewart is the third largest of New Zealand's many islands. Maori tribes first settled the island; later, European whalers and sealers arrived. Unlike its two larger sisters to the north, Stewart Island remains relatively remote and unpopulated with less than 500 people, most of them in and around the village of Halfmoon Bay. Electricity only recently became available on the island which has, intentionally or not, preserved an untouched atmosphere. Besides its intriguing isolation, our interest in the island lay in its rich variety of birdlife. Here could be found the world's greatest concentration of kiwis. In addition, penguins, shearwaters, cormorants, petrels, albatrosses and other seabirds nest on Stewart and the surrounding islands.

The Stewart Island Lodge, the only hotel on the island, was built in the 1880s and looked it. I arrived there before Lynette, only to learn that they had sold our room. The clerk blamed the travel agent and tried to shunt us off to an inconvenient and unattractive private residence, but she eventually found us a room in the lodge after I objected vociferously. It was Thanksgiving Day in the U. S., but, that evening, there was no turkey or pumpkin pie on the menu. Lynette tried the deep fried cod while I ordered an assortment of grilled vegetables. During dinner, we struck up a conversation with a dozen very friendly Kiwis from Dunedin. From the introductions, I gathered some of them were married couples, others weren't.

"Are you folks on holiday?"

"We are," responded a man who seemed to be somewhat of a group leader.

"Are you business associates, or friends, or what?" I ventured.

"We're in a share club," explained the same man.

"A shear club? That's funny, you don't look like sheep shearers."

The man exchanged puzzled looks with his friends. Then he saw the problem. "Oh, no. No. We're in an investment club, a share club!"

From my notes: *Stewart Island is a jewel. Beautiful mountains and rugged coasts, sheltered bays with half moon harbors, tall forests and deserted sandy beaches. The village of Half Moon Bay looks like it must have looked a hundred years ago. An old hotel, with a great bar and a good restaurant, and houses mostly occupied by families of fishermen. "The catch" is principally abalone and crayfish, and their price has been bid up so high on the world market that the locals can't afford to eat them. Only a couple of miles of roads and just a few cars.*

Lynette and I walked all of the roads and many of the hiking tracks. In a peaceful cove, we sat on a beach and watched two little blue penguins playing in the clear shallow water. While their wings were useless for flying, they gave the birds a remarkable agility under water, permitting them to change directions instantly and dart rapidly to wherever they chose.

With the folks from Dunedin, we chartered a small boat to take us to a beach where kiwis nested. Our only hope of seeing them would be at night. As we cruised off shore from the island, blue penguins bobbed in the low swells, and sooty shearwaters glided by, almost touching the water. Darkness had descended by the time our boat landed at a small jetty. Without flashlights, we groped our way through the thick bush, up and over a ridge running along a peninsula. Some of us had a brief glimpse of a brown kiwi along the way. We descended to the beach on the opposite side of the peninsula and saw blue penguins waddling across the sand to their nests in the bush. The group quietly explored the beach carefully, and before long we began seeing kiwis. The flightless birds easily tolerated our silent presence as, with their long slender beaks, they probed for amphipods and other small creatures feeding on rotting seaweed at the high tide line. Before long, we had opportunities to enjoy excellent views of at least four more brown kiwis. There was no moon, and the clear night was dark. Suddenly, at the far end of the peninsula, brilliant waves of light— first white, then blue, then pink—began rolling down from the ridge and over the beach, and for the next several minutes, we were treated to a spectacular display of Aurora Australis, the Southern Lights.

Kakas are native parrots with an olive brown back, a crimson rump, abdomen and nape, and a white crown. A waitress at the hotel restaurant told us they wakened her every morning at daybreak with their raucous, harsh "ka-aa, ka-aa, ka-aa calls." I arose early and walked to the next bay where she lived. First I heard them and then saw two of the birds. I returned for breakfast, and then we joined a charter boat that had a day of birding scheduled. The skipper took us to Ulva Island in Patterson Inlet where we walked through the rain forest for several hours and saw more kakas and a few tomtits, brown creepers, wekas and, foraging on the beach, variable oystercatchers. Then we paid a visit to a number of small islands with wonderful nesting colonies of sea birds including little and Stewart Island shags (cormorants), yellow-eyed and blue penguins, white-fronted terns and southern skuas.

From my notes: *Lynette thinks it odd that I can find such sublime enjoyment spending all day in a boat looking at birds, yet go to the trouble and expense of flying to and from the island just to avoid a one-hour ferry trip.*

After several perfect days, a steady rain greeted us our final morning on Stewart Island. Lynette's ferry, the Foveaux Express, left the island an hour and a half before my little plane. She was waiting for me at the airport in Invercargill. We visited the nearby fishing village of Bluff and then drove through the rain to Dunedin, the town about which Mark Twain reported,

"The people here are Scots. They stopped here on their way home to heaven, thinking they had arrived." We found an old Victorian mansion that had been converted to a bed and breakfast and checked in.

By morning, the rain had stopped, so we decided to take advantage of the sunshine and drive to the lovely Otago Peninsula, a finger of natural beauty extending northeast from Dunedin into the sea. We drove the Peninsula High Road, winding our way above precipitous cliffs and admiring the Pacific Ocean seascapes below. We stopped at a sheep station where we watched the animals being sheared. Lynette played with adorable two-day old brown lambs and bought several hand knitted sweaters made from hand spun, natural colored wool. Further along, we visited Larnach Castle, a fantastic baronial estate built in 1870s by an Australian businessman and politician. His story was complicated, but my recollection is that he killed himself after he learned that his third wife was having an affair with his son. At Tairoroa Head, the northern tip of the peninsula, we visited a breeding colony of royal albatrosses, enormous white birds with black wing-tips and eleven-foot wingspans. These pelagic, or oceanic, birds come to land only to breed and nest, and, otherwise, spend months at sea, gliding and soaring masterfully. They alight on the surface only to feed or when the sea is becalmed.

The next day Lynette led us on a walking tour of Dunedin. We visited the Renaissance style Dunedin Railway Station, a magnificent bluestone gingerbread structure, and the large Gothic inspired Presbyterian Church with its impressively tall spire. We toured an historic Victorian home and drank coffee and shared a scone under a huge statue of Robert Burns. That evening, we met some of the Stewart Island share clubbers for dinner.

We drove north and stopped in Oamaru, a town of stunning architectural homogeneity with scores of old limestone buildings constructed in the Greek revival style. The community's impressive architecture is a reflection of the wealth of the nineteenth-century goldrush era. After walking several of the streets, we drove west to Twizel, stopping in a marshy area bordering a glacial lake where Mike told us we might find the rare black stilt. I asked a ranger at the Mt. Cook National Park Visitor Center about the stilts, and she confirmed that they were there and suggested I also look for banded dotterels and wrybills while walking the marsh. We found the stilts and dotterels fairly quickly. I suspected the wrybills were beyond, across several shallow glacial streams, in the rocky glacial outthrow which looked like ideal nesting habitat for this bird. Lynette opted to pass on the wrybills when she saw me taking off my shoes and socks to wade across the icy cold streams, and, instead, returned to the car. I forded the streams and found three of the smallish gray and white shorebirds with the amazing unique bill that curves to the right, the only members of this species I have ever seen.

Mt. Cook was covered with clouds all morning, but the sky cleared around noon, and offered unobstructed views of New Zealand's highest mountain rising over 12,000 feet into the sky. We followed Lake Pukaki and then a portion of the eighteen mile long Tasman Glacier to Mt. Cook Village where we had lunch in the tea room of the luxurious hotel, The Hermitage, and then hiked a trail that afforded spectacular views of the park's surrounding peaks.

We drove north through scenic Mt. Cook Park and stopped at the Mt. Hutt ski field to look for New Zealand pipits (unsuccessfully). Lynette fixed sandwiches for lunch, and we stopped again at beautiful turquoise Lake Tekapo and walked to the tiny limestone Church of the Good Shepherd sitting all by itself on the lakeshore. We ate our lunch on a bench outside the little chapel and then entered it. Lynette pointed to the altar window in which Mt. Cook was dramatically framed.

After leaving the park, our route turned east through lovely rolling hills sprinkled with grazing sheep. Large lupine blossoms of various soft, pastel colors lined the roadside. Late in the afternoon we passed a beautiful farm, a sheep station, with a small sign that announced, "Diners and Overnight Guests Welcome." We checked in, cleaned up a bit, and then ordered a drink in the small bar. A friendly local couple who had come there for dinner introduced themselves. Later they joined us in the farm's homey dining room where twinkling lights reflected off the many colorful ornaments hanging on a large Christmas tree, and Bing Crosby sang carols softly in the background. Our dinner was lovely, and we sat for hours afterward talking with our companions. They owned a farm down the road where they raised cattle but were in the process of converting from cattle to deer. They both operated secondary businesses as well—she as a specialist in artificial insemination and he as an excavator. Much of our discussion involved politics. They complained about the growing influence in and ownership of New Zealand's economy by the Japanese. Without resentment, they acknowledged America's dominance in world affairs, expressing the opinion that someone needs to be the leader and America is the best choice since we had no designs on taking over other countries. We talked until 11:15 when they invited us to join them at a local establishment called The Blue Pub where they were going to meet a group of their friends. With significant regrets, we declined due to the lateness of the hour. We wished them well and walked to our cabin. The night was pleasant, and Lynette put her arm through mine.

"Did you want to go to the pub, Baby?"

"No, not really. I'm tired. Darwin, do you think we're getting old?"

Neo-Gothic Christchurch has been described as "the most English city outside England." Bisected by the River Avon, and with a skyline dominated by church spires, street names like Salisbury, Gloucester, Worcester, Cambridge and Manchester further betray the English influence on the city.

We checked into a lovely pink Victorian mansion that had been converted to a B&B and were assigned their largest and most elegant room. Lynette thought it was only right that our last few nights on the trip should be spent in luxury after all the primitive camping I had put her through the past few months. With a happy smile, she retrieved her New Zealand guide book, opened it to the section on Christchurch, and said it was time to begin her walking tour of the city.

During the next few days, we punted on the Avon, toured the Anglican Cathedral, the university and several old mansions, shopped at markets and browsed through antique stores, and strolled among the flowering trees and shrubs in the Botanic Gardens and on the pathways along the Avon. In historic Cathedral Square, the heart of the city, we listened to eccentrics and would-be politicians pontificating from soapboxes, watched old men playing chess with life-sized pieces, and heard the city's famous "Wizard" make his case for a world map with the southern hemisphere on top. We visited the Robert McDougal Art Gallery which featured works by New Zealand artists, the Canterbury Museum of Natural Science with its Maori exhibit and moabird gallery, and the International Antarctic Center, a fabulous collection of exhibits demonstrating exploration and scientific studies associated with Antarctica. In the mornings, we stopped for Devonshire tea, and, at night, we tried different restaurants, including one that offered an excellent and extensive vegetarian menu. Surprisingly, for it seldom happens, while eating breakfast at our B&B one morning, I met a man from Milwaukee who was also named Darwin. One afternoon we attended an Irish fair featuring competitions of little girls dancing in traditional costumes and of Gaelic drum and bagpipe bands. Another afternoon, we followed the scenic Summit Drive on the Banks Peninsula to the interesting old French settlement of Akaroa. Along the way, after weeks of searching for them, I finally found New Zealand pipits. They were foraging for insects among the roadside rocks.

Christchurch, New Zealand, December 7, 1994

From my notes: *Today, our last in New Zealand, Lynette walked us until our feet were sore. "Tomorrow we'll be sitting on that plane for a long time," she explained in response to my complaints. For the evening, we donned our best outfits, found a great restaurant where we ate a very slow dinner and got a little drunk on a second bottle of wine as we discussed our experiences over the past few months. I'm looking forward to returning to Wyoming. And to seeing Baby Abby, Krissie and Kirk. And, of course, Kiska.*

INTERREGNUM #3
Call It A Denouement?

Alice Springs, Australia, somewhere in the red desert, September 4, 1994

From my notes: *The moon will rise later; now millions of stars fill the dark sky. High in the south, Alpha and Beta Centauri point to the Southern Cross. An enormous, bright filmy cloud stretches across the night-time desert firmament—the Milky Way. A campfire burns in the distance. Around it dark figures move slowly, occasionally gesticulating—Aborigines, presumably passing along legends from the Dreamtime.*

Spent much of the day thinking about writing a book, bringing our odysseys together. Seeing the world has become an obsession occupying much of my adult life. These adventures began in 1973 and 1974—our young family driving a Volkswagen camper through Central and South America, Europe and Morocco. Alaska and Canada in 1987, Africa in 1988, and now Australia. Asia remains. When we return home, I think it will be time to begin writing.

Upon returning to Wyoming, I began, what was for me, the formidable task of writing this book. Notes and letters written more than twenty years before had to be located and organized. Some events recorded in notebooks remained in my memory as if they had occurred yesterday; others seemed distant and unfamiliar and had to be interpreted as best I could. For me, the act of writing was tedious. Usually I began working after breakfast and continued until dinner. Rarely did I produce more than three or four pages in a day. Most difficult was writing about my thoughts. Until now, my only published writing had been a series of three natural history books on Jackson Hole and Grand Teton National Park in which, for the most part, I merely regurgitated factual information gathered from my research and field work. This book, on the other hand, demanded much more, including the daunting necessity of laying out my personal and, sometimes, intimate thoughts and observations for anyone to see, a business in which I never grew comfortable. Nevertheless, I eventually transformed my notes and thoughts into the above account, setting the stage for the long awaited drive across Asia.

For some time, I had entertained the possibility that, once Lynette and I camped our way across Asia, we might become the only people who had traveled extensively by camper through every continent (except Antarctica which is virtually roadless). We had met many people over the years, especially Europeans, who had driven campers through several continents, but I had never heard of anyone who had traveled by camper through them all.

In January of 1995, I joined a friend of mine, David, and some of his friends whom I had not met before, skiing in Park City. These guys were dentists and physicians, dedicated professionals who, surprised at my having retired at such an early age, were curious about what I was doing with my life. Among other things, I told them about the continental drifting Lynette and I had done over the years. One of them, Chuck, startled me with an offhand comment.

"I used to know a guy who did that."

"Did what?" I asked, suddenly on guard.

"Traveled all over the world in a VW camper. I think it was back in the seventies."

"All over the world? Did he travel every continent?"

"Yes. I think so."

"Who is he?"

"Name's Coleman. Harry Coleman. Last I heard, he lived in California. I think I have his address back home. I'll send it to you."

True to his word, Chuck called me with Harry's name and address. The information was more than ten years old, but, with a few inquiries, I tracked Harry down and gave him a call. Sure enough, back in the early seventies, Harry and his girl friend spent two years driving around the world in a VW camper, traveling extensively on every continent. He had even written a book about the adventure. We talked for a long time, and I enjoyed sharing experiences with Harry, but I was a bit disappointed having learned that Lynette and I had been preempted.

"Harry, what you did and what we're doing really are different. You made the trip all at once, and we're doing it over three decades. But I'm kinda disappointed."

"Why's that?"

"Well, over the years I met a lot of people who had traveled extensively in campers. But, until hearing about you, I never met or heard of anyone else who had driven across all the continents. I was hoping that we might be the first, the only ones to do it."

"You are the only ones to do it."

"What do you mean?"

"You *are* the only ones, nobody else has done it... well, except for me."

Harry's book was out of print, but, with the help of our local library, I was able to locate a copy. Rather than a tale of his experiences, the book took mostly a "how to" approach, with lists of equipment, spare parts, and do's and don't's. Today, with the availability of terrific "how to" books on independent travel that cover virtually every country, such as those published by Lonely Planet, a book like Harry's would probably have limited interest. I never did learn the name of the girl friend who accompanied Harry in his globetrotting. In the book, Harry repeatedly referred to her, in the simple and eloquent vernacular of the seventies, as "The Fox."

Early in 1996, I carefully approached Lynette with the idea of camping our way across Asia the following year. I knew traveling for months in a camper no longer appealed to her. While she retained many fond memories of our African adventure, she also remembered the times when she was frightened to tears and the often terrible discomfort of unescapable tropical heat and third world primitiveness. Furthermore, she had little interest in leaving the daily Jackson Hole routine she enjoyed. While Australia had been a very pleasant experience for her, especially with Mike's family along, she knew crossing Asia would often be as uncomfortable as Africa and, at least potentially, dangerous.

For several months, off and on, we discussed the idea. In each conversation, her patent discomfort surfaced.

"Darwin, I dread the thought of it. I'm not the same person I was in the early seventies. The idea is so unsettling. My life is here."

"I know. But I have to do it. I don't want to look back on my life twenty years from now and say, "I wish I had done that.""

"Why don't you do it then. I understand how you feel, but I don't have to go along. You do it."

"Maybe I will. But I don't want to go by myself. I want you along."

"Where do you intend to go?"

"I'm not totally sure yet. I need to do a lot of research. I would probably ship a camper to Germany, drive it through the Baltic states to St. Petersburg and Moscow, then drive south through Eastern Europe and east across Turkey, follow the Silk Road across Central Asia, and then do the Indian sub-continent and Southeast Asia. Hopefully, we could spend time in China."

"OK Give me a proposal."

"What?????"

"Write up a proposal, Darwin. Describe what you intend the trip to be, and I'll think about it."

The traditional overland route across Asia used by drifters in the sixties and seventies began in Istanbul, ran east through Turkey, Iran, and Afghanistan, crossed the Khyber Pass into Pakistan, then followed the Grand Trunk Road through India and Bangladesh, and headed south through Myanmar (Burma) into Thailand and Malaysia. Political realities, however, rendered this route unlikely in early 1996. Iran and the United States had severed diplomatic relations, Afghanistan's borders were closed as the country waged a bloody civil war, and Myanmar's military leadership did not permit independent travel.

The disintegration of the Soviet Union, on the other hand, and the subsequent independence of the former Central Asian republics, opened another overland possibility that was even more interesting to me. From eastern Turkey, we could explore the mountainous Caucasus region (Georgia, Armenia and Azerbaijan), ferry the camper across the Caspian Sea, follow the Silk Road through Turkmenistan to Uzbekistan's magical cities of Bukhara, Samarkand and Tashkent, and then, provided Afghanistan reopened its northern border, drive south and east to the Khyber Pass. I had a contact in the Afghanistan Embassy in Washington who assured me that the government was making solid progress against the rebels and that the north would be secure by the end of the year. Myanmar remained a problem, but, if independent travel across that country continued to be prohibited, we could always ship our camper from Calcutta or Madras to Singapore and from there drive south to Indonesia and north to Thailand, Malaysia and the rest of Southeast Asia.

During the spring and summer of 1996, I researched the trip and developed a proposal for Lynette's consideration. I gave it to her in September along with a commitment that, if she decided to go along with me, she might choose to come home at any time or for any reason without any questions or second guessing from me. She read the proposal, considered it for a few weeks, and then agreed, if rather tentatively, to take up the drifting life once again.

For the next few months, I worked on visas and other travel arrangements. Early in 1997, the Taleban rebels gained control of much of Afghanistan, including the capital, Kabul, and closed the country to independent travel. While this disturbing development rendered crossing Central Asia impractical (the only route from Uzbekistan to Pakistan and India ran through Afghanistan), a new president had come to power in Iran and the hint of a growing detente between America and her former enemy encouraged me to look into the possibility of getting to Pakistan via Iran. These two countries wrap around Afghanistan and share a common border to the south. In addition, there was the possibility, if Iran didn't work out, of driving south through the Middle East and across the Arabian Peninsula, and then shipping our camper across the Arabian Sea to Pakistan or India.

With diplomatic relations suspended between the two countries, Iran doesn't have an embassy or consulate in the United States. The country does, however, maintain an Interests Section in Pakistan's Washington, D.C., embassy. In late February of 1997, I initiated contact with the Iranian officials and, without much encouragement from them, applied for visas. For the next four months, I ran up hundreds of dollars of telephone charges to the Iranian Interests Section, attempting to gain permission to travel through their country in a camper. Even though no one evidenced much interest in helping me, I talked with anyone who would listen. Often, when I tried to see what progress had been made on our visa applications, people would promise to follow up and then never call me back. Twice I was told to resubmit our applications. Rather than becoming discouraged, however, the intractability of the Iranian bureaucrats and their government inspired me to Herculean efforts. Getting Iranian visas became a quest. Perhaps they eventually concluded that awarding us visas might be the only way they ever would be rid of me, but, whatever the reason, in early July, just three days before we left Jackson Hole, Iranian visas for Lynette and me arrived in the mail.

From a letter to my mother: *Receiving visas for independent travel during a time when the U.S. and Iran do not maintain diplomatic relations, and doing so over the telephone, may rank near the top of any list of my life's otherwise modest accomplishments.* From my notes: *After months of frustrating effort, received visas for Iran. A lesser man would have given up long ago.*

Russia also made independent travel in a camper difficult. Visa applications required, among other impractical demands, that a schedule be attached which listed where the applicant would be staying every night during his or her stay in the country, certainly an unreasonable restriction for travel in a camper. On the other hand, Russian visas were readily issued for travelers on organized tours. Lynette read about a tour of European Russia that included a cruise from St. Petersburg to Moscow via a network of rivers, lakes, and canals and enthusiastically recommended it as an alternative to the confusing and difficult option of independent travel in that country. We decided to fly to Helsinki for a few days, and, while our camper was being shipped across the Atlantic, take Lynnie's Russian tour, and then ride by train through the Baltic republics to Germany where we would pick up our van and begin our camping trip through Eastern Europe and across Asia.

In March of 1997, I bought a new VW camper. The vehicle was manufactured in Germany and shipped to the U.S. where Winnebago did the camper conversion and made a number of improvements on the conversions that had formerly been performed by Westphalia. More important, the vehicle now was powered by a six cylinder, 139-horsepower engine, a dramatic improvement over the old underpowered vans of the past.

I found a freight forwarder in New York who had affiliates in Asia and the Middle East and made arrangements with him to ship our camper to Bremerhaven, Germany. Our family doctor brought us up to date on innoculations and supplies for our first aid kit. I arranged for international automobile insurance and, since the American Automobile Association no longer offered the service, contracted with the Canadian Automobile Association for a *Carnet de Passages en Douane*. The night before we left home, I reread Kipling's *The Man Who Would Be King*.

Chapter Seven
Nothing Is Forever: Asia

They call it Kafiristan. By my reckoning it's the top right-hand corner of Afghanistan, not more than three hundred miles from Peshawar. They have two-and-thirty heathen idols there, and we'll be the thirty-third and fourth. It's a mountainous country, and the women of those parts are very beautiful.

From: *The Man Who Would Be King,* by Rudyard Kipling

Lynette and Darwin, leaving Jackson Hole for Asia

Jackson Hole, Wyoming, June 30, 1997

We're off!

Lynette and I admired the poppies which had burst into full bloom in her garden. Nika sensed something was awry as she walked around the yard with us, wagging her tail as usual, but with a hesitating rhythm. Krissie and the girls had just left for town, and we took one last look at our log home in the mountains before we climbed into the camper and drove past our pole barn and down our long gravel driveway. Lynnie cried some, sad to leave.

The road ran north past the towering Tetons, through Grand Teton National Park, and then turned east and climbed out of Jackson Hole and over Togwotee Pass. Three hundred miles later we stopped for the night in Casper at the Izaak Walton League Campground. On our evening walk, we discussed Siberian Railway options for returning home at the end of the trip—from Beijing, we could take the Railway west through China, across Mongolia and Siberia to Moscow and then home. Or we could go Beijing to Mongolia to Irkutsk and then take the Railway east to Vladivostok and fly home from there.

July 1—Strong southwest winds gusted to 40 miles per hour and pushed us across Nebraska's panhandle, through the Sandhills. Further east, lovely farms dotted the rolling hills of Iowa. Each town, no matter how small, boasted a crisply maintained baseball field. No wonder Joe Kinsella was inspired to write *Shoeless Joe* and *The Iowa Baseball Confederacy*. Camp in Fort Dodge's lovely city park.

July 2—If Iowa were to disappear from the face of the Earth, I have to believe a significant portion of the world's supply of corn would go with it. Cross into Illinois and have lunch in historic town of Galena, home of U.S. Grant. In late afternoon, we arrive at Grammy Kathleen's apartment in Winnetka. Lynette will stay here while I drive east to visit my mother and then ship the camper. I'll return to Winnetka afterwards to help celebrate Grammy's 90th birthday.

July 3—The sun burst gloriously above the eastern horizon as I followed Lake Michigan's parabolic southern shoreline, down Sheridan Road through the Northwestern campus, and then along Lake Shore Drive past The Loop. I drove over the Chicago Skyway and through industrial Indiana, past Notre Dame's golden dome and on into the rural Midwest. Flat Ohio slipped by ever so slowly, and I found a run down campground near Pittsburgh.

July 4-7—Spent several days with Mother, friends, and relatives. Celebrated Independence Day at a family reunion in York and saw one of my favorite cousins for the first time in forty years. Mother and I took outings each day—went birding and visited a black-crowned night-heron rookery; looked for wildflowers and found yarrow, flax, wood lillies, fleabane, fireweed and poppies; met with her lawyer to take care of business; checked out the antique barns in the Amish country and ate several meals at Kuppy's Diner.

In Manheim, twice I walked unannounced into Mother's room at Pleasant View and found her singing and dancing to her recordings, a very welcome sight after the past two years of her difficult physical problems, and scenes I'll treasure for a long time. I hope she lives and enjoys herself for a few more years and pray she doesn't fall or have another stroke. Whatever happens, this is a visit I'll always remember.

July 8—I crossed the Verrazano Narrows about four hours after leaving Manheim and drove directly to the freight forwarder on Long Island. The ship's ETA in Bremerhaven was August 7. Then, at a campground on nearby Lido Beach, I removed the car's radio and stowed and locked it with the other equipment, supplies, and clothes to be shipped with the camper in various closets and compartments. Before going to bed, I had a beer with a group of firefighters and their families who were camping there and still celebrating Independence Day.

July 9—Under a cool and clear blue morning sky, I drank coffee and read the *New York Times*, waiting for the shippers to come to work. I drove past a shopping center with a Victoria's Secret, stopped and bought two flimsy nighties for Lynette to wear in the tropics. Later, at the freight forwarding office, I completed all the necessary paperwork with Neville, a genial Indian expatriate with lilting speech who seemed to be the manager. Neville gave me contacts to call in Delhi, Calcutta, and Bombay and confirmed that unleaded gas was available in India. He warned me to be careful of the water and to be aware of the awful drivers and then asked me to take along fifty dollars cash and a package of children's clothing to give to his former secretary who lives in Calcutta.

"Of course, but why don't you mail them, Neville? They'll get there a lot sooner."

"My friend, nothing of value ever survives the Indian postal system."

I left the camper in Neville's good hands and caught a cab to Kennedy Airport where I curled up in the passenger lounge with *Sophie's World*, more a primer on philosophy than a novel, and fell asleep sometime after 3:00 a.m. waiting for my early morning flight to Chicago.

July 10—Fly to Chicago's Midway Airport, take El to the Loop, Chicago Northwestern to Winnetka, and then crash for the afternoon in Gram's apartment.

July 11-12—Birded with Mike, Brock Sr. and Jr. (Mike's uncle and cousin) and Reed (a friend) and found black-billed cuckoos, Henslow's sparrows, grasshopper sparrows, and sedge wrens. Went to Howard's (Lori's father) retirement party. He seemed so happy to have his family and friends around him despite the terrible affliction that was spreading through his body. I never saw Howard again.

July 13—Happy Anniversary (34th)! Lynette's card assured me I was a "great catch." Our little celebration was properly overshadowed by Gram's 90th birthday party, a real blast! *Back in nineteen-ought-seven, a marvelous year, Little Katie O'Connor arrived with a tear.* Each of us wrote her a poem, and Krissie and Aunt Ann bound them attractively for her.

July 14—Uncle Brock (Lynette's brother) drove us to O'Hare and, along the way, explained that the facility's designation, ORD, was derived from the small town named Orchard which was razed to make room for what would become the nation's busiest commercial airport. We suffered a six hour layover at New York's JFK and then left at 9:30 p.m., in the dark, for Helsinki.

Within an hour of our departure, the northeast sky began to reveal the light of the next day.

July 15-17—A deep blue sky rose out of the sea beyond Helsinki Harbor where beautifully fresh produce was delectably displayed in the morning open air market. Enormous ferries rested at their moorings before making their crossings to St. Petersburg and Tallinn. Smaller ships waited to take sightseers among the Helsinki Archipelago lying outside the harbor.

Each day of our stay, Lynette led us on a different walking tour of the clean, bright city, and the weather was perfect. We visited the Olympic Stadium where I posed for a photo beside the statue of Paavo Nurmi, imitating poorly the classic running style of Finland's three time olympic champion. We strolled through the park and admired the flowers and birds and ate lunch by the monument honoring Jean Sibelius, the composer of *Finlandia*. We walked The Esplanade, toured the Orthodox Uspenski Cathedral with its marvelous altar screen and beautifully painted vaulted ceilings, ate several meals at a seaside pub filled with attractive Finns, and took the sightseeing cruise to the archipelago. Russian icons were featured in several shops, and we bought one of St. Nicholas covered by a brass screen and one of Mary and Jesus in a wooden box with a glass cover.

July 18—Up at 4:30 a.m., we walked to the railroad station and boarded the Sibelius for the six hour ride to St. Petersburg. Fireweed lined the rail bed, and we drank excellent coffee while watching the lovely rural landscapes speed by. Hours later, somber police officiously checked our papers at the Russian border, and the attractive farms that dotted the Finnish countryside were replaced by unpainted shacks. At the St. Petersburg station, I engaged a taxi to drive us to our hotel, the Grand Hotel Europa, arguably the best in the city. In the elegant lobby, Lynette was visibly excited. When she saw our stately room, she was ecstatic.

Nevsky Prospekt runs from the Neva River to the sea, crossing an area containing many of the city's shops, restaurants and most interesting sights. We walked the streets for several hours, admiring the fabulous pre-Revolution buildings most of which were in a terrible state of disrepair. Is this the famous workers' paradise? I bought several Matreoyshka dolls from a street vendor near the Hermitage. We stopped for a beer at an outdoor cafe, and I told Lynette that, oddly, I felt privileged to be here. It seems the people are enjoying their taste of freedom but still have one foot stuck in the mire of tyranny. At a pub for dinner, Lynette had Hungarian goulash while I enjoyed great sauerkraut and mashed potatoes.

July 19—Our morning city bus tour introduced us to St. Petersburg history up close and personal—the Peter and Paul Fortress where Peter the Great tortured his son and Dostoevsky, Gorky, Trotsky and others languished in prison; the Winter Palace from which tsars ruled Russia and in which is displayed (in the Hermitage) one of the world's greatest art collections; the Bronze Horseman statue of Peter the Great mounted on a steed rearing above the snake of treason; enormous and obscenely lavish St. Isaac's Cathedral with magnificent city views offered from its colonnaded gold dome; and St. Nicholas' Cathedral with its many wonderful eighteenth-century icons and magnificent, carved wood iconostasis (altar screen).

Our afternoon tour took us to Peterhof, or Peter's Palace, called "the Russian Versailles." Billed as the most impressive of St. Petersburg's splendid suburban palaces, Peterhof is now a vast museum featuring lavishly restored rooms and galleries. Possibly more interesting than the palace itself is *The Grand Cascade,* a spectacular assembly of gravity fed fountains and canals running through the palace's elaborate gardens. Back in the city, the evening's entertainment provided us with the highlight of this marvelous day when, at the Mariinsky Theater, the Kirov ballet performed *Swan Lake.* Afterwards, at the hotel, we were invited by a tour group from Arkansas to join them in the bar for a nightcap.

July 20—We toured the Russian Museum which featured the works of Repin and other great Russian artists, shopped in a flea market, visited a Lutheran church which had been converted by the Communists into an indoor swimming pool and was now being reconverted and restored, and stopped in a Roman Catholic church where singers were accompanied by a violin and a piano. We returned to the Grand Hotel Europa to see a display of incredibly exquisite Fabergé eggs, and then, in the afternoon, our group was transferred from the Europa to the good ship *Kirov* on which we would be sleeping for the next week. Lynette and I were invited by the Arkansas group to join them for meals at their table. During dinner, one of the women became agitated when her friend questioned the wisdom of funding the National Endowment For the Arts.

"Doing away with the NEA would be stupid! I'm tired of people trying to censor free expression!" she complained.

I found it hard to ignore her comment.

"When I go to the symphony, I don't see very many poor people. It seems possible to me that the people who benefit from the NEA are the affluent. In any case, I don't think you can have it both ways. You want government support for the NEA but call criticism of that support 'censorship.' Doesn't the First Amendment give us the right to criticize actions by our government?"

I felt Lynette's leg nudging mine under the table, her way of saying, "Shut up, Dumbo! You hardly know these people and you're already taking them on!"

July 21—We took a bus to Pushkin (Tsar's Village) and toured Catherine's Palace which was built by Rastrelli and added to by Charles Cameron. Then we visited Rastrelli's fabulous eighteenth-century Smolny Cathedral and Convent, the log cabin where Peter the Great lived during the construction of St. Petersburg, and the cruiser *Aurora* which fired the first shot of the Russian Revolution.

On the bus, somebody asked our chatty and knowledgeable guide, Elena, how the Russian people viewed the changes that had taken place since the fall of Communism.

"Young Russians love the changes, but the elderly have lost all their savings with the devalued rouble. They want to go back to the old ways. Socialism put Russia one hundred years behind the West."

This evening we attended a Russian folk music presentation with enthusiastic singing and athletic dancing. Dinner with the Arkansas folks. Very nice, but a little too much country club talk for me. I prefer living in the camper.

July 22—Spent the day at the Hermitage. Highlights include the Italian galleries, El Greco's wonderful *St. Peter and St. Paul,* the Rubens gallery, the marvelous seventeenth-century Dutch collection including masterpieces by Rembrandt and Hals, the Van Dyck portraits, and the fabulous "lost" impressionist collection.

A frank conversation with our guide who previously had been a guide with Intourist for many years:

"Elena, you are very open with your opinions about life and politics in Russia. Were you so openly critical of things before 1990?"

"In front of tourists? Of course not. But among ourselves, certainly. We guides sat in the kitchen, covered the phones with pillows, and, as you say in America, 'let it all hang out'."

Back at the *Kirov,* the Captain hosted a pre-departure cocktail party which was still in progress when the ship slipped away from the dock at 8:00 p.m. and plied its way up the Neva. Lynette and I remained on the deck until 11:30 p.m. when we sailed past the fort at Petrokrepost and entered Lake Ladoga, Europe's largest. The summer "night" was still light.

July 23—The *Kirov* negotiated its way through several locks and then stopped at a village. For several hours, while the others toured some of the homes, I wandered about the quiet streets, amused at the shy residents who stole puzzled glances at me looking into the trees with my binoculars. I identified a thrush nightingale and several whitethroats but received no more than a reluctant nod when I smiled and said hello to the people I passed. Later, when I asked Elena why the people were not more outgoing, she said the peasants prefer their privacy and don't need to be your friend. "Besides,"

378

she added, "they were conditioned under Communist rule not to talk with outsiders."

Wonderfully candid scenes of village life unfolded along the banks of the waterway—kids swam in the river, "babushkas" held babies and watched children playing, women pulled weeds from small gardens, and men fished from small boats and from the shore. Wooden houses were painted yellow, red, or blue. At night, fires illuminated campsites with tents, arrangements that appeared more permanent than holiday-like. Gulls foraged in the *Kirov's* wake, and once I saw a little gull, a species I had never seen before.

July 24—The ship entered Lake Onega and sailed north to Kizhi Island, a site of ancient pagan rituals. Russian colonists settled the island in the twelfth century and built Christian churches on the old pagan site. We visited the early eighteenth-century Cathedral of the Transfiguration, a fairy-tale-like gabled wooden structure with twenty-two onion domes, and toured the nearby, nine-domed Church of the Intercession which displayed the Cathedral's many icons. Several interestingly restored nineteenth-century peasant homes were open for inspection as well.

The *Kirov* retraced its path down the lake, now headed toward Moscow. On deck I chatted with a couple, the man a biologist from New York and the woman a travel agent from Israel. This evening, a handsome Danish couple joined our table. They live in Tallinn, Estonia, where she is Denmark's Vice-Consul. He travels quite a lot, teaching international business for the European Union. We danced the night away.

July 25—We continued southeast on the Volga-Baltic Waterway toward Moscow. The ship passed many picturesque villages, each with its own splendid onion-domed church dominating the scene, and threaded its way through many locks. Between the settlements, a mixed forest of pine, birch and fir trees lined the banks of the waterway. All along the way, children swam in the river, taking advantage of the perfect weather.

In the town of Goritzy, we visited the splendid fourteenth-century Kirilla-Belozersky Monastery, Russia's largest. According to legend, Kirill had a vision of the Virgin Mary in which he was told to build the monastery. According to tradition, Kirill was the same St. Cyril who, in the ninth century, devised the Cyrillic alphabet.

This afternoon, in the ship's salon, a professor from the University of Arizona gave an interesting lecture on Russian Totalitarianism. In the evening, the crew performed an amusing and entertaining talent show. A scence from *Swan Lake* danced by the waiters was hilarious.

July 26—The Volga River now flowed directly south toward Moscow. Onion-domed churches and monasteries popped out of each town that slipped by. Lynette and I attended two more lectures in the morning. About noon, the ship arrived at Yaroslavl, a historically fascinating town founded in the eleventh century by the Kievan prince, Yaroslav the Wise. We visited the seventeenth-century Church of Elijah the Prophet with its marvelous frescoes and icons, the Church of the Epiphany with its colorful tiles and wonderful carved iconostasis, and the twelfth-century Monastery of the Transfiguration of the Savior. On the way to the Officers' Club to see folk dances and music being performed, we crossed the town's main square, and, coming the other way, a man walked artlessly in nothing but his Jockey shorts.

Yaroslavl's streets bustled with shoppers and people going about their business. When I remarked to our guide, Tatiana, that the economy appeared to be vibrant, she indicated that was so, but that conditions before 1991 had been much different.

"There were no groceries or clothes to buy in Yaroslavl. People traveled in trains to Moscow to shop. One train was called the 'sausage train' because shoppers carried their groceries on it from Moscow to Yaroslavl and the train smelled like sausage."

"Tatiana, many of the people I talk to seem not to like Boris Yeltsin. Why is that?"

"Yeltsin was good at first. But now he is not a leader. He is too old. Russians want strong leadership. Perhaps democracy is not so important to them."

As we approach Moscow, Tatiana reflects upon the age-old conflict between the people of that Slavic city and those of European-oriented St. Petersburg: whether to look west to solve Russia's problems or to find answers within the Slavic traditions.

July 27—The highlight of our next stop in Uglich was the seventeenth-century, blue-domed Church of St. Dmitry of the Blood, which, according to legend, was built on the spot where Ivan the Terrible's son, Dmitry, was murdered by agents of Boris Godunov. Seven years after the treachery, Gudunov, the boy's advisor, became Tsar of Russia. We walked the Kremlin (seat of government) area and visited other historical buildings including the five-domed Transfiguration Cathedral.

Before 1991, consumer goods were either unavailable or in short supply in the Soviet Union. Now, especially in the cities, anything can be bought. Uglich's open air market offered endless varieties of clothes, shoes, food, appliances, and electronic equipment.

Much of Russia's uneven economy is beholden to the Mafia, a loosely knit network of many local organizations composed of former KGB agents and other thugs who deal in drugs and prostitution and provide "protection" for legitimate businesses. The Mafia bleeds substantial capital from the system, the bosses often sending hard currency to other countries for safe-keeping. The police are helpless or, possibly more often, guilty of complicity. Officials are unable to collect more than a minimum of taxes owed, and, generally, there is no rule of law. The government seems to be hamstrung, and it is not obvious how the country will extricate itself from this mess.

At dinner this evening, the Danish couple again joined us and the Arkansas group with whom, by now, we had become old friends. Later, in the ship's bar, Lynette was persuaded, incredibly, to participate in a hilarious talent show. She, Jerry, and Carol, as "Boris and the Spoofnicks," belted out a very funny song about life on the *Kirov*.

July 28—A city tour occupied our first day in Moscow. In Red Square, we visited the fabulous fairy-tale sixteenth-century St. Basil's Cathedral with its multi-colored domes and spires, and then toured the nineteenth-century GUM complex which houses more than a thousand shops. Many of the western world's most upscale names now operate shops in GUM where, prior to 1991, only empty shelves and drab merchandise greeted shoppers in the state-run stores. Lynette joined the group waiting in line to file through Lenin's Tomb at the foot of the Kremlin's wall. I had no intention of paying my respects to that despicable devil and returned to St. Basil's for another look.

For three-quarters of a century, the Soviet Union sowed misery and despair through much of the world. Happily, the Evil Empire's dreaded red banner with hammer and sickle no longer flies above the Kremlin, having been replaced by the red, white and blue Russian flag. We walked through the Kutafya Tower and the Trinity Gate Tower, 15th-century towers guarding the Kremlin's walls, into the fortress's interior and found ourselves surrounded by breathtaking symbols of the dramatic history of Russia. Eight hundred gun barrels captured from Napoleon's retreating army ring the yellow Arsenal which houses the offices of Russia's president. Five golden domes and four semi-circular gables crown 15th-century Assumption Cathedral, where most of the heads of the Russian Orthodox Church lie buried. The nearby five-domed, early 16th-century Archangel Cathedral for centuries served as the coronation, wedding, and burial cathedral of tsars. Ivan the Great's Bell Tower, 265 feet high, with its two golden domes and 65-ton sixteenth-century bell, is the Kremlin's tallest structure.

The Armoury, possibly the Kremlin's high point, contains a stunning array of treasures collected over the centuries by tsars and heads of the Orthodox Church. One room contains gold and silver objects, including the famous original Fabergé Easter eggs. Another room features jewel-studded thrones and coronation gowns. In another resides a collection of fantastic royal sleighs and coaches.

Late in the afternoon, our bus drove by a huge white building of unremarkable architecture. In 1991, Boris Yeltsin climbed onto a tank in front of the Moscow White House and inspired the opposition that aborted a coup attempt by reactionary hardliners. I found myself wishing I had been there.

This evening, we attended the Moscow Circus. I enjoyed the human acts—trapeze artists, acrobats, jugglers, clowns. But I was sad to see the humiliation of the tigers and elephants by their human trainers.

Our Moscow guide, Natasha, joined us for dinner. She seems even now to have one foot in the old days—"It wasn't all bad, you know." Natasha has been to India several times, to guide Russian tourists. She said these trips were provided by India as partial payment for Russian arms India could not otherwise afford.

Moscow seems more prosperous than St. Petersburg, and probably much more livable. It's cleaner, more modern, and not as much in a state of disrepair. The city is sprucing up for its 350th anniversary celebration. Reconstruction of old buildings may be the city's largest business!

July 29—Early in the morning, a bus drove our group sixty-five miles north of Moscow to the town of Sergiev Posad where the fourteenth-century Trinity Monastery of St. Sergius has played a major role in Russia's religious and historical past. The monk, Sergius of Radonezh, who gave spiritual impetus to the country's overthrow of Mongol Tatar rule, is now revered as the patron saint of Russia. The tomb of St. Sergius rests in the beautiful fifteenth-century Trinity Cathedral, the heart of the monastery. The tomb of Boris Godunov, the only tsar not buried either in Moscow's Archangel Cathedral or in St. Petersburg's Peter and Paul Cathedral, lies just outside of the monastery's wonderful sixteenth-century Cathedral of the Assumption, a fairy-tale structure with star-spangled domes.

Monks and nuns walk in deep meditation among the churches and chapels, museums, towers, and residences; and people pray inside the old walls of the monastery. This past Christmas, in anticipation of our coming here, I gave Lynette a handsome tree ornament that was a replica of Trinity Monastery. We considered this marvelous holy place to be among the top attractions of our trip. Lynette and I slowly and quietly explored the grounds and reverently entered the small fifteenth-century Church of the Descent of the Holy Spirit and listened to the beautiful *a cappella* music: (No musical instruments are permitted in Orthodox churches.) When we left the confines of the monastery walls, Lynette bought several more Christmas ornaments from street vendors in the town's market.

Back in Moscow, we visited the Tretyakov Gallery which boasts a spectacular collection of pre-Revolutionary Russian art (including Repin's finest masterpieces) as well as the finest collection of Russian icons in the world. The fifteenth-century *Holy Trinity* by Rublyov is regarded as Russia's greatest icon, and the twelfth-century Vladimir *Icon of the Mother of God*, is

Russia's most revered.

Tonight is our last on the *Kirov*. We had planned to travel the Golden Ring loop of old towns northeast of Moscow but now have decided to spend our two remaining days in Moscow. We're growing tired of churches.

July 30—How we managed to get stuck in the enormous 3,500 bed Hotel Kosmos, I'll never know. Prostitutes work the lobby, there is no air conditioning, and the women desk clerks are sour, nasty and unwilling to help. They don't smile and are short tempered and impatient. After being treated shabbily for the third time in a few minutes, I gave Lynette a look of frustrated bewilderment. She smiled and dubbed them "Sovietsky." (During our next few days in Moscow, each time holdovers from the old days behaved rudely, we smiled and, nodding our heads in agreement, pronounced them "Sovietsky.")

Moscow's Metro conveniently stops across the street from the Kosmos, the subway station entrance being located in the center of a thriving open air market. We descended the subway steps, consulted a map while waiting for the train, and headed for The Kremlin stop. After several stops, a transfer, and a few more stops, we emerged from the bowels of the city and walked a mile or so to the superb Pushkin Fine Arts Museum. In 1993, the authorities acknowledged that the Pushkin possessed much of the gold Henry Schliemann discovered at Troy and, two years later, they also announced the museum possessed sixty-three paintings by European masters that had been unaccounted for since World War II. The Pushkin's Impressionist exhibit alone justifies the visit, and the seventeenth-century Dutch and Italian Renaissance displays are almost as impressive.

Moscow's modern Ulitsa Arbat superficially looks like it could be a pedestrian promenade in any city. After walking into and among the many shops, Lynnie and I sat in a sidewalk cafe, drinking a cold beer in the warm sun. I couldn't help noticing the tall Russian girls who walked by wearing fashionable short skirts which properly revealed their long, slender legs. Lynette speculated that, one day, beautiful, skinny little Ana will look just like them. (Krissie and her husband, Kirk, a year before, had flown to Russia to adopt a five-year-old girl, Ana, and brought her back to Jackson Hole.)

For dinner, we tried an Italian restaurant, near the Pushkin, with comfortable seating on a pleasant outdoor patio. Lynette and I were talking about Schliemann's gold and our intention to visit Troy in September (when we would be drifting through Turkey). Suddenly, three expensive cars stopped in front of the restaurant. A dozen or so young men (who looked like they could have been Russian Mafia thugs) boisterously exited the black vehicles, laughing, shouting and gesticulating, trying to engender, it seemed, a "Look at me! I'm very important!" image. All the while they were fawning over an enormous fat guy who waddled into the restaurant, the only serene one in the bunch.

July 31—By now I had second thoughts about not going to see Lenin's mummy. The Soviets had gone to great lengths to preserve the butcher's remains, and I had an odd feeling of wanting to see what the fuss was all about. This morning, for the second time, Lynette waited in line to see the Bolshevik revolutionary, mostly to make sure that I did not carry through with my threat to spit on his tomb. As it turned out, enough guards were placed in strategic positions to dissuade anyone from behaving improperly. Besides, the walkway lies so far from the tomb that it is highly doubtful even the world's greatest expectorater could have defiled the old boy's remains. I did make a symbolic gesture, however, that made me feel good. When we reached the closest point to the casket, I surrepticiously licked my forefinger and then flicked a miniscule drop of the deposited substance in the general direction of that satanic box. Later, when I gleefully told Lynette of my private little coup, she said I was truly crazy.

City parks, surprisingly, are often remarkably good birding spots, precisely because of their location in the middle of what otherwise would be deplorable habitat to most birds. The green of the park provides an irresistable respite to an exhausted migrant which has been seeing nothing but miles of concrete and asphalt. With that in mind, Lynette and I made the long walk along the Moscow River to Gorky Park. It was immediately evident upon our arrival that, rather than birdsong, loud pounding music filled the air above the park, and "Characters of questionable intent" was by far the most common species we spotted. Disappointed, we spent little time in Gorky and soon retraced our steps along the river.

Lynette continued our walking tour through several run down but attractive neighborhoods. By now we are making progress in learning to read Cyrillic letters and getting better at interpreting street signs and finding our way around. We visited the serenely beautiful Novodevichy Convent with its marvelous golden-domed, red-brick tiered bell tower and sixteenth-century domed Smolensk Cathedral. The adjacent cemetery contains the remains of familiar Russian luminaries like Chekhov, Prokofiev, Rubinstein, and Shastakovich as well as Communist era political leaders like Kruschev, Gromyko, and Molotov. Our last night in Moscow, and Lynette found a fine, elegant restaurant where, with no rude interruptions from Mafia types, we drank excellent wine and dined slowly.

August 1—Across Prospekt Mira from the Hotel Kosmos, behind the Metro station, the All-Russian Exhibition Centre occupies two square kilometers and stands as a reminder of failed Soviet economic dreams. The complex of ostentatious pavilions and monuments previously known as the USSR Economic Achievements Exhibition, was built in the sixties to commemorate socialist success in the fields of technology, health, education and agriculture. Today those same pavillions house retail shops selling clothes, automobiles, and electronics products at prices determined by the market. A titanium obelisk with a rocket on top soars over three hundred feet high, a monument to Soviet space flight. A flea market of open air shops selling consumer goods unavailable under the Soviet system surrounds the base of the obelisk and stretches across the panoramic vista beyond. Lynette and I walked among the crowds of Russian women with children, and a few men, perusing the goods and bargaining with the proprietors. Here there was no sign of the Mafia, but we suspected, somewhere behind the scene, they were getting their cut.

Lynette and I bought wine, bread, and cheese to take along for dinner on the overnight train to Tallinn, Estonia and then caught a cab for Leningrad Station. That evening on the train, I wrote a letter to my mother in which I referred to our Russian granddaughter. From that letter: *We think of Ana often, and we have felt much more a part of what we have seen in Russia now that we have this little one.* Loud rapping on our compartment door wakened us at 4:00 a.m. Two Russian customs officials checked our papers perfunctorily, then we returned to the Land of Nod. But not for long. During the next two hours, we were wakened half a dozen times again by Russian and Estonian customs, passport and immigration types.

August 2—Tallinn leaves one with the immediate impression that Estonia might never have suffered under the Soviet yoke. The picturesque and masterfully restored Old Town evokes only the aura of the Middle Ages, and the scrubbed modern city retains no hint of the oppressive Communist occupation. We arrived in Estonia's capital mid-morning, checked into our hotel with its scrubbed Scandanavian appearance, and then began Lynette's city walking tour. The Viru Gate's twin towers flank the entrance to Old Town, only a few blocks from our hotel. We walked the cobblestone streets and visited the fourteenth-century Gothic Town Hall, several fourteenth-century towers, the sixteenth-century Fat Margaret bastion protecting the port-side entrance to town with its four-foot thick walls, fifteenth-century guild buildings, and houses of medieval German merchants, Toompea Castle where Parliament meets, fourteenth-century Gothic Puhavaimu Lutheran Church, and the Russian Orthodox Alexandr Nevsky Cathedral.

Shops displayed numerous Russian icons, treasures brought into Estonia during the Soviet era. Prices seemed surprisingly low in Estonia, giving us the impression that this might be one of the world's bargain places. Lynette bought two antique Russian samovars to be shipped to Krissie and Lori. Many people speak English, and economic and social conditions are infinitely better than in Russia.

August 3—At breakfast Lynette and I discuss the relative merits of traveling this way versus drifting in our camper. In the camper, many more interesting things seem to happen. I can see this in my notes—touring like we have been the past couple weeks, I tend to write about scenery, culture, architecture, etc., often duplicating information already contained in guide books. While traveling in the camper, on the other hand, my notes reflect our many experiences and my thoughts and observations. We're anxious to pick up our camper and start drifting!

Kadriorg Park lies about a mile and a half east of Old Town. With perfect weather, we walked through the pleasant, wooded park, where I heard and then saw an icterine warbler, to the Estonian Art Museum housed in the baroque Kadriorg Palace built in the eighteenth century for Peter the Great. Nearby, we toured the cabin Peter occupied during the construction of the palace. Then, in silent respect for their spirit of freedom, we sat in the park's empty Song Bowl natural amphitheater where, in September of 1988, more than 300,000 patriots sang out for independence in Estonia's Singing Revolution.

At Tallinn's railroad station, we talked with a backpacker from Ohio who taught physics in Madrid and was hoping to arrange for a Russian visa. Soon after our train departed for Riga, Latvia, Lynnie produced a small bag containing a bottle of wine, a baguette, and a piece of cheese. We kicked off our shoes, propped our feet on the compartment's facing seat, and enjoyed our supper.

Sometime later, the train stopped only for a moment at Tartu (Estonia). Two pretty little girls on the station platform looked into our window as our car slowly passed them. Lynnie and I waved at them, they smiled shyly, but didn't return the gesture. Further down the platform, the train came to a stop, and we could see the girls running to catch up to our car. I pressed my nose hard on the window. They saw me and laughed, then, coyly, looked away. One of them turned back toward us and waved. Then they both laughed and waved. The train pulled slowly away, and all four of us waved enthusiastically. The cutie-pies ran after us to the end of the platform as we all continued waving good-bye.

Darkness had fallen, and, with our street clothes on and our compartment door open, Lynette and I were lying down, reading, when the train stopped at Valka (Latvian border). Presently I heard a dog panting as it pattered down the aisle. Even with that warning, I sat up startled when a big German shepherd walked into our compartment and shoved its panting snout in front of my book. Fortunately, a soldier on the other end kept the leash short. The dog sniffed around our berths, found no drugs, and, after an official on the other end of the leash checked our passports, left.

August 4—The train arrived in Riga shortly after mid-night. A short cab ride took us to our hotel, a run-down seedy affair, which appeared to house more prostitutes than guests. How in the world did we come up with this flea-bag? After a few hours of sleep, I wakened to find Lynette crying. She wants to look for a nicer hotel closer to Riga's Old Town. With little difficulty, we found the very nice Hotel Riga, in the heart of Old Town, for the same price. Late in the morning, we began Lynnie's walking tour through interesting Old Riga, stopping at fourteenth-century Riga Castle, the early thirteenth-century Dom (Cathedral), several fifteenth-century houses, and the war-damaged but marvelously restored fifteenth-century Gothic St. Peter's Lutheran Church where we ascended its baroque spire and enjoyed splendid panoramic views of the city.

August 5—A bronze Lady Liberty stands atop of the Freedom Monument bearing the inscription, *For Fatherland and Freedom*. During the occupation of Latvia, the Soviets erected a statue of Lenin two blocks away and declared the Freedom Monument off limits. In 1987, 5,000 Latvian patriots assembled at the Monument illegally, and, thereafter, all rallies for Latvian independence focused on the Freedom Monument. Now an Honor Guard watches over the shrine day and night. Lynette and I paid our respects to the Latvian heroes who defied the Soviets by laying flowers at the base of the monument. Then we repaired to an open air cafe on the Daugava River for lunch.

The afternoon was lovely, and, after a perfunctory but pleasant tour of Makslas Muzejs (Fine Arts Museum), we spent most of it strolling lazily through Old Riga, where we looked into a few antique shops and stopped for sustenance in a festive beer garden on Doma Laukums, the old medieval square. Our train leaves for Vilnius (Lithuania) at 11:45 p.m.

August 6—Last night, at the Riga station, we learned there were no first class compartments. We shared with two men, which annoyed me more than it did Lynnie. She said she was too tired to care.

The train arrived in Vilnius at 7:15 a.m. After registering at our hotel, we showered and napped for two hours. Lynnie's inevitable walking tour took us to medieval Gedimino Tower, to Vilnius Cathedral where the heroic masses gathered in defiance of the Soviets during Lithuania's freedom campaign, to sixteenth-century Vilnius University, and to the Bishop's Palace which was occupied by Napoleon during his advance on Moscow and, ironically, in turn by Field Marshall Kutuzov when the Russians chased the retreating Napolean back to Paris. During lunch in a great little outdoor cafe, we agreed that Vilnius was very nice but that Tallinn and Riga were even better.

Vilnius is truly a city of churches, and, I suspect we saw them all—seventeenth-century St. Michael's and sixteenth-century St. Ann's, a masterpiece of Gothic architecture; the seventeenth-century Russian Orthodox Holy Spirit Church and the baroque Roman Catholic St. Theresa's, also seventeenth century; the baroque Holy Cross Church and the fourteenth-century St. John's, which the Commies adulterated during the occupation, converting it to a "museum of scientific thought." When it came to defiling religion, the Soviets defied gravity. Vilnius' oldest baroque church, St. Kazimieras, was converted to a museum of Atheism during the occupation. Can you imagine the arrogance? These diabolical tyrants weren't satisfied closing down the churches, they had to convert them to swimming pools and museums. But a museum of Atheism? The ultimate desecration! How stupid they were. Was it Lenin or Stalin who called religion "the opiate of the masses?" Wouldn't Communism have been stronger permitting the people to have their churches? Perhaps cracking down a bit on the church hierarchy would have been necessary, but the idiot butchers should have let the masses have their opiate. And their masses.

On January 13, 1991, Lithuanian president Landsbergis told the members of Parliament, "This could be the last session of the Parliament of the Lithuanian Republic. We have done everything we can and now we must stand with our people and see it to the end." Thousands of Lithuanians gathered outside behind concrete barricades to protect Parliament from marauding Soviet troops. Lynette and I walked to Parliament and silently threaded our way among the few remaining barricades, paying our respects to those heroes.

From a letter to my mother: *Can you imagine—knowing how swiftly and brutally Soviet tanks and troops put down the 1956 Hungarian and 1968 Czechoslovakian uprisings, these people had the courage to confront their oppressors and tell them to get the hell out of their country.*

August 7—At first, Lynette was very nervous on our bumpy two hour commuter flight from Vilnius to Berlin, clutching my arm and fighting back the tears. But she settled down after a couple of glasses of Rhine wine. We checked into our small, attractive hotel, confirmed our railway reservations to Bremerhaven in the morning, and spent the afternoon walking around Berlin's fashionable modern shopping area. We worked up an appetite and decided upon a lovely sidewalk cafe for dinner. Among the many automobiles and bikers passing by the cafe were quite a few people riding motor scooters.

"Lynnie, wouldn't it be fun to have a couple of Vespas? Can't you see us tooling around Jackson Hole?"

"If I had a Vespa, I'd probably have a head-on with a car." I caught the reference. Years ago, in Bermuda, we were riding motor scooters on a country road. We made a right turn, and, instead of staying on the left side in proper British fashion, she, by habit, steered to the right side and collided head-on with a car, flipping head over heels and luckily escaping injury.

August 8—The train ride from Berlin to Hannover revealed considerable contrast between the towns of the former countries of East and West Germany, with the latter, even now, appearing far more prosperous. We changed trains in Hannover and headed north to Bremerhaven where our camper had been unloaded from the ship, and everything seemed to be in order. Everything, that is, except one of the license plates was missing. This happened to us ten years before when we shipped our camper to France for the African journey. The artwork on our Wyoming license plates includes a cowboy on a bucking bronco, making it too tempting, I suppose, for a license plate collector to resist.

The woman who processed our paperwork directed us to a nearby campground on the Weser River. The campground restaurant served us a fair supper of beer, bratwurst, and fries, and then we spent most of the evening organizing the camper. Surprise! We brought too much *stuff!*

August 9—We drove into Bremen to stock up on groceries and found an open air market with marvelous fruit. We continued on to Potsdam, a three hundred mile drive, and camped by a canal near Sans-Souci, Frederick the Great's palace complex where, for several years, Voltaire became almost a permanent guest. While Lynnie fixed supper, I walked along the canal and found a red-backed shrike perched on a dead snag, grasping a big grasshopper.

August 10—We left for Berlin early and had continental breakfast in a sidewalk cafe on the Kurfurstendamm, a broad boulevard where fashionable people strolled past fashionable shops. Lynette said she felt at home, that this easily could have been Chicago's Michigan Avenue. Later we walked along the former East Berlin's Unter der Linden (Under the Lindens) from Alexanderplatz to the Brandenburg Gate. Allied bombing and Russian artillery fire severely damaged or destroyed much of Berlin in 1945. Enough remains with the restoration that has been accomplished in the area around the Reichstag, nevertheless, to comprehend the magnitude of Hitler's and Albert Speer's intent to make Nazi Berlin one of the world's architectural wonders.

After a look around Berlin's Tiergarten, we ate a lunch of bread, cheese and beer on a park bench at the seventeenth-century baroque Schloss (Castle) Charlottenburg, built by Frederick the Great's father for his mother, Queen Sophia Charlotte. Then on to Potsdam and Frederick the Great's park and palaces at Sans-Souci.

Why is there graffiti on every building in East Germany?

August 11—The Ukraine and Belarus embassies weren't set up to accommodate tourists' requests for visas. Instead I found a visa service that, for $370, could arrange for Lynette's and my visas in both countries. The catch was that processing them would take four days. We paid in advance as required, then visited the Rathaus where JFK declared, "Ich bin ein Berliner!" and shopped at a grocery store where we began buying and storing packaged food for use in the remote areas of Asia. Back at the campground, Lynette read a book while I went birding and found a family of great spotted woodpeckers, several crested tits, and a pair of nightingales.

August 12—A morning stop at the U.S. Embassy to pick up advisory reports on some of the politically dicey countries on our itinerary was, as we expected, pretty much a waste of time. The information on most of them was old and useless. (On our previous trips, information gleaned from other "drifters" was usually the most timely, accurate and useful.) Lynette requested and received a list of embassy and consulate addresses and phone numbers in the countries we would be visiting.

A gentle breath of wind stirred the surface of Wanssee Lake (near Potsdam), and a dozen bobbing gulls came about into the breeze. Lynnie spread a blanket on the shore, and, while we nibbled on sandwiches, terns hovered above and plunged into the lake. After lunch, on our walk around the lake, Lynette suggested we spend a few days in Dresden while we waited for our visas.

August 13—Pretty countryside and rather quaint towns characterized the leisurely drive south through East Germany. Storks foraged in the fields, undeterred by farmers working nearby with hand implements. In Meissen, we signed onto an interesting tour of the famous porcelain factory and then had a look at pieces offered for sale in their company shop. I mentioned to Lynette that, even at their discounted prices, everything seemed very expensive to me.

"Everyone sees things differently, Darwin. You paid $370 just to obtain permission to visit Belarus and Ukraine but complain about the price of a small piece of porcelain. Long after you forget about what you saw in those countries, I'll still be able to admire my little work of art."

Lynnie and I drank a beer on the cliffside patio (bierterasse) of a local tavern, enjoying the views of Meissen's fifteenth-century Gothic cathedral standing high on a hill across the valley and of the Elbe River below, flowing past the city with its fifteenth-century town hall and thirteenth-century Convent of St. Afra. We drove east along the Elbe to Meissen's attractive municipal campground. Polish Gypsies occupied most of the cabins and campsites, having come to town to participate in Meissen's summerfest celebration. When we drifted through Europe in the early seventies, the Gypsies had led a rather primitive life, living and traveling in horse drawn wagons. Evidently, things had changed in the past twenty-five years: these folks had parked Mercedes and BMWs next to their cabins and tents, and, having set up satellite dishes, were watching their TVs.

August 14—Prior to World War II, Dresden had been a major center of artistic and intellectual activity. Allied bombing in 1945 demolished the city's industrial capability and destroyed much of Dresden's Altstadt (Old City) as well, including its many famous churches and museums. Ongoing restoration since the war has gone a long way in bringing the city back to its former glory.

We walked for hours, admiring the marvelous rococo and baroque buildings. Lynnie was astonished by the stupendous rebuilding of the enormous Frauenkirche, a jigsaw puzzle-like project that required the reassembly of thousands of large stones. Standing in the courtyard of the Zwinger Palace, I was overcome by the restrained prodigiousness of the restored complex. We visited the Zwinger's Alter Meister (Old Masters') Museum and marveled at its galleries which included a wonderful Van der Meer and several great Rembrandts in the Dutch collection, Giorgione's *Sleeping Venus*, and Raphael's exceptional *Sistine Madonna*.

My aunt and uncle had lived in Germany after the war and brought my mother a small Dresden ballerina when they returned home. She was always very fond of the piece and, I remember, was so sad the day she dropped it. In a porcelain shop, I saw a similar ballerina and bought it for her.

August 15—Our passports, complete with Belarus and Ukraine visas, were waiting for us when we returned to Berlin. Back at our campground-sur-canal near Potsdam, I found a pair of black redstarts and a red kite.

August 16—The line of cars and trucks waiting to enter Poland stretched over a mile when we arrived at the border, but the officials moved everybody along expeditiously, and, within an hour, we were on our way to Posnan. That capitalism, including its oldest forms, had arrived in Poland was readily discernible. Scantily clad prostitutes lined the roadsides, aggressively and shamelessly gesticulating in an international language their desire for customers. Among the many retail shops that had apparently sprung up along the road in the past few years, night clubs and massage parlors advertised their products and services with graphically explicit signs. While it may be that truck drivers never had it so good, I cringed thinking about this new face freedom apparently had brought to Poland.

As the distance from the border increased, the frequency of roadside intrigues abated, and the charm and true beauty of Poland grew. Wooden windmills and picturesque churches and farms punctuated the rolling hills.

Birdlife was abundant in the varying habitats of mixed forests, ponds, marshes and wetlands. We arrived in Poznan in time to see butting goats of gold above the medieval town hall's clock herald the noon hour. We continued driving northeast through the legendary birthplace of the Polish nation, Gniezno, where, in the eighth century, the Polanian tribe lived in a fortified settlement and where the stout hearted Lech discovered the white eagle now symbolized on the Polish flag. Then, late in the afternoon, we crossed the Vistula River and arrived in medieval Torun, the birthplace of Copernicus.

August 17—Lynette's early morning walking tour of the Old Town (Stare Miasto) included the museum/home where the astronomer Nicolaus Copernicus was born in 1473, the fourteenth-century Gothic St. Mary's Church with its very high naves and fine stained glass windows, the fourteenth-century town hall with its large statue of Copernicus, the ruins of the Castle of the Teutonic Knights, and coffee at the town's McDonald's where the service was great and the bathrooms immaculate. The addition of cappucino to the menu didn't hurt. Torun boasts about its gingerbread, in my opinion, without good cause. The hard, stale treat tastes like cardboard. I'll take Lynnie's soft and buttery ginger cookies any time.

Driving in Poland is according to "Texas Rules." In rural Texas, there is an unwritten law that comes into play when driving on two lane highways with paved shoulders: when a car approaches from the rear, you must pull over and drive on the shoulder so it can pass. Also, do the same if you see one car passing another coming toward you. In Poland, the same law applies with a refinement: broken lines are painted on the shoulder when the law is in effect, solid lines when it isn't. I'm not very fond of this system which I find very stressful. You have to keep a constant lookout for following traffic, or the guy behind you thinks you're a jerk when you don't pull over. Worse, trucks barrel down the middle of the road occupying much of your lane, a dicey situation if you don't give way in time.

We followed the Vistula southeast and upstream to Warsaw where the beautiful river bisects the city. Here, Hitler's Nazi animals killed hundreds of thousands of Warsaw residents and systematically destroyed the city. Nevertheless, the reborn city has been masterfully rebuilt on the original foundations. What heroes there were in the Warsaw Ghetto and in the Warsaw Uprising at the end of the war! The indomitable spirit of the Poles in the face of adversity has been evident for centuries, but never more so than in the rebuilding of this city.

Lynnie's tour led us along The Royal Way past the seventeenth-century Royal Castle, the beautiful fifteenth-century St. Anne's Church, the seventeenth-century Radziwill Palace, and the enormous nineteenth-century Wielki Opera House. We visited the Frederic Chopin Museum and the

Church of the Holy Cross where Chopin's heart is preserved and then paid our respects at the tombs of Polish patriots like Cardinal Wyzinsky and Father Jerzy Popieluszko who resisted the Communist hardliners and gave sermons supporting the Solidarity Movement.

I registered at the Warsaw municipal campground.

"I am very sorry about the Romanians," the attendant apologized.

"The Romanians? What happened to the Romanians?"

"The Gypsies. They are from Romania, and they have taken over the campground. They are OK. They do not hurt anyone. But they are very dirty. There are two bathrooms. Here is the key for your bathroom. It should be clean. The Romananians are not permitted to use that one."

"How long will the Gypsies be staying?"

"Who knows? They have been here about one year."

"One year??? What do they do to make a living?"

"Many things. They steal, and they sell. They beg on the streets. Many things."

Gypsies surround our campsite. Some live in their cars, some in tents, some in small cabins with six bunks in a room. Women wash their clothes by hand. They seem very happy to me, and they obviously love their kids. In the evening, they sit in groups playing music, dancing, laughing and drinking wine or beer. Passionate people. The girls flirt with the boys. The boys primp, slick down their hair and wear spotless white shirts.

August 18—From Warsaw, we drove through the quaint Polish countryside to the Belarus border. Men and women cut and raked wheat and straw by hand with scythes and large wooden rakes. Horse drawn wagons hauled the harvest to run-down wooden barns next to dilapidated wooden houses.

An unmoving line of trucks ten miles long waited on the road for clearance into Belarus. We passed the trucks and miles later pulled up to the end of a line of cars. About ten minutes later, an official instructed us to drive to the head of the line. The line of cars turned out to be two miles long. Even with our good fortune, the official Belarus red tape took an hour and a half to complete. How long were all those others going to have to wait? Why did the man tell us to pull ahead? I wondered if it was because we weren't Poles, but other vehicles in line from countries other than Poland were not afforded the same consideration as we were. I'm sure I'll never know.

Like Ukraine and Poland over the years, history has afforded Belarus precious little independence. Greater powers interested in little more than gaining control over strategic terrain cared little for the fate of Belarusians. A fourth of the Belarusian population gave their lives in helping to defend Russia during World War II. Then after the war, the Russians displayed their graitude by purging or sending off to Siberia hundreds of thousands more.

Brest was described in our planning literature as "a lively and hectic border town." In our short experience, the town was anything but that. Our intent was to pay a brief visit to Brest, just to get a flavor of Belarus, and then return to Poland. We spent several hours walking the downtown pedestrian area and touring a few nice churches, including the seventeenth-century gold and white, St. Simon's Orthodox Cathedral. It is an understatement to declare that Brest is not a happy city. Our questions were answered perfunctorily, and not once did we see anyone smile or engage in relaxed conversation.

Brest Fortress was erected in the early to mid-eighteenth century to defend the city and was destroyed in the 1941 German attack. The ruins of the fort have been converted to a memorial to the defenders which, in itself, is admirable. The disservice, however, is the ponderous, heavy-handed architectural nightmare typical of the Soviet style. At the entrance to the memorial, loud recordings of explosions emanate from a large star-shaped opening in an enormous concrete slab resting on the fort's original brick wall. Within the fort, a gigantic carved soldier's head emerges from a massive rock outcropping, and a tall, slender metallic obelisk stretches without meaning into the sky, all of this accompanied by an amplified dirge blasting from hidden loudspeakers. Why didn't the brutes just plant a few gardens with flowers, erect a respectable historic plaque, and otherwise leave the ruined fort as it was?

Back at the border, I took it upon myself to drive ahead of the long queue of vehicles, an action which bothered no one noticeably but Lynette and me. For some reason, we apparently had the right not to wait in line. Officials processed our papers quickly, and, a half hour later, the charming rural countryside and quaint villages of Poland were flying by our windows.

Nearing Lublin late in the afternoon, we stopped to ask a man directions to the town's Botanical Gardens campground. He told us not to go there.

"This campground is not safe. It has been taken over by Romanians and Bulgarians. Gypsies, you know."

He sent us south of town to the Marina Campground where "Germans and English go." We followed his suggestion, and, on the drive to Marina, I saw a car coming down a hill toward us out of control. I pulled off the road as far to the right as possible. The car slid through a curve in the road, did a 360 degree spin, skidded right and then left, and, now beside us, had slowed just enough to steer out of trouble. The unfazed driver smiled and waved enthusiastically as he drove by and then accelerated. Somewhere I read that the rate of traffic fatalities in Poland is one of the highest in the world.

Perhaps we should have camped with the Gypsies. Here (Marina Campground) the bathrooms are filthy and the showers have only cold water. I'm afraid the campgrounds in Eastern Europe, unlike those in the

Western Europe, will continue to be pretty grim. I hope they don't bum Lynette out too much.

August 19—The weather continues to be marvelous. We spent the early morning walking the narrow, crumbling streets of Old Lublin, exploring Market Square with its sixteenth-century Town Hall, the town's fourteenth-century wall and gates, the sixteenth-century baroque Cathedral, and Lublin Castle. After having a leisurely cup of coffee in an outdoor cafe, we continued on to Zamosc, a lovely old Renaissance town largely unchanged since the sixteenth century and reminiscent of Latin America with its long arcades surrounding Rynek Wielki, the large central square. Both Lublin and Zamosc are very nice towns mostly untouched by tourism.

We called Mike on his birthday. It made Linnie a bit sad to be so far from home. We walked to the camper for her sunglasses "to hide my puffy eyes," and returned to Rynek Wielki where we sat under an umbrella and drank a beer. We leave for Ukraine in the morning.

August 20—Early this morning a long line of vehicles waited to cross the border into Ukraine. Obviously, they had been there all night. We were not terribly motivated to go to Ukraine, especially after our rather uninspiring visit to Belarus. Certainly, we didn't intend to wait in line all day and night or even longer. But I had a friend who enjoyed receiving post cards from exotic places and whose mother grew up in Ukraine, and I kind of wanted to send him a card from Lviv, the supposedly interesting and historic capital of Western Ukraine. So I thought it was worth a try to see if the mysterious advantage that allowed us to enter and leave Belarus without waiting in line would carry us into Ukraine. Not very optimistically, I pulled into the left lane and began passing the line of waiting cars and trucks, threading my way in and out of oncoming traffic. When I reached the border post, an obviously perturbed soldier hurried to my window and proceeded to berate me in a language I didn't understand but with gestures that very clearly instructed me to return to the end of the line. We had gotten as close to Ukraine as we ever will. I turned the camper around, as he instructed, and retraced our route.

"Are you upset we're not going to Ukraine?"

"Lynnie, there ain't a country in the world, other than the good ol' U.S. of A., that I'd wait that long to get into."

With great charity, Lynette didn't remind me of the money and time spent waiting for Ukraine visas.

We headed west toward Krakow and stopped for the night at a municipal campground in Tarnow. The young woman at the reception desk spoke English. In response to my questioning about where she learned to speak the language so well, she explained that she had studied English philology at the University of Lublin. Lynnie later had to tell me that philology was the study of language. We had the campground to ourselves until dusk when a Polish family arrived for the night. Lynnie and I were drinking a glass of wine quietly when she observed that we're not meeting anyone on this trip. She's right. Unlike camping in Western Europe, where people from all countries travel in campers, we are meeting very few campers in Eastern Europe. It is a bit lonely.

August 21—Krakow is one of Poland's most historically significant cities and probably its most beautiful since this medieval cultural and intellectual center luckily escaped the wartime destruction to which most of the rest of the country was subjected. We found a campground nearby overlooking the Vistula. It turned out to be the cleanest and best run operation we've seen since entering Eastern Europe. We drove into the city, parked and walked to Rynek Glowny, Europe's largest medieval town square, where, in 1794, the great patriot Tadeusz Kosciuszko inspired an armed uprising for Polish independence. Above the sixteenth-century Cloth Hall, we toured the National Museum containing the works of many Polish artists, including some of Jan Matejki's great historical paintings. In the Cloth Hall shopping arcade, I bought a chess set and Lynnie found beautiful traditional dresses for our granddaughters.

We ate lunch at a castle overlooking the city and then drove to Auschwitz and Birkenau, two Nazi concentration camps where a million and a half Jews perished. How could those butchers do it? I was too young to be aware of the Nazi horrors, but I was around to witness the excesses of Communism. I watched politicians and journalists making excuses for the expropriation of freedom and even for genocide in much of the world. These apologists went on to argue that some countries were better off under Communism. How could anyone come to these places where unspeakable horrors took place daily and make excuses for the equally evil Communist thugs?

When things go wrong in a free society, eventually we know about it and respond. The unfettered ability to criticize and to generate ideas corrects wrongs. Under totalitarianism, when things go wrong, they don't get corrected—there is no room for the ideas and opinions that force the corrections.

I look around these places and think many Germans must have known—doctors, military officers, business owners, ordinary workers. Was the price they had to pay too high? What each of us would have done is hard to say. I hope, had I been there, I would have been one to stand up and be counted.

The pollution in Krakow is awful. Those Soviet bastards cared nothing about the environment. Wherever they were, the result was an ecological disaster.

August 22—Rynek Glowny glows with an irresistible magnetic attraction. The old market square is the commercial and social center of the city. We returned there to continue our city walking tour, beginning with the four-teenth-century Church of Our Lady which dominates the northeast corner of the square and features a trumpet call from one of its towers each hour. Around the other side of the Cloth Hall, we drank coffee in the cafe at the base of the fourteenth-century Town Hall Tower. Then we visited two thir-teenth-century monastic churches, one Dominican and the other Franciscan, across the street from the latter of which was the Episcopal Palace where Cardinal Karol Wojtyla lived until he became Pope John Paul II.

We returned to our camper and found a large steel lock on its left front wheel. None of the international *No Parking* signs was posted, but a man explained that a sign posted a block away explained in Polish that parking in that area was reserved for vehicles with special permits. Seven or eight cars had already been parked there before we arrived, and I suspected nothing. I found a policeman who, after I paid the fifteen-dollar fine, removed the lock.

Back at the campground, a French family with a VW pop-top van was parked next to us. They live in Brittany and are on holiday for a few weeks. The father, having lived with a family in Iowa while studying as an exchange student in the U.S., speaks English with not more than a trace of an accent. This morning, they saw our camper parked downtown, pulled in next to us, and, after spending a few hours walking around Krakow's Old Town, returned to their camper and also found a lock on its front wheel. The French family reminds us of our family drifting through Europe in the early seventies. Their son is 9 and daughter 6, the same ages Mike and Krissie were then. The difference is, they have a third child, a 4-year-old daughter. While Lynnie fixed dinner, I walked to a marsh between the campground and the Vistula and found wood sandpipers high-stepping through the shallow water and several water rails, one of them attempting to eat an enormous dragonfly.

August 23—Poland's border with Slovakia traces the rugged ridges of the dramatic Tatra Mountains, the highest peaks of the Carpathian Range. The attractive mountain town of Zakopane serves as a popular ski resort in win-ter and a hiking and climbing center in summer. We registered at an immac-ulate campground beautifully and conveniently located in a streamside mixed forest within easy walking distance of town. Our timing is good since the town's Folklore Dancing Festival begins today.

We walked into town past a number of Zakopane's traditional houses which are constructed of square logs with bright chinking and trimmed with ornate designs. A path from the campground to town passed through a bustling, open air market with lovely fresh produce where, on our return to the campground, we re-stocked our camper's larder. In town, the festival was in full swing. We stopped to see some of the dancing competitions and other street acts, visited some of Zakopane's landmarks including an old wooden church, and rode a funicular railway to the top of Mt. Gubalowka where we hiked one of the ridge trails.

The campground bar was empty. One man sat on the patio outside, warming himself in the late afternoon sun. He waved at us when we walked by, and Lynnie, thinking he looked lonely, suggested that we join him for a brewski. Heinrich, the brother of the woman who owned the campground, was seventy-eight years old but looked not a day over sixty. He had been in the Polish army during the war, most of which he spent in England as a Military Policeman. After a bit, a German couple, friends of Heinrich, joined us. We became acquainted over a beer or two. Then we turned to some serious drinking. Heinrich set before us a concoction of chocolate tea laced with a local product, the name of which I forget, but the formulation of which was 95% alcohol and 5% something else.

The five of us walked into town to a local restaurant that had been operating in the same old log building since 1870. The decor seemed the same as it must have been a hundred years ago with old plank floors and tables and low beamed ceilings. Our friends ordered an assortment of regional dishes for us to try for dinner, during which a trio of local musicians, two playing violins and one a cello, sang traditional songs. In deference to Lynette and me, they even gave Yankee Doodle Dandy a good try. After dinner, several local couples danced expertly to the trio's rather arcane folk music.

August 24—Leaving Zakopane, our route climbed into the mountains to the border post at Polana Palenica. From here, a trail leads six miles to Morskie Oko, the largest lake in the Tatras, and a concessionaire offers popular horse cart rides to a lakeside teahouse. We paid our fare and joined the other passengers on the bouncy, hour and a half long ride up the mountain. Morskie Oko means "eye of the sea." The name is derived from a legend which describes an underground passage connecting the lake with the Adriatic. As promised, the marvelous views across the lake make the trip worth while, and, in the teahouse, we drank coffee and snacked on "bigos" (sauerkraut with pieces of sausage) and apple pastry. We walked down the mountain to our camper and then made an easy border crossing into Slovakia.

Slovakia is distinguished by its natural beauty, unspoiled medieval towns, rich folk traditions and, compared to much of Europe, a refreshing lack of tourists. Our narrow road twisted through Tatra National Park's rugged granite mountains which reminded Lynnie of the Tetons. We stopped for brief walks around the attractive mountain resort towns of Stary Smokovec and Strbske Pleso. We registered at a fine campground in the mountains near Tatranska Lomnica and then drove into the pleasant town where we strolled among the cheery residents, drank a beer in the warm afternoon sun, and watched young people folk dancing in the garden of an elegant old spa hotel.

August 25—Levoca was settled in the thirteenth century and survives today substantially unchanged. We approached the town's medieval fifteenth-century walls, entered the Old Town through the Kosice Gate, and visited the historic buildings around the original Market Square. A few miles to the east, we drove into Spissky Kapitula, a walled thirteenth-century ecclesiastical settlement, and followed a street lined with picturesque Gothic homes to the thirteenth-century St. Martin's Cathedral with its two imposing Romanesque towers and Gothic sanctuary. Then we visited the ruins of spectacular thirteenth-century Spissky Hrad. It was from this castle, Slovakia's largest, that the heroic defenders of the Spis region repulsed the fierce Tatars in 1241.

The drive south toward Hungary took us through lovely East Slovakia with its quaint villages and picturesque countryside. We crossed the border at Kral and drove the few miles to Szilvasvarad, the center of Hungarian horsebreeding where prize-winning Lipica horses are bred. There were no horses at the town's racecourse, so we went to the stables adjacent to the Horse Museum, arriving there ten minutes after their four o'clock closing time. An officious guard, insisting the facility was now closed to the public, refused to let us walk near the stables where we easily could have seen several of the horses. Just as we began to drive away from the stables, three carts, each being pulled by two Lipica horses, drove up to the stables. I switched off the car, and the guard seemed disappointed in our good fortune as we watched the grooms unhitch and care for the horses.

We stopped for the night at a municipal campground in Eger. Nearby, a small restaurant was carved into a cliff and boasted a menu of local fare. We sat at an outdoor table and ordered a carafe of red wine. The evening was pleasant, and the wine tasted good after a long day of driving, so we decided to give dinner a try. Colorfully dressed musicians roved among the tables on the patio playing Hungarian folk music. Lynette became a bit uncomfortable, however, when they lingered at our table longer than she thought necessary. Hand-in-hand, we slowly walked back to the camper and discovered I had locked the keys in the car. I searched in vain under the van for a spare key I was certain I had put somewhere in a magnetic key box. Lynnie called my attention to a small sliding window that had not been locked. It was too far away from any door, however, to reach a lock. Several spaces away from us, a German couple sat outside their camper watching their two little children playing. I explained our situation to the couple, and asked if we could borrow their small son for a few minutes. They laughed and readily agreed. I boosted the boy through the small window, and we all clapped and cheered when he unlocked and opened the door. As for the boy, he was shy at first, but then he seemed proud to be chosen for such an important task, and, finally, he was especially pleased at the Milky Ways Lynnie gave him to share with his sister. We always carry chocolate for such emergencies!

August 26—A golden oriole wakened me, screaming harshly at something that was annoying him. We were a bit slow getting up this morning, the red wine from last night apparently taking its toll, but, by mid-morning, we were well into Lynnie's walking tour of the interesting baroque city of Eger. We admired the many palaces and churches and climbed the hill to Eger Castle where, in 1552 the Hungarians repelled the Turks. After watching a political rally in the town's central square, we bought groceries at a splendid open air market and then drove to The Valley of Beautiful Women (Szepasszonyvolgy) where we tasted wine in several of the many caves and bought a liter of their famous "Bull's Blood" for sixty cents.

Szentendre (St. Andrew) sits on the Danube, twelve miles north of Budapest. The picturesque town has become a favorite for artists, and, while the winding streets and old buildings have a certain charm, I think there may be more tourists here than in the collective remainder of Eastern Europe. We visited the interesting Kovacs Margit Museum of decorative ceramics featuring Hungarian folk-art and, from an old Catholic church, we admired hilltop views of the town and the Danube. Here at our campground on the Danube, Lynette went to bed early, convinced she is still feeling the effects of cheap Hungarian wine.

August 27—Budapest bills itself as the Paris of Eastern Europe, certainly with some, if not total, justification. The Danube divides the city, with Buda featuring the historic castle district and Pest boasting the fashionable Vaci utka shopping area. We stopped early this morning at the Romanian and Iranian embassies to see if either country experienced any recent developments that would affect our travel and then at the American Express office for mail. Later, at Pest's City Park, we toured the Museum of Fine Arts with its marvelous European collection, the nineteenth-century neo-Renaissance State Opera House, and St. Stephen's Basilica with its 315-foot dome and where the right hand of the founder of Hungary, St. Stephan, is enshrined.

We drove to downtown Pest and parked in the last available space in a cul-de-sac. I bought a two hour parking ticket from the well-marked machine on the street and placed it on the dashboard. When we returned, one-half hour later, our camper was nowhere to be seen. My heart sank to the pit of my stomach. I looked around and saw a cab driver walking toward me. He told us the police had towed the van away because it was parked in a wheel-chair space. He pointed to a sign that, in Hungarian, designated that one space for the handicapped. He said he knew where the cops had towed the car and offered to take us there. The cab had no meter, and I followed our route on my map, quickly discovering we were taking the long way. When we arrived at the police impoundment area, the cabbie asked for $40. By now I suspected what had happened: Since we had only been away from the car for a half hour, the driver had called the police as soon as we left knowing he would get the fare when we returned.

I handed the cabbie $15 and said that was all he was getting. He was furious, insulted my ancestry, and drove off. I paid the police $45 to get the car back and drove off in a funk, ready to get the hell out of Budapest. Lynnie's cooler head prevailed, and we drove to Buda Hills where we found a lovely campground nestled in a wooded canyon.

The nighttime lights of Budapest are spectacular. A glass or two of wine and dinner had put me in a better mood, and I readily agreed with Lynette to drive back into the city. Buildings on both sides of the Danube, including Parliament and Buda Castle, are outlined in light as are the river bridges, including the very elegant lines of Chain Bridge. This day now ended on a far better note than seemed likely a few hours ago.

August 28—A beautiful morning accompanied our visit to Old Buda. We toured the fifteenth-century Palace of Buda Castle with its wonderful collection of Hungarian art and the Mathias Church where Liszt composed the *Hungarian Coronation Mass* for the crowning of Austria's Franz Josef and his wife, Elizabeth, as king and queen of Hungary. We visited St. Stephen's equestrian statue and Fisherman's Citadel which offers splendid views of Parliament and the Danube. We wrote the children while sipping cappuccino in an outdoor cafe, and I thought of Lynette's father who had, years ago, regaled us with stories about his experiences in Budapest before the war.

A short drive south from Budapest took us to Lake Balaton where, on a lovely, sandy beach, we found a large campground full of Hungarians on holiday. We did our laundry by hand and then walked on the beach. Later, after enjoying dinner at a colorful local restaurant, Lynnie took me by one stroke in a game of miniature golf.

August 29—The Tihany Peninsula stretches a good portion of the way across Lake Balaton. We caught the first ferry (7:40 a.m.) across the strait and then continued east to the Hungarian *puszta*, the Great Plain where Hungarian cowboys tend their forked-horn gray cattle, and nomadic shepherds watch their twisted-horn sheep.

At Kiskunsag National Park in the Bugac *puszta*, we stopped to see a whip-snapping cowboy holding long reins that stretched to each of five horses, gallop at full speed while standing with each foot on the back of two rear horses, the other three horses in the lead. Several cowboys galloped full speed and drank beer from a pilsner glass without spilling it while others performed tricky demonstrations with whips. The rains came just as the show finished, and we were drenched by the time we walked the two miles back to the camper.

Sitting in a campground in Cserkeszolo, we still had some drying out to do, but the "bull's blood" tasted good. German campers surrounded us, the popularity of this area due to its nearby thermal pools. I suppose these folks don't want to pay Baden-Baden's prices.

August 30—We drove through pastoral scenes that could have been painted by Millet—rolling hills where the grain was being harvested by men with scythes and women with wooden rakes. The rain continued as we drove toward Romania. Lynette was concerned—we had heard that the Hungarian-Romanian border crossings were interminable, the campgrounds awful, and the drivers worse.

Whatever the experience of others, we made the border crossing smoothly in less than an hour. In the Romanian mountains, we wound our way over deteriorated muddy roads being worked on with manual labor and concluded that these roads were too bad for even the worst drivers to take chances on. Then we pulled into a beautiful Dutch-owned campground that was only a year or two old and had marvelous facilities. We drank good Romanian wine and ate excellent local food at the campground restaurant. This isn't such a bad introduction to Romania!

August 31—Cluj-Napoca, the capital of Translyvania, traces its history back two thousand years. Over the centuries, the town came under the control of the Dacians, Romans, Goths, Huns, Petchenegs, Tatars and Hungarians. On a rainy Sunday morning, it was with some difficulty that we found a legal money changer hidden away on one of Cluj's narrow back streets. We drove around the Piata Unirii (Town Center) with its huge equestrian statue of the fifteenth-century Hungarian ruler, King Matthias, and inspected several of the town's fine medieval churches and buildings. The rain continued, and so did we, driving on muddy mountain roads, to Sighisoara, a beautifully preserved medieval town and the birthplace of Vlad Tepes the Impaler, better known as Count Dracula. The local campground was closed, so we checked into this small hotel, and I'm in a pissy mood.

After traveling through a good chunk of the Communist world, I am amazed that American journalists let these guys off the hook for so many years. They actually tried to make it sound like Communism was a better system for some of these countries. Why didn't they tell us that, under Communism, these countries had fallen a hundred years behind the western world? That they were able to keep it going only on the backs of the peasants, by taking their land and depleting their natural resources? That the Soviet (Evil) Empire was an ecological disaster? That they ravished the human spirit? We heard the steady drumbeat against dictators the west tolerated or propped up, but hardly a word about guys like the Romanian megalomaniac, Nicolae Ceausescu, who didn't give a damn for the people but created a kingly lifestyle for himself and his family, bankrupted the country by lavishly spending on ridiculous architectural projects, and, in the name of development, ecologically destroyed the Danube Delta. These guys screwed the masses, screwed the environment, and screwed beauty, creativity and the soul. Where the hell were all the journalists? I don't feel so good—I've had too much "blood of the bull." And Princess Diana is dead.

September 1—We walked around Brasov's charming medieval square and, on the way out of town, stopped at Brasov's charming McDonald's. I still didn't feel well and thought a large vanilla milk shake might help. Lynnie and I sat in the sun which was shining for the first time in days, slowly sipping our drinks, when a couple with two teenage children walked across the parking lot to our camper. They were a missionary family from Wisconsin who had been in Romania for five years. During our conversation, the father suggested we drive through Bulgaria as fast as possible.

"They'll steal your car and everything you have. The place is terrible."

In Risnov, we visited the ruins of a marvelous fourteenth-century hilltop castle and then continued south to a beautifully restored fourteenth-century fairy-tale castle in Bran. Tourist merchandise in the small town's shops would lead you to believe Bran Castle belonged to Count Dracula, but other sources indicate there is no evidence Vlad Tepes ever lived there.

September 2—The castle was closed yesterday until this morning, so we walked around town and talked with a group of Aussies traveling in camper vans. I felt lousy last evening, and, lying in the camper, endured terrible abdominal pains. I kept trying different positions without any relief. Miraculously, about 1:00 a.m., the pain was gone.

I arose early and, while waiting for Bran Castle to open, walked around the area to see what birds were about. In a filthy garbage strewn yard behind a government building, I saw considerable bird activity, including several hyperactive Bonelli's warblers. An official-looking man approached the building and, when I asked permission to enter the yard to look for birds, smiled and said of course I could. Ten minutes later, a bulky looking woman walked over to me and, unceremoniously, told me to leave the premises. I told her about the man giving me permission, and she became infuriated. So I left.

Lynnie and I toured Bran Castle unaccompanied and at our own pace. We saw all the rooms one would expect in a medieval castle, and they were furnished in authentic period furniture. A woman caretaker took us into her confidence and led us to several off-limits rooms where, she claimed, some of the furnishings belonged to Vlad Tepes himself.

Our route followed the Prahova River as it tumbled down the rugged slope of the Bucegi Mountains to the ski resort town of Sinaia. We visited the Sinaia Monastery and Peles Castle, a fabulous German Renaissance palace that Ceausescu turned into a private retreat for him and his Commie pals. Then we continued south to Bucharest only to find that the municipal campgrounds were closed for the season. In the most elegant section of a town that screamed for elegance, we drove into the grand entrance loop of the glitzy looking Hotel Sofitel. Inside, I explained to the room clerk that we were on a seven or eight month journey across Eastern Europe and Asia, that the two Bucharest campgrounds were closed for the season, and that we needed a safe place to park for the night. The clerk led Lynette and me to the bell captain and explained the situation to him. The bell captain told us to feel free to use the hotel's rest rooms (which were immaculate, modern and included showers) and then took us to the parking attendant and instructed him to let us enter and leave the gated area at will. I gave the captain five dollars, and he seemed ecstatic. Later, Lynnie learned from the desk clerk that a double room went for $300 per night.

People in Eastern Europe, with exceptions, are not outwardly friendly. Is it their nature or is it a product of living under generations of oppression? From a letter to my mother: *The people (in Eastern Europe) generally are surly and unfriendly.* So far, this trip has been interesting but not a whole lot of fun. Hopefully Turkey will be better.

September 3—"Everything is as expected in America," was the response of a Russian exchange student to a sponsor who had wanted to know what the boy liked best about his stay in the U.S. When pressed to elaborate on what he meant by that, the student explained that things work properly—toilets flush, lights go on, engines start and water flows when a faucet is turned. Such is often not the case in Russia and Eastern Europe. They build new facilities but don't maintain them, and, soon, nothing works.

Bucharest boasts tree-lined boulevards, parks with lakes, and many monuments and public buildings. But the city is mostly ugly. The streets are dirty and dangerous, the parks and lakes and fountains are strewn with garbage, and the buildings and monuments are repulsively prodigious and impersonal. Certainly Bucharest has many redeeming qualities and a few interesting buildings and sights, but I found none of the old world charm or

Parisian flavor suggested in some guide books. Lynnie and I walked through a large debris-strewn city park where not even the children smiled, and the waiter who served us wine in an open-air cafe was surly.

While the country's economy was foundering and the peasants were starving, Ceausescu expropriated their meager resources to build gigantic monuments to socialism. Lynette and I stared aghast at the Stalinesque enormity and sterility of Ceausescu's House of the Republic in which this champion of the proletariat intended to house the Communist party and Romania's government. Making room for the monstrosity, sadly, required the demolition of many fine historic buildings. On the streets converging like spokes into the House of the Republic, Ceausescu constructed rows of plush apartment buildings to house the *nomenklatura*, the privileged few of the bureaucracy. Unlike many of the world's Communist leaders, however, Romania's butcher received his just desert. On December 23, 1989, Nicolae Ceausescu and his wife, Elena, after standing trial before the people of Romania, were executed by a firing squad.

Two mile long Friendship Bridge spans the Danube and connects Giurgiu, Romania, with Ruse, Bulgaria. To our relief, the border crossing was smooth and easy, taking less than an hour. Lynette waited in the camper while I went to a shop to change money. Several boys wanted to wash our windows and proceeded to do so even after Lynette told them the windows were fine as they were. I returned as two of them climbed on the front bumper with their sponges. I chased the boys away and could see Lynnie was near tears.

We drove east toward the Black Sea through pleasant countryside and poor, backward villages. We stopped first to see the twelfth-century Shumen Fortress and then again at Madara where an eighth-century relief of a horseman spearing a lion is carved into a cliff. At Varna, we experienced the luxury of reading street signs in Latin as well as Cyrillic and easily found our route leading south along the gorgeous Black Sea coast. At Slanchev Bryag (Sunny Beach), we registered at a campground on the sea. We took a swim, then, while Lynnie fixed supper, I walked along the sandy beach and saw Mediterranean and yellow-legged gulls sleeping in the afternoon sun, pygmy cormorants drying their wings, a pair of little ringed plovers each standing on one leg, and Isabelline wheatears foraging for sand-dwelling insects. Now a million stars fill the sky, and, in a pavilion down the beach, I can see Gypsies dancing to their happy music.

September 4—On a sunny, cool morning, we explored ancient Nesebar which traces its history back to when it was the sixth-century BC Greek settlement of Mesembria. Today Nesebar is primarily a fishing village, but remnants of second-century AD walls and the ruins of a fifth-century AD church may easily be seen in the small town which occupies a rocky peninsula connected to the mainland by a narrow causeway. Many medieval buildings remain, including St. Stefan's Church which dates from the eleventh century. Architecturally, St. Stefan's preserves the unique Nesebar Style of white stone and red brick layers forming its walls, striped arches spanning its rectangular columns, and ceramic rosettes decorating its facades. Narrow cobblestone streets wind through the picturesque town past houses with stone foundations and timber upper construction jutting over the streets. The sea is visible from almost anywhere in town. We stopped for coffee and watched foraging oystercatchers come in and out of focus as the surf pounded the rocky coast, propelling its spray between us and the morning sun's rays.

Continuing south, we entered Burgas on a road with two southbound lanes, the right one marked for exit only. A speeding car behind me began blowing his horn without stopping, apparently wanting me to pull to the right so he could pass. I didn't want to exit and the traffic was such that it would have been dangerous to pull over, so I continued as I was. He continued blowing his horn and, about a hundred yards further along, he found enough room on the left to pass, yelling at me as he went by. I flipped him an internationally known gesture, and he hit his brakes so I would catch up to him. As I pulled to his side, he pointed a hand gun at my face. I pressed the gas pedal and lurched ahead of him. He sped up as well, and we approached a fork in the road just as he was catching us. I hit the brakes, allowing him to speed past us. The fork was upon us, and, when he committed to the left, I took the right fork.

What an experience! This was a clean cut looking kid. Certainly we have run into nice people in Eastern Europe. But, generally, from Russia to Bulgaria, these people have been unfriendly at best and surly and malevolent at worst. To the extent this is true, is it the result of living under regimes of fear? That is, don't be friendly, you never know who might be listening. Or does it have something to do with might makes right? If you have the power, screw anyone who steps in your way.

We entered Turkey, and, what a difference! With the exception of one arrogant border official, everyone has been friendly and helpful, expecting nothing in return. Drivers are polite, villages seem much more prosperous, and things seem to work and are better cared for. We registered at a campground near Istanbul's airport. Tonight the moon is of fingernail proportions, and, in an imitation of Turkey's flag, Jupiter is resting just outside the crescent. An augury of pleasant times in Anatolia?

September 5—We spent the morning cleaning the camper. A Polish backpacking free-lance photographer had set up his camp next to us. He had only a mosquito net covering his sleeping bag which was stretched on the ground. He was returning to Poland after a photography assignment in India, Pakistan and Iran. During a description of his travels, he told us he had been harrassed pretty badly in Tehran. He had made arrangements to go into downtown Istanbul and asked us to keep his film canisters in our camper for safety, a request we readily agreed to.

After the Pole left, Lynette began crying. His problems in Iran brought her worse fears to the surface. She said she just can't come to terms with going to Iran. I hugged her, and she apologized for losing it again.

"Darwin, I'll go home. You go on by yourself. I know you need to do this." Then she went to the bathroom to wash her face. In the few minutes she was gone, I quickly decided crossing Asia is not worth it. Lynnie has made a great effort over the years to indulge my drifting urges, but now she's frightened to death. How much do I want to cross Asia versus just wanting to complete the dream? I've done enough harm to our marriage. No more.

When Lynnie came back to the camper, she was still trembling.

"Lynette, I don't want to go on by myself. I love you. The only way I'm going anywhere is with you."

"But you need to do this. You can't stop now."

"Yes I can... believe me. I was thinking while you were washing your face. I have a proposal for you."

"Not another proposal?" she laughed.

"Here's what I'm thinking. Let's continue doing Turkey. It's safe, interesting and it should be fun. When we get to Cappadocia, depending on what you're thinking, we can do one of three things: Head east and take the camper through Iran. If you still don't want to do that, we can drive south through the Middle East and ship to India from the Arabian Peninsula. If that's not appealing, let's give up on driving across Asia. We'll drive back to Greece or Italy or Spain, wherever we want to go. Maybe, if we want to, we'll spend the winter there. Or maybe we'll ship the camper home and hop-scotch across Asia by plane. Or maybe we'll just go home. Whatever the case, we're not doing anything unless you really want to do it... and, anything we do, we do it together!"

Lynette felt much better, and so did I. Whatever we end up doing, all of this has still been a good story. I feel a bit like I imagine Frank Wells, the Disney exec, felt when, in the book *The Seven Summits*, he was faced with the choice of climbing Everest or losing his wife. To him, it was an easy decision—he loved his wife. To me, it's just as easy. I love Lynette. (I just hope that now I don't die in a helicopter crash.)

This afternoon we hired a cab to take us to the medieval Grand Bazaar, an enormous covered market which is divided into souks selling carpets, jewelry, clothes, books and almost anything else. We first started seeing Muslim minarets in Bulgaria, now they dominate the skyline. The cab driver wound his way through the colorful and crowded narrow streets past the fifteenth-century Beyazit Mosque, the fourth-century Forum of Theodosius, and Istanbul University. Lynette bought a gold charm for Krissie and harem slippers with pointed toes for our granddaughters. With the pressure off of driving through Iran, we both had a splendid time.

I tried to fill the camper's propane tank and learned that the fittings used to do so in Asia were different from those in Europe. With nothing in it for him, the friendly and very helpful owner of the propane filling station where we had stopped sent one of his men with us to a garage that could change our fitting. It's difficult to imagine that kind of helpfulness happening in Eastern Europe. We made arrangements to have the work done tomorrow.

Back at the campground, an overland truck full of Aussie women has just arrived. As I write, the Sheilahs are setting up camp, and the Faithful are being called to prayer.

September 6—I left the car at the garage to install an adapter for the LPG (propane) system, and Lynnie arranged for a tour of Istanbul tomorrow. We washed our clothes by hand and enjoyed a day of relaxation and reading. I picked up the camper—$115 to install the adapter, including a full tank of propane.

September 7—Driving in Istanbul is not for the faint of heart or for anyone in a hurry. Traffic is heavy, and the streets are narrow. Happily, the tour Lynnie chose included our being picked up by a mini-van which arrived at the campground at eight o'clock. Our first stop was the sixth-century Aya Sofya (St. Sophia) which was built by Justinian and, for a thousand years, was Christianity's largest church. Across the street sat the sublime Blue Mosque which was built in the seventeenth century by Sultan Ahmet I. Six slender minarets and numerous domes grace the exterior. We removed our shoes and admired the luminous blue tiled walls and the hand woven carpets on the floor. Then we visited the Hippodrome, the scene of third-century chariot races, with its obelisk of Theodosius, a 3,500-year old column from Egypt's Temple of Karnak, and, in the nearby sixteenth-century palace of Suleyman the Magnificent's son-in-law, toured the Turkish and Islamic Arts Museum with its impressively illuminated Korans, exquisite carpets, and other historical *objets d'art* from Turkey's past.

Our young guide, Turget, was a knowledgeable Moslem who carefully explained points of interest and responded eagerly and in detail to our questions about his religion. This was a part-time job for him while he studied economics at the university. Turget talked readily about himself and his life. At the time, he was pining mightily over a woman he loved. For some reason of which the young man claimed to have no clue, her parents had forbidden the girl to see him.

After a fine lunch of local specialties, we toured the sprawling and fortified, fifteenth-century Topkapi Palace with its exhibits of priceless porcelain and silverware, its lavishly decorated rooms, its treasury of diamonds, emeralds and gold, and its shrine of Holy Relics containing the Prophet Mohammed's cloak, samples of his teeth, hair and footprints, and, of course, his sword. Our next stop was the Suleymaniye, the grand sixteenth-century mosque complex where Suleyman the Magnificent and his wife are entombed. Finally, we visited a government run carpet weaving company. The operation began with silk being extracted from the worms' cocoons and then spun into thread. The thread was then dyed with natural colors, dried, and mounted on looms where skilled women hand wove splendid silk carpets, often spending years on the same piece of art.

September 8—Perched atop the narrow peninsula extending south from Gallipoli, Ataturk and his heroic soldiers defended the Dardanelles and Istanbul from a larger and equally heroic, but poorly commanded, force of Australians, New Zealanders and Brits. We visited the well cared for monuments and cemeteries above Anzac Cove and, with tears in our eyes, paid our respects to the many who died from both sides. What a bloody and horrible battle! The older I am, the more of a pacifist I become. Why did all those Anzac boys have to die fighting for the British? Why did the Turkish boys have to die for the Germans?

A short ferry ride took us from Eceabat across the Dardanelles to Cannakkale. At a gas station, we chatted with a backpacker from Alabama who had ridden his motorcycle from South Africa around the Middle East to Turkey. He intended to ride through Eastern Europe and finish his trip in Scandinavia. We continued south along the beautiful Aegean coast and stopped at a campground on the beach. Happier than we had been on the whole trip, we walked on the beach and found a marvelous local restaurant. We ordered a bottle of wine and sat outdoors, listening to the muffled sound of the surf and watching the sun set over the Aegean. People were laughing, and the waiter was impossibly friendly and nice. He led us into the kitchen to meet the cook and sample the numerous choices of local fare offered this evening.

"Now," Lynette smiled when we returned to our table, "I'm having fun. The Turks are so friendly. We're meeting some people along the way. The weather is great. And the beaches are superb."

September 9—The ruins at Troy indicated to me that Priam's city had to be far too small to accommodate the cast of many thousands Homer described in *The Iliad*. Nevertheless, I was moved by the experience of walking through the archeological levels discovered by Heinrich Schliemann in the 1870s, especially Level VI, the generally accepted scene of Ilios, the Troy over which the epic battle was waged. Here warriors from the Mycenean kingdoms conducted a ten year siege to extract revenge for the abduction of Menelaus' wife, Queen Helen of Sparta, by Priam's son, Paris. I stood outside Priam's walls remembering Homer's descriptions of the fearsome battles and visualized "Achilles of the Great War Cry" dragging Hector's lifeless body to the Achaean camp. I thought the site's museum was quite good and instructive, even though, outside of it, the all too apparent, life-sized replica of the Trojan horse was a bit "kitschy."

We drove south along the Aegean Sea coast to Behramkale, where, more than 2,000 years ago, Aristotle looked from the mountaintop Temple of Athena across the sea to the Greek island of Lesbos, and, today, Lynette and I did the same. We carefully descended the steep hill to Behramkale's small, picturesque *iskele* (fishing port) where we camped on the beach below a hillside sprinkled with Roman ruins. Our late afternoon walk under the coastal cliffs produced a number of birds we had never seen before, including Kruper's and rock nuthatches, sombre tit, blue rock thrush, rock bunting, and the elusive Orphean warbler, which, as its coarsely unpleasant song betrays, must have derived its name from something other than an Orphean ability to create beautiful music. On the way back to our campsite, we stopped at a restaurant on the pier and, watching the sun set on Lesbos' western slope, enjoyed a dinner of marvelous local food. All in all, a wonderful day!

September 10—With beautiful weather continuing to hound us, we drove to Ayvalik, crossed a causeway to an island and found another lovely place to camp on the beach. Our alimentary canals seemed to be rebelling a bit against the delicious but oily and rich Turkish food, so we settled for a supper of canned corn soup and fresh bread in the camper.

September 11—South of Ayvalik, a flock of more than a thousand greater flamingos foraged in a coastal estuary. Their bills, legs and flight feather edgings colored by the carotene in their diet created a shimmering pink aura connecting the impressive but colorless salt flats expanse with the deep blue early morning sky.

The ancient ruins of the Acropolis of Pergamum, a small but cultured and powerful Alexandrian kingdom, lie on a hilltop outside the modern city of Bergama. Lynnie and I climbed over the many temples and other buildings and sat on a wall from where we saw the Aegean Sea in the distance. I glanced across to another section of wall and, perched in a rocky cavity and staring at me with large yellow eyes was a little owl, a small diurnal species no more than eight or nine inches high which not infrequently may be found in the nooks and crannies of ancient rocky ruins.

We continued south along the coast through Izmir (ancient Smyrna and birthplace of Homer) to Selçuk, the town closest to the remarkable ruins of Ephesus. We found a campground situated in a grove of lime trees, home to a family of Syrian woodpeckers, and discovered our arrival coincided with the beginning of the International Air Exposition which Turkey was hosting. Selçuk was to be the scene of the parachuting competition, and teams from many of the participating countries were staying at this campground. The scene was colorful and festive as the grounds were being prepared for the evening's dancing and partying. Lynnie and I walked to the ruins of the Temple of Artemis, one of the Seven Wonders of the Ancient World, a deteriorated and unreconstructed site that unfortunately does nor reflect in any apparent way its original splendor. Back at the campground, a rug merchant sold us an old and splendid, hand-woven silk rug at a price he claimed was extraordinarily low for each of the following reasons that he offered at various times throughout his sales pitch. Take your pick: 1. His monthly payment was due to the bank. 2. We were his first sale of the evening, and it's important to get the first one out of the way, because it brings you luck for the remainder of the evening. 3. His brother recently moved to Chicago and has been treated very well by Americans, and he wants to reciprocate.

September 14—Much of our morning was spent watching parachuters making spectacular dives from small aircraft high in the sky. One contestant plunged so close to the ground without his or her parachute opening that he or she disappeared behind a small hill without, as far as I could see, the chute ever opening. Fortunately, we didn't hear any sirens or see any signs that someone had bitten the dust, so to speak, so we chose to believe that the diver's chute opened in time behind the hill.

Ephesus can be traced back at least 3,000 years to its Greek origins when it was a dominant city in the Ionian Confederation. Later, in the period of Roman ascendancy, Ephesus was the capital of Asia, and today many of that ancient city's buildings are remarkably preserved or restored. It is one of the world's most impressive sites of antiquity. The ancient amphitheater is one of the world's largest—capable of seating 24,000 people. Lynnie and I walked among the houses of the affluent on Marble Way and visited outstanding structures such as the Fountain of Trajan, the Celsus Library, and the Temple of Hadrian.

On the drive south to Bodrum, we met an English couple in a camper. This fellow intends to drive across Asia to Singapore. After touring Turkey, his wife plans to go home to England and then fly back to join him in India. Unfortunately, he won't be leaving for Iran for two more months. Too bad. Would have been a good companion if we do choose to cross Iran.

In Bodrum, we visited the site of the Tomb of King Mausolus which is another Wonder of the Ancient World. Over the years, we've been to five of the seven locations—Mausolus' tomb, the Colossus of Rhodes, the Pyramids at Giza, the Temple of Artemis, and Olympia's Statue of Zeus. (We're missing Nebuchadnezzar's Hanging Gardens of Babylon and the

Lighthouse at Alexandria.) We walked to the fifteenth-century Castle of St. Peter which was used by the Crusaders in the sixteenth century, drank a beer or two in the warm afternoon sun, and found a campground on the beach. We sat by the sea eating dinner as a wedding party arrived at the restaurant. People danced to love songs late into the night, and we discovered the *macarena* has made it to Turkey.

September 13—The two and a half hour ferry ride from Bodrum to the village of Datca passed the Greek island of Kos (and crossed an imaginary line where Turkey's Aegean Coast gave way to its Mediterranean Coast.) We camped on the seashore, spending the afternoon cleaning the camper, our clothes and us. I also attended to a recurring problem. Frequently we have been stopped by police for not having a license plate on the car's front bumper. Weary of trying to explain what happened to our second plate, I simulated a European style license plate by affixing our numbers in black tape to the white area where the camper's second plate would have been mounted. Luckily, the finished product looked very much like one of those generic black and white European plates. (For the rest of the trip, we were never stopped again.)

September 14—From the picturesque yachting harbor of Marmaris, we could look beyond Turkey's rugged coastline and across the turquoise Mediterranean to the Greek island of Rhodes. We stopped in the pleasant farming town of Koycegiz for lunch and then in riverside Dalyan where we saw Lycian tombs carved in cliffs above the river. In Fethiye, we inspected more Lycian tombs carved in rock walls. Further south, in the picturesque formerly fishing, now yachting, village of Kalkan, after a fine dinner at a restaurant on the beautiful harbor, we camped in the parking lot of the yacht club.

September 15—In Kas, we walked around the quayside square and then the large open air market where Lynnie and I had our shoes repaired. In Kale (ancient Myra), we visited the twelfth-century Church of St. Nicholas where Father Christmas is allegedly entombed, more Lycian tombs, and the marvelous ruins of a Roman theater. Nearby, we toured the ruins of ancient Phaselis which occupy three small, beautifully wooded bays.

The coast curved north, and our highway clung to the mountains rising directly from the sea. Near Antalya, we stopped for the night at a basic rundown campground that looked like it was built by a relative of the protagonist in Mosquito Coast. An inspection of the grounds revealed sculptures constructed from junk, a tree house covered by overgrown vegetation, signs with confusing instructions, and facilities that didn't work. A swampy creek filled with snakes, frogs and garbage ran slowly along the edge of the campground. I heard the chattering of kingfishers and spotted two species (white-breasted and European) working the banks of the sluggish drainage.

September 16—Antalya's marvelous Kaleici (old town), with its narrow, winding streets, offered few parking places. We drove slowly through the colorful bazaar area, looking for an empty parking space, and, when a young man asked if he could be of help, I allowed him to direct us through a gate into a small parking area behind his family's rug emporium. The eldest son in a family of carpet merchants with shops in New York, Germany and Istanbul as well as Antalya, the young man had attended Rutgers, we weren't surprised to learn, as fluent English rolled off his tongue with a distinct New Jersey accent. Inside the family's well stocked shop, two of our friend's brothers brought us tea while they showed us a splendid selection of lovely silk carpets. We felt a little bad in that, while we were tempted by more than a few, we didn't buy any. We visited the town's famous Yivli Minare (Grooved Minaret) and the immense, second-century Hadriaynus Kapisi (Hadrian's Gate) and then strolled along Antalya's picturesque, ancient Roman harbor where we enjoyed a light lunch in a very pleasant outdoor cafe.

Lynnie and I apparently had not had our fill of the fascinating Greek and Roman ruins which are liberally sprinkled along the Turkish coast. We stopped about ten miles east of Antalya to see the ruins of Perge which included an ancient stadium and theater capable of seating, respectively, 12,000 and 15,000 people. Then we continued to Side, the ancient Mediterranean slave market and pirate base, where we toured the temples of Apollo and Athena, public baths and a fine amphitheater. Late in the afternoon, we found a campground on the beach. This evening, while we were sitting on the beach talking, Lynnie noticed the left edge of the full moon had become very fuzzy looking. Soon it was obvious that an eclipse was taking place. With our binoculars, we watched for hours as the shadow of the Earth grew across the moon, covered it completely, and then withdrew.

September 17—In thirteenth-century Konya, a poet named Mevlana Rumi founded an Islamic mystical order of pious mendicants who, as a part of their worship, performed whirling dances. Present day Whirling Dervishes are seldom seen in public, so Lynette took special notice this morning when, in Side, she saw a poster advertising a performance by the dancers this very night at the second-century Roman theater in nearby Aspendos. We bought tickets and arranged to be picked up at our campground and taken to Aspendos. Then we visited several carpet shops and strolled through the village and along the beach.

This evening, we sat on a broad limestone step, watching several thousand people filling up Aspendos' ancient open-air theater, perhaps the best preserved of any in the world. Jupiter hung at its zenith directly above us while a full moon rose above the proscenium's backdrop just as the dancers whirled onto the stage. For the next hour, the audience sat mesmerized as the graceful performers gradually increased the speed and wildness of their dance, and the leaders' chants grew louder and more frenzied. After a time, the seemingly exhausted dervishes entered an almost sudden and rather anticlimactic deceleration, bringing themselves and the audience to near quiescence, and then slowly spun their way from the stage.

Lynette had been very keen on seeing the Whirling Dervishes perform their ritual, and the Aspendos venue only enhanced her enchantment. On the bus ride back to our campground, she compared the experience favorably with seeing Aida performed at the Baths of Caracalla in Rome. Groggily, we fell into the camper at 1:30 a.m.

September 18—A long day of driving took us over the rugged, photogenic coastal mountains and up onto the Anatolian Plateau, Turkey's heartland. Red-footed falcons in considerable numbers perched on posts, rocks, and shrubbery, resting for the next enervating leg of their migration. We admired some of the Seljuk architecture in Konya and stopped for the night at a campground in Aksaray. A young Dutch couple, P.J. and Claudia, were the only other campers there. They invited us to join them for coffee this evening. Lynnie brought along a box of cookies. They were about Mikey's age now, my age when we were drifting through South America and Europe in 1973 and 1974, and were on their way to Africa. He and several siblings had been running their parents' business, but he sold out to them after tiring of management style disagreements.

September 19—A short drive east from Aksaray took us into Cappadocia, an area of Turkey famous for its villages carved out of remarkable formations of volcanic rock. First we visited Kaymakli, a fantastic underground rock city. Bus loads of tourists had the same idea as we did, and the resulting long lines of curious people proceeded very slowly through the cavernous underground rooms. Some of those more impatient began to get a little ugly, so, at our first opportunity, having seen enough, Lynnie and I ducked through a room marked "No Entry" and doubled back to the entrance.

We crossed the Kizilirmak (Red River) to Avanos where we bought groceries and checked out the pottery for which the town is known. We continued to Uchisar, a town carved into and hanging onto the rocky slopes of a mountain peak, and then, in the Zelve and Goreme valleys, toured the homes, stables, churches and other buildings early Christians carved into the peculiarly shaped volcanic tuff formations. Cross-shaped frescoes painted twelve hundred years ago remain relatively undisturbed on some of the stone walls.

In the village of Goreme, we talked with another young man from a family of rug merchants. He is expecting word today from Michigan State on whether he has been accepted into a program which will allow him to complete his Ph.D. We looked at a few rugs and then drove to a marvelous campground high on a hill. We registered, got ourselves organized, and then helped a German couple reposition their caravan which they were planning on pulling through the Middle East to Egypt for the winter. I set up our lawn chairs while Lynnie poured the wine, then we kicked up our feet on a fence rail, watched acrobatic alpine swifts foraging on the wing, and admired the view over the Goreme Valley.

"This is a nice place, Darwin."

"It is. What a view!"

"Yes, it's lovely. Everything looks so biblical."

September 20—I wakened at daybreak to an odd sound—like a motor turning on and off, almost a hissing noise. I opened the camper shade and, less than a hundred yards away, a red and white hot air balloon drifted down a drainage toward the Goreme Valley. I nudged Lynnie, pointed to a yellow and blue balloon now drifting by, and we scampered out of bed, hurried out of the camper, and counted twenty-seven colorful balloons at varying heights and distances drifting into the valley. Later, we learned that the Hot Air Balloon Competition of Turkey's International Air Exposition was taking place in Goreme.

If there were any "drifters" on their way to Iran, we were now in a part of Turkey where we might be likely to meet them. We spent the better part of the morning visiting a half dozen campgrounds in the area to try to find someone planning on driving across Iran and Pakistan to India. No luck. Everybody was either spending the winter in Turkey or was headed for the Middle East and Egypt.

In Goreme, we stopped to see if the young man had received word from Michigan State. He wasn't there, but his cousin said he had indeed been accepted and that he had gone to Ankara for consultation with government authorities. Lynnie and I found ourselves looking at a few rugs, and soon "Uncle" introduced himself to us. Uncle smiled.

"My friends, how may I be of service to you?"

"My friend," I reciprocated, "thank you for your kind offer. If you do not mind, we only want to look at your lovely rugs."

"Of course! You are my first customer today. If I can find a rug for you, even a very small one, I will make you a very low price, even if I lose money. You see, in Turkey, a man's first customer brings him luck." He smiled warmly and seriously.

All of this, of course, was by now familiar. These guys all went to the same sales school. But Uncle had refined his pitch to an art, and I sensed amateur hour was over.

"I understand. With your permission, we will continue to look at your exquisite rugs to see if there is one we cannot live without."

Uncle wrinkled his brow, took each of us by the arm and pulled us closer, lowered his voice to a confidential tone, and then the rug selling turned serious.

"My Brother... My Sister... You are very lucky. I am ready to sell below my cost. I need the money. I bought a new delivery van, and now I must make a large payment."

"Yes, my Brother." I expressed a grave face and entered the mood. "I only wish that I could be of assistance to you. Your rugs are beautiful, and we would be eternally proud to have even a small one in our humble home. But I have very little money. Your Sister has already bought a rug in Turkey, and the purchase relieved me of all my spare cash."

All the while, young people were offering us tea, then beer, and then a sublime carry-out supper of local specialties from my Brother's restaurant next door. Even an Efes beer tray for Lynette's back-home bona-fide brother, Brock, who has an extensive beer tray collection. When the long afternoon was finished, we had spent a lot of dough on six gorgeous rugs. Most of what had been said, I'm sure, was Turkish malarkey. But Lynette and I were happy and very fond of our new rugs. We had enjoyed spending the afternoon in a shop that was an authentic old caravanserai and had been in our Brother's family for many years. It was a very nice experience, probably mostly malarkey, but nice nevertheless.

September 21—The other most likely place to find "drifters" headed for Asia was in Turkey's capital, Ankara. The drive there took most of the day, and we found a municipal campground that was mostly deserted. I walked around the area looking for birds, spotting migrating blackcaps and warblers. The campground guard who didn't speak English was curious why I was looking into the trees with binoculars. I showed him my bird book by way of explanation. Later, at dusk, the guard came to our camper, asked to see the bird book, opened it to the section on owls and motioned for me to follow him. We walked across the lawn to a large tree, and he pointed to several owls perched on a limb. I walked around the base of the tree and, looking up among its branches, counted a dozen roosting long-eared owls.

September 22—Most of the day in Ankara was occupied by visits to embassies and visa paperwork. At the U.S. Embassy, we requested updated travel information on Asian and the Middle Eastern countries. We applied for visas at the Syrian Embassy and there met a young American backpacking couple, Rene and Otto, on their way to Africa. Syrian and U.S. embassy officials were apparently in the midst of what Otto called a "diplomatic pissing contest," necessitating several trips back and forth between the two embassies which were a fair distance apart. Our plight was further complicated in that an American couple sympathetic to Iraq had obtained Syrian visas in order to enter Iraq (visa not required if entry is made from Syria), which with Cuba and Libya is one of three countries for which U.S. passports are not valid. The U.S. officials were concerned others might do the same. Because the clerk in the U.S. Embassy didn't seem to have the authority to give us the letter of introduction that the Syrian Embassy demanded as part of our visa applications, I asked to talk with her boss. Harvey, the Vice-Consul listened to our request and agreed to give us a letter of introduction. He signed the letter, started to hand it to me, then hesitated.

"I have to ask you something."

"What is it, Harvey?"

"Are you going to Iraq?"

"Are you kidding? Depend on it, Harvey. We're not going to Iraq."

Our understaffed campground would soon be closing for the season, possibly explaining why the water heater had not been fixed in the women's shower room. Lynnie and I were taking showers in the only two stalls in the men's shower room when a Frenchman entered and couldn't understand why he couldn't take a shower in the stall I had just finished using. After a bit, he understood the problem, laughed and said he would return later.

September 23—We met René and Otto for coffee before going to the Syrian Embassy to pick up our visas. As a very young boy, Otto had been adopted into a family with five other children. Because Krissie and Kirk had recently adopted Ana, I was especially interested in the subject of adoption. Among other questions, I asked Otto if he ever felt the urge to learn who his biological parents were and perhaps even try to meet them.

"I know who my parents are. They are the ones who have always loved me. I love my parents. There is no one else."

Lynnie has pretty much decided to continue on to India with me. The only question remaining was whether to go through Iran and Pakistan or through the Middle East. We visited the embassies of Iran and Pakistan and inquired about safety, unleaded gas availability, and other factors which would be useful in making our decision. I called Mike and asked him to check on the Internet, including Lonely Planet's web site, for current travel information on Asia and the Middle East.

Back at the campground, we're the only campers tonight. Far fewer people seem to be traveling overland in campers than there were twenty-five years ago. Most of the overlanders are backpackers. The line of people waiting with us for visas at the Syrian Embassy included Otto and Rene, a South African gal, two Kiwis (New Zealand), and a guy from Canada. Only

Lynnie and I were traveling in a camper. The others were all backpacking.

September 24—At breakfast Lynette suggested we visit the Saudi Arabian Embassy. Our understanding was that Saudi visas were issued only in Jordan, but she had pretty much decided upon the Saudi route to India and wanted to see what information the embassy might offer. We were surprised upon our arrival not to have to wait in line to see someone. An employee asked if he could help us, and, when I told him we were interested in visiting Saudi Arabia, he led us directly to the First Secretary's very large and plush office. Hisham Ali Al-Naili stood behind his large polished desk, bowed slightly, and welcomed us with a smile.

"Please. Have a seat." He gestured toward two chairs in front of his desk. "Will you drink tea with me?"

Mr. Al-Naili answered our questions thoughtfully, inquired about our interests in visiting his country, and suggested many places for us to see. We asked him whether we had to wait until we arrived in Jordan to apply for visas. He laughed and shook his head.

"Of course not. May I have your passports?"

We discussed Saudi customs, and he compared them with practices in the States. I also inquired about the availability of unleaded gas in Saudi Arabia, and Mr. Al-Naili assured us that, in his country, only unleaded gas was sold. Twenty minutes after we had arrived, our passports were returned with Saudi visas. We thanked Mr. Al-Naili profusely.

"Mr. Wile, before you go. Will you agree to do one thing for me?"

"Of course... anything!"

He handed me his card.

"When you return to America, will you write to me and tell me candidly what you thought of my country?"

Our next stop was the embassy of the United Arab Emirates. With Saudi visas in hand, we knew the UAE visas would be almost automatic. An official took our applications and politely requested we return the day after tomorrow for the visas.

Back at the campground, the German couple we had met in Cappadocia, Peter and Lara, had arrived. The four of us ate supper in their caravan and compared our respective travel plans. He had recently retired from a large printing company where he worked as a typographer. They intended to spend the next few years living in their caravan, drifting to new places as the spirit moved them.

September 25—Four thousand years ago, Hittite tribespeople lived on the site now occupied by Turkey's capital. The Anadolu Medeniyetleri Muzesi (Anatolian Civilizations Museum) boasts the world's best collection of Hittite and Assyrian artifacts. We toured the museum and walked through

Ankara's historic Old Town with its half-timbered houses mounted on old stone foundations. From Ulus Square, we climbed the hill on which the Kale (Citadel) is perched, stopping at a fruit and nut market and a number of carpet and *kilim* shops along the way. Then we visited the impressive and grand Mausoleum of Ataturk, the military, civic and political genius who, in many ways, is responsible for Turkey's twentieth-century modernity.

I have not been feeling a hundred per cent the past several days, experiencing a mild version of the abdominal pain I experienced that night in Bran, Romania, when we camped below Dracula's Castle. Vanilla milk shakes, for some reason, seem to provide relief. Even in Turkey, McDonald's knows how to make vanilla shakes, so each afternoon we sit at one of Mac's outdoor tables while Lynette drinks coffee and I indulge myself with a vanilla shake.

This afternoon, a particularly pleasant and sunny one, we found ourselves again at McDonald's, talking with a fellow from Holland who had set up his tent next to us at the campground. As a young boy, he had lived for a few years with his family in New Zealand, and now he had left home with the intention of backpacking his way across Asia and back to New Zealand to seek his fortune. He was quite interested in riding with us across Iran and Pakistan to India, but, unfortunately, he did not have visas for those countries. It would have been an interesting possibility, but we can't wait for another week or two or even longer to see if he can get visas. During our conversation, with no provocation, a detestable bee alighted on Lynette's leg and stung her, leaving a painful welt.

September 26—Lynnie and I looked at each other over the breakfast table. I smiled. She said, "Let's go to Saudi." We opened our maps and quickly made plans to drive south through Syria, Jordan, Saudi Arabia, and the U.A.E. from where we will ship the camper to India. Perhaps we will fly to Sheraz, Iran, from Dubai while the camper is being shipped. We might also drive to Pakistan from India to see the Lahore area.

In Ankara, we picked up our visas at the United Arab Emirates. Unable to read what it said in Arabic, I turned to the woman, puzzled.

"What does it say?"

"Your visa allows multiple entries for six months at a time, and it is valid for ten years."

"Really? That's incredible. How much do I owe you?"

"The visas cost nothing."

"Wow! You folks know how to make a tourist feel welcome!"

We enjoyed lunch with Peter and Lara at a great Italian restaurant, hugged them good-bye, and drove south past Tuz Golu, an enormous salt lake, to Aksaray. We registered at the same campground where we stayed eight days ago. I'm disappointed we can't make the traditional trans-Asia journey, but things change. The past couple of weeks, Lynette has become more enthusiastic about the trip each day, and that's so important. She's been in the shower too long, so I'll go check on her since we're the only campers here. Her leg is swollen from the bee sting at McDonalds yesterday.

September 27—We drove southeast to Tarsus, where Antony and Cleopatra first met and became an item, and which was also the birthplace of St. Paul. Further east, above the fertile Adana delta, a blackbird flew with a purpose, while, far higher, a falcon that was smaller than but otherwise looked like a peregrine, a hobby, glided swiftly on a course perpendicular to that of the blackbird. Suddenly, the hobby turned downward, evinced three rapid and powerful beats of its long, pointed wings, then partially folded them and entered a deadly hundred mile an hour stoop aimed at the hapless blackbird. The high level drama was over in seconds when the falcon struck its prey a lethal blow with its clenched feet, snatched the bird with its powerful talons and beat its way into the distance.

The road curved south to Iskenderun (old Alexandretta) where The Great One defeated the Persians and Jonah was liberated from his three day ordeal inside a whale. Along the way, a blue-cheeked bee-eater foraged for insects on the rocky shores of a Mediterranean bay. Rain began pouring steadily when we stopped in Iskenderun for groceries and continued into the evening. We found a campground on the sea south of town. A young Aussie couple, Julia and Dean, arrived soon after us, and, to escape the dreary weather, the four of us repaired to a local pub for fish and chips and an evening of beer drinking.

September 28—Biblical Antioch enjoyed a depraved reputation which induced St. Peter, the rock-like apostle on which Christ said he would build his Church, to try his hand at converting the wayward locals to Christianity. We drove through old Antioch's modern incarnation, Antakya. On the outskirts of town, we visited Senpiyer Kilisesi, the small church carved, fittingly, into a rock cliff where St. Peter preached to the corrupt Antiochans.

Crossing into Syria was a complicated affair. A business thrived at the border which provided guides to usher foreigners through the bureaucratic tangle of paperwork. A smiling young man approached us when I stopped at the spot designated by a Syrian soldier.

"Hello, Friend! I am your guide. I will take you through this terrible mess."

"How much will your services cost?"

"Oh, nothing. I do this to welcome you. If, at the end, you think I have been of assistance, perhaps you will give me something small."

The fellow knew exactly where to go, what short cuts to take, and whose palms to cross. He got us through the mess in thirty-five minutes.

"How much do I owe you?"

"Whatever you think I was worth, my friend."

Our passport stamps and car insurance cost $69, three bribes cost $8, a total of $77. I thought ten percent might be appropriate, so, with an appreciative smile, I gave him $8.

"Thank you, my friend, but that is not enough. I worked very hard for you."

"OK. Here's another $2, but that's all I'm paying." He was very upset, or at least acted like he was. As I pulled away, he raised a clenched fist in the air and yelled.

"Americans always give me much more!"

Turks exuded cordialness and hospitality. Syrians aren't so forthcoming. Here women wear veils and dress in black, and children wear military style uniforms to school. In Turkey, restaurants and shops are ubiquitous, and people are happy. My first impression of Syria is vastly different. Everyone is so serious. Perhaps St. Simeon is to blame.

Near the village of Daret' Azze is the ancient Qala' at Samaan (Basilica of St. Simeon). The enormous church sits on the spot where, in 423 AD, St. Simeon climbed to the top of a pillar and sat there until his death thirty-six years later. How's that for establishing a serious tradition? The village advertised a small campground which wasn't much more than somebody's walled back yard. I knocked on the large wooden gate, and a boy who appeared to be in his early teens let us in and collected our money. He said his name was Hahmad, and since Lynnie and I were his only customers, told us to park wherever we pleased. We chose a spot away from the large house to which Hahmad was walking, apparently his home, on the porch of which sat an old fat man with a beard and a dreadful countenance. The boy had just stepped onto the porch when the gaffer began yelling and tried to hit him with a switch. Hahmad jumped away, easily eluding the attack. Presently he came back to us, curious about our rig. He hung around and became greatly amused watching Lynette trim my hair, my first haircut during the past three months. When she finished, I pointed toward a water faucet on the wall of the small outdoor shower and bathroom.

"Hahmad, can I wash our camper over there?"

"Let me do it for you."

"How much do you charge?"

"Two dollars."

I parked the camper next to the faucet. Soon Hahmad was back with a hose.

"My grandfather wants me to charge you four dollars."

"That's too much, Hahmad."

"I will do it for two dollars. But don't tell my grandfather."

The boy sprayed the car and began wiping it with his hand. I told him to wait a minute and, from the rear of the camper, retrieved a bucket, soap and a sponge.

"I will help you, Hahmad."

Soon after I paid the boy, I heard his grandfather yelling and berating him. Hahmad ran away from the house to the far corner of the yard. I waited a few minutes and then joined him, only to witness his tears.

"Hahmad, your grandfather is having a bad evening. Our car now looks very good for our journey. Thank you for making it so clean." I gave him another two dollars. "Here is a bonus for good work. But don't tell your grandfather."

September 29—Gardens and trees grace the banks of the Orontes River (Nahr al 'Assi or Rebel River) as it flows through the pleasant town of Hama. From the ruins of a citadel on a hill overlooking the attractive town, Lynnie and I counted seven "norias," wooden water wheels, the largest of which was sixty-five feet in diameter. Built hundreds of years ago to irrigate the surrounding farmland, the picturesque norias still turn slowly in the current, groaning under the weight of their liquid burden. We visited the Grand Mosque and shopped for groceries in Hama's Old Town market, then continued south through rural villages whose homogeneous mud brick buildings were tinted in the prevailing earth color of the area—red, brown or gray. The landscape appeared as it must have for many generations, marred only by billboards and statues promoting the ubiquitous image of Hafez al-Assad (the leader of the Arab Ba'ath Socialist Party and Syria's President since 1971) and equally omnipresent human trash, especialy thousands of plastic bags littering the countryside. Among the countless ways in which humans have forsook their custodial responsibility of Mother Earth, the invention of free, disposable plastic grocery bags ranks at the top.

While planning this trip, I had hoped to avoid the fuel problems we experienced in Africa nine years before where the U.S.'s emissions control systems were a mystery to mechanics and a non-factor to gasoline suppliers who offered only leaded fuel. Until we left Turkey, we had no trouble finding unleaded gas for the camper. Syria, on the other hand, had only recently begun supplying unleaded at a few of their gas stations. We filled up at such a place on the outskirts of Aleppo but were now getting low on fuel as we entered the crossroads city of Homs. We tried several gas stations with no luck and then asked a traffic policeman for directions to a station selling unleaded. He conferred with his partner, then, with hand signals, indicated he would ride in the rear of the camper and show us the way. We filled our tank with the rather rare fuel and returned the helpful fellow to his post. Grateful, I tried to pay him for his services, but he declined the cash with a sincere air of propriety. He did accept, however, two chocolate bars Lynette offered for him and his partner.

Perched strategically on a mountain pass thirty miles west of Homs, the huge Crac des Chevaliers (Qala' at al-Hosn or Castle of the Knights) was built by the Crusaders in the twelfth century to accommodate a garrison of 4,000. The classic fortress has survived its 800 years almost intact with thirteen towers accenting the castle's formidable outside wall. A second wall which surrounds and protects the citadel's vital inner buildings is separated from the outer rampart by a moat. We climbed the winding road to the castle and explored the surrounding rural countryside. A small campground near the castle was undescribably filthy and contained a group of desperate looking characters, so we returned to Homs and registered in a hotel.

September 30—The road to Palmyra led east from Homs past villages whose occupants live in beehive-shaped mud brick houses. Here minimal rainfall supports sparse vegetation which permits these desert fringe dwellers to eke out a subsistence economy of sheep and goat herding. Further east in the desert itself, permanent villages give way to tent communities of nomadic Bedouins, scenes out of *National Geographic* with shepherds tending their herds and riding their donkeys and camels.

Palmyra's historic location as a desert crossroads gave the caravan town great strategic value. The Assyrians controlled Palmyra for a thousand years, then Greek rule prevailed during the first three centuries AD. Queen Zenobia came to power in 267 AD when her husband, King Odenathus, died suspiciously. Ambitious Zenobia quickly got the attention of the Roman emporer, Aurelian, when she sent 70,000 Palmyrene troops first to occupy Egypt, and then to invade Asia Minor, actions tantamount to taking on the Romans. Those moves got the attention of Aurelian who sent the mighty Roman legions to retake Egypt and then Palmyra itself.

Palmyra is one of the most impressive ruins in the world. Better yet, the remote location of this famous oasis far out in the Syrian desert protects it from the tourist hordes. Lynnie and I explored the more than 125 acres of Palmyra's ruins which have been extensively excavated and restored, and we could easily imagine what life must have been like there in the second century AD. The Great Colonnade, Palmyra's column-lined "Main Street" ran almost a half mile from the town's Monumental Arch to the Funerary Temple. We zigzagged our way among the columns and intersections, along the way admiring an impressive amphitheater, the once bustling Agora (marketplace), the Senate, and a number of tombs and temples. All the while, on a hill in the distance, we could see the Qala' at ibn Maan, a seventeenth-century Arab fortress looming over the valley. Several species of birds inhabited the ruins, including little owls perched in rock cavities, mourning wheatears foraging the sparse grass for seeds, hoopoes probing the ground for grubs and insects, and a flock of blue-cheeked bee-eaters darting from one ruin to another.

Later in the afternoon, we registered at the Zenobia Hotel which permitted camping in their parking area. Then we walked into contemporary Palmyra and visited the ethnographic museum which contained statuary from old Palmyra as well as displays of more recent desert civilization. We walked around the town's colorful market and shopping district. In one shop, Lynette bought a black silk *abayya*, required dress for Saudi Arabia, and I bought a few *kafirs* (Arab headdresses). We then carried a bottle of wine to the ruins and watched a marvelous sunset.

Filled with millions of stars, the desert firmament stretched above the outdoor patio restaurant of the Hotel Zenobia. We sat with a Swiss couple who had camped their way through Italy, Greece, and Turkey and now planned to return home through Bulgaria and Romania. Too bad! Only half-joking, I recommended they consider returning the way they came.

October 1—A lesser kestrel hovered above the immense courtyard, and the early morning sun's pink rays penetrated between the lines of gigantic columns into the magnificent, massive Temple of Bel. From the temple's steps, we looked out over the ancient city and imagined the thousands of people going about their business. Then we set off into the desert toward Damascus and, in the middle of nowhere, saw a juvenile black stork totally out of his range and habitat. It seemed pretty stressed. We stopped for the night at a campground north of Damascus where, upon our arrival, P.J. and Claudia, the Dutch couple we had camped with weeks earlier in Aksaray, greeted us. We were celebrating our reunion over a glass of wine when two motorcycles roared into the campground ridden by another Dutch couple who were on their way to South Africa. They joined us, and pretty soon we had a party going.

October 2—Damascus dates back to 5000 BC and may be the world's oldest continuously inhabited city. The Persians, Greeks, and Romans all took a turn at ruling Damascus. Saul of Tarsus (St. Paul) experienced his revelation on the road to Damascus and then, in that city, was converted from a persecutor of Christians to a follower of Christ. In the Old City, we visited St. Paul's Chapel where Christianity's first major theologian escaped a plot to kill him by being lowered in a basket over the Damascus city walls. Sections of the wall still remain. We toured the third-century Temple of Jupiter and the eighth-century Omayyad Mosque and inspected the shops in the crowded and bustling Souq al-Hamadiyyeh (covered market). We walked along Via Recta (Straight Street) past the Roman Arch and visited the twelfth-century, red-domed Mausoleum of Saladin and the black and white Azem Palace with its interesting Museum of Syria.

The red Syrian desert turned brown as we crossed without incident into

Jordan. Not far from the border lies the beautifully preserved ancient Roman city of Jerash. We walked an impressively colonnaded street past the Nymphaeum (city fountain), the Triumphal Arch, the 15,000 seat Hippodrome, the second-century Temple of Zeus, and the unusually oval-shaped Forum.

In the hills outside of Amman, we stopped on the side of the road to eat lunch. A woman and her son invited us to their house for tea, but we declined. In Amman, unleaded gas was readily available. This capital city of Jordan reflects its American queen. No longer do we see women only in traditional Moslem dress. Some are completely western in their appearance. There are no police or armed guards on the streets as there were in Syria. Almost as important, we found a marvelous Safeway supermarket. King Hussein waved at us as his motorcade passed, and we received permission from the Carlton Hotel to camp in their parking lot. This evening, we ate dinner in a superb Lebanese restaurant that had been recommended to us. Walking home from the restaurant we smell the lovely fragrance of Jasmine.

October 3—Safeway has everything an American could want! We restocked our pantry and then drove across the treeless plateau on which Amman sits to the fertile valley of Wadi Seer to visit the ruins of Qasr al-Abd (Castle of the Slave). In the desert habitats of the Middle East, birds we have never seen before are showing up each day—today we added red-rumped swallow, masked shrike, and Finsch's wheatear to our "life-list." The nice desk clerk at the Carlton Hotel offered us a suite at the price of a double, so we decide to splurge tonight. We walked downtown and enjoyed a simple dinner of *shurmas*, sandwiches of lamb shaved from skewers and other finger food bought from street vendors.

October 4—On its way south, the King's Highway crosses a number of high desert plateaus, periodically making dramatic descents into spectacular canyons which stretch far inland from the sea, and then, painfully twisting and climbing, returning to another high plateau. Once, we were listening to a taped lecture on religious Baroque music in which Handel's *Messiah* was being analyzed. Just as the Hallelujah Chorus was nearing its climactic end, Lynette gasped, "Look at that!" An absolutely spectacular canyon cut inland from the west. We decided Handel deserved an encore, so we stopped for lunch on a precipice looking over the gorge. While the immortal chorus wafted over the abyss, we watched the canyon's monochromatic vistas changing color—gray, pink, yellow—and ate our sandwiches. Less impressed by the moment, a half dozen blackstarts foraged fearlessly on our crumbs.

On the drive south, we stopped to see the ruins of Machaerus, Herod's fortress perched high on a hill where John the Baptist was beheaded, as well as Kerak and Shobak, two crusader forts that once were a part of a chain of such forts stretching from Aqaba on the Red Sea to Turkey. We arrived at the hillside campground overlooking the town of Petra late in the afternoon. Julia and Dean, the young Aussie couple we had met in Iskenderun was enjoying the view and a beer on a terrace outside the campground's bar. Dean offered to buy our first if we joined them.

October 5—The Nabateans ruled much of Jordan and Arabia for several centuries before the Romans came. Their spectacular capital city of Petra was built in the third century BC but became lost and remained undiscovered until the nineteenth century. Elaborate temples, palaces, storerooms, stables, tombs, and houses were carved into cliffs of solid rock, and, in Petra, the Nabateans controlled the trade routes between Damascus and Arabia.

With Julia and Dean, we walked a mile and a half through the dramatic *siq*, a high narrow rift cutting through the mountain that protects the city. Black robin-sized birds with orange flight feathers, Tristram's grackles, whistled from the cliffs above, sounding more like a short wave radio tuning in than a bird. As we approached the *siq's* end, the monumental Khazneh, or Treasury, came into view in all its enormity. I focused my binoculars on the high columns and openings carved into the cliff face and saw Sinai rosefinches hopping about the rocky ledges and rock martins swooping in and out of the many cavities.

The four of us spent the morning exploring the ruins of magnificent temples, tombs, an 8,000 seat amphitheater, a monastery, and many other buildings. The area was extensive and contained a variety of desert vegetation in which I saw scrub warblers, white-crowned black wheatears, and desert larks. Then we ate lunch at a small outdoor cafe near the Temple of the Winged Lions from where we could see fan-tailed ravens riding the cliffside thermals. At the edge of a nearby *wadi*, a red-breasted flycatcher perched on a dead snag, resting between his frequent insect forays. Closer to the restaurant patio, Palestine sunbirds, small birds with curved bills and splendid, glossy dark blue and purple plumage, extracted nectar from the many flower blossoms.

Julia and Dean followed us into the desert to see Wadi Rum, a Bedouin settlement surrounded by sheer *jebels* (mountains) rising from the sandy valley floor. From here in 1916-1919, T.E. Lawrence (of Arabia) led the Arab Revolt against the Turks. After finding a secluded spot in a wide canyon, we set up camp for the night and then hiked into the mountains. Brown-necked ravens soared on the afternoon thermals. Suddenly, I caught a glimpse of a streamlined flash in the periphery, turned and found a speeding raptor in my binoculars, a sooty falcon speedily gliding effortlessly along the edge of a cliff, presumably searching for an unsuspecting passerine going about its business below.

It's a pleasant night to be camped in the desert. The four of us sat out late, drinkin' wine, talkin' travel, and watchin' a meteor shower.

October 6—The town of Wadi Rum turned out to be disappointing. It's no longer a small village of Bedouins living in goat-hair tents. Tourism, even the relatively small amount of it that reaches this far into the desert, has changed all that. The tent village is more of a concrete slum now with a bunch of hustlers trying to lure you into one desert adventure or another. I suppose tourism has its advantages, at least for the resourceful few, but it plays hell with traditional cultures. Lynnie said that the populace had lost its "Bedouinity."

With Julia and Dean, we returned to King's Highway and drove south to Aqaba on the Red Sea, Jordan's only port. We needed gas but soon determined, contrary to what we had been assured by several people in Amman, there was no unleaded gas being sold in Aqaba. Three stations had carried the precious liquid until a few weeks ago, but had stopped doing so because of minimal demand for the more expensive fuel. The Hotel Aqaba operated a campground, so our Aussie friends and we registered there. We bought some beer, repaired to the beach, and did some snorkeling while we considered what to do about our gasoline problem.

October 7—Lynnie and I did our laundry and then drove into town in a *bela rsas* (unleaded gasoline) quest. We revisited each station that had carried it in the past to see if anybody had any ideas. One especially friendly merchant named Ali had a son-in-law who was Saudi Arabian and lived across the border in Haql. Ali telephoned his son-in-law, only to learn that gas stations in Haql did not carry unleaded gas and that the nearest Saudi location where unleaded gas possibly was sold was 200 miles away in Tabuk, no closer than Amman. This, sadly, contradicts what Mr. Al-Naili told us at the Saudi embassy in Ankara.

I spent much of the day trying to solve the problem. Another very friendly merchant, Said Al-Helo, eventually came up with a solution for us. He arranged to have four-twenty liter cans (about 21 gallons) brought to us from Amman in a private car. The shipment should arrive at his shop by 9:30 tomorrow morning.

October 8—After breakfast, we joined our merchant friend, Ali, at his shop for tea. Before long, Said, the merchant who arranged to have the gas transported from Amman, stopped his car in front of the shop and joined us. We made some small talk while waiting for Said's tea. I thought he seemed rather glum, but I was afraid to ask about the gas. His tea came. He took a sip and moistened his lips.

"My friend."

"What is it, Said?"

"I'm afraid my news is bad. The people in Amman say it is bad to carry gas in a car. Very dangerous."

I'm crestfallen, too disappointed even to reply. I looked at my feet for a moment and then glanced up at Said. Incredibly, he wore a big smile.

"No! No, my friend. I make a joke! In my car is 80 liters of *bela rsas*. We will fill your car after we have tea."

Said helped me pour the gas into our camper, then we walked to his shop to settle what I owed him. As it turned out, his brother had driven the gas from Amman to Aqaba overnight. His brother's five-year-old son, Oman, is in the hospital in Amman undergoing kidney dialysis.

"Said, is this not a very expensive procedure?"

"Yes, my brother and his wife cannot afford this problem. However, we are a big family. My other brothers and I are paying the bills."

We called the brother at the hospital to see how the boy was doing, and, before long, we were all on the phone with one another. Lynette talked to the boy's mother who invited us to their home when we return to Amman, and I talked to Oman, who, when I was about to hang up, told me he loved me. Lynnie and I gave Said more than he wanted for the gas and asked him to buy Oman a present from us.

With a full gas tank, we drove south along the Gulf of Aqaba to the Royal Jordanian Diving Center where we proceeded to engage in some serious snorkeling in some of the world's best coral, the Yamanieh Reef. As we had been led to believe, the varieties of coral and fish (also water snakes) were diverse, interesting and exciting. Later in the day, thoroughly soaked by sun and sea, we set up camp on the beach about a mile north of the diving center.

A couple from Holland stopped by soon afterwards and asked if we minded their sharing our beach for the night. We didn't, of course, and soon we were also sharing the startling sunset, a marvelous balmy breeze, a couple of bottles of wine, and an evening's conversation. Not much younger than we are, he's an artist and she teaches languages. They recently bought a small, tumbledown, eighteenth-century home in Spain and now planned to return there to renovate it. These folks are vintage "drifters," veterans of a number of trans-Sahara camping trips in Libya, Tunisia, Algeria, and Morocco. Lynnie remembered we had a canned Danish ham which the Saudi border officials surely would confiscate if it was found in our car, so she invited our Dutch neighbors for a supper of ham sandwiches. They accepted and contributed a fine salad, and I found another bottle of wine that was far better off being drunk now than being discovered in the morning at the border.

October 9—While the Saudi border officials were properly friendly and polite, they were surprised to see Americans at this border crossing and positively astonished that we carried ten day visas permitting us to go wherever we chose. One man indicated that such freedom of travel by non-Moslems was highly unusual. However impressed they were by our liberal travel permits, they were not a bit dissuaded from assuring themselves that we carried no food, drink, or literature capable of contaminating their society. For some reason, I escaped the strip-search that Lynette was forced to endure. The car and its contents, on the other hand, were thoroughly searched, their going so far as to raise it on a lift to inspect all the underparts. I fully expected them to grill us about the vast selection of drugs in our medicine kit, but, curiously, the inspector gave it only a perfunctory glance and a shrug.

In Haql, we stopped for groceries and, at a gas station, inquired about unleaded gas. The owner insisted that unleaded was unavailable in Saudi Arabia. He said that "Super" was the only grade produced in the country and that it did not contain very much lead. If he's right, our next tankful will be Super, and we'll see what happens to the camper's catalytic converter. Our road curved to the east and slowly climbed through the dry, rugged and dramatic Jabal Ash Shifa range of mountains. Every so often a Bedouin tent or two would appear, and, inevitably nearby, a herd each of camels and goats. Unlike Wadi Rum, there wasn't a tourist in sight. At Tabuk, I asked the Tabuk Sahara's desk clerk, a young man from India, for permission to camp in the hotel parking lot. He paged the manager, a friendly man from Tunisia, who gladly agreed to our request. In responding to my inquiry regarding how he liked living in Saudi Arabia, the Tunisian became visibly disturbed.

"Of course, I am paid well."

"Does your wife like it here?"

"My wife stays in Tunisia. This is no place for a woman. I go home to see her each six months."

One guest, a Saudi businessman named Khalid, was curious about our situation, especially that our visa permitted us to travel virtually anywhere in the country. With such freedom, he suggested we take the route east via Ha'il, since it traversed a portion of the Nafud, one of Saudi Arabia's two great sand deserts. This way, he said, would be far more interesting than continuing south to Medina and then east to Riyadh. He agreed that unleaded gas was not available in Saudi Arabia and said he was certain Super would not render our catalytic converter ineffective, that Super contained only minute levels of lead. I'll believe it when I see it. With a sinking feeling, I filled the tank with Super and fervently hoped the griffin vulture sitting on the light post wasn't a harbinger of doom.

Lynette is required to wear her *abayya* anytime she is in public. She says the heat is making her miserable. Certainly this country's treatment of women doesn't help her comfort level.

From a letter to my mother: *Daytime temperatures soar, and Lynette finds the social rules for women even more oppressive than the heat. She is required to wear an "abayya," a black silk gown covering her entire body except for her face and hands.*

October 10—The Arabian Peninsula has been one of the world's great historical stages. Today, ruins from many of the acts dot the arid landscape. We drove south through Taima where, for ten glorious years, twenty-five centuries ago, the city served as capital of the Babylonian Empire. A restored city wall, a palace and a large well are among many sites dating to that time. Less than a hundred miles to the southwest lies Madain Salah with a history dating back to the Midianites of the *Old Testament* and fabulous two thousand-year old Nabatean ruins almost as impressive as those of Petra.

At the village of Jaharah, we turned east toward Ha'il and entered the sandy expanse of the Nafud. Only a few small towns interrupt the breathtaking, endless desert. Men tend their camels and wear flowing white robes with red and white checked *kafirs* (headresses), and women wear black *abayyas* and black veils. Lynette's *abayya* is too big for her, so, in the middle of nowhere with not another person within miles, she takes it off and, with needle and thread, makes the necessary adjustments.

At one point the wind whipped up for an hour or so and our visibility decreased considerably. What we thought might be evidence of a sand storm brewing soon settled down, fortunately. The blinding noon day sun reappeared and the sky turned blue. We were stopped at four police checkpoints. While the friendly officials waved the local cars through, they stopped us and each time performed a quick, perfunctory search, mostly, I assume, out of curiosity. Saudis seem to drive either large, expensive black sedans, Isuzu Troopers, Land Curisers, or small Toyota pick-up trucks and old clunkers. So far no evidence of catalytic converter problems.

The Al-Saud family has ruled Saudi Arabia for most of the past 250 years. For a few years at the end of the nineteenth century, however, they lost control to the Al-Rashid family. Mohammed Bin Rashid pushed the Al-Saud out of Riyadh and controlled the Najd (Central Region) from Ha'il until he died in 1897. Within a few years, the Lion of Najd, Abdul Aziz Bin Abdul Rahman Al-Saud, drove the Al-Rashid out of Riyadh, and, by 1932, his family controlled all of Arabia and named the country the Kingdom of Saudi Arabia. We visited the mud brick Al-Qashalah fortress where Abdul Aziz quartered his troops after seizing Ha'il from the Al-Rashid clan. Then we arranged to camp in the parking area of the Al-Jabalene Hotel which Mr. Khalid recommended yesterday in Tabuk.

October 11—Jubba, the only sizable village in the Nafud, lies 60 miles northwest of Ha'il and boasts one of the country's great archeological sites, 5,000-year old Thamudite rock carvings. Fascinated by the always interesting and often spectacular scenery, we pick our way slowly along the difficult road into the remote Nafud. Camels roam among wind-sculpted, pink sand dunes searching for sparse vegetation. Only occasionally does a sign of humanity interrupt the otherwise desert wilderness—a Bedouin tent or a goatherd tending his flock.

At first glance, the desert appears lifeless. Close inspection of wadis, however, reveals scrubby vegetation in the usually dry stream beds. Where there's vegetation, there are insects. And where insects thrive, so do larger animals in the food chain. I saw movement under an acacia and focused my binoculars on several gray Arabian babblers picking their way along the similarly gray sandy soil. Several species of larks foraged on the ground along the roadway—Temminck's horned larks, desert larks, and much larger hoopoe larks.

We retraced our route back to Ha'il and then continued southeast through Saudi Arabia's irrigated agricultural belt (mostly wheat) to Riyadh, the country's immaculate, modern capital. The sprawling city is confusing and difficult to navigate, and is made especially more so by all the signs being written in Arabic script. We were tired, having driven well over 400 miles from Ha'il, and, unable to reconcile our map with the Arabic signs, quickly became lost. We gave up all hope of finding a place to camp and instead checked into a hotel. I walked to a nearby Safeway for provisions while Lynnie waited in our room. She had lost much of her interest in Saudi Arabia and did not want to be subjected to the heat and humiliation of having to wear an *abayya* to the grocery store. I bought a broiled chicken, French fries, salad, and cold drinks, and we ate supper in our air-conditioned room. She was ecstatic!

October 12—The small oasis of Dir'aiyah lies on the outskirts of Riyadh. Here are the walled ruins of old Dir'aiyah, the historic capital of the Al-Saud family. We visited the site's museum and then several of the restored buildings including the Mosque of Al-Turaif, the defensive Tower of Feisal, and the palaces of Salwa, Fahd, and Abdullah Bin Saud, Thunayyan Bin Saud, and Sa'd Bin Saud.

We stopped at the enormous camel market east of Riyadh, an interesting city in itself with all the characters one would expect in an Arabian camel market, but the really serious trading would not begin until tomorrow, so we continued east toward the Al-Hasa Oasis at Hofuf. Our route traversed the superb carmel-colored dunes of the Ad Dahna desert. About fifty miles west of Hofuf, the car suddenly bucked and coughed, and the yellow "Engine Alert" light flashed on for a few seconds. So Saudi Super's "very low" lead content may be catching up with us.

Lynette was beside herself during the afternoon. She's afraid that leaded gas will cause us to be marooned in the middle of nowhere and she'll have to wear her accursed *abayya* forever. We drive the rest of the way to Hofuf with no further signs of trouble. I registered at a hotel where the desk clerks spoke English and then called the VW service manager in Dhahran. He assured me that the car would not stop running and that the worst possibility would be a ruined Catalytic converter. He recommended our continuing to Abu Dhabi where there is a large, well-stocked VW dealer, and where, he promises, the gas is lead free.

Lynnie and I took a walk along King Abdul Aziz Street to Hofuf's heralded souk. We wandered through the many shops, inspecting wonderful Bedouin jewelry and weavings, but she didn't have her heart in it. On the way back to our hotel, we stopped at a bank to change money. We had just walked in the front door when a uniformed guard hurried to us and asked Lynette to leave and go through the women's entrance where she would be able to sit in a waiting room until I completed our business. Her tears of anger, humiliation, and sadness flowed freely during our walk back to the hotel. Lynnie is hot and distressed and ready to go home. Late this evening, I called, Klaus, the trusty VW service manager in Idaho Falls. He concurred that leaded gas would ruin the catalytic converter, but we could be assured the car would continue running.

October 13—The United Arab Emirates is a confederation of seven sovereign shaikhdoms, each with its distinct character. Before oil was discovered here in the '60s, the cities of the Emirates were small backwater settlements. Today Abu Dhabi and Dubai, in particular, are modern and vibrant and very accepting of westerners and their ways.

We drove 438 miles among white sand dunes and along the turquoise Arabian/Persian Gulf without a whimper from the camper. The service manager from Dhahran was correct—we crossed the border into the United Arab Emirates and pulled into a large, modern gas station where only unleaded fuel was sold. Lynnie shed her *abayya,* and we were both in a much better mood. We arrived in Abu Dhabi just before sunset and checked into a Sheraton Hotel. Lynnie's spirits soared! I made an appointment at the VW dealer's service department for eight o'clock tomorrow morning.

October 14—The VW dealer performs all the appropriate service. Pleasant surprise—our catalytic converter is fine. With relatively low lead content, the few tanks of gas we bought in Saudi Arabia apparently did no damage. Who knows why the "Engine Alert" light flashed on? The modern eight-lane highway landscaped with palm trees and flowering vegetation runs eighty-five miles, connecting Abu Dhabi and Dubai. Perhaps it was planned for some other future situation, but today the beltway carried an incredibly light traffic load. Lynette commented that Land Cruisers rather than Mercedes seemed to be the transportation of choice among Arabs from the UAE. In Dubai, we drove immediately to the freight agent with whom we had arranged to ship our camper to India and made an appointment for tomorrow. Then we stopped at Air Iran to see about visiting Shiraz and Persepolis while the camper was being shipped to Bombay. Later we drove to a Holiday Inn hotel/shopping center complex where we arranged to camp in the parking lot.

Lynette was still in a funk trying to decide whether she wanted to continue on to India. The shopping center included a McDonald's, so we went there for supper to discuss our options. First, we could ship the camper and fly ourselves home. This would permit us to hopscotch our way across Asia if we chose, stopping in various interesting cities of our choosing. We thought the problem with this alternative was that she would feel guilty, and I would be regretful. Second, Lynnie could go home and I could continue on by myself. The problem with this, I would be very lonesome without her and might not want to complete the trip. Third, we both go on, and Lynette would be frightened and unhappy. For sure, Lynette didn't want to fly to Iran, even for a few days. We talked about my going there and her staying in Dubai a few extra days. We postponed any decision until we met with the freight forwarder and saw what the shipping schedules to India looked like.

October 15—Sleep came slowly and was frustratingly ephemeral last night. At first, the heat was unbearable. The all too occasional and too brief soft whisper of wind felt marvelous. It reminded me of hot, sticky nights spent in the Susquehanna River valley as a boy, before air conditioning, soaked in perspiration and rolling from side to side for hours. Suddenly, about 2:00 a.m., a howling wind whipped up carrying so much sand that our surroundings beyond a few feet from the camper were totally obscured. Then came lightning, thunder, heavy rain, and then, incredibly icy hailstones the size of golf balls! This meteorological phenomenon raged for about an hour, blessedly cooling the night air for another hour before the oppressive heat retook the night.

Lynnie felt a bit better this morning and, after visiting the shipping agent, decided to continue to India. Then, at Air Iran, while I was inquiring about schedules and hotels, she became visibly upset. I quickly scotched going to Iran. She obviously didn't want to go, and I didn't really want to go without her. Later, at Air India, while we were waiting for the attendant to issue our tickets to Bombay, she said the thought of wearing an *abayya* another day was about to send her over the edge.

We finished our business and spent the afternoon sightseeing. We visited the nineteenth-century house of Sheikh Saeed who was ruler in the

1930s and the grandfather of the emirate's present head of state. Then we toured the Dubai Museum and the early nineteenth-century Al-Fahaidi Fort where, in the early evening, pallid swifts darted among the city buildings foraging for insects.

October 16—About a hundred miles southeast of Dubai, the Buraimi Oasis lies in the remote Al Qafa desert, straddling the border between the United Arab Emirates and Oman. The UAE area of the oasis wraps around a peninsula of Omani territory and is called Al-Ain. The camper will not be leaving for several more days, so we set out for Al-Ain early this morning. After a scenic drive through the desert, we spent the day touring the oasis, visiting several mud-walled forts of classical Arabian design. One of the forts housed the Al-Ain Museum which I was not permitted to enter because today it was open only to women. We wandered about the livestock souk and the camel market and then drove across the border into Oman where we toured several more forts and checked out the shops in the Buraimi Souk.

Back across the border in Al-Ain, we set up camp in the hillside parking lot of the Intercontinental Hotel. We relaxed on our folding chairs, eating the supper Lynnie had prepared. Beautiful turquoise plumed rollers perched on nearby posts. We talked while the sun set and then finished a bottle of wine while the full moon rolled across the black sky. The evening cooled a bit, and we retired, leaving our small table and chairs outside the camper.

October 17—In the morning, our table and chairs were gone. We washed and vacuumed the camper and packed for our trip to Bombay. On our return drive to Dubai, we stopped a few miles south of the city at Khawr Dubai, a marvelous wetlands where we saw thousands of waders and other birds, including a number of new species such as lesser and greater sand plovers and spotted eagles. This evening, we ate dinner at a fine pub and then repaired to the bar at the Sheraton Hotel where there were more Moslems (men only) than Christians. What a sight with white-robed drinkers belly-up to the bar!

October 18—Indian men wearing turbans and robes hustled from one office to another, only to wait in line again, at the colorful Dubai docks. An agent from the shipping company led us through three hours of complicated bureaucratic hassle required to ship the camper to Bombay. Finally, we drove the van to the loading area. A tall, slender man with a long, stringy beard looked through our papers, smiled, then gathered his flowing robe and ducked his turban as he climbed into the camper and drove it over a ramp and into a steel container. We watched as other workers blocked the car's wheels and otherwise prepared it to ride safely on the potentially rough seas. After they sealed the container, the agent drove us downtown where we first checked into a hotel and then walked along Dubai Creek. Slender-billed and great black-headed gulls and Caspian and little terns soared over-head while colorful *dhows* and water taxis plied their way up and down the creek.

Steve Stolarz had been a Marine guard at several U.S. embassies. A civilian now, he worked for the freight forwarding company and was handling the shipping of our camper to Bombay. We met him for dinner at his favorite pub where he told us about his interesting life the past few years as a bachelor expatriate in Dubai. He said he was now thinking about moving to Australia, mostly because of a potential romantic interest he had there. As we parted, he gave us his card and we gave him our hotel information in case of questions or changes in the camper's shipping status.

October 19—Lynnie and I walked down Beniyas Road to the highly acclaimed Cafe Mozart for breakfast. Tables were filled with important-looking businessmen reading the morning paper over cappuccino and croissants. We strolled through the Deira Souk, spending much time in the extensive gold souk. With modern skyscrapers as a backdrop, we explored the exciting, colorful waterfront where *dhows*, lateen rigged sailing vessels that have been used by Arabs for many centuries, lined up at the piers. Nubian laborers loaded and unloaded merchandise that was being traded with Iran and other Gulf countries. Unique among its Gulf neighbors, Dubai's wealth emanates from trade rather than oil. As the sun dropped behind the city's Old Souk across the Creek, Lynnie and I sat on a bench eating finger food, fascinated by dockside scenes that were largely unchanged from ancient times.

October 20—Maharashtra is one of India's largest and, economically, most important states, and Bombay is its capital. We arrived at the bustling international airport early in the evening and hired a cab to take us on a long and very slow drive through Bombay's crowded and colorful streets. We entered the area called Colaba, drove past the famous yellow basalt monument, The Gateway of India, and stopped in front of the Fariyas Hotel where a tall, bearded Sikh doorman wearing a red and gold turban and a red and white frock coat opened our door, smiled, and bowed. Unfortunately, I felt too bad to enjoy much of any of this.

October 21—I had a terrible night of abdominal pain—like that night in Romania, only worse. The hotel arranged for me to go to the Kalajot Hospital, a rather primitive and somewhat unclean operation, where I was assigned a cardiologist, Dr. Ashok Thawani, who gave me a complete examination and found that my "white count" was high and that I had malaria. Strangely, and suddenly, in the middle of his examination, I felt much better.

He gave me medication to cure the malaria and, in response to my questions, told us that he worked at this "hospital for the poor" because his family was "quite wealthy" and he didn't need the money. He gave me his card and suggested I call him in the evening if the severe pain returned. On the way back to the hotel, Lynnie and I remembered that malaria had been present in Ha'il (Saudi Arabia). We were not aware of that fact before going there and had not begun taking our preventive medication until after we left Ha'il. Well, wherever I picked up the malaria, I feel much better now that I know what my problem is. The medication will cure the problem, and I can continue the trip. I'm still puzzled, however, since my symptoms seem quite different from anything I have ever heard about malaria. Oh well, blood tests don't lie.

Back at the hotel, there was a message from Steve Stolarz—the ship has been delayed for two weeks. Rats! Lousy news! If that wasn't bad enough, I went to the bathroom, and, when I looked down, my stream looked like cherry juice. I called Doctor Thawani to tell him about this development, and he said to bring in a sample in the morning.

For the first time, I'm ready to give up. Lynette isn't having fun.

"This isn't like it was in the seventies." She reminisced. "I liked moving from camp to camp, not sleeping in parking lots of hotels."

"I know. I liked the hippie life much better than this." I feel like everything is stacked against me, that I've been beaten from every direction. Do I really want to do this so much?

October 22—First thing this morning, I took a sample of blood red urine to the hospital. Doctor Thawani had not yet arrived, but the desk nurse told me to leave the sample with her and come back in two or three hours.

To kill some time, we took a leisurely walk along PJ Ramchandani Marg (Strand Road) past the Gateway of India and stopped for coffee in the fabulous Taj Mahal Hotel. Then we continued down Shivaji Marg, crossed Wellington Circle and toured the Jehangir Art Gallery and the Prince of Wales Museum with its splendid archeological and natural history exhibits.

Later in the morning, we returned to the hospital. Doctor Thawani greeted us in his office with a smile.

"Good news, Mr. Wile. You don't have blood in your urine."

"No blood in my urine? What do you mean?"

"Here, look at the report."

The report he handed me had my name at the top. Under *Blood In Urine?*, the word "negative" was entered. Under *Color of Urine?*, it said "pale yellow." I looked at Lynette, and she was as nonplused as I was. The container of urine I had left with them looked like cherry juice. Somebody had mixed up the samples! Now I wondered if the same thing hadn't happened with my blood tests and whether I really had malaria.

We didn't dispute the findings and, instead, returned to the hotel. We reminded each other that our agreement had always been on these trips, if either of us has a serious medical problem, we come home. Lynette is afraid to continue traveling with me being sick. I don't know if my problem is serious, but I feel awful and I'm peeing blood. I've had it.

I called Steve Stolarz in Dubai and explained our situation. He said he would make all the arrangements to re-route the camper to Seattle rather than Bombay. He called back later and confirmed the VW should arrive in Seattle in less than a month. I hope it makes it OK. Next I made reservations to fly home five days hence on Cathay-Pacific with layovers in Bangkok and Hong Kong.

This is the sixth time we've set out to traverse a continent in a camper and the first time we didn't make it. Things seem so different now from twenty-five years ago. Iran, Pakistan, Afghanistan, Burma—the list of dangerous destinations has mushroomed all over the world. I don't feel so bad about quitting. Africa was chock full of physical challenges—digging out of sand and mud, navigating diabolical roads, sandstorms, car problems. We handled them with aplomb. The kinds of political problems staring at us are quite different—we have little control. All of that is a pain in the ass. And now, bloody urine. I don't think I will regret quitting. But it makes me sad. I think I'll feel better after seeing Bruce and Ralph. (My family doctor and urologist.)

October 23—The doorman at the Fariyas Hotel had arranged for a taxi driver to give us a tour of Bombay. This turned out to be a good way to see the hot, steamy city which was jammed with traffic and a navigational nightmare. We visited Chowpatty Beach and observed worshippers at a gaudy but fascinating Jain temple. In Malabar Hill's Hanging Gardens, we snapped photos of fearsome cobras swaying hypnotically to a charmer's eerie flute melody as they rose out of reed baskets. Then we stopped at the nearby Towers of Silence where a Parsi sect of Hindus lays their dead out in the open to be picked over by vultures and other scavengers. We stopped at the Mahalakshmi Temple and the *dhobi ghat*, Bombay's municipal open air laundry where every day, in rented tanks and troughs, thousands of men wash and thrash tons of clothing and bed linen from all over the city and lay it on the pavement to dry.

October 24—"A driver!?" Lynette and I exclaimed, looking at each other. We had taken a very early flight to Delhi with the intent of spending a few days touring the area, including Agra and Bharatpur. We thought we had rented only a car; now the rental agent informed us a driver came with the deal.

"Where is our driver?"

437

The agent smiled. "I am he! Call me 'KK'."

KK suggested that we would have enough time to tour Delhi upon our return to the city and that we should leave for Agra immediately. Before too long, we were beyond Delhi's city limits and traveling east on the Grand Trunk Road, the historic artery that runs from Amritsar to Calcutta and dates back to Mughal times, and that was described by Kipling as India's "river of life." All the marvelous splendor of Indian life indeed unfolded along the roadside—women wearing their colorful saris, top-heavy double-decker busses leaning and wanting to topple, more bicycles than cars, a cow sleeping undisturbed in the center of the highway, villages with open air markets, old men thrashing wheat by hand. Such an overcrowded country! Water birds thrived in open wetlands—egrets, herons, cormorants, darters, dabchicks, ducks, ibises, and at least three species of storks. Stilts foraged on the mudflats and lapwings in the fields. Four species of vultures soared on the thermals, waiting, I suppose, for the next road kill. Kingfishers, bee-eaters, rollers, hornbills, and mynas all went about their business in a variety of habitats.

Several hours later we crossed the Yamuna River and entered Agra from where, in the sixteenth and seventeenth centuries, the Mughal emperors ruled India. After registering at our hotel, we drove to Agra Fort. Emperor Akbar began building this magnificent fort in 1565, and construction continued through the reign of Shah Jahan, Akbar's grandson. Massive walls and a wide moat surround the fortress-city which includes Shah Jahan's audience halls, the Nagina Masjid (Gem Mosque), a Ladies' Bazaar where merchants sold their wares to ladies of the Mughal court, the sumptuous Jehangir's (Akbar's son) Palace, and Shah Jahan's beautiful, white marble private palace, the Khas Mahal.

Emperor Shah Jahan's beloved wife, Mumtaz Mahal (Chosen of the Palace), bore fourteen children before dying in childbirth. Heartbroken upon her death, Shah Jahan built the Taj Mahal, one of the world's most marvelous structures, in her memory. The main building is perfectly symetrical and is topped by a large Oriental dome rising 200 feet above the structure's ten thousand-square-foot platform. Four 133-foot high minarets rise from the platform's corners. Precious gems are set in the brilliant white marble construction material to form delicate decorative patterns and inscriptions from the Koran. The Taj Mahal has been described as "the most extravagant monument ever built for love."

An afternoon thunderstorm came and went, leaving an assortment of pleasant aromas wafting from the many flowering trees as Lynnie and I stood in line outside the Taj's red sandstone entrance buildings. Tiny green and yellow coppersmiths uttered their metallic calls from thick shrubbery, and red-vented bulbuls darted flycatcher-like into the open after insects. Scores of chatty Indian women wearing their ever-flowing saris, a profusion of beautiful colors, made the wait pleasant. Inside the walls, the beauty and grandeur of the Taj emanated from every perspective in the post-thunderstorm subtle pink light. By any measure, Lynnie and I agreed, the Taj Mahal ranked among the most beautiful, most dramatic, and most memorable wonders we have ever seen. We took our time wandering about the grounds, absorbing the magic of India and the country's defining shrine.

On our walk back to the car, we were besieged by beggars, rickshaw drivers and persistent hawkers of merchandise. I don't know what malady I'm hosting, but it leaves me always feeling poorly. So I wasn't receptive to the barrage of annoying attention and found myself lashing out verbally in response to their endless supplications. Now I regret my impatience. The kindness, gentleness, and generosity of the Indian people have been everywhere apparent. I have never been among nicer people. For example, KK's resources are meager by our standards, but he never passes a begger, and we pass many of them, without finding a spare coin or two to give him.

October 25—The Keoladeo Ghana National Park near Bharatpur is one of the birding world's great sanctuaries. We intended to spend the day birding at the park, and a staff member at our hotel in Agra had arranged for a naturalist/guide to meet us there. Arun Bhatt lives in Bharatpur and was waiting at the entrance gate when we arrived. He lived up to his advance billing and was very knowledgeable about Keoladeo and the local birds. The park also was worthy of its reputation with a variety of habitats producing an equal variety of birds. In five hours, we found about 100 species, more than half of which I had never seen before, including yellow spoonbills, bronzewinged jacanas, coucals, white-cheeked bulbuls, chestnut-headed tit-babblers, Indian tree-pies, spotted owlets, and collared scops owls. This was a pretty special experience for me, and Lynnie too sang Keoladeo's praises. On the way back to Agra, I asked what her favorite sightings were.

"Ohhhh..., probably the little green bee-eater and the bronze-winged jacana."

"Really?"

"Yes, I'm into irridescence."

Fatehpur Sikri lies about halfway between Bharatpur and Agra. The palace complex is preserved intact today, more than four hundred years since it was built by Emperor Akbar. The Mughal ruler abandoned the city after only fifteen years because of an unreliable water supply. KK brought along a friend from Agra named Gyp who was very knowledgeable about the history of Fatehpur Sikri. With Gyp as a guide, we entered the palace complex through the 175-foot high Buland Darwaza (Gate of Victory) and toured the Jama Masjid (Dargah Mosque), the tomb of Shaikh Salim Chishti (the saint who foretold the birth of Akbar's son) where even today childless women come for inspiration, the Palace of Jodh Bai with its architectural blend of Muslim cupolas and Hindu columns, and the tiny but elegant palace (Birbal Bhavan) built for Raja Birbal, Akbar's favorite courtier. We explored the large, enclosed courtyard Karawan Serai (Caravanserai) that accommodated visiting merchants, the Golden House palace of Akbar's Christian wife (Maryam), and a number of other palaces, buildings and monuments.

KK drove away from the city and stopped the car on a nearby hill. We got out and looked back toward Fatehpur Sikri. The sun had dropped low in the sky, and, in the early evening light, the reddish-brown sandstone ruins had been transformed into a shimmering, soft pink apparition.

October 26—KK's English is limited, but during the several days we have spent together, we have all gotten pretty good at communicating. He has shared many of his thoughts and experiences with us and has tried to explain Hindu ways. During this time, we have learned KK is a good man who is devoted to his wife and four children. On the drive back to Delhi, Lynette asked how he met his wife.

"Our's is not a love marriage. Our parents arrange this marriage when we are children."

"You did not love your wife when you married her?" Lynette asked carefully.

"No. When we marry, I not know her much. She very young than me."

"Do you love her now, KK?"

"Of course. I love her much now. She is everything to me. She is my life."

KK gave us the cook's tour of his city including, in Old Delhi, the Kashmir Gate, the seventeenth-century Fatehpuri Mosque, and a Jain temple. We visited Shah Jahan's Lal Qila (Red Fort) and his Jama Masjid, India's largest mosque, and then walked among the gardens of Bahai's splendid Lotus Temple.

This evening, we flew from Delhi back to Bombay where we transferred from the domestic to the international terminal. We managed a few fitful naps while sitting most of the night in the terminal's uncomfortable chairs, waiting for our Cathay-Pacific flight to Bangkok. Lynnie received sad news when she called Krissie to tell her we were coming home. Gabriel, Lynnie's beautiful young palomino, died of colic yesterday. She finished the call rather abruptly and began weeping.

"Gabe's dead."

"Oh, Lynnie, I'm so sorry..." I embraced my baby, my heart breaking for her.

"I don't have much luck with horses, Dar." (Several years before, her dun horse, Peaches, had to be put down after breaking a leg.)

Krissie was crying when she broke the news to her mother. Lynnie asked me to call her back and tell her how sorry we were we hadn't been there to deal with the situation instead of Krissie having to do it.

October 27—Long flight to Bangkok on very accommodating airline, Cathay-Pacific. Registered at hotel, arranged for tours next two days, and napped. This evening inspected the many stalls at the open air market near our hotel.

October 28—Toured Bangkok's exotic temples and palaces—including Wat Phra Kaew (Temple of the Emerald Buddha), the Grand Palace, Wat Pho (Temple of the Reclining Buddha), and Wat Traimit (Temple of the Golden Buddha). Our guide is good and interesting, but it just isn't the same as driving through the country in our camper. I've lost my enthusiasm, and I feel terrible. I'm ready to be home. At a clothing store, Lynette selected a dress pattern and material and arranged to have a dress made.

October 29—Our guide drove us through the Thai countryside, past rice fields and salt fields. We toured a coconut processing operation where Alexandrine parakeets foraged in fruit trees and purple-rumped sunbirds extracted nectar from flowering shrubbery. Then she drove us to the floating market at Klong Dammoen Saduak where buildings rest on stilts, and waterways serve as streets. We toured the town in a long boat powered by a long-handled motor, the same type of craft used in the James Bond film, *The Man With The Golden Gun*. Children waved and jumped from their houses into the muddy water, and, at the market, women sat in long dugout canoes selling vegetables, flowers, clothing, and other wares. Lynnie bought silk robes for our four grandchildren.

October 30—We lay over in Hong Kong for six or eight hours and take a city tour. Now our plane is taxiing to the takeoff runway. The magic of 1974 is certainly gone. I want to be home. Strange, we'll cross the International Dateline this evening and arrive in Los Angeles yesterday. Long flight ahead. I don't think the antibiotics are working—I feel like malaria is winning the battle.

Jackson Hole, Wyoming, Sunday, November 1, 1997—

Lynnie and I returned to Jackson Friday night. My doctor, Bruce Hayse, was able to see me early Saturday morning. He ran a number of tests which showed I was anemic, severely dehydrated, and apparently carrying a systemic infection. He expressed doubt that I had malaria but, otherwise, was unable to diagnose my problem. He recommended I check into the local hospital immediately and undergo an ultrasound test.

By mid-afternoon yesterday, I learned that my gall bladder was swollen, infected, contained stones, and that I also had giardia. There was no indication of my having had malaria. Lynette was also diagnosed with giardia.

This morning, Sunday, my gall bladder was removed. After the operation, Bruce stopped to see me in the hospital.

"Well, Darwin, you had me fooled."

"How's that?"

"I didn't know what your problem was, but I would have never guessed it was your gall bladder."

"Why not?"

"You're not the right profile."

"What's the right profile?"

"Overweight female."

"Do me a favor, Bruce."

"What is it?"

"Tell Lynette I'm getting in touch with my feminine side."

POSTSCRIPT
Jackson Hole, Wyoming, October 6, 1998—

Before long, Lynette and I recovered completely from our maladies. I've spent much of the last year working on a thoroughly enjoyable project, reviewing notes taken during our years of continental drifting and putting them into this chronology. I had written a journal on each of our adventures, knowing that someday I might want to write a book. After finishing each trip, I returned to the conventional life, putting my journal away for another day. Until I began writing, I have never reviewed any of these notes. You can imagine my pleasure when, for the first time in twenty-five years, I read and re-lived the year and a half when our family of four drifted through South America and Europe in a Volkswagen camper. That alone is payment enough for my effort in completing this project.

Most of us set goals or, at least, have a vague idea of what we want to do with our lives. Seeing much of the world in a camper has been something of a dream of mine for the past thirty years. This last trip across Asia was to have been the culmination of that dream. When our family drifted through South America and Europe in the seventies, the experience was sublime. A year ago, sitting in a Bombay hotel room, Lynnie and I knew that magic was gone. Twenty-five years had passed, during which time, the world had changed, and so had we. We just wanted to come home.

Now, a year later, I sit here and wonder what happened to the dream. Crossing Asia has been left undone, the dream unfulfilled. Does it matter? It depends upon the day. I know now that crossing Asia in a camper is simply out of the question for Lynette. Had we done as she suggested in 1974, taken another year and continued as a family drifting through Africa and Asia, she would have led the charge. However, at this time and in this world, she cannot do it.

Where this leaves me, I'm not sure. I know I don't ever want to find myself saying, after it's too late to do anything about it, "I wish I had done that." Sometimes I want to go back so much it hurts. I sit and wish Lynnie could enjoy the drifting life as she did in the seventies. She can't. So then I think about shipping the camper back to Asia and making the trip by myself. But the thought of being without Lynnie for a long time is depressing. At best, travel without her wouldn't be fun. At worst, I'd be miserable, call it quits, and come home. Then there's the question of Lynette's thoughts. What if I have to choose between finishing the dream and keeping Lynnie? Like Frank Wells, for me that's an easy decision. I love Lynnie. So, I don't know what I'll do. I'll keep thinking about it.

APPENDIX
Whatever Happened To............?

Sharing adventure, adversity, good times, and interesting experiences usually forges friendships. Lynnie and I were fortunate to have met and/or traveled with many people who became our friends. Friendships, however, need a modicum of ongoing contact to prosper. Otherwise, time, distance, and our evolving lives often find these relationships fading into nothing more than pleasant memories. As Ed Brennan would say, "That's life its damn self!" Nevertheless, the circumstances which we shared with the people below were rather special, and, I like to think, if I picked up a phone and called any one of them or vice versa, the friendship would immediately be revived.

Over the years, we have lost contact with many of the friends we met drifting. With a few of them, fortunately, we remain good friends. In order of their appearance in the book's narrative, the list below relates what we know today about these people based upon any contact we had subsequent to traveling with them.

SOUTH AMERICA

Jennifer and Eric Walker—In 1975, we received a post card from Colorado telling us they had returned to the university.

Maria—For several years, Krissie corresponded with her friend, Maria, from the Lima Golf Club. There was a time when Maria was thinking about visiting us in Illinois. Then her letters stopped and Krissie's letters went unanswered. We assumed Maria passed away.

Dori and Karl—For twenty-five years, we have remained friends with Dori and Karl Zuchold, corresponding regularly and occasionally visiting one another. They live in the San Francisco area. Karl is the chef at a women's club, and Dori teaches classes on porcelain art.

EUROPE

Rosemary and Russ—After spending a few more years in Paris, Rosemary and Russ now live in Connecticut. Mike's pal, Jeff, is a chef; Krissie's friend, Cindy, and her husband live in Europe; and my little buddy, Scott, is at Harvard Law School.

Matsons—After meeting them in Vienna, our friends from Oregon turned up three more times in Europe (Naples, Rome, and Madrid). In 1975, we received a note letting us know they were back home in Oregon.

Dee and Ian Christensen (also Sally and Rod)—We received a note in 1975 telling us about their travel experiences after leaving us in Greece. They successfully drove across Asia and returned to their home in Australia.

Mother—While Helen Wile has slowed down a bit physically, she remains as mentally sharp as ever. She lives in a personal care facility in

Manheim, Pennsylvania, where she listens (and sometimes dances) to her music. She counts her time spent drifting through southern Europe as one of the highlights of her life.

Gail and Ian—While Lynette and I never heard from our Australian (and our Canadian) friends with whom we drifted in Spain, Mother did. Gail wrote her once after she and Ian returned to Australia.

Maureen and Rob—For several years Mother corresponded with Maureen and Rob after their return to Vancouver. She has not heard from them in recent years.

ALASKA

Rollie "R.V." Wagner—I received a note from the folksy Oklahoman after returning to Jackson in which he reminded me to send him a copy of anything that gets published about our drifting which, of course, I will do, if anything ever gets published.

Jean and Dick Newell—We have remained friends with Jean and Dick over the years. Retired, they now live in Yuma. We have visited each other several times, and Jean and I still enjoy taking wildflower and bird walks together.

Fred and Sara Machetanz—Alaska's greatest artist is entering his tenth decade and, as far as I know, still painting. We receive a Christmas card each year from Sara and Fred.

Ed Rasmussen—I've seen my college buddy several times since our trip to Alaska. I'm hoping to take him along on a birding trip to Attu, the westernmost of the Aleutian Islands.

Barb and Ed Brennan—Our good friends who helped preserve Lynnie's sanity in Alaska and Africa continue to live in Belleville. We see each other regularly and even manage to travel together now and then.

Nancy McGuire—I returned to Nome a few years ago, on the way to a birding trip on St. Lawrence Island, and had a pleasant and interesting visit with the salty owner of the Nome Nugget.

AFRICA

Jan and Juul—In June of 1988, we received a long letter from our Dutch friends, with whom we crossed the northern Sahara, describing their experiences as they drifted south through Mali, Senegal, and Guine Bissau. From that letter: *Sometimes it seems that it has been a wonderful dream, but when we look at the pictures, and read our diary, we know that it has been true.* Jan and Juul married in August, and we corresponded for another year or so.

Heidi and Luis—Our Austrian friends returned home, and, for a few years, we exchanged Christmas cards with them.

Stefan, Johann, Thom, Margot, and Jurgen—We never heard again from the lovable rogue, Johann.

Within a year after our return to Wyoming, Thom sent us photos from the trip and brought us up to date on his and Margot's circumstances.

Stefan reported that profits on cars were so attractive that he made three more trips across the desert in 1988.

In December of that year, Jurgen wrote to tell us he would be touring the United States with his wife, Karin, and young son, Dominik. He wanted to fly to Jackson for a visit and buy our camper, if it was for sale. Jurgen's family arrived in April of 1989 and stayed with us in Jackson for ten days. They toured the western U.S. in the camper and then drove to Charleston, S.C., from where the VW was shipped back to Germany, the fourth trans-Atlantic crossing for our former travel-home. The last time we heard from Jurgen was in August of 1989. From that letter: *Now we have a lot of good and unique remembrances about the wonderful landscapes and the people in West-America. We think very often... our stay at your house, and the nice times in your society, also the riding with your horses... I say special and thousands thanks for your help to start a good trip and give us a nice home... I, Karin and Dominik love you and your home!*

Tams Ngeri—The Nigerian immigration official who spent days helping us obtain Cameroun visas sent several cards thanking us for books we had sent to him. In November of 1989, we received a letter in which Tams described very difficult economic and social conditions being faced by the people of Nigeria. We never heard from him again.

Wilfried—The backpacking Austrian with whom we crossed the African "jungle" sent us a note from South Africa in August of 1988. From Zaire he hitched his way through Uganda, Kenya, Tanzania, Malawi, Mozambique, Zimbabwe, Botswana, and Namibia. Wilfried also reported that, in Cape Town, he ran into Mary Donald, the woman from Alabama who traveled with us on the Zaire River boat, and that she planned to hitch her way north through West Africa. From Wilfried's note: *South Africa is a nice place but not 'Africa' what I am looking for—so I am going up to Nairobi—and then decide what's next.*

Anar and Bjorne—From Nairobi, the brothers from Iceland intended to turn north, head down the Nile, and then work their way across Asia.

One day in August of 1989, I was painting our pole barn. From my perch high on a ladder, I saw a large, vintage car turning into our long, gravel driveway. I didn't recognize the rusty old Mercury chugging noisily toward me and, assuming it was somebody who needed directions, I dismounted the ladder to see if I could be of help. When I saw Anar and Bjorne smiling from behind the bug covered windshield, I called Lynette, and the four of us embraced and danced and laughed and screamed.

From Africa, they had hitched across Asia (and reported that they favored the Thai girls above all others), flew to Alaska (where they bought the cheapest car they could find) and drove down the Alcan Highway. The boys stayed with us for a week or so, a great visit during which we tried to give them a taste of the American West, including Jackson Hole's Saturday Night Rodeo and western swing dancing at the Million Dollar Cowboy Bar. They especially liked donning their jeans and cowboy hats and, in their words, "riding off into the sunset" on our horses. Later that year, we heard from them that they were trying to land jobs in Los Angeles.

Karin and George—After returning to Jackson Hole, we corresponded with K&G regularly. For their part, sometimes Karin did the honors, other times George. Some excerpts from one of George's letters, written in July of 1988, when they lived in Johannesburg:

Dear Darwin and Lynnet,

We have made it to South Africa. I am sat here writing to you, watching 'Breakfast TV' drinking tea, eating cheese on toast, all very sivalised!! What!! A bit different from waking on the boat, sweeping maggots off the deck, before running the gountlet of crocs and afs to get a shower... The last time we sore you was that camp site in Kenya, 'yuk', well we went to Tanzania... I had to go to the police station for hiting a Scotch man who was causing trouble, next we went to Malawi 3 weeks later, after a fantastic time, and some buetiful people, we went to Zambia, where we came close to trouble again (exit quick) on to Zimbabwe where it was to much. We stayed two days at vic falls then, on our way to Bulawayo, we stopped for a drink at wankie colliery. It took us a week to get away... we eventually sold our Wilbur (Land Rover), in Bulawayo, for 12,000 zim dollars, and bought S.A. rand 6000 which is about $3,000 US. Not bad for a Land Rover that cost me 700 pounds in England, and took 28,000 miles across Africa. It is not enough to come to US with so we are going to work here untill we have about $6000 US that should last us a bit... Did Lynn have a nervous breakdown. Ha Ha only joking... Well folks thats a lot for me to write, I hope you can understand it, cos writing wasn't my best subject at school... we are always talking about you.

Love,

George & Karin xxxxx

P.S. Karin is still bird spotting. Thanks Darwin. I might have to buy her a book now.

About a year later, G&K were living in Durban. From one of Karin's letters: *We got your letter and have been very lazy about writting back... I hope you are still keeping fit and happy and hope your both loving each other... hope to get over there as soon as possible... we are both working yes working for a living. I'm waitressing... (not doing bad on tips with my chatter they can't get away without tipping.) George is rigging and pipe fitting and doing very well. We have not fallen out since Zaire and are very happy still. We love and miss you both...*

On June 26, 1992, Karin and George drove an old camper into our driveway in Jackson Hole, two days before Krissie's wedding day. Just as they promised, they had come to see us!

Joe Glik—The man from St. Louis, who was astonished at my tattered physical appearance in the remote Serengeti and who offered to share his room if the lodge was unable to accomodate Lynette and me, recently showed up in Jackson Hole as unexpectedly as he had in Tanzania. Just this past summer (1998), I was walking across the parking lot of the Teton Pines Golf Course and spotted Joe emerging from a car driven by his son Bobby. I waved at them, and Joe's first words rang with recognition, "Darwin, you look better than the last time I ran into you!" Joe and his two sons had come to Jackson Hole to fish for cutthroat trout.

Bob and Gloria Volpa—After a few more years in Cairo, Bob retired and the Volpas moved to Vancouver Island where they still live. They travel frequently, and Bob writes books and places their investments with Norm Kastner, one of our friends from Belleville whom Bob met at the Lake Manyara Lodge.

Rashid—We received several letters from Rashid updating us on his family's plans to move to Canada. In October of 1989, Rashid wrote that they had received their immigration visas for Canada and would be leaving Kenya in January. A year later, Rashid called from Canada. He had landed a good job, and Johnnie was doing well in their community's fine school.

AUSTRALIA

Alexandra Katherine Wile—Our little granddaughter, who technically began her days in Australia, now lives with Zach, Lori and Mike in Redmond, Washington, where Mikey runs Polaris, his own computer consulting business. He and Lori talk about leaving sometime in the next year or so on a camper trip to Alaska or South America. They've invited Lynnie and me to join them.

ASIA

Arkansas Group—Lynette and I were disappointed when we learned that we would not be able to attend Al White's 70th birthday party in Pine Bluff, Arkansas. Not only had we become very fond of Al and his friends on the St. Petersburg to Moscow boat trip, but the week-long party also promised to be the social event of the year, beginning in Pine-Bluff and ending in Little Rock, and including hundreds of participants. Al spent much of his life pounding drums in jazz groups, and jazz musicians from all over the country would be coming to Arkansas to join in the festivities. Unfortunately, the party was scheduled for February when Lynette and I were planning to be drifting somewhere in Southeast Asia.

As events unfolded, my infected gallbladder rendered possible our attending Al's party after all. We hopped a plane to Dallas, drove to Pine Bluff, joined in on possibly the gayest birthday celebration I've ever been a part of, and had a joyous reunion with the Arkansas travelers.

Julia and Dean—We exchange Christmas cards with our Aussie friends. They are now living in London.

P.J. and Claudia—One day in June of 2000, our Dutch friends showed up on our doorstep in Jackson Hole, their large old Mercedes motor home parked in our driveway. We joined them in Alaska in September of 2000.

Other Wind Canyon Book & CD Titles

Aerial Drug Wars: The Story of U.S. Customs Aviation by Henry M. Holden — The first-ever account of this secretive and remarkably effective organization. Includes a photo/video CD-ROM disk. Stunning, previously-unreleased video clips & photos, details of secret missions, specific interdictions and foreign engagements.

Aero Albums by Kenn Rust and Paul Matt — 20 volumes, each 48 pages, 64 to 95 photos in each volume. Wide variety of Pioneer, WWI, Golden Age, WWII and aviation history articles. Many 3-view drawings, profiles and illustrations.

Aeronca's Golden Age by Alan Abel, Drina Welch Abel and Paul Matt — Details the events leading to the Aeronautical Corporation of America from early 1900s through WWII. Emphasis on C-2, C-3, C-1, Model K and Model L, Aeronca 7AC "Champ", and 11AC "Chief". Includes factory photos. Also details people, facilities and manufacturing operations.

Aviation Heritage Airplane CDs organized by Alan Abel and Drina Welch Abel — Each CD in this series includes 300 to 630 photos and 3-views. Titles include all Paul Matt scale drawings on 4 CDs, Grumman Aircraft Archive 1, Grumman Aircraft Archive 2, WWII Fighters, Fighters & Attack 1945-1975, WWII Bombers, Bombers & Support Aircraft 1945-1975, and Airplane Magazine Ads of the Golden Age. Each image can be cropped, enlarged, zoomed-in and printed.

The Blue Ghost: The Ship That Couldn't Be Sunk by Art Giberson — History of aircraft carrier *USS Lexington*, from her birth to WWII exploits during which she destroyed over 1,000 planes and sunk or damaged almost 1 millions tons of shipping. She has recorded more arrested landings than any carrier in Navy history.

Bonanza Around the World by Dennis Stewart — 1994 around-the-world air race by group of private pilots. Some were serious racers, others participated for the sheer adventure. Extraordinary journey where strange alliances developed and political expectations did not always turn out as planned.

Cessna's Golden Age by Alan Abel, Drina Welch Abel and Paul Matt — Looks at the Cessna Aircraft Company through the struggling years of the Depression & WWII, including details of people and manufacturing operations. Emphasis on Primary Gliders, Airmasters, T-50 Bobcats, Waco CG-4A Gliders (Cessna-built) and Cessna 120 and 140 airplanes.

The Corsair & Other Aeroplanes Vought by Gerald Moran — The story of Chance Vought and his struggles to build a business. His designs went on to great fame as he broke into the field of naval aviation. With the Corsair biplane in 1926, a name and heritage began. The F4U Corsair was developed after WWII broke out and became a beloved legend.

Crosswind by Patricia Valdata — A novel about a young woman's discovery of the unique and satisfying private world of soaring, as she rebounds from personal tragedy. A reader thinks about his/her own life, and the combination of choices and circumstances that put us where we are.

The DC-3/C-47 Encyclopedia - Photos, Videos Facts & Fun by Henry M. Holden — A 2-disk multimedia CD-ROM presentation. Articles, data bases, complete construction list, tables. 800 photographs and 50 minutes of archival video.

Exploring the Monster by Robert Whelan — Mountain lee waves and the rotors which so often accompany them comprise one of the most powerful, and least known, forces in nature. Vertical ascent and descent rates exceeding 2,500 feet per minute, rotors with vertical & horizontal accelerations exceeding +/-15Gs.

Eyes of the Fleet - A History of Naval Photography by Art Giberson — The officially-commissioned history by the National Association of Naval Photography. It traces the history of naval photography from 1914 to the present, highlighting the many talented and colorful photographers. Action photos taken over the decades by some of the Navy's best.

Florida: The War Years 1938 - 1945 by Joseph & Anne Freitus — Preparations for war affected the entire country, with Florida being particularly active. Florida had 6 military bases in 1941, but had 227 by 1944. Details specific bases, men & women and activities, wartime industry, military aviation, blimps, POW camps.

Goodyear & Formula One Air Racing 1947-1967 Volume One and Volume Two (*1967-1995*) by Robert Hirsch — Learn how this exciting sport caught on, the early players and governing organizations. These books track technological developments which allowed faster speeds and greater safety. Over 1,000 photographs, 162 scale drawings.

Halfway Home! by Jeff Justis — An experienced and skillful pilot, Dr. Justis's (and his wife's) world changed dramatically when their instrumentation failed and they crashed blind at 9,500 feet on Greenland's ice mass. Describes his preparations, what went wrong (and then right), and some fascinating characteristics of Greenland's icecap.

Just For the Love of Flying by Betty Rowell Beatty — About an incredibly modest and accomplished aviator, who at age 32 in 1954 traveled the length of Africa in an Auster Aiglet landing in 54 places during the 6-week flight. No radio, no ELT, no GPS. Just maps. Reminiscent of Beryl Markham.

The Legacy of the DC-3 by Henry Holden — The highly acclaimed comprehensive history of the people and events behind the DC-3/C-47, affectionately known as the Gooney Bird. Personal accounts of DC-3s flying themselves and hauling everything imaginable. 500 photographs and illustrations.

The Luscombe Story by John Swick — A history of aviation pioneer Don Luscombe and the Luscombe Aircraft Company, and all the planes from the Phantom through the Silvaire to the Sedan. A detailed history with production tables, serial blocks and serial numbers, military contracts, flight tests, rare photographs, and 3-views with complete specs.

Paul Matt Scale Airplane Drawings Volume One & Volume Two by Paul Matt — These internationally-acclaimed drawings include airfoils, templates, dimensions, specs, cross-sections and color schemes. Includes drawings from Pioneer, WWI, Golden Age, WWII, Classic and Modern eras. Vol. One includes airplanes A through G. Vol. Two: H – W.

Photojournalist by Art Giberson — Ty Stephens is a Navy photojournalist with impressive credentials, a reputation to match and a "nose" for being where the story is, who receives transfer orders to Vietnam under suspicious circumstances. An adventure novel whose main character is as complex as he is interesting.

Roosevelt Field by Joshua Stoff and William Camp — Roosevelt Field was the center of the aviation world of the 1920s and 1930s. Lindbergh's historic flight to Paris began from Roosevelt Field. The book traces 40 years of uninterrupted aviation history, from Glenn Curtiss' arrival with his pusher biplane in 1909 through the closing of the field in 1951.

Ryan Broughams and their Builders by William Wagner — The story of T.

Claude Ryan and Ryan Airlines, Inc., Ryan Flying Co., B.F. Mahoney Aircraft Corp., Mahoney-Ryan Aircraft Corp., Ryan Aircraft Corp., and Ryan Mechanics Monoplane during the 1920s-1930s. Includes the M-1, M-2 Bluebird, B-1 Brougham, B-3 and B-5 "Doodle Bugs," B-7 and C-1.

The 20th Century As I Lived It by L.D. Gleason — This 97-year-old author recounts his recollections of that remarkable century. He skillfully weaves his own family and career details within the changing settings from WWI, to pre-Depression days, through the Great Depression, WWII and the postwar period. Interesting insights into political, social & economic events.

Upcountry Odyssey by Frank Bostwick — At age 68 the author biked solo from southern Florida to the Canadian border. A wonderful journey with tense moments, to be sure, but this story dispels myths about age-related limitations, and describes a country rich in human and natural resources and beauty.

Waco, Symbol of Courage & Excellence Volume One and Volume Two by Fred Kobernuss — Vol. One is a comprehensive history from 1910 to 1925, and includes the development of the Waco "Cootie," Waco 4, Waco Five, Waco Six, Waco Seven and Waco 8. Vol. Two includes history from the 1920s into the 1930s, with emphasis given to the Waco Nine, Improved Waco 9 and Waco 10. Many rare and previously-unpublished photos.

The Wichita 4 by Bruce Bissonette — New perspective into Clyde Cessna, Walter Beech, Lloyd Stearman and Jake Moellendick. These self-taught entrepreneurs developed an industry in the design & production of airplanes, establishing standards in engineering & production. Their successes made Wichita "The Air Capital of the World" in that era.

The Wild Blue by Walter Boyne and Steven Thompson — Classic *New York Times* Best Sellers List novel about life in the Air Force and viewed to be the "book of record" on the opportunities, struggles and achievements available to those who love aviation and combine this love with an Air Force career.

A World Flight Over Russia by Brad Butler — In 1992 a group of private pilots circumnavigated the world in their small aircraft. This occurred at a moment in history when the Soviet empire had just unraveled, and the area was reeling from the shock waves. Spectacular b/w and color photographs. Tour of top-secret Star City (not on maps).